S0-BJG-157

WOMEN AT WORK IN THE
DEUTERONOMISTIC HISTORY

Society of Biblical Literature

International Voices in Biblical Studies

General Editors
Monica J. Melanchthon
Louis C. Jonker

Editorial Board
Eric Bortey Anum
Ida Fröhlich
Jione Havea
Hisako Kinukawa
Sam P. Mathew
Néstor Míguez
Nancy Nam Hoon Tan

Number 4
WOMEN AT WORK IN THE
DEUTERONOMISTIC HISTORY

WOMEN AT WORK IN THE DEUTERONOMISTIC HISTORY

Mercedes L. García Bachmann

G. Allen Fleece Library
Columbia International University
Columbia, SC 29203

Society of Biblical Literature
Atlanta

Copyright © 2013 by the Society of Biblical Literature

All rights reserved. No part of this work may be reproduced or published in print form except with permission from the publisher. Individuals are free to copy, distribute, and transmit the work in whole or in part by electronic means or by means of any information or retrieval system under the following conditions: (1) they must include with the work notice of ownership of the copyright by the Society of Biblical Literature; (2) they may not use the work for commercial purposes; and (3) they may not alter, transform, or build upon the work. Requests for permission should be addressed in writing to the Rights and Permissions Office, Society of Biblical Literature, 825 Houston Mill Road, Atlanta, GA 30329, USA.

Scripture quotations labeled NRSV are from the New Revised Standard Version Bible (London, HarperCollins Publishers), copyright © 1989 by the Division of Christian Education of the National Council of the Churches of Christ in the USA.

SBL Hebrew Fonts and BWHEBB and BWTRANSH PostScript® Type 1 and TrueType fonts Copyright ©1994-2013 BibleWorks, LLC. All rights reserved. These Biblical Hebrew fonts are used with permission and are from BibleWorks (www.bibleworks.com).

Library of Congress Cataloging-in-Publication Data
García Bachmann, Mercedes L..
   Women at work in the Deuteronomistic history / by Mercedes L. Garcia Bachmann.
       pages cm. — (International voices in biblical studies / Society of Biblical Literature ; volume 4)
   Includes bibliographical references and indexes.
   ISBN 978-1-58983-755-3 (paper binding : alk. paper) — ISBN 978-1-58983-756-0 (electronic format) — ISBN 978-1-58983-761-4 (hardcover binding : alk. paper)
   1. Women—Employment—Biblical teaching. 2. Women in the Bible. 3. Bible. O.T. Deuteronomy—Criticism, interpretation, etc. I. Title.
   BS1199.W7B33 2013
   221.8'3054—dc22
                                    2013004947

To my family

To my faithful friends,
those close by and those far away

They know what they mean to me.

TABLE OF CONTENTS

ACKNOWLEDGEMENTS

Scholarship is both a very lonely activity and a collective enterprise, as one enters into an ongoing dialogue with colleagues, both living and "printed" ones. The "printed" friends are recorded, to the best of my memory, in the footnotes and bibliography. The people I would like to thank for their help are too many to be included here by name. Thus, only a few names will be publicly acknowledged in these pages.

Going back some years, I am indebted to the Lutheran World Federation and the Evangelical Lutheran Church in America for a scholarship; and to the Lutheran School of Theology at Chicago for their teaching and accompaniment, which turned me into an accredited scholar (1994-1999). I hold fond memories of classmates, teachers, school personnel (especially those at the International Office), and friends who became family outside the school. I have no words to express my gratitude and respect for my advisor, the late Wesley J. Fuerst, for his unfailing support and his generous advice throughout the whole program. In order not to forget any name, at this time I would like to express my thanks to my friends Carolyn Leeb and Mark Bartusch for sending me copies of their own books. My special thanks to my good friends Ahida Pilarki and Alejandro Botta, who always manage to electronically send me any material that may seem important to my work. That is just one way in which their friendship shows.

Three professors who do not belong to LSTC, but who generously gave of their time to guide me, deserve my special thanks. These are the late Prof. Tikva Frymer-Kensky (University of Chicago), Prof. Edward Campbell, Jr. (from McCormick Theological Seminary), and Prof. André LaCocque (Chicago Theological Seminary). Professor Phyllis Bird has mentored me since those days, and I would like to express publicly my debt to her. In particular, chapter 7 of this book owes much to Prof. Bird: not only from publications on prostitution in the Bible, but also for her careful reading of vast portions of chapter 7 (any remaining mistakes are mine alone, however).

It took me more than a decade to come back to my dissertation, resume research and turn it into a book. That would have been impossible without the sabbatical year 2010 granted by my school, the Instituto Universitario ISEDET at Buenos Aires (Argentina), for which I am most grateful.

Part of the time was devoted to refresh my knowledge of German and to get bibliography for this book, and to work with a colleague. No words could adequately convey my gratitude to a good friend of mine, Ms. Renate Murmann, who helped with all types of logistics, organization, contacts, hospitality, and plain friendship during my time in Germany. In terms of the financial support for that project, I am deeply indebted to OKR Johann Schneider (Evangelische Kirche in Deutschland), to OKR Oliver Schuegraf (Vereinigte Evangelisch-Lutherische Kirche Deutschlands) and to Dr. Claudia Jahnel (Mission EineWelt). My special thanks to Ms. S. von Aderkas, Ms. J.-O. Hong, Mr. H. Grünwedel and Ms. A. Müller for their kindness during my stay at Collegium Oecumenicum (Munich). Likewise, Prof. Renate Jost, her assistant Mr. J. Leipziger (and his wife Ms. Binder) from Augustana Hochschule-Neuendettelsau went beyond courtesy during the week that I spent at their premises, invited by MissionEineWelt. The highlight of that Sabbatical was my stay as guest professor at the Catholic theological school of the Westfälische-Wilhelms-Universität in Münster. Prof. Marie-Theres Wacker was much more than my hostess in ways beyond words. Also her assistants Ms. A. Nutt, Ms. S. Feder, Ms. L. Leibold, and Ms. D. Albers took good care of me in several ways, which showed me the best of German hospitality. Thank you very, very much. And a special word of recognition goes to the several libraries staffs for their help in finding my way from my own insights to catalogue cards, and stacks.

I relied on friends related to the oriental institute of the University of Buenos Aires on matters related to Egypt. I thank especially for explanations and bibliography Prof. Alicia Daneri, Ms. Virginia Laporta, and Ms. Graciela Gestoso Singer.

My former student and now colleague Mr. R. Darío Barolin read part of the material and made useful suggestions. My cousin Mr. Javier Elizalde and my friend Mr. Raúl O. Denuncio helped me with that feared ally, my computer. Finally, my colleague at school Ms. María A. Roberto undertook the preparation of the Scriptures index—a task too arcane for me, which she carried on with patience and humor. Thank you again.

My acquaintance with the SBL has developed from a humongous event at the beginning of my graduate studies (when I was still struggling to understand "American English" and find my way with Chicago public transportation) to an association of people as rare as me (biblical theologians are not the most common profession around!), to which I am proud to belong. In this regard, the International Cooperation Initiative ranks first and Prof. Ehud Ben Zvi and his team deserve recognition for carrying it on. Access to the depository of online books has been particularly helpful, not only for this book but for teaching as well.

In terms of completion of this book, some people were instrumental and deserve my utmost gratitude. The first one in chronological order is Prof. Monica Melanchton from India, a good friend who encouraged me to seek the SBL as a publisher for my book. She answered many questions before I dared to bring my manuscript to critique. My warm thanks goes also to Prof. Louis Jonker, general editor with Prof. Melanchton of the *International Voices in Biblical Studies* series of the SBL; and to my colleague and friend, Prof. Néstor Míguez (Latin American regional editor), for having accepted my manuscript. At least two anonymous readers made very helpful suggestions, for which I am indebted (and sorry for the several editorial English mistakes they had to endure). Finally, an extra word of recognition goes to Ms. Leigh Andersen for her copyediting. The work that is now presented would be far less enjoyable were it not for their commitment.

My last word of thanks goes to God for the many opportunities throughout my life to experience joy, communion, and salvation—that same Deity who appears through the life of so many women and men in the Scriptures; and for the many people, whose names do not appear in these pages, who have made and make me feel I would not want my life to be other than it is.

Mercedes L. García Bachmann
February 2, 2013

ABBREVIATIONS

The following abbreviations have been used in addition to those for journal titles and series found in the *SBL Handbook of Style*:

ANE	Ancient Near East
B.C.E.	before the common era
BDB	Brown, Francis, S. R. Driver, and Charles A. Briggs. *A Hebrew and Aramaic Lexicon of the Old Testament*. Oxford: Clarendon Press, 1968.
CD	Codex Hammurabi
Dtr	Deuteronomist/s
DtrH	Deuteronomistic History
ed.	edition
Eng	English
JB	*New Jerusalem Bible*, 1985 [cited 19 February 2013], http://www.catholic.org.
JPS	Jewish Publication Society (Bible translation and commentary)
KB	Koehler, Ludwig, and Walter Baumgartner. *Hebräisches und aramäisches Lexikon zum alten Testament*. 3rd rev. ed. by Walter Baumgartner and Johann J. Stamm. 4 volumes (I. Leiden: Brill, 1967, II. Leiden: Brill, 1974, III. Leiden: Brill, 1983, IV. Leiden, New York, Copenhagen, Köln: Brill, 1990).
LXX	Septuagint
MT	Masoretic Text
NRSV	*New Revised Standard Version* Bible
Rev.	revised

INTRODUCTION:
ON FEMALE LABOR IN THE HEBREW BIBLE

"Non-formal economies" is an expression used in my country to speak of those economic sub-systems not belonging to a recognized business. Because they are too low in the socioeconomic scale to afford paying taxes and because they do not fit into the welfare system, nobody protects the rights of people involved in such economic activities. Countless men, women, and children are unable to succeed in a given socio-economic system, falling into the gaps and—although an active part of their society—becoming expendable in the eyes of many. And being symbolically expendable, their lives are literally spent in brothels, sweatshops, child pornography, prostitution, and other modern enslaving systems, while the world watches impotently or just looks away.[1]

This is not a new phenomenon. The biblical record is filled with "expendables," people who are economically dependent and thus bound to work for others and/or depend on others' good will: foreign slaves, indentured Israelites, daily laborers, artisans, prostitutes, women and children with no man to protect them.[2] Israel's very beginnings are traced back to being expendable in

---

[1] Of course there were and are dissenting or alternative voices. To take one example close to us, liberation theology has been instrumental in reminding the church that God's evaluation of people is not that of the status quo, which deems expendable anyone who does not conform to its game, but, on the contrary, that God chooses those despised by society to carry on God's plan. Only recently has liberation theology started to go beyond general socio-economic and political categories and focus more particularly on the socio-economic, political, and theological consequences of injustice and oppression for women.

[2] The *Oxford Dictionary Online* (n. p. [cited 1 September 2011] Online: http://oxforddictionaries. com/view/entry/m_en_gb0959850#m_en_gb0959850) defines "work" as, 1) "activity involving

1

Egypt and delivered by YHWH. The location of people in genealogies and the distribution of land according to tribes intended to provide Israelites with socio-economic and political protection. It is evident, however, that working one's own land and being free Israelites was the ideal to which they clung, but the writers were also aware that not every family could attain these—not even those families that had enjoyed, for several generations, a privileged position.

HOW DID I COME TO THIS BOOK

My research on female labor is born out of a conflation of concerns, intersecting at the junctures of gender and class; to be more precise, an awareness of the number of biblical stories in which dependent women (also men) perform some task and immediately vanish from the story. There are several examples throughout the narratives. The Pharaoh's daughter and Naaman's assistants (Exod 2; 2 Kgs 5) are just two such instances of dependent women and men, both at a riverside, engaging in actions that will affect their own lives and nations. Like so many narrative characters, what they do is not their everyday task (take an ark from the waters or convince their master to follow Elisha's advice). On the other hand, to be available to their master or mistress and follow orders was certainly in their job description.[3] Since also the Deities commanded and were obeyed by kings and prophets (or so these claimed), following orders does not say much about work in ancient Israel.

Ascription of honor and shame are social instruments, used by the dominant culture to reward those who comply with its criteria and control those who think otherwise. What is honorable is not homogenously accepted, not even within a given culture. There would be several elements of a culture shared by most of its members; others would be less agreed upon, and finally, even those values mostly accepted would be challenged or rejected by certain sub-cultures.[4] The dominant view, evident in the Deuteronomistic History (DtrH) and other biblical writings, ascribes honor to those in good Yahwistic standing (observers of ritual and other religious laws and regulations), ties to prominent families, possession of land, respect for those higher in the hierarchy and, particularly for women,

---

mental or physical effort done in order to achieve a result"; and 2) "work as a means of earning income; employment." The latter is the one adopted here by the word "work."

[3] There are both Israelite and foreign examples and also other, more dramatic, war-related examples, such as Saul's armor-bearer (see 1 Sam 31:4, where the Hebrew term is כלי נשׂא, not עבד) or the female servant who passes information to David during Absalom's revolt (השׁפחה, 2 Sam 17:17).

[4] People who worshipped the Queen of Heaven, for instance, deemed not "YHWH alone" worship in the same way as Jeremiah (or a priest) would—and for them it was also a matter of honor-shame. Other examples are not religious, such as underdogs tricking the powerful and even the Gibeonites tricking the conquering Israelites. Jargon, regional differences, women's defiance of males (Queen Vashti), and several other factors would have challenged the prevailing honor system.

sexual purity, avoidance of males other than their family members, and seclusion.[5]

I found in most scholarly (and popular) descriptions of ancient Israelite women too much uniformity; they looked too much as today's middle class.[6] As I read for my dissertation on women in ancient Israel and these expectations on their "shame," I could think of many situations in which that was just not possible. Would the slave, the courier, or the midwife, to name only a few, have been able to stay "inside" their own domestic, secluded space? Would they have been able to, or allowed to, observe even the taboos related to menstruation?

A model cannot take in every exception or it would no longer be a model. One could, of course, explain this silence by stating that those women would not have been able to keep their shame (shame understood in the preventive sense of guarded sexual behavior) and therefore would be "out of the game." That would certainly be possible in a system in which so much emphasis is set on control of bodies. Yet, even that answer leaves many open questions. Suppose the biblical writers would have answered me by stating there was no positive shame but staying securely inside, protected by their males. Would that be it? Would that be all there is to say in assessing or evaluating each of these women? Could it be possible that the biblical texts would assess those women with other standards than those upheld by what we usually call "honor-shame in the Mediterranean world"?

It is my contention that, together with this dominant view of the male urban elite, there are also sub-cultures of the peasants and other poor who uphold other values, such as working hard, being upright, cooperative with other poor, and shrewd with those in power and, in the case of women, taking as much control of their reproductive capability as possible.[7] This I will try to lay bare to my readers, so that a more nuanced model can be achieved.

---

[5] On virginity see Tikva Frymer-Kensky, "Virginity in the Bible," in *Gender and Law in the Hebrew Bible* (ed. Victor H. Matthews, Bernard M. Levinson & Tikva Frymer-Kensky; Sheffield: Sheffield Academic Press, 1998), 79–96; as an economic asset, see Victor Matthews and Don C. Benjamin, *Social World of Ancient Israel, 1250–587 BCE* (Peabody: Hendrickson, 1993), 176–86; Karen Engelken, *Frauen im Alten Israel: Eine begriffsgeschichtliche und sozialrechtliche Studie zur Stellung der Frau im Alten Testament* (BWANT, 7th series, 10; Stuttgart: Kohlhammer, 1990), 5–16.

[6] Other scholars have also raised their concern on this pairing, perhaps more so in what pertains to the Hebrew Bible and its milieu than to the Greco-Roman world. Susan Brayford, "To Shame or Not to Shame: Sexuality in the Mediterranean Diaspora," *Semeia* 87 (1999): 164, contends that "although honor is almost always an important criterion in assessing the male characters, shame, in its positive sense, is not always a major factor in female characterization. Pentateuchal texts, in particular, do not represent consistently the value accorded to positive female shame in the *Mediterranean* [the *cultural* milieu that most closely corresponds with the values of the dominant Hellenistic culture in the later centuries B.C.E. and early centuries C.E.] model of the honor/shame code."

[7] Previous work with lower-class, hard-working women, mostly coming from the countryside, had taught me how different their shared values were from those of the middle class with which I was

A LONG, LONG ROAD

In the following pages I reproduce the long road travelled in order to arrive at these affirmations, starting with the semantic field of work and continuing with a very sketchy overview of terms for professions/occupations in the Hebrew Bible in general. My intention in offering this panoramic outlook that signaled the beginnings of my research is to explain some of the decisions made along the road and to encourage others to proceed further. It will become evident that there are many more terms and texts than thought at first; on the other hand, they do not yield much information. Far more serious for an academic study, they are scattered along the whole Hebrew Bible, thus belonging to diverse literary genres, times and locations, and theologies. It is not the same to speak of Abraham's slaves as of Nehemiah's "donated ones"; it is not even the same to look at the anti-monarchic context of the perfumers mentioned in 1 Sam 8 or at Esther's (literal) immersion in ointments for the king's contest. Ezekiel's use of "pornoprophetics" does not say the same thing about harlots as a law does. Examples are abundant, but the point is clear. One could simply make some kind of enlarged dictionary entry and enumerate all instances of each term and perhaps even do some short reflection on them. That would be helpful for further work on "work" and is what comes up below.

Finally, this panorama will help one understand my choice of the Deuteronomistic History. I am well aware that the term "DtrH" itself will put some people off. I am not inclined to deal with the historical problems involved in each of these book's composition and transmission, on how many editors there were, and so on. Yet, they are somehow present in some assumptions needed to proceed: Is there a 'DtrH' with a particular theology or is each book to be read on its own? Are there common theological and ideological traits in this block of material? In the particular issue under discussion, there is not much to be gleaned from Deuteronomy in terms of female workers. Mentioned are dependents of different types (slaves in Deut 5:12; 15:12–18; captive wives in Deut 21:10–14; and a mention in passing in the list of curses, Deut 28:68). The only term for a professional is the זונה in a law against using her wages for temple vows (Deut 23:19). Thus, taking Deuteronomy to 2 Kings or Joshua to 2 Kings does not make a weighty difference.[8]

Since I needed a corpus large enough to find female workers within a frame of reference, this was my choice. And it has the added value of depicting various

---

familiar. The fact that they did not adjust to the middle-class model (not to speak of upper-class!) did not mean they did not live, interact, and judge each other and reality by a certain value system not shared by other social classes. I thank them for widening my horizon and my theology.

[8] The DtrH is a composite work produced in the Persian period, in which earlier sources are perceptible to a certain degree. For the sake of convenience, I will refer to "the Dtr" to indicate the post-exilic editors who are, in fact, the authors of the text we have. This is not to deny earlier sources, but in the end, the late editors decided which ones to leave in, which ones to modify, and which ones to erase.

scenarios, from the countryside to the city, from the foundational moment of the settlement/conquest to the exile, from the private home or family to the court; from the heroes and heroines to the worst actions human beings can do to each other.

My interest is also not philological, so I have tried not to get jammed by the terms themselves, although that is where I have started to look for women. Discussion of harlots will make this tension especially evident, as in the last years several scholars have contested this traditional meaning of the participle זונה. Since my study is the worker and not the term, I selected those instances of the term that seemed to apply to such a study.

A SHORT GUIDE TO THIS ROAD: THE BOOK'S ORGANIZATION

The noted Assyriologist Ignace Gelb begins his article by saying, "The term 'slave' can be discussed, but not defined."[9] Definitions of slavery and of several other social categories are tied to methodological and conceptual problems, which are discussed below. To ideological positions and differences in training among modern scholars one has to add the fact that the sources themselves use the same words (אמה, שפחה, and עבד) to refer to several different types of legal conditions of people. I have tended to translate them with the term "slave," although sometimes a difference with the "indentured servant/slave," the one under temporary debt-slavery, is made. That biblical Hebrew does not make this difference (as far as we know) should be kept in mind, for it would thus save us from some missteps and it would remind us that their social and legal perception of their contemporaries is, at best, different from ours. Since indentured slaves were from the same society as their creditors and were meant to work only for some years, they held some rights, particularly if society foresaw that after the period of servitude they would again be fellow Israelites in good standing. So, in theory at least this social difference cannot be philologically perceived.

"Dependent" is used here to generally describe a person who is under the authority of another in economic terms; a person who is economically or socially dependent on another and thus not his/her own master. Dependency does not have to do with the legal aspect (free, hired, or enslaved person), but with the relation between the one who offers the service and the one who pays for it, be that a person or an institution, and whatever type of payment is implied. Dependent is used to translate נערה (or נער), when in service in a household other than her own, because her status is not clear in the text, while her economic and social dependency are.

Chapter 1 lays bare the main assumptions and choices made in this study in terms of the body of research, methodology, and the lens through which I read.

---

[9] Ignace Gelb, "Definition and Discussion of Slavery and Serfdom," *UF* 11 (1979): 283. His description is more fully quoted in chapter 3.

In the second chapter, I acknowledge the enormous debt I have to many scholars, especially in those areas less recognized in the footnotes. Chapter 3 looks at the conditions under which women labored in ancient Israel; conditions generally shared with their sister neighbors from Egypt and the Levant and condensed in terms such as "peasantry," "agrarian society," and "slave" or "unfree." In chapters 4–7, I discuss the different clusters of terms. Here I look first at the non-specific field of slavery, servant hood, and dependency, where the terms just mentioned in the paragraph above appear. Then I discuss the Deuteronomist's world of workers, organized into those ignored and those acknowledged. Finally, the last chapter offers some concluding reflections.

Having come to the end of this book, I am still convinced the subject matter is worth further research and discussion, and I hope in the coming years more will be done in this area. I recognize the difficulties in following the material across several sections, yet it is the best that I found between an over-generalization that would say nothing and an over-concentration on one term or one biblical book. Indeed, even taking such a large body of material, one needs to go to other texts, biblical and extra-biblical, in order to glean some insights. That makes it look disorderly, but hopefully also interesting.

THE SEMANTIC FIELD OF "WORK"

With an ancient body of literature in which the female segment of society is often included in masculine terms, the extremely common verb עבד, "work," "toil," "serve" would be the first choice in a research on work. Apart from the fact that it does not differentiate between the more general connotations of "do, make" (including service to a Deity) and the more particular one of "work (for wages)", there is no feminine noun or verbal form from עבד.

Psalm 104:23 uses in parallel the nouns עבודה and פעל. The subject is the generic אדם, thus *NRSV*'s "people": "People go out to their work and to their labor until the evening." Who are these "people"? Are women included? Presumably, although the only appearance of this noun with a feminine suffix, happens in a prophetic utterance in Jer 50:29, where the term כפעלה refers to Babylon.

As a verb, פעל appears pursed in first person singular in a woman's mouth, only in Prov 30:20: "This is the way of an adulteress: she eats, and wipes her mouth, and says, 'I have done no wrong.'" This proverb does not refer to work and therefore, adds nothing to the semantic field under survey.[10] The noun appears in Ruth 2:12 with a second feminine singular suffix. Although the context of the conversation is one in which Ruth is clearly attempting to bring home an income, in Boaz's praise of Ruth, the noun seems to refer in a more

---

[10] Contrast with the only other instance of the same verbal form, פעלתי, in Job's prayer in 34:32.

general sense to all her actions in favor of her mother-in-law and not just to her work at Boaz's field.

There is yet another verb שרת, "to minister," less frequent than עבד, and it also has a cultic and a secular connotation.[11] It is used, for example, of Joseph, Joshua, Elisha, Aaron, and priests, and Samuel ministering at the sanctuary. In its denotation of secular service it is applied to only one woman, Abishag the Shunammite (1 Kgs 1:4, 15); in its religious sense, it is not explicitly applied to any woman.[12]

This short survey alerts us already that there is much to disentangle before we can have a fairly complete view of such an important item in life as work. Thus, words usually translated "slave," "maidservant," "girl," or the like (אמה, שפחה, and נערה) are the next choice in looking at women subject to someone's authority, working for others. These terms cover a wide range of people, some of whom were economically bound but legally free. This raises the additional problem of establishing appropriate categories in translating terms to another language and culture and where ancient Israel's social categories are largely unknown to us.[13]

"SLAVE OR FREE?" IS NOT ENOUGH

I started from the assumption that עבד is parallel to אמה and שפחה, and נער is parallel to נערה. In the case of אמה and שפחה, this correspondence is not morphologically evident. And, as it will be discussed below (chapter 4), we do not even know whether and how these two terms differed from each other; both appear in parallel to the masculine עבד.[14] Thus, reasons to assume that these terms serve as descriptors of "women in situations of social, economic and legal dependency," serving in multiple capacities (often including bearing children from their masters) come from the texts themselves, centuries-long translations of these terms in the Bible, and modern research.[15] Just as with עבד, the legal status of these women is uncertain.

---

[11] In its non-cultic use it is said of eunuchs in Esth 1:10 and of the king's commanders in 1 Chr 27:1, to take only some examples.

[12] KB IV. 1532–33.

[13] Students of "slavery" in antiquity in the ANE and the Greco-Roman world disagree even on whether these were slave societies or not. Since each definition is disregarded by other scholars, and there are more exceptions to any rule than one would want to see, the reader will soon realize that any term has to be used very loosely. See chapter 1 for methodological issues and definitions used here; previous scholarship in chapter 2; and description of peasantry, slavery, and indentured work in the ANE and the Greco-Roman world in chapter 3.

[14] For example, both versions of the Decalogue enumerate עבד with אמה among those belonging to the household; and Gen 12:16 and other texts record עבדים ושפחת side by side as possessions.

[15] Phyllis A. Bird, review of Karen Engelken, *Frauen im Alten Israel, JBL* 112 (1993): 320, quoting Engelken.

This reinforces the realization that any definition will always have sufficient exceptions to question its validity, and that looking at female labor in the Bible requires much more than looking at terms for "slave." It also requires imagination and the courage to cut clean at some points. It is not mine to say whether I hit the mark. What I can say is that this is a vast field in which there is much to be done and also much we will probably never be able to know.

Women other than those called שפחה ,אמה, and ערה also worked in the ANE. I have found in the Hebrew Bible about twenty-five feminine nouns or participles denoting what we would call professions or occupations (see Charts IV to IX).[16] Many of these occupations are also attested for men, with no explicit criteria about division of labor across gender, age or status lines. Other terms are only mentioned in feminine; and still other, masculine (mostly plural) terms, could in theory include women as well. These terms attest to the variety of tasks women assumed, besides their daily household chores. And one may also imagine there were many others not attested in the sources available to us.

In her analysis on sex and gender in ancient Mesopotamia, Julia Asher-Greve contends that social stratification was ascribed by "rank, status, profession, occupation, etc." The "second sex" comprised five categories, ranging from "family women" to "[p]rostitutes, tavern keepers, seductresses, witches and magicians, foreign women [whose s]ocial status depends on occupation, behavior or circumstances."[17] In the Hebrew Bible one finds mentioned, among others, female slaves, bakers, cooks, harlots, perfumers, child-care providers, messengers, and women who are said to draw water for herds, spin and weave, wail and sing. Masters also had a wide range of women at their disposal for sexual service: the so-called "concubines" (secondary wives?), captive brides, slaves, and "loose" women. Their dependency determines their inclusion among lower-class people—their dependency being not only legal but, more importantly, socio-economic, as those women provided sexual and reproductive services besides other, regular household tasks. In other words, except perhaps for the very rich families, everyone worked, from the *paterfamilias* to the least of the slaves. Would every dependent woman be expected also to produce offspring for the household and perhaps pleasure for the master, if thus required?[18] It is hard to give a definite answer; probably—as

---

[16] I do not claim to have been thorough; there was no list available to me (except for the list on professions recorded in the Ras Shamra publications) and it is fairly easy to overlook some text or term. To these difficulties one must add that the number also varies according to criteria adopted in reference to *hapax legomena*, relational terms (like the "concubine") and other dubious cases.

[17] Julia M. Asher-Greve, "Decisive Sex, Essential Gender," in *Sex and Gender in the Ancient Near East: Proceedings of the 47th Rencontre Assyriologique Internationale, Helsinki, July 2–6, 2001* (ed. Simo Parpola and R. M. Whiting; Helsinki: Neo-Assyrian Text Corpus Project, Institute for Asian and African Studies, University of Helsinki, 2002), 16. Seductresses and foreign women are not exactly professions (or, perhaps, seductresses were, but how to find them?), so they are left out.

[18] In the laws on forbidden sexual relations in Lev 18 there is no prohibition of a master-slave relation, which might indicate that they were not considered close kin. Tikva Frymer-Kensky, "The

is the case also today—there were all kinds of masters, mistresses, and situations.

Women appear working for their own households and at other peoples' households, both for private ones (especially in Genesis) and for the great institutions; but most of the time they are only very generally located.[19] The running of a household depended on its particular characteristics (how many nuclear families and single people it included, whether it was urban or rural, how close to a well or to a valley it was, whether it had flocks or not, whether there were many elderly or children, and so forth). According to its size and to its owner's means, it could count a large or a small number of slaves, foreigners, and other dependents, who attached themselves to the household in exchange for basic needs. Other services were supplied by exchange or hiring, such as midwifery, wet nursing, gleaning, pottery, perhaps shepherding and sheep-shearing.

THE POLITICAL, THE RELIGIOUS, AND THE SERVICE REALMS

From all terms for female labor mentioned in DtrH, this study deals only with those serving household needs, as opposed to religious and political occupations, which have a different setting.

> While there is sufficient documentary evidence with which to reconstruct the composition of the state households of Mesopotamia, there is very little evidence with which to reconstruct the composition of the temple and palace households of the united and divided kingdoms of Israel, although archaeological finds and various biblical accounts do give some indication of the various administrative offices created by David and Solomon and the extent and composition of their palace economies.[20]

While many of the women to be studied are related to the palace household, they do not serve a political position, much less an office. Religious and political

---

Family in the Hebrew Bible," in *Religion, Feminism, and the Family* (ed. A. Carr & M. Stewart Van Leewven; Louisville: Westminster John Knox, 1996), 64 has noted, however, that they also miss the father-daughter incest prohibition.

[19] Sophie Kauz, "Frauenräume im Alten Testament am Beispiel der Siedlung," *lectio difficilior* (2/2009), n. p. [cited: 28 August 2011]. Online: http://www.lectio.unibe .ch/09_2/pdf/kauz_ frauenraeume.pdf, studies the different locations of women both in nature and in enclosed areas.

[20] Gregory Chirichigno, *Debt-Slavery in Israel and the Ancient Near East* (JSOTSup 141; Sheffield: JSOT Press, 1993), 113. See also Ignace Gelb, "Quantitative Evaluation of Slavery and Serfdom," in *Kramer Anniversary Volume: Cuneiform Studies in Honor of Samuel Noah Kramer* (ed. B. Eichler, with the assistance of J. Heimerdinger and Å. Sjöberg. AOAT 25. Kavalaer: Butzon & Bercker, 1976), 195 on Babylonia: "Our information about the composition of households is best for the temple households, in terms of both quantity and quality. Less known are the crown, or state, or royal households, while our information about private households of individuals is quite limited."

occupations also serve the community, but at more particular times and ways, such as singing or wailing for family occasions, consulting spirits, prophesying, and negotiating political decisions as a prophetess or a wise woman. A queen might have had political weight (Athaliah or Jezebel come to mind), but in the biblical texts the title מלכה is conferred only upon a foreign queen—the Queen of Sheba—or upon a Jewish woman in a foreign court (Esther).[21] A second title, גבירה, Lady or Queen-mother, was conferred upon very few women in the Bible, and at least one of them was later deprived of it, because of alleged affiliations to Asherah (1 Kgs 15:13 = 2 Chr 15:16).[22]

The שפטה "judge" (Judg 4:4) and the אשה חכמה "wise woman" are related to offices of justice, law, and political mediation, אשה חכמה is used in the Hebrew Bible for two types of women, the recognized and honored political leader of her community, who uses her intelligence, speech, and ability in political matters (2 Sam 14; 20; cf. Judg 5:29), and the skilled craftswoman (Jer 9:16 [following Hebrew verse numbers], Exod 35:25).[23]

Some prophetesses (singular נביאה) are recognized as community leaders at different points in Israel's life. Their role seems to have been political as well as religious, like those of male counterparts.[24] Besides those individualized by name, 2 Kings mentions the prophetic communities, literally "the sons of the prophets" (2 Kgs 2:3–15; 4:1; 6:1, see further, chapter 7) and Ezekiel derides "those (women) who prophesy" (13:17).[25] Even without answers it is worthwhile wondering in what ways women were part of the particular

---

[21] Athalya Brenner, *The Israelite Woman: Social Role and Literary Type in Biblical Narrative* (Sheffield: JSOT Press, 1985), 17. A. Leo Oppenheim, *Ancient Mesopotamia* (rev. ed. comp. by E. Reiner; Chicago: University of Chicago Press, 1966, 1977), 104, states "As for the king and his family, one should note first that the term 'queen' was only applied to goddesses and those women—in fact, only the queens of the Arabs—who served as rulers. The chief wife (called with deferential circumlocution 'she-of-the-palace') and the royal concubines lived, at least at the Assyrian court, in a harem guarded by eunuchs."

[22] Brenner, *Israelite Woman*, 17. Recognized as גבירות are Jezebel (2 Kgs 10:13), Maakah (1 Kgs 15:13), King Jehoiachin's mother (2 Kgs 24:15), and an unnamed wife of an unnamed Pharaoh, Tahpenes (1 Kgs 11:19–20). Tahpenes is usually taken to be her personal name. Cf. K. Kitchen, "Egypt and Israel During the First Millennium B.C.," in *Congress Volume, Jerusalem*, (ed. J. Emerton; VTSup 40; Leiden: Brill, 1986), 109: "the best and simplest interpretation is to take it [*taḥpenes*] as for *Tah(emt)panis(u)*, 'the Wife of the King', i.e. 'queen' in Egyptian." Finally, another term translated "(queen-)consort" in Ps 45:10, Neh 2:6, and perhaps in Judg 5:30 is שגל. Its Aramaic cognate appears in Dan 5:2–3:23. Nowhere are these women given a name or a more detailed location. For references to סגל, M. Garsiel, "Puns upon Names as a Literary Device in 1 Kings 1–2," *Bib* 72 (1991): 382; Brenner, *Israelite Woman*, 19 (although there is a mistake in her quotation).

[23] Brenner, *Israelite Woman*, 33–45. Robert Gordon, "A House Divided," in *Wisdom in Ancient Israel: Essays in Honour of J. A. Emerton* (ed. J. Day, R. Gordon & H. Williamson; Cambridge: Cambridge University Press, 1995), 97.

[24] *KB*, II.662. Exod 15:20, Judg 4:4, 2 Kgs 22:14, 2 Chr 34:22, Isa 8:3, Neh 6:14.

[25] Wilda Gafney, *Daughters of Miriam: Women Prophets in Ancient Israel* (Minneapolis: Fortress, 2008), 107–9.

communities to which their male relatives belonged, and how much and what kind of participation they had in them.[26]

Women in some function variously translated as "mediums" or "necromancers" אבות in parallel to ידענים (usually translated "wizards," but the stem is ידע "to know") appear in a few texts, all very polemical against idolatry.[27] Since the texts are clearly against their existence one cannot know much about their occupation, but the very need of repeated religious reforms to rid the land from them attests to their popularity. The first of these terms appears also in 1 Sam 28:7 "a woman of mastery in divination," אשת בעלת־אוב, a medium, someone to speak to Samuel's spirit on behalf of Saul. Judging from this particular narrative, economically such women were not at the lowest echelons of society, even though banned by the king.[28]

Still in the realm of religious practices, one finds "devotees," both male and female, mentioned as a pair or alone, in narratives and in laws. The feminine term/s, קדשה/ות, are usually translated "hierodule/s" or, worse, "sacred prostitute/s" in secondary literature.[29] Their social status is obscure; however, representing non-orthodox religious practice, and being women with no apparent male in charge of them, they must have endured a strong pressure to conform to the system, at least at some periods—if we may believe the narrator on that. On the other hand, the very fierceness of Dtr's crusade against them speaks of their

---

[26] See F. Charles Fensham, "The Son of the Handmaid in North West Semitic," *VT* 19 (1969): 312–22; B. Cutler and J. Macdonald, "The Unique Ugaritic Text UT 113 and the Question of 'Guilds,'" *UF* 9 (1977): 13–30, T. Yamashita, "Professions," in *The Ras Shamra Parallels* (ed. L. Fisher, D. Smith & S. Rummel; AnOr 50; Rome: Pontificium Institutum Biblicum, 1975), 2.41–68.

[27] The meaning of אוב is uncertain. The other stem is traced by *BDB*, 396 to ידע, hence "familiar spirit (prop. either as *knowing, wise* (acquainted with secrets of unseen world), or as *intimate acquaintance* of soothsayer)—*familiar spirit* ...)." See Lev 19:31, 20:6; 1 Sam 28:3, 9; 2 Kgs 23:24, Isa 8:19,19:3.

[28] After having sought Samuel's spirit and receiving an announcement of doom, Saul is devastated; this unnamed woman prepares a fattened calf she owned, a sign that she was not among the poorest. See Pamela Tamarkin Reis, "Eating The Blood: Saul and The Witch of Endor," *JSOT* 73 (1997): 3–23 who contends the meal she prepares is not "motherly protectiveness" toward an appalled king to be killed, but a sacrifice for self-preservation. Be it as it may, she is rich enough to offer a calf.

[29] "Sacred Prostitute" has become a widely accepted designation for the קדשה, despite the lack of evidence for such a concept and the growing research against it. See Ch. Virolleaud, "Les Villes et les Corporations du Royaume d'Ugarit," *Syria* 21 (1940): 151: "*qdšm* XI 73; XII 1; XIII 1 (?), 'les saints'; voir *Syria*, XVIII, 164, 1.2 où les *qdšm* sont nommés après les *khnm*, comme dans RŠ 8208 (*Syria*, XVIII, 166, 1.2) et ici même: no. XII 72–73;" Phyllis A. Bird, "The End of the Male Cult Prostitute: A Literary-Historical and Sociological Analysis of Hebrew *qādēš-qĕdēšîm*," in *Congress Volume, Cambridge, 1995* (ed. John Emerton; VTSup. 66; Leiden: Brill, 1997), 37–80; Athalya Brenner, *The Intercourse of Knowledge* (Leiden: Brill, 1997), 148–9; Renate Jost, "Hure/Hurerei (AT)," *WiBiLex* 2011, n.p. [cited 3 June 2011]. Online:www.wibilex.de/stichwort/Hure/.

popularity in Israel, where the קדשים and the women weaving for Asherah are found even at the temple precincts![30]

Particular occasions in the life of Israel were accompanied by music, dancing and singing, as Deborah and Barak do (Judg 5:1, ותשר, *qal* imperfect feminine singular of שיר, for Deborah and Barak) and Miriam (and Moses) had done as well (Exod 15). Other notable pieces of the Hebrew Bible are presented as songs, from the Great Song (or Song of Songs) to Isa 5. People also performed for entertainment (David for Saul, for example, מנגן, 1 Sam 16:14–23). Women probably sang to their children or among themselves and—according to parallels taken up by anthropologists—they were mistresses in the art of humorous and ironic public performing, as a few hints throughout the Bible indicate.[31] Particular occasions, such as victorious return from war (הנשים המשחקות, 1 Sam 18:7) were also celebrated by organized groups of women. Judges 11 recounts the origins of a yearly ritual performed by (young) women in memory of Jephthah's daughter. There was also a different type of singer, the מקוננות, "wailing women" (Jer 9:16), a profession which implies the creation of the *qînâ* as much as its performance. In DtrH, only David is credited with this creative act, intoning a lamentation for Saul and for Jonathan, which he orders to be taught to the people (2 Sam 1:17–27), and another lamentation for Abner (2 Sam 3:33).[32] Would these performances have been "secular"? I am thinking, for example, of the dancing women abducted during their celebration in the vineyards (Judg 21:21) or, at Saul's and David's victorious homecoming from their battle against the Philistines, when הנשים מכל־ערי ישראל "the women from all the towns of Israel came out to sing ..." (1 Sam 18:6).[33]

---

[30] The masculine singular appears in Deut 23:18; 1 Kgs 14:24, 22:47; plural in 15:12; 2 Kgs 23:7; Job 36:14; feminine singular: Deut 23:18; Gen 38:21–22; plural in Hos 4:14; most of these texts are in polemics against idolatry, in texts associated with the Dtr.

[31] As Brenner points out in *Israelite Woman*, 46, women sang and told stories to their children at bedtime from time immemorial, and even if their stories were not recorded, they may very well have also told them in settings more public than their children's bedside. F. Van Dijk-Hemmes, "Traces of Women's Texts in the Hebrew Bible," in *On Gendering Texts: Female and Male Voices in the Hebrew Bible* (ed. A. Brenner & F. Van Dijk-Hemmes; BIS; Leiden: Brill, 1993), 32–43 (victory songs), 43–48 (mocking songs).

[32] Female musicians are further discussed in chapter 5.

[33] Since there was no such a sharp distinction between the "secular" and "religious" realms, I decided to include singers in my analysis. I have done otherwise with the secondary wives or "concubines," many of whom are either related to the patriarchs or are located in Saul's or David's court. The decisive question is whether the lexeme belongs to the semantic field of family or to work. Traditionally, the term פילגש has been translated "concubine" and understood to be a slave who bore children to the master. Recent scholarship has promoted her. Naomi Steinberg, "Social Scientific Criticism: Judges 9 and Issues of Kinship," in *Judges and Method* (ed. Gale Yee; Minneapolis: Fortress, 1995), 51 stresses the economic independence of a marriage involving a פילגש: "a concubine was a woman whose continued presence within the family was not dependent upon economic arrangements. Typically, a concubine was a secondary wife, whose involvement with the husband represented a secondary union, both in terms of being an additional wife and of having a lower status than the legal wife." A final example is that of Andrew Hill's proposal, "On

Although often unrecognized, proximity of women to blood, birth, sickness, and death makes it very likely that the same women who helped as midwives were also healers and advisors, prepared the dead for burial, and perhaps even directed the burial rites, especially since corpses were polluting.[34]

In her study on women in ancient Greece, Sarah Pomeroy gives additional reasons for woman's involvement with mourning.

> Women's association with rituals concerning the dead is still customary in Greece. Women have always been freer than men to indulge in displays of emotion, and are therefore more impressive participants at funerals. The washing and dressing of the corpse has certain analogies to the caring for infants; the cycle of life takes us from the care of women and returns us to the care of women.
> As a realistic consideration, kinswomen had the most cause to be deeply grieved at the death of their male relatives, for the lives of women lacking the protection of men were truly pitiful.[35]

Whether more emotional, more unprotected by the social system, more flexible to perform in different circumstances, or more barred from the official ritual practices—for whatever reason, women seem to have occupied this niche throughout cultures and times, being needed, respected and also feared and suspected. What we call in general "sorcerers" (health practitioners and religious specialists) belonged probably to every social stratum and served those around them: examples range from King Saul seeking a medium he himself had banned to Rebekah seeking an oracle to understand what was going on in her womb.

Societies are neither static nor internally compartmentalized and, even though our written sources reflect a particular moment of their flow, there must be room for exceptions, for the unknown and also for overlapping categories. To this we must add that we are dealing with religious material, even when looking at mundane issues. To try to classify some of these events into "cultic" and "secular" is to beg the question. Yet, it is a titanic enterprise to deal with every single instance and, my focus being on lower-class women (as far as we can identify them), some of them had to be left out. Here again, categories are porous and a good case could be made for the opposite decision than the one I

David's 'Taking' and 'Leaving' Concubines (2 Samuel 5:13; 15:16)," *JBL* 125 (2006): 129–50, who explores the evidence for these royal concubines to have been local, Jebusite princesses, who could not leave the state during Absalom's revolt and cross the river with David.

[34] Susan Starr Sered, *Women as Ritual Experts* (New York: Oxford University Press, 1992) on religious practices by elderly women among Orthodox Jews today; K. van der Toorn, *From Her Cradle to Her Grave* (Sheffield: JSOT Press, 1994), 138–40; see also his remarks about official and popular religion, 141–45.

[35] Sarah Pomeroy, *Goddesses, Whores, Wives, and Slaves* (20th anniversary ed. New York: Schocken, 1995), 44.

have made, be it to leave in or out a certain category. We are making informed guesses, I am painfully aware ... and sometimes not even that informed!

SUMMING UP

This review only shows that women worked in several occupations; it does not show which of these women were free and which ones were bound, and although a more detailed study will give some clues, there are texts which do not allow for a decision for one or the other possibility. Even if we could decide on the matter, their situation varied as to degree of self-determination, political and social climate, and other factors. In any case, all women belonging to a household were subject to a male authority. All found themselves restricted in their exercise of authority, from the king's wife to the widow.[36] There were also "loose women," women unattached to a patriarchal household, about whom much is still controversial.

The particular characteristics of extra-biblical primary sources from the ANE[37] and the ideological focus of the Dtr make even more formidable the challenge of drawing a model that considers lower-class women.[38] Yet, since in pre-industrial societies there is no division between private life and state affairs, many political events are located in the palace household, and family affairs invite a political reading.[39] Behind Dtr's reflection on history there is a large host of support staff, especially in the court, who carry out many required and expected tasks, among them, harvesting and gleaning, grinding and cooking, fetching water and preparing baths, spinning and weaving, healing the sick and washing the dirty, consulting with spirits and preventing the evil omens from affecting their beloved ones, recording events, burying the dead and keeping

---

[36] I mean it literally. See Tamar under Judah's authority (Gen 38) or Tamar, the daughter of David, who remained secluded after being raped. We do not have biblical examples of beggars, but they would have been even more severely restricted by those above them. I also mean this affirmation symbolically: the texts themselves restrict women's authority and power by several means: ideological diminishing, erasure of their deeds or their names, exemplifying them as evil or disobedient.

[37] Biblical and extra-biblical sources on female labor and socio-economic structures in the ANE are discussed in chapter 3. Main methodological problems in this area are the use of material from one society to explain another (i.e., to what extent were societies in the ANE similar to each other?), and the lack of parallel material for comparison (there are no contracts from Israel, no narratives from Mesopotamia).

[38] Chapters 4–6 look at every pertinent text within the DtrH, and contrast them with other pertinent material. Dtr's focus is on the fall of the monarchy because of royal disobedience to YHWH. The poor and dependents do not score high in his attention, although they are not despised either. They just don't matter. See further my concluding chapter.

[39] Gerhard Lenski and Jean Lenski, *Human Societies* (New York: McGraw-Hill, 1974), 228, explain "the proprietary theory of the state." This theory shows how preindustrial societies ignore a separation of state and private affairs on the part of the ruler, thus explaining the use of economic surplus as it pleases him/her, often for enjoyment by those close to the ruler (especially family).

their memory alive. These people are taken for granted rather than recognized, because the writers' interests lie elsewhere, and because the elite class was accustomed to being served. These mostly anonymous women (there were, of course, many men in similar situations) who worked for others, who are sometimes mentioned only in one verse, and who have gone unrecognized in DtrH and in modern scholarship, despite their contribution to the socio-economic system (and as secondary characters to narratives): these women constitute our focus.

At a time when society starts to recognize that women carry a heavier economic and social burden than men do, that women do not share equally in decision making, and that women are all too often subject to violence and humiliation, theology is called to take up those it has so far forgotten, and to enlarge the picture of what service and faithfulness mean. Perhaps then there will be no more "little women."[40]

---

[40] That was part of the title of my dissertation, taken from Louisa M. Alcott's famous novel ("'Little Women': Female Labor in the Deuteronomistic History" [Ph.D. diss., The Lutheran School of Theology at Chicago, 1999]).

CHAPTER 1

THE CHALLENGE OF STUDYING
WORKING WOMEN

This work is an exegetical study from a liberation feminist perspective. It is "exegetical" in its broadest and primary sense of bringing out what the text offers (at least, something of it), starting with translation. I have been taught since my first classes in seminary that even YHWH makes options. Why should I not, then? Exegetical work goes beyond the traditional historico-critical methods into a feminist hermeneutic. "Feminist" evokes differing feelings and is variously defined and it thus requires further explanation.

> According to its self-understanding, feminist exegesis of the Christian Bible of the First and New Testaments situates itself where exegesis and feminism intersect. Biblical exegesis here means the historical and literary, scholarly interpretation of the Bible within the overall framework of Christian theology. ... "Feminism" here refers to the determined movement in recent times of women seeking to come free from the judicial and economic predominance of "fathers" and also from the psychic and ideological tutelage of men.[1]

---

[1] Marie-Theres Wacker, "Historical, Hermeneutical, and Methodological Foundations," in *Feminist Interpretation: The Bible in Women's Perspective* (ed. Louise Schottroff, Silvia Schroer, and Marie-Theres Wacker; Minneapolis: Fortress, 1998), 36. What is new about it is the consciousness by the scholar about his or her location; it has always been present and it has always determined people's perspective, but it had not been recognized. See Frank Crüsemann, *Der Widerstand gegen das Königtum: die anti-königliche Texte des Alten Testament und der Kampf um den frühen*

This definition stresses feminism as a movement, allowing it to grow or decrease with flexible boundaries. It is also useful because it looks at this movement as addressing, among others, economic and ideological boundaries. For the present study this means that a feminist standpoint not only prioritizes women as the focus of attention, but also as the hermeneutical principle by which secondary literature is also appropriated. This is the first characteristic of this study.

A second characteristic is that it focuses on a segment of ancient society not easily identifiable, namely, female laborers. And, among these, women who are found in menial occupations in households that are not their own, in service-type work, and women who produced at home to increase their means. Many of them were slaves; others were free Israelites from the lower economic echelons of society working as dependents. In order to try to disentangle how workers are perceived in the Bible, at the intersection of exegetical and feminist studies there is the need to also add to the picture the socio-historical approach, which is thus defined by Wacker.

> First, the approach implies the abandonment of writing history centered around great names or the winners in favor of a historiography of everyday life, of the "little people." Second, it submits to scrutiny exegesis that turns a blind eye toward power, thereby affirming power and, concomitantly, the existential appropriation of Scripture rooted in the advocacy of a purely individualistic piety. Instead, the social-historical approach recalls the political dimensions of faith that cannot forego the analysis of power in church and society. Third, and related to the two preceding points, the approach implies critical reflection on the social location of one's own interpretation. These three aspects offer the prospect of taking up the social-historical interpretation of Scripture as a liberation-theological exegesis and of recommending it from a feminist point of view.[2]

The social-historical and the feminist approaches to the biblical witness are the backbone of this study.[3] In order to determine what it meant to belong to female labor in Israel, one has to examine the socio-economic organization of the ANE, including questions about who were free people and who were not; whether different groups were treated differently in different aspects of life

---

israelitischen Staat (WMANT 49; Neukirchen-Vluyn: Neukirchener Verlag, 1978), 4–9, especially 6, n. 40–41.

[2] Wacker, "Historical, Hermeneutical, and Methodological Foundations," 77. One should note that feminist scholars have not, so far, developed new methodologies, but they have appropriated existing ones, and used one or combined some of them, according to the questions they seek to answer.

[3] German-speaking scholarship uses the terms "social-historical approach." This is not a problem, provided that in the social analysis one does consider the economic factor. Since here the expression "socio-economic conditions" is often mentioned, the two expressions should be seen as synonymous.

(legally, economically, socially); how this affected women's lives; and what determined someone's social location.

THE BODY OF RESEARCH

The Introduction mentioned briefly some of the major problems regarding the body of research chosen, namely, the lack of information in the Hebrew Bible about women in general and the social location of lower-class women in particular; the need to pick pieces of information here and there and still have an incomplete picture on the ANE; and the lack of corresponding Western concepts for those in the ANE. We immerse ourselves now in some of these complexities.

LIMITATIONS IMPOSED BY THE SOURCES

Although women are found in the Bible working in a variety of occupations, terms denoting socio-economic dependency are scattered throughout it, some of them with a predominance in certain books or in material attributed to early sources. Scholars have delved into the semantic fields of poverty and social classes, but there remains much to be discovered. With regard to the semantic field of female labor, a pattern of occurrence of אמה in the E material and שפחה in the J material of the Pentateuch has long been recognized. Recently Leeb showed that נער and נערה appear only in the oldest traditions.

> With two arguable exceptions, the appearances in the Tetrateuch (נער 31 times, נערה 9 times), all come from material which is "non-P". The words are not found in Leviticus at all. Within the Former Prophets (נער 142 times, נערה 14 times), the words occur exclusively in material drawn from Dtr's sources rather than from apparent expansions and insertions by the editor(s) themselves. ... The pattern of distribution leads to the conclusion that these words were used by the earliest "tellers of tales" rather than by compilers and editors.[4]

These studies, touching more or less explicitly into the vexing issue of sources and transmission of traditions, are helpful in that they help explain variation within a concept or between concepts, yet they do not allow much insight into what they meant. Neither the Priestly redactors nor the Deuteronomists or the Chroniclers were ethnographers; their interests lie in reading historical events from the past to understand their theological present

---

[4] Carolyn Leeb, *Away from the Father's House: The Social Location of na ʿar and na ʿarah in Ancient Israel* (Sheffield: Sheffield Academic Press, 2000), 20. I take the chance to express my thanks to her for sending me a copy of her book.

and to prescribe behavior. The many women and men who supported the system with their labor are taken for granted, not brought to the center of the scene. Certain terms proved to be particularly evasive, partly due to lack of a detailed context against which to understand the concept involved, and partly due to the fact that women in occupations pertaining to the household usually appear out of the expected context, that is to say, out of the context where a certain task is expected to be carried. The סכנת is a good example (1 Kgs 1:1–4). Her designation as personal assistant is inferred from her service to David, while the dialogue that eventuates in her selection makes clear that what David's men were looking for was a virgin to sleep with him, keep him warm and prove or disprove his potency.[5]

Two other challenges merit mention. One is the lack of an answer to the question of the relation between designations for bonded and dependent people (אמה, שפחה, and נערה) and designations for particular occupations. The question arises because there is hardly any overlapping between these two semantic fields.[6]

WHERE DO DESIGNATIONS FOR BONDED WOMEN AND FOR OCCUPATIONS INTERSECT?

One could think that unfree women, when referred to according to their legal status, would be אמה, שפחה, and נערה and would otherwise be working as midwives, prostitutes, or singers. This reconstruction would find support in studies on slavery in other societies. In Greece, for example,

> [w]ith little exception, there was no activity, productive or unproductive, public or private, pleasant or unpleasant, which was not performed by slaves at some times and in some places in the Greek world. The major exception was, of course, political: no slave held public office ... (though slaves were commonly employed in the "civil service," as secretaries and clerks, and as policemen and prison attendants).[7]

Palace archives from Nuzi, to take one more example, also make reference to several occupations performed by people who received rations in exchange for their work. The following professions, mostly attested for men, are recorded in the Nuzian archives.

---

[5] Leeb, *Away from the Father's House*, 126–28, demonstrates how it is characteristic of the נער and נערה to be at the threshold, in and out, but mostly doing nothing. This insight applies also to other characters, as just stated about the סכנת.

[6] The only exceptions are some women whose status shifts between אמה and פילגש, such as, the unnamed woman in Judg 19 and the patriarchs' "secondary" women.

[7] Moses Finley, "Was Greek Civilization Based on Slave Labour?" *Historia* 8 (1959): 147.

The archives [of the royal descendent Šilwa-Tešup] contain large lists of personnel who received rations of barley, cloth, or oil. Some plowmen who till the fields are mentioned, but most of the personnel were either those performing personal services for the households or textile workers, of which many were female....

In the Palace Archives, in addition to higher administrative officials, a wide variety of professions is attested [Mayer 1978]: scribes, cultic personnel, male and female singers (usually coming from Aššur and Ḫanigalbat), messengers, physicians, millers, brewers, bakers, cooks, potters, wood and metal workers, leather workers, smiths, bowmakers, gardeners, fishermen and poultry breeders or fowlers, male and female weavers and spinners, carpet manufacturers, heralds, manufacturers of ointment, barbers, nurses, fullers, preparers of oil, and a number of Hurrian professional names not yet translated.[8]

Lest one thinks the Mesopotamian information is clear-cut in comparison to the biblical one, scholars working on the sources themselves recognize they are confusing.

They [handicraft laborers] belong rather to that class of persons, distinguished by Diakonoff [1972, 1976] and Gelb [1972:88], whose "status between free, semi-free, and unfree is not quite clear." They should be called servants or personnel under "patriarchal authority of the king as head of the household; from his household they could receive either rations in kind, or land allotments ... on condition of service" [Diakonoff 1972:44].[9]

Behind these affirmations there is a deep net of ancient obscure categories, which prevent us, scholars in the twenty-first century, from understanding them. What exactly were chattel slaves? What does it mean in practical terms to be "under patriarchal authority of the king as head of the household"? Likewise, one often finds in commentaries assertions that slaves had to be released so that they could join an army. We lack any law or narrative that would allow (or prevent) slaves to join the local armies. At least from Nuzi, Babylonia or Egypt one knows which palace personnel received rations for what type of activity,

---

[8] Gudrun Dosch, "Non-Slave Labor in Nuzi," in *Labor in the Ancient Near East* (ed. M Powell. AOS 68. New Haven: American Oriental Society, 1987), 230–31. Quoting W. Mayer, *Nuzi-Studien I: Die Archive des Palate und die Prosopographie der Berufe* (AOAT 205/1, 1978).

[9] Dosch, "Non-Slave Labor in Nuzi," 231. Quoting IgorM. Diakonoff, "Slaves, Helots and Serfs in Early Antiquity," in *Wirtschaft und Gesellschaft im alten Vorderasien* (ed. J. Harmatta & G. Komoróczy. Budapest, 1976), 45–78; Ignace Gelb, "From Freedom to Slavery," *CRRA* 18 (1972): 81–92, and "Socio-Economic Classes in Babylonia and the Babylonian Concept of Social Stratification," *CRRA* 18 (1972): 41–52.

while there is no way to compare terms for slave with occupations in the Bible.[10] Thus, as far as possible, this study refuses to give people a boxed-in status. The reader will often find loose ends, but they reflect the state of the art in studies where gender and class play a key role.

In the last ten to fifteen years there has appeared a bulk of feminist studies questioning the accuracy of traditional translations of terms such as נַעַר and נַעֲרָה, qadištu/קְדֵשָׁה or זוֹנָה. Some of these claims are actually older (and were made by male writers) but only now are they weighty enough to start to be considered among scholars, even though not yet "malestream." These studies have enlarged our knowledge, challenged our prudence and biases, and fed our imagination. And they pose another challenge. If we take for instance, Leeb's contention that the terms נַעַר and נַעֲרָה indicate someone outside the *paterfamilias'* protection; and we take Stork's contention that the זוֹנָה was the unmarried woman, outside a patriarchal household, what would be the result when these (and other) accurate insights are set one next to another? Are they synonymous terms? Regional variations? Is the נַעֲרָה category a social one, while that of זוֹנָה is legal? The other way around? Neither? I am unable to say and can only point at an area that requires further investigation.

ADVANTAGES TO CHOOSING DTRH

At first sight, DtrH might seem an odd choice for studying female labor. Figures such as the matriarchs and their servants, or prophets like Amos, with their call to social justice and mending of oppressive deeds might seem a wiser choice. However, the Torah is—narratively speaking—too narrow to provide enough data about women and occupations in general. While slaves and secondary wives are common in Genesis, and two of the three references to the midwife (מְיַלֶּדֶת) occur in this book, several other terms do not occur. Furthermore, while Genesis might contribute to the general picture, it bristles with complications, for instance in terms of dating, of sources, and of location of customs and laws *vis-à-vis* ANE law codes known to us. And its focus after 11:27 is on a childless couple (and their descendants after they overcome barrenness) who migrate seeking land, descent, and their God's blessings is too provincial.

The monarchy in Israel is the period when the gap widened between an urban elite of the politically and economically privileged and the increasingly drained peasants. There are plenty of other witnesses to this process in the pre-exilic prophets and some proverbs and the DtrH itself. On the other hand, the

---

[10] These two sets of terms are discussed in chapters 4 and 5 respectively, and although some conclusions about them will be collected in chapter 6, the fact remains that we have no explanation for the absence of more overlapping between them.

elite had the leisure and the means to sponsor theological and wisdom reflection, and thus books like the Psalms, Proverbs or Qoheleth are ascribed to David and Solomon. The monarchy is then the period to be explored, a period directly or indirectly covered by the former and latter prophets, wisdom literature, and DtrH. Among these, DtrH offers some advantages over other sources. It contains narrative material, which thus allows for a sample of terms inserted in believable contexts. Other types of material include speeches, laws, formulae, fables, a chronologically-defined period, and a distinctive theological perspective.[11]

Parallel to the monarchy in DtrH runs the remembrance of YHWH's redemption of Israel from slavery in Egypt, with the consequent exhortations to treat each other as "brother" among Israelites. While this is undoubtedly present in DtrH, equally present is the reality of slavery and indentured servitude (which could eventually turn into permanent slavery, cf. Exod 21:2–6; Deut 15:12–18), in the face of which all one hopes for is that one gets slaves but does not become one. This is the way slavery is seen throughout the ANE, yet the combination of these two seemingly opposite themes is prominent in the Dtr school.

Biblical stories are set up in a scenario that seeks to create an appropriate atmosphere for the message they want to convey. Here narratives have an advantage over ration lists or contracts, for instance. They provide the reader with a more colorful picture, which had to be credible to the original audience. This is not to imply that everything the story contains should be taken as historically true; the ancient audiences themselves knew better than that. Stories use convention and require also imagination.

AN INTRIGUING COMBINATION OF TERMS

I wish to raise yet another difficulty detected as I studied the different texts, which, like these just mentioned, involves more than translation. A close look at the several terms for female workers (and corresponding masculine terms, when appropriate) shows that many of them appear in two syntactically different forms; the question to be discussed is whether these lexemes are semantically

---

[11] See Moshe Weinfeld, *Deuteronomy and the Deuteronomic School* (Oxford: Clarendon Press, 1972), especially 326–8 on the remembrance of slavery and Weinfeld's and others' papers in Duane L. Christensen, ed., *A Song of Power and the Power of Song* (Winona Lake: Eisenbrauns, 1993); G. Gerbrandt, *Kingship according to Deuteronomistic History* (SBLDS 87; Atlanta: Scholars Press, 1986); B. Halpern, "The Centralization Formula in Deuteronomy," *VT* 31 (1981): 20–38; and Naomi Steinberg, "The Deuteronomic Law Code and the Politics of Cult Centralization," in *The Bible and the Politics of Exegesis: Essays in Honor of Norman K. Gottwald on the Occasion of His Sixty-Fifth Birthday* (ed. D. Jobling, P. Day, and G. Sheppard; Cleveland: Pilgrim, 1991), 161–70. Also Norbert Lohfink, *Theology of the Pentateuch* (Minneapolis: Augsburg Fortress, 1994), 227–89 treats themes of the book of Deuteronomy, although none directly related to our texts.

identical or not; and when the answer to that question is "no," try to discern what would be the difference.

Since most Hebrew terms identified for performers of an action are participles (often *qal*, also *nipʿal*, *piʿel* or *hipʿil*), here the ones under consideration are those in which the participle is acting as noun, not as verb. Many are determined by the article, such as "Miriam, the prophetess" or "where the prostitutes wash themselves." There is a second form, in which the participle acts syntactically as adjective to the corresponding noun for "person" (shortcut for אשה, איש, נשים, and אנשים, with or without a definite article). I have not seen much written on this construction, although it is not easily searchable. The closest remark appears in Tammi Schneider's commentary on Judges. Speaking of Deborah, she states about אשה:

> The term is problematic because the decision as to which meaning to translate is, as always, a function of the translator's interpretation of the text. Since little work has been done on how the noun *ʾiššâ* functions and is used in word plays, it is not always clear how to translate the noun in each context. In the above translations [quoted by her from Boling's *Judges*, *JPS*, *KJ* and *RSV* Bible translations] the translators view this noun as modifying the following noun "prophetess" *nabî'ah* [*sic*] by making it feminine. While this may be its function, the noun used for prophet is already in the feminine form. The noun must function, at the least, as emphasizing the femaleness of Deborah or her status as prophet, a title rare for women in the Bible.[12]

In her masterpiece on prostitution in the Bible, published in 1989, Phyllis Bird doubted any possibility of differentiating both uses of the participle, זונה and אשה זונה and, to my knowledge, nobody has proved her wrong.[13] After examination of all instances of participles indicating occupation or profession, alone or in apposition to "woman/en," I am convinced *there is* a difference between both constructions. I cannot say whether the difference stems from chronological or geographical (regional) distance; from various economic conditions; whether one became more loosely used or, on the contrary, it became a technical term stemming from a general designation; or whether one eventually replaced the other. I even realize that the evidence does not lend itself easily to explanations and classification; otherwise it would have been noted earlier.

---

[12] Tammi J. Schneider, *Judges* (Berit Olam. Studies in Hebrew Narrative and Poetry; Collegeville: Liturgical Press, 2000), 64–65.

[13] Phyllis A. Bird "'To Play the Harlot,'" *Missing Persons and Mistaken Identities* (Minneapolis: Fortress, 1997), 221–25 and more shortly in "Prostitution in the Social World and the Religious Rhetoric of Ancient Israel," in *Prostitutes and Courtesans in the Ancient World* (ed. Christopher A. Faraone and Laura K. McClure; Madison: University of Wisconsin Press, 2006), 56 n.5.

What are the reasons for positing a difference between both lexemes? The first reason, although a minor one, is the economy of words of the Bible. Why add "person" when the participle is enough? Secondly, Naomi Steinberg's work on אלמנה, אלמנה אשה and אשת־המת (all terms usually translated "widow") makes me think that, eventually, a different meaning or at least a clearer gradation will be discovered for other constructions.[14] Finally, once the suspicion that there is a difference is on one's mind, one notices certain trends. I am aware of the danger of circular reasoning here, and thus, to be on the safer side, I call them only "trends" and submit my hypotheses hoping for further discussion and, eventually, for a clearer understanding. Seven examples follow, not all equally weighty, on these forms:

SEVEN CASES OF SYNTACTICAL VARIATION

אשה זונה *and* זונה — *"Loose Women" and "Prostitutes"*[15]

- Legal material uses זונה (a harlot's wage or a dog's price as vow payments to the temple, Deut 23:19).[16]
- Pay for sex. The term "wages" (אתנן) only appears associated with a זונה, never with אשה זונה or with any other professional, male or female.
- As term of comparison, זונה appears in stories or proverbs comparing with another person/s, except for the "אשה זונה's forehead" comparison of Jer 3:3.

---

[14] Naomi Steinberg proves that these three terms denote women whose husbands are dead, yet they convey different categories of "widows." Naomi Steinberg, "Romancing the Widow: The Economic Distinctions between the *ʾalmānâ*, the *ʾiššâ-ʾalmānâ* and the *ʾēšet-hammēt*," in *God's Word for Our World: Biblical Studies in Honor of Simon John De Vries, Volume I* (ed. J. Harold Ellens, Deborah L. Ellens, Rolf P. Knierim, and Isaac Kalimi; 2 volumes; JSOTSup; London: T&T Clark, 2004, 327–46. The version quoted here is from *Women and Property in Ancient Near Eastern and Mediterranean Societies: Conference Proceedings, Center for Hellenistic Studies, Harvard University.* Edited by Deborah Lyons & Raymond Westbrook. Center for Hellenic Studies, Trustees for Harvard University, 2005, n. p. Cited 25 Nov 2010. Online: http://www.chs.harvard.edu/wa/pageR?tn=ArticleWrapper&bdc=12&mn=1219.

[15] These points and most of the texts mentioned here are further studied in chapter 7, so here only an outline of my arguments is offered. The term appears both with full and defective spelling; in all DtrH instances it is fully spelled, except for both occurrences in 1 Kings. In general I have used the full spelling in order to differentiate the participle from the stem.

[16] The only other lexemes for female occupations in the legal corpora are: i. those for slaves, including sabbatical rest, manumission of debt slaves, non-manumission of slave-wives, etc.; the right to eat during the land's sabbath (Lev 25:6); sex with a slave (Lev 19:20); and ii. terms such as אבות, קדשה and others of (male and female) functionaries of forbidden non-Yahwistic practices (Deut 23:18; Lev 19:31; 20:6, etc.).

- זונה is used in a variety of stories and literary genres, even though it is not always clear whether the woman so named is a harlot or a fornicator.
- זונה (אשה) + "house of" appears several times in slightly different forms, most of them in Josh 2 and 6.
- Those who are "single mothers" are always called אשה זונה, never זונה alone: the two women in 1 Kgs 3:16, Jephthah's mother Judg 11:1.

In short, there is a strong tendency to use זונה alone, when its connotation is that of a sex worker and אשה זונה when the woman is more probably a "loose woman" in the sense of a woman living outside a patriarchal household (or perhaps erring from the household, "זונה-ing") even when she is a mother.[17]

הנצבים and הנצבות — Workers on Duty

Several (nip ʿal) plural participles of the stem נצב (+ preposition על) appear on occasion with the meaning of someone standing or posted with a purpose.[18] Often they function as nouns: ועזריהו בן־נתן על־הנצבים "Azariahu the son of Nathan was over the officers" (1 Kgs 4:5); or the notice that "These officers provided for King Solomon" וכלכלו הנצבים האלה את־המלך שלמה (1 Kgs 5:7).They also appear in compound formulas, except that they are built with other nouns or participles and not with איש or אנשים. One of these cases is 1 Sam 22:17, where the participle accompanies another participle acting as noun: "the guard stationed by him" (ה)רצים הנצים עליו.[19] These examples show this participle, at least when determined and alone, has a connotation of an identifiable body of professionals at the service of the king. The only example of the feminine participle is also somehow related to an institution, even though the exact nature of that relationship is unclear to me. First Sam 4:20 uses הנצבות in allusion to the midwives, "the women who attended to" Phineas's widow as she bore a son, named him, and died. Were these professionals or ad hoc neighbors and relatives?

הנשים) הצבאות) — The Women in Service

Still another participle can be added to this list; curiously, the feminine plural of צבא shares in this phenomenon of appearing both with and without the noun

---

[17] See further below, chapter 7. As mentioned, not every appearance of the terms is clearly explainable.

[18] *BDB*, 662: "**1.a.** *station oneself, take one's stand,* for definite purpose; … **b.** *stand = be stationed* (by appointment, or in fulfillment of duty)…; **2.** *be stationed = appointed* over… Hence **3.** Pt. as subst. *deputy, prefect* …"

[19] "The guard" is literally those who run, רוץ; and נצב על has the meaning of being appointed, thus "stationed." Another case appears in Ruth 2:6–7, where Boaz's supervisor is called "the dependent in charge of the reapers" הנער הנצב על־הקוצרים.

נשים. Like the one just listed, the immediate meaning of the stem is not an occupation, but a formation of people serving in some orderly fashion: "serve at sacred tent" (*BDB*). In the feminine it appears in 1 Sam 2:22 (הנשים הצבאות) and Exod 38:8 (הצבאת); curiously, once with the noun and once without, once written *plene* and once defective. Even more curious is the fact that the three cases of the masculine participle have it as appositional to האנשים (Num 31:42) and to הגוים (Isa 29:7–8, twice).[20]

The next three examples are all texts introducing a person or group not previously mentioned in the narrative. In all three, the participle accompanies the noun אשה or נשים. As seen above, by itself this fact does not indicate much: in other presentations of new characters the participle alone is used and there are also second mentions (Ruth 2:7) in which a noun for "person" is used. Thus, no theory can be based solely on this fact.

הנשים המשחקות — *The Women Performing*

Another participle feminine plural, denoting—if not professionals, at least a skilled group—appears in 1 Sam 18:7: הנשים המשחקות, from the stem שחק, "to play, make sport, leap." On eight occasions the verb is used to say something of a man/men and twice of pre-creation Wisdom in Prov 9, but in no other text with this combination.[21] Since the context is one of joyful celebration with singing and dancing, it is usually translated "the women sang" or something similar; it could equally be "the female performers" (who gathered *ad hoc*?)

אשה נביאה — *A Woman Prophetess*

These words are said of one woman in the Hebrew Bible, in her introduction to the biblical story: ודבורה אשה נביאה אשת לפידות היא שפטה: "Deborah, a woman, a prophetess, a fiery woman, she was a judge" (Judg 4:4).[22] Four other prophetesses are mentioned and in all the determined noun הנביאה is used (none with אשה and, strangely, none undetermined either). Most commentaries see this seemingly unnecessary mentioning of Deborah as female and prophetess but do not pay much attention to its significance. The welcome exception is Schneider's quotation reproduced above.

Additionally, the following parallel might be of interest here. The only instance of the masculine noun with a similar construction appears in Judg 6:8,

---

[20] Both verses in Isaiah are ambiguous, for the participle could be adjectival or verbal in meaning.

[21] On music, see chapter 5.

[22] I follow here Renate Jost's translation, *Gender, Sexualität und Machtin der Anthropologie des Richterbuches* (Kohlhammer: Stuttgart, 2006), 353: "Und Debora, eine Frau, eine Prophetin/ war eine Frau von Fakeln (war die Frau Lapidots)."

where "YHWH sent a man, a prophet, איש נביא to the Israelites" to announce punishment. This is an anonymous prophet who disappears from the text after delivering his message. I have not been able to find any other instance of this construction.

אשה מינקת — *Breast-feeding Woman*

This is the last text that might be of importance in discussing Schneider's "how the noun *ʾiššâ* functions" question, plus our own question "how it modifies the participle to imply a meaning lost to us." The last piece of evidence is the well-known story of Moses' upbringing by his own mother. In that story, Moses' unnamed older sister offers to look for a wet nurse from the Hebrews, who might suckle the baby. The sister's question to Pharaoh's daughter is, "Shall I go and call for you an אשה מינקת from the Hebrew women?" (Exod 2:7). Obviously, it is unnecessary to indicate that a woman is implied, for (apart from the fact that only women suckle) the participle is itself feminine in form. Finally, in Gen 35:8 the participle accompanies a proper name, Deborah, Rebekah's wet nurse ותמת דברה מינקת רבקה.

אשה פילגש — *"Concubine" and Other Loaded Terms*

Finally, there are some non-participles of which it is arguable whether they belong or not to the semantic field of labor. One ambiguous term is פילגש, usually translated "concubine," yet more accurately secondary (second-class?) wife.[23] The point of interest here is that it acts in the same way as the constructions studied above. פילגש/ים appears only as a noun, for example, in 2 Sam 5:13 and in 1 Kgs 11:3; in both cases the narrator reports (David's and Solomon's) acquisition of numerous wives. Seen together, these two are especially interesting, for they combine two forms in one breath and also in reverted order from each other: " … David took more concubines and wives, ונשים פלגשים (2 Sam 5:13) and Solomon "had 700 princesses נשים שרות and 300 concubines פלגשים" (1 Kgs 11:3). Noticeable is the inversion in the regular order from major to minor, "wives and concubines" in 2 Sam 5:13. To be noted also is the redactor's use of the noun "women" נשים to introduce only one of the groups and his omission in the second category. Are these ellipses?

The construction נשים פלגשים appears in 2 Sam 15:16; 20:3 in reference to the ten women left behind by David. In other texts, like Judg 19–20, both forms, with and without the noun for "person," appear (altogether, eleven times in these chapters), with preponderance of the single form (+ suffix) פילגש.

---

[23] The ambiguity stems from the fact that many of them were also slaves; and others, like the ten פילגשים left by David in his flight from Absalom (and even worse, the one related to a Levite in Judg 19), are not treated with the respect due to wives.

Thus, there seems to be no rule here, except that the introductory remark uses the complex form.

Yet another case is that of the adjective חכמה "wise (woman)" which sometimes works syntactically as noun (for instance, in Jer 9:16, where it comes as a parallel term to מקוננות, the mourners) and which indicates a professional counselor, a mediator, or some other political office.[24] However, I bring it up here because in the two stories in which a counselor or mediator is a main character in a narrative, she is presented as "a wise woman from" (Tekoa or Abel-Meholah): the adjective is accompanied by the noun אשה (2 Sam 14:2; 20:16). This is exactly the opposite trend to what I observed in the texts of the זונה (אשה)! Is that due to the nature of the adjective as opposed to that of the participle? Is there a reason or is it only happenstance? Does that mean that they acted on an ad hoc basis, as needed, and did not hold a permanent office under a tree?

SUMMING UP

I see a problem here but cannot solve the puzzle alone. Most of these participles appear both functioning alone as nouns and in compound formulas functioning as adjectives or appositions to those nouns. It must be recognized also that this is not a thorough analysis of all participles in biblical Hebrew; the ones noted here (by myself) are traced as companions to the nouns אשה and נשים, and reflected upon. Other terms or other combinations might still be further noticed.

The relatively small number of examples and their erratic behavior make it too difficult to systematize them with any degree of reasonability, for there is practically an exception to every rule one attempts to set. The terms זונה and אשה זונה appear often enough to allow for some observations, even though there remains much to be confirmed or rejected. There is a tendency to use זונה with a more technical sense than אשה זונה; the reasons are never stated and there are also—as discussed in chapter 7—numerous borderline cases, such as Rahab in Josh 2.

In some stories, the construction "person + participle" seems to be somehow related to the liminal status of the person on the verge of becoming that which the participle denotes (wet nurse, prophetess or something else) or

---

[24] Claudia Camp, "The Wise Women of 2 Samuel: A Role Model for Women in Early Israel?," *CBQ* 43 (1981): 14–29; *Wisdom and the Feminine in the Book of Proverbs* (Decatur: Almond, 1985), 120–123; Adele Reinhartz, "Anonymity and Character in the Books of Samuel," *Semeia* 63 (1993): 117–41; Katheryn Pfisterer Darr, "Asking at Abel: A Wise Woman's Proverb Performance in 2 Samuel 20," in *Women of the Hebrew Bible and Their Afterlives* (ed. Peter S. Hawkins and Lesleigh Cushing Stahlberg; vol. 1 of *From the Margins;* Sheffield: Sheffield Phoenix, 2009), 102–21.

someone acting ad hoc or on an amateur status, something approximately similar to what we call today "appointed." Or perhaps it would indicate the turning point from being amateur to being paid or something in that line. If this is true, what the young sister was saying in Exod 2 was something like "May I call a woman who is about to work as (thus become) a wet nurse?" Or, again, I might be totally wrong and it might only be acting as appositional, "a woman, namely, a wet nurse" (or whatever the case).[25]

Finally, for some types of participle, whose primary meaning is not that of a profession, no clear rule appears. One of them seems to offer both forms as variants to each other (there are only two examples, however). Likewise, I cannot find a rule for the use or avoidance of the noun אשה or נשים accompanying the noun פילגש/ים.[26] Strictly speaking, it is not a term for a profession and it is a noun, not a participle, and perhaps that adds a difficulty to the already difficult task of understanding its meaning.

In short, I can only point to the puzzle. Rather than being right, I would be happy if this issue is taken up and further discussed and refined.

METHODOLOGIES USED IN THIS WORK

SOCIAL-HISTORICAL CRITICISM

Working on issues of class and women in the Bible often implies attempting several tries with no evident result, and this is one fact the scholar has to consider. Societies are not isolated bricks, but organizations of people in touch with each other, influencing each other, copying from each other and whenever possible conquering each other. A quick look at the biblical material of any period shows this interaction in culture, commerce, marriages, treaties, and vassalage. Each society, in turn, changed according to several factors, only some of which they could control. As one writer put it, one "must resist the tendency to objectify Israel's social system into a static and monolithic hypostasis. It developed unevenly, underwent change, and incorporated tension and conflict. It was a frame for human interaction in which stability struggled against change

---

[25] As taken by *GK*§131.

[26] In Judg 19, the compound nouns אשה פלגש open the narrative. And again, the two "wise women," the counselors called upon to solve a political crises in the book of Samuel are first introduced as אשה חכמה and yes, in these cases it is the only introduction, so no example of חכמה alone appears later (perhaps that is due to the fact that the latter is an adjective?). So far, one could posit a theory on the use of אשה to introduce a narrative. My theory is ruined, unfortunately, by a counter-example in 2 Sam 3:7, where Saul's concubine Rizpah is introduced for the first time and only פלגש is used: ולשאול פלגש ושמה רצפה בת-איה.

and change eroded away stability."[27] The same struggle between stability and change happened in cross-cultural encounters. To this fact, one has to add the chronological and cultural distance between the cultures reflected in the biblical texts and our own.

While the ANE as a region had several states, each with its particularities, they shared basic aspects.[28] This allows the scholar to compare societies which are close by in time and in characteristics and to show that, given cross-cultural evidence, this or that fact could very well have also occurred in the society studied, although it may not be proved. To take one example, there is no definite evidence for temple slavery in Israel, since no contracts or ration lists have been found so far; thus, the several עבדים and the נתינים, who *are* mentioned, could be anything from ministers or priests to chattel slaves. The most one can say is that, considering the amount of work needed in a huge organization like the Jerusalem temple, considering biblical evidence supporting increasing impoverishment of the peasantry, and the role temples and slavery played in similar, neighboring societies, it is *very possible* that the same system applied to the Jerusalem temple.[29] Whether slaves or not, people's living and working conditions in the ANE did not solely depend on their legal status of free, semi-free, or slave.[30]

SOCIAL-SCIENTIFIC CRITICISM

Use of social models drawn from present-day rural Mediterranean cultures has been welcomed by some and rejected by other scholars. Models are perceived as an external imposition on the texts, and distant in time. This is true and it has to be weighed in the argument. On the other hand, all exegesis done today is equally distant in time, and for most of us foreign in culture as well, but that has

---

[27] Norman K. Gottwald, "Sociological Method in the Study of Ancient Israel," in *The Bible and Liberation: Political and Social Hermeneutics* (ed. N. Gottwald. Maryknoll: Orbis, 1983), 27.

[28] For instance, their basic socio-political organization with a state organized around a walled city, which was the political, military, and religious center; surrounded by farming land, which was the main source of income and of wealth; a deity as patron or patroness, with his or her temple, which was both a religious and an economic institution; slaves and dependents owned by the palace, the temple, and families, who were in charge of agriculture, building projects, daily errands, household tasks, and other duties according to their number, location, and the particular needs of that society.

[29] Dandamaev, *Slavery in Babylonia from Nabopolassar to Alexander the Great (626–331 BC)* (rev. ed. DeKalb, IL: Northern Illinois University Press,1984), 547–57; Isaac Mendelsohn, *Slavery in the Ancient Near East* (New York: Oxford University Press, 1949), 99–106.

[30] This argument does not invalidate the concern on the side of ANE scholars for how scholars from other fields use their findings. See Julia Asher-Greve, "Feminist Research and Ancient Mesopotamia: Problems and Prospects," in *A Feminist Companion to Reading the Bible* (ed. Athalya Brenner & Carol Fontaine; Sheffield: Sheffield Academic Press, 1997), 222–24.

not hindered scholars from making all kinds of statements, many proved to be just wrong.

Models are unavoidable, because the mind constantly produces or adopts models to represent and capture reality, choosing from several impressions. In fact, one does not choose whether to use models or not; our choice "lies in deciding whether to use them consciously or unconsciously. If we use them unconsciously, they control us, we do not control them."[31] It follows that review of available scholarship on any biblical theme in a sense can be seen as review of unconsciously- or consciously-used models, the difference being that consciously-used models can be carefully monitored. What criteria are necessary, then, in a biblical model? Since a model intends to explain some object unknown or not understood, it has to be cross-cultural, abstract, and large enough to facilitate comparison yet take into consideration all fundamental aspects of the modeled "thing." It should not contradict basic aspects of the society or object studied as known from other models and methods, or otherwise it must be able to demonstrate faultiness in earlier approaches. Finally, if it intends to be accepted as a social-scientific project, its "application ... should be acceptable to social scientists (even if they disagree with the validity of the enterprise)."[32]

Not surprisingly, the so-called "Mediterranean Basin culture" model has encountered much enthusiasm among North-American biblical scholars. One reason for this enthusiasm is the need to make sense of widely different (that is, for the North-Atlantic world) cultural attitudes, approaches, and presuppositions evident in the biblical writings. While some of this model's insights are accurate (I will shortly review the ones useful for this work), they are also too general, since they include cultures

> along all shores of the Mediterranean Sea, the Middle East even to Afghanistan. Furthermore, the honor-shame model has been identified in cultures which are very distant at least geographically from the Mediterranean basin, such as Nicaragua and Japan. Honor-shame as a pair seen to apply to the whole Mediterranean basin served an epistemological purpose in the 1960s, when anthropologists were looking for common models. Today there is an increasing awareness that "emphasis on honour/shame as typically Mediterranean takes

---

[31] T. Carney, *The Shape of the Past: Models and Antiquity* (Lawrence: Coronado, 1975), 5.

[32] Bruce Malina, "The Social Sciences and Biblical Interpretation," in *The Bible and Liberation: Political and Social Hermeneutics* (ed. Norman K. Gottwald; Maryknoll: Orbis, 1983), 22, mentions these and some other conditions.

much for granted," especially in covering with one stroke several age, sex, and class groups.[33]

Several cautious voices have also arisen from within the North-Atlantic academic milieu itself. In view of these, some of its followers have recently attempted to rejuvenate it. After acknowledging some valid critics to it, Zeba Crook, for instance, states: "Yet, despite the obvious strengths of Malina's model, it is starting to show signs of its age and might benefit from some changes that would increase its heuristic power and longevity."[34]Another modification to the model is that by Susan Brayford, who explores some narratives in Genesis and compares them with the Hellenistic model (including their LXX version). She shows that, contrary to those later expectations, some women in the Hebrew text (starting from Eve) have a concern for *their* sexual desire and their own needs (children and recognition),which would be improper of shameful = modest women (according to the Hellenistic [male] ideal). In other words, important women in Genesis follow a different honor-shame code than that identified as "Mediterranean."[35]

Especially harsh are some voices from anthropologists having done research within that same "Mediterranean Basin" area. A Portuguese anthropologist is even harsher. I bring up his reflection because it helped me understand why this model has become so trendy even though it has been so much modified, refined, and even rejected:

Are the Algarve mountaineers more like Moroccans than like *minhotos*? Are Andalusians more like Tunisians than like *gallegos*? ... Are Greeks more like Egyptians than other Balkan peoples? My answer is that the notion of the Mediterranean Basin as a "culture area" is more useful as a means of distancing Anglo-American scholars from the populations they study than as a way of

---

[33] Alison Lever, "Honor as a Red Herring," *Cultural Anthropology* 1, no. 2 (1986), 86. See Ken Stone, *Sex, Honor, and Power in the Deuteronomistic History* (JSOTSup 234; Sheffield: Sheffield Academic Press, 1996), 42, for a review and bibliography.

[34] Zeba Crook, "Honor, Shame, and Social Status Revisited," *JBL* 128 (2009): 592. My interest lies elsewhere so I will not dwell long on this issue; yet, seeing the fate of the Pentateuchal sources theories after so many modifications, I wonder how long can this model still hold its pace without turning into something else.

[35] Brayford, "To Shame or Not to Shame." See also M. Herzfeld, "Honour and Shame: Problems in the Comparative Analysis of Moral Systems," *Man*, New Series 15 (1980): 339–51, already from 1980, doubting *"whether 'the Mediterranean' necessarily or usefully constitutes a discrete cultural zone"* and proposing *"(a) to examine each terminological system as an independent whole in its local setting; (b) to elucidate the relationships between such systems within each linguistic area before proceeding to wider cross-cultural comparisons."* (abstract, article unavailable to me).

making sense of the cultural homogeneities and differences that characterize the region.[36]

Another reason for bringing up his reaction is that his approach, training, and his own social and cultural location place him on the other side, so to speak: he belongs to that culture and that region and resists being catalogued or, should I say, "over-homogenized." If only for that, it is a voice to be heard. "Over-homogenization" is my main critique of the model as well: that is what one finds when one reads what has been published and thought of lower-class women. In other words, the model is applicable to the "typical" Israelite mistress of her household, but it serves not the slave, the prostitute, the midwife, and several other women. Exposition of pertinent arguments and contributions will be mentioned in order to state what aspects of the model are useful in studying lower-class women.

Peasantry. From studies on rural pre-industrial areas, the model of peasantry has emerged, proving to be a valuable tool in understanding an organization of people sharing particular socio-economic and cultural characteristics in spite of time and space differences. For the ANE, China, Mexico, and Poland to share social, economic, and cultural characteristics, of necessity these have to be *very* general. In the last years, "peasantry" has come under serious discussion amongst anthropologists and ancient economists.[37] A very recent article in one of the leading biblical journals starts, precisely, with such doubts:

> Perhaps no social-scientific concept has had a greater impact on historical Jesus research than the common one of "peasants" as a distinct socioeconomic and cultural human type. This result is despite the fact that there is at present no consensus among social scientists on the issue of "whether a distinctive category of peasantry can be identified both conceptually and empirically."[38]

The article is concerned with its use in New Testament scholarship, but it is still applicable. In her open questioning of this model, what Mattila does is bring to light, precisely, the question about methodology. Roland Boer has proposed a model of "Sacred economy" in which the state appears "in response to the conflict between the village commune and the city-temple complex."[39] In his view, it is not the state which oppressed and exploited the peasants, but the city-

---

[36] João DePina-Cabral, "The Mediterranean as a Category of Regional Comparison: A Critical View," *Current Anthropology* 30 (1989): 399.

[37] Peasants' living and working conditions within an ancient agrarian society, such as any in the ANE, are discussed in chapter 3.

[38] Sharon Lea Mattila, "Jesus and the 'Middle Peasants'? Problematizing a Social-Scientific Concept," *CBQ* 72 (2010): 291.

[39] Roland Boer, "The Sacred Economy of Ancient 'Israel'," *SJOT* 21 (2007): 30.

temple(s) and thus, the sacred component of such an economy should not be underestimated. Boer's additional contribution is his review, in the first part of his paper, of Marxist Russian ANE scholars whose works are not generally accessible. Although I for one would have wanted to know more about those scholars and not just a quick mention of their insights, it is at least an attempt to build a bridge between them and Western scholarship.

Very helpful in understanding the complexity and ideological weight of the discussion on "peasantry" or even "peasantness," was for me Bernstein and Byres' introductory article to their joint enterprise, the *Journal of Agrarian Change*.[40] In it, they review the discussion on these pertinent questions, with special reference to a previous journal, the *Journal of Peasant Studies* (to which they were also closely related). If I have understood the current discussion correctly, there are challenges to the concept itself as well as to its application to long-gone, ancient societies. The discussion is partly due to the fact that "peasantry" is ideologically charged from its very beginning. It responded to a Marxist-Leninist egalitarian model. Thus, some contend, it cannot be uncritically used as if "peasantry" were a homogeneous social class where families enjoyed their own household and had the same goods as every other family. Challenging though such a discussion might be, it belongs to a wholly different field and it cannot be reproduced here.

Perception of Goods as Limited. The limited nature of goods applies not only to water, food, and other natural resources, but to incalculable goods as well. Honor, happiness, well-being are all limited. This is an important concept not because of its anecdotal character to many modern readers, but because one acts towards limited resources very differently than if they were unlimited. Just as industrial Western societies waste natural resources as if they were unlimited, pre-industrial Mediterranean societies preserve cultural resources as if they were limited.[41] All eligible members of the community got a share of the good in question, for instance honor, and each one tries to increase it at the expense of others, while at the same time trying to prevent their own honor from being diminished by transference to another person, who is shamed. In general the model is tested in public challenges between males, as there is a gender division

---

[40] Bernstein, Henry & Terence J. Byres. "From Peasant Studies to Agrarian Change," *Journal of Agrarian Change* 1 (2001): 1–56. I gather from their article the *Journal of Peasant Studies* appeared for the last time in July 2000.

[41] Bruce J. Malina and C. Seeman, "Envy," in *Biblical Social Values and Their Meaning: A Handbook* (ed. B. Malina & J. Pilch. Peabody: Hendrickson, 1993), 56: "The perception of limited good is the socially shared conviction that the resources enabling a community to support itself are in finite supply and that any disruption of the social equilibrium can be only detrimental to community survival." Notice that this handbook has an entry on thrift, but none on work.

in the understanding of honor-shame.[42] Public challenge requires that both parties be conversant with their own status and that of others in the community, so as to act properly and acquire further honor.

Honor. "Honor is a claim to worth that is publicly acknowledged,"[43] thus requiring a claim from an individual and the community from whom recognition is expected. Depending on its source, honor is ascribed or acquired. Ascribed honor belongs to the person because the person belongs to a certain clan and family, with lineage, land, gender, religion, and probably also military and ethnic records, while acquired honor is also shared by the family, but it is subject to sudden events and to whether or not expectations are fulfilled.[44] Honor is also related to land and work. In a study on Greek writings about "the poor man," Neyrey contrasts the daily worker τένης, who might not know what the family will eat tomorrow, with the poor πτωχός, who lost the family property and honor and has to beg.[45] Neyrey's conclusions on the relation between land and honor seem to apply to what we know from the OT:

1. Honour and shame are closely related to wealth and loss of wealth respectively.
2. In antiquity, wealth and honour were not individual possessions such as we see in the personal fortune of John D. Rockefeller, but the property of the family or kinship group. When a family lost wealth, its status and honour were threatened.
3. Although most people had meager possessions and low status, there were families or kinship groups who could no longer maintain their inherited status in regard to marriage contracts, dowries, land tenure and the like.

---

[42] Such a division is in effect part of the biblical idea. However, it has become the only part twentieth-century social models highlight, with detrimental effects on woman's assessment, as will be discussed below. See Saul M. Olyan, "Honor, Shame, and Covenant Relations in Ancient Israel and Its Environment," *JBL* 115 (1996): 201–18, T. R. Hobbs, "Reflections on Honor, Shame, and Covenant Relations," *JBL* 116 (1997): 501–3.

[43] J. Plevnik, "Honor/Shame," in *Biblical Social Values and Their Meaning* (ed. Bruce J. Malina & John Pilch; Peabody: Hendrickson, 1993), 95. More widely quoted is J. Pitt-Rivers' definition, *The Fate of Shechem, or The Politics of Sex: Essays in the Anthropology of the Mediterranean* (Cambridge Studies in Social Anthropology. Cambridge: Cambridge University Press, 1977), 1: "Honor is the value of a person in his [*sic*] own eyes, but also in the eyes of his [*sic*] society. It is his [*sic*] estimation of his [*sic*] own worth, his [*sic*] claim to pride, but it is also the acknowledgement of that claim, his [*sic*] excellence recognised by society, his [*sic*] right to pride."

[44] Thus the importance of the genealogist in an oral culture, because all these events have to be remembered and updated in the people's memory.

[45] Jerome Neyrey, "Loss of Wealth, Loss of Family, and Loss of Honour: The Cultural Context of the Original Makarisms in Q," in *Modeling Early Christianity: Social-scientific Studies of the New Testament in Its Context* (ed. P. Esler; London: Routledge, 1995), 141.

Loss of wealth translated into lower status, which meant loss of honour (Hobbs 1989b: 293).[46]

For the present study what matters is that patrimonial land (Hebrew נחלה) and family honor were closely linked together, determining the honor of every member, and committing every member of the family to work for its upkeep and protection. In this sense, shame as a value contrary to honor is still a positive value, in that it is "sensitivity about one's own reputation, sensitivity to the opinion of others."[47] However, as seen below, when people lose land and have to find their value in another element, sensitivity about one's reputation is still present, but it is linked to other values, which become the source of honor within that subculture.

Honor, Shame, and Women. Many scholars find a second dimension of acquired honor, which is gender determined. Statements like the following one are current among biblical scholars who follow the Mediterranean model on honor and shame.

> One can speak of honor and shame of both males and females specifically as they pertain to those areas of social life covering common humanity, natural groupings in which males and females share a common collective honor: the family, village, city, and their collective reputation. However, actual, everyday, concrete conduct that establishes one's reputation and redounds upon one's group is never independent of the gender or moral division of labor. Actual conduct, daily concrete behavior, always depends upon one's gender status. At this level of perception, when honor is viewed as an exclusive prerogative of one of the genders, then honor is always male, and shame is always female. Thus in the area of individual, concrete behavior (and apart from considerations of the group), honor and shame are gender-specific.[48]

According to this model, honor means for man the ability to keep up with expectations of good behavior, righteousness in dealing with others, care of the weak members of the community, participation in communal activities, and any other particular aspect which his culture would say is proper for an honorable man. The *paterfamilias* has the additional responsibility of guarding the acquired honor of every member of the household, as expected according to age,

---

[46] Neyrey, "Loss of Wealth," 140. Reference to T. R. Hobbs, "Reflections on 'The Poor' and the Old Testament," *ExpTim* 100 (1989): 293. Neyrey's study of Greek sources for both terms obviously does not apply to Israel in the OT.

[47] Bruce J. Malina, *The New Testament World: Insights from Cultural Anthropology* (rev. ed.; Louisville: Westminster John Knox, 1993), 50.

[48] Malina, *The New Testament World*, 51.

gender, and place in the family, since honor belongs to the family, not the individual. While certain conduct is honorable for both sexes, honor = shame obliges a man to defend his honor and that of his family, and a woman to safeguard her purity. Yet the concepts of honor and shame also extend to the point where they are no longer synonymous, and at this point they lose their ethical value. Shame, no longer equivalent to honor, as shyness, blushing and timidity is thought to be proper to women, even though it no longer constitutes virtue, while honor, no longer equivalent to shame, becomes an exclusively male attribute as the concern for precedence and the willingness to offend another man if provoked.[49]

Thus, while for men positive actions and values equal a gain of honor, for women shame rather than honor defines the expectations set on them. "The female domain is that of shame in the sense of focal concern for honor ....It is ... presupposed and then maintained as a veil of privacy and of personal and sexual integrity. Shame is therefore not associated with strength or wisdom or courage, but rather with privacy, reserve, and purity."[50] Thus, woman is expected to keep her ascribed honor, expressed in guarding her sexuality. While a man takes action in acquiring further honor, the most a woman can do according to this definition is to defend hers. And what better place to safeguard woman's honor but at home? Let the man go out into the dangerous world, while the woman remains secluded, protected from other men. This type of argument is seen as typical of societies in which men dispute each other's honor by trying to use each other's women, including the biblical world, and it started well before the "Mediterranean Basin culture" model became popular:

> It is the man who acts outwardly and represents the family. Behind him stands the woman, whose sphere is in the house and within the circle of the family, and who does not appear independently in public. An exception is made by the *hetæras* (designated in the translations as "harlots"). They do not follow the laws of women fulfilling their appointed task, but, leaving the normal sphere of women, they converse freely with men.[51]

---

[49] Pitt-Rivers, *The Fate of Shechem*, 20–21. In other words, for a woman to lose honor it is necessary that a man who has no right to her sexuality takes it from her, and so augments *his* honor. This model will be further evaluated below.

[50] Plevnik, "Honor/Shame," 96.

[51] J. Pedersen, *Israel, Its Life and Culture* (London: Oxford University Press, 1926), 44. Pomeroy, *Goddesses, Whores, Wives, and Slaves*, 169–70: "... the Roman matron bore sole responsibility for the management of her town house, and although her work was mainly the supervision of slaves, she was expected to be able to perform such chores as spinning and weaving. ... Household duties did not hold a prominent place in a woman's public image: the Roman matron could never be considered a housewife as could the Athenian. In fact, the writer Cornelius Nepos, who lived in the 1st century B.C., states in his 'Preface' that the principal contrast between Greek and Roman women is that the

Looking at the model proposed in Pedersen's statement one has to ask to what extent Pedersen is faithful to biblical models. There are biblical women appearing independently in public. Rebekah, for example, speaks with a foreigner at the well, apparently unaccompanied; a similar setting (the well) serves other stories (like that of Jethro's daughters encountering Moses). Several women in Proverbs encounter men; in fact, Wisdom and Folly are depicted as calling out to their banquets at crossroads, the market, and other places. Ruth speaks to the dependent in charge of Boaz's fields and to him as well, and Boaz's instructions not to molest her indicate, precisely, that, *at least for many women*, there were ample opportunities, many of them unpleasant, of interacting with unrelated males. Pedersen's quotation is a clear example of a possible misunderstanding when a model is applied uncritically, assuming "the laws of women fulfilling their appointed task," which the harlots do not follow, when in fact as far as the biblical text is concerned those "appointed tasks" are nowhere appointed. So, here there is also an (unchecked) model being applied. A more useful approach is that from Laniak, who sees in the book of Esther a well of "a multifaceted description of the dynamics of honor and shame in the exile."[52] My main reason to prefer his approach is his avoidance of sexual purity as a key concept in understanding societies in which ascription of honor is important.

While it is true that the biblical world shows a division of work along gender lines, such a division is far from explicit, because people in the Bible usually do not work when they are on stage, so to speak. Most biblical men, especially in the prophetic and wisdom literature, meet, talk, marry and beget children, write God's words, go to battles, to sheep shearing, die, offer sacrifices, have dreams, but they hardly chop wood, till the ground, or carry grain to the market. *Their slaves* do menial tasks. And the text hardly takes time to tell what was the male or female slaves' job description.[53] But even if that information were available to us, it would still not account for other instances in which a woman who is *not* a slave exercises an occupation, where neither she nor the occupation is dishonorable. The prophetess, the wise woman, or the singer would be some of the cases in point, in which their very profession would

---

former sit secluded in the interior parts of the house, while the latter accompany their husbands to dinner parties." This is not the place to enter into full discussion of the relationship between patriarchal systems and woman's seclusion, but its importance for woman's safety at home and outside should not be overlooked.

[52] Timothy S. Laniak, *Shame and Honor in the Book of Esther* (Atlanta: Scholars Press, 1998), 14.

[53] For instance, Ruth gleans until she marries Boaz, and while the נערות and נערים continue to work in the fields so that Boaz and his family can eat, once Ruth is not there anymore, they disappear from the story. See Leeb, *Away from the Father's House*, 42–67, 126–30 on some of the occupations in which male or female servants appear, and 68–90 on males in battleground.

put them in contact with men and women not belonging to their immediate family.

Yet a more serious concern, raised by many anthropologists, is the pairing of honor and shame as comparable categories. This second concern bares stronger weight on our study. "If shame and honour are indeed a pair, shame should provide as good a starting point as honour," reasons Unni Wikan.[54] A perusal of works that use these categories affirms her conclusion. In any of the languages heard around the Mediterranean, including the Middle East, "shame" has multiple meanings, going from faulty behavior to serious breach of custom, and it is widely used in every-day speech. Honor is used by anthropologists but not by the people they study, at least in colloquial. Finally, while shame refers to an act and does not automatically disgrace a person, "honor" connotes an essence, hardly perceivable in everyday behavior.[55] Thus honor and shame are not a suitable pair, and while both terms connote important elements and will thus be kept in this study, they are not intended as mirror images, especially not with the meaning anthropologists have ascribed to them: increasing honor for men, increasing shame for women.

Honor, Shame, and Class. Two important issues are raised by this gender division in matters of honor. First, if male honor concerns the material support of the family, how does one account for the numerous women who worked outside the home? One could argue that they are all shamed because of their notoriety, or in turn that only the ones whose sexuality was improperly used were shamed. One may suppose they sought an extra income because their male relatives failed to provide for their families; or because they were rebellious enough to seek an occupation outside; or they were forced because they became war captives, and so on. Considering all these possibilities, males immediately related to them should lose as much of their honor for "allowing" their women to go public or for not being able to provide for their sustenance.[56] These concerns point to the need to further study how social values work for different social classes and legal situations.

---

[54] Uni Wikan, "Shame and Honour," *Man* 19 (1984): 636.

[55] See Wikan, "Shame and Honour," 635–39 (theory), and 639–49 (field work in Oman); Sally Cole, *Women of the Praia: Work and Lives in a Portuguese Coastal Community* (Princeton: Princeton University Press, 1991), especially 77–86 (discussed below). I thank Carolyn Osiek for reference to the latter.

[56] This perception that the male has failed in his obligation when the female has to go out to work ran strong till recently among lower middle-class and traditional groups here at home. Both men and women were brought up to marry and live on the man's salary, but the country's economic situation has obliged them otherwise. On the other hand, lower-class people have always known what it means to work outside home.

The second issue raised by this gender division has to do with the anthropologists who drew up the model. As defined by Pitt-Rivers or Peristiany, shame is practically the only way in which Mediterranean women are evaluated, but that is a largely male perception of the female, acquired by males through field work conducted among males. For sure it is not the way women see themselves, and, as this study shows in the following chapters, it is also not the way many men saw women, at least in the biblical narratives. Wikan, for instance, presents a case-study in Oman, in which a married woman who is well-known in the neighborhood for her adulteries would be the perfect case to prove Pitt-Rivers's model. However, the anthropologist discovers that, although her *actions* are regarded as "not good," and shameful, she as a *person* is "always friendly and hospitable, does not gossip, is kind and helpful. Only in this one respect is she not good (*muzēna*)."[57] There is surely a sense of shame which is only connected to the woman's sexuality, and which is accepted by both men and women, but this is regarded as action, not personal quality. Her value, her honor, remains especially high among the neighborhood women, who draw their sense of worth from the people who know who they are and value friendship, hospitality, and mutual care. On the other hand, men draw their sense of value from a multiplicity of relations, many of them quite anonymous, and therefore how they behave is the most important fact.

There are two worlds, the public one of men, and the semi-private one of women, each with a different concept of what is honorable. Or, rather, there are several worlds:

> There is the multitude of small women's worlds in which men also figure, but marginally and in partial capacities as husbands, brothers, sons etc., and there is a single large world of the men which also embraces women, but in their partial, male-relevant capacities, as mothers, wives, daughters, sisters etc. Both worlds contain standards for both men and women, but one as embraced by men, and the other as embraced by women. In the male world, females are interesting mainly in terms of their sexual trustworthiness, because this is where they so strongly affect the lives of men. In the female world, hospitality and a number of other qualities are highly relevant and have priority.[58]

Several other contributions to methodological models could be added here, but one is especially important. Based on her fieldwork in a Castilian village, Alison Lever contests this honor-shame model because it reflects the interests and ideology of the dominant social class or group.

---

[57] Wikan, "Shame and Honour," 640.
[58] Wikan, "Shame and Honour," 645. See below Cole's conclusions, which run in the same line.

The existence of patriarchal control at a general level is not necessarily apparent at the level of individual couples. A wife may have more economic power than her husband due to higher earnings or inheritance, and this has often been the case in San Santiago. So, whereas women are restricted in the "public" life of the pueblo they may have greater power than the husband within the marital relationship, and they may also have better knowledge of the world outside the pueblo from selling embroideries. Neither men nor women saw women's earning more as an ideal; in the context of the pueblo, if this happened it usually meant the woman was working extremely hard at both paid and unpaid work, while her husband had no useful role. It is important to remember that, though there may be gender antagonism, there is also cooperation between men and women. Husbands and wives have common interests in maintaining the household as an economic unit and in raising the children. This requires coordinated effort.[59]

These models are important for our work, because they alert the scholar to proceed very carefully with his or her assumptions about Israelite society, especially since what is left of it in the written witness overwhelmingly reflects the ideology of upper-class males.

A different approach appears in several studies which intend to show that women played an active role side by side with men in society. They do not directly challenge the Mediterranean model, but show that the woman-as-victim-of-man, as object-of-shame guarded at home, should be corrected. Carol Meyers sees an egalitarian society with gender division during Israel's settlement. In her analysis, gender division means that procreation and food gathering and processing (women's realm) were seen as equally important as building terraces or defending one's territory (men's realm), not only during the planting or collection season, but in order to survive until next season.[60] Gender-

---

[59] Lever, "Honour as a Red Herring," 94. Notice how the study suggests that the richer a man the more possibilities he has to keep women isolated, while a poor man finds himself in such financial constraints that, not only is he unable to make the same requests of his women, but they know better what is going on in the village. Lever, 86–94, also evaluates instances of lip service on the part of those subordinated, from children who are unhappy with their obliged obedience to their parents to conflicting political views between labor workers (in favor of strikes) and the dominant ideology of conformism of their employers, who see strike as immoral.

[60] Carol Meyers, "Procreation, Production, and Protection: Male-Female Balance in Early Israel," *JAAR* 51 (1983): 569–93. In "Domestic Economy of Early Israel," in *Women's Earliest Records from Ancient Egypt and Western Asia* (ed. B. Lesko; BJS 166; Atlanta: Scholars Press, 1989), 276, she states "The implications of this reconstruction of female roles in early Israel, in which a situation of near parity of female and male contributions existed and in which females exerted control over significant tasks and over numbers of persons, becomes clear when the context we have delineated is set against the analytical opposition of domestic and public realms found in much of the social scientific discussion of female roles and status."

differentiated roles did not automatically mean different value perceptions for women in their society. Naomi Steinberg states that

> men and women in ancient Israelite society performed as social actors in a much more complicated and interdependent fashion than has heretofore been suggested....
>
> Our Western prejudices may actually limit the data that is collected because the questions asked in cross-cultural studies on women reflect our ideological biases.... The public/political world of men is deemed more meritorious and status-laden than the private/domestic world of women.[61]

Steinberg goes directly to the point when she speaks of the public or political world, the man's world, as the only one worthy of notice, while the domestic or private one, more connected to women, goes unnoticed, or if it is noticed, it is not considered "work" even today. As long as record of events, past and present, is only made from an androcentric perspective, the picture will be incomplete and distorted, because it will value events and occupations only according to one segment of society, wrongly taking their view as representative of the whole, ignoring other segments.

Scholars are trained to ask "the right questions." But right or wrong is determined by the tradition of the particular discipline, a tradition still largely shaped by males. Reflecting on issues of feminism and research in Mesopotamian studies, Julia Asher-Greve sees a false dichotomy male-female as part of the incomplete picture created by looking only at males from a male point of view. On the basis that "feminist philosophers attack paradigmatic dualism and either/or categorization, claiming that those are neither normative nor universal," Asher-Greve started to review her own scholarly assumptions.

> My study of women in ancient Sumer was based on the either/or model, that is, if it is not male then it must be female. Depictions of persons whose dress and features were apparently ambiguous were still pressed into a two-gendered system, or the visual object was interpreted as of low artistic quality, perhaps of provincial origin. The implication that (provincial) artists were gender blind never occurred ....
>
> The evidence led to new interpretations. An analysis of gender in mass produced seals in the late Uruk period (c. 3100-2900 BCE) revealed that, although there is a division of gender and work or tasks, this gender division is not very rigid; women occasionally do men's work, like herding, and occupy positions as overseers of groups. But it was not always important to the Sumerians to specify gender. The tasks or roles of a group (and, occasionally, of an individual) are sometimes more important than gender differentiation. In

---

[61] Naomi Steinberg, "Gender Roles in the Rebekah Cycle" *USQR* 39 (1984): 175–76.

some instances a task like weaving, herding or fishing is sufficient to indicate which gender was associated with that work.[62]

Asher-Greve offers three important thrusts for this study. First, the combination of a feminist viewpoint, fed by insights from feminists from other disciplines, and serious review of her own scholarship. Secondly, she stresses that new viewpoints produce new questions and new interpretations; finally these new interpretations mean that, judging from the seals examined, Sumerians were more focused on the tasks than on the performers, and although there was a gender division of work, it was superseded when there was a need to have the work done. A cursory comparison of Asher-Greve's and Meyers's results is sufficient to demonstrate that with a new set of questions, provided by disciplines other than biblical exegesis, pioneering work is being done on new interpretations of available sources. These interpretations show a more nuanced and richer picture of life and gender relations in antiquity.

A last example is the work of a student in anthropology, who tested some of the scholarly assumptions in reference to honor/shame and gender division of labor in a small fishing village, Vila Chã, in Northern Portugal. Families in the village have a basic division of labor, which consists of fishing and caring for the boats by men, while women sort and sell fish, mend nets, harvest seaweed for fertilizers, rear children, have a garden and animals for their own, complement the income by hiring their labor to land-owning farmers, do the basic household chores, and keep the accounts of all that was earned and spent. However, since life is always so precarious, the economic advantage of the whole family comes before gender rigidity, with the end result that roles are often occupied by every possible hand.

All men went to sea, but some women also went to sea; women controlled the seaweed harvest; but, when called upon, men assisted their wives with this work; and, while domestic tasks were performed primarily by women, men also assisted with cooking and were active in child rearing. Women were able to replace men and men were able to replace women in the tasks associated with both the fishery and the domestic work of the household. At the same time, however, women were responsible for the tasks of commodity distribution and household management that defined their economic autonomy and authority in the maritime household.[63]

---

[62] Asher-Greve, "Feminist Research and Mesopotamia," 234–35.

[63] Cole, *Women of the Praia*, 66. Women appear to have gone to fish with their fathers and brothers regardless of the need to do so. If a poor family did not have sons, then the daughters would have a more active role, fishing with their father, and obtaining their state license to fish at the age of fourteen (Cole, *Women of the Praia*), 67. Some kept fishing well into pregnancy and into seniority (66–74). At times of economic hardship in Portugal men left their families and migrated alone to

From Sally Cole's study, the following conclusions are important on the question of honor/shame as understood to have applied in the Mediterranean basin. On the one hand, Cole observed the typical double standard in the moral evaluation of male or female as to their sexual behavior, which expects a particular type of shame only from the woman. However, it was not seen in relation to her virginity, but to heavier consequences for women, especially in case of a child born out of wedlock.

> Expressions about vergonha [shame, shyness] are used daily to refer to both men and women, except in the area of sexuality, where vergonha is expected of women but not of men. A girl was taught to have vergonha because she must maintain control over her fertility. Should she become pregnant, it was she who would assume responsibility for the child's needs or become a burden to the parental household.[64]

On the other hand, as seen in previous examples, the maritime village shows a subculture of poverty, hard work, and cultivation of kinship as more important for survival and friendship than are sexual mores. In this framework, the younger were advised "to avoid selecting marriage partners from households known for laziness, slovenliness, or drunkenness. This is to say that, among the maritime households of Vila Chã, property was rarely a factor in the choice of a marriage partner," and the same applied to sexuality-related factors, such as virginity or being the daughter of a single mother.[65]

Brazil and to Mozambique with the purpose—often forgotten after a while—of sending money back home. This situation, only indirectly acknowledged by the biblical writers, must have been common at times; furthermore, it would be similar to what happened at home when men went to war, to corvée or hired themselves out to meet ends. Cole does not detect any sense of shame because of these changes in traditional positions; women just took up additional responsibilities.

[64] Cole, *Women of the Praia*, 83. Cole, 59–62 also records that in other aspects of life theirs was a more lenient position, seen for instance in that the child is not discriminated against, but is taken as part of the maternal household. When the child reaches marriageable age, he or she joins the "marriage-pool" of the poor people, like any other fisherman or woman. For the pregnant woman's parents this type of situation gives them also the expectation that this daughter will remain close to her home and care for her parents when they grow old, rather than migrate.

[65] Cole, *Women of the Praia*, 48. On p. 46–54 Cole studies the Roman Catholic parish records of marriage for 1911–59. The parish is formed by two very different, conflicting groups, namely, the maritime village and the land-owning farmers. The latter are richer, buy fish and seaweed from the fisherwomen, hire them for labor, and when in winter there is hunger lend them a cup of flour or sugar. Cole finds very different patterns between these two sub-cultures. For instance, the fishermen and women belong to the poorest class, value hard work and thriftiness, and marry other poor, while the farmers prevent their children from mixing with these poor, confine their women to their own home or relations, and try to marry their children to other land-owners.

Cole's contribution for us consists in demonstrating that when research focuses on women themselves, interviewing and observing them instead of having them interpreted by men, their own perception of themselves, of their value and values, comes out much more nuanced. They reveal a whole world in which they see themselves as active participants and contributors. This is only fair, since they are active participants and they do contribute to society at least equally with men. This is an important consequence, because it does not deny the typically patriarchal double standard in sexual matters, but at the same time it does not perpetuate the valuation of woman only or primarily in terms of her roles of mother and wife.

Cole's research coincides in many aspects with those of Wikan and Lever discussed earlier in showing other trends in anthropological studies, and especially showing once again how much results depend on the scholar's approach and biases. Together with contributions coming from the application of feminist questions to disciplines related to the ANE (reviewed in the following chapter) these studies support and affect the work undertaken in these pages.

IDEOLOGICAL CRITICISM

One other method of biblical criticism—ideological criticism—is incorporated into this work, but not to its full potential, as that would have enlarged considerably the scope of this research. According to Yee, ideological criticism "entails ... an extrinsic analysis that uncovers the circumstances under which the text was produced and an intrinsic analysis that investigates the text's reproduction of ideology in the text's rhetoric."[66] Ideological criticism implies reading between the lines, or against the grain, trying to get to the writer's point of view and possible reasons for his/her way of depicting a situation, and at the same time it also questions how the history of scholarship and how particular traditions of scholarship have understood and used a text and its ideological message to serve their own interests. This is not to blame one group over another. As stated earlier in reference to the use of models, no one is free from ideological positions and biases, which, unless checked, are just transferred into the text.

Briggs traces the origin of ideological criticism to the very beginnings of historical criticism, to nineteenth-century Germany, because biblical criticism

---

[66] Gale A. Yee, "Ideological Criticism: Judges 17–21 and the Dismembered Body," in *Judges and Method* (ed. Gale A. Yee; Minneapolis: Fortress, 1995), 150. She adds in n. 9, "In addition to investigating the text's production and reproduction of ideology, ideological criticism can also study how the text is received/read in the *consumption* of that ideology."

originated in ideological dissatisfaction with the current political system, and it was used for the purpose of challenging it.

> Biblical criticism has therefore a double character: it is a means simultaneously for creating ideology and for ideological critique ... Critical methods were crucial to the self-assertion of the middle class because they gave it ammunition to fight the claims of the older authoritarian aristocratic cultures that *they* were the natural and necessary order of things. Instead, as critical methods could be used to demonstrate, the feudal order was grounded in aristocratic and monarchal self-interest and fostered a way of life now outmoded in and restrictive of an industrial society. Of course, Marx was going to turn critical methods against the bourgeoisie itself.[67]

On the other hand, Newsom acknowledges also its post-modern character: "While it is true that ideological criticism in general begins as a phenomenon of high modernism (in its early Marxist forms), it is now practiced with a deep sense of the contextualized nature of truths and of the way in which all texts can be deconstructed to reveal conflicting claims and implicit contestations for power."[68] Ideological and other forms of post-modern criticism have thrived in the last years because of the increasing dissatisfaction of scholars with historical criticism, and because of the increased pressure on the part of minority groups to uplift voices other than the dominant one, to prevent the taming of the text, and to call attention to the use of ideology also by those who defend the monopoly of a specific biblical interpretation.

> The point here is that biblical texts are also social productions, that is, they emerge out of very particular social and material settings, and as a result they simultaneously preserve and promote certain views about power relationships and social identity. In short, biblical texts take sides in ideological debates, debates which usually center around issues of power where literature becomes a form of public discourse seeking either to challenge or to defend the way in which people are socially constituted.[69]

Like all sub-disciplines of biblical exegesis, ideological criticism looks at the general picture from a particular standpoint, namely, one intended to

---

[67] S. Briggs, "The Deceit of the Sublime: An Investigation into the Origins of Ideological Criticism of the Bible in Early Nineteenth-Century German Biblical Studies," in *Ideological Criticism of the Bible*, 2.

[68] Carol A. Newsom, "Reflections on Ideological Criticism and Postcritical Perspectives," in *Method Matters: Essays on the Interpretation of the Hebrew Bible in Honor of David L. Petersen* (ed. Joel M. LeMon & Kent Harold Richards; Resources for Biblical Study; Atlanta: SBL, 2009), 542.

[69] Renita Weems, "'The Hebrew Women Are Not Like the Egyptian Women': The Ideology of Race, Gender and Sexual Reproduction in Exodus 1," in *Ideological Criticism of the Bible*, 26.

challenge the *status quo* and to move people to justice. Ideological criticism is particularly helpful when one asks whose interests are being served by a certain depiction of society, of women, and of work.[70]

BORROWING FROM EXISTING MODELS

Having made explicit the body of research and the main methodologies, it is time to review some models, establishing their usefulness for us. The one we prefer is a model in which power is seen as a continuum, with shades of gray, rather than black and white compartments.

THE "CONTINUUM OF POWERLESSNESS" MODEL

Gerda Lerner's work is a history of the relation of women to history. That means, on the one hand, women have made history from its very beginning, while on the other hand history writing has ignored woman's contribution and participation. Lerner traces the beginning of patriarchy to the submission of woman's sexuality, beginning with Mesopotamia at a time before history writing, private property, and classes. Thus, as city-states grew and empires formed, submission of their women and submission of enemies were not foreign to each other, but the two sides of the same coin. This is how she sees the beginning of the process.

> The appropriation by men of women's sexual and reproductive capacity occurred *prior* to the formation of private property and class society. Its commodification lies, in fact, at the foundation of private property ...
>
>   Men learned to institute dominance and hierarchy over other people by their earlier practice over the women of their own group. This found expression in the institutionalization of slavery, which began with the enslavement of women of conquered groups ....
>
>   Women's sexual subordination was institutionalized in the earliest law codes and enforced by the full power of the state. Women's cooperation in the system was secured by various means: force, economic dependency on the male head of the family, class privileges bestowed upon conforming and dependent

---

[70] The matter is, however, far more complicated, as Newsom's analysis, for instance, shows ("Reflections on Ideological Criticism and Postcritical Perspectives," 542–44). For there are several different understandings of the words "ideology," "(false) consciousness," "power," or "reality." My preferences lie with those who see "ideology" as somehow similar to a political worldview, in the sense that an ideology explains how the world works, who is "in" and who is "out," who deserves better, and so forth.

women of the upper classes, and the artificially created division of women into respectable and non-respectable women.[71]

Lerner locates people in interrelated spheres, each partly overlapping with neighboring ones. This creates a continuum within which concubinage, slavery, prostitution, and the suppression of goddess worship are landmarks in the making and maintaining of the patriarchal system. They are not isolated phenomena, happenstance events, but pieces of the same machinery. To say it differently, everyone is part of the same system, which has on one extreme the *paterfamilias par excellence*, the only god and patron of that system (in this case, YHWH for Israel), and on the other extreme the dispensable, with the women always below the men of the corresponding social group (unprotected widows, lepers, prostitutes too old to attract clients, perhaps beggars). The fact that society is a continuum has consequences for social studies: nobody is totally independent from all the others. On the other hand, there are recognizable social classes, but these boundaries between classes are formed by overlapping groups. Women of one group might be better off socially in relation to the next social class, yet there are men from the next social group who hold more authority than those women. Lerner's model, which I have nicknamed "the continuum of powerlessness" in deference to women, challenges those studies which look at women, in this particular case in the ANE, as if they had all lived the same way, had enjoyed the same privileges, suffered the same discrimination, and shared a uniform world view.

THE "DISTRIBUTION OF POWER AND PRIVILEGES" MODEL

Gerhard Lenski approaches social stratification with the question "Who gets what and why?" and develops a model of distribution of power and privilege among social classes, which varies according to the particular types of society. He finds five main distribution systems (and a variety of hybrid ones): (a) hunting and gathering; (b) simple horticultural; (c) advanced horticultural; (d) agrarian, and sub-variation of maritime societies, and (e) industrial societies. It should be noted that Lenski strongly supports categories of class which are not extremely precise, but are rather broad in scope. This is an approach to stratification which we welcome, as we find ourselves unable to discern in the biblical narratives a very exact system of social stratification.[72]

---

[71] G. Lerner, *The Creation of Patriarchy* (New York/Oxford: Oxford University Press, 1986), 8–9.

[72] G. Lenski, *Power and Privilege: A Theory of Social Stratification* (Chapel Hill: University of North Carolina Press, 1984), 73–84, sees society as formed by several classes divided according to their position in terms of power. Sex, race, age, income, education, lineage, and other factors

For a typical agrarian distribution system, Lenski proposes a graphic summary, in the form of a diamond truncated on the basis, in which the upper apex is disproportionately taller than the horizontal axis, and the lower one is truncated, so that the basis is broader than a regular diamond figure. At the bottom are the expendables, followed by the unclean and degraded. Then, the largest section, where both axes meet, is occupied by peasants, and smaller groups of artisans at the bottom and merchants going up. Lenski describes its main characteristics as follows.

> First, it should help to make clear that the classes within agrarian societies cannot be thought of simply as a series of layers superimposed one on the other. On the contrary, each covers a range of the distributive spectrum, and what is more, each overlaps certain others to some degree. Second, this diagram may serve as a reminder of the inaccuracy of the familiar pyramidal view of societies, which ignores the depressed classes at the very bottom of the social order and minimizes the degree of inequality (which, incidentally, is still minimized by the diagram shown here; it would require a spire far higher and far slenderer than these pages permit to show accurately the relationship between the upper classes and the common people). Finally, this diagram may help to make clear that there is a *continuum* of power and privilege, not a series of separate and distinct strata in the geological sense of that term.[73]

Lenski and Lerner undertake very different projects, have different agendas, and look at issues from different disciplines. Yet they agree in seeing power and its distribution as a continuum among groups, which overlap at some points but are also clearly distinctive, and at this conjunction is where our study meets theirs.

THE "WOMEN AND CLASS IN ANTIQUITY" MODEL

James Arlandson goes into Luke-Acts in order to find out what Luke meant by Jesus being "destined for the falling and the rising of many in Israel, and to be a sign that will be opposed," as Simeon announces (Lk 2:34, *NRSV*) and Mary sings (1:46–55), and how that applies to women, since it has long been recognized that Luke favors poor and women in his gospel.[74] With the help of extra-biblical sources, Arlandson tests Lenski's model and classifies all women

---

determine people belonging to different classes as power applies to them in various degrees. If, considering all these facts, one still tried to have very precise social classes, then there would be millions of social classes, each with a small number of people. This is what is meant above by the lack of a "very exact social stratification" in biblical narratives.

[73] Lenski, *Power and Privilege*, 285.

[74] James M. Arlandson, *Women, Class, and Society in Early Christianity: Models from Luke-Acts* (Peabody: Hendrickson, 1997), 1–13.

in Luke-Acts, accordingly, into the following seven categories. First, the governing classes, divided into ruling families and prominent women, followed by the retainers and religionists. Then two groups run parallel in the graphic, namely, the rural group formed by peasants and the urban group, divided into landowners, merchants, artisans, and crowds. The fifth category is that of the slaves, followed by the unclean and degraded, divided into sick people, demonized, prostitutes, and ethnic people, and last of all the expendables, divided into widows and persecuted people.[75] Except for the crowds and the demonized, who are not prominent (if they appear at all) and the persecuted, who seem more difficult to categorize in the Hebrew Bible, the remaining groups fit quite well what we know of its class systems.

Arlandson's study is most valuable for biblical studies in that it shows how a model from the social sciences can be applied if there are other sources available, (for instance, the Gospel, the book of Acts, and primary and secondary sources for the classics). Arlandson pictures society as a quadrangle (rather than Lenski's diamond) with an enlarged area covering those from merchants to slaves, rural and urban, and still leaving room on the bottom for the unclean, degraded, and expendables. As Arlandson explains, the graph cannot be fully appreciated because it would not fit into the page width, since "the population in the widest portion was far more numerous than [his] model is able to show. The right side of the L [the horizontal axis of his quadrangle], representing the rural sphere, is longer than the left side [the vertical axis], representing the urban sphere, because most Mediterraneans lived outside the large metropoleis and in small towns and villages."[76] Arlandson's model shows that society comprises several factors, not only governing and governed, and rich and poor, but it is also comprising those pure and impure, and those needed (workers) and expendable (those the system can do without). The latter were worse-off in comparison to slaves in the Greco-Roman society, even if slavery was harsh and well-spread. Just who comprised the "expendables" is, however, hard to say for "expendable" is a relative concept, not a fixed category: Who decides who is expendable? What are the criteria? In Arlandson's scheme they are those who could not work and thus were less taken care of than slaves; it is well known, however, that even slaves were expendable. Discussing barley rations from Mesopotamia, Daniel Snell states that:

> An important group of texts records the rations of groups of women who had been "dedicated" to temple-managed weaving establishments and shows that

---

[75] Arlandson, *Women*, 124–126. See 24–112 (governing classes, retainers, urban and rural, slaves, degraded, and expendables).

[76] Arlandson, *Women*, 23.

the women died off at an appalling rate; in these cases bureaucrats must have decided that since they were dealing with women and children whom no one else wanted in their households, it did not matter how long they lived. And the work being demanded of them, though important for the economy of the Mesopotamian state, was not so skilled that replacements for workers could not be easily found.[77]

This example shows the cruelty of the concept of "expendable" and what I mean by it being a relative concept. Evidently, in the relation between economics and children's and women's lives, economics primed. Unfortunately, this is still reality.

DEFINING CLASS

Our working definition is adopted from Gerhard Lenski, whose model has just been discussed. He makes a distinction between class, which he defines as "*an aggregation of persons in a society who stand in a similar position with respect to some form of power, privilege, or prestige*," and power class, which he defines as "*an aggregation of persons in a society who stand in a similar position with respect to force or some specific form of institutionalized power*."[78] Although Lenski's definitions are broad and imprecise, they seem to fit well with the very vagueness of ancient data when it comes to classifying people.[79]

ELEMENTS IN A WORKING MODEL

The reader will notice how often the only answer we have is "we do not know." To lack of descriptions in the sources, which would make one understand how

---

[77] Daniel C. Snell, *Flight and Freedom in the Ancient Near East* (Culture and History of the Ancient Near East 8; Leiden: Brill, 2001), 35. I had no access to the printed book; chapter 2 is available online, quotations here are from this version. Cited 21 September 2011. Online: http://books.google.com.ar/books?id=sxvk2iGhcioC&printsec=frontcover&dq=snell,+flight+and+fr eedom&hl=es&ei=qhFfTdWxHIP88AbjhomoDA&sa=X&oi=book_result&ct=result&resnum=1&ve d=0CCwQ6AEwAA#v=onepage&q&f=false.Just one more example from the other extreme of the social ladder to illustrate what I mean by "relative" (it could also be relational): any political revolt may take many lives deemed expendable by those with the political decision and the military power to kill. Thus, the relationship between those in power and those revolting determines who are expendable and killed. Those killed, seen from the other side, may be victims or even martyrs, and are not necessarily poor, downtrodden or socio-economically fallen out of the system (I am thinking of the Maccabean revolt, for instance).

[78] Lenski, *Power and Privilege*, 74–75.

[79] Lenski, *Power and Privilege*, 219–230 (governing class), 243–248 (retainer class), 248–256 (merchant class), 256–266 (priestly class), 266–278 (peasant class), 278–280 (artisan class), 280–281 (unclean and degraded classes), and 281–284 (expendables).

things worked, one has to add lack of an adequate model focusing on women and asking what were the class powers, statuses, and locations they were in. This is a project far more ambitious than one single study can accomplish. What follows is just a beginning.

The models reviewed converge in their claim that society is a continuum and should not be seen as a compartmentalized layer of isolated classes. In pre-industrial societies in which there is social stratification, people know where everyone belongs. But that belonging is not into upper-class or lower-class only, there are several little circles overlapping each other in several ways. This view of society is more accurate and it better reveals the women this study is intent to bring out of their confinement.

Economic dependency is connected to social dependency, but they are not the same. Social dependency is determined by many other factors, such as legal status, marital status, family ties, ritual purity, education, age, and beauty. Thus, within female labor one would have found free women and indentured servants, women bound permanently to the court, temple, and a family household, women seeking daily labor or seeking hiring on a more permanent basis, women working as collateral at the creditor's household in payment for interest on loans, women sold as concubines or slave-wives, and women taken to a harem as wives or as servants. The list could go on, but the variety of situations and the difficulties in classifying them is clear.

Society can be represented in a graphic in many different ways and here I trust my readers' imagination. For me it would be enough simply to superimpose, as if working on a computerized presentation, certain colored graphics for men and for women onto Lenski's truncated diamond figure. If we tried to imagine what such a superimposed colored graph would look like, we would find that the female color tends to fall to the bottom and is therefore more concentrated where the unclean, degraded, and expendables lie. The graph for males would follow the opposite direction toward the top. I would still want to imagine that a large part of this middle section would be shared by both colors in approximately equal proportions. Then, merchants and retainers would move toward a male-dominated top, headed by the priestly and the governing classes.

SUMMING UP

From the findings on female labor discussed below, a graphic on women would have to consider these aspects. First, in none of the categories for women are top markers achieved, showing that women as power groups are always at a disadvantage to men: there is a glass ceiling preventing them from achieving the top.

It would have dotted lines or blurred boundaries to show that many questions are not addressed by sources from the ANE and thus, there must be room for elusiveness. For example, Lenski and Arlandson rightly depict, starting from the top, the governing class, retainers, priests, artisans, and merchants. While there is evidence in our sources for queens, priestesses, prophetesses, oneiromancers, rich women selling their production, and some types of artisans, the evidence is insufficient to determine what Sjoberg calls "similarly valued objective criteria," which would be shared within the same class.[80] This means that, while one can locate the merchants or the priests as a *group* in a certain location in the social spectrum, according to what the ANE sources tell us about them in general, one cannot pin down its women.

Class is comprised, according to Sjoberg, of a large group of people who occupy the same position in reference to different aspects of life.[81] This means that dependency would be one of various facts in determining people's location. People who shared the same labor situation, (for example, that of working for a master) would not share among them every other aspect of life (such as education or ethnicity).To state it differently, social models which look at the three-layer class system (upper, lower, and outcasts) are helpful and accurate in that there were three layers, and apparently quite distinctive layers. Those models, on the other hand, do not specify how the situation of economically dependent women differed from the situation of racially different women (foreigners, especially from enemy groups), or from that of beggars or poor widows. These women—and many other—would share in their need to work for others, but their social location would vary.[82] While it would have been simpler to study only women from one of these social classes, biblical texts lack

---

[80] G. Sjoberg, *The Preindustrial City* (Glencoe, IL: Free Press, 1960), 109: "For us, a social class is a large body of persons who occupy a position in a social hierarchy by reason of their manifesting similarly valued objective criteria. These latter include kinship affiliation, power and authority, achievements, possessions, and moral and personal attributes. Achievements involve a person's occupational and educational attainments; possessions refer to material evidences of wealth; moral attributes include one's religious and ethical beliefs and actions; and personal attributes involve speech, dress, and personal mannerisms." On 142 n.1 he states that his is an adaptation of Talcott Parsons' model, *Essays in Sociological Theory* (Glencoe: Free Press, 1957) 171–172.

[81] Sjoberg, *Preindustrial City* (110–137) sees preindustrial societies divided into three distinctive social strata, i.e., the upper class, which is urban, despises manual work, and controls wealth, land, education, politics, military paraphernalia, and religion; the lower class, found both in the cities and the villages, comprising skilled and unskilled labor (harvesters, artisans, animal drivers, ditch-diggers), merchants, secondary bureaucrats (political, religious, and military), and peasants; and outcasts, usually ethnically different from the upper and lower classes, comprising several groups whose services are needed while their performers are despised and scorned (such as slaves, "night-soil carriers, leather workers, butchers, many barbers, midwives, prostitutes, dancers, lepers, etc.") and expendables (lepers, widows, perhaps beggars).

[82] See Martin Whyte, *The Status of Women in Preindustrial Societies* (Princeton: Princeton University Press, 1978), 167–184.

examples for many occupations listed by Sjoberg (or Lenski)—not to speak of the lack of class markers.

A model focusing on women in the ANE would include variables of fertility, age, beauty, ritual purity, and marital condition among others.[83] These variables might have affected men's lives at some point, but they affect women's working possibilities in powerful ways. Beauty or pregnancy, for instance, could determine a woman's location in certain jobs, and her ritual impurity (menstruation) would have prevented her from certain tasks; in many societies, rituals and healing activities are in the hands of post-menopausal women. Thus, the model would not be a static one, but it would change form and color, showing woman's different statuses through time and life stages.

A model focusing on women in the ANE would value them for their socio-economic, political, and cultural contribution to society, not for their virginity or sex appeal.

Finally, the model would have to leave room for "the forgotten laborer," for the woman whose life was left unrecorded, and also for the "unknown" woman, the woman of whom we know so little that we cannot count her in. Their labor, however, made a difference in society, and that should not be written off.

---

[83] Jo Ann Hackett, "In the Days of Jael: Reclaiming the History of Women in Ancient Israel," in *Immaculate and Powerful: The Female in Sacred Image and Social Reality* (ed. Clarissa W. Atkinson, Constance H. Buchanan, and Margaret R. Miles; Boston: Beacon Press, 1985) 17–22 reviews questions posed by the New Women's History (in this case, to the Bible); particularly on pp. 18-19 the contributions from feminist anthropologists and marxists historians.

CHAPTER 2

ON THE SHOULDERS OF OUR PREDECESSORS

"If we stand tall, it is because we stand on the shoulders of those who were there before us," says an African traditional proverb.[1] These words are intended to acknowledge the enormous debt I have with many more people than we may here recognize.

Since this study stands at the intersection of several fields, each with a broad scholarship in its own right, a review of work bearing upon this research would take a whole book or otherwise be necessarily eclectic and limited. I will refer only to major contributions to this study's understanding of lower-class women, addressing other studies as we go.[2] The review is itemized into: feminist and gender studies (including studies on ANE women); biblical studies; social-scientific studies; studies on labor; and studies on slave, semi-free and unfree workers.

---

[1] Heard from Dr. Musimbi Kanyoro, then Secretary for the Women in Church and Society Desk of the Lutheran World Federation, at her opening speech to the International Consultation on Women, Geneva, October 1995.

[2] A difficulty encountered repeatedly in this dissertation is that of appropriate terminology for the people studied. For the sake of simplicity, "lower class women" will be used at times to refer to social class, although many factors within any class should be considered. "Working women" and "female workers" are used as synonyms, to refer to women who exchanged a service for pay, regardless of occupation and legal status. In the same vain, "work" refers to productive work exchanged for a payment, either by wages, goods (oil, flax, etc.) or supplying of basic needs (lodging and food). Finally, "dependent" is used in general to refer to people serving in a dependency position in a household other than their own, for example the נער/ה/ים/ות and captive women whose exact status is unknown. Although an encompassing term—if there was one—would have aided in clarity, on the other hand it would had obscured the variety of aspects found in the texts for women who worked for others.

FEMINIST AND GENDER STUDIES

Like every evolving discipline, what started as "women studies" eventually developed into what are today gender studies and feminist studies with their many emphases and sub-disciplines. The term "women studies" is ambiguous: it may include studies by women, about women, and for women and it need not promote gender awareness; thus, I try to avoid it. "Gender studies" covers several aspects and, to many, seems to be too mild. "Feminist" is troublesome and loaded. Troublesome because there is no English inclusive term for the different tracks (Anglo-Saxon feminists, African-American womanists, Latino "mujeristas," Latin American Feminist Liberation movements, and others). Loaded because certain clichés remain ("they hate men," "they want to throw men out and take their place") even among women who are aware of the injustices the patriarchal system inflicts upon them. It is obvious that we have here a conceptual problem. Despite these drawbacks, I personally identify myself as a feminist scholar and hope that the issue will not be bothersome to my readers.

The point of including this sub-section here is to recognize the colossal debt to so many women (and some men) who sought to change hegemonic scholarship by putting a small stone on that seemingly smooth way. It has also the intention of warning unaware readers that, even though this is a long path already, it is still in the making. And finally, it shows what have been my main tools. Scholars in tune with gender issues have used all types of methodologies and approaches, from the new literary criticism to post-modern epistemological and philosophical insights. It is eclectic, because it tries not to be too narrow in its focus and also because it is young and alive. At times it might look chaotic and it is so, indeed. In this section I will only mention those studies which were foundational to my research and which, for a variety of reasons, are not quoted often in the next chapters.

In the introduction to the volume she edited, Beth Alpert Nakhai tells how the American Schools of Oriental Research started a section on *World of Women: Gender and Archaeology*. Perusing through the Association's program books, she had discovered there were more papers dedicated to pigs than to women. The anecdote is funny and telling. I have not traced entries on female workers, but would bet that they do not fare much better today. "Women" in all categories, yes; in that sense we have outnumbered the pigs.[3]

Some years ago, it was still possible to make an overall review of the production of "women studies" on biblical themes. Today that is no longer

---

[3] Beth Alpert Nakhai, "Introduction: The World of Women in the Ancient and Classical Near East," in *The World of Women in the Ancient and Classical Near East* (ed. Beth Alpert Nakhai; Newcastle upon Tyne: Cambridge Scholars Publishing, 2008), ix.

possible. There are several general dictionaries, commentaries on particular books, feminist journals, theses and dissertations, and scattered articles on almost any subject related to women and to gender issues.[4]

On gender awareness, at least two names deserve recognition as pioneers in bridging the gap between archaeological and biblical studies. Carol Meyers's *Discovering Eve* was instrumental in this sense, as she challenged traditional readings of Gen 2–3 and recovered the social context of Iron Age Syro-Palestinian (Israelite) settlers. In this context, slaves are not noticeable. Therefore, though an important contribution, this book is not much quoted.[5] The other name comes from Europe: Silvia Schroer, part of a research team located in Switzerland, has studied for years iconography from the ANE with an impressive production still going on.[6]

Together with the late van Dijk-Hemmes, Athalya Brenner is author of a collection of essays exploring signs of gender authorship of a text, regardless of its actual writer. This book is an important work, because it moves the discussion from the dubious possible male or female author, to male or female voices, which *might* or *might not* have proceeded from male and female writers respectively.[7] An earlier little book also by Brenner, *The Israelite Woman*, also deserves attention especially because of her concern with social roles. In the first part of the book she chooses six Israelite models for women in occupations: prostitutes, prophetesses, queen-mothers, singers and poets, wise women and magicians.[8]

---

[4] It feels almost luxurious to be able to find so many works with a feminist (in the broad sense) lens. The following books and collections deserve my gratitude for their quality and for their pioneering character. Phyllis Trible's most impressive one is *Texts of Terror: Literary-Feminist Readings of Biblical Narratives* (Overtures to Biblical Theology, Philadelphia: Fortress, 1984). The texts she dealt with have almost no incidence on my research and thus are not quoted. Carol Newsom & Sharon Ringe, edited *The Women's Bible Commentary* (Louisville: Westminster John Knox, 1992); Athalya Brenner edited the Feminist Companion to the Bible, First and Second Series (by now, more than twenty volumes published since 1993); very useful also is the volume edited by Athalya Brenner and Carole R. Fontaine, *A Feminist Companion to Reading the Bible*. In Germany, Luise Schottroff and Marie-Theres Wacker edited the *Kompendium feministische Bibelauslegung* (Gütersloh: Chr. Kaiser-Gütersloher, 1998). Fortunately, several collections have started to be published as well.

[5] Carol Meyers, *Discovering Eve* (New York: Oxford University Press, 1988). Meyers has also written abundantly on other subjects more pertinent to my research, such as music; see bibliography.

[6] From Schroer see especially her *Images and Gender: Contributions to the Hermeneutics of Reading Ancient Art* (ed. Silvia Schroer; Fribourg/Göttingen: Fribourg Academic Press & Vandenhoeck & Ruprecht, 2006), product of a conference held under her auspices in 2004.

[7] Brenner & van Dijk-Hemmes, *On Gendering Texts*.

[8] Brenner, *The Israelite Woman*. Her study only partly overlaps with the women studied here.

Another work on sexual violence against women should be mentioned, also because it is not much quoted below.[9] Renita Weems has called attention to the relationship Ezekiel and Jeremiah make between idolatry on the part of the whole Israelite community—notably the leading men of Judah—and sexual violence against women.[10] This study is one of the first available on the effects of religious language, in this case in the prophetic corpus, on women and their sexuality.

Issues of gender and class, religious condemnation, violence and sexuality intersect especially in such difficult issues as prostitution. While sociology helps understanding it not as primarily moral or even sexual, but as a form of commercial activity with particular characteristics, it is a form of commerce to which women and children resort when no other form of work is available and even coerced. And here is where the moral aspect comes to play. Not to condemn the prostitute, on the contrary: to condemn a system that oppresses women, coerces them to prostitute themselves to survive, forgets to condemn the patrons and the "pimps," and despises her—after using her body. Some very different studies have been published, which look at the socio-economic conditions by which women became impoverished and had to prostitute themselves in order to survive, and relate this socio-economic reality with the biblical text. Their starting-point is totally different from that from Julia Assante, Irene Riegner and others who have questioned the meaning of "harlotry" for זנה. One might say these scholars take the traditional translation of the word to be true and have gone to the texts from their Christian social engagement. Phyllis A. Bird starts from the assumption that women had hardly any possibility outside prostitution if they were not under a "father's house." Therefore, one has to look at the whole social system rather than the women by themselves, even if the texts are sometimes unclear as to their everyday situation.[11]

Tânia Vieira Sampaio studies the first chapters of Hosea looking at Gomer as a woman who, like so many women around the world still today, has *become*

---

[9] Speaking of violence against women, in recent years several commentaries on the book of Judges have appeared. Mieke Bal's *Death and Dissymmetry: The Politics of Coherence in the Book of Judges* (Chicago: University of Chicago Press, 1988), opened the way to addressing the tremendous thrust toward death in this book. Tikva Frymer-Kensky has also a very interesting article comparing fathers, mothers and children in Genesis and Judges ("The Family in the Hebrew Bible"). More recently, Renate Jost's *Gender, Sexualität und Macht in der Anthropologie des Richterbuches*, is particularly helpful in addressing these issues from an anthropological standpoint. It should be noted that this biblical book yields little for our search and thus these works do not appear often in the footnotes.

[10] Renita Weems, *Battered Love: Marriage, Sex, and Violence in the Hebrew Prophets* (Minneapolis: Fortress, 1995).

[11] See below my bibliography, especially "The Harlot as Heroine" and "'To Play the Harlot': An Inquiry into an Old Testament Metaphor." More on her work below in chapter 7.

a prostitute, has *come* into a situation of prostitution. It is not her "essence," so to speak, but her status due to the straits the family is suffering. In fact, she claims, it is the elite men, the priests, who exercise prostitution against the land and its people. The main reasons for that situation are social unrest, increasing concentration of land in fewer hands, and farmers' impoverishment due to war, luxury, and other expenses from the state, which exhaust them and constrain them to seek other ways of surviving.

Finally, Avaren Ipsen has just published her dissertation on texts about sex workers in the Bible.[12] The most interesting and moving aspect of her book is the fact that her insights come from working in the San Francisco (USA) area with sex workers and having herself been brought up in a suspected family. The hermeneutical principle that reality colors our reading is well proven as they read these stories through their own experiences of suffering, violence, poverty, and discrimination in a way others are unable to see. Yet, both the readers and the read-about sex workers engage in their society, seek to escape the hardship which burdens them, and devise ways to trick the system. They are victims of a perverse social structure, but they are more than victims; they are at the same time subjects of many of their decisions, to a higher or lesser degree, just like we are.

ANCIENT NEAR EASTERN STUDIES FOCUSING ON WOMEN

Coming from the ANE studies that are not about the Bible, there are some collections of articles and some very important books. The series Rencontre Assyriologique Internationale has a few issues specifically on women and on gender from different international meetings.[13] From the 1980s there are already some very useful books by Barbara Lesko on Egypt, and by Sarah Pomeroy on Hellenistic Egypt and on Greek women. Like their biblical colleagues, they opened up the way for further discussion and exploration of issues of gender. In 1993, Gay Robins published her *Women in Ancient Egypt*. Her conclusion is that "the main roles of Egyptian women were to bear children, to run the household and manage its economy, to help accumulate wealth through the exchange of surplus goods (often of their own production), to weave textiles which were fundamental for clothing, and to produce flour and bread basic to the Egyptian diet."[14]

---

[12] See below, bibliography on Vieira Sampaio and Avaren.

[13] J.-M. Durand, ed., *La Femme Dans le Proche-Orient Antique* (1987) and *Sex and Gender in the Ancient Near East* (2001).

[14] Robins, *Women in Ancient Egypt* (Cambridge: Harvard University Press, 1993), 190–191; idem, "Some Images of Women in New Kingdom Art and Literature," in *Women's Earliest Records*, 116.

These are all very important and often quoted books on this subject. I would consider these the pioneering works on women in those lands and cultures. Happily, these are not the only ones available today. Among studies on women in the Greco-Roman world, Pomeroy's *Goddesses, Whores, Wives and Slaves* is a classic. Less well-known but equally necessary is her work on Hellenistic women in Egypt.[15] Here she compares their social, economic, and educational situation to that of women in Greece, and concludes that the egalitarian character of the Egyptian culture is to be credited for the more advantageous situation of women in Hellenistic Egypt vis-à-vis Athenian women. Eva Keuls' *The Reign of the Phallus* follows the path earlier taken by Pomeroy, paying special attention to misogynist constructions of women in Greek myths, art, religion, and philosophy, which has so much permeated Western thinking to date.[16] In recent years, several publications have appeared on the Greek and Roman world; treating them in detail or even delving into the material deep enough to make meaningful comparisons would entail a much larger enterprise than possible at this point.

BIBLICAL STUDIES

This section evaluates studies with a strong emphasis on biblical texts themselves, unlike Mendelsohn's and other studies, which do not do biblical exegesis. Exegetical studies on each of the books covered by this work have been consulted, and they appear in the bibliography. Even to list every pertinent article on the specific texts dealing with slavery would be too long to be profitable.[17] Speaking in general terms, compiled studies, such as works on sociology and the Bible or women and the Bible (some are discussed in chapter 2), on labor, or on cuneiform and biblical laws were particularly helpful in a field where references do not abound.[18]

---

[15] See my bibliography.

[16] Eva Keuls, *The Reign of the Phallus: Sexual Politics in Ancient Athens* (New York: Harper and Row, 1985). I thank Edgar Krentz for bringing this book to my attention.

[17] See Dean Miller, "Biblical and Rabbinic Contributions to an Understanding of the Slave," in *Approaches to Ancient Judaism: Theory and Praxis* (ed. William Green; BJS; Missoula: Scholars Press, 1978), 189–99; J. van der Ploeg, "Slavery in the Old Testament," in *Congress Volume: Uppsala 1971* (ed. H. S. Nyberg et al.; VTSup 22; Leiden: Brill, 1972), 72–87; Victor Matthews, "The Anthropology of Slavery in the Covenant Code," in *Theory and Method in Biblical and Cuneiform Law* (ed. B. Levinson; JSOTSup 181; Sheffield: Sheffield Academic Press, 1994), 119–135; N. Lemche, "The Hebrew Slave. Comments on the Slave Law, Ex. xxi 2–11," *VT* 25 (1975): 129–44; "The Hebrew and the Seven Year Cycle," *BN* 25 (1984): 65–76; and Hans W. Wolff, "Masters and Slaves," *Int* 27 (1973): 259–72.

[18] See, for instance, *Judges and Method* (quoted above); *Gender and Difference in Ancient Israel* (ed. P. Day. Minneapolis: Fortress, 1989); *Families in Ancient Israel* (ed. L. Perdue, J. Blenkinsopp, J. J. Collins, & C. Meyers; Louisville: Westminster John Knox, 1997). Especially helpful is *Labor in*

Gregory Chirichigno studies debt-slavery in Israel through the laws on manumission in Exod 21:2–11, Deut 15:12–18 and Lev 25:39–54. His analysis is especially valuable in a detailed study of the laws involving debt-slaves, an increasingly common situation among Israelites from the monarchy onwards.[19] I am unaware of other, more recent large studies that would address directly the subject of slavery as a subject in itself.[20]

Carolyn Pressler contested studies on Deuteronomy which claimed a particular concern in this book for woman's interests. Studying the Deuteronomic family laws (which exclude slaves) she shows that laws aim at order and harmony within the extended family. Order protects in the first place the *status quo*, which is to say, it prevents changes in society which would disrupt traditional structures and privilege, and thus laws protect first and foremost the *paterfamilias*.[21] Pressler concludes that

> the laws presuppose the dependence of women within male-headed households and the subordinate role of women within the family. The laws aim to support the stability of the family by undergirding hierarchical, patrilineal family structures. They also protect dependent family members. Their efforts to protect dependents do not, however, fundamentally challenge the hierarchical family structure.[22]

---

the ANE (quoted above). Its value lies not only in contributions from experts on various cities and periods, but also in their repeated assessment that the difference between slave and free is often blurred in the sources. On legal issues see Raymond Westbrook, *Property and the Family in Biblical Law* (JSOTS 113. Sheffield: Sheffield Academic Press, 1991), especially chs. 2 (Jubilee laws) and 7 (dowry); E. Otto, "Rechtssystematik im altbabylonischen 'Codex Esnunna' und im altisraelitischen 'Bundesbuch'. Eine Redaktionsgeschichtliche und rechtsvergleichende Analyse von CE §§ 17; 18; 22–28 und Ex 21,18–32; 22,6–14; 23, 1–3.6–8," *UF* 19 (1987): 175–97; D. Daube, *Studies in Biblical Law* (Cambridge: Cambridge University Press, 1949). Meyers' *Discovering Eve* is an example of the use of anthropological insights to study biblical texts.

[19] Chirichigno, *Debt-Slavery*, quoted above.

[20] There are papers on particular laws, of course, but no books; there are also indirect references, including last decade's hot debate principally between John van Seters and Eckart Otto. Since the Covenant Code is involved in the discussion, one may argue that these have a bearing on the subject of slavery; they do, but only indirectly. See John Van Seters, *A Law Book for the Diaspora: Revision in the Study of the Covenant Code* (Oxford: Oxford University Press, 2003) and Eckart Otto, review of John Van Seters, *A Law Book for the Diaspora: Revision in the Study of the Covenant Code*, *Review of Biblical Literature* [http://www.bookreviews.org] (2004).

[21] Carolyn Pressler, *The View of Women found in the Deuteronomic Family Laws* (Berlin: De Gruyter, 1993); Elizabeth MacDonald, *The Position of Women as Reflected in Semitic Codes of Law* (Toronto: University of Toronto Press, 1931); Shalom M. Paul, "Biblical Analogues to Middle Assyrian Law," in *Religion and Law: Biblical-Judaic and Islamic Perspectives* (ed. E. Firmage, B. Weiss, & J. W. Welch; Winona Lake: Eisenbrauns, 1990), 333–50.

[22] Pressler, *View of Women*, 1.

Another useful publication is a collection of articles where several well-known scholars in the field reflect on gender and law in the ANE and Israel.[23] In this collection Pressler takes up again her concern and challenges traditional scholarship for its broad-sweep assumptions about women.[24] Pressler's main question, "How do these laws treat women in the roles of 'wife,' 'daughter,' 'widow,' and so forth?" can be deepened by asking how do laws treat female slaves, slave-wives, child guardians, prostitutes, weavers, and other workers. Even a cursory look at the biblical law codes shows the scarcity of references to women in general and to professionals in particular; further research on them is still needed.[25]

Among those who look at the effect of the legal material on women, Tikva Frymer-Kensky deserves consideration as a leading voice. I deeply regret her untimely death. Her scholarship is an example of the integration of biblical and ancient Near Eastern issues with a critical, yet passionate, eye for women and for the Divine.[26]

Finally a word about a study on the servant motif published in 1950 by Curt Lindhagen. He endeavored to illumine the image of the suffering servant in Isaiah by providing biblical and extra-biblical background on the connotation of the term עֶבֶד ("slave" or "servant"). Our work was not conceived as a feminist companion to Lindhagen's, but in a sense it may be so seen: several female suffering servants, in whom to see YHWH at work, can be found in the biblical stories to be explored below.

SOCIAL-SCIENTIFIC STUDIES

Unlike the relation of biblical studies to gender and feminist studies, which is still unappreciated by many, two other methodological interactions have a long history behind them, namely, those of biblical exegesis with anthropology and

---

[23] See Raymond Westbrook, "The Female Slave," in *Gender and Law in the Hebrew Bible and the Ancient Near East* (ed. V. Matthews, B. Levinson & T. Frymer-Kensky. JSOTSup 262. Sheffield: Sheffield Academic Press, 1998), 214–238. I thank Alejandro Botta for referring me to this book.

[24] Carolyn Pressler, "Wives and Daughters, Bond and Free: Views of Women in the Slave Laws of Exodus 21.2–11," in *Gender and Law in the Hebrew Bible* (ed. Victor H. Matthews, Bernard M. Levinson, and Tikva Frymer-Kensky; JSOTSup 262; Sheffield: Sheffield Academic Press, 1998), 150. See in the same collection Eckart Otto's indirect response to her, "False Weights in the Scales of Biblical Justice: Different Views of Women from Patriarchal Hierarchy to Religious Equality in the Book of Deuteronomy," 128–46, taking a much more positive view of the laws. True, he does not deal with family laws but with laws on participation in religious events... and he (like everybody else) looks at them from his own social, male location.

[25] See also S. Schroer, "Toward a Feminist Reconstruction of the History of Israel," in *Feminist Interpretation*, 87–88.

[26] She was also very generous with her time and wisdom on my last stages as a doctoral student, back in 1998 in Chicago, for which I feel privileged.

with sociology. The next sections explore major contributions for our study coming from these two disciplines.

Since the biblical text reflects a foreign and long-gone society, in a sense neither sociology nor anthropology have in the Bible an object to be studied first-hand, and they often overlap in studying phenomena such as prophecy, family structures, power or violence. In this regard, Naomi Steinberg's study of the Pentateuchal narratives is pioneering in that she uses what in North America is known as "the social-scientific analysis," which is "the general methodology of social anthropology, a discipline concerned with social organization, and the subdiscipline of household economics, an approach that examines family units."[27] She manages to integrate gender issues into them. This makes sense, since gender affects deeply social organization and economics. The Pentateuchal kinship narratives are not immediately relevant to my concern, however, and therefore this work of hers is not quoted below.

First, anthropology has been instrumental in disclosing a variety of family systems, which constitute a preoccupation and determine many biblical events. To mention just one such example, the narratives about Saul, David, and Solomon—which are families whose stories are narrated more minutely than others—are a mixture of state-related affairs with family affairs, because hereditary monarchies are based even more on family conflicts and negotiations than are other families.[28] Dependent women were especially affected by social practices. Slaves who became the master's concubines and bore him children could hope for an improvement in their social position.[29] Anthropological insights on the importance of the patrilineal system of inheritance show how added women, and especially their sons, could be inserted into the family and participate in its rights and responsibilities.

Finally, insights from anthropologists working in Mediterranean societies are often used, especially by students of the New Testament. Among them, names like Bruce Malina, John Pilch, Victor Matthews and Don Benjamin are

---

[27] Naomi Steinberg, *Kinship and Marriage in Genesis: A Household Economics Perspective* (Minneapolis: Augsburg Fortress, 1993), 1.

[28] Most evident family affairs are Saul's offer of his daughters to David, David and Jonathan's covenant, David making Mephibosheth his client, David giving the Gibeonites seven grandchildren of Saul, and all the violence—Dinah's rape by her half-brother and Absalom's vengeance upon Amnon, Absalom's revolt, and Solomon's rise to the throne and his disposal of his brother—stemming from David's possession of Bathsheba and murder of Uriah.

[29] Judging from Exod 21:7–11 there were—at least in the ideal framework of the law—certain restrictions on the owners, which ensured the slave-wife some security. How important that really was and how much slave owners observed their responsibilities towards slave-wives is far from clear. Here we should listen to Susanne Scholz's warning in her *Sacred Witness* (Minneapolis: Fortess, 2010), 53–82, that when women were given and taken, that is rape, even if they were slaves.

well-known, but are by no means the only ones.[30] Since claims made especially by Pitt-Rivers and Peristiany in the 1960s form the basis of a supposed Mediterranean dyad of honor and shame, which has serious effects on women and which is contested in this work, this particular use of anthropology was explored in detail in chapter 1.

STUDIES ON LABOR

Studies on labor available to me have been few. Those at hand are helpful in what they provide, but it would be an exaggeration to say that they are the basis of my work. There is nothing that I know of that would treat female workers in a comprehensive way. Perhaps difficulty of the theme should be partially blamed for this dearth, since it intersects at too many disciplines.

Dictionary and encyclopedia entries have not offered much in this line either, perhaps for the reasons just stated; and collective works usually forget the topic as well. Nonetheless, there are two articles to mention. One is Bernhard Lang's "Arbeit (AT)" in *WiBiLex*, "the scholarly Internet Bible lexicon" from the German Bible Society. He starts with a Medieval painting on Adam and Eve, which somehow sets the tone of the article; it looks generally at its characteristics related to men's and women's areas of work, at forced labor, and Sabbath rest. The second one is an article by Warburton on work in Egypt. This one helped me by opening the depths of the Egyptian bureaucracy and helping me imagine that at least some of those occupations could be in female hands: I had never thought of confectioners or bitumen collectors!

One useful collection of papers is that edited by Marvin Powell on labor in the ANE, which is further discussed in the next sub-section, as it deals with definitions of slavery. It does not focus much on women, unfortunately (it is twenty-five years old, at that time androcentrism wasn't even an academic concern). It does bring, on the other hand, a panoramic view as scholars reflect on working conditions in the different kingdoms and periods they survey.

---

[30] Some of the most comprehensive books and articles are B. Malina & J. Pilch, *The New Testament World*; (already quoted); K. C. Hanson, "BTB's Reader's Guide to Kinship," *BTB* 24 (1994): 183–94; C. Osiek, "Slavery in the Second Testament World," *BTB* 22 (1992): 174–79; idem, *What Are They Saying about the Social Setting of the New Testament?* (rev. ed. New York: Paulist Press, 1992); Victor Matthews, "Social Sciences and Biblical Studies," in *Honor and Shame in the World of the Bible* (ed. Matthews and Benjamin; *Semeia* 68; Atlanta: Scholars Press, 1996), 7–21; Matthews, "Honor and Shame in Gender-Related Situations;" Olyan, "Honor," 201–18; K. Stone, "Gender and Homosexuality in Judges 19: Subject-Honor, Object-Shame?" *JSOT* 67 (1995): 87–107. I have included some more recent contributions (Zeba A. Crook, "Honor, Shame, and Social Status Revisited" and Brayford, "To Shame or Not to Shame").

In this section are included only major works about the surrounding cultures, which shed some light on the issue of unfree laborers, with all its ambiguity. Other studies of a more general nature or more particularly on terms or texts are dealt with in the corresponding sections (such as dancers in Egypt or Enkidu's introduction into civilization by Shamhat in the Gilgamesh epic). Inevitably, some references to these definitions and ambiguities are also made in the next chapter, as slavery's particular characteristics are discussed.

A classic work is that by Orlando Patterson, *Slavery and Social Death*.[31] This is a sociologist's work, which takes into account much material from the ANE, but leaves also some very weak spots. His greatest contribution to this issue is to offer a general view of the phenomenon beyond particular aspects in each culture. One can then try to apply his insights concerning social death, loss of rights (including rights to family ties, to life itself) in a particular culture or text.

There is also the very useful collection of essays, *Labor in the Ancient Near East*, published in 1987. When one takes the first sentence by its editor, M. Powell, one learns it stems from a conference on "Non-Slave Labour in Antiquity."[32] Yet, its introduction by Diakonoff deals with the conceptual and methodological difficulties to define "slave" and, therefore, "non-slave." I do not imply these scholars made a mistake; the dissonance comes from the field itself. One of the difficulties lies, precisely, on definitions. If hard pressed, most students of labor in the ANE would agree that the "term 'slave' can be discussed, but not defined."[33] Igor Diakonoff explains this dilemma in this way:

> I do not know whether to define it as a juristic or social mentality, but, in any case, for the Babylonians, the Hittites, the Ugaritians, the ancient Hebrews, and other Near Eastern peoples, "slave" is not an absolute, but a relative, concept. ... everyone who has a "lord" is automatically the "slave" of that lord. No person is without his or her lord (human or divine) and, thus, as was already noted in antiquity by Herodotus and again by Marx, everybody is someone's slave.[34]

---

[31] Orlando Patterson, *Slavery and Social Death: A Comparative Study* (Cambridge: Harvard College, 1982). See further below(chapter 3), as I discuss social conditions affecting women.
[32] Marvin Powell, "Editor's Preface," *Labor in the Ancient Near East*, vi; cf. in the same volume Igor M. Diakonoff, "Slave-Labour vs. Non-Slave Labour: The Problem of Definition," 1–3.
[33] Gelb, "Definition and Discussion of Slavery and Serfdom," 283.
[34] Diakonoff, "Slave-Labour vs. Non-Slave Labour," 1–2.

If slavery is a relative concept, then so is "freedom."[35] Understanding slavery to be relative—which to modern readers might be exasperating because of its inherent ambiguity—has the advantage of preventing them from approaching the text with a preconceived idea about the meaning of the term "slave" in it. Sources are unclear on the connotations of the terms they contain. Aside from this difficulty, there is a diversity of variables to consider in a definition of slavery, including ownership of and right to sell a person, legal status (which varied with circumstances), and ownership or use of the means of production. Formulation of a comprehensive and consistent picture of slavery has resulted in different solutions.

Soviet scholars have been prominent in the study of slavery, because of the Marxist theory that slave societies represented one stage in the development toward a free, classless society. Their interest is permeated by issues concerning ownership of the means of production and economic coercion, which in turn have proven to be a bone of contention among Soviets, because

> an "unusual abundance and variety of forms of socio-economic relations" was characteristic of antiquity and ... slavery was only one form of personal dependence and extra-economic coercion [1969:6f.,23]. "In antiquity a slave could in certain cases find himself [*sic*] in the same or even better circumstances than a free man. And, on the contrary, a man could be legally free and at the same time in a state of severe dependence, subject to coercion and oppression" [1969: 23].[36]

Unlike a sociologist's point of view, Muhammad Dandamaev looks at it from his specialization as a Marxist orientalist; he defines slaves as a legal class within society, as persons "recognized as such [slaves] by enforced law, the property of other persons, of collectives, or even of a 'deity,' but not necessarily an article of commerce, not necessarily deprived of the means of production or even legal capacities, not necessarily persons oppressed in a cruel way."[37] Note, however, that the items included by him as "not necessarily so" point to the

---

[35] Norbert Lohfink, "*Hofšī*" in *TDOT*, 5:117, quoted by Snell, *Flight and Freedom*, 29n.36.

[36] Dandamaev, *Slavery in Babylonia*, 72–73. References to K. Zel'in, *Formy zavisimosti v vostochnom Sredizemnomor'e ellinisticheskogo perioda* (Moscow, 1969, unavailable to me). From Dandamaev's analysis (p. 70–75) of the history of the disagreements between Soviet Orientalists, there appears to have been two major understandings of ancient societies based on diverse understandings of Marxist-Leninist social categories, namely, the "slaveholding" mode of production and the "asiatic" mode of production. Unfortunately, Dandamaev does not explain in detail these two modes or their difference, and consequently the interested reader would have to search for them elsewhere.

[37] Dandamaev, *Slavery in Babylonia*, 73–74. He further states, "However difficult the problem of social classes in Babylonia may be to grasp, for us it is at least possible to distinguish in the second and first millennia two estates in particular: persons enjoying full rights and slaves in the Classical sense of the word, who are clearly contrasted with one another in the legal texts." (75–76).

variety of conditions and of possibilities. It is well-known amongst students of these societies that several ancient social categories have proven very difficult to understand and to be translated into modern concepts: "slave," "free," and "citizen" are notorious, although by no means unique (many terms referring to social status, especially those for women, are currently under discussion). From our perspective, Muhammad Dandamaev's main contribution lies in his detailed study and recording of hundreds of contracts from the Neo-Babylonian period, a period more in accordance with DtrH's final redaction than with the monarchy Dtr reflects upon. His analysis provides a broad basis upon which one can draw conclusions and make informed guesses about Israel, especially since biblical witnesses from this period retain only a particular focus on the theological reflection of the exiled Jewish community and do not expand on its impact on those fallen into poverty, slavery or war.

Applying Marxist categories to the Mesopotamian sources, Igor Diakonoff concluded that there were three social classes, which roughly coincide with the groups contemplated in the Codex Hammurabi. These are those "sharing property rights in the means of production but not partaking in any process of production" (citizens); those "sharing property rights in the means of production *and* partaking in the process of production in their own interests" (semi-free peasants or helots); and those "devoid of property in means of production and taking part in the process of production in the interest of others" (slaves).[38] However, other scholars do not find these categories so clear-cut:

> The last category [*wardum*, slave] is uncontroversial, but the first two have proved extremely hard to define precisely, it is possible that by *awīlum*, a free citizen was meant, as opposed to *muškēnum*, "royal retainer/palace dependant" (Diakonoff 1971) ... Chattel slaves, by contrast, pose no problem of definition: they were marked either by a special hairstyle or some kind of tattoo which it was a crime to change or remove.[39]

Moses Mendelsohn's book is widely quoted, because he compares slavery in Israel and in the ANE and provides a basic platform from which to proceed reflecting on the phenomenon of slavery, the type of analysis missing in Dandamaev.[40] Less well-known are Mendelsohn's articles on particular legal

---

[38] Diakonoff, "Slave-Labour vs. Non-Slave Labour: The Problem of Definition," 3.

[39] Amélie Kuhrt, *The Ancient Near East, c.3000–330 BC* (2 volumes; London: Routledge, 1997 [repr. 2003]), 1:114.

[40] Mendelsohn, *Slavery in the ANE*, quoted above; see also his "The Conditional Sale into Slavery of Free-Born Daughters in Nuzi and in the Law of Ex 21, 7–11," *JAOS* 55 (1935) 190–195; "The Canaanite term for 'Free Proletarian,'" *BASOR* 83 (1941): 36–38; "State Slavery in Ancient Israel," *BASOR* 85 (1942): 14–17; and his "The Family in the ANE," *BA* 11 (1948): 24–40.

aspects, such as the biblical חפשׁי, "client" (or freed person, depending on the translation accepted) or the Nuzi contracts of sale of daughters for concubinage (discussed in chapter 4). His view of slave conditions is gloomy; the slave in the ANE was legally

> a chattel. He was a commodity that could be sold, bought, leased, exchanged, or inherited. In sharp contrast to the free man [*sic*], his father's name was almost never mentioned; he had no genealogy, being a man without a name. In the Sumerian period the slave is simply referred to as *sag* "head," *sag nitá* or *eri*(*d*), "male slave," and *sag geme* or *sag munus* "female slave."
>
> The female slave, like her brother, the male slave, was treated as a commodity. She was leased for work, given as a pledge, handed over as a part of a dowry, or presented as a gift to the temple. In addition to her routine duties as a maid servant, she was subject also to burdens peculiar to her sex. Ownership of a female slave meant not only the right to employ her physical strength, but also, and in many cases primarily, the exploitation of her charms by the male members of her master's household and the utilization of her body for the breeding of slave children. The highest position a female slave could achieve was to become a child-bearing concubine to her master, and the lowest, to be used as a professional prostitute.[41]

Gelb's classification of dependent groups in Babylonia on the basis of "function as reflected in their utilization in service and production" is very useful because it avoids criteria which only lead to further dilemmas.[42] He sees dependent productive classes ascribed to large enterprises (agriculture, mining or industry), carried by semi-free serfs and unfree slaves; and service labor "employed full-time in a menial domestic capacity, mainly in private households," performed mostly by foreign slaves.[43] Gelb's research on the great households as economic units is also helpful in that it provides a clearer idea about what life was like, for instance in the temple of Eanna in Uruk, with its storage rooms, craft personnel, slaves, cattle, and tools, and gives insights the Bible does not provide on the functioning of the Jerusalem temple.[44]

---

[41] Mendelsohn, *Slavery in the ANE*, 34, 50.

[42] Gelb, "Definition and Discussion of Slavery and Serfdom," 283.

[43] Gelb, "Definition and Discussion of Slavery and Serfdom," 294.

[44] Gelb, "Household and Family in Early Mesopotamia," in *State and Temple Economy in the Ancient Near East* (ed. E. Lipiński; 2 volumes; OLA 5–6; Leuven: Departement Orientalistiek, 1979), 1:1–97. Our information about the composition of households is best for the temple households, in terms of both quantity and quality. Less known are the crown, or state, or royal households, while our information about private households of individuals is quite limited. The temple acquired its slaves mainly from indebted families and house-born slaves, and thus had to be more careful about their casualties. A small household would take care of its slaves because of the investment they represent, but it would not conduct accounting in the same way as one of the great institutions. On the other hand, while the city-states might have kept records of their slaves, they had

Kuhrt's analysis on women in this same period is a good supplement. Against Mendelsohn and Dandamaev, she suggests that female temple slaves enjoyed some advantages over privately-owned ones, because

> slave-girls in households frequently bore children to their owners (note the fact that household-slaves are usually identified by the name of their mother only) and had, one assumes, little chance of either fending off their master's advances nor any legal claims on their owner as a result of bearing him children ... Because of their reproductive and sexual function, moreover, those who were beautiful were highly prized (CT 22,201;202), and lost their value as they aged.
> ...
> By contrast, female temple slaves were less vulnerable to sexual advances as of right since their owners were institutions, and as they were inalienable temple-property their age, physical attributes, state of health etc. could not affect their market-value and hence insidiously influence (in that respect, at least) the regard which they were accorded. A significant difference between temple and private slaves is that temple-slaves were almost always identified by their patronymic suggesting the existence of a regular family-structure among this group.[45]

Institutional conditions such as obedience to a master or a great institution would have affected every slave; if the slave was lazy, for instance, a private owner would have tried to remedy it sooner than a supervisor in the temple, likely also a slave. Kuhrt calls attention to particular aspects in which the type of ownership had different consequences for a woman because of her gender. Since in Babylonia temple slaves could not achieve manumission or be sold to an individual, manumission or sale could not be used as coercive elements. Unlike the slave owned by a man, the temple slave's value was not tied to her beauty, age, or reproductive capacity.

Resources on women in the ANE, as reflected in ancient written documents (sales, adoptions, marriages, lists),[46] in pictorial documents (Nineveh reliefs, the

---

easy access to replacement of slaves through prisoners of war, and thus could afford being careless about accounting. See also his "Prisoners of War in Early Mesopotamia," *JNES* 32 (1973): 70–98; and "Approaches to the Study of Ancient Society," *JAOS* 87 (1967): 1–8.

[45] Amélie Kuhrt, "Non-Royal Women in the Late Babylonian Period: A Survey," in *Women's Earliest Records*, 231.

[46] Rivka Harris, "Woman in the ANE," in *IDBSup* (ed. K. Crim. Nashville: Abingdon, 1976), 961–62. Of importance are also her "Independent Women in Ancient Mesopotamia?" in *Women's Earliest Records*, 145–56, and "The Organization and Administration of the Cloister in Ancient Babylonia," *JESHO* 6 (1963): 121–57, where she studies the institution of the *nadītu* women, priestesses related to the temple. M. Roth, *Babylonian Marriage Agreements, 7th–3rd Centuries B.C.* (AOAT 222; Neukirchen-Vluyn: Butzon & Bercker Kevelaer/Neukirchener Verlag, 1989).

Enheduanna disk, figurines),[47] and in religious documents (myths, poems)[48] have been widely used in understanding the situation of women in preparation for this work. These studies are important for the possibility of comparing women's lives in diverse contexts, for the example they set of collection and analysis of resources based on material that is scarce in quantity and ideological in quality (just as the biblical material is) and for the advantage many of them have as evidence, since bas-reliefs, pottery or contracts could not have gone through successive redactions, unlike narrative material. Archives are one possible source of unadulterated information, if correctly interpreted and assessed, although they do not offer us a complete, encyclopedic or archive-like information on each issue they treat.[49]

Egypt. With respect to Egypt, a general picture is even less clear, because of the stereotypical tendency of tomb depictions, focusing on the owner, who belongs to the upper-class, and describing ideal situations in life. Information about

---

[47] P. Albenda, "Woman, Child, and Family: Their Imagery in Assyrian Art," in Durand, *La Femme*, 17–21. Her article "confines itself to the depictions of Western Asiatic women in the Iron Age, circa 880–625 B.C., specifically to their occurrences in Neo-Assyrian art. The most important source for this subject remains the monumental stone reliefs which covered the walls of Assyrian palaces at Nimrud, Nineveh, and Khorsabad." She finds evidence of gender division of roles for instance in the location of boys with the men in the depiction of deportees coming from Judea (p. 19): "Upon one series of wall reliefs where Judean families are seen departing from the embattled city of Lachish, an event that occurred in 701 B.C., teenage boys and girls are separated from one another and wear garments similar to those worn by the respective parent behind whom they march. This implies the existence of a social structure which dictated that, once having attained a certain age, boys were considered part of the male population and could no longer remain with female members of the family in public." See also J. Asher-Greve, *Frauen in altsumerischer Zeit* (Bibliotheca Mesopotamica 18; Malibu: Undena, 1985); Ilse Seibert, *Woman in Ancient Near East* (Leipzig: Edition Leipzig, 1974); J. Reade, "Was Sennacherib a Feminist?" in Durand, *La Femme*, 139–45.
[48] W. Lambert, "Old Testament Mythology in Its Ancient Near Eastern Context," in *Congress Volume, Jerusalem 1986* (ed. J. Emerton; VTSup 40; Leiden: Brill, 1988), 124–43; "Goddesses in the Pantheon: A Reflection of Women in Society?" in Durand, *La Femme*, 125–30; J. Asher-Greve, "The Oldest Female Oneiromancer," in Durand, *La Femme*, 27–32; Tikva Frymer-Kensky, *In the Wake of the Goddesses* (New York: Free Press, 1992); Gregorio del Olmo Lete, *Mitos y leyendas de Canaán según la tradición de Ugarit* (Madrid: Cristiandad, 1981); Thorkild Jacobsen, *The Treasures of Darkness* (New Haven: Yale University Press, 1976); Samuel N. Kramer, "The Woman in Ancient Sumer: Gleanings from Sumerian Literature," in Durand, *La Femme*, 107–12.
[49] Foster, "Notes on Women in Sargonic Society," in Durand, *La Femme*, 55, comparing several archives with different man to-woman of varying ages ratios, concludes: "The singular absence of girls in the Me-ság records, as well as the rarity of old men and women, point to the existence of family relationships beyond accountability, more so than a first perusal of the records might lead one to expect. To some extent, therefore, administrative texts can assist in reconstructing non-administrative roles and functions, for both men and women referred to in them." Foster's analysis is significant in that it shows once again how incomplete data are and how little understood are the function and form of structures (in this case families) within the great households.

peasants is therefore less reliable, and the picture about semi-free and unfree laborers, and especially about women, remains necessarily incomplete.

> Over-formalised even for the peak of the Old Kingdom, it [the evidence] cannot make allowance for changing conditions as society developed [Helck 1975:134–138]. It is too heavily biased towards the necropolis, depending on the idealised information the king and officials chose to leave in their inscriptions, and relates basically to the state and the estates of great officials, providing little information about lower or middle classes of society. For instance, even the terms on which the peasantry worked the land are not clear; whether they paid a portion of the produce to the estate holder, which seems likely in the Egyptian environment [cf. Baer 1962], or whether they worked for rations or wages. Economic life outside the great houses is effectively undocumented, which does not mean it did not exist. However, the general picture is likely to be correct, of patronage and provision working downwards through society from the king, in return for labour and service working up from the lowest peasant.[50]

In 1952, Abd El-Mohsen Bakir published his thesis on slavery in Egypt. He only defines slavery after an analysis of the social and economic conditions of the country, because these determine social needs. Agriculture was the main economic activity, for which the yearly blessing of the Nile was needed, and periodic work on its banks and canals was required. Several forms of compulsory work were in force, slavery being one of them.[51] Corvée in general included people whose main activity was not agriculture—like priests—unless specifically exempted by a royal decree. The economic need produced a strong corvée system, the attachment of certain people to the land as serfs, and the use of foreigners as slaves. With this key information as background, Bakir defines slavery. It is to be noted that, even though he defines "slave" using the Roman law definition, he starts by quoting a sociologist who supports ambiguity rather than precision:

> "As the distinctions between different forms of slavery are indefinite, so must there be an indefinite distinction between slavery and serfdom, and between the several forms of serfdom. Much confusion has arisen in describing these respective institutions, and for the sufficient reason that the institutions themselves are confused."[6] The truth of this observation of Spencer's strikes the student of Slavery in Pharaonic Egypt very strongly. We shall use the term "slave" in the sense it has acquired under the influence of Roman law, to mean a person owned by another in the same way as any other chattel, so that he [sic]

---

[50] Christopher Eyre, "Work and Work Organisation in the Old Kingdom," in *Labor in the ANE*, 40.
[51] A. Bakir, *Slavery in Pharaonic Egypt* (Cairo: Institut Français d'Archéologie Orientale, 1952), 1–2.

may be used as his [*sic*] owner pleases and be disposed of by sale, hire, and so forth.[52]

It is evident to the reader that boundaries between categories for free and slave remain blurred also with regard to Egypt. That people were bound is not doubted; the difficulty lies in pinning down precise differences between groups.

Ugarit. Here, two important works deserve mention. The first one is Eleanor Amico's dissertation on the status of women at Ugarit according to their roles in family, public, economic, and religious life. Although twenty years old already, the value of her work for us can be seen in her use of questions posed by feminist anthropologists, by which she manages to extract valuable information on women at Ugarit from scarce material. Second, her work shows a world of female workers, even if many are conspicuously absent from the sources.[53]

The second book is Hennie Marsman's dissertation, comparing the social and religious status of women in Ugarit and Israel. Her main conclusion is that similar groups from each society were, in general, in the same position:

> I have demonstrated that by and large, leaving aside minor differences, the social and religious position of women was the same in Ugarit and Israel, and as far as I was able to ascertain, in the ancient Near East as a whole. Everywhere women were subordinated to men, even though women belonging to the upper classes often enjoyed somewhat more freedom than other women.[54]

Marsman examines the evidence looking at the social position of women, especially in the family, and the religious position, wondering whether monotheism or polytheism did make any difference in the lives of the women, as presented in the available literary and non-literary sources.

There is yet another book with the promising title of *Ugarit at 75*. This book is blind to females: no single mention of "women" and only four of "female," of which only one refers to a female name.[55] I have found no entry on

---

[52] Bakir, *Slavery in Pharaonic Egypt*, 6–7, quoting H. Spencer, *Principles of Sociology* (1885–1896), III, 472.

[53] Eleanor B. Amico, "The Status of Women at Ugarit" (Ph.D. diss. Madison, University of Wisconsin-Madison, 1990). Other contributions are apparent throughout the chapters, especially in trying to determine the connotation of a given term: Hbr קדש/ה, usually translated "sacred prostitute" in Deut 23:18, the title of סכנת (personal attendant) applied to Abishag the Shunammite in 1 Kgs 1:2–4 (discussed in chapter 6), or the connotations of the phrase "...בן" ("son of") in the light of Ugaritic guilds (discussed in chapter5).

[54] Hennie J. Marsman, *Women in Ugarit and Israel: Their Social and Religious Position in the Context of the Ancient Near East* (Leiden: Brill, 2003), 738.

[55] Edited by K. Lawson Younger, Jr. (Winona Lake: Eisenbrauns, 2007), it is the product of a conference under the auspices of the Mid-West Branch of the American Oriental Society and the

"labor" and hardly any on "work." So, this collection did not help me much. A much more interesting approach is that by Marguerite Yon, *The City of Ugarit at Tell Ras Shamra*, brought to my attention by Wilfred Watson:

> M. Yon, *The City of Ugarit at Tell Ras Shamra* (Winona Lake 2006; translation by G. Walker and B. Schmidt of M. Yon, *Cité d'Ougarit sur le tell de Ras Shamra*, Paris 1997) is based directly on archaeological evidence. Especially significant are "Artifacts Illustrating Official and Everyday Life" (pp. 123–172) as well as sections of the "Description of the Tell" (pp. 27–122), notably on the residential quarter, the lower city and the tombs.[56]

I have only been able to check on the pages of the book available on the internet, which are most of what Watson calls "especially significant." Thus, I can only say that the book's layout catches the eye, with several pictures and lists of available material described and located, such as this one:

24. Miniature figurine of a musician   RS 24.400
1961, South Acropolis, tomb 3464   Damascus Museum (inv. 3602)
H. 5.4 cm. sculpted in the round in hippopotamus ivory (this object is similar to a small lyre-player found at Kamid el-Loz, Lebanon … This miniature figurine represents a kneeling person, sitting on his/her heels, holding either a tambourine or a pair of cymbals.[57]

Again, one cannot make much out of this evidence in terms of who would have played where, what was the purpose of the figurine and so forth. Yet, it is primary evidence from which to work further. And aesthetically, it is delicious to be able to see a good picture of what otherwise is only written about. Although Watson's review article has been very helpful for so many references on works in several languages, it is not on women and gender, much less on female laborers, but on daily life—an area traditionally ascribed to women, no doubt. Yet, that particular focus does not help much in differentiating workers from household ladies; furthermore, "daily life" includes also male gendered activities, such as fishing and hunting.

Mid-West Region of the SBL, held in 2005.
[56] Wilfred G. E. Watson, "Recent Work on Daily Life in the Ancient Near East," 94; Marguerite Yon's, *The City of Ugarit at Tell Ras Shamra* (Winona Lake: Eisenbrauns, 2006) is partially available online; quotations here are from this version, since I have had no access to the printed book. Cited 2 September 2011. Online: http://books.google.com. ar/books?id=2YWQZ6x56dAC& printsec=frontcover&dq=Yon&hl=es&ei=IdJiTbj1HsP88AbszeHsCw&sa=X&oi=book_result&ct= result&resnum=5&ved=0CDwQ6AEwBA#v=onepage&q&f=false.
[57] Yon, *City of Ugarit*, 139.

The Greco-Roman World. Views of conditions of slavery in the Greek and Roman empires are as divergent as those among Assyriologists on the ANE. The following are some of the most representative writers.[58] William Westermann believes there was a great fluidity of statuses among Greeks between free and slave, the number of slaves was low, and there were no revolts, because of possibilities to acquire one's freedom by borrowing money. He considers that, since slaves in Greece could live far from their masters, and choice of location was characteristic of a free person, some slaves were "one-quarter free, or three quarters free."[59] Studying the same period, Moses Finley arrives at opposite conclusions, for instance with regard to numbers of slaves and slave revolts. Finley believes there were revolts, but they did not progress because of external reasons. He sees slavery ("roughly the status in which a man [*sic*] is, in the eyes of the law and of public opinion and with respect to all other parties, a possession, a chattel, of another man") as one extreme in a continuum.

> If we think of ancient society as made up of a spectrum of statuses, with the free citizen at one end and the slave at the other, and with a considerable number of shades of dependence in between, then we have already discovered two lines of the spectrum, the slave and the serf-like *oikeus* of Crete. At least four more can easily be added: the helot (with such parallels as the *penestes* of Thessaly); the debt-bondsman [*sic*], who was not a slave although under some conditions he [*sic*] could eventually be sold into slavery abroad; the conditionally manumitted slave; and, finally, the freedman [*sic*]. All six categories rarely, if ever, appear concurrently within the same community, nor were they equally significant in all periods of Greek history. By and large, the

---

[58] See also Joseph Vogt, *Ancient Slavery and the Ideal of Man* (Cambridge: Harvard University Press, 1975), 211–217, and K. Bradley, *Slavery and Society at Rome* (Cambridge: Cambridge University Press, 1994), 183–185, who have bibliographical suggestions. These two scholars stand at opposite extremes in their view of slavery conditions, with Vogt stressing the more humane aspects of it, while Bradley sees it more as a form of social control. Worth noticing also is G. deSte.Croix, "Slavery and Other Forms of Unfree Labour," in *Slavery and Other Forms of Unfree Labour* (ed. L. Archer. London: Routledge, 1988), 22–23. He adopts definitions of slavery, debt-slavery, and serfdom from the Slavery Convention held by the League of Nations in 1926, and the Supplementary Convention on Slavery organized by the United Nations in 1956.

[59] William Westermann, "Slavery and the Elements of Freedom in Ancient Greece," in *Slavery in Classical Antiquity: Views and Controversies* (ed. M. Finley. Cambridge: Heffer, 1960), 31."Greek society was, of course, a slave society. Its slavery was of a type unfamiliar to Europeans and Americans in the last two centuries. It had no color line. (Therefore, *pace Aristotles*, it had no single and clearly defined slave race or slave caste.) The person enslaved might well be one-quarter free, or three quarters free. ... There was an astonishing fluidity of status in both directions, from slavery to freedom as from freedom to slavery. This it is which, in large measure, explains the absence of slave revolts in the Greek classical period."

slave proper was the decisive figure (to the virtual exclusion of the others) in the economically and politically advanced communities[60]

These scholars see as typical of slavery the owner's exercise of the powers attached to ownership, and conversely the bound person's inability to exercise his (and her?) free will. As happens also with some students of slave conditions in the ANE reviewed earlier, stress is not laid on the legal aspect of slavery but on the exercise of power. This is a very important point for this study, because, as will be repeatedly seen, the quest for the legal aspect of the problem only answers part of the question of the social status of women. These scholars' political, social, and economic positions, including gender, age, race, training, and other biases affect their perception of the sources; it happens to anybody, the difference being made by our degree of consciousness or blindness to our own biases.

In summary, comparing material from different areas and epochs it is clear that, starting already from the institution of slavery, certain phenomena appear repeatedly while they might have had local idiosyncrasies as well. All these societies shared certain common features, such as being agrarian societies, traditional in their beliefs, polytheistic by conviction or by practice (Israel), ready to conquer their neighbors and if possible, avoid being conquered, and patriarchal in their structure. On the other hand, geographical, historical, ethnic, cultural and religious differences existed; some of them became powerful empires while other city states either disappeared or survived but at great costs. it should be stressed that, despite complaints about the scarcity of the sources, biblical scholarship gains enormously from studies about neighboring cultures, because the volume and the detail of their primary sources exceed anything available from ancient Israel and offers a wide-lens perspective.

Concluding Remarks

In the light of the areas surveyed above one might conclude that feminist studies, with their many particular aspects, from the North-Atlantic and from other regions of the globe, have started a journey from which there is no return, and which everyone is invited to join. In this endeavor, I have enlisted allies from other disciplines, especially ANE history and archaeology, and anthropologists' and sociologists' insights.

The careful reader will find an imbalance in my sources: some are far more abundant than others; very recent works are not many or are incomplete, depending on what has reached the internet. This is due to practical reasons,

---

[60] Moses Finley, "Was Greek Civilization Based on Slave Labour?" 147.

such as the impossibility to purchase every article that one finds quoted in
secondary literature, the limited access to online resources by our libraries,
geographical distance from the North-Atlantic academic centers, and others. In
particular, I regret not to have found more material from scholars from the
peripheries, especially women living and reflecting in Africa, Asia, Latin-
America and the Caribbean, and women from minority groups in the North-
Atlantic world.[61]

My intention is not to bring the Dtr or any other biblical witness to court;
rather, it is to join biblical conversations from a particular, feminist, Latin-
American, liberation (and evangelical) perspective, informed by the social
sciences and with the purpose of including in the picture those in ancient Israel
whose toil allowed the sages to sit down and reflect theologically.

---

[61] Access to academic resources, both as readers and as writers, is not easy for those of us who work
far from the North-Atlantic universities. Here I would like to express my heartfelt thanks to some
good friends who have provided access to some fundamental materials, otherwise unavailable.

CHAPTER 3

SOCIETY'S CONDITIONS AFFECTING WOMEN'S LIVES IN ANCIENT ISRAEL

When leaders of a society make a decision, and especially if it proves to be the wrong one, it affects every sector of that society, but not in equal measure. If a decision has economic consequences, the weaker sectors of the economic spectrum pay for them more dearly than the better-off sectors, because they have less room for maneuvering and because usually those who take those (wrong) economic decisions look after their own interests—and they do not belong to the poor. This means that surplus distribution, land distribution, natural disasters, and other factors very much affected poorer families, without giving them resources to palliate their effects on their lives and the lives of their families. Lenski's model (discussed in chapter 1) is particularly helpful for this analysis, because it is based on power and distribution systems.[1]

The first part of this chapter will discuss the main characteristics of agrarian societies; all the ANE societies were of this type. Since each social category is the subject matter of other disciplines or sub-disciplines (anthropology, archaeology, political and social sciences, and so forth), and is controversial in these sciences, here only a few items will be presented. In the second part of the chapter, main items related to slavery will be quickly reviewed. Slavery was

---

[1] Lenski, *Power and Privilege*, 90–93.

(and it still is, although not any longer legal) an important socio-economic institution, which they faced daily.

Our discussion in previous chapters showed that there is a basic consensus among scholars that many people in the ANE were not free citizens. But when one moves from that basic consensus, many disagreements remain, due to differences in definitions, in training, in views on how particular conditions applied to a certain society (that is, whether privately-owned slaves had a harder or easier life than temple slaves), in understanding society (terms apply to a wide range of legal status, from free to chattel-slave), and finally due to the imprecise nature of the sources, such as narratives in the Bible, abundant temple or state archives from Mesopotamia for one period and practically no archives for another period, and ambiguity in the sources themselves.

There is not enough evidence to say how many women worked in ancient Israel, in absolute or relative numbers. Peasants usually have to supplement their income with other earnings in order to make ends meet, especially in times of hardship. Thus a number of people, men, women, and children were bound to some form of dependency, social and economic, which could go even to permanent slavery. They belonged to the lower class and found their honor, protection, and self-determination compromised by being away from their own household. As is still the case, women had the additional burden of not being able to keep their sexual favors if so required by their masters—a situation that would only rarely have happened to men.[2]

Biblical texts pertinent to this study will be dealt with later on; thus, here they will only be quickly mentioned if at all. The present chapter gives an overview of the socio-economic conditions in the ANE focusing on what would have affected women in a particular way. Then in chapter 4 all texts in DtrH (and several additional ones) in which any of the words for "female slave" or "dependent" play a role will be discussed. The following chapters will leave aside the question of their legal status and look at yet another set of texts.

GENERAL CONDITIONS OF LABORERS IN AGRARIAN SOCIETIES

"PEASANTRY" AS A CONCEPT

In the last years, "peasantry" has come under serious discussion amongst anthropologists, as already mentioned. Warnings by scholars from several disciplines against too uncritical, romantic, or populist views of "peasantry" are

---

[2] I do not rule out the possibility of molestation of males, including rape, but it would not have been as common as that toward females. Lack of honor, protection, and self-determination applies also to men away from home.

well taken. Challenging though such a discussion might be, it belongs to a wholly different field and it cannot be reproduced here.

If "peasant" denotes someone who belongs to a certain social class, "farmer" refers to the occupation of running a farm, including land cultivation, animal and tree husbandry and so forth. And, as it is not the same to be "peasant" or "farmer," it is not the same to belong to "peasantry" or to live in an "agrarian" society. Perhaps we can still take advantage of some of the classical definitions of "peasantry," with the proviso that they would apply to the larger segment of the "Israelites" but not to everyone and certainly not with the implication that every family possessed exactly the same economic resources and facilities as all others in their social class.

Peasants are "small agricultural producers, who, with the help of simple equipment and the labour of their families, produce mostly for their own consumption, direct or indirect, and for the fulfilment of obligations to holders of political and economic power."[3] The first part of this definition stresses peasantry as those possessing a family-owned business—the farm—whose production goes to consumption by the family itself, and to meet financial obligations: the "peasant family farm [is] the basic multi-dimensional unit of social organization."[4] The farm is a productive organization as well as home, where social relations, upbringing, training, and other events happen.

> The peasant unit is thus not merely a productive organization constituted of so many "hands" ready to labor in the fields; it is also a unit of consumption, containing as many mouths as there are workers. Moreover, it does not merely feed its members; it also supplies them with many other services. In such a unit children are raised and socialized to the demands of the adult world. Old people may be cared for until their death, and their burial paid for from the unit's stock of wealth. Marriage provides sexual satisfaction, and relationships within the unit generate affection which ties the members to each other.[5]

It is hardly surprising that people living and working on their own farms would have collectivistic, rather than individualistic personalities.[6] In the household most people would spend literally their whole life: children grow, are

---

[3] Theodor Shanin, "Introduction: Peasantry as a Concept," in *Peasants and Peasant Societies: Selected Readings* (ed. T. Shanin. Oxford: Blackwell, 1987), 3.

[4] Shanin, "Introduction," 4.

[5] Erik Wolf, *Peasants* (Englewood Cliffs, N. J.: Prentice-Hall, 1966), 13.

[6] Bruce J. Malina, "Understanding New Testament Persons," in *The Social Sciences and New Testament Interpretation* (ed. R. Rohrbaugh. Peabody: Hendrickson, 1996), 46–9; Wolf, *Peasants*, 61–62 (multiplicity of dyads, such as sexual dyad, mother-child, brother-sister, child-father); 66–73 (relationship between preference for nuclear or extended family, and natural and economic conditions).

socialized, learn all there is to learn about life, and, even if later some move away, they will still be part of the same agrarian culture for their whole lives.[7] The land is the basic economic asset of the whole household under the authority of the *paterfamilias*.[8] Within a single household, scholars presume, there would be several families living together: husband and wife/wives and their unmarried children, and eventually other members, such as "grandparents, the families of grown children, (since postmarital patrilocal [based on husband's family] residence must have been very common), an adopted child or adopted children, a divorced adult daughter who had returned to the paternal homestead, male and female servants or slaves, and other dependents."[9]

From the archaeological field, reports by A. Faust and S. Bunimovitz both affirm and contradict these assumptions. On the one hand, they confirm his statement that the urban upper class was able to afford larger (and lavishly decorated) households and—presumably, since these do not appear in the archaeological findings—higher numbers of dependent personnel. On the other hand, they also show an overwhelming predominance of larger (four-room) houses in the rural areas as opposed to the regular, smaller, urban houses.[10] The presupposition is that the former harbored extended families, while in the urban settings nuclear families were the norm, except for the richer families.

From what has been stated, it is clear that "household" is a different concept from "family." Both are closely related in an agrarian society, since people far from, or deprived of, their kin (who are regularly living in the same household or close by) would lack honor, safety, reference, identity, and probably shelter and wealth as well, and could be easily abused.[11] "Household" has several meanings; it

---

[7] H. Inhetveen & M. Blasche, "Women in the Smallholder Economy," in *Peasants and Peasant Societies*, 29. Studies in a region in Germany in the 1970s show that "although, as a rule (in about 85 per cent of all cases), women had to leave their farm of origin upon marriage to face the often difficult process of reorientation on the husband's farm, the wives of smallholders identify extraordinarily strongly with 'their' farm."

[8] There are a few biblical examples of families headed by a mother instead of a father, but they are exceptional, and it is not clear whether they are independent or how they related to the household of which they were part. See C. Meyers, "'To Her Mother's House': Considering a Counterpart to the Israelite *Bet 'ab*," in *The Bible and the Politics of Exegesis*, 39–51.

[9] Joseph Blenkinsopp, "The Family in First Temple Israel," in *Families in Ancient Israel*, 52. I would add to his list single aunts (more unlikely, also uncles). Terminology for kinship is porous in the Hebrew Bible, with terms applying very differently, even within a single book. See also Frymer-Kensky, "Family," 55–73. Sjoberg, *Preindustrial City*, 157–163 states, however, that this ideal form of extended family applied only to the upper-class, especially the royal family, who had the means to foster it (land production and urban facilities) and who also had in the extended family and inter-family alliances an added means to control power and resources, and to protect each other.

[10] Avraham Faust & Shlomo Bunimovitz, "The Four-Room House: Embodying Iron Age Israelite Society," *NEA* 66 (2003) 25–27.

[11] This lack is, precisely, one of the characteristics of slaves; see Peter Garnsey, *Ideas of Slavery*

extends in meaning to cover social groupings ranging from a small family household living under one roof to a large socio-economic unit, which may consist of owners and/or managers, labor force, domestic animals, residential buildings, shelters for the labor force, storage bins, animal pens, as well as fields, orchards, pastures, and forests.[12]

It is no wonder, therefore, that land would be the main symbol of security, honor, and wealth. But precisely because home and production are so closely tied together, when the economic situation is precarious the whole family is in danger, because there are few external sources of income. This can be seen in some of the biblical stories where drought and poverty are acute, in the eighth-century prophets and their critique of the social and commercial exploitation of fellow Israelites, in proverbs that acknowledge precariousness of life, in the overall attitude of security deposited on the land, and in several extra-biblical documents, such as legal corpora.[13]

Financial Obligations

The second part of Shanin's definition stresses peasants' obligations. As "small agricultural producers, who ... produce ... for the fulfilment of obligations to holders of political and economic power," farmers are bound to financial obligations to those holding power over them, for the fulfillment of which they need to produce a "rent fund."[14] In fact, according to Wolf, "[*i*]*t is this production of a fund of rent which critically distinguishes the peasant from the primitive cultivator*," because peasants belong to a larger political and economic

---

from Aristotle to Augustine (Cambridge: Cambridge University Press, 1996), 1, on slaves in the Greco-Roman world. "A slave was property. The slaveowner's rights over his slave-property were total, covering the person as well as the labour of the slave. The slave was kinless, stripped of his or her old social identity in the process of capture, sale and deracination, and denied the capacity to forge new bonds of kinship through marriage alliance. These are the three basic components of slavery." Franz Steiner, "Enslavement and the Early Hebrew Lineage System," in *Anthropological Approaches to the Old Testament*, (ed. B. Lang; London: SPCK; Philadelphia: Fortress, 1985), 21–25, explores this disruption of the relation of lineage when slavery occurs in the story of Joseph (Gen 47–48).

[12] Gelb, "Household and Family in Early Mesopotamia," 3.

[13] Raymond N. Whybray, *Wealth and Poverty in the Book of Proverbs* (JSOTSup 99; Sheffield: JSOT Press, 1990), 11–23 (vocabulary), 27–31 (threat of poverty).

[14] For the sake of clarity, "economy" should also be defined. Since this is not my field of expertise, I rely here on the work of anthropologist Michael E. Smith, "The Archaeology of Ancient State Economies" (*Annual Review of Anthropology* 33 (2004): 74, who has worked on ancient economies and ancient urbanizations. Smith chooses "the 'substantive definition' of the economy as the provisioning of society (entailing production, exchange, and consumption) rather than the 'formal definition' of the economy as the allocation of scarce resources among alternative ends ... [because] the substantive definition has greater applicability in cross-cultural analyses."

organization, within which they exchange food for certain services (cultural, religious, political, protection), while the "primitive cultivator" of an horticultural society belongs to an autonomous group, with no ties to a larger organization.[15]

In his review on the archaeology of economies and criticizing Polanyi's "simplistic triad of reciprocity, redistribution, and market exchange," Michael Smith prefers to speak of "transfers" rather than rent: "At least five relevant categories of transfers exist: allocation within the unit of production ...; gift, without expectation of return (from the family level to international diplomacy); taxes (obligatory transfers from individuals to the state); tribute (wealth transfers between states); and theft and plunder."[16] This seems to be a nuanced enough view, and it also allows a glimpse into a world in which women and non-elite also had a role to play, either as victims (of plunder, for instance) or as subjects (of gift-preparing, gift-giving and perhaps even gift-receiving).

Scholars disagree on what came first: advancements in technology and in crops resulting in concentration of people, or concentration of people needing more food. The end-result is a structure in which more advanced technologies (the metal plow or the wheel) yield more abundant crops and thus, people need not always wander, farms can be permanently established and a surplus is produced. Once farms are established, farmers gain a surplus of time for other occupations (such as crafts and engineering), and of crops for emergencies. In other words, as Warburton states clearly, sedentarization means harder work:

> From the start, the sedentary way of life increased the labor burden as house construction and maintenance were supplemented by sowing, harvesting, and herding, at least for those obliged to work in the fields. These activities also increased the scope of production, spurring the manufacture of new tools. Pottery and sedentary life transformed storage, opening up new possibilities for wealth, and above all providing opportunities for a new elite class.
>
> All of this increased the risk of loss since the sedentary villages were concentrations of immovable wealth, which states could either expropriate as taxes or remove as booty, if thieves could be kept at bay. Only the institutions and their representatives in the elite could guarantee or offer protection of property from neighbors or marauders. In return, they assumed a right to

---

[15] Wolf, *Peasants*, 10. There are three funds farmers need to produce (9–10): the replacement fund is the amount and time set aside for replacement of granaries, roofs, fences, clothing, and other works needed in the farm throughout the year; the ceremonial fund is that reserve with which to entertain social relations with other households, including eventual weddings and dowries or other special events, which are likely to happen within a year; finally the fund of rent is "a charge, paid out as the result of some superior claim to his [the peasant's] labor on the land."(9)

[16] Smith, "Archaeology," 84.

expropriate, which in turn led to increased production, and thus made more work.[17]

Although there is wide agreement on the effects of these elites on the peasants, each scholar uses different categories and concepts to explain them. Roland Boer takes Regulation ("Marxist-Althusserian") theory and speaks of "theo-economics" as the tension between "regimes of allocation" and "regimes of extraction."[18] He agrees that the basic economic unit was the village or *"village commune,* as both a kinship and economic unit"; and that there was a gradual process of class differentiation whereby "a much smaller ruling elite, comprising tyrants, religious professionals and other hangers-on were based in the temple city complex," holding wealth, political connections, the necessary technology of war, and the ideological apparatus to sustain their undertakings.[19] Thus fortresses, temples, palaces, and other large buildings are conceived and realized. Here again there is a clear difference with advanced horticultural societies, where most of the crop yield stays within the immediate environment, and where large engineering is missing.[20] These obligations were a constant source of friction between the village and the center, and a constant drainage for the private households, especially the smallest ones. Warburton attributes the down-keeping of grain prices and poverty of farmers to the institutions' leverage:

> The institutions were not only run by the bureaucrats, but utterly dependent upon them. The key to understanding the economy was the capacity of the institutions to determine employment and investment strategies by controlling agricultural production. It was the agricultural production that produced the surplus allowing the institutions to invest in textiles, and it was the institutional agricultural surplus that kept grain prices low, so as to ensure rural poverty among small-holders. It was the scribes who assured that the whole functioned; they formed an essential part of the elite, with vested interest in increasing their own wealth and the strength of the institutions.[21]

When one adds to this picture possibilities of food and grain shortage because of drought, poor harvest, locusts, war, or other facts, one has a sense of

---

[17] David A. Warburton, "Working," in *A Companion to the Ancient Near East* (ed. Daniel Snell; Oxford: Blackwell, 2005), 169.

[18] Boer, "Sacred Economy," 39–44.

[19] Boer, "Sacred Economy," 35, 43. Where Boer's analysis differs from others is in his ascription of the elite-function and class formation to the religious center and not to the state.

[20] Lenski, *Power and Privilege,* 192–94. It should also be said that Lenski makes a strong emphasis on the overlapping between some advanced horticultural societies and agrarian societies.

[21] Warburton, "Working," 172. It is unclear whether by "the institutions" he means also the religious ones; presumably he does.

how frail the situation was for farmers in antiquity.[22] The reason for bringing to the picture these obligations, characteristic of agrarian societies, is that they are usually only implied in the biblical texts, but they need to be brought into the picture, as they form an important component in the lives of the women with whom this study is concerned.

Characteristic of agrarian societies is also the occurrence of urban settlements, estimated from five to ten percent of the total population, although one should not think in terms of megalopolis and the very use of the term "city" is misleading. Sjoberg estimates that in the pre-industrial world even cities of more than 25,000 inhabitants would have been rare.[23] Wolf, on the other hand, prefers to take as characteristic of the agrarian system not the city *per se*, but the relation of several villages into a larger community with a center of power, a system he calls "the state."

> Not the city, but the state, is the decisive criterion of civilization and it is the appearance of the state which marks the threshold of transition between food cultivators in general and peasants. Thus, it is only when a cultivator is integrated into a society with a state—that is, when the cultivator becomes subject to the demands and sanctions of power-holders outside his [*sic*] social stratum—that we can appropriately speak of peasantry.[24]

Note the idiom of power. One can appropriately speak of peasantry when the cultivator's integration into a society with a state equals the cultivator being subject to demands and sanctions by the power-holders outside his or her social stratum. In other words, the agrarian social system is based upon a mass of farmers who become "peasantry," who suffer what another sociologist calls *"the 'underdog' position—the domination of peasantry by outsiders."*[25] Although farms are breadbaskets of the whole system, distribution mechanisms work in such a way that farmers are the ones who usually absorb any loss. In theory, return mechanisms are provided—otherwise the urban elite would not be able to exploit indefinitely the peasants. The system is supposed to provide roads and

---

[22] Chirichigno, *Debt-Slavery*, 142. "[T]he rise of debt-slavery and the alienation of land in Israel, as in Mesopotamia, can be attributed to insolvency among free citizens that was caused by various interrelated socio-economic factors, including taxation, the monopoly of resources and services among the state and private elite (i.e., rent capitalism), high interest loans and the economic and political collapse of higher kinship groups. That the development of debt-slavery and the alienation of land were similar in each of these societies can be attributed to the similarity in the kinship structure of the various tribal societies that made up the population of these agrarian states and the development of these tribal groups into state societies."

[23] This opinion is held by Sjoberg, among others. See *Preindustrial City*, 83, and Lenski, *Power and Privilege*, 198–200. Other scholars think some of the largest preindustrial cities had up to a million inhabitants.

[24] Wolf, *Peasants*, 11.

[25] Shanin, "Introduction," 4.

military and religious security for the whole country. However, return occurs in such a way that primary resources (grain, seed, greens, fruit, animals, dairy products, oil, wine) flow from the farm to the urban center with little compensation the other way around, since the surplus goes to buildings, road, and architectonic embellishments which mainly benefit urban elites. Peasants also lose their young people to the urban centers, especially those who have no possibilities of inheritance.[26]

These are not the only disadvantages peasants suffer. The peasants' "political subjugation interlinks with cultural subordination and economic exploitation through tax, rent, corvée, interest and terms of trade unfavourable to the peasant."[27] Additional disadvantages come from high interest rates for loans, the ever-present possibility of natural catastrophes and wars, and increasing loss of patrimonial land on the part of the peasants and concentration of that land in fewer hands, either privately or by institutions, such as the crown or temple.[28] In short, even for those who owned the land they toiled, abundance and leisure were utopic. Of course, there was much for which to be thankful, as well as much in which to rejoice: a good harvest, rain in due time, good weather, people singing or telling stories, religious festivals, and much more. But there was always the phantom of hunger, war, and death hovering over people and land. The soil entailed much toil and little result—as anybody familiar with Gen 3 already knew.

Warfare. In the ANE, states were at war with neighboring states (defensive or offensive) or in internal strife during much of their existence, since there were

---

[26] Sjoberg, *Preindustrial City*, 114, notes that only in the urban location are there possibilities for advancement in the intellectual realm, thus people who would be interested in these fields, who wanted "a better life" would seek the city. These are important data for the social location of any people, as one has to add uprootedness from the countryside to other adjustments. In the cases studied in the next chapters, in which women are not intellectuals consulting libraries, one does not know for sure whether these women came from the countryside because of lack of resources at home, or because of slavery, but in the majority of the biblical texts women appear in urban settings, which is where the court and temple are.

[27] Shanin, "Introduction," 4.

[28] According to Mendelsohn, *Slavery in the ANE*, 23: "The average rate of interest charged in Ancient Babylonia was 20–25 per cent on silver and 33 1/3 per cent on grain. The Hammurabi Code maintained this rate and threatened those who charged a higher interest with the forfeiture of the loan." Again, 25: "Assyria had no fixed or average rate of interest. In Late Assyria the usurer had a free hand in determining the rate of interest he wished the borrower to pay. Interest on money varied from 20 per cent to as high as 80 per cent per annum.... There were two other kinds of loans current in Babylonia and Assyria; loans granted without interest (by the temple and the landlords to their tenants), and loans on which interest was charged only after the date of maturity. In the latter case the interest was enormous. In Ancient Babylonia 100 per cent was charged; in Neo-Babylonian times we find 40 per cent and also 100 per cent; in Assyria it reached 100 per cent, and 141 per cent. In Nuzi the average interest rate seems to have been 50 per cent."

no neutral political fora to determine international boundaries, rights, and conflict-resolution, nor was there a democratic distribution of power to ensure internal cooperation between different parties. In fact, Lenski considers that *"warfare* was a chronic condition in virtually all agrarian states."[29] This means that those who master military technology, political maneuvering, and wealth profit further. Always, according to this scholar, it is also a determinant in producing social inequality through the development of a military elite.[30] Constant warring means that as long as the state is victorious against its neighbors, it increases in size, redistributes land as reward to those most loyal and heroic, and promotes population mixing by relocation of population. But it often means also murder of males and pregnant women, rape of women, and sale into enslavement of defeated groups. Conversely, if the state loses the war, its people will be depleted of their land, killed, raped, or enslaved.[31]

Warfare is a vast area covering ideological, military, technological, economic, and other aspects of a state's organization which must be treated only briefly here; but it needs to be quickly brought up because it is clearly present throughout the OT and also because it has a large bearing on women.[32]

> Early in the monarchy foreign policy becomes a source of increasing military activity. Once the Philistine threat is dealt with during the reign of David, attention is turned to Israel's neighbours and the king invades the Transjordan, subduing Moab, Ammon and Edom (2 Sam 8:1–14) ....
> Also early in the years of the divided monarchy, foreign policy entails constant warfare between Israel and Judah over the control of the lucrative "Benjamin saddle," the highway linking the coastal trunk road (the Via Maris) with the Jordan Valley and the Kings' Highway (1 K 15:16).[33]

Supported by extra-biblical studies on the effects of war on armies and on their victims on the enemy's side, T. R. Hobbs shows how a war meant wounded and deformed (surviving) men, starvation during siege, polluted water supply, diseases, slaughtering, destruction, and deportations. The ANE was not an exception to these maladies. Although Hoffner asserts that in Hittite society captives enjoyed a higher status than slaves, he mentions several texts that allude to the allocation of captives to their captors, mainly high officers and

---

[29] Lenski, *Power and Privilege*, 196. He even states that there is evidence for internal strife when there were no external ones.

[30] Lenski, *Power and Privilege*, 193–94.

[31] Lenski, *Power and Privilege*, 194–97 on agrarian systems and warfare in general.

[32] Even if there were periods of peace and prosperity, external enemies, wars and the curse of the sword are integral part in the story of Israel's life already since Gen 4, although not all are inter-state wars yet.

[33] T. R. Hobbs, "An Experiment in Militarism," in *Ascribe to the Lord: Biblical and Other Studies in Memory of Peter C. Craigie* (ed. L. Eslinger & G. Taylor; JSOTSup 67; Sheffield: JSOT Press, 1988), 471.

vassal-kings; for instance, those instructions from a king that, should a city under their authority rebel, they are to "kill all its fighting men, send the remaining captives (NAM.RA) to the king, and keep for themselves the captured livestock."[34] Particularly notorious in his review of data available up to 1997 are the instructions relating to "blind" or to blinding prisoners, as well as their work allocation in mills.

Textual findings from Babylonia also attest to desperate attempts by sieged populations to ensure that, as they sold their children, they would be fed in exchange for work.[35] A different, even gloomier picture is depicted in 2 Kgs 6:24–30, when two mothers present their case to king Jehoram of Israel, one demanding that the other woman submit her child to be eaten, as they had agreed to do, and as they had done on the previous day with her own child. Furthermore, there were also side-effects on the local economy, with technological specialization by the state in order to produce required chariotry and weaponry, loss of males at least during part of the year, the need to provide for their families, especially if they died, and the continuous drainage of resources (grains and other food, clothing, wood, metal) from the countryside to the urban centers. Further consequences were the relocation of land ownership, and with the pauperization of the farmers (their children in the war, their women alone, their grain in the king's granaries or destroyed by the enemy), the increase of debt slavery and serfdom, that is, of peasantry occupying and working what had been their own land for the benefit of others.[36]

In his article on the impact of the Assyrian invasion on other lands and peoples, Elat reports that during this empire's hegemony, Judah increased considerably its population, while the lands to the north, corresponding to "Israel," dramatically decreased, leaving formerly important cities and villages unpopulated. He supposes such a phenomenon (not unique to Israel) may have been due to "the Assyrian policy of exploiting the economic and human resources of the countries which had been annexed as provinces" and the increase of Judah as a consequence of immigration.[37]

---

[34] Harry A. Hoffner, Jr., "The Treatment and Long-Term Use of Persons Captured in Battle according to the Maşat Texts," in *Recent Developments in Hittite Archaeology and History: Papers in Memory of Hans G. Güterbock* (ed. H. A. Hoffner, Jr. & A. Yener; Winona Lake: Eisenbrauns, 2002), 63; on allocation of captives to vassal-kings or to the king, 63–66; on allocation of prisoners to grinding mill (and allusion to Samson), 68–70.

[35] Dandamaev, *Slavery*, 170, referring to A. Leo Oppenheim, "'Siege-Documents' from Nippur," *Iraq* 17 (1955): 69–89.

[36] T. R. Hobbs, "*BTB* Readers Guide: Aspects of Warfare in the First Testament World," *BTB* 25 (1995): 83–84 on the effects of war, and bibliography. The concept of "holy war" does not affect militarism. G. Jones, "The Concept of Holy War," in *The World of Ancient Israel* (ed. R. Clements; Cambridge: Cambridge University Press, 1989), 299–321.

[37] Moshe Elat, "The Impact of Tribute and Booty on Countries and People within the Assyrian

One should also do good in listening to Ames's reflections, for we do not have direct access to ancient warfare nor to its impact on people:

> ... war is a *construct* of the academic imagination.
> ... war is a *phenomenon* that scholars attempt to identify, evaluate, and explain.
> ... war is *mediated.* Those who study ancient Israelite war and its representations in the Hebrew Bible do so indirectly;
> ... war is all too *human,* and a scholar makes a significant contribution by thinking about ancient Israelite war as a human as well as an Israelite phenomenon. We study the events and traditions of antiquity because they have present value.[38]

What I find especially meaningful from his reflections is the last quotation. We do not study war, poverty, slavery, and other unpleasant features because of a morbid interest, but because these are human phenomena and they tell us something about human nature, often also about human representations of the Divine. We can learn from them about ourselves, our own disordered, sinful world and, hopefully, try to avoid their pitfalls in order to make this world a better place.

In summary, agrarian societies are generally characterized by these elements: (a) family households (both home and business) producing mostly for their own consumption and for obligations toward an elite, with land husbandry as their main occupation, and an "underdog" position *vis-à-vis* the political elite; (b) urban centers where the administration of the state is concentrated (retainers), disenfranchised people gather and the elite have their residence; (c) rise of a labor force unattached to the land, seeking better occupational opportunities (including harvesters, artisans, carpenters, prostitutes, slaves) or just survival (the "expendables," such as beggars, handicapped, aged and sick people, widows, foreigners); and (d) a state which exacts from the peasants labor (corvée and slavery), armed service, and taxes, and allows a minority to climb socially due to use of military technology necessary for their wars, connections with the religious establishment, wealth, education, and political influence. Within each social class, there operated also the hierarchy of age, sex, family, and, wherever applicable, race. Thus there was created not only a hierarchy within the hierarchy, but also a complex social web, within which people were expected to behave and respond to each other in specific, prescribed ways, quite obviously because of status markers.[39]

Empire," *AfO* 19 (1982): 247.

[38] Frank R. Ames, "The Meaning of War: Definitions for the Study of War in Ancient Israelite Literature," in *Writing and Reading War* (ed. Brad E. Kelle & Frank Ritchel Ames; SBL Symposium; SBL: Atlanta, 2008), 29–30.

[39] Sjoberg, *Preindustrial City,* 125–32 explores how manners, dress, and speech vary among social classes in several societies. Unfortunately most of these signs within the biblical world are lost to us,

Not all characteristics of an agrarian society are perceivable in the available sources. However, a model is not a detailed description that fits every society, but an organization of available material in an imaginable, coherent, picture. With this model as background, the discussion can move on to labor conditions for unfree people in the ANE.

Unfree Labor in the ANE

It is clear that not every family could maintain the biblical ideal of having their own inheritance and live freely out of its produce. There were people who were free to work their own land; people who had to sell themselves or their land for a time (indentured- or debt-slaves) and people who either had had land and lost it or never met the requirements to be a member of "the people." And there were those who had too many older brothers and got no inheritance. These all needed to survive. This means that the first distinction to be made is between labor for oneself and labor for others, the latter implying "not only that 'others' take some of the fruits but also that they customarily control, in direct ways, the work that is done and the manner of its doing, whether in person or through agents and managers."[40]

In his classical work on the institution of slavery, sociologist Orlando Patterson defines it as *"the permanent, violent domination of natally alienated and generally dishonored persons."*[41] This is a useful definition, as "natally alienated" does not necessarily mean slave-born. Natally alienated means, according to his study, that slaves have lost their claim to birth origins, both their own ancestry and to offspring. The often emphasized biblical theme of being "son of" or "daughter of" takes on new light when one sees who would have been associated with its deprivation, and how would that have affected, for instance, a young woman. Corroboration for this assertion is found in Wilcke. He supposes sources attest to people sold because of debts "in cases where the person sold (so far all are male) is qualified by his patronymic indicating that a free person is sold into slavery and where a profession is mentioned."[42] In other

---

as they are non-written. A few remain, such as bowing down to a superior, and golden clothing as a sign of royalty.

[40] M. Finley, *Ancient Slavery and Modern Ideology* (New York: Penguin, 1983), 67.

[41] Patterson, *Slavery and Social Death*, 13.

[42] Claus Wilcke, *Early Ancient Near Eastern Law: A History of Its Beginnings: The Early Dynastic and Sargonic Periods*. Rev. & enlarged version. Winona Lake: Eisenbrauns, 2007 [2003]), 57. It has been only partially available to me online. Cited 8 November 2012. Online: http://books.google.com.ar/books?hl=es&lr=&id=nwlbg0MqmYoC&oi=fnd&pg=PA7&dq=claus+wilcke,+Sargonic&ots=wf2Zj6sMm5&sig=iW3iU4h2uk2YPPvDUS3V2Pm9nS8#v=onepage&q=slave&f=false.

words, they have no more claim to family or "pedigree." Nor to honor. Nor, in the end, to life. For *powerlessness* defines them according to Patterson:

> Perhaps the most distinctive attribute of the slave's powerlessness was that it always originated (or was conceived of as having originated) as a substitute for death, usually violent death. ...
> The condition of slavery did not absolve or erase the prospect of death. Slavery was not a pardon; it was, peculiarly, a conditional commutation. The execution was suspended only as long as the slave acquiesced in his (*sic*] powerlessness.[43]

To his focus on "the slave" it is necessary to apply, as Gerda Lerner does, the feminist focus: it is not the same "his powerlessness" as hers: "With typical androcentric focus, Patterson subsumes female slaves under the generic "he," ignores the historical priority of the enslavement of women, and thereby misses the significant difference implicit in the way slavery is experienced by men and women." By "ignoring the historical priority" she means that men were predisposed "to enslave women before they had learned how to enslave men."[44]

The fact that the Sumerian terms for slave are "the composite signs *nita* + *kur*, 'male of a foreign country,' and *munus* + *kur*, 'female of a foreign country,' indicating that the first humans to be enslaved in Ancient Babylonia were captive foreigners"[45] does not necessarily contradict her insight. For there are complex and interrelated processes by which groups consolidate power and privilege within a given society and vis-à-vis their neighbors. It is amply recognized, also, that conquered women were enslaved earlier than men, who were killed.

Slavery is one of the most important social and economic institutions. It ensures accomplishment of work requiring a cheap and coordinated workforce, which cannot be done by single persons or families (work in agriculture, mining, building, running large households). It is done through the incorporation, voluntary or compulsory, of people who are deprived of claims of power, honor or rights, in exchange of whose work their basic needs are covered. And, when women are enslaved and "their" males are alive, it is a further means to humiliate them and prove them unable to care for "their" women. On the other hand, in particularly harshly socio-economic times, unlike the hired laborer the slave was an investment made by the master and needed to be protected; thus, slaves were better off than hired laborers, beggars, and other "outcasts."[46]

---

[43] Patterson, *Slavery and Social Death*, 5.

[44] Lerner, *Creation of Patriarchy*, 80 and 87.

[45] Mendelsohn, *Slavery in the ANE*, 1.

[46] Among those Dtr has especially in mind as needing social protection are the sojourner, the poor, and the Levite, and not the slaves (see Deut 24:10–15, 17–21). Since slaves are granted Sabbatical rest among other rights (Exod 20:10, Deut 5:14), one may suppose that their absence from other lists implies that they were supposed to be fed, clothed, and sheltered by their owners.

In her history of patriarchy, Gerda Lerner attributes the feasibility of slavery to the conjunction of several factors, such as surplus of food, a hierarchical organization, a state that ensures that those who are enslavable will remain enslaved, and an ideological frame that makes it possible to differentiate a certain people, or a group within a people, as those who can be cast out and made to obey on a permanent basis. Food surplus and its channeling to the city is typical of agrarian societies; hierarchical organization is typical of the patriarchal family; and a state that ensures slavery is clearly recognizable in the Israelite monarchy. There remains to be seen to what extent the ideological frame that justifies the *status quo* is traceable in DtrH. This is not our primary goal and thus it will not be fully pursued, but at least is a component of the picture and deserves to be kept in mind.[47]

There is agreement that Mesopotamian society could be divided, according to the ownership of the means of production, into three classes which basically reflect those found in the Code of Hammurabi.[48] Careful analysis should be exercised, however, since "[i]n practice, the men of the Ancient Orient, especially the letter writers and administrators ..., did not think in well-defined legal categories."[49] In view of such difficulties, perhaps we should take Diakonoff's remarks,

> If ... we wish to find some unifying principle in this variety, then it is to be found in the division of ancient society into three classes, according to their respective position in regard to production and to property in the means of production ... Taking the term "slaves" in this sense [a class devoid of property in the means of production and taking part in the process of production in the interests of others], we will probably have to concede that the only real non-slave labour in the ancient world is the labour of the "free" peasantry, the "sons of the town," on their own land, i.e., community land. All the rest would be some form of slave labour[50]

"Some form of slave labour," which would leave aside any attempt at classifying the terms found in our sources according to these categories. One thing is sure: behind every expression about "some form of slave labor" there would have been a whole ladder of men, women, children and elderly people with diverse degrees of power and privilege. Diverse and, often, dwindling. A recent book on

---

[47] Lerner, *Creation of Patriarchy*, 76–100.
[48] These were those who owned the means of production and therefore would have worked on their own; those who held land allotments or herds in exchange for service to the land owner (temple or palace) and were semi-free, and those who were slaves, owned institutionally or, less often, privately. See above, chapter 2.
[49] Diakonoff, "Slave-Labour vs. Non-Slave Labour," 3 (categories on pp. 2–3).
[50] Diakonoff, "Slave-Labour vs. Non-Slave Labour," 3.

ancient Mesopotamian legal material by Claus Wilcke sheds light on this same discussion. According to one of his reviewers,

> In the area of personal status, Wilcke cites texts distinguishing "free citizens" from slaves via Sumerian terminology denoting status levels slightly beneath those of "full citizens" (Sum dumu-gir₄ [51]). Further, the two Sumerian words for "male slave" (ir₁₁ and úrdu.d) both use the signs NÍTA x KUR, suggesting to Wilcke that "mountain man" was the original meaning. Private persons and institutions own slaves, while a Sargonic tablet of unattested origin gives higher status to slaves who are "house-born." The individuals most responsible for creating new slaves are not politicians but desperate family members, particularly mothers forced to sell offspring for food and shelter (56).[51]

The last assertion deserves further discussion, yet we are not going to take issue with it at this point. Wilcke reports that "more than a third of the relevant documents deal with the creation of slavery by family members, the heads of the nuclear families selling off other members of their family. This is then basically a social problem stressed by the fact that (widowed) mothers selling their offspring form the largest groups of sellers."[52] Of particular interest for us in this reflection is the confirmation of existence of acquired and house-born slaves (the latter with higher social status) and gender-determined poverty (my term, the widows being the main sellers of their children) as the main cause for slavery.

This short review shows that the question of slavery has to be answered in terms of social location and description of function, rather than in terms of definition. This approach seems to be warranted by the lack of clear-cut definitions and by the fact that in women's lives other issues mattered more than these. We now proceed to explore, as much as sources allow, those institutions which owned people's work.

MODES OF ACQUISITION OF SLAVES

Slavery feeds itself from several sources, with predominance of one or more, according to a constellation of factors, including societies' preferences and beliefs. Patterson talks of two main modes of social death, intrusive and extrusive. His classification brings light to heated discussions among biblicists and Assyriologists on the proportion of foreign slaves to native ones for the

---

[51] Michael S. Moore, review of Claus Wilcke, *Early Ancient Near Eastern Law: A History of Its Beginnings: The Early Dynastic and Sargonic Periods*, RBL 2008 [http://www.bookreviews.org], 2. Wilcke refers to an Old Sumerian source in which the house born slaves are counted with the master's (other) children and not the slaves, "suggesting that they were children born to the head of the family by a female slave." (55).

[52] Wilcke, *Early Ancient Near Eastern Law*, 56.

period and society they study. The intrusive mode imports slaves from other peoples through war and commercial acquisition. In this system the slave is the foreigner who is roughly integrated into the master's society, but always remains an alien. The slave "did not and could not belong because he [*sic*] was the product of a hostile, alien culture .... On the other hand, the slave was symbolic of the defeated enemy, the power of the local gods, and the superior honor of the community."[53]

The second mode is extrusive, making slaves from within by a process of exclusion of people who are charged with some type of unlawful or sinful act, thus losing membership in their own community. "The dominant image of the slave was that of an insider who had fallen, one who ceased to belong and had been expelled from normal participation in the community because of a failure to meet certain minimal legal or socio-economic norms of behavior."[54] Besides giving clear, sociological terms to differing approaches on the part of scholars, Patterson's contribution at this point of the discussion is the possibility of asking (although there is probably no answer) whether within a given society one mode of acquisition (which means also the mode of falling into slavery) had a higher social status than another. This is not always possible to answer, but some scholars have developed some general models about conditions of life for foreign slaves and for enslaved natives. Gelb's terse description draws up lines of differentiation.

> In conclusion, the main characteristics of slavery and serfdom in different areas and periods are as follows:
> Unfree chattel *slaves*, foreign born, without family life, without means of production, employed full-time mainly in *service type of labor* in "primitive societies" and, mainly in private sector, in Ancient Near East, Athens, Rome, and Americas.
> Semi-free *serfs* (Mesopotamian *guruš*, Spartan helots, etc.), native born, with family life and with means of production or without family life and without means of production, employed part-time or full time mainly in *productive type of labor*, mainly in public sector, in Ancient Near East, Mycenaean and Homeric Greece, later Sparta, etc., India, China, etc., but not in Athens, Rome, and Americas.[55]

---

[53] Patterson, *Slavery and Social Death*, 39. See Lerner, *Creation of Patriarchy*, 76–81, 257–8 on how these conditions affected women worse than men.

[54] Patterson, *Slavery and Social Death*, 41.

[55] Gelb, "Definition and Discussion of Slavery and Serfdom," 294. Gelb bases his classification of Mesopotamian dependent classes on "function as reflected in their utilization in service and production."

Time and again the Hebrew Bible makes a difference on how Israelites and foreigners are to be treated. Enslaved fellow Israelites are to be treated as hired laborers and released after a period of time, unless they choose to become permanent slaves (Exod 21:2–6). Biblical laws accept only the intrusive mode, while the extrusive one is reserved for debt-slavery, which, at least in theory, would have had different conditions attached to it.[56] The different treatment of foreigners from Israelites seems to be due to the notion that slaves are perceived as not belonging to the same people, because if they did, they would have to be treated with kindness and fairness. Deuteronomy 15 shows a clear differentiation in language between the member of the community who is in need (את־רעהו ואת־אחיו "his neighbor and his brother," Deut 15:2–3) and the foreigner (נכרי); Lev 25:44–46 boldly states that foreigners can be treated as slaves, unlike any "fellow Israelite" (בני־יישראל איש באחיו). These laws presumably mean a more humane treatment and the right to participate in the cultic community together with those who were in better socio-economic conditions. Thus when a biblical story refers to Hagar as the Egyptian slave, one can imagine that such a qualification implies the possibility—certainly exercised by Sarai—of abusing her, since she was her property, and Hagar did not have fellow Hebrews or her own kin living among the Israelites to protect her rights; nor was she to be released in a few years to become her mistress' equal as an Israelite.

MANUMISSION OF SLAVES

Manumission is the release of a person from the condition of slavery, achieved by a variety of procedures, not all of which are available in any one society, however. Among those deemed most widespread by students of slavery, the ones considered in this study are those that seemed to us to be more pertinent to sources from the ANE.

Postmortem Manumission. The origin of this type of manumission can apparently be traced to slave sacrifices at the master's death, allowing the master to get to the underworld with adequate help and honors. Human sacrifice was later changed into manumission of slaves who took care of the burial.[57] Since Ugaritic and Mesopotamian myths often have the gods, goddesses, and human

---

[56] Dandamaev, *Slavery*, 179 mentions a Babylonian document in which "the son of an insolvent debtor became a temple slave, and it is clear that such slaves could not be redeemed or freed. Consequently, the transformation of slave debtors, who formed an intermediary social group, into slaves in the true sense of the word was possible." Dandamaev's "intermediary social group" refers to a third group between a free Babylonian whose son is given as security, and permanent slaves such as temple slaves, namely, the debt-slave.

[57] Patterson, *Slavery*, 219–28.

heroes go down into the pit with their servants, perhaps this form of manumission happened in the ANE, but it is not recorded as such.[58]

Cohabitation. This form of manumission is especially important, because it affects women in more direct ways than the other types. Codex Hammurabi §171 prescribes this mode of manumission for the slave and her children begotten by the master at the master's death. From the Jewish colony at Elephantine there is evidence for the manumission of one woman and her daughter, begotten by her master.[59] Apparently, Hagar and Ishmael were sent away in Gen 21 on the basis of this right to manumission. As Sarna notes, however, this right had its disadvantages as well.

> Abraham ... undoubtedly recognized Ishmael as his legitimate son, a fact repeatedly attested by a variety of earlier texts (16:15; 17:23, 25f.) and affirmed here (v. 11) as well as later on (25:9,12). Did this status assure Ishmael automatic inheritance rights even after the birth of Isaac? Sarah's formulation of her demand and the extreme length to which she was prepared to go point to an affirmative answer. The laws of Hammurabi (par. 170f.) and of the still earlier Lipit-Ishtar (par. 25) implicitly make inheritance rights a legal consequence of the father's acceptance of the infant as his legitimate son. There is no doubt that Ishmael was entitled to a share of Abraham's estate. The key to Sarah's demand lies in a clause in the laws of Lipit-Ishtar where it is stipulated that the father may grant freedom to the slave woman and the children she has borne him, in which case they forfeit their share of the paternal property (cf. Judg. 11:1–3). Sarah is asking Abraham to exercise that legal right (cf. 25:6).[60]

---

[58] Mendelsohn, *Slavery in the ANE*, 16–18 records contracts from Nuzi, by which Habiru immigrants, "being unable to find employment, entered 'of their own free will,' singly or with their families, into the status of servitude" (16) in exchange for their basic needs. Although there are a few documents from which it is known that a Habiru could leave if he/she left another Habiru in his or her place, Mendelsohn states (17–18) that "the man or woman who 'enters' the house of a master must remain there as long as the latter lives. In case of desertion the Habiru becomes subject to the most cruel punishment." These contracts should probably not be considered a post-mortem manumission; yet the Habiru's obligation was terminated by the master's death.

[59] Dandamaev, *Slavery in Babylonia*, 444, records the existence of manumission, made in the presence of a judge or by contract, so that no further claims could be made on the freed slave; he also quotes (on p. 447) E. G. H. Kraeling, *The Brooklyn Museum Aramaic Papyri: New Documents of the Fifth Century B.C. from the Jewish Colony at Elephantine* (New Haven: Yale University Press for the British Museum, 1953) no. 5: the military colonist Mešullam son of Zakkur makes free his wife-slave and the daughter she bore to him while he is still alive.

[60] Sarna, *Genesis* (JPS Torah Commentary; Philadelphia: JPS, 5749/1989), 146–47 and 361 n.4: "For Lipith-Ishtar, par. 25, see ANET, p. 160; for Hammurabi, par. 170f., see ANET, p. 173 ...." Sarna considers quite possible the meaning of "divorce" for the verb גרשׁ in v. 11. G. von Rad, *Genesis* (rev. ed. OTL. London: SCM, 1972), 233 speaks of "Hagar's expulsion"; Claus Westermann,

There might have been other children in this situation behind some biblical stories, but the information we gather about slaves and freed slaves is always very scant.

Adoption. Adoption of a slave is an economic arrangement by which people who do not have heirs (or cannot count on them) adopt a slave on the condition that the slave cares for the master's or mistress' needs until his or her death, after which the slave is free and eventually inherits from the owner. A typical case occurs among the *naditu*s, priestesses who belonged to the Babylonian upper class and who could use their part of the inheritance (i.e., what would have been their dowry) for businesses and for their living expenses. "The hundreds of *naditu* texts are mainly business documents: contracts of sale, lease and hire. With few exceptions it is a *naditu* who buys houses and fields, leases out fields, houses, and plots of land, and hires out her slaves as farm hands"[61] and yet, there was another side to their independence and business opportunities, since these high-class women and priestesses

> had to care for themselves when they grew old and perhaps feeble, for this was not a function of the cloister administration. Dozens of adoption texts remain which tell of *naditu*s adopting slaves, males and female, or younger *naditu*, many of whom were their relatives, to care for them when they grew old.
>
> The community of *naditu*s represented an alternative kinship structure, especially in the area of funerary obligations. It was a sisterhood that served in many ways as a substitute for natal kin who may well have died and forgotten about their sequestered aging relatives. And yet a basic reason for the establishment of the cloister was to ensure the integrity of the paternal estate.[62]

There are examples from Babylonia where a master writes a document agreeing to manumit the slave in exchange for care until he dies, stating that the son whose responsibility it was to take care of his father could not, or did not want to take it.[63] And Bakir states that in Egyptian records emancipation appears only "in the 'Adoption Papyrus' of the XXth Dynasty" of Egypt, a text in which the mistress, who already bore children, declares that her children will have no claims in the future on the adopted and manumitted slaves. In other words, that claims to her adopted and manumitted slaves will die with

---

Genesis 12–36: A Commentary (Minneapolis: Augsburg, 1986), 339.

[61] Harris, "Independent Women," 152; "Organization," 121–57.

[62] Harris, "Independent Women," 152, 154–55.

[63] Dandamaev, *Slavery in Babylonia*, 438–52, discusses available evidence, but he states that information about manumission is scant for many periods of Mesopotamian history. K. R. Veenhof, "A Deed of Manumission and Adoption from the Later Old Assyrian Period," in *Zikir Sumim: Assyriological Studies Presented to F. R. Kraus on the Occasion of his Seventieth Birthday* (Leiden: Brill, 1982), 359–85.

the mistress.[64]Apparently Abraham's complaint to YHWH for his lack of offspring in Gen 15:2–3 would imply the elsewhere attested custom of adopting a slave as heir, in order to ensure one's care in their old age and after death. As von Rad puts it, "the conclusion to v. 2 is absolutely untranslatable (we do not know the meaning of *mšk*, and *dammešek* cannot be translated 'the Damascene.')." Since "Eliezer" appears in this corrupted text and nowhere else, one may assume that Abraham's intention is to adopt his servant as heir, but the point should not be stressed too much.[65]

Political Manumission. This is a mode that operates out of a decree or decision taken by a higher organization than the individual master of the slave, with or without the master's consent. The most common reason for such a political move was, according to Patterson, the need to recruit slaves for warfare when the law or custom did not allow the slaves to carry weapons.[66] In the ANE there are examples of political manumission, which usually have to do with the increasing imbalance between rich and poor. In Babylonia we find the institutions of the *mēšarum* and *andurārum*, which occurred whenever the monarch deemed them necessary, usually on the second year of his rule.

> While *andurāru* was the specific state of 'release', the misharum act was a general decree by the king which included as its major component acts of release, but of course of classes rather than individuals. ...
>
> The misharum act had three main effects: the cancellation of taxes, the cancellation of public and private debts and/or arrears, and the introduction of miscellaneous reforms. A natural consequence of the second was the release of persons in debt-bondage and the return of lands seized for debt. ...
>
> The misharum acts, therefore, were acts involving an element of desperation which, like price-fixing regulations, attempted to curb the worst effects of an economic condition without approaching the underlying causes thereof. They were, of course, only temporarily effective, as their very repetition proves.[67]

---

[64] Bakir, *Slavery in Pharaonic Egypt*, 123.

[65] von Rad, *Genesis*, 183–84; see also Sarna, *Genesis*, 112, 382–83. On adoption in the ANE, Mendelsohn, *Slavery in the ANE*, 50–52.

[66] Patterson, *Slavery and Social Death*, 234–35. In the case of Jer 34 one could surmise that male Israelites were liberated with the intent of adding them to the defense, but women were also manumitted.

[67] R. Westbrook, *Property*, 45, 45–46, and 47 respectively. See Moshe Weinfeld, "'Justice and Righteousness'—מִשְׁפָט וּצְדָקָה—The Expression and Its Meaning," in *Justice and Righteousness: Biblical Themes and Their Influence* (ed. H. Reventlow and Y. Hoffman. JSOTSup 731. Sheffield: Sheffield Academic Press, 1992), 238 "the word מִשְׁפָט וּצְדָקָה, and especially the phrase מִשְׁפָט

And in the Bible we find the institutions of the Sabbatical and Jubilee years, which served the same purpose of reinstating justice by commutation of debts (therefore, restitution of debt slaves to freedom) and redistribution of land.[68]

Contractual Manumission. Finally, slave owners could free their slaves. This is how I understand Abraham's sending Hagar and Ishmael away in Gen 21, even though the narrative lacks a description of such a procedure.[69] Also biblical laws on manumission (Exod 21:1–6; Deut 15:16–17) contemplate both options for the indentured Israelite (according to the Deuteronomy version, also Israelitess). That he may choose to stay as a permanent slave because "he loves his wife" given by his master indicates that they could also have opted to leave after six years: option to stay is the exception that needs legislation. The ceremony prescribed would probably have contractual enforcement or serve as such.

Manumission laws appear also in the Covenant Code, Deut 15 and Lev 25. Since the biblical material is scattered throughout different books and laws and narratives contradict each other, it is impossible to deal with them thoroughly without writing another book.[70] At this point what is important to remember is that the laws make a distinction between foreign slaves and indentured Israelites; that they make gender differences when her sexuality is involved; and that they foresee release of debt slaves. Since the Hebrew uses the same terms for all types of slaves (and even for servants who would not have been slaves), it is not always clear what kind of situation they envision and what kind of manumission.

This concludes the sub-section on manumission. The variety of forms and of attestations for the ANE speaks of society's mechanisms through which some of its slaves are re-integrated into society, usually staying close to their former masters. Although Greco-Roman society has not been discussed here, it comes to mind in a special way when one thinks of freedmen and freedwomen. One reason for their importance then is that slave numbers were much higher than in the ANE, making significant also the number of freed people.

וצדקה, does not refer to the proper execution of justice, but rather expresses, in a general sense, social justice and equity, which is bound up with kindness and mercy."

[68] As Westbrook, *Property*, 47 notes, the Mesopotamian *mēšarum* was rather unpredictable, and consequently they intended to avoid the social and economic speculation that would have come with their announcement or periodic implementation. The biblical institutions, on the other hand, were cyclical, thus predictable. It is not clear how well these devices worked, or if they were ever put into practice. See also S. Kaufman, "A Reconstruction of the Social Welfare Systems in Ancient Israel," in *In the Shelter of Elyon: Essays on Ancient Palestinian Life and Literature in Honor of G. W. Ahlström* (ed. W. Barrick & J. Spencer; JSOTSup 31; Sheffield: JSOT Press, 1984), 277–86.

[69] Patterson, *Slavery and Social Death*, 219, mentions abundant examples from Babylonia.

[70] At any rate, some of these laws are dealt with in chapter 4.

RUN-AWAY SLAVES

This is, evidently, a social preoccupation in the laws that have survived. Institutions, political systems, and patriarchal households invested in the smooth running of the institution and every leak in it would have been fought as much as possible. It looked otherwise from the workers' side, of course. The Assyriologist Daniel Snell has looked at this issue. He wonders that so little has been written about what "appears to be a prime example of a way into the world of the illiterate masses and their relation to labor management schemes of the elites."[71]

The laws on protection of runaway slaves leave room for much discussion, since they do not define what kind of slave was eligible: Israelites ("your brothers") coming back from abroad? Foreign slaves who had run away and had been caught were given asylum?[72] Considering Codex Hammurabi §280–281, Deut 23:16–17 [Eng 15-16] probably only applied to Israelites who had managed to return to Israel from foreign locations or, according to de Vaux, to foreigners seeking refuge in Israel. He thinks it would not apply to Israelites, fleeing neither from Israelite masters, nor from foreigners. "It seems then that the law must deal with a foreigner coming from abroad and admitted to Israel as a *ger* or a *toshab*. Extradition would be refused and all the Holy Land would be considered a place of refuge, in the spirit of Is 16:3–4."[73] Besides these laws, there is evidence to the contrary as well. One might think of Hagar running away with Ishmael (Gen 16); of Pharaoh refusing to let the oppressed Israelites leave to worship YHWH and, of course, Philemon in the New Testament. These confirm the statement above, that runaways were returned to their masters, at least those belonging to individuals. That enslaved laborers tended to run away is also attested in other Babylonian witnesses. From these, a study offered by Brinkman in a Festschrift for F. R. Kraus is especially appropriate here. He offered a preliminary study on laborers' lists around the city of Nippur during Middle Babylonia (fourteenth-thirteenth centuries B.C.E.). He studied the terminology used to refer to laborers in the rosters available, which are comparatively abundant. These classify people according to "(a) the sex and age of the individual; and (b) his or her health or confinement status (if either was or

---

[71] Snell, *Flight and Freedom,* 31.

[72] Mendelsohn, *Slavery in the ANE,* 4, 63–64 quotes Codex Hammurabi §§280–281, which "provide that if a slave be bought in a foreign country, and after having been brought to Babylonia it be discovered that he had formerly belonged to a Babylonian master, then, if the slave be a native Babylonian he must be freed unconditionally ... If, however, the slave be of foreign birth, he must be returned to his former owner."

[73] R. de Vaux, *Ancient Israel: Its Life and Institutions* (New York: McGraw-Hill, 1961), I. 87.

had been in any way abnormal)."[74] Both data are interesting, even though Brinkman himself alerts us that his conclusions are very provisional, subject to further study and eventual unearthing of additional material. Here what concerns us is the confinement status. Since rosters served the purpose of knowing how large the work force was and having a control over rations provided, those who had previously served but were not any more active are also enlisted, either as dead, impaired, excused ("on the road"), fettered, or "escapee." As Brinkman concludes,

> It is obvious, especially from the frequent mention of escapees, that these persons labored under constraint. It is also apparent from some types of account texts that gross numbers of personnel were of concern to higher officials; couched in phraseology vaguely reminiscent of that employed in cattle accounts, some personnel records reckon chiefly debits and credits in terms of numbers of "offspring" (*ildu*), "returned escapees," "escaped," "dead" almost like inventories of possessions. But there are many questions yet to be answered. Do these rosters depict a single uniform social or economic class within society? Were these persons slaves? Were they serfs, or could they be shifted from place to place as a mobile work force? What was their economic role in society, and how does their function compare with that of free workers? … Were many or any of them originally prisoners of war?[75]

What is only an entry into a very old record cannot answer these really interesting questions. However, much can be gleaned from records, as also Snell shows. His study on runaways (not only in ancient Mesopotamia, but that is the segment of this study that interests me more) throughout different periods, places, and types of material shows that it was fairly common to escape, especially from the large institutions, but no large numbers of escapees are recorded until the *ḫapiru* in the Middle Babylonian period (1500–1200).[76] That could mean either that working conditions were not that bad or that it was in the interest of the bureaucrats who recorded (and who held responsibility for those workers) not to call attention to absentees (including runways and dead workers).[77]

TYPES OF LABOR

The last section discussed legal statuses of people. This section will deal with types of labor according to location of service. "Laborer" here connotes unfree,

---

[74] John Brinkman, "Sex, Age and Physical Condition Designations for Servile Laborers in the Middle Babylonian Period," 2.

[75] Brinkman, "Sex, Age and Physical Condition," 7–8.

[76] Snell, *Flight and Freedom*, 58.

[77] Snell, *Flight and Freedom*, 37–40, 46–49.

and probably also semi-free people, especially servants and specialized workers whose legal status is unclear.[78] Scholars divide slaves into state-, temple- and privately-owned; they can also be divided into those owned privately or by the great institutions. Although the relationship of the temple and the particular city and/or empire to which it was connected differed according to times and circumstances, both owned and distributed land in exchange for revenues, drew their income from taxes and offerings from the population, acted as loaners, had jurisprudence on legal issues, received people as donation or as booty, and also hired out people for particular projects.[79]

> By far the most important employer in the Ur III period was the state, whose influence was felt in every area of activity, from agriculture and animal husbandry through craft industries such as weaving, milling, and the working of metals, wood, leather, and reeds to administration of the state, the provinces, and the individual cities.
> Second in order of importance were the temples. They too possessed large estates devoted to agriculture and animal raising and employed large numbers of craftsmen, officials, and administrative personnel.

---

[78] Ration lists are not complete and do not give details (for instance, differentiating between slaves and semi-free workers). For instance, there are temple archives and a few particular archives, but so far no palace archives have been found for Babylon. In Israel, no ration lists or letters by kings ascribing prisoners to certain officers (as in Hittite discoveries) have been unearthed. Thus, lists are not exhaustive, so that what can be said here applies to certain periods and places and is reliable for those periods and places, but not further. They serve us to speculate on what could have happened to slaves in Israel.

[79] Bibliography on this subject is quite extensive. See for instance, on temples as business organizations, M. Silver, *Economic Structures of the Ancient Near East* (Totowa, NJ: Barnes and Noble, 1986), 7–8. On Sumer, Adam Falkenstein, *The Sumerian Temple City* (Los Angeles: Undena, 1974); Igor M. Diakonoff, *Structure of Society and State in Early Dynastic Sumer* (Los Angeles: Undena, 1974); and Muhammad Dandamayev, "State and Temple in Babylonia in the First Millennium B.C.," in *State and Temple Economy*, 2:589–96. On Ugarit, Michael Heltzer, "Royal Economy in Ancient Ugarit," in *State and Temple Economy* 2:482–94 (particular male professions). He finds no clear differentiation between court and palace economies (p. 496), "It appears that, in Ugarit, there was no exact definition of the royal economy. The temple personnel, the administrative personnel, the military men, with their duties, obligations, and privileges, were also royal dependents (*bnš mlk*). All these people were connected with the *gt*, receiving there deliveries and '*ubdy*-fields. However, the *bnš mlk*, according to their professional groups, were distinguished from the peasants of the village communities." On Egypt, J. Janssen, "The Role of the Temple in the Egyptian Economy during the New Kingdom," in *State and Temple Economy* 2:505–15. On the other hand, Roland Boer, "Sacred Economy," 36, asserts that "*the temple-city complex is not the same as the state*. Rather, the state arises in a tension between the village commune and the temple-city complex."

> The number of persons engaged in work for private parties is extremely
> difficult to estimate, because so few private documents from this period have
> survived.[80]

Waetzoldt gives us a vision of what it meant to live in a society dominated by a
powerful and prosperous state; Israel/Judah rarely achieved what would be a
"prosperous" state, even though at times they imitated the great institutions of
their neighbors. So, perhaps one can apply these words at a smaller scale.

STATE LABORERS

By "state laborers" is meant personnel ascribed to the palace or to enterprises
under the king's control, such as mining, agricultural endeavors, either for the
crown or leasing crown lands, building projects which were too large to be
privately undertaken (such as the Nineveh palace, roads, perhaps even temples
or canal digging), and in general in the everyday tasks of the palace household.[81]
Main modes of incorporation of state slaves are conquest (intrusive mode in
Patterson's terms, see above), and indebtedness to the state through tax evasion
or theft, and perhaps loans for agricultural emergencies (extrusive mode), while
biological reproduction kept the number of slaves more or less constant. This
seems to have applied to the whole area, regardless of who were the winners or
losers. Moshe Elat affirms it was so in Assyria throughout the empires, even if
the king did not go himself to battle.[82]

Bakir finds in Egypt "a fundamental rule that the captured become in the
first place human chattels of the king,"[83] who assigns them to temples, private
individuals, or palace activities, according to needs.

> No distinction seems to have been made between those who had been slaves
> and those who had been freemen in their own countries. This is clear from:
>   (1) "[List of booty brought from this place] as an entire army: princes, 3; their
> wives, 30; men seized, 80; male and female slaves ... and their children, 606"

---

[80] Cf. Hartmut Waetzoldt, "Compensation of Craft Workers and Officials in the Ur III Period," in
Labor in the Ancient Near East (ed. Marvin Powell; AOS 68; New Haven: American Oriental
Society, 1987), 117.

[81] Mendelsohn, *Slavery in the ANE*, 92 starts his section on state slavery speaking about the fate of
prisoners at Akkad: "It was these enslaved war prisoners who, with the assistance of *corvee* gangs
and hired free laborers, constructed roads, dug canals, erected fortresses, built temples, tilled the
crown lands, and worked in the royal factories connected with the palace. They labored under the
supervision of overseers and were housed in special barracks; and their names, ages, and land of
origin were duly recorded in slave registers. Among the tasks assigned to these inmates were
activities in the weaving, brewing, and general work departments of the palace..."; 93–95 (Assyrian,
Babylonian and Egyptian slavery), 95–99 (Israelite).

[82] Elat, "Impact of Tribute and Booty," 244, 249 n.6.

[83] Bakir, *Slavery in Pharaonic Egypt*, 109.

(2) "I (*i.e.* the king) equipped it (the *pr* of the god) with captured male slaves..."[84]

Also Hittite documents studied by Hoffner show that the king had prerogative over war captives. He states that when "a designation is given, it is that they were brought 'to H̲attuša,' but occasionally it is to the king's 'house,' that is, to his personal estate." He further affirms: "On some occasions, the king relinquished his right to the captives and allowed his troops to take them as semi-free servants."[85] Whether people thus uprooted faced a harsher or more lenient treatment, is very hard to say. It would probably have depended on the particular conditions encountered by the prisoners at their master's place, as well as the particular occasion in which they were taken prisoners: the harder they fought and the more they wounded the winners, the harsher their treatment after the battle or the siege.

Since the king was responsible for the booty as chief military leader, and he was also responsible for those large projects that required—and perhaps produced—slavery, such as canal digging, emergency repairs in canals, dikes or buildings, pyramid or temple construction, stone-quarrying, mining, security and police, and agricultural work in crown lands, it makes sense that the king would have the right of disposal of the war booty, giving to the temple or to individuals as many or as few slaves as he wanted to. Furthermore, one characteristic of agrarian societies is the absence of clear boundaries between what pertains to the state and what pertains to its king, so that taking slaves for his administration, for agriculture, or for his own personal service would have been about the same.[86]

In the DtrH, Solomon is especially credited with having subdued neighboring peoples and having submitted these to forced labor (and his own Israelite people to corvée) in all kinds of labor, from mining to building the Jerusalem Temple, the palace for his Egyptian wife, embellishing his palace, and so forth.[87] Rather than product of war, Solomon's achievements are presented as

---

[84] Bakir, *Slavery in Pharaonic Egypt*, 110.

[85] Hoffner, "Treatment," 63; see also his "Daily Life among the Hittites," in *Life and Culture in the Ancient Near East* (ed. Richard Averbeck, Mark W. Chavalas, & David B. Weisberg; Bethesda: CDL Press, 2003), 106–7.

[86] Lenski, *Power and Privilege*, 210–19, especially 215–16.

[87] This information appears in 1 Kgs 3–11, but one should not take it at face value. These same chapters induce a careful reader to raise questions concerning his wisdom, his success vis-à-vis Hiram or the Pharaoh, and his kingdom's prosperity for the whole people. His "prosperous" kingship cannot be viewed aside from the Northern tribes' upsurge in chapter 12, whose primary motifs are not religious but socio-economic. See, for instance, Jerome T. Walsh, "The Characterization of Solomon in First Kings 1–5," *CBQ* 57 (1995): 471–93; David Jobling, "'Forced Labor': Solomon's Golden Age and The Question of Literary Representation," *Semeia* 54 (1991): 57–76; and Nadav

the result of his wisdom, especially commercial and diplomatic wisdom. At any rate, whatever the degree of truth of these statements, they confirm the information gleaned from extra-biblical sources, that the king had the right to submit people to forced labor and allot them according to his needs and whims.[88] With the monarchy there also raised prophetic voices which saw in the system an opportunity for a few families to increase their profits, while many Israelites were increasingly impoverished (Judg 9, 1 Sam 8, Amos 2). Even Dtr's review of Solomon's reign, with all its glamour, shows signs of conscripted labor, of a widening gap between those related to his entourage and most other families (especially in the North), and consequently, of increasing unrest among the tribes (1 Kgs 5:27–32 [Eng 5:13–18], 9:15–28, 11:26–28).

TEMPLE LABORERS

Here again "laborers" implies bound people, ascribed on a permanent basis to a temple, which held at least certain ownership rights over them. Temple slaves had distinguishing characteristics from other slaves. The main one is that, since their owner was the Deity of that particular temple, manumission seems to have been much harder if at all possible.[89] Main sources of slave acquisition were war prisoners, and dedications of slaves by owners, of free children by their parents or—in the case of orphans or exposed children—by those who had found them. Several documents attest to these dedications as a way to save children from starvation in times of crisis: "A document of the time of Nabonidus from Uruk is of great interest. According to this document at a time of famine in the land, a woman whose husband had died dedicated two of her young children to the Eanna temple to be slaves and marked or branded them. The text noted that the children were given to the temple so they would not die of starvation."[90] Other reasons, equally dramatic from the personal perspective, could lead people to

---

Na'aman, "From Conscription of Forced Labor to a Symbol of Bondage: *Mas* in the Biblical Literature," in *"An Experienced Scribe who Neglects Nothing": Ancient Near Eastern Studies in Honor of Jacob Klein* (ed. Yitschak Sefati *et al.* Bethesda: CDL Press, 2005), 746–58.

[88] See further in chapter 5 under "Hidden Women" on מס and מס־עבד.

[89] According to Dandamaev, *Slavery in Babylonia,* 179, at least in Babylonia they could never be manumitted; see also Mendelsohn, *Slavery in the ANE*, 99–106. Bakir, *Slavery in Pharaonic Egypt*, 80 speaks of the protection of temple slaves by the Pharaoh, so that no one could remove them and make them work elsewhere. Bakir does not mention whether they could be manumitted. In Isa 44:5 there is mention of writing on the hand ליהוה "Belonging to YHWH," a mark to denote possession; see on this, Mendelsohn, *Slavery in the ANE*, 49. On the other hand, Lev 27:1–7, a late appendix to the book, contains a price list for dedications to the temple, apparently for people's redemption through money.

[90] Dandamaev, *Slavery in Babylonia,* 173. The text alluded to is YOS 6 451:5–6.

promise a child to the temple. First Samuel 1 tells the story of Hannah's dedication of her firstborn to the temple were she to overcome her barrenness.

Neo-Babylonian documents attest also to legal disputes on slave property. One document from Uruk from 532 B.C. (YOS 7 66), for instance, refers to a slave given by her owner to the Eanna temple. Her owner died and his brother took the slave, who bore three children in his house. The temple finally allowed the man to keep her while he lived but set conditions—among them that her owner was not to live with her or marry her off—and after the man's death she would be transferred back to the temple.[91] Contracts such as this document the life of a woman alternatively owned by two men, for (both of) whom she bore children, and her transferal to another slave system, which she and her children could not leave. How many more people experienced this type of bargaining over their own bodies is not known. It also shows what has been also suggested, that female slaves belonging to a temple compound fared better on a daily basis than women subject to a male owner.

Other factors, belonging to the macro-economy and not just to a man's desires or rights, must be considered as well. Depending on the amount of work needed and the resources available, temples hired free laborers or hired out their own slaves to the state or to individuals. And, judging from the lists available, and apparently depending on the ratio of work:workers:food, institutions undernourished certain "supernumerary" groups (not coincidentally, women and children), who were also non-specialized workers and thus, easy to replace.

At any rate, no dependent was overfed. A study based on Sumerian texts from Lagash during the Ur III dynasty is of particular interest here. Waetzoldt estimates yearly ration allotments, and concludes that they were kept at survival values for most of the workers, both hired workers with permanent jobs, and slaves. Other scholars reason that these probably were also assigned land or lived close to their own land and supplied their nutrition with their own production. Waetzoldt also shows that women were systematically paid less than men.

> Among the crafts, masculine occupations are represented by——among others—copper smiths, gold and silver smiths, reed weavers, wood workers, leather workers, bakers and cooks, potters, malters, brewers, shipwrights, basket makers, rope makers, and fullers, as well as scribes. Grinding grain, pressing oil, and weaving were female occupations.
> Most male craftsmen, including scribes, received a barley allotment of about 60 liters (60 sila) per month, though sometimes this varies from 40 to 60

---

[91] Dandamaev, *Slavery in Babylonia*, 409. Laura D. Steele, "Women and Gender in Babylonia," in *The Babylonian World* (ed. Gwendolyn Leick; New York: Routledge, 2007), 308–11 studies this and other documents in which a female slave is claimed by more than one party.

liters. Clearly, 60 liters per month was regarded as the normal allotment for a grown man, because porters, doorkeepers, herdsmen, date palm gardeners, boat pullers, as well as men who worked in gardens or in the boat and ship center all received this same amount.

Then as now, women were paid distinctly less than men, a phenomenon that is already attested for earlier periods in documents from Ebla in northern Syria and from presargonic Girsu in the State of Lagaš. The normal barley allotment for women ranged from 30 to 40 liters per month.

The disparity between the compensation of men and women appears in an even crasser light when one considers that a man could rise very high in the scale of compensation, whereas women workers always remained on a relatively low level.[92]

From Waetzoldt's analysis one can conclude that, although hired workers might have been legally free, the system prevented them from saving resources and climbing in the socio-economic ladder, and so apparently in everyday life they were as bound as slaves were.[93] This situation very likely applied to other kingdoms as well. The Bible does not contain any ration list with which to compare their situation with the one at Lagaš; however, even free Israelites knew hunger and starvation from time to time.

Temple slaves worked mainly in agriculture and in business; apparently very few of them worked in animal husbandry or in crafts:

The temple administration had to turn to the labor of free artisans many times in the course of a year, employing jewelers, brewers of beer, bakers, leather workers, blacksmiths, bronzesmiths, carpenters, architects, weavers, bleachers, builders, potters, engravers of seals, launderers, and others, as hundreds of documents attest.[94]

At Mari there is evidence of male and female scribes of several types. Pearce mentions a group of ten female scribes, nine of whom, judging from their rations, are estimated to have been slaves at the harem. Typically, evidence of women in general, slaves or free, is not abundant, thus it is impossible to assess whether they were rather common or not. Evidence at Mari "is limited to one fragment of a vocabulary text by one Belt-remanni in the Old Babylonian period. Female counterparts to diviners, physicians, performers, and artists are

---

[92] Waetzoldt, "Compensation," 121–22.

[93] Waetzoldt, "Compensation," 123: "Workers in the lower pay scales must have been especially hit by reductions in rations, because the lowest of these was Beven in normal conditionsB very near the subsistence minimum." Compensations seem to have been partly based on the people's need to survive and not only on performance, as everyone, from toddlers to grandmothers, received an allotment.

[94] Dandamaev, *Slavery in Babylonia*, 302.

all attested. But their activities, too, are overshadowed by those of their male counterparts."[95]

Biblical evidence for temple slavery is rather scant. The נתינים, "donated ones" are mentioned in the post-exilic lists of returnees, but it is not clear whether their status as consecrated necessarily means slavery. The information is scant and it only tells us of their services, not of their legal status (1 Sam 2:22, 2 Kgs 23:7). Since "guilds" were hereditary and for life, since pre-industrial societies do not have high social mobility, and since parents teach children their occupation, it is very likely that also in Israel slaves donated to the temple would not be manumitted.[96]

Two oblique references might be brought here as possible references to women permanently ascribed to the Jerusalem temple, perhaps as donated or enslaved. Josiah's reform included throwing out and destroying non-Yahwist cultic objects, including Ashera's paraphernalia. Second Kings 23:7 mentions the "women" who wove for Ashera in the very temple compounds. And one of Ezekiel's visions includes, also at the northern gate of the temple, women who sat (ישבות, or dwelled?) there, who wept for Tammuz (Ezek 8:1). While the traditional understanding is that these women were Israelites living elsewhere and coming to worship, I do not see why the reference could not be also to women ascribed to the temple on a permanent basis.

PRIVATE LABORERS

From Neo-Babylonian times two archives were found, covering the Murašu and the Egibi families, which held several businesses and personnel.[97] Slaves were assigned to all types of work, depending on their training (if they had any), the size of the household, age, sex, and other factors. Slaves worked in domestic tasks (cooking, fetching water, weaving, grinding grain), in attendance to the

---

[95] Laurie E. Pearce, "The Scribes and Scholars of Ancient Mesopotamia," in *Civilizations of the Ancient Near East* (ed. Jack M. Sasson; vol. 4; New York: Scribner, 1995), 2266.

[96] "Guilds" is within quotation marks because of B. Cutler and J. Macdonald's warning (indicated already as they begin their study) that they should not be confused with associations thus called in the Middle Ages. More on these brotherhoods in chapter 5.

[97] Dandamaev, *Slavery in Babylonia*, 19–20. "The majority of the documents from the Egibi archive was composed in the area of Babylon and its suburbs, but a few were written in other cities where members of the Egibi family possessed real estate or were engaged in business. Unfortunately, documents from the Egibi archive are scattered among the most diverse museums and publications. The archive of Murašu was discovered in its entirety in a single room and for this reason was published more connectedly. This archive consists of 730 tablets in all, a large part of which are beautifully preserved .... Almost all the texts are dated to the reigns of Artaxerxes I and Darius II. The earliest tablet was written in 455 and the latest in 403."

master and/or mistress (especially during traveling or warfare), in agriculture, care of animals, handicrafts, and administration.[98] Women were also hired out as prostitutes, wet nurses, taverners, and beer brewers, and in addition to their daily work, some of them were taken by the master as concubines, or bred with slaves to produce more slaves for the master. Dandamaev affirms that "in the Neo-Babylonian period brothels already were called 'the place where they know slave women.'"[99] Records of female slaves from the Neo-Babylonian period also include a weaver, brewers, a baker, and a wet nurse.[100]

At times a slave (generally male) was sent to learn the craft with a craftsman, often a slave himself, although there are contracts of one female slave learning the crafts of weaving, and another slave working as brewer for the temple and paying her *quitrent* (her earnings) to her master. Apprenticeship seems to have been inconvenient and therefore rare, because (at least from the contracts from Babylonia) it could take up to six years, during which the master had to support his slave and got nothing in exchange.[101] According to Dandamaev's report, the range of specialties was quite wide:

> Twelve contracts have been preserved which concern the training of slaves in various trades: leatherworking and shoemaking, seal engraving, weaving, sack making, bleaching of clothes, a special type of weaving, baking or cooking, carpentry, house building, bread or food peddling, as well as a number of other trades, the nature of which is not sufficiently clear.[102]

At this point it is important to remember that, in talking about craftsmen and possibly craftswomen, one cannot always find in the sources a clear

---

[98] Mendelsohn, *Slavery in the ANE*, 92–98 (state slavery), 100–6 (temple slavery), and 106–17 (private slaves in agriculture and industry.)

[99] Dandamaev, *Slavery in Babylonia*, 133, mentioning Nbk 409:5–6. On 135 he states, "It is evident from the documents examined above that Nabu-ahhe-iddin of the house of Egibi, and later his son Itti-marduk-balatu, placed their slave women engaging in prostitution at the disposal of various persons for three sūt (c. 18 liters) of barley a day [n.73] or turned them over to a brothel, the keeper of which apparently paid the master of the slave three-fourths of the earnings." [n. 73, "It has already been mentioned above that the daily pay of an adult worker (free man or slave) was one sūt of barley. In UCP 9/I I 53, the monthly payment for cohabitation with a slave woman is ten shekels of silver, at a time when the yearly wages of an adult worker consisted of twelve shekels."] Recently prostitution in the ANE has been much discussed, see below, chapter 7.

[100] See Dandamaev, *Slavery in Babylonia*, 295."According to Camb 330 and 331, a slave woman who paid her master quitrent was engaged in brewing beer;" and 296 "A baker was sold with three other slaves, including a nursing child, for five minas of silver." J. Greenfield, "Some Neo-Babylonian Women," in *La Femme*, 75–80.

[101] Mendelsohn, *Slavery in the ANE*, 116, "the apprenticeship period lasted from two to six years, a period during which not only did the slave not bring in any profit, but the owner had to spend money for his upkeep." Dandamaev, *Slavery in Babylonia*, 297–99.

[102] Dandamaev, *Slavery in Babylonia*, 279.

distinction between free and unfree ones, and thus one can know that these were the professions available, but not who did what.

> Even in the Neo-Babylonian period, however, slave labor did not play a decisive role in the handicraft industries and was in no position to supplant free labor … The documents refer both to artisans in general (ummânu) and persons in specific branches of production in the artisan trades: craftsmen who wove mats of reeds, goldsmiths and silversmiths, leather workers, launderers, blacksmiths, bronzesmiths, oil pressers, carpenters, bleachers, barbers, weavers, builders, architects, potters, bakers, beer brewers, engravers of seal, and others.
>
> The number of free skilled artisans was far greater than that of slave artisans.[103]

Scholars agree that there is an imbalance in the ratio of trained men and women, but few pause to ask why. First, in a patriarchal system there is the general preference for males, and since most owners and supervisors of the great institutions were male, they would have prioritized male apprenticeship over female. Female slaves seem to have been more profitable to their owners in sex-related jobs, as slave breeders, wet nurses, or prostitutes, and probably in service-type occupations related to the household. Comparing the roles of female and male slaves in the Late Babylonian period, Kuhrt attributes the lack of visibility of women in the sources to an imbalance in the investment by masters in female's specialization. Thus they would be mainly confined to a few house-located occupations, for which there was no need of special training or need of contracts:

> [W]hile one can see slave owners investing in their male slaves by having them apprenticed as barbers, shoemakers, bakers, and smiths, there is only one instance where a female slave was set up in business in this way, probably as a tavern-keeper (Camb. 330; 331). Similarly, although slave-women do appear as owners of land (Dar. 470) and acting as agents for their owners, attestations of them in these roles is quantitatively tiny compared to male slaves. … they never have seals in contrast to some of the prominent, wealthy male slaves of this period; indeed there seem to have been no similarly well-endowed slave-women. A frequently attested way in which female (as well as male) slaves were used was either to secure loans or work them off in their creditor's house (*antichresis*). But the most striking method by which female slaves were exploited (both by private owners and temples) was to hire them out to brothels (Nbk. 409) or individuals (Nbn 679) as prostitutes, the fee paid augmenting the

---

[103] Dandamaev, *Slavery in Babylonia*, 299–300.

income of their master or that of the god/goddess to whose house they belonged (UCP 9/1 1 53).[104]

As to the biblical accounts, although many professions are casually mentioned in the Bible both for males and females, we are not told how people acquired their mastery, nor who were slaves and who were hired workers. Temple עבדים (slaves or servants) are mentioned in a few texts, but their status is unstated. Narratives attest to slaves as part of private and royal households. However, due to the character of the biblical account, there is lack of evidence of other aspects present in Babylonia, for instance contracts, particular conditions of slavery, possibilities of manumission, apprenticeship or wages charged for their "use" by third parties. Furthermore, there is increasing doubt as to the narratives historical character.

OTHER FORMS OF UNFREE LABOR

Two other forms of unfree labor should be recognized as part of the labor force in antiquity. One is helotage or serfdom; it consists of the attachment of the peasant to the land, not to a master. This is an intermediate form of freedom, since peasants were sold and bought with the land, they were probably obliged to obey the master, could not leave their land, and had to supply an amount of grain (and perhaps other services) to the owner of the land. They seem to have comprised the majority of peasantry in Babylonia. It is unclear whether and to what extent it pertained also to Israel. However, the wider the social gap between the urban elite and the peasants, the more possibilities that helotage became an option. Helotage has the advantage of allowing the peasants to stay in what used to be their land, and it provides for the new owners more reliable labor than slaves, as it usually works on the basis of the payment to the owner of a percentage of the yield.[105]

Another typical form of unfree labor is the corvée, which is a different institution from slavery. Corvée is a compulsory service for the state on the part of the citizen. Depending on the state and the period, it could involve military service, agricultural work, and many other forms. One of the types of corvée mentioned in many documents is that of the *ilku*. According to a recent work on the Nuzi texts,

---

[104] Kuhrt, "Non-Royal Women,"232–33.
[105] Petr Charvát, "Social configurations in Early Dynastic Babylonia," in *The Babylonian World* (ed. Gwendolyn Leick; New York: Routledge, 2007), 259 mentions the "serfs," who at times entered into this institution more or less voluntarily out of debts, as one of the two groups of underprivileged during the Early Dynastic Sumerian, the other being the prisoners of war.

> *ilku* is one tax amongst several levied in the Nuzi region. Not all these taxes are
> clearly understood. Nevertheless, it appears certain that some taxes were
> payable in goods, while others were paid in labor. Obligatory military service is
> implicit throughout the Nuzi corpus, although a term for this service is
> curiously lacking. The *ilku* has been seen as involving such military service, at
> least some of the time. However, the only specific descriptions of the *ilku* are
> agricultural labor for the government (text #37), the manufacture of textiles
> (text #72), and other non-military labor (text #37). Another text, text #73, may
> even imply that the *ilku* is specifically non-military in nature. Thus, the *ilku* is a
> labor tax, predominantly—probably exclusively—of a non-military sort. The
> *ilku*, in short, is a corvée.[106]

For us, the most interesting aspect of this quotation from Maidman is the
fact that this type of tax, like several others, involved work rather than monetary
compensation. It is unclear whether at any time and in any society, women also
had to do some corvée (it appears that 1 Sam 8 refers to corvée, but it could also
mean permanent employment of young men and women by the palace). At any
rate the poorest households must have felt the impact of the males leaving for a
period of time for corvée, even if they did not have to serve themselves.[107]

This concludes the section on types of slaves attested in different documents
throughout the ANE. The review is not exhaustive, but it affords a background
against which to look at women in the Bible, several of whom were perhaps
dependents but not legally slaves.

CONCLUDING REMARKS

While land-owning was the ideal for Israel, it often fell short of the mark and
people had to take all kinds of measure to survive. Western categories of "lower-
class" or "upper-class" do not fit the ancient material as one might wish. Thus a
model had to be used which would prove valuable for testing information from
the ANE sources about socially and economically dependent women. Whether
"economically dependent" is the best term to define them is left for the reader to
decide. For lack of a better term, it is used here for those women who had to
work because of financial or social constraints, from those who had to hire
themselves out as harvesters in order to help out their own families, to those
taken away as war booty, to some place far from home. All these situations were

---

[106] Maynard Maidman, *Nuzi Texts and Their Uses as Historical Evidence* (ed. Ann K. Guinan;
Atlanta: SBL, 2010), 164.
[107] Isaac Mendelsohn, "Samuel's Denunciation of Kingship in the Light of the Akkadian Documents
from Ugarit," *BASOR* 143 (1956): 17–22; "On Corvee Labor in Ancient Canaan and Israel," *BASOR*
167 (1962): 31–35.

rather common in a world where war, famine, and other maladies occurred frequently; a world in which slavery was an accepted institution and a kind of "social security" system.

Several themes relevant to slavery and indentured servitude have been focused upon, such as the difficulty in differentiating slave from indentured statuses, slave conditions in one of the great institutions and in family households, and manumission. Other themes have not been touched upon, such as ransom of prisoners, family life and hardships, branding or marking of slaves, chain gangs, punishment and torture of slaves, and conditions of slavery as reflected in legal non-biblical evidence. Although these certainly were part of reality for many throughout every slave-holding society, they do not constitute major themes in the biblical analysis of lower class women in DtrH. Slavery was a widespread economic institution, which provided labor in exchange for basic survival needs. Its origins are very much related to the need to dispose of people who would have otherwise died (war prisoners, criminals, starving people), and to the need to have cheap and coordinated labor as well. Disgusting as it is to us today, slavery was a social mechanism through which much labor was channeled in practically every society and among societies. One should also remember that slavery was not the only form of unfree labor in antiquity, and that the term has to be loaded with many conditions and characteristics, from the slave who rose to be manager of the master's estate and enjoyed considerable power, honor, and commodities, to the foreigner who died in the mines or sick. Most information conveyed by our sources applies to males or in general to "slaves" or even "servants." The picture concerning women is, if anything, worse than that of men, because of the high imbalance in the use of power and of the added sexual discrimination—facts which, incidentally, still apply.

CHAPTER 4

FEMALE SLAVES AND DEPENDENTS

Chapter 1 looked at the difficulties in establishing a model that contemplates women and social stratification in ancient Israel, and chapter 3 reviewed the political and socio-economic conditions which led many women throughout the ANE to work in multiple occupations and locations as slaves and indentured servants. When an army managed to have a city surrender or be taken, the most privileged sectors of society (if not killed) were deported and located elsewhere, while the people of the land were left to work it and pay high tributes.[1] Although conditions might have varied depending on social groups and conquerors, the customary situation of labor in one's own household, for one's inheritance, could very easily be drastically disrupted: the mistress could become slave to a foreigner, and the farmer, tenant of his own land (Isa 47; Deut 30:15–20). Conversely, if one's king conquered another, there would be foreigners being brought in, and displaced people seeking refuge. It should not be surprising, then, that the Bible is aware of the fact that a number of women worked for others. What should be surprising is that scholarship in general has paid so little attention to the contribution females made to their society in socio-economic, cultural, and religious terms, and to the matter-of-factness of the Bible on this issue. In her overview of woman in the OT, Phyllis Bird states that

---

[1] See Albenda, "Woman, Child, and Family," 17–21.

Man in the Old Testament recognizes woman as one essentially like him, as a partner in pleasure and labor, one whom he needs, and one who can spell him weal or woe. From his point of view—the only point of view of the Old Testament texts—the woman is a helper, whose work as wife and mother is essential and complementary to his own. In a sense she completes him—but as one with a life and character of her own. She is his opposite and equal.[2]

His opposite and equal: in working conditions as well? Although there are several examples of occupations both for men and for women, from the texts it is impossible to know whether they would work together or under the same conditions, since often both terms do not appear together, and when they do, they do not describe any activity. Due to power distribution, social location and especially valuation were not the same for both sexes, woman always behind man in her corresponding group.[3]

This chapter will study women whose occupations are unknown, but who are in a position of dependency of a master. In some narratives these women play a key role, while in others they are barely referred to, as part of the scenario. The study will not be able to determine an exact social or legal location for each of them, because there are no elements in the texts for such a decision. It will provide as accurate a location for a particular woman or group as possible. Since the material is not historical but theological, there is more basis to locate the writer's view and presuppositions than the women he mentions.

In the first section, we will look at the semantic field of female slavery in the Hebrew Bible. This is a large section, including different genres and topics. This section will comprise two major items and several sub-sections. Section I will take a look at the pertinent texts, in which the lexemes for female slave or servant appear in DtrH. The latter part of this section will look at these concerns through the legal corpora of the Hebrew Bible. Not all laws will be studied, but only those which would somehow answer any of the leading questions, "What do laws tell us, if anything, about female labor? What about their ascription of honor?" It is, nevertheless, a large sub-section.

Because one leading question is whether we can trust the lexemes so translated to mean "slave" (regardless of the several connotations "slave" would

---

[2] Phyllis A. Bird, "Images of Women in the Old Testament," *Missing Persons and Mistaken Identities* (Minneapolis: Fortress, 1997), 45.

[3] See Waetzoldt, "Compensation," 121–2; Robins, *Women*, 101–6. Women were used as sexual objects and harassed to a degree that men were not, simply because the ones in power could exert it over their subordinates and, as it still happens today, the overwhelming majority of those in power were males (Potiphar's wife, on the other hand, used power in the same way as many males did). Also down the social ladder, men could still harass women in a lower standing, as Boaz implies (Ruth 2:8–9). We cannot, therefore, put a woman in the same social location as a man who did the same occupation.

have, i.e., permanent or debt-slavery, slave-wives, concubines, servants, and so forth), Section II of the chapter looks at texts in which some terms, particularly אמה, are used in an argument with an ideological intention of diminishing the honor of the opponent. The section comprises examples of self-abasement, as an insult toward another person in direct speech and in an argument about a third party not involved in it.

SECTION I: WHEN DO אמה, שפחה, AND נערה MEAN "SLAVE"?

The two terms for female slaves are אמה and שפחה, while נערה refers in several stories to a woman in a dependent position, but not necessarily a slave. All these have in common their economic dependency, their lack of power, and the precariousness of their situation and rights.

Both אמה and שפחה appear with a literal and a figurative meaning in reference to several women (see Charts I–III). From their lack of rights and power claims one can infer that some were slaves, for example, Hagar, Bilhah or Zilpah, whom their mistresses gave to the masters. In other cases the information is so scant that not much can be drawn from it; the Levite's concubine (Judg 19) is one example: her status remains totally unclear despite so much telling about her.

The study will first look at all appearances of the terms שפחה, אמה, and נערה in DtrH, divided into two categories: (a) instances where the term might be taken literally, which are the ones which will then be studied in more detail, and (b) instances where the term is used by a woman in self-reference as a polite manner of speaking. It will soon be noticed that there is no instance of נערה with the latter sense in the Hebrew Bible.[4]

אמה. The term אמה appears in DtrH in reference to:

- Abimelech as son of one אמה (Judg 9:18), according to Jotham;

- the concubine of a Levite (Judg 19) by the narrator;

- women in front of whom David dances (2 Sam 6:20, 22) by Michal.

It is also used figuratively of the following women, each speaking of herself as אמתך to a male superior:[5]

---

[4] Where אמה or שפחה appear in category b), the literal meaning of the term is ruled out because the use of אמה or שפחה in those instances is a social convention, unless also the context/narrator qualify her as a slave. But this is not the case in any of the texts in DtrH.

[5] See chart II. These instances do not concern us here, because they do not provide any information about the social location of lower-class women. They only tell us that, as men use עבדך, women use שפחתך or אמתך to place themselves in a clientele position in reference to a superior, which in all

- the wise woman of Abel (2 Sam 20:17) to Joab;

- Bathsheba (1 Kgs 1:13,17) to David;

- Two single mothers in court (1 Kgs 3:20) to Solomon.

Finally, the following women use *both* אמה and שפחה to speak of themselves to a male superior, also with figurative meaning:

- Hannah, to YHWH and to Eli, the priest (1 Sam 1:11[x3], 16);

- Abigail (1 Sam 25:24–41) to David;

- the wise woman of Teqoa (2 Sam 14:15,17) to David.[6]

Laws concerning participation of slaves in religious festivals, and Abigail's servants traveling with her, are to be taken literally. In other cases it is not immediately clear whether the connotation of אמה is literal or not, because there is an element of disdain that needs to be considered before a decision can be made; these are the stories of the Levite's concubine, Jotham's characterization of his half-brother Abimelech as the son of one such woman, and the women in front of whom David dances.[7]

שפחה. The term שפחה appears sixty-two times in the Hebrew Bible, also with a literal and a figurative meaning, and applied to a variety of women.[8] In DtrH, it occurs in the following texts:

- a slave as a possession in general (1 Sam 8:16; 2 Kgs 5:26);

- an unnamed slave who helped during Absalom's revolt (2 Sam 17:17);

- Israel in general becoming prisoner (Deut 28:68).

It is used by the following women, each speaking of herself to a male superior,

---

these instances is a man or YHWH, never another woman. In fact in the whole Bible there is no instance of a woman addressing another woman in this way. עבדך never used for an equal, always someone placing himself in a subservient position, see Curt Lindhagen, *The Servant Motif in the Old Testament* (Uppsala: Lundequistska, 1950), 71. On patronage in general, see *Patronage in Ancient Society* (ed. A. Wallace-Hadrill. London: Routlegde, 1989), especially A. Wallace-Hadrill, "Introduction," 1–13; Richard Saller, "Patronage and Friendship in Early Imperial Rome: Drawing the Distinction," 49–62, and Keith Hopwood, "Bandits, Elites and Rural Order," 171–87.

[6]Outside DtrH, Hagar (Gen 16), and Bilhah and Zilpah (Gen 30–31) are referred to alternatively by both terms, and Ruth does likewise in self-reference.

[7] There is no instance of the use of שפחה or נערה in this sense by a third person.

[8] S. Mandelkern, *Veteris Testamenti Concordantiae Hebraicae atque Chaldaicae* (ed. F. Margolin; Graz: Akademische Druck- und Verlangsanstalt, 1925), 1222. Lindhagen, *Servant Motif*, 43, quotes Fleischer (*Biblischer Commentar über das Alte Testament* [ed. C. Keil & F. Delitzsch; Leipzig: Dörffling und Franke, 1870–1879, 9 vols.], 3. 78, n.1) on the etymology of the term שפחה, "ejaculate: a woman into whom a man ejaculates his seed > a woman slave, sexually at the disposal of her master."

in addition to the women who use אמה and שפחה, already listed:

- the medium at Endor (1 Sam 28:21–22), to Saul;

- a widow of the "children of the prophets" (2 Kgs 4:2), to Elisha;

- the woman of Shunnem (2 Kgs 4:16), to Elisha.

All texts of the first group—Deut 28, where the background warning is defeat in war or slavery; the texts where female slaves are mentioned in a list after the children and the male slaves, and the unnamed servant who served as broker during Absalom's revolt—can be taken literally, since there is no ideological interest against them. The women of the second group situate themselves in relation to a man, as before, but in contrast to instances of "אמתך," there is no woman addressing YHWH by שפחתך.⁹

נערה. The term נערה appears in a series of occurrences which dictionaries generally divide into two major groups: "girl, damsel," from a girl to a widow, and "attendant, maid"; however, נערה is a term that responds to a categorization of status, not age, thus rendering dictionaries' classifications inaccurate.¹⁰ In DtrH, נערה is used only by third persons in reference to:

- some women at the well (1 Sam 9:11), mentioned by the narrator;

- the Shunammite (1 Kgs 1:2–4), mentioned by David's attendants (v. 2) and the narrator;

- women abducted for the Benjaminites (Judg 21:12), mentioned by the narrator;

- a girl taken by the Arameans (2 Kgs 5:2), mentioned by the narrator;

- Abigail's attendants (1 Sam 25:42), mentioned by the narrator.

In this case the question is not whether the term can be taken literally, but what it refers to, and in which instances it can be equaled to a slave or dependent woman.

Even a quick review of the lists above shows that the information about female slaves is scant and scattered. There are several mentions in passing in the

---

⁹ Whether the use by women of אמה to pray to God is a reason to make an אמה higher than a שפחה is hard to say. There are no parallel uses with terms for males that could help in discerning this question.

¹⁰ Even if we stayed with the traditional classification, *BDB*'s is inaccurate in including the girl in 2 Kgs 5:2,4 under "girl, damsel," since, as verse 2 explicitly says, she is a slave-girl. Leeb's book addresses, precisely, the question of the meaning and social location of these men and women.

deuteronomic laws,[11] two stories in Judges with a high content of violence, family instability and political implications for the institution of the monarchy (Judg 9 and 19–21);[12] two stories that each involve an argument between a woman and David (1 Sam 25 and 2 Sam 6:20–23);[13] a woman related to David in his old age, Abishag (1 Kgs 1:2–4); an unnamed slave who helped during Absalom's revolt by passing on information (2 Sam 17:17); a few sayings where female slaves are part of the package of possessions (1 Sam 8:16; 2 Kgs 5:26; Deut 28:68); and finally a girl taken captive by the Arameans (2 Kgs 5:2).

As already stated, no block of biblical text conveys much information, because the writers' focus was neither on an ethnographic account of their society, nor on women *per se*, especially not on lower-class women.[14] This unclarity in the relation between שפחה, אמה, and נערה is part of the larger problem of irretrievable lives throughout history. Despite these difficulties, several theories have been proposed to explain the mutual relation of אמה and שפחה, and although this seems a hopeless task, a short review follows in order to explore the main possibilities proposed so far. In an article published in 1958, Jepsen proposed a double thesis, that "1) שפחה ist das noch unberührte, unfreie Mädchen, vor allem im Dienst der Frau des Hauses; 2) אמה ist die unfreie Frau, sowohl die Nebenfrau des Mannes, wie die unfreie Frau eines unfreien Mannes, eines Sklaven."[15] In support of אמה as slave or as concubine, he turns to six cases where the expression בן־אמה appears (and to some other examples as well). Jepsen's claim would explain the absence of בן־שפחה (supposing for a moment it is not happenstance): the woman's role as concubine would be expressed by אמה not by שפחה. The problem with this theory (and any other, for that matter) is that it is unable to explain accurately the mix of terms, for instance, to speak of Hagar, Bilhah or Zilpah as both אמה and שפחה.

---

[11] Only the laws of Deut 15:17 deal with issues of slavery proper, the others include the slaves among those persons with the right to participate in the religious festivals.

[12] Judges 21 (the abduction of the young virgins for the Benjaminites) is presented as the consequence of the horror narrated in Judg 19. In Judg 21 נערות does not refer to slaves, but to women abducted, who were not protected by their *paterfamilias*.

[13] Abigail's attendants move to David's household with her when she becomes his wife; Michal's argument with David implies his impropriety in exhibiting himself in front of אמהות.

[14] For instance, when Naaman the Syrian general is afflicted with leprosy (2 Kgs 5) it is an Israelite נערה who tells Naaman's wife about the prophet in Israel; when David flees Jerusalem because of Absalom's coup, it is a נערה who goes out of Jerusalem to tell two men, who in turn will tell David, what is going on in the city. Yet, these would not have been their everyday tasks. R. Alter, *The Art of Biblical Narrative* (New York: Basic Books, 1981), 67–68 attributes this function to the "biblical preference for direct discourse [which] is so pronounced that thought is almost invariably rendered as actual speech, that is, as quoted monologue." From a sociological point of view, the slave, because of her liminality, can come and go more easily than her mistress without incurring in the danger of pollution or death, because she is already socially dead.

[15] A. Jepsen, "'Amah' und 'Schiphchah,'" *VT* 8 (1958): 293.

Engelken sees a concentration of אָמָה in the major prophets, the legal corpora, and wisdom literature, and of שִׁפְחָה in Genesis and the books of Samuel.[16] She suggests the אָמָה represents a dependent who is closer to the household, and therefore higher in the social ladder than the שִׁפְחָה, who should be rendered as slave.[17] Recently, Edward Bridge has tried again to discern different meanings between both terms and concludes that they are synonyms, with patterns of preference "אָמָה is preferred in legal contexts and שִׁפְחָה is preferred in Genesis. Outside Genesis, only אָמָה is used in marital/conjugal contexts."[18]

In summary, attempts to differentiate between these have failed to achieve consensus so far. Engelken's suggestion is correct in regard to שִׁפְחָה as generic for female slave, appearing in texts such as the curses in Deut 28 or Jeremiah's accusations to the men of Jerusalem (Jer 34). In turn, אָמָה would refer to the maidservant (it would be the occupation, not the legal status), thus explaining why it would be closer to the family. Or one could hypothesize that originally one of the terms referred to the foreign (שִׁפְחָה), permanent slave who was attached to the family (notice that שִׁפְחָה is from the same stem as מִשְׁפָּחָה), and the other one to the indentured-servant (אָמָה); as debt turned people increasingly into permanent slaves, terms were undistinguishable. This would explain why אָמָה is used for the laws that allow their participation with the family in the feasts.[19] Except for the fact that only אָמָה is used to address God, and that there seems to be a more general tone to the שִׁפְחָה (for instance in the curses in Deut 28) they seem to be very close in meaning, and their relationship remains unclear. Perhaps at a certain stage they had different meanings, or originated in different geographical locations, but later use rendered them undistinguishable from each other.[20]

---

[16] Engelken, *Frauen im Alten Israel*, 128. Both terms appear in Genesis (even referring both to Hagar, for instance), Exodus, Leviticus, Deuteronomy, Judges, 1 and 2 Samuel, Psalms, and Ruth. אָמָה appears also in 1 Kings, Nahum, Ezra, Nehemiah, Job; שִׁפְחָה appears also in 2 Kings, 2 Chronicles, Isaiah, Jeremiah, Joel, Esther, Proverbs and Qoheleth. Engelken, 130–32, has also attempted a social differentiation of both terms on the basis of the apparent closeness of the אָמָה to the family, while שִׁפְחָה would belong to a lower rank of slaves, probably living in barracks.

[17] Engelken, *Frauen im Alten Israel*, 166. She also discusses Eissfeldt''s attempt (*Einleitung in das Alte Testament* [3rd new rev. ed. Tübingen, 1964], 243) to use both terms to delineate Pentateuchal sources, ascribing אָמָה to E and שִׁפְחָה to J. Jepsen's proposal makes more sense than a source criterion (131).

[18] Edward J.Bridge, "Female slave vs female slave: אָמָה and שִׁפְחָה in the HB," *JHS* 12 art. 2 (2012), n.p. [cited 22 January 2013]. Online: http://ejournals.library.ualberta.ca/index .php/jhs/article/view/16440/13145.

[19] However, in Gen 21 אָמָה is used of Hagar the Egyptian, which invalidates this hypothesis.

[20] I thank Carolyn Osiek for the suggestion of different regional origins. Perhaps Dandamaev's conclusions, *Slavery in Babylonia*, 89, which refer to the similar enigma in Mesopotamian material,

Thus, starting from the premise that both terms are not distinguishable any more, they will be studied thematically. The advantage of this proposal is to focus on the situation of women, rather than on philological differences between terms of unknown origin. This study calls attention to particular points, which are of importance for the location of these women. It also asks the texts questions concerning their ideology of class and gender. Since the study is thematical and not linguistic, it will start with occurrences of the terms meant to be literal, and then proceed to terms used by the writer to build his historiography. That section is called "Why These Ones Are Not Slaves."

A CLOSER LOOK AT THE PERTINENT TEXTS

נערה — *When There Is No Paterfamilias*

Traditionally the terms נער and נערה have been given a multiplicity of meanings, originating in their presumed age or life stage ("girl of marriageable age," "youth") or their supposed occupation ("servant," "squire," "maidservant," "prostitute").[21] Some years ago, Carolyn Leeb challenged these interpretations, and looking carefully at the social location of people called by either of those two terms, she found that "the common social location that these characters all share is neither age nor marital status nor 'social class' .... Rather, what these characters share is the situation of being 'away from their father's house,' beyond the protection and control of their fathers, while not yet master or mistress of their own households."[22] In other words, whether slave or free, young or old, servant at a household or promised heir to Abraham, people in very different stages of life found themselves temporarily or permanently being in the נער category. By providing a strong basis from which to locate the נערה/תו, as women in a precarious situation of lack of family and even physical protection, Leeb illuminates the present inquiry into the status of women who might have not been slaves but were dependent on a master. Leeb started by

---

are applicable to our problem: "This word [amtu/ GEME $_2$] already occurs in documents from the Old Babylonian period. Slave women who are called amtu are sold...and pawned... amtu also appears as a synonym for qallatu, another term designating the female slave [see NRVU 67 and Nbn 391, on the one hand, and NRVU 391 and Nbn 391, on the other, where the same slave woman is called in one place amtu and, in another, qallatu]."

[21] Main supporters of these hypotheses and discussed by Leeb, *Away from the Father's House*, 15–20 are H-P. Stähli, *Knabe-Jüngling-Knecht: Untersuchungen zum Begriff Naʿar im Alten Testament* (ed. J. Becker & H. Reventlow. BBET. Frankfurt: Lang, 1978); J. Macdonald, "The Status and Role of the Naʿar in Israelite Society," *JNES* 35 (1976): 147–70; W. Mayer and R. Mayer-Opificius, "Die Schlacht bei Qadeš: Der Versuch einer neuen Rekonstruktion," *UF* 26 (1994): 321–68; Lawrence Stager, "The Archaeology of the Family in Ancient Israel," *BASOR* 260 (1985): 1–35, with the consequent perpetuation of the image of the נער as a young adult of a prominent family, a "knight."
[22] Leeb, *Away from the Father's House*, 41. I have already referred to her work in chapter 1.

grouping references to the נער in a cluster of functions, which are more determined by the place where they appear than by what they do—which is the reason why there have been so many translations and interpretations for one term.

> Perhaps the most important [observation about נערים who are servants] is how seldom the biblical text actually reports them *doing* anything. The most prominent feature of their activities seems to be their presence: they are "with" other characters, they are taken along, they are sent and left behind, they speak and are spoken to, but often the real work of the narrative is performed by other characters.[23]

In the Hebrew Bible there often appear נער/ה/ים/ות as indicators of their owners' status and honor, as "someone to talk to."[24] The נער's location was lowly and vulnerable, and that of the נערה likely lower than that of the male, and especially vulnerable in terms of her sexuality.[25] A majority of נער/ה/ים/ות are servants located in the domestic, the agricultural, and the cultic settings, staying at one place or travelling with the master or mistress. In the book of Ruth, Boaz has נערים and נערות among his workers, from harvesters to overseer. At least some נער/ה/ים/ות enjoyed a degree of power, within the limits imposed by the fact of not being *paterfamilias*, of course: Gehazi (Elisha's נער), Ziba (Saul's נער), and this unnamed supervisor of Boaz are examples. There is no similar נערה recorded as personal assistant to a prophet or king's advisor; there is, however, an outstanding נערה, Abishag the Shunammite (1 Kgs 1:1–4).[26]

---

[23] Leeb, *Away from the Father's House*, 42.

[24] They indicate their owners' status, and not the other way round. This means that a master with several servants who go on errands, prepare food, bring information, fight with him, is a powerful man in his society. This does not make the נער powerful or important, as scholars believed earlier. Part of the confusion with נערים as important military warriors is that the status of the masters whom they serve has been transferred by commentators to them. See Leeb, *Away from the Father's House*, 43 (status indicators), 43–44 (anchor points, someone to talk to), 44–45 (serving and standing by their masters, and conduits of information between "inside" and "outside"); 45 (traversers of thresholds).

[25] Leeb, *Away from the Father's House*, 44–62 (domestic), 62–66 (agricultural), and 66–67 (cultic).

[26] Among those identified by name Gehazi appears in several stories in 2 Kgs 4:8 through 8:1–6, in one of which there is also a נערה קטנה, a "small dependent" (2 Kgs 5). Most dependents go unnamed, such as Abraham's (Gen 18:7), Nabal's (1 Sam 25:8, 14–19) or the Levite's (Judg 19). Ziba is also an interesting narratological character, in that he is named, he himself has slaves and children (he is far from being a boy), he maneuvers in order to get the best he can out of circumstances (especially during Absalom's revolt), yet not only he remains a נער throughout the text, but "[w]e know nothing about his family or ancestry, his home town or ethnicity, nor about how he came to be in the service of Saul." (Leeb, *Away from the Father's House*, 62). Whether legally

A cluster of texts have נערים in the military setting. Due to a particular understanding of 1 Kgs 20:13–22 and of the account of the battle of Kadesh, this particular type of נער has been ascribed the status of a particular military troop. This group of נערים has only an indirect bearing on the issues of this study, and therefore a detailed discussion of this misunderstanding will not be found here.[27] For the present study it is important in that it corroborates the picture drawn from other sources in the previous chapter, in which it was seen that many young men, whose families could not provide them with inheritance, and especially those who contracted debts, left home in order to find means of survival other than farming. Again, there is no biblical parallel to this type of service by a נערה. They might as well have been the "your sons" and "your daughters" taken by the king about whom Samuel had warned (1 Sam 8).

In the narrative which culminates in Abigail becoming one of David's wives (1 Sam 25) Nabal plays a particular role, hinting at social tensions between well-established landowners and נערים who found it increasingly difficult to settle on their own. Nabal's foolishness does not prevent him from ideologically seeing society from his class location, where he represents those who are landlords and try to control resources. When David's men request provisions from Nabal, he airs his view of them as servants who have abandoned their masters, men coming from who knows where, facts previously implied by the narrator in 1 Sam 22:1–2, and exemplified in 1 Sam 23–27, where David's band of run-aways נערים used the wilderness both to take refuge from Saul's men, and to loot the cities of the region.[28] Although a full discussion of these chapters is not in order here, they point to a society already in economic distress, where people leave home because of debts, families move to the fringes of society, and villages in the region are looted, producing further misery and slavery.

As one reflects on how "big" names like Isaac, Moses, and Samson were put in the position of נער due to the lack of protection by a *paterfamilias,* one can very well imagine how much more a nobody like the girl taken captive by the Arameans was vulnerable. The following pages review נערה/ות in their different capacities in DtrH.

---

free or slave, he certainly enjoyed a certain degree of power, as he had his own family and slaves of his own.

[27] Leeb, *Away from the Father's House,* 68–90; Hopwood, "Bandits, elites, and rural order," 171–9.

[28] We have chosen some of these examples because of the connections with this study: Ichabod's birth is the only instance in the whole DtrH in which a woman is portrayed in delivery, with women attending to her (below, chapter 5); Ishmael's and Hagar's dismissal (Gen 21) is at the same time their manumission (above); Moses' delivery is connected to his own mother's hiring as his wet nurse, a story in which a contract is most clearly implied (Exod 2). Finally, Samuel's dedication has been considered as well (see above, chapter 3).

נערה/ות as Servants. Only three examples fall into this category in DtrH. The first one is Abishag, a נערה full of mysterious features, who serves King David in his old age (1 Kgs 1:1–4, see below chapter 6). The second is the נערה קטנה of 2 Kgs 5, and the third example is 1 Sam 25:42, where נערים (male servants or mixed group? probably the former) save an explosive situation by reporting to Abigail her husband's foolish words to David; after her husband's death, five נערות travel accompanying Abigail to David's palace, where they all join his harem (one wife and five workers), after which they vanish again.[29] Signs of the focus of the Dtr are the economy of information about the women and the fact that all, except for the small dependent of 2 Kgs 5 end up in David's court. As to the unnamed שפחה who helped pass on information during Absalom's revolt (2 Sam 17:17), she was already part of David's palace. Although her precise location is not established, it would be easy for her to spy for David if she belonged to the domestic service in the palace. The text does not give any information about her.

Two Types of Women, One Type of Experience. Second Kings 5 is the story of Elisha's healing of Naaman's leprosy. Naaman had learnt about this man of God through a נערה קטנה, an unnamed Israelite girl who had been taken captive in the conflicts between Aram and Israel and was serving at Naaman's household. The girl serves as a tool by conveying information so that the story can continue, and is never mentioned again. Since the story is not interested in her conditions, location, daily tasks or even in her name, all the text tells us is that she had been taken from Israel.

Later in the chapter there is a confrontation between Elisha and Gehazi, after which Gehazi leaves punished by a skin-disease because of his defiance of Elisha's instructions. During that confrontation Elisha asks Gehazi a rhetorical question by which he states that charging goods from Naaman was wrong: "Is this the time to accept money and clothes, olive orchards and vineyards, and sheep and oxen, and male and female slaves (שפחות)"? (2 Kgs 5:26). Lists in the Bible are presented according to their maker's interest. To denote a man's family the list would start with his sons and daughters and then include male and female slaves (women invariably after the corresponding males, thus denoting their lower status: עבדים ושפחות), and finally animals.[30] Since 2 Kgs 5:26 is

---

[29] Leeb, *Away from the Father's House*, 127 notes that their function is that of ensuring the mistress's honor by acting as "chaperones;" once Abigail is under David's protection, they are (literarily) disposed of.

[30] When lists are concerned with possessions, slaves (עבדים ושפחות) are mingled with flocks, camels and donkeys; but when the focus is on family, Dtr starts with offspring, then slaves (עבדים ואמהות) and then animals (Gen 32:6). Both Exod 20:17 and Deut 5:21, when referring to the prohibition against coveting, start their list with house and fields, and then follow the order already

concerned with possessions, the list starts with silver and fields, the most precious ones, and ends with female slaves, the least valued goods. Lists reflect social values, hierarchy, and order and, like genealogies, vary according to needs and social mobility of the society that keeps them; lists where slaves appear follow a basic structure of male first—female second. The conditions in which these particular slaves found themselves cannot be explored, as the rhetorical question does not imply nor expect any particular location further than being possession.

נערות *at the Well.* First Samuel 9 recounts Saul's anointment as king of Israel. In search of their lost mules, Saul and his נער seek directions to "the seer." They meet נערות who direct them to the prophet later identified as Samuel. The text does not say whether these women coming out to fetch water (נערות יצאות לשאב מים) are free women at risk or dependents working at someone else's household.[31] When other narratives of encounters at a well involve a woman, these will become important characters and are all free. This does not mean only important characters fetched water, on the contrary: only the important ones are recorded in the texts.[32] One might suppose that both free and slave women would gather at the well, depending on the household needs and on the mistress's own preferences to go herself or send a servant to the well, if she had a servant. Thus, no decision can be made about the status of the women in 1 Sam 9. One should also take into account that, according to the tale told in Josh 9, the whole population from Gibeon was enslaved by the Israelites, becoming hewers of wood and fetchers of water, both for the congregation and the temple, forever.

נערות *as Free Women at Risk.* This is another category Leeb has shown is present in several biblical texts. In DtrH the Levite's concubine and the women abducted with the purpose of replenishing the tribe of Benjamin (Judg 19–21) are among the strongest examples of women who find themselves unprotected to

---

seen: male and female slaves (עבדים ואמהות), animals.

[31] Few other texts have women at a well: Hagar, a (runaway and later freed) slave in Gen 16 and 21, Jethro's daughters whom Moses meets (Exod 2:16) and Rebekah in her encounter with Abraham's slave (Gen 16:7; 24:29–42), and in the NT, the Samaritan woman who talks to Jesus (John 4). Leeb, *Away from the Father's House*, 135–136 includes Rebekah and the women in 1 Sam 9 among free women at risk. The Samaritan woman in John 4 is also free, otherwise there would be no concern about her marital status.

[32] As Abraham's servant approached the well at Nahor, at "the hour when the women come to draw water" (Gen 24:11), he met Rebekah. The term used there is שאבות, *qal* plural feminine participle of the verb שאב "to draw water," which also appears in Deut 29:10 and Josh 9:21–27 (the wood-cutters and water-drawers conquered by the Israelites and made permanent slaves).

the point of abduction or gang rape and dismemberment. They are very sad stories, but do not add much to our survey.[33]

This concludes the study of the status of the נערה/ות. Leeb's analysis is most valuable in showing their overall characteristic of dependency and vulnerability due to lack of protection of the *paterfamilias* regardless of their legal or socio-economic status. Their dependency and vulnerability by being away from home explains why this term includes women (and the same applies to men, of whom, as seen, there are many examples in the Hebrew Bible) who belonged to several different socio-economic classes, ethnic groups, and legal statuses. Those who were free still were at a high risk of ending up serving at someone else's household (the little one at Naaman's household, 2 Kgs 5:1), being seduced (Dinah) or being abducted (the women mentioned in Judg 21). There seems to be no substantial peculiarity in Dtr's treatment of these women as opposed to texts outside DtrH. Although from these texts we learn very little about particular persons, they are important in providing background material to understand how some free Israelites became bound.

Whatever the reasons for these men and women to have found themselves outside the realm of the *paterfamilias'* protection, the fact remains that in a patriarchal society woman's sexuality belongs to men, and an unprotected woman is in serious trouble, no matter what her legal status is. Today little seems to have changed. The news reports daily on women and children who suffer greatly and often die out of feminicide, violence by male relatives and former partners, sexual harassment, pornography, assault, gang rape, rape as war weapon, and other crimes that show that female bodies are still considered to belong to a male. This is not surprising, since patriarchy is still well and strong.

אמה *and* שפחה *Used Literally: Bound Women*

Previous sub-sections explored an important social category, that of people away from their sources of protection and honor. This sub-section explores texts where the terms for bound women are to be understood literally. In the texts we are dealing with, אמה is only used literally in the laws allowing household slaves the rights to participation in the religious festivals, and the right of the master that his property not be coveted by neighbors (Deut 5:14, 21; 12:12–18;

---

[33] The status of the Levite's secondary wife of Judg 19 is less clear than that of the women abducted later, but seems also to be that of a free person: it took some months for the husband to move to her father's house to convince her to return with him; an unlikely behavior if she was a slave wife (and her father lives in a wealthy house and can afford much banqueting). In texts outside DtrH, unnamed נערות appear as servants in Prov 9:3; 27:27; 31:15; Job 40:29. It is never used by women to speak of themselves.

16:11–14). No other instance of אמה in DtrH seems to be intended to mean literal slaves.

The second term, שפחה, refers to slaves as a possession in general and to servants of particular households. The amount of material from DtrH itself for each of these two groups is so small that it would not justify subsections. שפחה/ות appear in texts in which they are spoken *about* (not *to*) as one would speak of any other object, in matters such as what would be the cost exacted by the monarchic system for the people (children, male and female slaves, vineyards, tithes, 1 Sam 8:11–18), or the consequences of not obeying YHWH in terms of going into slavery (Deut 28:68).[34] Texts do not mention whether these would be Israelites or foreigners.

A CLOSER LOOK AT PERTINENT TEXTS OUTSIDE DTRH

This is as much as can be said about bound labor in DtrH. Study of texts in other bodies within the Hebrew Bible put some more color on the issue, but their general approach to the institution of slavery remains the same. One typical text would be Gen 20, where Abraham mediates in favor of Abimelech's wives and slaves (אמהות), whose wombs had been closed because of Sarah ("every womb of Abimelech's house" 20:17–18).[35] Abimelech's position as king and the various hermeneutical possibilities of terms such as "his house" and "אמהות," make it very difficult to determine whether the writer is thinking of Abimelech's personal family (primary wives and "slaves" in which case his family situation would be similar to Jacob's) or whether "all the wombs of the house of Abimelech" means the whole kingdom, every free household of Gerar, in which case his situation would rather resemble that of the Egyptians at the time of the plagues, when they suffered national catastrophes because of YHWH's chosen ones. In verse 14 another list of possessions, this time gifts from Abimelech to Abraham for the sake of Sarah, includes animals and the already familiar עבדים ושפחות. Note that the term is not the same as used to refer to Abimelech's slaves in his house (אמהות v. 18); the narrator made an intentional choice of terms by using שפחה to mean "slaves" as a generic term implying owned people, and אמהות for Abimelech's household's slave-wives or concubines.

---

[34] Beginning the final section of the book, Deut 28 reinforces the terms of the covenant between YHWH and Israel. Commentaries disagree on the origin of its parts. Most agree on its similarity with Mesopotamian treaty formulas, especially considering the disproportionate amount of text dedicated to curses over blessings. In its present setting, v. 58–68 form another section with a new introduction on v. 58. The terrors of war end up with what Gerhard von Rad, *Deuteronomy: A Commentary* (OTL. Philadelphia: Westminster, 1966), 176 calls "a divine liquidation of the whole history of salvation" with Israel's return to Egypt for no rest.

[35] Of the three parallel stories, only in this one is the host's "punishment" connected with barrenness. Gen 12 has "severe plagues" and Gen 26 does not mention any immediate consequence.

Servants of Important Characters. This sub-section includes, within the DtrH, only one case: the unnamed שפחה in 2 Sam 17:17, who helped pass on information to David's troops during Absalom's revolt. This woman would leave the palace unnoticed and report events to David's men. The most interesting aspect of this woman is that she is given the characteristics of a נערה; she is unnamed and immediately disappears from the story; she trespasses boundaries and is depicted outside rather than in the household. Conversely, *in this text* the שפחה is not said to have been given as dowry, is not used to give the master offspring, and is not a possession in general. She might have been all of these things, but Dtr only uses her ability to trespass the threshold, an ability which is typical of נערים and נערות, as Leeb has shown.[36]

Outside of DtrH other servants of important characters—aside from the נערות—appear in the Genesis narratives. In narratives which focus on surrogate mothers they retain both their status of slave and inclusion into the family. Hagar, Zilpah, and Bilhah are servants to the mistress and slave-wives to the master.[37] The treatment of Hagar by Sarah and Abraham poignantly reflects this double status and it is far more developed in the narratives than the stories of Zilpah and Bilhah.

Hagar. Hagar appears in two different chapters: Gen 16 (attributed to the J tradition) calls her Sarah's שפחה; Gen 21 (E) calls her Abraham's אמה. There have appeared several good studies on Hagar, restoring her to her deserved position of matriarch. The following notes look at what her story tells about slavery.

Hagar's story embodies the ambivalence in the slave between her being a person and her use as a commodity, as well as the ambivalence between her role of slave to Sarah and secondary wife to Abraham (אמה), although her status of secondary wife (or slave-wife) was not enough to ensure his generosity toward the mother of his child, even if by law he was not bound to give her anything.[38]

J. Waters struggles with some of the very questions that motivated our study, namely, why is there no feminine noun from the verb עבד "serve" to talk about women? Why two nouns and what is the difference between them? In his book, he looks at Hagar's story from an African American perspective, using

---

[36] Leeb, *Away from the Father's House*, 126–128.

[37] When Rebekah travels to marry Isaac her wet nurse (מינקת), Deborah, travels with her. There seem to have been many situations like this, when the services of a slave changed in kind.

[38] "The dual status of the slave given as a wife is well expressed by the Old Babylonian contractual formula: 'A is a slave to B (first wife); a wife to C (husband).'" Westbrook, *Property*, 153–4, and 154 n.1: "CT 4 39a.9–11; CT 8 22b.5–6; CT 48.6–8. In none of these contracts, however, does the slave appear to have been acquired by way of dowry."

three main arguments: 1) the political power of Egypt over Palestine at the time Abraham and his family are thought to have lived (2000–1720 B.C.E.) argues for the improbability that Egypt would have given its own citizens as slaves to foreigners; 2) the constant mixing on the part of Western Euro-American theologians of J and E sources. If Gen 16 and 21 are studied on their own, he argues, Hagar's depiction varies, being Abraham's wife in one tradition, and an Egyptian slave in the other; and 3) that Hagar is the first real matriarch, being the only woman who receives a promise similar to that received by Abraham.[39] Waters's challenge to Western Euro-American theology is welcome and to be celebrated. Especially his third point is well taken and it has been recognized particularly by women embracing gender and class studies.[40] On the point that affects our research more directly, however, I do not understand his view that an Empire would not have also produced slaves. He states,

> The Abrahamic period in Israel is usually designated as lasting from 2000 to 1720 B.C.E. This is the time of Egypt's Middle Kingdom, during which period the areas of Damascus (Syria) and Canaan remained under the domination of Egypt. This is also the time of the twelfth dynasty in Egypt. Since Egypt was in a strong military position at that time, it certainly would not have allowed its citizens to be held as slaves by those who were under its domination. As a

---

[39] John Waters, "Who Was Hagar?" in *Stony the Road We Trod: African American Biblical Interpretation* (ed. C. H. Felder. Minneapolis: Fortress, 1991), 198–199. Waters, 189 argues for an original tradition in which Hagar was a free Egyptian, wife of Abraham; tradition which suffered a later Israelite re-shaping which made a slave of her. Although not all his arguments are convincing to me, his effort to call attention to elements which point at Hagar's depiction as a free woman (arrangement for an Egyptian wife for her son, her independence, her condition of being the only real "matriarch," and the flavor of the story, as he calls it) should be taken into consideration in order to see the tension between these two traditions, the fluidity of a woman's status, and how scholarship is slowly being recognized as biased.

[40] Here is just a sampler of scholars from different social locations: Elsa Tamez, "The Woman Who Complicated the History of Salvation," in *New Eyes for Reading* (ed. J. Pobee & B. von Wartenberg-Potter. Geneva: WCC, 1986), 5–17; Maricel Mena López, "Raíces Afro-Asiáticas en el mundo bíblico. Desafíos para la exégesis y hermenéutica latinoamericana," *RIBLA* 54 (2006)17–34. Cited 4 September 2012. Online: http://www.ribla.org/; Milton Schwantes, "Hagar and Sarah," in *Faith Born in the Struggle for Life: A Re-reading of Protestant Faith in Latin America Today* (ed. D. Kirkpatrick. Grand Rapids: Eerdmans, 1988), 76–83; Trible, *Texts of Terror*, 9–35; Renita Weems, "Do You See What I See? Diversity in Interpretation," *Church and Society* 82 (1991): 28–43; Mary Callaway, *Sing, O Barren One: A Study in Comparative Midrash* (SBLDS 91. Atlanta: Scholars Press, 1986), 18–23; Savina Teubal, *Hagar the Egyptian: The Lost Tradition of the Matriarchs* (San Francisco: Harper & Row, 1990), 235–50; Jo Ann Hackett, "Rehabilitating Hagar: Fragments of an Epic Pattern," in *Gender and Difference in Ancient Israel* (ed. P. Day. Minneapolis: Fortress, 1989), 12–27.

matter of fact, most of the slaves in Egypt during the Middle Kingdom were Asiatic.[41]

The historical setting concerning Egypt has no weight on the question of the enslavement or not of an Egyptian citizen. If we stay within the narrative, Abra(ha)m is no "nobody" and is given abundant gifts—including slaves—from the Pharaoh's treasures for the sake of Sara(i). If one follows that line, one could argue that Hagar was a princess given by Pharaoh but Abraham and Sarah oppressed her disregarding her high origins; a fact not only possible, but mirrored by Joseph's treatment in Egypt during his first years.

Be it as it may, that does not help much in considering the biblical slaves. It seems to me that an empire's economic or political power does not automatically translate into making all of its members rich and independent. Lenski argues for a social model in which several factors determine a person's social standing, so that there are larger areas but there are also overlapping sections between them. Social categories are porous, not bunker-like compartments. That means that someone might be more highly regarded, even though belonging to a theoretically lower category, than someone else in an upper social ladder, namely a young, female Egyptian. Intersections of race, class, gender, age, and other factors sometimes operate in mysterious ways, depending on power, authority, privilege, and gender. What really matters to me is not who Hagar "really was" but how Waters can, from his own experience as an African American scholar, contribute his voice.

Focusing on Hagar as both אמה and שפחה, the following aspects should be highlighted. First, her social location is extremely complex; she is a foreigner, a slave, a surrogate mother, mother of a prospective heir to the patriarch, a run-away slave who returns, a freedwoman, and the only woman to receive from YHWH a promise similar to that of Abraham. Second, it is fundamental to look at the story with an informed perspective as to what slavery was. For instance, much as we can sympathize with her today, and be indignant about how YHWH makes her come back to her mistress Sarah (16:9), a runaway slave was unprotected and she would have been returned to her master and punished, even if pregnant.[42] Perhaps Sarah's harshness at her actually was

---

[41] Waters, "Who Was Hagar?" 189.

[42] Mendelsohn, *Slavery in the ANE*, 59: "Outside the master's house, the slave was as defenseless as a stray animal." See 58–64 on penalization for harboring a fugitive in several societies and also *Legal Aspects of Slavery in Babylonia, Assyria and Palestine: A Comparative Study (3000–500 B. C.)* (Williamsport: Bayard, 1932), 37–42. Frymer-Kensky, "Family," 61–62 argues that in Genesis YHWH intervenes to moderate the *paterfamilias'* authority (in Judges there is no such divine intervention any more). In this case, YHWH seems to be also moderating the bitter struggle between women for a future, as their security lies on the *paterfamilias'* choice of an heir.

Sarah's plan to make her run away, so that, when returned to her, she could lower Hagar's status back to what Sarah believed Hagar was, that is, her slave, and a foreigner at that. If this is true, then YHWH's intervention, although painful and humiliating for Hagar at the moment, intended to protect her and to lead to her eventual freedom. Many commentaries see YHWH's command to return to her mistress as oppressive. It is oppressive, but not because of the command to return, but because the text does not question slavery, seeking only better conditions within slavery. However, Hagar's dismissal in Gen 21 should be read as her manumission. Slaves could not just go away; they were either kept and passed as inheritance, sold (including their ransom sale if that was possible), or manumitted by their owners.

The stories of Bilhah and Zilpah appear to be less dramatic, but this is largely due to the fact that Hagar is a rounded character, she speaks, she conceives, she looks at Sarah with contempt, she flees, she returns, she names YHWH, she gets a promise as only Abraham gets. Bilhah and Zilpah are "everyday characters," with no glamour, but with burdens and discrimination. With regard to their historical reality, one should remember that almost anything that can be said about any of them has to be carefully weighed, because there are many aspects of the patriarchal narratives—including slave conditions, legal procedures and more generally possible date and place of origin of the narratives—which are open to discussion.

Another source of speculation is the story of Moses' delivery from the waters, where the focus is right at the center of power. Engelken sees a hierarchy of women surrounding Pharaoh's daughter: first the עלמות whom Engelken understands as courtesans of higher rank in the palace (*Hofdamen* or *Palastfrauen*), who served as companions to important women, played music, and in general were part of court life. Then there are נערות who attend to her, and finally the אמהות, belonging to the service personnel, of a lower rank; or at least one אמה, the one to get into the water and catch the basket Exod 2:5.[43] Engelken has a point in that Moses' sister, an עלמה, would not have had such a direct access to Pharaoh's daughter had she not belonged to her entourage, but her location is still far from clear.

In summary, the perception of the slave as possession in texts outside the DtrH does not differ drastically from our understanding of Dtr's depiction of women. The book of Genesis's concern with the matriarchs' barrenness shows

---

[43] Engelken, *Frauen im Alten Israel*, 44–46. Nevertheless, many questions remain unanswered, such as the fact that no עלמה appears walking together with Pharaoh's daughter, that there is no עלם with a high rank in the OT to support Engelken's claim (Engelken acknowledges this lack of evidence). A more serious fact against Engelken's argument is the absence of the עלמה from 1 Sam 8:11–18, where they would make a strong parallel to "your sons," who are made captains of hundreds and fifties, if they belonged to the upper echelons in court. Nevertheless, as scholars struggling with social categories in ancient sources know, there is still much that we cannot prove.

up in their slaves being brought in to fill in the blank, even in Abimelech's kingdom (Gen 20). Stories set in a foreign court (Exod 1, Esther) focus on the important character they accompany rather than on the נערות or אמהות themselves. No data are provided about their everyday situation, ethnicity, names, or any other element that could locate them socially, a fact that, again, speaks more of the redactors' concerns and interests than the women.

This concludes the study of texts in which—in our view—the terms for "a female servant or slave," אמה, שפחה, and נערה, are intended to be read literally.

Biblical Legal Material

This section will study some of the laws in the Hebrew Bible concerning slaves.[44] Laws tend to be taken as if always applied, while a careful cross-examination of the biblical testimony itself raises questions on their application. Further complications come from the fact that often what is preserved is a general statement, while we miss the details of its application. Thus one cannot be sure whether keeping the Sabbath, for instance, was meant as a legally-enforceable law. It is true Israel was both a religious and a legal community; so the question is even more pertinent: Was a certain statement with an apodictic or casuistic formulation enforced as binding to the community or was it a theological statement?

Study of the concrete and the philosophical implications of law are a field in and of itself, of which at this point it is possible to grasp only some basics. Israel must have applied more laws or precedents than the ones written down in the Hebrew Bible while others must have been inapplicable as laws (not to covet the neighbor's wife or goods: how to prove that in court?).[45] Thus, laws can be taken as a thermometer of what society deemed as valuable and desirable, and dangerous and undesirable. As Carolyn Pressler states, one can focus "on assumptions and ideals about women expressed by the laws, not on legal practice."[46] A review will help see how society valued its least protected members.

---

[44] This section is included in this chapter and not in the next one because much of the legal material concerning slaves in general is located mainly outside DtrH.

[45] Furthermore, their temporal and spatial location (where and when they were written down and perhaps put in practice) is unclear; debate about mutual dependence of the different codes (and the related question of the date of the Covenant Code, the Ten Words, the Dtr Code, and the Holiness Code) is still heated. See, for instance, the first remarks by Mark Leuchter, "The Manumission Laws in Leviticus and Deuteronomy: The Jeremiah Connection," *JBL* 127 (2008): 635–6, who considers they are "in relative temporal proximity to each other."

[46] Pressler, "Wives and Daughters," 148.

Basic socio-economic and religious rights of masters and slaves are mentioned in:[47]

Masters' and slaves' rights	Exod 20:17, Deut 5:21 (coveting)
	Exod 21:20–21, 26–27, 32 (assault)
	Lev 25:6 (food on Sabbatical year)
	Deut 23:16–17 (run-away slaves)
Religious rights and obligations	Exod 20:8–11, Deut 5:14–21 (Sabbath)
	Deut 16:9–12 (Weeks)
	Deut 16:13–15 (Booths)
	Deut 12:12–19 (Offerings)
Manumission (debt-slaves)	Exod 21:2–6 (all, on 7th year)
	Deuteronomy 15 (all, on 7th year)
	Lev 25:39–42, 47–55 (on Jubilee year)
Non-manumission (foreign slaves)	Lev 25:44–46 (foreigners)
Slave wives	Exod 21:7–11 (rights)
	Deut 21:10–14 (war captive)
	Lev 19:20–22 (sexual relation)

Legal codes in the Bible leave uncovered other areas, such as what legally defines a slave, which of these laws applied to indentured servants, which ones to chattel-slaves and which ones to both.[48] Only some of the most pertinent laws will be discussed here.

Assault of Slaves. This issue receives special attention in the Hebrew Bible. It appears in Exod 21:26–27, often interpreted as sending free a slave who has lost

---

[47] See Chirichigno, *Debt-Slavery*, 147, who organizes the laws into ten groups, to wit: manumission (male slaves), marriage and manumission (female slaves), sex outside marriage, coveting, assault, Sabbath, sabbatical year, offerings, feasts, and miscellaneous laws.

[48] According to the *Oxford Dictionary Online* ([cited 7 July 2011]. Online: http://oxforddictionaries .com/view/entry/m_en_us1241057#m_en_us1241057.005), "be indentured to" is "bind (someone) by an indenture as an apprentice or laborer"; while "indenture" refers to the formal contract or agreement by which a person is bound to service. And "distrain" is "seize (someone's property) to obtain payment of rent or other money owed." I am not sure whether all scholars use both with this sense or even to what degree they are taken as synonyms. In the case of debt slavery, the "indentured" would be the one bound, perhaps the *paterfamilias*, while he could put his wife or children to work at the distrainer as distrainees to pay for the family's debts. In other cases it could be the same person who was indentured and distrainee. On Greek parallels see Westermann, *The Slave Systems of Greek and Roman Antiquity* (Philadelphia: American Philosophical Society, 1955), 137.

an eye or a tooth because of assault by the master (or mistress). Interpretation of this law is disputed, partly due to the fact that both foreign slaves and indentured Israelites are called by the same Hebrew term. A society that owns slaves has to provide the system with the means to keep the masters in control. The law in Exod 21:26–27 can be interpreted in two different ways. One is to understand it as a limitation of the power of the master in punishing his male or female slave. Another one, which we find more convincing, understands this law to apply only to indentured servants. If one compares Exod 21:26–27, which sets a slave free if his or her eye or tooth is knocked out by the master, with 21:20–21, which only punishes the master if the intention of killing the slave can be presumed by the death of the slave at the master's hands, there appears to be an imbalance that is difficult to explain if both laws applied to the same type of slave.

According to Westbrook, the law in v. 26–27 applies to a "distrainee" working at the "distrainor's" until the debt is paid. S/he suffers a loss of an eye or a tooth at the hands of the creditor. The two parties' families reach an agreement: s/he goes free with no right to further claim against the creditor for the loss to the face, and the debt is cancelled, with no further claim against the debtor, for the damage done on the distrainee. However, there are further consequences if the debt-slave dies out of the punishment:

The death has occurred of a debt-slave while in the service of his creditor.
There are several possibilities.
1. He dies of natural causes. In that case there is no liability on the creditor/master, who may still claim his debt. This is dealt with in CH 115, but not in the biblical law.
2. He died as a direct result of mistreatment. This is dealt with by both codes. The debt-slave's father/master/relative is entitled to vicarious revenge or ransom, the latter not being stated expressly, but fixed by CH 116 in the case of a debtor's slave. CH adds forfeiture of the debt, which is not mentioned in the much more terse biblical formulation.
3. He died apparently of natural causes, but there is evidence linking it to a previous beating. This is a difficult case, dealt with expressly by the biblical law alone, but hinted at in CH 116, where the debtor's right to revenge is stated to depend on his ability to prove the causal connection ("the master of the distrainee shall prove it against his creditor"). In this intermediate situation where the evidence is ambiguous, the biblical law effects a reasonable compromise, precluding revenge but providing a penalty equivalent to a fixed ransom by way of cancellation of the debt.[49]

---

[49] Raymond Westbrook, *Studies in Biblical and Cuneiform Law* (CRB, 1988), 100. See also E. Otto, "Aspects of Legal Reforms and Reformulations in Ancient Cuneiform and Israelite Law," in *Theory and Method in Biblical and Cuneiform Law* (ed. B. Levinson. JSOTSup 181. Sheffield: Sheffield

One has to notice that the law contemplates certain rights for the Israelite in debt-bondage, and it explicitly does so for the man and the woman on equal terms. Notable is also the fact that these situations foresee, if Westbrook is right in his interpretation, that the slave has someone (a father, master or relative) who is able to exercise the right of revenge or ransom. In case slaves were foreigners and they were far from home, this would have been very hard to accomplish.[50]

What would have been the implications were the distrainee an unmarried daughter? If the text considers the possibility of losing an eye because of punishment, and even dying in the hands of the distrainor, her sexual usufruct by the master or another person for the master's profit can be assumed even if not attested in the laws. If and when that daughter was freed because of her lost eye, what opportunities awaited her, being poor, lacking an eye, and very likely, also her virginity? Would such a woman have any other possibility than secondary marriage (or staying unmarried at home?) or some type of dependent situation from then on? Regrettably, the laws do not respond to these questions, and we are left to imagine how society would act.

Three Test-Cases on Women

Three biblical laws deal with special situations concerning bound women; special situations because "the various laws that treat of extramarital sex evidence a strong feeling in Israel that sexual intercourse should properly be confined to marriage, of which it was the essence (Gen. 2:24) and the principal sign. Thus the victim of rape, the slave girl, or the female captive taken for sexual pleasure, must become, or must be treated as, a wife (Exod. 21:7–11; Deut. 21:10–14)."[51] To these two texts mentioned by Bird, may we add Lev 19:20–22, concerning the compensation to a male whom a slave had been assigned but became pregnant from another one before the owner took possession of her. Laws concerning sexual offenses in Deut 22:13–29 do not pertain, because they apply to free women, not to (en)slave(d).[52]

Exodus 21:7–11.[53] This law starts with a reference to the immediately preceding

---

Academic Press, 1994), 181–85.

[50] With Leuchter, "Manumission Laws," 637–38 and others, I take the six/seven years of Deut 15:1–18 as the length for debt-slavery in Israel.

[51] Bird, "Images of Women in the Old Testament," 24–25.

[52] See Pressler, *View of Women*, 21–43.

[53] Here it is understood that Exod 21:2–6, like Deut 15:12–18 and Lev 25 apply both to male and female debt-slaves, provided the female was not bought for concubinage, as in Exod 21:7–11. For further discussion on these laws see MacDonald, *Position of Women*, 50–65 on Biblical law codes; Pressler, "Wives and Daughters," 147–72; Joe M. Sprinkle, *"The Book of the Covenant": A Literary*

law in 21:2–6, in which conditions for release of indentured male slaves after six years of service are set. Verse 7 states that the procedure for male indentured servants at the term of their service will not apply to the אמה. She does not leave unless her owner is unable to meet particular conditions.[54] Since they present some difficulties, several explanations have been offered on the meaning of these verses. The major difficulty lies in the meaning of אמה both for regular female slave and for "(slave)-wife" or "concubine." Because of this ambiguity, some scholars think that v. 7–11 applied only to certain females, taken as slave-wives, while the general law (v. 1–6) applied to, at least, certain women unattached to a male.[55]

A second difficulty is that the law has "packed" three different situations into a few verses. It is not easy to disentangle them. And, to add to the difficulty, one of the three rights the אמה is to keep (v. 10) is a *hapax legomenon*.

That the law understands the woman as unfree may be gathered from its attachment to the previous law in v. 2–6) and by her description and restraint in v. 7. Scholars split in two main groups: those who believe she is a wife and the law "pertains to the sale of a young girl by her father to a purchaser who must ensure her with a marital status"[56] and those who believe she is a slave bought to become a concubine. We review briefly most arguments in favor of each position.

Approach (JSOTSup 174; Sheffield: JSOT Press, 1994); David Daube, *Biblical Law* (Cambridge: Cambridge University Press, 1947), 47–53; Nahum Sarna, "Zedekiah's Emancipation of Slaves and the Sabbatical Year," in *Orient and Occident: Essays Presented to Cyrus H. Gordon on the Occasion of His Sixty-fifth Birthday* (ed. H. Hoffner, Jr. *AOAT* 22; Butzin & Bercker: Kevelaer/Neukirchener Verlag: Neukirchen-Vluyn, 1973), 145–6 for a list of similar elements in Jer 34 and Deuteronomy; Yairah Amit, "The Jubilee Law—An Attempt at Instituting Social Justice," in *Justice and Righteousness* (ed. H. Reventlow and Y. Hoffman. JSOTSup 137. Sheffield: Sheffield Academic Press, 1992), 55; Westbrook, *Property*, 51–7.

[54] Thus Pressler, "Wives and Daughters," 160; Shalom M. Paul, *Studies in the Book of the Covenant in the Light of Near Eastern Law* (VTSup 18. Leiden: Brill, 1970), 56–61. Slightly different, Sprinkle, 53–54 comments: "I take שארה, normally translated 'flesh', as not just 'food'—any slave would be fed—but butcher meat (cf. Ps. 78.20, 27; Mic. 3.3 for this sense of שאר, which for the ancient diet was a delicacy, a 'choice food'. If שאר is metonymy for 'choice food', it followed that כסות ('covering') should imply more than mere clothes (which would be provided any slave), but rather 'fineries,' clothes as befits a master's wife. The third item, the *hapax legomenon* ענתה, is uncertain in meaning, but 'cosmetics,' is an attractive guess." Sprinkle's proposal presupposes the אמה as a concubine of a higher rank than a slave who would be provided clothes, food, and oil.

[55] Pressler, "Wives and Daughters," 167, posits the case of widows, divorced women, and other unprotected women, who would not be the wives mentioned in v. 3 and even less in v. 7. She makes a strong case based on the fact that all legislations include both male and female bound people on equal terms.

[56] Paul, *Studies*, 53.

All in favor of a wife? Isaac Mendelsohn used a particular type of contract from Nuzi, known as the "Daughter and daughter-in-law-contract" to understand what this law is about. The Nuzi contracts contain several possible conditions of the particular sale, e.g., "(a) to be married to her master, (b) to be married to her master's son, (c) to be sold as a wife to a free-born man outside of the family, (d) not to be given as a wife to a slave, and (e) to be given as a wife to the owner's slave."[57]

In the light of the Nuzi contracts, the biblical law appears to say that if upon her puberty the owner does not want her for himself, he can: a) only sell the girl back to her family (which is unlikely to happen, since they had sold her, probably out of financial need); b) he can give her to his son and then (depending on the interpretation) "he shall deal with her as is the practice with free maidens"[58] (or give her the status of a daughter until the son takes her); or c) he can take on another wife, in which case the rejected wife still holds rights (whether she stays as a concubine or not and whether her rights include sex or not, depend on that *hapax*!). Only when none of these applies she goes free.

Shalom Paul also interprets the law as relating to a girl sold as a wife; the law prevents her husband from easily getting rid of her. Since she is a wife, she remains in the family or returns home. Paul amply demonstrates that the *hapax* ענה (ענתה) means "oil or ointment."[59]

Also Elizabeth MacDonald, in one of the earliest works on women and legal codes, locates this אמה as a second of three types; she comes very close to seeing it as a marriage, noting her possible right to divorce:

> The second type of ʾama appears in Ex. 21. She was sold by her father (vs. 7) doubtless for his debt, and became the property of the one who bought her ... He could take her as a wife, but if she was "evil" in his eyes he could not sell her to foreigners but had to let her be redeemed .... Hers is the only case in the codes where the woman had even a pretence to the right of divorce. It was recognized that she had definite conjugal rights and if, when another woman was taken, these were denied her she could leave her master and he then forfeited what he had given for her (vv. 10–11). The later law of Deut. 15:12 ff. reads as though it applied to this particular type of ʾama, but in the earlier period this woman, under ordinary circumstances, was evidently kept for life (vs. 7, contr. CH §117)[60]

---

[57] Mendelsohn, "Conditional Sale into Slavery," 191–92.
[58] Paul, *Studies*, 55, shows this is the meaning of this technical term.
[59] Paul, *Studies*, 56; see examples of this formula on 57–59. Following him, B. Childs, *The Book of Exodus*, 469 takes the three stipulations as "critical examples ... which might threaten her status." Although he considers Paul's arguments for translating the *hapax* as oil "impressive," he prefers the "traditional conjecture" as conjugal rights.
[60] MacDonald, *Position of Women*, 61–2.

Gregory Chirichigno is very reluctant to consider this woman a slave. He rather sees her as a woman getting into marriage: "[T]his law should not be compared with these institutions [chattel slavery], but rather this law should be understood as an attempt to guarantee to a girl who is sold as a wife those rights that were normally afforded to daughters who were married in the customary manner."[61]

All in favor of a slave? As Raymond Westbrook and others have pointed out, a close comparison between Exod 21:7–11 and the Nuzi contracts as Mendelsohn proposes is problematic, the main reason being that the Nuzi contracts are adoption contracts in which the biological parents of the adopted girl ensure her future right not to be obliged to get into prostitution. Thus, comparison with those sources is misleading. Taking the position that nothing in the biblical terminology suggests marriage, Westbrook considers her to have been sold because of debts with the sole purpose of becoming a concubine, i.e., to be used for sexual and reproductive purposes (which is why she does not go free on the seventh year). If the master decides to give her to his son, she must be treated as a daughter, which would mean, not to be given in the meantime to other males: "The law insists that her master must in the interim give her the standing of a daughter within the household, not a servant, because the purpose of the contract is that she provide sexual and reproductive services, not labour."[62] Here careful analysis is needed, for it would be very easy to misread Westbrook: Is he reading her position as a concubine as giving her the right not to work? In my opinion, this is a matter of emphasis. Since Westbrook's is on the reproductive aspect of this type of אמה, he puts a bit too much emphasis on the contrast:

> The right of redemption revives only if the purchaser fails to abide by the special purpose of the contract—if he fails either to consummate the assignment himself (*qere*) or to assign her for the concubinage altogether (*ketib*). In either case, the purchaser has treated the contract as one of ordinary servitude, not concubinage, and has denied the slave-woman the possibility of gaining the protection available to a concubine through motherhood.[63]

For, why should the master keep a woman only for that purpose and not make her work at the same time (at least between pregnancies), and since, as Westbrook himself claims (and I agree), the concubine's children would have no rights of inheritance and would be slaves? It is hard to imagine, if we are speaking of concubinage within slavery and not of marriage. He himself sees it

---

[61] Chirichigno, *Debt-Slavery*, 251. See also his review of scholarship, especially notes on 186–92.

[62] Westbrook, "Female Slave," 219; see also 222.

[63] Westbrook, "Female Slave," 219.

in these terms when, referring to v. 11, he rightly points out that "rations are the stuff of servants and dependents, not wives."[64]

In short, one can agree that a woman would be acquired with the purpose of producing children and that her family could have claims against the master if he failed to give her the opportunity. I could also imagine that a concubine would have the right not to do physically hard labor while pregnant or the right not to be obliged to prostitute herself, but I have my doubts that concubines would not have to work—everybody worked!

Somewhere between those extremes, Carolyn Pressler takes a cautious approach to the Nuzi materials, assessing their value not in their immediate application to the biblical text, but "in that they suggest the range of purposes for which daughters might be sold and the range of contractual provisions and protections that might be imposed," a suggestion that Westbrook would probably accept as well.[65]

Pressler also rightly noted that the text uses אדון rather than בעל, אמה rather than אשה, and מכר rather than נתן, all signs of a purchase/sale transaction, and not of a marriage. She further states that elsewhere אמה is first of all a bondswoman, whose conditions depended on the particular type of contract.

> "Elsewhere in the Book of the Covenant, ʾamâ is used in the general sense of 'bondswoman' (Exod. 21.20–21, 26–27, 32; 23.12). In fact, with one exception (Lev. 19.20), ʾamâ is used for 'bondswoman' in all Pentatuechal [sic] laws; in none of the other laws does the term refer to a slave wife. It seems likely that ʾamâ, used in the context of law, is a general term meaning 'bondswoman.'"[66]

What is clear is that this אמה is a girl sold by her parents under certain conditions, who thus enjoyed the advantages of a rather secure marital life in whatever legal capacity, and was spared worse conditions (being sold to third parties and, probably, prostitution or multiple breeding). Prevention of her exploitation as a prostitute seems to have been the main reason on the parents' side for this type of contract in Nuzi and probably in Exod 21, while her work and procreation were in the interest of her owner and thus, could not be legally prevented.[67]

---

[64] Westbrook, "Female Slave," 236–37.

[65] Pressler, "Wives and Daughters," 154, notes that the main asset of a girl was her sexuality and reproductive capacity, and therefore conditions varied according to circumstances, but she could not go free because then the purpose of her sale (sexuality) would be defeated, at least for her owner.

[66] Pressler, "Wives and Daughters," 163.

[67] Mendelsohn, "Conditional Sale," 192.

Leviticus 19:20–22. This law deals with the not altogether uncommon situation of sexual use of a female slave by someone else than the one(s) allowed. The text is unusual in several ways, which affect its translation.

> If a man lies down with a woman (a lying of seed), and she is a slave previously (designated) for a man (והוא שפחה נחרפת לאיש) and she has not been ransomed or given her freedom, there shall be an indemnity (בקרת); they will not be put to death for she had not been freed.

There are several particularities here. One rarity is the addition to שכב of שכבת־זרע which, according to Baruch Levine, is "the literal Hebrew formula for impregnation."[68] Considering that slavery is an economic institution, one has to ask about the reason for that addition to שכב, and what are its legal implications, since a slave's offspring belonged to her master. However, nothing is said about the offspring, either because that was not the concern in this law or because it was clear enough to the legislators.

A second peculiarity is the *hapax legomenon* בקרת, here translated "indemnity" or "compensation" on the basis of Akkadian *baqrum / pirqum*.[69] Other scholars opt for "inquiry" (*NRSV*). What would be the reason for an inquiry: to determine whether her child be claimed by someone else, for instance, the father's owner (if he was a slave)? To find out whether she consented? Hardly. The law is concerned with compensation to her owner and to the one she had been promised (or sold) to, not with the woman's rights or, even less, her feelings.

The expression שפחה נחרפת, in which the *nip'al* participle works as adjective to שפחה, is also uncommon and difficult. I have followed Levine's proposal to understand it as "previously or already" from Akkadian "to be early." Since it is acting as adjective to שפחה and the expression לאיש interferes between her and her freedom, "in advance" does not refer to the fact that it happened prior to her freedom ("has not been ransomed nor given her freedom") but it refers to "to a(nother) man." Levine translates in a similar manner, but he understands it otherwise: "On this basis, *neḥrefet* would mean 'assigned in advance,' that is, in advance of redemption or manumission." He relates this law with the one on female debt-slaves (Exod 21:7–11). According to to him, when masters found a legal truce so that they did not comply with either

---

[68] Baruch Levine, *Leviticus* (JPS Torah Commentary; Philadelphia: JPS, 5749/1989), 130 however, translates it as "have carnal relations" both in 18:20 and 19:20.

[69] With Levine, *Leviticus* 130 and G. Wenham, *The Book of Leviticus* (NICOT; Grand Rapids: Eerdmans, [1979] rep. 1992), 270 n.20 who notes that the same word appears in CH §279 as compensation for a claim against a slave. Gerstenberger, *Leviticus: A Commentary* (OTL; Louisville: Westminster John Knox, 1996), 260, also translates as compensation but does not support his translation. Cf. M. Noth, *Leviticus* (London: SCM, 1965), 137,who chooses "inquiry".

of the three requirements set up in v. 8. Although in theory she should not have been sold out of the family, he asserts Exod 21:8

> does not prohibit such arrangements as would involve another Israelite man. The latter would redeem the girl by a payment to her master and take her as his wife.
>
> The situation projected in our passage is as follows: An Israelite slave girl … was pledged by her master to another Israelite man. The designation had already been made, but had not been finalized by payment to the girl's master or, possibly, the man had not yet claimed his bride. …
>
> In parallel circumstances, Exodus 22:15–17 stipulates that one who seduced a free maiden who was not yet pledged as a wife had either to marry her himself or pay her father …In our case, the option of marriage was ruled out because the girl had been pledged to another man. The man who had had carnal relations with the girl had to pay an indemnity to her master to compensate him for his loss.[70]

Levine's interpretation is ingenious and has the advantage of weaving together several different laws on the same subject—or should we say object. But are they really on the same object? I am not sure; I would not reject his explanation, while at the same time calling attention to the fact that this slave is a שפחה and not an אמה (as in Exod 21:7–11).[71] Neither would she be a "Hebrew slave" if Leviticus is coherent with its own theology in chapter 25 which, on the other hand, enumerates slaves using עבד and אמה, not שפחה.[72]

As already discussed, there is as yet no consensus on the meanings of אמה and שפחה and especially on the difference/s between them; the אמה seems to have been slightly better off. With regard to this point, all references to manumission (included the adjective "freed" חפשי) are for the אמה, except for an extraordinary event. Jeremiah 34:9 is about a covenant to let free their Hebrew slaves: לשלח איש את־עבדו ואיש את־שפחתו העברי והעבריה חפשים. Perhaps the fact that it is a proclamation of liberty (דרור, v. 8) would explain that the ones who would not ordinarily be freed, are freed. Perhaps the שפחה

---

[70] Levine, 131. He and several scholars follow E. A. Speiser, "Leviticus and the Critics," appeared in *Yehezkel Kaufman Jubilee Volume* (ed. M. Haran. Jerusalem: Magnes, 1960]), 34–36, and in *Oriental and Biblical Studies* (Philadelphia: University of Pennsylvania, 1967), 128–31, taking נחרפת from an Akkadian cognate, *ḫarāpu* "to be early, arrive in advance," from which he translates "in advance;" (pages 130 and 208 n.24, quoting *CAD*, s.v. *ḫarāpu* A).

[71] Pressler, "Wives and Daughters," 158–9, notes this is the only Pentateuch law in which אמה is not used for the female slave.

[72] On the manumission laws in Lev 25 and their relationship to the Deuteronomic laws and to Jer 34, see Leuchter, "Manumission Laws"; Bernard M. Levinson, "The Birth of The Lemma: The Restrictive Reinterpretation of the Covenant Code's Manumission Law by the Holiness Code (Lev 25:44–46)," *JBL* 124 (2005), 617–39.

belonged to a class of slaves who would ordinarily not be manumitted. Perhaps, we do not know.

Coming back to Lev 19:20–22, the law has in common with other laws the fact that it addresses conflicting interests of free males and, like many of them (such as the law on the pregnant woman who is accidentally hit and miscarries, Exod 21:22–24 or the unbetrothed free girl whose virginity is taken, 22:15–17, referred to by Levine) the beneficiary is not the woman directly affected in her body, but a male's honor or business. It also resembles adultery in that the woman's sexuality had been previously designated to another male, but adultery legislation does not apply: "they shall not be killed." At the same time, the law has in common with other laws affecting slaves the fact that the offender is not held guilty further than for a guilt offering at the sanctuary and a monetary compensation. In any case, whatever the relationship of this law to the other ones on female slaves, on female sex and on bodily assaults or consent (nowhere it is said whether she consented or not), it is clear that the only "benefit" for the girl is that she is not punished because it is presumed that she did not have a choice in the use of her sexuality; or said otherwise that her body, including her consent to its use, does not belong to her. As Westbrook remarks, "ownership implied the exclusive right to exploit the sexuality of a female slave. Accordingly, the law protected her owner against unauthorized use of her by a third party."[73] This would be a situation common enough for women to merit a law; a situation male slaves did not suffer, at least apparently. Of course, one cannot rule out homosexual rape against slaves. Perhaps it was a very unusual situation; perhaps it was so tabooed that it did not make into the laws—or both.

Then and now, it is so sad that assault to underprivileged men and women of all ages, to the most vulnerable members of society—particularly children, teenagers and elderly—be executed on one of their most treasured but also most vulnerable assets, their sexuality. Then and now, there is also the danger that the system would let the culprit get away very easily.

Deuteronomy 21:10–14. This law appears to address my last concern by ensuring certain rights to a young woman taken as booty among the prisoners of war—a time to mourn and in the end, either marriage forever to her captor or emancipation. One should see it in the light of a prisoner's fate, where violent death, death by starvation, thirst or sickness, forced labor, compulsory exile, and rape happened often. In this light, Deuteronomy tried to cut short suffering and humiliation of those defeated and set some rules for those receiving new wives

---

[73] Westbrook, "Female Slave," 223. Gerstenberger, *Leviticus*, 274 n.38 calls attention to similar attempts in today's society to exonerate the perpetrator as easily as possible, turning down the rights and interests of the least privileged in society.

at home. This law does not say so much about women as about men who would have conquered others and their social setting at home: What is appropriate sexual and family behavior for an Israelite when he conquers another nation?[74] One can also perceive behind the law the hope that their own women, if survivors of military defeat, would be spared as much humiliation and sexual assault as possible.

One cannot but wonder what it would have felt like to be married to one's enemy, having lost her whole family, house, friends, and community. The fact that she is "a beautiful woman" whom the soldier would want to marry, and that she mourns her father and mother, probably indicates a very young girl, still living at home. What would "being taken as wife" mean in concrete terms? The law looks at her as a survivor of an enemy, defeated in war and noticed because of her beauty from among other captives. I take it that she would remain a captive bride or, at least, a defeated foreigner, no matter her marital status. As Pressler points out, this provision serves the interests of the free Israelite man and his family (perhaps other wives) by stipulating a period of one month, during which she has to go through certain rituals, before the captive woman becomes her captor's wife. One could imagine that besides allowing her grieving and mourning for her beloved ones, it would have been a time to closely keep an eye on her and make sure her behavior would be acceptable to the family and she would not attempt to escape (the context would make it rather difficult any escape, having conquered her people and killed its men: to whom should she run?).

This law is particular in that its insertion in Deut 21, together with other laws concerning familial harmony, shows that, while the captive was considered as part of the family, it is also a war law.

> Deut[eronomy] 21:10–14 belongs to a group of Deuteronomic laws concerning warfare. The introduction of the law ... refers explicitly to battle, and ties the law firmly to chapter 20, a compendium of war laws which begins with precisely the same phrase. Deut[eronomy] 21:10–14 is also linked to the other war laws by similarity of content, in that it concerns warriors and captives, and by similarity of form, in that most of the war laws take the 'if-you' form.
>
> Deut[eronomy] 21:10–14 belongs equally to the Deuteronomic family laws, however. It is connected to them by content, in that it concerns marriage and

---

[74] As I write, there are news reports on hundreds of women abducted for human commerce in sex (pornography and prostitution). Their first period in captivity is called in the criminal jargon "softening" and it consists of gang rape and drug inducement in order to soften their resistance to their new fate, according to witnesses and news information. This says much about the length to which this criminal business goes; about how profitable it is; how little is accomplished in combatting it; and about the human (lack of) quality of those in charge of this dirty job. Perhaps the law sought to forbid an Israelite this type of behavior, which dehumanizes both the victim and the victimizer.

divorce. The motive clause found in v. 14 ... is found also in the law concerning the violation of an unbetrothed girl (Deut 22:29), further linking the law to other Deuteronomic family legislation. Finally, the law is followed by two family laws.[75]

Several of its points remain unclear and find all kinds of explanation, such as the significance of the rites later associated with her mourning her family, and the significance of "humiliate her" (עניתה) in such a text.[76] While some scholars understand this law as an example of Dtr's "humanization" of the treatment of captives, others are more mindful of the position of the weakest in this scheme. Thus, Washington asks about the location and authorization of abuse:

> What sort of abuse does the text refer to in the expression עניתה? Does this refer to the devastating circumstances of the woman's original capture, the destruction of her home, killing of her family, and forcible removal of her person? Or does it refer to the woman's subjugation to ritual denigration in the captor's household, followed by compelled sexual penetration? Is the woman humiliated by the decision to dismiss her after marriage, or perhaps by the man's choice not to go through with the marriage after bringing her to his household?
>
> There is a slight protection for the woman in this law. The primary effect of the law is to assure a man's prerogative to abduct a woman through violence, keep her indefinitely if he wishes, or discard her if she is deemed unsatisfactory, above all, perhaps, if she proves to be pregnant by another man. By authorizing the violent seizure of women, this law takes the male-against-female predation of warfare out of the battlefield and brings it to the home.[77]

Washington's analysis hits the point: warfare is now at home. Even though the language is that of family, her status within the household is debatable as to her working conditions. And it is precarious, as the law itself foresees. As Carole Fontaine expresses, "Force her into marriage if you will, but should it not turn out as desired, leave her some small honor—let her go free to beg on the streets, or hire herself out for more exploitation, or become a prostitute. After all, niceties must be observed if the conscience of the victor is to be at rest."[78]

---

[75] Pressler, *View of Women*, 9.

[76] Westbrook, "Female Slave," 235, thinks that "the captive woman is initially a slave, marriage makes her a free person, but subsequent termination of the marriage revives her previous status: her husband becomes her master again, and therefore can in principle sell her as a slave. The law forbids him to do so."

[77] C. H. Washington, "Lest He Die in the Battle and Another Man Take Her: Violence and the Construction of Gender in the Laws of Deuteronomy 20–22," in *Gender and Law*, 207.

[78] Carole R. Fontaine, *With Eyes of Flesh: The Bible, Gender and Human Rights* (The Bible in the Modern World 10; Sheffield: Sheffield Phoenix Press, 2008), 69.

Another Case of Spoils of War

In Judg 5 Deborah sings of Sisera's death and depicts his mother waiting for him. She imagines his delay produced by the distribution of the spoils, including רחם רחמתים, "a womb, two wombs" (v. 30). From the poem it is impossible to know what the writer (who uses Sisera's mother as his voice) means by רחם רחמתים, except that the context of war and the specific mention of spoils no doubt point to some type of object the soldiers will divide among themselves, and since the word's literal meaning is that of womb, it makes sense to understand them as females taken to be prisoners, slaves, captive wives as in Deut 21:10–14, or women to be raped and left as part of the ruins of the destroyed city.[79] Whatever their later fate, women are named here by the organ they are most precious for, which also defines them sexually as none other does, whether for pleasure or to produce children as slaves.

> The result is a victory song in which Deborah, a woman, a mother in Israel, sings about another woman, Sisera's mother, who sings (this is a poetic text) about women being raped in war. By means of this song within a song, not only Sisera's mother's voice but also that of the good mother, Deborah, is appropriated to advocate the male ideology of war in which rape is taken for granted as a weapon of terror and revenge. This is not Canaanite ideology; it is male ideology.[80]

In reading a patriarchal text, one should be especially wary of the use of women to justify the patriarchal practice of abducting and raping them as a sign of victory and power. As Exum notes, there is here a male using several female voices to condone woman's rape.

In summary, masters could treat and maltreat their foreign slaves, male or female, as it pleased them, for they were their private business. If they assaulted a slave to death (Exod 21:20–21), the slave's family had the right to blood revenge; but this right could have been exercised, if at all, if the family lived close by and got news of his or her death—and if they could somehow go through the process without losing even more. Experience tells people without financial support—and here we are speaking of people whose relative was a slave—that power and influence go together with money. Although Lev 25:44–46 makes a philosophical distinction between the indebted "brother," the Israelite man or woman, who is to be treated as a hired worker, and the foreigner, such a distinction lacks a specific semantic field and it is not always

---

[79] KB, IV, 1136: "ein, zwei Frauenschösse = eine, zwei (kriegserbeutete) Frauen, Beischläferinnen (Soldatensprache)." Because of this implied meaning, I have located them in chart I. They could also be seen as ideological—depreciative—terms and thus go into chart II.

[80] J. C. Exum, "Feminist Criticism: Whose Interests Are Being Served?" in *Judges and Method*, 74. Cf. a different reading of the female voice in this text by van Dijk-Hemmes, "Traces," 44.

easy to know to whom would the laws apply. Laws concerning female slaves' sexuality allow a glimpse into family life and at the same time into property handling, as for the overwhelming majority of women their sexuality belonged to a male. Although laws can be seen as attempting to protect the weakest segments of society, a closer look shows that laws are in the first place concerned with the preservation of order and authority of the *paterfamilias* and of the established Israelite free family. Frymer-Kensky starts her section on women and war with very pertinent words: "The laws of Deuteronomy begin to see women as objects when they consider marital or sexual relations."[81] With these words we finish our section.

SECTION II: WHY THESE ONES ARE NOT SLAVES

This section will look at texts where a term is used with the ideological purpose of implying low social status for the person thus called, not because she was literally a slave but in order to enforce a value or explain an action intended to be accepted. An ideology seeks to present a coherent depiction of reality by choosing which elements or people will be highlighted, which will be downplayed, and which will be ignored (the poor, handicapped, colored, innovators, foreigners, women, the environment, "progress" and so on), so that those holding that ideology—whether in power or a minority, intentionally or not—justify peace, war, subversion, resistance or other actions. As one writer puts it, "Ideology *constructs* a reality for people, making the oftentimes perplexing world intelligible; it is not, however, the actual state of affairs in its entirety. While helping people understand or make sense of the world, ideology concurrently masks or represses their real situation or standing in the world."[82] The very fact that the people here studied are normally treated as "servant" or "slave" by translations and commentaries attests to how effective the ideological depiction resulted. We include them here so that it becomes clear why they should not be included (in a study on slavery or lower class women).

Naming Oneself "שפחתך (אני)" *or* "אמתך (אני)"

The most obvious use of this device is so common that it goes usually unnoticed. It is used by any person in self-abasement when, in an encounter with another person—always a male in the biblical examples—the one using the terms "I am your slave" asserts his or her willingness to "lose face" in favor of the one granting him/her a favor, gift, etc. (superior-inferior); it is not a

---

[81] Tikva Frymer-Kensky, "Deuteronomy" in *The Women's Bible Commentary* (ed. Carol A. Newsom & Sharon Ringe; Louisville: Westminster/John Knox, 1992), 55.
[82] Yee, "Ideological Criticism: Judg 17–21 and the Dismembered Body," 148.

competitive relationship among equals.[83] It is ideological because, first, the person who thus declares him/herself is in a social position close enough to the other one as to have to declare that s/he is willing to be in an inferior position (otherwise there would be no need to assert it); secondly, biblical and extra-biblical examples point at many important characters thus debasing themselves, who are aware of the serious consequences a wrong movement on their side might bring, and speak not from a literal position of slavehood, but with the intention of pursuing certain goals. Thus, there is no example of a slave using it, because there is no need to mark difference.[84] This is most obvious in the case of the wise women of Tekoa and Abel, who are political negotiators; in other instances—Abigail's dialogue with David, Hannah's with Eli, or the woman of Shunem's plea to Elisha—the woman is in a humble position due to her need, while at the same time her need makes the strongest argument in her favor.[85]

Outside the DtrH the book of Ruth would be worth studying on this issue, particularly the connection between Ruth's use of נכריה, "alien" in 2:10 and שפחתך "your slave" in 2:13 to enlist Boaz in her plans. A similar connection, this one between אמה and the foreign woman, appears also in two stories in Judges (8:31–9:18 and 19), where Abimelech's mother and the unnamed concubine of a Levite are presented as alien to their husband's household and as אמהות.[86]

When a woman is named "אמה" not by herself but by a third person, the reader has to find out if there is an ideological motive for the speaker to use אמה in a diminishing way or whether there is another explanation for her being called אמה.[87] Three stories from DtrH will be studied here. It will be shown that

---

[83] Non-biblical examples of self-abasement on the part of men abound for instance in the Amarna letters, where the vassal king calls upon his Egyptian sovereign both debasing himself, and expecting the promised help from the powerful overlord. See, Lindhagen, *Servant Motif*, 7–13 (Amarna parallels), and different examples in Edward J. Bridge, "Self-Abasement as an Expression of Thanks in the Hebrew Bible," *Bib* 92 (2011): 255–273. C ited 22 January 2013. Online: http://www.bsw. org/Biblica/Index-By-Authors/Self-Abasement-As-An-Expression-Of-Thanks-In-The-Hebrew-Bible/470/.

[84] One possible exception (depending on one's interpretation of his status) is Ziba, who had been Saul's נער. In 2 Sam 9, David restores Mephibosheth, son of Jonathan, to a client of his, and confirms Ziba's attachment to Saul's house. In the successive dialogues in this chapter, first Ziba and later Mephibosheth refer to themselves as (David's) "עבדך." Considering Ziba's role, it is likely that he was a dependent, but not a slave. Otherwise, Ziba would be the only slave to state his dependent status to his own master.

[85] See above a list of women who use this device; H. McKay, "She Said to Him, He Said to Her: Power Talk in the Bible *or* Foucault Listens at the Keyhole," *BTB* 28 (1998): 46–48.

[86] K. Nielsen, *Ruth: A Commentary* (OTL. Louisville: Westminster John Knox, 1997), 60.

[87] See Crüsemann, *Widerstand*, 19–54; Z. Weisman, *Political Satire in the Bible* (Atlanta: SBL, 1998), 25–36; Katie M. Heffelfinger, "'My Father Is King': Chiefly Politics and the Rise and Fall of Abimelech," *JSOT* 33 (2009): 277–292; and Ken Stone, "How A Woman Unmans A King: Gender Reversal and The Woman of Thebez in Judges 9," in *Women of the Hebrew Bible and Their*

in two of them—Abimelech's kingship, and the concubine of the Levite—the text uses "אמה" and "פילגש" to create a correlation between their lower status and their condition of being foreign women. The story of Michal's confrontation of David is different, since "אמה" is not used by the narrator about one of the main characters, but by both main characters in their confrontation with each other.

Using "Son of a Slave" as Insult

Abimelech's Struggle for Kingship. Here attention will be focused on Abimelech's lineage, since that is where the אמה appears, rather than on the whole story of this king. Abimelech's paternal side is composed of brothers in the symbolic number of seventy, whom he kills on one stone; and on his maternal side, Shechemites who comply with his desire to be king and pay dearly for it. What is the meaning of Jotham's accusation of the Shechemites for having chosen the בן־אמה rather than a son of Gideon? It is precisely on this accusation where attention has to focus.

The story is already prepared by the narrator in 8:29–32; Gideon's house with his "seventy sons" is contrasted with the outsider, the פילגש from Shechem who also bore him a son. Everyone in the story takes for granted this difference between the seventy and the one. First, Abimelech presents himself to his kindred in Shechem with the alternative "that all seventy sons of Jerubbaal rule over you, or that *one* rules over you?" (9:2). The text presents the same logic in the Shechemites' acceptance of Abimelech and in their compliance in the murder of the seventy. Finally, since Jotham speaks of the seventy sons on one hand (who are *Gideon's* sons) and of the son of the slave on the other—as if Abimelech was not Gideon's son—implies that, at least for the "legitimate" brothers, Abimelech does not count as heir to Gideon.[88] Since Judg 8:31 witnesses to Gideon's recognition of Abimelech as his son, by renaming him, the factor that determines his not being considered one of Gideon's (eligible) sons has to be related to who is his mother.[89]

Robert Boling points out that whenever שׂים שׁם is used instead of the more common ויקרא לו to denote someone's naming (as in 2 Kgs 17:34, Neh 9:7, and Dan 1:7), it implies a re-naming. Since naming has a performative power, re-naming implies a new identity, as all cases pointed out by Boling show. In Abimelech's case there is no trace of the name given originally by his mother, thus only his re-naming by "Gideon the Yahwist" remains. However, since there are here two different family lineages, that of Gideon and his house, and the

---

Afterlives, 71–85.
[88] Matthews and Benjamin, *Social World of Ancient Israel*, 67–81.
[89] R. Boling, *Judges* (AB. Garden City, NY: Doubleday, 1975), 162.

maternal Shechemite tradition evidenced in her first naming him, and then bringing him up far from Gideon's house, it is not far-fetched to suppose certain tensions between clans as well as between endogamy and exogamy—to the extent that such categories apply in Judges. In light of this tension, the question remains, is this אמה a slave? Is Abimelech a son of a slave or a "son of a …"? That is, is it literal or an insult? Boling does not decide for or against her designation as implying low status.

Charles Fensham compares appearances of בן־אמה and cognates in Ugarit, the Amarna letters, and the Hebrew Bible and concludes that in the social realm אמה means a slave woman, in the political realm, a city in a vassalage relationship with a more powerful city and king, and in the religious realm a woman who places herself under the protection of the Deity.[90] Fensham finally opts for the literal sense of slave in this text. He sees him in a situation similar to that of Ishmael, the son of a manumitted slave claiming his right to a share in his father's inheritance … only that he claims the wrong share!

> ben-ʾămātô, the son of his handmaid, the third person suffix referring to Gideon. ... might have been used to show the citizens of Shechem what kind of social status their king has. They have elevated the son of a second-wife, from his menial position of ben-ʾāmāh to that of a king .... If Abimelech was the son of a second-wife, we must accept that with the death of Gideon he received manumission and thus became free. It is, however, but natural, in the circumstances described in Judges, that his brother should refer to his previous lower status. Like in the case of Ishmael, Abimelech is denoted as the son of a handmaid, a status that does not allow him to inherit his father's position, but only part of his property. By accepting the kingship of Shechem he usurped a position which was not legally intended for him.[91]

Naomi Steinberg submits Judg 9 to a social-scientific scrutiny and concludes that the key issue to which the chapter originally spoke is how manipulation of kinship lines can lead to disaster, rather than unity among the tribes. Abimelech manages first to kill his own brothers and then to divide the Shechemites, his own people, into several factions, all of whom seek their own political or economic advantage but end up defeated or dead.[92] How does the fact that his mother is called an אמה affect the picture, considering Abimelech's use of his family for his own advantage? Steinberg asserts that in circumstances like the ones depicted in Judg 9, the concubine was not primarily bound by economic reasons.

---

[90] Fensham, "The Son of a Handmaid in Northwest Semitic," 319.
[91] Fensham, "The Son of a Handmaid in Northwest Semitic," 319.
[92] Steinberg, "Social Scientific Criticism," 51–53, argues for such an original meaning of the chapter, which a later Dtr hand re-interpreted in the light of the exile by adding the parable to the 'historical' events.

[A] concubine was a woman whose continued presence within the family was not dependent upon economic arrangements. Typically, a concubine was a secondary wife, whose involvement with the husband represented a secondary union, both in terms of being an additional wife and of having a lower status than the legal wife. Her function was to provide sexual enjoyment in a situation where the man already had offspring by his primary wife. If he did not have a child by his primary wife, a man could take a secondary wife to produce a child.[93]

Steinberg is certainly right with regard to the affirmation that since the אמה in Judg 9 (and to a certain extent also the one in Judg 19) relied on her own kindred rather than her husband's, her economic security could not depend on her husband.[94] However, Steinberg's statement should not be generalized about woman's economic independence. Women became secondary wives, concubines, and slaves because of their families' economic hardships, loss of virginity, and other reasons that prevented their families from a more advantageous marriage arrangement. Since Abimelech is able to get to the elders of Shechem through his maternal family, it is true that in *her* case she had an economic independence from Gideon because of her family's wealth. Before this particular case is generalized even for the biblical פילגשים, further studies are necessary.[95]

Later in her analysis Steinberg poses a very important question which she, unfortunately, does not develop. "How does analysis of Judges 9 shed additional light on the process of assuming economic independence from a power structure that disadvantaged the underclasses?"[96] It is clear from the satire and from the events narrated in this chapter that Abimelech and his family in Shechem expected to get advantages from each other, expectations which soon turned into death. Looking at the political and economic game between both parties, and considering that Abimelech's mother is in the midst of it (even if never present in the story, she is the link between both parties and the reason of the initial "deal"), it would seem that this particular אמה was not a poor woman, for at least she belonged to a family with political connections, who was willing to use them for the בן-אמה's sake.

In the light of these internal clues, and considering that it is Jotham who calls her אמה, while the narrator calls her פילגש, there are different solutions to

---

[93] Steinberg, "Social Scientific Criticism," 51.

[94] Steinberg, "Social Scientific Criticism," 51.

[95] The same caution applies to Steinberg's affirmation that the פילגש's main task was sexual pleasure, especially since she does not provide any evidence. The Levite's פילגש (Judg 19) also had a wealthier father than husband, see below.

[96] Steinberg, "Social Scientific Criticism," 53.

this problem. One is to consider it a disrespectful naming on the part of Jotham, in order to diminish his half-brother. Another one is to consider that she was a slave and Abimelech got his manumission at Gideon's death. Still another possibility is to assume that אמה and פילגש are synonyms, implying a secondary wife, either living on her own or with her family.

There is still one more possibility, which would make sense for the אמה of Judg 9 as well as the one in Judg 19. From the Babylonian laws we know that women were allowed a fairly large amount of freedom in conducting their own businesses.[97] Laws become tighter, however, when it comes to regulating woman's sexuality, including divorce. Women were not allowed to initiate divorce, and men, according to Codex Hammurabi, were allowed it in one circumstance. The one given reason for which a man might divorce his wife was if she misbehaved generally, neglecting her home and "belittling" (or neglecting) him. Apparently the Babylonian standard for the wife was high, for if found guilty of these indiscretions she was dismissed empty-handed, or her husband could take another wife and lower the erring one to the position of an *amtu* (Akkadian cognate to the Hebrew אמה; Codex Hammurabi§141).[98] In the light of this situation, it could be possible to explain why secondary wives like Gideon's or the Levite's are called both פילגש and אמה they were not slaves, but for whichever reason, they did not stay at home by their husband's side, but returned to their paternal home. Characterizing the woman degraded to the position of an אמה "the erring one" is telling in this regard.[99]

Judges 19: The "Concubine" of a Levite

Judges 19 is a text even more studied than the previous one.[100] Unlike Judg 9, the אמה is in the center of the story, although she remains unnamed and mute,

---

[97] MacDonald, *Position of Women*, 25.

[98] MacDonald, *Position of Women*, 18–19.

[99] See also Engelken, *Frauen im Alten Israel*, 99. Since a thorough study of the Babylonian laws adduced by E. MacDonald is not possible here, the explanation just submitted needs to be further tested.

[100] See, among others, Engelken, *Frauen im Alten Israel*, 88–95; Bal, *Death and Dissymmetry*; Yairah Amit, "Literature in the Service of Politics: Studies in Judges 19–21," in *Politics and Theopolitics in the Bible and Postbiblical Literature* (ed. H. Reventlow, Y. Hoffman & B. Uffenheimer. Sheffield: JSOT Press, 1994), 28–40; Koala Jones-Warsaw, "Toward a Womanist Hermeneutic: A Reading of Judges 19–21," in *A Feminist Companion to Judges* (ed. A. Brenner; Sheffield: Sheffield Academic Press, 1993), 172–86; J. P. Fokkelman, "Structural Remarks on Judges 9 and 19," in *Shaarei Talmon: Studies in the Bible, Qumran, and the Ancient Near East presented to Shemaryahu Talmon* (ed. M. Fishbane & E. Tov. Winona Lake: Eisenbrauns, 1992), 33–45; S. Niditch, "The 'Sodomite' Theme in Judges 19–20: Family, Community, and Social Disintegration," *CBQ* 44 (1982): 365–78; D. Penchansky, "Staying the Night: Intertextuality in Genesis and Judges," in *Reading Between Texts* (ed. D. Nolan Fewell; Louisville: Westminster John Knox, 1992), 77–88.

and hardly talked to; in fact the only time she is directly addressed, it happens at a time when she is apparently dead already (v. 27–28).[101] Otherwise the narrator, her father, her husband, their host, and again the narrator and the Levite speak about, not to, her.[102] There are too many issues related to the purpose of Judges, to intertribal war, to the need of having a king and fundamentally to gender violence, which make it impossible to deal with this text in depth in a few pages.

Key elements in this chapter for the present discussion are the use of אמה and נערה for the woman in Judg 19, where אמה very likely points at a slave-wife or secondary wife. From the Levite's location she is a "stranger;" not a foreigner in the real sense, but a woman who does not belong in the remote parts of the hill country of Ephraim, and who surely shows her ability to get back to Bethlehem of Judah. In all likelihood אמה refers, together with the use of זנה to describe her behavior, to a wife who embodies the type of female conduct patriarchy cannot tolerate: Judg 19:2 states that she, his "concubine" פילגשו, "fornicated" against him ותזנה עליו and went away from him. Like Rahab in Joshua and some unnamed women in Judges, whom also the name זונה is given, the use of that stem to characterize her behavior says much about the text's understanding of "loose women," not sex workers (see below, chapter 7).

As mentioned in the discussion of Abimelech's mother, a woman who had had pre-marital sex and did not marry was in a very precarious situation in terms of marriage arrangements with another man. Boling points out that the father in Judg 19 dwells in a house where they can feast endlessly, while the Levite's home is a tent.[103] If these are signs of socio-economic status, then she belonged to a well-off family, and she had to enter into a poor marital arrangement (evidenced in the use of פילגש and אמה, and in the tent home). While the text does not give details, it could have been because of an event earlier in her life (loss of an eye, loss of virginity), which disqualified her for a better marriage arrangement.[104] If that was the case, especially if it had to be with her sexuality,

---

[101] With Boling, *Judges*, 276, by *homoioteleuton*.

[102] The master is also called a Levite residing in the remote parts of the hill country of Ephraim (19:1) and is also characterized as her "husband/man" (איש) in v. 3, as "son-in-law" (חתן) in v. 5, and as "master" (אדון) is servant in vs. 11–12 and of his concubine in vs. 26–27, after she has been raped and comes to the threshold. In v. 28 when he speaks to her and there is no answer, "the husband/ man" (איש) departed home. Other characters are "the נערה's father" and the נער who travels with him. Leeb, *Away from the Father's House*, 140–42 notes this uncommon way of speaking of the host and father, as well as textual overtones from Deut 22 of the phrase אבי הנערה.

[103] Boling, *Judges*, 275.

[104] I mean any event that implied her loss of virginity, from consented pre-marital sex to rape or even debt-bondage, during which she was unprotected and after which she was disqualified for a good marriage. Staying in the scenario of the book, where there is constant danger of external and internal war and conquest, she could earlier have been subject to abduction without marriage, as the women in Judg 5:31 and in 21 were. Considering her father's comfortable living, these seem unlikely

this would be an example in which the woman's honor is related to her sexual purity.[105]

Using אמהות *in an Argument*

The story of Michal's confrontation with David (2 Sam 6:16, 20–23) needs to be seen in the light of David's rising at the expense of Saul's falling dynasty, of which Michal is one of the last survivors. The ark is finally coming to Jerusalem, and the procession dances and celebrates, with David at its head. Michal observes his behavior from a window and despises him, and as soon as David comes in, she tells him how shameful his behavior was, exposing himself in front of the אמהות עבדיו, the female servants or slave women who belonged to David's male servants. David responds that they understand better what is happening than she does. Both Michal and David use "אמהות" for a comparison, to press their point, both taking for granted their lowly status. The question is whether their lowly status is an ideological construct or social reality. Since Michal brings it up and David uses it for his own response, the question one has to ask is what kind of contrast Michal intended.[106]

Largely due to their own ideas on purpose and structure of the books of Samuel, scholars are divided as to the relation of verses 16 and 20–23 to the rest of the chapter. In the canonical text v. 20–23 serve as epilogue to the location of YHWH's ark at Jerusalem, yet they may very well have had an independent origin. P. K. McCarter takes a moderate position on the traditio-historical aspects of this pericope.

> In view of its editorial function ... and its present inclusion in the Deuteronomistic assemblage of materials in 5:11–8:18, it is safest to think of it as part of an ancient document—perhaps affiliated with the original story of David's rise, perhaps not—taken up by a Deuteronomistic writer precisely because of the thematic link it provides in the larger narrative.[107]

Frank Crüsemann sees the origin of the story in a joke that laughs at David's problems with women, but which is innocuous enough not to seriously threaten him.[108] He calls attention to the wordplay between the verbs קלל and

---

possibilities. But the point is to recognize that there were several occasions in which a woman could be induced to sex or raped and then her future marriage possibilities were smashed.

[105] It is true also that Lev 21 forbids priests to marry certain women; so perhaps some of those proscriptions were the reason she became a פילגש and אמה and not an אשה, wife.

[106] The parallel story in 1 Chr 15 gets only to Michal's disparaging in her heart. I deal with this text as evidence for musicians and performers in chapter 5.

[107] P. Kyle McCarter, *2 Samuel* (AB. Garden City: Doubleday, 1984), 188.

[108] Frank Crüsemann, "Zwei alttestamentliche Witze: I Sam 21 11–15 und II Sam 6 16.20–23 als Beispiele einer alttestamentlichen Gattung," *ZAW* 92 (1980): 225 considers that since the last word favors David against Michal in his view of how to be glorified, the origin of the joke has to be in a group

the infinitive נגה, on the one hand, and כבד on the other hand. He is also right in perceiving ironic tones in Michal's initial complaint—more insinuated than plainly stated—that David's behavior has sexual overtones (exhibitionism?) in front of the women, while the end of the story leaves open the implication that David did not have any more sexual contact with Michal.[109]

Adele Berlin studies the women who play the main roles in David's life not as historical figures, but as narrative characters of different depth. Her analysis shows that Michal and her brother Jonathan play inverted roles in the narrative of David's rise. Michal asserts her feelings for David (earlier of love, in this text of contempt), lowers him through the window, lies for him, and has no children; Jonathan helps him in a less physical way, makes a covenant with him and has his offspring sitting at David's table long after he is dead. On the other hand, David uses Michal's feelings but does not reciprocate them (at least narratively speaking), while his love for Jonathan is very openly expressed. These verses deny Michal feminine traits, fertility and even beauty: "Not only is this [verse 23] the culmination of the disappointment in her life, and a hit that the husband who never loved her now stopped having marital relations with her, but ... it suggests that Michal never filled a female role, or at least the role that the Bible views as the primary female role."[110] To her analysis I should add that Michal never uses "your servant" in David's presence; she rather stands on an equal footing with him. Could this be the reason why she loses her battles?

Rolf Carlson builds his argument on the basis of an article by Porter claiming that the ark had been brought to Jerusalem during the *sukkot* festival, a time of fertility renewal rites, popular among the Canaanites, embraced by David.[111] That politics and religion are mixed is not new, and that Michal might

that is close to David.

[109] Crüsemann, "Zwei alttestamentliche Witze," 226. It will soon become obvious that scholars are divided in their interpretation of Michal's barrenness: many assume it implies that David did not have sexual relations with her any more, while many assume YHWH's punishment of Michal. See chapter 5 on musicians.

[110] Adele Berlin, *Poetics and Interpretation of Biblical Narrative* (Winona Lake: Eisenbrauns, 1994), 24–25.

[111] Rolf Carlson, *David, the Chosen King: A Traditio-Historical Approach to the Second Book of Samuel* (Stockholm: Almqvist & Wiksell, 1964), 95, states: "The main theme of the *sukkōt* festival is the restoration of fertility, and it is also this which especially characterizes the last passage of 2 Sam. 6, which is described in 'disintegrated' *sukkōt* terms. He [J. Porter, "The Interpretation of 2 Samuel vi and Psalm cxxxii," *JTS* 5 (1954): 161–73] further supposes that the 'maids' (*'ămāhōt*), with whom David says in v. 22 that he intends to seek 'honour' (*'ikkābēdāh*) are to be regarded as temple prostitutes, similar to the *kōṭārātu* of the Ras Shamra texts. These 'daughters of rejoicing' at the same time filled a musical function in the cultus; the same has been taken to apply to the *'ămāhōt* of 2 Sam. 6:20, 22 .... *Kabod* implies 'first and foremost the possession of sons', as Pedersen puts it; Porter's interpretation of David's statement in 6:22 as referring to a rite of *hieros gamos* with 'his servants' maids', v. 20, does full justice to this aspect. Nor can it be ruled out that David's desire to

have had different religious traditions than David is also likely. Where Porter's and Carlson's arguments are unconvincing to me is in the connection between the *sukkot* festival and Michal's barrenness as the main argument of the chapter; and for that purpose making the אמהות of 2 Sam 6:20 sacred prostitutes![112]

The אמהות Michal refers to are not sacred prostitutes. But are they slaves or not? The reader can only know Michal's intended connotation, namely, these אמהות עבדיו *are* lowly. McCarter implies the ideological character of the text by speaking of "Princess Michal" as an "aristocrat" who looks at these women from high above her. "As one king's daughter and another's wife she does not hesitate to refer to all the young women of Israel, whether slave or free, as the 'maidservants' or 'wenches' of the king's subjects; thus there is no reason to suppose that 'the noblewomen of the free Israelites are excluded from the offensive remark' (Cruesemann, 1980: 226)."[113] What matters in Michal's eyes is that the king of Israel should behave according to a certain protocol, which includes not "making an exhibition of himself under the eyes of his servant-maids, making an exhibition of himself like a buffoon!" (v. 20, *JB*).[114] Michal's problem is not that David did so in front of women, since he had a whole harem already, and there is no instance in which a woman confronts her husband about his sexual affairs. Michal's criticism is that David danced in front of "servants," improperly flirting in front of lowly persons. David, on the other hand, perceives as the main issue not any possible sexual connotation of his behavior, but that he is humbling himself in the presence of YHWH, a fact Michal is unwilling to see or to accept. David has Dtr's and YHWH's support—Dtr's by his initial comment against Michal ("she despised him in her heart"), and YHWH's indirectly, since opening wombs is YHWH's prerogative in the Bible, and those are the final words about Michal.[115]

All that can be stated on the social location of these אמהות is that, since in the end they are a pawn in a chess game between Saul's falling dynasty and

---

win 'honour' with these has similar implications."

[112] It is an unsustainable position for these reasons among others: a. It lacks evidence in the biblical texts; אמהות never has the meaning of sacred prostitute, and in any event אמהות עבדיו requires explanation, which they do not provide. b. קדשה, the term usually—and wrongly—translated "sacred prostitute," does not appear in 2 Sam 6:20–23; and, as McCarter, *2 Samuel*, 189, points out, "the context and details of 6:1–15, 17–19 reflect not a cultic reenactment but a historical ceremony of the sort that traditionally marked the introduction of a national god into a new capital city. Sacred marriage had no part in such a ceremony."

[113] McCarter, *2 Samuel*, 187.

[114] Several commentaries highlight the difference in expectations between Michal's מלך and David's נגיד; see A. Campbell, *Of Prophets and Kings: A Late Ninth-Century Document (1 Samuel 1–2 Kings 10)* (CBQMS; Washington: Catholic Biblical Association, 1986), 57; H. Hertzberg, *I & II Samuel* (OTL. London: SCM, 1964), 281.

[115] Indirectly because YHWH does not speak directly, but Dtr, so to say, co-opts YHWH by stating that Michal remained barren.

David's rising one, their real status in the story cannot be known. Since they are referred to in relation to their masters or husbands, David's עבדים, I would suppose they are either wives or slave-wives to David's officers, both of whom, wives and officers, had diverse ranks. At any rate, they did not rank high in the eyes of Michal, David, nor the narrator, as they all build on their alleged low status.

CONCLUSION TO "אמה" AND "שפחה" USED IDEOLOGICALLY

When a free woman uses "אמתך" or "שפחתך" to show respect and obedience to a higher-ranking man, she is observing a social mechanism to deal with statuses and behaviors which can be dangerous if not controlled. Women like Abigail, Ruth, Bathsheba, or the wise women of Tekoa and Abel use this mechanism with precision and ease, and succeed in their enterprises. Similar ideological use of the term was perceived in Judg 9, where אמה and פילגש are both used by a third person for a secondary wife. The unnamed concubine of Gideon (Judg 8:31–9:18) is particularly singled out as outsider, a quality that is used by her son and his enemies alike in their dealings between Abimelech and her family from Shechem. She appears not to have left her home country and family, thus contributing to a cultural separation between her and her family (including her son) on one hand, and Gideon's other wives and sons on the other.

The unnamed woman of Judg 19 is also singled out as foreign to the remote areas of the hill country of Benjamin, where her husband dwells. Of course the story contains much more than this single issue, yet it is telling that the only two texts in the whole Hebrew Bible in which both פילגש and אמה are used referring to the same woman are Judg 8:31–9:18 (Gideon's "wife"), and Judg 19 (the Levite's "wife") and in both stories אמה reflects a woman who was more than a slave, whose family of origin was financially well-off, (and received her in their midst), and who were somehow alien to their male partners.

In the discussion between Michal and David, both use "אמהות" to speak of a group of people, not to them. In that sense, this text is similar to Jotham's use of the term to disregard his half-brother Abimelech and the Shechemites who took him as their king; unlike Judg 9, in 2 Sam 6:20–23 there is no narrative framework from which to extract much information about the אמהות. From an ideological reading of Michal's and David's positions it became clear that no matter how honest or concealing Michal might have been in her understanding of kingship and protocol, David, Michal and Dtr all share the view that the אמהות are lowly in status, while on the other hand neither David nor Dtr appreciate Michal's confrontation of the chosen king. No reason is given to support their mutually-shared assumption, whether they are lowly because they are slaves, because they belong to the common people, or because they dance in the streets. It is also unclear the degree to which their low status is shared by David's officers or servants, the immediate referent of these "servants." Consequently, to consider that their lowly status depended on their sexuality requires a huge leap from text to interpretation.

CONCLUDING REMARKS

The previous chapter examined conditions many women found themselves in throughout the ANE, such as being in more vulnerable conditions than men in a similar situation (lower pay, lack of specialization, and often also in the use of their sexuality for profit).[116] Although not all these facts are clearly recognizable in the Hebrew Bible, there are hints that differences applied, as the following examples taken from references studied earlier show. One finds in DtrH a Ziba who handles property and slaves, is politically astute and ends up with a huge share of what had been Saul's property. There is no female counterpart to Ziba. The female character that gets closest to David is Abishag the Shunammite, but she is literarily far less developed (she does not talk, does not act on her own) and she does not get any promotion, even if—as will be demonstrated below—the only biblical סֹכֶן is a high officer of the king.[117] Another hint comes from Nabal's and Abigail's household, whose dependents rise and fall within one verse. Yet, whereas the נְעָרִים save the situation by reporting to Abigail her husband's words to David, her five נַעֲרוֹת only accompany Abigail in her journey, and do not utter a word.

When a female slave appears in a list of possessions, she always appears after the male slave, and even if in stories the slave is used for extraordinary tasks, one can assume she still performed her everyday tasks (producing offspring, chaperoning the mistress, or carrying information about Absalom's revolt would not have been her only tasks!), all signs of her low status. Another

---

[116] There are no data for lower payment in Israel, since no ration lists have been found outside Lev 27:1–7, in which women are always rated lower than men. However, since chapter 27 is a late appendix to the book of Leviticus, its "information" cannot be used as a source with any certainty. See J. Milgrom, "H_R in Leviticus and Elsewhere in the Torah," in *The Book of Leviticus: Composition and Reception* (ed. Rolf Rendtorff & Robert A. Kugler; Leiden: Brill, 2003), 26–9; A. Ruwe, "The Structure of the Book of Leviticus in the Narrative Outline of the Priestly Sinai Story (Exod 19:1–Num 10:10)," in *The Book of Leviticus: Composition and Reception* (ed. Rolf Rendtorff & Robert A. Kugler, with the assistance of Sarah Smith Bartel; Leiden: Brill, 2003) 69 n.34 notes that, thematically, it belongs to Num 1–10. It is also true that, archaeologically, there is an overwhelming majority of (עֶבֶד)-seals with masculine names and very few examples of feminine names, a sign that less women held high official positions.

[117] One also finds male slaves like the Egyptian whom David found, who had been left by his owner three days earlier because he was sick (1 Sam 30:11–15), for which there is no parallel story either.

example is the use of women for achieving offspring, a theme that is more developed in the Genesis obsession with children.

Finally, some laws concerning slaves and indentured servants show equality of rights in men and women: going free if they get a knocked tooth or eye, and—in Deuteronomy—going free on the seventh year of servitude. This points to a basic view of indentured male and female Israelites as equal. On the other hand, laws concerning woman's sexuality (Lev 19:20–22, and Deut 21:10–14) also show a difference in treatment between men and women.

This chapter attempted a two-fold approach. The first one was to look directly at bound women, organizing the references into those for slaves and indentured servants (אמה/תו, שפחה/תו), dependent women away from paternal protection (נערה/תו), and captive women (רחם/תים). Besides these categories in which one expects to find lower-class women, a section was also added in which the ideological use of terms to diminish a person was evaluated. This ideological use presents instances of self-reference, in which both אמה and שפחה appear, and instances of use of אמה to disqualify another person, either by direct application of the term (2 Sam 6:20–23, Judg 19) or by its application to someone's mother (Judg 8:31).

The range of occurrences throughout most of the biblical books, paired with the scarcity of information about their conditions and activities, merits some reflection. In order for a society to function, everyone has to keep his or her place, and this applies to free citizens, males and females, children, slaves, animals, and institutions. An important part of keeping one's place is the division of work and how one contributes to the good of society. Since a woman is expected to work, there is an implicit recognition of the woman's contribution to society, even if more is taken for granted than positively stated. This recognition does not make distinctions between free Israelites, foreign slaves or indentured servants. It just takes for granted that there are tasks to be performed, and that women could do them well and did them well.[118] In fact, women like the one depicted in Prov 31:10–31 show more household productivity than all the slaves put together![119]

Speaking about household tasks, there is no single pattern of household locations, unlike other occupations discussed in the following chapter, the

---

[118] In her book *Discovering Eve*, Meyers approaches the settlement period with a similar view, which eventuates in equality between men and women, and gender division of tasks. Meyers seems to understand the evidence from the book of Judges as corresponding to a chronologically early period in the history of Israel.

[119] The reason seems to be that, although it pertains to the slave's position to work, her master or mistress does not acquire honor from their industriousness, but from possessing them, while an industrious wife is a source of honor for the husband at the gates and for her children, at least according to this poem.

majority of which occur in the palace. It is obvious that stories where servants appear, especially if there is more than one, are located in wealthy households, such as those of Abraham, Abimelech, Nabal or Boaz. Some of them are related to King David, although not necessarily in the palace (the woman who helped spy during Absalom's revolt) or the dialogue between Michal and David about his dancing in front of the women when the ark was brought to Jerusalem (2 Sam 6:16, 20–23). There are also women who appear alone in the story. Thus one cannot know how many dependents households usually had (in Naaman's household, for example, only one appears, 2 Kgs 5).

On the other hand, precisely because they are taken for granted, the amount of information that one can collect on life conditions of female labor is surprisingly small, starting from the fact that they very seldom appear in what the reader would expect to be their working location (doing laundry, baking bread, fetching water, cooking, grinding grain). Summarizing the information collected in this chapter, what can be said is that in DtrH slaves and dependents are found as part of the household, on the road carrying information, at the well carrying water or accompanying their mistress. Much more than that is left to the reader's imagination.

Many of these economically dependent women were socially low. These are permanent slaves, probably foreign and with no rights. Others were socially better off, due to their being Israelites, even if indentured. For some of them being a slave-wife or a concubine might have been a bonus in their social location, but one should not presume too much, because social locations were determined, as discussed in chapter 1, by several elements. The worth of these women, what would ascribe them honor, is not explicitly stated. Yet, it does not have to do with their sexual purity. Sexual purity is not the main quality of an enslaved woman, whose whole body, at any rate, belongs to her master. By the very assumption that they are where they are needed and they do what they are expected to do, slave and dependent women are assessed as reliable workers.

CHAPTER 5

HIDE AND SEEK: MISCELLANEOUS WOMEN

This chapter is very important for the overall study of laborers in general, for the range of occupations is far larger than the texts of the Hebrew Bible recognize. In the case of women, it is especially important that their contribution to the economy be recognized. Not only is biological reproduction important for a society's survival, but it involves economic aspects as yet not recognized by most people, involving child rearing and education, fetching water, feeding and caring for everyone (especially the males, the elderly and the sick), and a variety of domestic tasks which would make an enormous difference in household budgets, were they to be paid.

Since this chapter intends to concentrate on hidden workers and the parameter is the DtrH, it includes three sections rather independent from each other. First, I will review those texts in the DtrH in which masculine plural lexemes are used to denote groups deemed to be related to servitude by the texts themselves or by secondary scholarship. It will be clear that there are many which could have included women. We just cannot know. We do know that most occupations were taught from parent to child and eventually taken up from them; and that many groups were explicitly hereditary, like the priesthood and some prophetic companies. Furthermore, experience also tells us that when an undertaking is run by the family, all its members help in some way and often those invisible know and do as much as the "head" of the business does, for instance, in handicraft or administration. Since we do not know, it could be that we are only overviewing the semantic field of work and not its female laborers.[1]

There are several areas where ignorance of female contributions is most evident, especially because of their importance in the life of any community, namely, birthing children and nourishing (people and domestic animals), tool making, textile industry, and some form of bartering and of commercial activities.

a) midwifery has been and still is an area in which women have traditionally held a prominent role as health-care workers and conception counselors before and during pregnancy, through birthing as obstetricians and as neonatologists. While Genesis and Exodus include some of the most interesting narratives in which there is a midwife at work, DtrH totally omits mentioning her—in fact, they are hardly mentioned at all in the rest of the Bible and the Ugaritic materials as well! Yet, there are plenty of occasions recorded in which men beget children.

b) nourishing (in all senses) is another area traditionally ascribed to women. Food and drink preparation is here understood starting from grain and water. Except for the butchers or cooks and bakers listed in 1 Sam 8:13, they are notably absent, especially those persons who did the basic tasks needed for feeding many. Apparently it was mostly women who prepared their most popular and safest drink—beer. It is strange to me that there is not even a participle or noun for these professionals, neither male nor female, nor for inns or taverns, and this in the whole Hebrew Bible.

c) tools in order to build houses, threshing floors, cisterns, terraces, and other buildings; tools for boats, wine and oil presses, pottery and crafts making, for plowing and sewing, carving and cutting instruments, processing food required ability, know-how and often, strength. It is usually assumed most of this work was made by men and not women. However, at least "domestic pottery" must have been included among female household tasks.[2] We do not hear much about this in the DtrH, except for general terms including metal workers or artisans (see 2 Kgs 24:14, החרש והמסגר).[3]

---

[1] Charts VIII and IX present these terms.

[2] Also, domestic grinding, as evidenced in tools found in kitchens (although also in temple complexes). Jennie Ebeling and Yorke Rowan, "The Archaeology of the Daily Grind: Ground Stone Tools and Food Production in the Southern Levant," *NEA* 67 (2004): 113, suspect gender bias is one reason of their neglect by most scholars. For a good review of research on ground stone tools and also on their neglect, Jennie Ebeling, "Archaeological Remains of Everyday Activities: Ground Stone Tools in Bronze and Iron Age Palestine," in *Life and Culture in the Ancient Near East* (ed. Richard Averbeck, Mark W. Chavalas, & David B. Weisberg. Bethesda: CDL Press, 2003), 311–17 (on state of research), 317–22 (tools uncovered).

[3] Actually, the first thing that we hear in DtrH of is their *absence*: according to 1 Sam 13:19 "no smith was found throughout the land of Israel." Another expression is וכל-חכם בכל-מלאכה "every (man? person?) wise or skillful in any manner of work" (1 Chr 22:15, *JPS*). Studying Late

d) textiles is a fourth area of work, probably involving women, from preparing the yarn and spinning to sewing and dying, at home and professionally. Goddesses and women held the emblematic spindle as both a working tool and a sign of femininity. Some luxury items appear in the written sources as specialties from certain regions, and archaeological remains also tell us about workshops or cities specializing in this craft—although they do not tell us whether women or men were the specialists, of course.

There is not much evidence for female participation in other areas, at least not that we know of (in masonry and some other building-related activities, in mining, in transportation, and in scribal activity, for example), although some exceptions may be brought up: there is one allusion to Rachel in Gen 29:9 as "shepherdess" (רעה); and there is at least one text in which "daughters" are rebuilding the walls of Jerusalem under Nehemiah's leadership.[4] As to scribes, considering the high rate of illiteracy in general, and supposing that those who knew reading and writing were from the elite, I surmise they used their abilities for personal purposes and at times even put them in the service of others (Letter writing? Contracts or agreements? Poetry transcription?); however, it is hard to believe that they would hold a recognized post in court or temple. On the Mesopotamian evidence, Marsman makes the following affirmations: "Through the centuries female scribes are occasionally mentioned. Still, women who exercised this profession were rare. ... And it would seem that in general those women who acted as professional scribes served only women."[5] Nemet-Nejat looks at it, however, with an awareness of its social side:

Bronze Age Metallurgy in Denmark Janet Levy, "Gender, Heterarchy, and Hierarchy," in *Handbook of Gender in Archaeology* (ed. S. M. Nelson; Lanham: AltaMira, 2006), 227–28, calls attention to two things: (a) the different processes and skills needed in order to produce a high-quality product, some of which are not gender-determined; and (b) gender biases from researchers and informants as parallels are drawn from today's possibly similar organizations. The book is only partially available to me thorough the web [cited 10 September 2011]. Online: http://books.google.com .ar/books?id=EtlQUpgo2cEC&printsec=frontcover&dq=Handbook+of+gender+in+archaeology&hl =en&sa=X&ei=vcsFUcOZLee-
0QHVwoGgCQ&ved=0CCoQ6AEwAA#v=onepage&q=Handbook%20of%20gender%20in%20arc haeology&f=false.

[4] Nehemiah 3:12. Return with Ezra and the rebuilding of Jerusalem under Nehemiah are extraordinary events, in which representatives from each tribe and group did participate, in a kind of new conquest/settlement reminiscent of the earlier one under Joshua. Thus, it is both extraordinary and natural that each family would have someone. Just as there was land for daughters when there were no sons, there was participation in the wall building in some extraordinary cases. This is not to say that women would not help build their own homes; I mean they were probably not professional masons.

[5] Marsman, *Women*, 411. Robins, *Women*, 111, states that there is not one Egyptian document that can be proved to have been either written by or for a woman to read it independently from a male.

Though scribes were usually men, there were women scribes in Old Babylonian Mari and Sippar –some were even the daughters of scribes. Literary prayers, laments, and lullabies have been attributed to queens and princesses. Scholars know the names of at least ten female scribes from Mari. Nine of them were slaves; they received small rations, indicating the low regard in which they were held. Slaves with scribal skills were sometimes given to princesses as part of their dowries. At Sippar cloistered women, celibate devotees of the sun god Shamash and his consort, Aya, served as scribes for their own cloister administration.[6]

On the other hand, one should be careful not to indiscriminately project later restraints on every period and every location. Samuel Meier asserts that "[a]lthough the evidence for female scribes spans the period from the end of the third millennium to the first millennium B.C., identifying female scribes is problematic. In the earliest period, there was no gender marking in Sumerian to distinguish women from men in occupations which both shared..."[7] He wonders further what processes lay behind the conception of female Deities as patronesses for scribes in Mesopotamia and in Egypt and their (at least less recorded) participation in these societies.[8]

With regard to the Bible, the only, very weak evidence, is mention of the בני־הספרת, "the sons/children of the female scribe" (most translations take it as a personal name, Hassopereth, Ezra 2:55), whose name could have originally been that of the profession.[9] This is not to say that women did not compose poetry, mostly orally but even in writing; however, the scribal profession seems to have been too much oriented toward preserving the tradition or ensuring the smooth administrative ways, and too close to political and religious power to have been open to women—but I hope to be proved wrong.

e) commercial activity by a woman in the Bible is best evidenced in Prov 31:10–31. In several letters from Mesopotamia, the trend seems to have been that the husband would travel and the wife would remain at home, control the production, send her husband the products and expect him to send the money back home, which was sometimes a heroic enterprise to succeed![10] The women

---

On the other hand, the title *seshet* "female scribe" occurs rarely in documents from the Middle Kingdom, and belongs to someone who is wealthy.

[6] Karen Nemet-Nejat, "Women in Ancient Mesopotamia," in *Women's Roles in Ancient Civilizations: A Reference Guide* (ed. Bella Vivante; Westport: Greenwood, 1999),108.

[7] Samuel Meier, "Women and Communication in the Ancient Near East," *JAOS* 111 (1991): 541.

[8] Meier, "Women and Communication," 543–4.

[9] Tamara Cohn Eskenazi, "Out from the Shadows: Biblical Women in the Postexilic Era," *JSOT* 54 (1992): 36, quoted also by Marsman *Women*, 429. Similarly, there are the בני מחול (1 Kgs 5:11), "the children of Mahol," a term (מחול) meaning "music."

[10] The situation of a wife whose husband left for business for a long time (and sometimes even tarries to send money home) is also reflected in letters, such as those from the old Assyrian period, discussed by Steele, "Women and Gender," 303–4.

from these letters or from Prov 31 were not poor women, but mistresses of their households, running a business. Perhaps merchants (the "Canaanite" in Prov 31:24) would regularly come by, acquire the products from the village and sell those from other areas. Travelling and lodging was neither easy nor safe and, for what we gather, it was extremely expensive. Estimations by specialists indicate that most products were sold within a distance that to us would be regional at most. "In fact, the degree of commercialization is one of the crucial axes of variation in ancient state economies; the type of political organization is another." This archeologist of ancient economies further states that

> Economies with low commercialization have limited marketplace distribution of goods and services, but land and labor are not commodities. Government control of many sectors of the economy is strong, but typically a small independent commercial sector of merchants and marketplaces does exist. These economies are often of limited spatial scale.[11]

Thus, by "large-scale commercial activity" is meant commercial enterprise in an area larger than the immediate villages. A different picture is that of "small-scale" commercial activity, such as selling fresh fish or vegetables (and perhaps bread and some other produce) to other quarters of the city or to the next village, either individually or in local markets. At least one tomb scene from Egypt depicts a local market at the city port, in which a woman sits and sells some produce.[12] This type of activity is also well attested by anthropologists working in small villages around the world. The starving widow in 2 Kgs 4:1–7, who was on the brink of selling her children because of debts and had plenty of oil to sell after the miracle would be one (circumstantial?) example.[13]

Thus, many reasons make it improbable that certain occupations would be regularly carried out by female professionals when they involved large-scale logistics, especially travelling. But the same activities (selling or bartering, pottery making, record keeping, health care) were carried at home or for neighbors at the small-scale or domestic level—equally effectively, I would guess, for they knew their neighbors.

---

[11] Smith, "Archaeology," 78, 79.

[12] Discussed by Teresa Armijo Navarro-Reverter, "La vida de las mujeres egipcias durante la Dinastía XVIII," *Boletín de la Asociación Española de Orientalistas* 38 (2002): 133–34. Cited 8 September 2011. Online: http://www.cervantesvirtual.com/obra/la-vida-de-las-mujeres-egipcias-durante-la-dinasta-xviii-0/.

[13] Circumstantial in the sense that we are not told how they made a living daily; so, perhaps they did sell some produce regularly (Vegetables? Olives? Almonds? Figs?); the prevailing drought would explain why they were in dire poverty. On the other hand, since her deceased husband belonged to a company of prophets of YHWH, they might have been supported by the other prophetic families or from the State. We just do not have this information.

Loops in our sources like those noted here may be partly due to the accidents of archaeology and time; also, they might have been so common that nobody cared to record them; or we might be missing this information because of mistranslations and misunderstanding of terms. Whatever the reasons, these deserve further exploration, as far as that is possible without forcing the evidence too much.

After looking for women hidden under general masculine plural terms, Sections II and III will look at occupations for women which, for particular reasons, do not fit into my classification. These include (Section II) Dtr terms referring to women doing certain tasks for which terms are not quite profession-like, such as "attendants" or terms common enough to be realized regularly, but which DtrH attributes only to the religious realm, such as "weavers" and "music performers."[14] Finally, in Section III come the notable absentees from DtrH. There, I will concentrate on those aspects which could be considered "work," that is, not performed only for one's own household, where there are reasonable traces that they were performed by women, but they are ignored.

On the practical level, this is a rather slippery chapter, for it seeks to bring to light what was not meant to be said—perhaps not intentionally, only because of the redactors' own interests and biases. It has therefore a tentative character; hopefully, time will either confirm these assertions or give us more material to work with.

SECTION I: WOMEN HIDDEN IN OCCUPATIONS DENOTED BY MASCULINE TERMS

This section studies terms referring to groups with the masculine plural form. As stated in the Introduction, biblical Hebrew uses עבד and שרת for "work, toil, serve," as well as "minister at the sanctuary." The noun עבד "servant, slave" appears more than seven hundred times in the Hebrew Bible, with two basic milieus, secular and religious, all of them for males. We know that at least one instance of שרת indicates a woman. Then, does the term עבדים include women in any text? The answer will vary, but at least sometimes it is affirmative, as in these few examples:

> "Moses summoned all Israel and said to them: You have seen all that the LORD did before your eyes in the land of Egypt, to Pharaoh and to all his servants and to all his land" (Deut 29:2, *NRSV*)

---

[14] Music-making includes different words and several texts. About half of them fall outside the DtrH and those within do not indicate clearly to what extent they were professionals. It seemed to me that it would be more fruitful to treat them as a semantic field, in a block, even though some term would, technically, belong to other sections of this chapter or the previous chapter. It has been especially hard to decide where to locate weavers, musicians and bringers of news (messengers).

"King Jehoiachin of Judah gave himself up to the king of Babylon, himself, his mother, his servants, his officers, and his palace officials. The king of Babylon took him prisoner in the eighth year of his reign." (2 Kgs 24:12, *NRSV*)

Besides "servants" עבדים, there are several other terms, which usually go unnoticed. Many of them are mentioned in passing. In Jer 51, for instance, YHWH recounts destruction of several groups by Babylon, addressed in second masculine singular: "By you, I will smash the shepherd (רעה) and his flocks … the farmer (אכר) and his team (of oxen) … governors and deputies" (v. 23). While רעה is attested once in feminine (Rebekah), the term אכר "farmer/s" appears seven times, all masculine and, notably, six of them in the prophetic corpus.[15]

There are also all those groups said to have become enslaved by the Israelite/Judean victors from the time of the "conquest" on; there are also several brotherhoods returning to Yehud with Ezra and Nehemiah, whose legal status is unclear, but were hereditary and ascribed to the large organizations. Finally, there are a few other lexemes not clearly translatable, belonging to the semantic field of unfree servitude.

Among the groups that came back from Babylon one finds the נתינים, "devoted ones" and the בני עבדי שלמה, "descendants (or company) of Solomon's servants" (Ezra 2:43, 55 // Neh 7:46, 57, etc.) and, if Albright was correct, also a guild of temple musicians, the בני מחול "members of the orchestral guild" (1 Kgs 5:11).[16]

These seem to be designations for hereditary groups bound to the great institutions, which then must have included women, even though the terms are only masculine in gender. Scholars have shown that many laborers for the great institutions in Babylon lived with their own families and were enlisted as such, if sources are correctly interpreted. Other groups, like the Babylonian *nadītu*s, were priestesses who lived secluded in cloisters (but they were not slaves, on the contrary).[17] Thus, it would not be far-fetched to suppose there were women considered female workers by the great institutions themselves.

It is hard to assess how much these institutions influenced the social organization of their time. Likewise, it is hard to make generalizations about its

---

[15] And mostly in late texts, see 2 Chr 26:1; Isa 61:5; Jer 14:4; 31:24; 51:23; Joel 1:11; Amos 5:16. Commenting on the latter, James L. Mays, *Amos: A Commentary* (OTL; Philadelphia: Westminster Press, 1969), 98 reflects on the ironic character of farmers and vinedressers called upon to bury their expropriators.

[16] Eng: 4:31. On the בני מחול see W. F. Albright, *Archaeology and the Religion of Israel*, 127 (quoted by Baruch Levine, "The Netînîm," *JBL* 82 [1963]: 212 n.28). Both the Chronicler and Qoh 2:8 recognize male and female singers (mentioned together); I deal with musicians below.

[17] Harris, "Organization," 121–2; Dandamaev, *Slavery in Babylonia*, 547 n.113.

unfree servants and guilds along several centuries, and even more, about their female members. Yet, even if these groups were not slaves, and even if they did technically exclude women—that is, if their wives and daughters did not belong to the labor force—still labor for these institutions affected women's lives, especially when it was imposed on people (by corvée or to pay off debts for loans, for instance).

What do we know of each group? Not much individually, but they give us a panorama of ancient life and social relationships.

נתינים — *Those Donated*

The נתינים are generally regarded as temple slaves. Considering the extent and economic function of temples, and their need for workers in agriculture, husbandry, textiles, water, bread making, and all priestly daily duties, it is not far-fetched to state that temples had slaves. Although no decisive answer on this issue can be found in the Bible, considering neighboring societies the possibility cannot be ruled out. Leviticus 27, a chapter appended to the Holiness Code, regulates the transference of vowed property to the temple, including persons, animals, and immovable property.[18] Probably most of these devoted persons or objects were redeemed by silver, but others might have been given to the temple and thus become its property. Leviticus 27 specifies the monetary value of women to be redeemed, so it considers the possibility of "נתינות"—even if unrecorded.

Levine demonstrated the close historical and linguistic parallels between the נתינים and the Ugaritic guild of the *ytnm*, who were cultic personnel, but not slaves.

> An investigation into the formulation of personnel lists both at Ugarit and in the biblical sources results in the following analysis: The formula *bn X* means: a guild member (or royal official) identified in terms of a) a patronymic, b) a derivative place name, or c) a skill by which the guild is known. This analysis would apply in every respect to the list of *netînîm* in Ezra 2, wherein the *bn X* formula is used.
>
> We thus have a comparative argument for the guild character of the biblical *netînîm*: 1) An historical relationship existed between the Ugaritic and biblical guilds. 2) Biblical records list personnel in the same manner as do Ugaritic lists. 3) The cultic guild structure of biblical Israel is patterned after the Ugaritic model, which might have been the Canaanite model as well. Both

---

[18] Gerstenberger, *Leviticus*, 19. Levine, *Leviticus*, 193 points out that "the verb *hipli?*, with a final *alef*, is a variant of the verb *palah*, with a final *heh*, a verb whose meaning is clearly known: 'to set apart.' The term *neder* here refers to the substance of the vow, to what is pledged, not to the original pronouncement of the vow; hence the preferred translation 'votary offering.'" (and 213 n.1 and 2).

biblical and Ugaritic sources indicate clearly that the *ytnm-netînîm* were part of the guild system of their respective societies.[19]

Levine's comparison of the formula בֶּן־ ("son of") for a guild member at Ugarit and in the Bible, and the parallel between these two societies in terms of temple personnel is important for this study.[20]

חטבי עצים ושאבי מים — *The Wood Hewers and Water Drawers*

Nehemiah 11:3 mentions also the בני עבדי שלמה, who, according to Rabbinic tradition, were descendants of the Gibeonites (Josh 9), whom David made slaves—an inference which, Levine points out, does not find support in the biblical text. In Levine's opinion, the position that the בני עבדי שלמה were state slaves is wrongly inferred from 1 Kgs 9:15–28, where two different groups are mentioned: those levied and enslaved from the native population, and a group from the Israelites, who were Solomon's "'warriors, *his royal officers*, his commanders, his *šālišîm*, and the captains of his chariotry and cavalry.' *ᶜabdê Šelômô* of vs. 27 are to be identified with the 'royal officers' of vs. 22, and not with the levies of 20."[21] Levine is right in pointing out that Josh 9 says nothing about the בני עבדי שלמה who returned with Nehemiah. On the other hand, there is merit in the rabbinic tradition, because it picks up a lost trend and ties it to another textual cord, so to speak, creating a semantic knot. Joshua 9 tells how the Gibeonites managed to make the Israelites let them live, despite YHWH's commandment to annihilate every people on the land. Since the Israelites had given their word, they made a compromise: they let them live but made them "hewers of wood and drawers of water (חטבי עצים ושאבי מים) for the congregation and for the altar of the LORD, to continue to this day, in the place that he should choose" (*NRSV*). Hewing trees and fetching water would be heavy tasks for the women; however, women have been (and still are whenever these tasks are still done manually) responsible for fetching wood and water to ensure cooking, cleaning and heating. Hewers alone, presumably males, appear in other texts, such as Deut 19:5, Jer 46:22 or Ezek 39:10. But these are about all the occurrences of this stem חטב I. With regard to water, most scenes at a well in the Hebrew Bible involve women, not men. There, they meet prospective

---

[19] Baruch Levine, "The *Netînim*," 212.

[20] Levine, *"Netînim,"* 207–12. The main concern of Levine's paper is to claim that the נתינים and the בני עבדי שלמה were temple guilds but not slaves, and had been free also in pre-exilic times. While his argument for these groups as guilds is well-taken, discussion about their slave status requires far more information than there is available and is therefore debatable. See also Wilfred Watson, "Archaic elements in the language of Chronicles," *Bibl* 53 (1972): 204–5, 11.1, where he adds to Levine's list of parallel temple guilds at Ugarit and the Bible.

[21] Levine, *"Netînim,"* 209.

husbands, future kings, and even the Messiah (John 4). Notice also the indication of a customary way, לְעֵת צֵאת הַשֹּׁאֲבִים, literally "the time of the going out of the female (water) drawers" (Gen 24:11).[22]

But not everything was so safe there, as these three very interesting stories tell us. The first encounter at a well between Moses and his bride-to-be (and all her sisters) results in Moses defending them from the shepherds, so that they would not be harassed and would not have to wait until every male had watered his animals: "An Egyptian man saved us from the hand of the shepherds and he even drew water for us and watered the flock." (Exod 2:1). That this was extraordinary is evident in their father's inquiry about the reasons why they had returned unusually early. A second interesting little piece of information is provided in the book of Ruth, when Boaz instructs her (at that time, a daily worker at his field) that she is allowed to drink water drawn by his נְעָרִים when she is thirsty (Ruth 2:9), rather than having to fetch water for herself and for other workers. This indicates a kind gesture on his side, just as several others in this story. Finally, 2 Sam 23:16 and its parallel in 1 Chr 11 tells us of three men breaking through the Philistines' stronghold and fetching water from the well at Bethlehem as a sign both of their courage and their commitment to their lord David. This is a male story, for it has to do with warring and proving their faithfulness, rather than with water itself.

Perhaps we should apply the proverbial "Solomonic wisdom" and split these two occupations, so that Gibeonite men would be hewers and Gibeonite women would be water fetchers. After all, the "mother of the water fetchers" is Rebekah, with an enthusiasm and a strength hard to emulate (see Gen 24). She is the first one of whom the verb "fetching (water)," שָׁאַב is used and the one who takes on most of its occurrences![23]

The expression "hewers of wood and drawers of water" could have become a *merismus* indicating "from the first to the last chattel," for it appears with a similar connotation in Deut 29:9–11, the only other text apart from Josh 9 in which both occupations come together: "You stand ... all of you before the LORD your God—the leaders of your tribes, your elders, ... your children, your women, and the foreigners ... from the hewer of your wood to the one who draws your water—to enter into the covenant of YHWH..." At any rate, often the whole family lends hands in a task assigned its head, so that it can be done more quickly and with less effort by the one in charge. It would not be out of the blue to state, therefore, that several women were involved in these two lowly

---

[22] Marsman, *Women*, 406, also thinks "Drawing and carrying home a vital commodity like water was a task both men and women could and did perform in the ancient Near East. However, as is the case up to the present day in the Orient, women were normally supposed to fetch the water a household needed from the well."

[23] It is also true that, according to Exod 2:17–19, the well could turn the battlefield between men and women, perhaps when there were too many herds around. The verb used there is a rare one, דלל.

tasks, when we accept the narrator's story that the entire people became slaves to Israel "until this day," when we look at how many important women appear at a well, and when we realize that, although the text uses the masculine plural participles, it never states only the men were enslaved.

בני עבדי שלמה — *The Company of Solomon's Servants*

Levine is also right in that certain עבדי שלמה were officers and not slaves, an argument strengthened by their descendants being mentioned together with other families who came back from exile. On the other hand, 1 Kgs 9:21–22 is not annalistic, but it is an ideological justification of Solomon's actions, and it should not be taken at face value. Elsewhere DtrH warns about the financial cost for the Israelites of the monarchy, in which officials, chariotry, and cavalry, the same offices Levine insists were not slaves, are depicted as the high price of having a king—and they are exacted from the people, at any rate. Levine is right in that they were not legal slaves, but the great institutions were based on labor (most of which cannot be said to have been given willingly by the farmers), whether called בני עבדי שלמה or not.

Mendelsohn believes that, in time, these groups were merged; unlike Levine, he takes the נתינים to have been temple slaves:

> Under the new ecclesiastical order established by Nehemiah and Ezra, the *benê ʿabdê šelômô*, consisting of the descendants of the enslaved Canaanites to whom in course of time other foreigners were added, were merged with the *netînîm*, the temple slaves. The end of independent statehood marked also the end of state slavery.[24]

And Sara Japhet has noted that, unlike other groups, the בני עבדי שלמה are not taken up in Chronicles. There seems, thus, to be biblical corroboration of Mendelsohn's point.[25]

מס and מס-עבד — *Those Submitted to Forced Labor*

Besides the בני עבדי שלמה, the term מס appears in reference to forced labor, for instance in a law concerning a city that submits to Israel's terms and is not destroyed, to peoples whom Israel could not drive out of the land, and in a few texts, to an officer in charge of labor gangs.[26] A second expression related to this

---

[24] Mendelsohn, *Slavery in the ANE*, 98.
[25] S. Japhet, *I & II Chronicles* (OTL. Louisville: Westminster/John Knox, 1993), 208.
[26] Deuteronomy 20:11 (a city that surrenders), Josh 17:17, Judg 1:28–35, 2 Sam 20:24, 1 Kgs 4:6, and 2 Chr 10:18 (those whom Israel could not drive out of the land), and Exod 1:11 (Egyptian bondage on Israel).

one but not exactly synonymous, is מס־עבד, which appears only three times, two of which, Josh 16:10 and 1 Kgs 9:21 pertain to this discussion.[27]

Mendelsohn sees מס and מס־עבד as two parts of a three-fold institution of state slavery, together with the בני עבדי שלמה. He reduces מס־עבד to 1 Kgs 9:21 and its parallel in 2 Chronicles, and dismisses the appearances in Gen 49 and in Josh 16:10.

> The term *mas* is employed in a three-fold sense: (1) when used in reference to conquered nations, particularly to Canaanites, it means "payment of tribute"; (2) when used in reference to Israelites it means *corvée*; and (3) *mas ʿōbēd* means "total slavery." The term *mas ʿōbēd* is found three times: Genesis 49:15, Joshua 16:10, and I Kings 9:21. Disregarding the *ʿōbēd* in Genesis 49:15 as a poetical exaggeration of Issachar's fate, and the *ʿōbēd* after *mas* in Joshua 16:10 as inconsistent with the numerous statements dealing with the same subject that use only *mas*, the term *mas ʿōbēd* in I Kings 9:21 leaves no doubt of its real meaning: The Canaanites were reduced by Solomon to *mas ʿōbēd* "state slavery," in contradistinction to the Israelites, whom he did not reduce to the status of *ʿabādîm* "slaves" (I Kings 9:22, II Chron. 8:9), but merely made them subject to the *mas corvée* (I Kings 5:27).[28]

R. de Vaux translates מס־עבד as "servile levy," a distinction from מס which seems to have been more a literary device than a reflection of reality during the monarchy.

> We may question this distinction, by which the redactor tries to exempt the Israelites from a burden (cf. [1 Kgs 9] v. 22) to which they had in fact been subjected, according to the early documents of 1 K 5:27; 11:28. But the important point is that he adds (1 K 9:21) that the Canaanites remained slaves 'until this day'. In his time, therefore, at the end of the monarchy, there were State slaves, whose institution was ascribed to Solomon.[29]

More recently, Nadav Na'aman has traced the meaning of the term מס־עבד and confirmed these divergent connotations. In the earliest sources it indicates, just as in 1 Kgs 9:15–22, "men conscripted for activities far from home." Later, it became "placed in bondage," usually through the construction היה למס but

---

[27] A. Soggin, *Joshua* (OTL. Philadelphia: SCM, 1972), 162–163 (translation), 180 (commentary). 1 Kgs 9:21–22 is considered a late addition, especially because of its contradictory information with early texts. See J. Gray, *I & II Kings: A Commentary* (London: SCM; Philadelphia: Westminster, 1963), 222 for example: "Certain statements in this passage suggest that they were drawn from royal annals, e.g. vv. 11b, 14 .... The account of events leading up to Jeroboam's revolt (esp. 11.29; cf. 5.13) contradicts the statement that only the Canaanite subjects of Solomon were put to forced labour, hence vv. 20–22 is also probably a late gloss." Similarly J. Montgomery, *A Critical and Exegetical Commentary on the Books of Kings* (ICC. New York: Scribner's, 1951), 210.

[28] Mendelsohn, *Slavery in the ANE*, 97, 149.

[29] de Vaux, *Ancient Israel*, II. 89.

also למס ... שים or למס ... נתן, "expressed by the liability for conscription in the service of the conqueror" or, in other words, being levied, far from home (again) but this time because of forced displacement by the conqueror.[30]

This short review supports the contention that there was state slavery in Israel, even if details about its function, technical terms, and even internal organization are unclear. State slaves provided the necessary workforce for large state projects, such as building cities, fortresses, roads, temples or mining, which would have been too costly for private enterprise (and too costly for private owners in terms of the slaves' lives lost in the enterprise, while the state could always wage war against neighbors, buy slaves or adjust the corvée system). The Dtr makes no issue of submitting foreign peoples to slavery—it is either that or being submitted to slavery, depending on faithfulness to YHWH. On the submission of Israelites by Israelites, the DtrH is more ambiguous. On the one hand, it "clears" Solomon by stating that he made slaves only of the Canaanites. On the other hand, he sees the great discontent of the Northern tribes at Solomon's hardship on them (a heavy yoke) as the reason for their secession. What is not explained is how the system worked and neither מס nor מס־עבד are explicitly mentioned.[31]

בני־הנביאים and חבל־נביאים — The Company of the Prophets

When a very poor widow, on the fringe of losing her sons because of debt-slavery, cried to Elisha for help, she referred to her deceased husband as עבדך אישי "your servant my husband" whom Elisha knew "feared YHWH" (עבדך היה ירא את־יהוה), 2 Kgs 4:1–7. Although both depictions could be only secondary evidence, together with her presentation at the beginning of the verse as "a wife of the men of the sons of the prophets" or, in better English, "the wife of a member of the company of prophets" (v. 1a, *NRSV*), they point to a guild of prophets or at least a group of prophets associated with Elisha (and with Elijah, see 2 Kgs 2). This mention is not alone. Part of Saul's confirmation as God's chosen king was an encounter with a band (חבל) of prophets coming down from a regional sanctuary and falling with them into a prophetic frenzy (1 Sam 10:10–13). These prophets may or may not have been only males.[32]

---

[30] Na'aman, "From Conscription," 753. G. Chirichigno, *Debt Slavery*, 118 believes the foreigners on whom Solomon imposed מס־עבד *mas ʿōbēd* forced labor, "either worked for longer periods of time or they (more likely) became the permanent possessions of the king (e.g., semi-free), a status that parallels that of the Israelites in Egypt."

[31] For instance, questions about which Israelites were recruited, who enjoyed exemption from corvée, how long corvée took, whether every family was recruited, whether it was a one-time event or periodical, and whether women were subject to it and in what ways and capacities.

[32] Gafney, *Daughters of Miriam*, 42 considers 1 Sam 10:11 and 19:20 (להקת הנביאים) refer to guilds.

One should not dismiss female prophetic participation too easily, since the ancestors of prophecy are two mothers, Miriam and Deborah, and both are highly honored in their leading role as singers and musicians, like these prophets.[33] Wilda Gafney finds in the Bible three kinds of prophetic guilds, to wit:

> In regard to gender, there are three guild groupings of prophets attested to in the Hebrew scriptures: (1) those that are presumed to be all male because of masculine plural descriptors and a lack of delineated female presence—most references to the disciples of the prophets, *beney hannevi'im*, fit into this category; (2) mixed-gender groups such as the guild in 2 Kings 4 in which women are present as the conjugal partners of male prophets and possibly as prophets themselves; and (3) all-female guilds—the vilified community of female prophets, *hammitnabbe'ot*, in Ezekiel 13 is the exemplar.[34]

As already discussed, there were several women closely related to music, worship, prophecy and especially to divinatory and magic practices deemed "abominable" by pure Yahwists, while others, like this widow, seem to belong to a group in good standing with Yahwism. At any rate, my main point in this section is to call attention to the possible "wives of members of companies of prophets" like the starving widow saved thanks to Elisha's advice, who may have been involved in prophetic activity as part of hereditary guilds.

יליד (ה)בית — The Home-Born

Especially difficult to locate is the יליד (ה)בית because the phrase can be literally translated "the child/ren of the household," including both free and unfree children; but it can also be interpreted as those born in the household of a slave mother, and/or those rescued from exposure and brought up in the household, who would also have been slaves. When Abraham is ordered that every male of his house be circumcised, YHWH says, "When he is eight days old, will be circumcised every male in his generation, one born in the house and one acquired by money from every foreigner who is not from your own seed." (Gen 17:12). While here "born in the house" seems to include free and enslaved and is contrasted with those coming from outside, most translations use "home-born slave."[35] Similarly, the law on those allowed to eat from the sacred donations stipulates that the person acquired by a priest with his money and the

---

[33] Marsman, *Women*, 556, quotes Carol and Eric Meyers' work on Zech 12:12–14, where mourners are mentioned especially. See also below, on singers.

[34] Gafney, *Daughters of Miriam*, 119.

[35] Less ambivalent is Jer 2:14, because there is no contrast, but parallelism: "Is Israel a slave? (עֶבֶד), one house-born (יליד בית)? Why has he become plunder?"

one born in his house may eat (Lev 22:11). Here again, the home-born are paired with the ones bought from without.

According to Willesen, יָלִיד (or plural יְלִדֵי־) only appears in conjunction with terms denoting a particular group, never occurring in conjunction with a gentilic, for which בֶּן־ is used.[36] Willesen concludes that "the root *yld* always implies subordination and dependence, and in our compounds the second elements only assert to whom or what the person in question was born and therefore subordinate. In face of this we cannot claim that the notion of subordination is constituted by the compound, but it is implied in the word *yālīd*."[37]

The disappointed king impersonated in Qoheleth enumerates, among his many (and senseless) riches, "male and female slaves (עֲבָדִים וּשְׁפָחוֹת), and home-born slaves (children of the house בְּנֵי־בַיִת, Qoh 2:7), herds and flocks." Perhaps the difference in vocabulary is due only to the particularities of this book and the meaning intended would have been exactly the same as the יְלִדֵי־בַיִת. Were there a difference, it would not be between free or unfree, judging from their place in this list. Here again, the porousness of language points to the inclusion of slaves as part of the household in which they grew, to the denial of an identity as adult for the slave, and to the subordinated role children played even in their own families. Indirectly, they attest also to foreigners being bought and incorporated into the household. Many of these must have been women.

שָׂכִיר — *The Hired Laborer*

The adjective שָׂכִיר, "hired," appears ten times in legal texts in the Torah. The information one may glean from these is scant, but it seems to apply both to Israelites under indentured work (Lev 19:13) and to foreigners (they are not allowed to partake of the holy, see Exod 12:45, Lev 22:10); and they were among the poorest (see Deut 15:18; 24:14). Besides these instances, the term appears three times in the Joban poetry. There is also a handful of appearances in the prophets; these share the same impression as to their precarious situation (see especially Jer 46:21). Even though the only feminine term does not refer to a person (Isa 7:20), nothing precludes the presence of women among the poorest

---

[36] F. Willesen, "The *Yālīd* in Hebrew Society," *ST* 12 (1958): 192–3.

[37] Willesen, "The *Yālīd* in Hebrew Society," 197–98. Notice 198 n.10 (in brackets in the quotation above): "P. HEINISCH, *Das Sklavenrecht in Israel und im alten Orient* (Studia Catholica 11/1934–5), stresses the fact that the concept of slavery in the ancient Near East was not that of our time. 'It was paternal refuge for the impoverished and a sanctuary for conquered aliens,' NORTH, op. cit. [*Sociology of the Biblical Jubilee* (AnBib 4/1954)], p. 135."

who had to hire themselves out, perhaps in the hope of not having to fall into permanent slavery.

חפשי — *The Client*

The adjective חפשי should also be mentioned here, a term that appears in the texts concerning release of slaves, and in a few poetic texts, and is usually translated "freed." Niels Lemche, however, has suggested that the חפשי —at least the one in 1 Sam 17:25—was a client of the king, getting sustenance, rather than exemption from taxes, from the royal household. The issue deserves a study of its own; for the present discussion what matters is that a חפשי would have been in a precarious situation, either economically (if a semi-free peasant, or a manumitted slave) or socially (if a temple slave or a client) and would not have been among the privileged rich or independent. Furthermore, considering the Deuteronomic injunction to give lavishly to the debt-slave who leaves you (Deut 15, esp. v 18), one may assume a clientship relationship, even if only informally stated in our sources.[38] Even though the adjective appears only in masculine (singular and plural), at least in Deut 15:12 it includes women: "if your brother, a Hebrew man, or a Hebrew woman is sold to you ... you shall let him [or her] go free" (חפשי).

SUMMING UP

Were women part of all these groups? There were, for sure, daughters, wives and mothers of those enslaved men from the groups so indicated (servants, prisoners subject to forced labor, Canaanites). In my opinion, women related to these groups were also bound workers, although we do not have information on them. There were also women donated as votaries to the temple and, obviously there were women amongst those "born in the household" and—judging from ANE sources—some were freed and some remained slaves forever.

What cannot be ascertained so clearly is that they worked in the same occupations as their husbands or fathers. Since slavery is a social and economic

---

[38] The main difference between master-slave and patron-client relationships is that the latter is (at least in theory) a voluntary association, although it is doubtful that an indentured slave, for instance, who was to start anew, would have other options. See Ralph W. Klein, *1 Samuel* (WBC 10; Waco: Word Books, 1983), 178; McCarter, *1 Samuel* (AB; Garden City: Doubleday, 1980), 304. On patronage see R. Saller, "Patronage and Friendship in Early Imperial Rome: Drawing the Distinction," *Patronage in Ancient Society* (ed. A. Wallace-Hadrill. London: Routledge, 1989), 49–62; Mendelsohn, "The Canaanite Term for 'Free Proletarian,'" *BASOR* 83 (1941): 36–39; "New Light on the *Hupšu*," *BASOR* 139 (1955): 9–11; E. R. Lacheman, "Note on the Word *Hupšu* at Nuzi," *BASOR* 86 (1942): 36–37; Lemche, "חפשי in 1 Sam. XVII 25," and "The Hebrew and the Seven Year Cycle," 71–72 and 72 n.29; Frank S. Frick, *The City in Ancient Israel* (Missoula: Scholars Press, 1977), 98, 151–52, n.111.

institution, I am inclined to believe that the majority of these women were also ascribed to groups or guilds, so that control was easier. I suggest that, the more public the profession and the more related to issues of purity, the lesser probabilities to find there female workers. For instance, men who prepared the animals or the bread for daily sacrifices at the temple would more likely be controlled by functionaries (priests?) and would have been restricted from women for the sake of purity taboos.

SECTION II: DTRH REDACTORS FALL SHORT OF THE MARK

My title for Section II is accurate, even though not very academic. In this section I look at hints within the DtrH about tasks regularly realized by women—and specialized women—in which none of the terms for female occupations dealt with in last chapter is used, nor is it totally ignored (those come in Section III). Sometimes these women are mentioned in passing, as "the women who were doing so-and-so" and sometimes they are depicted only within the religious realm.

נצבות(ה) *and* הנשים הצבאות — *Women on Duty*

Starting from Josh 1, only one birth is recorded in the DtrH: that of Ichabod, son of an unnamed woman and a deceased paternal line (1 Sam 4). He is the only survivor of the priest Eli's lineage. His mother is a theologian, as we will see soon; so the narrative becomes important in itself. As YHWH had announced, Eli's two sons Hophni and Phineas died in battle against the Philistines. Eli died when he heard the news and fell from his chair on his neck, and the ark of God was lost.

> His daughter-in-law, Phineas' wife, was pregnant and about to give birth. And she heard the news that God's ark had been taken and that her father-in-law and her husband had died. And she bowed down and delivered, for her labor pain came suddenly. As it was time for her death, the women attending her (הנצבות עליה) said to her "Do not fear, for you have borne a son." (אל־תיראי כי בן ילדת) But she did not answer, paid no heed. And she called the baby Ichabod ("Where is the Glory?"), saying "The Glory has departed from Israel because God's ark has been taken," and because of her father-in-law and her husband. And she said "The Glory of Israel departed, for God's ark has been taken." (1 Sam 4:19–22)

Her story shares a common theme with that of the matriarch Rachel: delivery of a son, the woman/en attending comfort her with the announcement of the son's birth, the mother names the son and dies.[39] The main differences are that Rachel is having her second son, who will be Jacob's favorite ('Do not be afraid; for this one is also a son' אל־תיראי כי־גם־זה לך בן, Gen 35:17),while Phineas's unnamed widow seems to be delivering her only child. The second difference is the theological statement put in her lips, as a foil to Rahab's earlier statement on God's power—only that this time it is not a foreigner and that power has departed from the land. Still a third difference is the use of different terms to refer to those attending the woman in labor. Rachel is helped by one midwife, המילדת while Hophni's widow has attendants around her, הנצבות עליה. Even a cursory reading of these similar stories shows attendants fulfilling the same tasks for the woman about to deliver. There is, however, more to say about this circumlocution for "midwife" in 1 Sam 4.

The Constructions הנצבים and הנצבות[40]

The verb is a *nip ʿal* plural participle of נצב, on whose meaning dictionaries agree:

> The basic sense of the Niphal stem of *nāṣab* is well illustrated in God's order to Moses to "stand (i.e., station himself) by the river's brink" to meet Pharaoh (Ex 7:15) .... The Niphal ptc. with the article occurs in Ruth 2:5, designating a certain servant 'that was set over' the reapers.
>
> The passive sense of the Niphal is more evident in those cases where stand is equivalent to "be stationed" by appointment or in fulfillment of duty. Hence we find Samuel "standing as appointed over" (*ʿōmēd niṣṣāb*) the company of prophets, in I Sam 19:20. The participle is used as substantive, "deputy, prefect," in I Kgs 4:5,7, and 27 [H 5:7], 45:16 [H30]; 9:23; II Chr 8:10. The usage in I Sam 19 indicates the verb *naṣab* has a more specific, technical connotation than its synonym *ʿamad*.[41]

This quotation looks at three very important and related characteristics of this verb: to station oneself to fulfill a task, to be appointed in fulfillment of duty, and to be a prefect. All of them point to responsibility and duty in the face

---

[39] See S. Schäfer-Bossert, "Den Männern die Macht und der Frau die Trauer? Ein Kritischer Blick auf die Deutung von אין – oder: Wie nennt Rahel ihren Sohn?," in *Feministische Hermeneutik und Erstes Testament: Analysen und Interpretationen* (ed. H. Jahnow et al. Stuttgart: Kohlhammer, 1994), 106–25.

[40] See also chapter 1 on the different combinations of "person" + participle.

[41] *Theological Wordbook of the Old Testament* (ed. R. Harris, G. Archer, Jr., & B. Waltke; Chicago: Moody Press, 1980), II.591; GK III.675, "sich hinstellen," "hingestellt sein, stehen," and "fest sein"; *BDB,* 662, includes to station oneself and to take one's stand for a definite purpose," as discussed in chapter 1.

of a task, and none less than Moses, Samuel, and David's officers are brought as example. However, does נצבות have the same connotations of God-given duty and responsibility that the dictionary finds in males? Is it dissolved when applied to a woman in the Bible? These questions seek to address two issues. The first is to alert to scholars' biases, for instance in failing to give equal value to men and women described with the same Hebrew word (as is the case with the *nip'al* of נצב). The second issue is to further address the realization made in chapter 1, that there is a difference in meaning between occurrences of the participle as noun and as adjective to another noun for "person."

In Samuel-Kings, the masculine plural (always *nip'al*) appears often with the denotation of "chief officers" or a "guard" around their commander. It appears as a military term, for instance, in 1 Kgs 4:7 in reference to Solomon's twelve "district governors,"[42] who provided food for the king on a monthly-based system. It also appears in Ruth 2:6–7, where Boaz's supervisor and reporter is called "the dependent in charge of the reapers" הנער הנצב על־הקוצרים. As discussed in chapter 1, most combinations of a term for "person" (here הנער) with the participle for a function or profession (הנצב) might indicate a less formal (or the beginning of a) working relation than the participle alone would convey. This particular instance would either contradict my theory of a kind of *ad hoc* status or it would indicate that this נער did not have a permanent position as supervisor at Boaz's service.

The masculine participle הנצב appears in compound formulas of the type "person + participle" similar to the one just seen in Ruth 2:6–7; yet, unlike other cases noted in chapter 1, they are built with participles or nouns other than אנשים/איש. One of these cases is 1 Sam 22:17, where the participle accompanies another participle acting as noun: ויאמר המלך לרצים הנצבים עליו "The king spoke to the guard stationed by him."[43] The feminine of נצב appears in reference to Hannah (1 Sam 1), and to Wisdom (Prov 8:2).[44] Hannah certainly had a purpose as she stood stationed in the temple, expecting a blessing

---

[42] Thus translated by Na'aman, "From Conscription," 750. Other examples are 1 Kgs 4:5; 5:7. The verb also means "to stand with a purpose" but not necessarily appointed to any function: Moses and Aaron stand or wait נצבים in the supervisors' way, Exod 5:20 or YHWH stands beside Jacob in his dream, Gen 28:13.

[43] "The guard" is literally those who run, רוץ; and נצב על has the meaning of being appointed, thus "stationed."

[44] *BDB*, 662. Compare with Hannah's self-presentation to Eli the priest in a previous chapter: "I am the woman who stood beside you …" אני האשה הנצבת עמכה (1 Sam 1:26). It might be just chance that one is used as adjective to the noun אשה; however, chances are that there is more to it here, that Hannah is not "stationed with any appointed duty" and that is implied by the use of the noun אשה and avoidance of the preposition על. The feminine הנצבה appears in Zech 11:16 speaking figuratively of sheep standing firm in contrast to feeble ones, but it is a dubious case, and the image connotes the quality of firmness, but not of purpose or task. Cf. also Ps 45:10.

from Eli that would confirm God's willingness to listen to her sorrows; yet, a purpose is not an office or an occupation. Is that the reason why she uses the formula הַאִשָּׁה הַנִּצֶּבֶת "the woman who stood ..." (1 Sam 1:26)? Hannah is not "stationed with any appointed duty" and that may be implied by the use of the noun אִשָּׁה and avoidance of the preposition עַל. Lady Wisdom, calling people from the hills to learn from her is more assertive in her task. A task not explicitly said to be ordered by God, but which, considering her supernatural origin, in itself bears weight in terms of responsibility.[45]

Then, were these נִצָּבוֹת attending to Phineas's widow professionals or *ad hoc* neighbors and relatives? Could women from the priestly families become unclean by attending a birth or would they have called at least one outsider, a professional who was at any rate contaminated by blood because of her profession?

Perhaps the difference in terms lies in that מְיַלֶּדֶת implies a "certified" practitioner who walked with the couple from the start (before conception), while הַצָּבָאוֹת (those standing by her) refers to female neighbors or friends, who came to support her during delivery, due to the absence of the midwife. Perhaps it was Dtr's preference to use הַצָּבָאוֹת in 1 Sam 4:19–22, while both terms were equally used as synonyms. Or perhaps, taking Frank Frick's insights concerning the use of terms for "poor" in DtrH, the writer wanted to avoid the explicit term "מְיַלֶּדֶת."[46]

There is a second lexeme to be briefly mentioned. It appears a few chapters earlier, where the reason for the impending destruction of Eli's lineage is mentioned (1 Sam 2:12–36). The priest at Shiloh, Eli, would not correct his wicked sons, who would lay with "the women who served at the entrance to the tent of meeting" (v. 22, *NRSV*) הַצֹּבְאוֹת פֶּתַח אֹהֶל מוֹעֵד הַנָּשִׁים. The plural participle (feminine in form) of צָבָא is very common as "troops" and the noun is well known from the expression "YHWH Sebaoth." Thus, its connotation is that of people gathered in order and for a purpose, not just any aggregation. The same participle is also used in Exod 38:8, apparently for the same (otherwise unidentified) "guild" or association, located at the entrance to the tent of

---

[45] This is not the place to enter a discussion about Lady Wisdom as divine or not, but at least one can state that she is eternal, since time and space belong to creation, and she is "pre-creational." Camp, *Wisdom and the Feminine*, 129 notes the indirect but interesting connection between wisdom standing at the gate where justice is administered and Boaz's words telling Ruth that she is recognized as a woman of valor by all the people at the gate.

[46] Frank S. Frick, "*Cui Bono?*—History in the Service of Political Nationalism: The Deuteronomistic History as Political Propaganda," *Semeia* 66 (1994), especially 80–83, 88–90, shows how one of Dtr's strategies for taking sides with the political and religious upper class is by avoiding (or using with a different meaning) biblical vocabulary for "poor." Note, however, Lohfink's study on the use of poverty terminology in Deuteronomy, "Poverty in the Laws of the Ancient Near East and of the Bible," 44–47, where "the stranger, the orphan, and the widow" are distinguished from the אֶבְיוֹן or the עָנִי.

meeting. There are several obscure data, such as what were the functions of these women ascribed to the tent of meeting, how did they belong (Election? Selection? Hereditary? Priests' daughters?) and what was their descriptive name. We know very little indeed.[47]

In short, the occurrence of the two participles הצבאות and הצבאות "(the one/s) standing with a task" has added important evidence concerning the presence of women at certain posts as opposed to casual standing, even if usually unrecognized by the texts and most translations.

As will be discussed in chapter 6 concerning women who take care of royal children, stories of childbirth only appear in the Hebrew Bible when some extraordinary, dangerous event happens. Otherwise, writers overlook a moment which was so fundamental, for the woman involved, for the newborn, and for her husband and immediate family, as it involved high life-risk, a new member of the family and a prospective heir.

Pregnancy and childbirth are among the few moments mentioned in the biblical tradition when a woman has particular, gender-determined needs, and these are hardly mentioned in these texts. And when mentioned, it is with a circumlocution. Many other needs are not gender distinct, such as consumption of oils, food, or mourning rituals.[48] Still, there is no particular information as to whether women used other services, for instance the advice of wise women or prophetesses on economic or family issues, or the use of a young virgin to keep warm an elderly woman in a way comparable to that performed for David in 1 Kgs 1.[49] We do not even hear whether kings' daughters also had "nannies" to look after them, or only (some) sons did. These are some of the hidden women whom we have only partially identified.

מבשׂרת — *Bringers of News*

It is usual to find in commentaries assertions that it was expected (thus honorable) for women to remain inside their home, while men would go freely between cities, and among families, negotiating and performing the political, socio-economic, cultural, and religious tasks. If this is so, one would not expect to find female messengers or "bringers of news," for it would belong to their job

---

[47] See my "La ley y el orden. Una apreciación del material legal y cultual en el libro del Éxodo," in *Relectura del Éxodo* (ed. I. Gómez Acebo; Bilbao: Desclée de Brower, 2006), 254–58.

[48] Jephthah's daughter inaugurates a ritual to which "the daughters of Israel" would go every year for four days (Judg 11:40). This is a particular female event, but it does not mention any particular leader. One might also imagine some type of rite of passage when a woman reached menopause, as in many societies menopause frees women to participate in ceremonies tabooed to her during menstruation or childbirth.

[49] It is not attested of other men either.

description to have to be out of home.[50] According to some scholars, bringers of news were one of the important political functionaries in the ANE, for some of their tasks were to call people (men?) to corvée service, restore runaway slaves to their owners, and other unpleasant tasks on behalf of their lord, usually the king.[51] Studying the commercial exchange between Egypt and western Asia during the Late Bronze age (*ca.* 1500–1350 B.C.E.), Graciela Gestoso Singer states that the Amarna correspondence offers a wide range of tasks. While conveyance of messages was one of them, messengers' most important responsibilities were those related to the diplomatic political realm:

> Sus funciones más importantes fueron: 1) llevar la correspondencia diplomática; 2) comunicar mensajes orales; 3) actuar como lector de los mensajes reales, proveyéndosele—a veces—de un "intérprete" (ac. *targumannu*); 4) llevar regalos reales; 5) conducir y presentar ante el rey a las jóvenes entregadas por los países dominados; 6) acompañar a la hija de un rey extranjero, prometida como esposa real; 7) recolectar el tributo para el faraón, y 8) informar acerca de la situación política de los países extranjeros.[52]

More focused on conscription, another scholar states:

> The office of *'al hammas* "in charge of the levy" is functionally similar to that of the herald (*nāgiru*) in Mesopotamia … The herald performed different functions in different historical periods in different kingdoms, but conscripting workers to forced labor was basic to his job (Sassmannhausen 1995:129–36). Hence, his activities are sometimes associated with the verb *šasû* "call, exclaim," or the noun *šisītu* "a cry, proclamation" (CAD Š/2, 147, 152).[53]

Thus, it entailed more responsibility than bringing back and forth messages and news. It was, somehow, "double-duty" or "double-edged," a sort of ambassador responsible for the king's commands' observance. This would have

---

[50] I took the expression "bringer of news" from Pamela Tamarkin Reis, "Killing the Messenger: David's Policy or Politics?" *JSOT* 31 (2006):171. It avoids misunderstanding with the other term, the מלאך; I use both here.
[51] Snell, *Flight and Freedom*, 49–50.
[52] Graciela Gestoso Singer, *El intercambio de bienes entre Egipto y Asia Anterior: Desde el reinado de Tutmosis III hasta el de Akhenaton* (Ancient Near Eastern Monographs/Monografías sobre el Antiguo Cercano Oriente. 2nd ed.; Buenos Aires: SBL/Centro de Estudios de Historia del Antiguo Oriente, Universidad Católica Argentina, 2008), 72 (with bibliography).
[53] Na'aman, "From Conscription," 750; ref. to L. Sassmannhausen "Funktion und Stellung der Herolde (NIMGIR/*nāgiru*) im Alten Orient," *Baghdader Mitteilungen* 26, 1995. The quotation ends with a footnote 6 on the same page: "The office of the *nāgiru* was sometimes equated with that of the biblical *mazkir* (Fox 2000:110–21). However, as suggested by Avishur and Heltzer (2000:42–46), the task of the *mazkir* might have been similar to that of the title holder *mnēmōn* in Classical Greek. He was probably a private secretary of the king and among his tasks was memorizing of the political, juridical, and administrative affairs of the kingdom."

made them very unpopular, for sure. I concur with Tamarkin Reis, however, that the "killing of the messenger" is what we would today call an "urban myth."[54]

In the Bible, messengers (root בשׂר) are especially common in the books of Samuel (six texts), in post-exilic prophetic literature and in a few Psalms. In the DtrH we find them often spreading good or bad news about battles (see 2 Sam 18:19), deaths of kings and other leaders (see 1 Sam 4:17 on Phineas and Hophni, Eli's sons; 1 Sam 31:9// 1 Chr 10:9 on Saul and his sons).[55] This is a task that might induce rage, sorrow, or misconception; it is for a trustworthy person:

> Messengers announcing the results of a war appear in the Bible in a standard way: the main protagonists receive the report of the battle which was decided in their absence. The messenger, therefore, connects the battlefield and the leader who did not participate. By means of his report, therefore, the messenger influences the actions and responses of the main protagonist, and may change the course of history.[56]

The verb is used, for instance, when Adonijah and his companions want to know what is the loud noise they hear coming from Jerusalem; here it is not a professional messenger, but a priest who brings the news (1 Kgs 1:42–43). There seems to have existed, however, a profession of female messengers, at least in Mesopotamia and in Israel. Marsman states that they served women. It makes sense, since they would be accessible to important women needing to convey messages, would be trusted to keep confidentiality, and would be able to come and go into the women's quarters. And they would probably be able to come and go more unnoticed than military or royal messengers.[57]"Several professions were regarded as male jobs, although they were sometimes occupied

---

[54] Tamarkin Reis, "Killing," 167.

[55] There is much discussion on whether the stem denotes only good news. Galpaz-Feller, "David and the Messenger – Different Ends, Similar Means in 2 Samuel 1,"*VT* 29 (2009):199 notes that the verb "usually appears in the Bible, and in the cultures of the Ancient Near East in the context of good tidings. The only time the term *mebasser* [*sic*]appears in the Bible in connection with bad news is in the account of the fall of Eben-ezer, 1 Samuel 4:17." Based on the addition of the adjective טוב in some texts, Tamarkin Reis, "Killing," 168–172, prefers a neutral connotation.

[56] Galpaz-Feller, "David," 200. Reliability, is, to Tamarkin Reis, "Killing," 172 the main characteristic of a מבשׂרת over against someone who recounts or tells, "the teller" (המגיד) who "can relay either information or misinformation."

[57] Marsman, *Women*, 411. Galpaz-Feller, "David," 202 notes in reference to 1 Sam 4:12 and 2 Sam 1:2: "In both accounts, the narrator dwells on the messengers' outward appearances. These descriptions of the messengers retard the tempo of the plot, while at the same time alluding to the messages and to their essences." It could be supposed, then, that perhaps they had some distinctive attire, so that they would be recognized once inside the city. On the other hand, maybe not: in these two stories they do not have a uniform in common, but dust on their head and torn clothes.

by women. Often the women in these professions worked for other women. This seems to be the case with female scribes and female messengers."[58] This being so, it is all the more noticeable that Isa 40, with its hope for a new beginning after the exile, uses the image of the messenger of YHWH's good tidings to Jerusalem. And it is a מבשרת (pi ʿel feminine singular) who is twice called to task:

> Upon a high mountain, get you up, O messenger (of/for) Zion (מבשרת ציון)
> Lift up with strength your voice, O messenger (of/for) Jerusalem (מבשרת ירושלם)[59]
> Lift it up! Don't you fear! Tell the towns of Judah: "Look here! Your God!"
> (Isa 40:9)

Perhaps, as suggested by some scholars speaking of ANE gender representations, what really mattered was the function and not the performer, so that both may be invoked within a few chapters: in Isa 41:27, affirms YHWH, "... to Jerusalem I give a מבשר herald (of good tidings)."

> But who is this herald? And why is she feminine? She is clearly a complement to the male herald (מבשר) in 52:7, and thus cannot be identified in any simple sense with Zion/Jerusalem. But she also cannot be separated from other female figures associated with Zion: the "daughter of Zion" of 1:9, the "inhabitant of Zion" (יושבת ציון) of 12:6 etc, and hence the motif of Zion as the spouse of God. The "herald of Zion" may then be an aspect of Zion that is returning to itself, just as God is in v. 3. But the voice of the prophet is also summoning, or claiming, a female counterpart to itself, as if it cannot speak, at least for the moment, except in this disguise. ...
> The herald of Zion/Jerusalem (מבשרת ציון...ירושלם) is presumably human as well as female, in contrast to the ambiguously divine voices in the first part of the passage; at any rate, she is not disembodied. The human quality of the voice is emphasized through the transposition of בשר to מבשרת ציון.[60]

McEvenue goes even further and posits a female author/prophetess as Second Isaiah. Thus, it would make sense to represent herself as מבשרת for that is, precisely, her call.[61] It has long been recognized the "female-sensitive"

---

[58] Marsman, *Women*, 467. Below we address very briefly the scribal profession.

[59] Since nouns or participles of this form do not present differences between the absolute and the construct states, the two parallel constructions, מבשרת ציון and מבשרת ירושלם, may be read as double vocatives or as construct nouns.

[60] Francis Landy, "The Ghostly Prelude to Deutero-Isaiah," *BibInt* 14 (2006): 350–51.

[61] Sean McEvenue, "Who Was Second Isaiah?," in *Studies in the Book of Isaiah: Festschrift for Willem A. M. Beuken* (ed. J. van Ruiten & M. Vervenne; Louvain: Leuven University Press, 1997), 221–22.

tone of the Exilic Isaiah. Based on this fact, Marsman reasons, "It is therefore remarkable, but not problematic that YHWH had a female messenger."[62]

Besides the text just reviewed, a feminine plural participle determined by the article appears in Ps 68:12b: המבשרות צבא רב: "the women that proclaim the tidings are a great host" (JPS). There is general frustration with this Psalm in its entirety, its meaning, bad state of preservation, and other vexing issues. Adding to that the fact that we are focusing only on half a verse, we cannot make much out of this evidence. Verses 12–15 "may be an old, badly preserved victory hymn of the descriptive type, similar to Judg 5:19, 30."[63] Most authors do not comment on the messengers at all. And when they are not ignored, there is much disagreement on the particular referent in the Psalm to these female bringers of good tidings. Some refer them to the doves mentioned in verse 14, thus precluding any human female messenger. Marvin Tate, for instance, translates "A great host of messengers give the (good) news" and explains:

> (1) "the great host" is in apposition to the participle; (2) the news in this context is good, and consists of the material in vv 13–15; (3) we need not think of the messengers as women (though they should not be excluded absolutely) … because is collective. In the *Comment* I accept the interpretation of Eerdmans and Keel that the messengers are the doves of v 14, which has the merit of gender (fem.) between "messengers" and "dove."[64]

Also James Limburg translates "great is the company of those who bore the tidings," without reference to their being female or anything else, except (in his explanation) that "The psalm continues to speak of God with a variety of pictures. Here the Lord gives a command, the armies are victorious, and the enemies run away. The women, who have been staying home caring for the flocks, have the joy of dividing up that which was captured."[65] His comment on the joyous women sharing the spoils among themselves and their families reminds (like other elements in this Psalm) of Judg 5, especially as Sisara's mother comforts herself for her son's delay by thinking the men are splitting

---

[62] Marsman, *Women*, 429, quoting Gruber, "The Motherhood of God in Second Isaiah," *RB* 90 (1983): 354. To be noted is the early date at which Maier Gruber recognized the use of female metaphors to represent the Divine in Isaiah. See also Katheryn Pfisterer Darr, "Two Unifying Female Images in the Book of Isaiah," in *Uncovering Ancient Stones: Essays in Memory of H. Neil Richardson.* (ed. Lewis M. Hofpe; Winona Lake: Eisenbrauns, 1994),17–30; Helen Schüngel-Straumann, *Denn Gott bin ich, und kein Mann*, 57–62; and J. F. A. Sawyer, "Daughter of Zion and Servant of the Lord in Isaiah: A Comparison," *JSOT* 44 (1989): 89–107.

[63] Erhard Gerstenberger, *Psalms, Part 2, and Lamentations* (Forms of the Old Testament Literature XV; Grand Rapids: Eerdmans, 2001), 39.

[64] M. Tate, *Psalms 51–100*, 164 (translation on 126).

[65] J. Limburg, *Psalms* (Louisville: Westminster John Knox, 2000), 226 (translation on 223).

"one womb, two wombs" among the soldiers.[66] Luis Alonso Schökel and Cecilia
Carniti, on the other hand, notice that they are a "host," a specialized, numerous
corps, which could very well indicate a feminine profession, giving examples
from Isaiah: "*mbśrt* puede ser femenino de oficio, como en Is 40,9; 52,7 (cf.
qhlt). Los/las mensajeros/ras son muchos, son un cuerpo especializado
numeroso, para llevar la noticia rápidamente a todos."[67] In short, interpretations
vary greatly on what the מבשׂר(ו)ת means. If the scholars just quoted are right,
what can be safely stated is that there is biblical and extra-biblical evidence that
there were female messengers. It stands to reason that, because of lack of safety
in the roads, because of gender ascription of tasks, and other reasons, they would
be less numerous than their male companions and would serve primarily
women's needs. This is Marsman's conclusion as well:

> The same mechanism [that in general those women who acted as professional
> scribes served only women] might be true for female messengers. Although
> compared to their male colleagues female messengers (*mārat šipri*) are few in
> number, they are attested in various periods of Mesopotamian history. Usually
> women would employ female messengers, but sometimes they used male
> messengers.[68]

A short mention deserves also an effective but unprestigious messenger serving
king David. She was a female slave (השפחה) who carried information about
Absalom's revolt for David (2 Sam 17:17), coming out of the palace and
reporting to Jonathan and Ahimaaz daily; here, again, this was an *ad hoc* task,
not her occupation, and the verb used is נגד "tell," not בשׂר. At any rate,
perhaps experiences like this one—and the presence of prophetesses—allowed
the poets at least to imagine that a bringer of good tidings could be a woman.
Since that is the only acknowledgment they receive from the Dtr, I leave them
hidden among the male corps.

מנחם(מים) — *Comforter(s)*

Perhaps this is a good location to introduce yet another occupation, namely, that
of the comforter, מנחם, *pi'el* participle from נחם. My reason to include them
here and not further below in Section III is mainly the fact that, professionally
speaking, perhaps it was not indispensable; that is to say, it may have been more
the loving service of friends, relatives and neighbors than a profession. מנחם is
often spoken of YHWH toward a human being, in first-person prayers or by a
prophet (Ps 23:4; 71:21; 119:82; Isa 63:13). And because of massive destruction

[66] On this text see the wonderful study by F. van Dijk-Hemmes, "Traces," 43–8; see also above,
chapter 4 on war captives.
[67] Luis Alonso Schökel & Cecilia Carniti, *Salmos* (2 vols.; Estella: Verbo Divino, 1992), 1:884.
[68] Marsman, *Women*, 411.

and death, it is more an absence perceived as needed or wanted than a presence. Comforting beloved ones in mourning often meant sitting with them in despair and silence, as they performed loud cries and wept, wearing sackcloth, refraining from ointment, and sitting in dust.

That at least certain men (perhaps also women?) carried at times this function on an official, diplomatic capacity is clear from 2 Sam 10:3 and its parallel 1 Chr 19:3, where the "messengers with condolences" (*NRSV*) are מנחמים, the "comforters" (*JPS*); non-biblical sources support this as well.[69]

In the Hebrew Bible there is no instance of a feminine participle, although Jacob receives his sons' and daughters' comforting attempts as he learns of Joseph's (supposed) death, Gen 37:35. There are also several plurals, which could include women. At any rate, there is not much more to say about this occupation as it pertains to women's realm, except that because of the typical war dynamics, women and children were more often left alone in the destroyed cities to comfort each other and find ways to survive and to mourn their imprisoned or killed men (in the Bible, Lamentations is especially poignant).

(טוה) *and* ארג *— Spinners and Weavers*

Virtually every commentary on daily life in ancient Israel includes some lines on these activities as typical of women of each household and I would not be the one to contest this. Carol Meyers asserts:

> Women's networks in small agricultural communities function in several important social and economic ways. The nature of women's daily routines in ancient Israel would have been dictated by the division of labor by gender. Women and men each had certain prescribed, gender-specific tasks as well as some that they shared. Most of women's regular tasks involved food preparation (transforming raw products, such as grain, olives, and grapes, into bread, oil, and wine), textile production, and some horticultural work.[70]

A book on daily life published that same year makes a similar assertion:

> Traditionally, weaving was a woman's job (Prov 31:13, 19), although sometimes men were also involved in this activity (Isa 19:9). The different sizes of the loom weights strongly suggest that different types of fabric were woven. Bone spatulas discovered in archaeological excavations imply that Israelite weavers were familiar with pattern weaving. This is corroborated by

---

[69] Xuan Huong Thi Pham, *Mourning in the Ancient Near East and the Hebrew Bible* (JSOTSup 302; Sheffield: Sheffield Academic Press, 1999), 19–20. She also recalls Anath's mourning for Baal according to these Deities' Canaanite poems.

[70] Meyers, "Everyday Life in Biblical Israel: Women's Social Networks," 197–8.

several references to weaving with gold and silver threads (Exod 39:3) and by references to dyed fabrics (Judg 5:30).[71]

And the list could go on, with more specific commentaries about Egypt, Mari, Babylon, and so forth. It is thus all the more noticeable that neither the stem טוה, "to spin" nor ארג "to weave" appear very often at all. Actually, the texts quoted by Borowski are about all there is to find in the Bible.[72] And since they are all very diverse in literary genres and in historical origins, they do not lend easily to further comparison.[73]

The stem טוה appears in only one text, Exod 35:20–29, telling how the whole community, women and men, everybody with a willing heart and skillful, was involved in making the tabernacle in the desert: כל־אשה חכמת־לב "Every skillful woman spun with her hand (טוה, vs.25–26, only occurrences of the verb) and brought in that which (was) spun" מטוה. Since they spun in colors other than the natural linen or wool ("in blue and purple and crimson yarns and fine linen," *NRSV*) they also dyed their yarns. Spinning and weaving were part of the skills women would have learned.[74] Two names are recorded as specialized craftsmen for the Tabernacle hangings: Bezalel, a Judahite, and Oholiab, a Danite, of whom it is said that he was "engraver, designer, and embroiderer in blue, purple, and crimson yarns, and in fine linen" (Exod 38:23, *NRSV,* חרש וחשב ורקם).[75]

Weaving, ארג, is attested only thirteen times in the Hebrew Bible, but whenever the participle has the connotation of a professional weaver (mostly in a fixed comparison, see Isa 38:12, 1 Sam 17:7, 2 Sam 21:19, 1 Chr 11:23, 20:5)

---

[71] Oded Borowski, *Daily Life in Biblical Times* (Atlanta, SBL: 2003), 32.

[72] Isaiah 19:9b is ambiguous, as a perusal of some translations will make evident. There is no verb, so many translations take the first one as doing double-duty and provide a synonym. Here there is a *hapax legomenon* feminine plural שׂריקות, *śĕrîqôt* which *BDB,* 977 takes as adjective "combed, of flax" from שׂרק I, but several translations take it as a double parallel to ארגים (both in meaning and as a masculine-feminine word-pair) for female workers: "and the carders and those at the loom will grow pale" (*NRSV*); "and they that weave cotton, shall be ashamed" (*JPS*).

[73] This is the reason why, after much pondering, I decided to include the whole item on textiles in this chapter and not with the words appearing in DtrH studied in the previous chapter. For the only occurrence in it, 2 Kgs 23:7 puts them as a religious activity (and rather as an aside commentary), much like the other text during the desert narrative, in which women are said to spin and weave. While either location would be possible, it is noteworthy that no mentioning of weavers appears in the whole village-like setting of Joshua-Judges nor in court. Their hiddenness prevails, in my view, over the milieu in which they are located.

[74] Phyllis A. Bird, "Women (OT)," *Missing Persons and Mistaken Identities,* 59. On the use of חכם for "skilled" see Brenner, *Israelite Woman,* 33–34, 44–45; Gordon, "A House Divided," 100.

[75] The first noun, "blacksmith or silversmith," חרש is rather common. The second one חשב is uncommon with this sense of "designer." Its basic meaning is "to devise" and thus it appears often in *nip'al* with the meaning of "deemed." The last one, רקם, is almost exclusive of these chapters in Exodus, in which the building of the Tabernacle is discussed.

the masculine singular is used. Of the only two feminine occurrences, one tells of Delilah's weaving Samson's locks into the web, from which we only learn that she was a dexterous weaver (Judg 16:13). The remaining one will be considered soon. Two other texts should be mentioned, although their meaning (and thus, pertinence) is doubtful and their contexts do not ensure a clear translation. One is David's curse on Joab because of his murder of Abner. After his disclaimer, David curses his whole progeny with never-ending discharge and leprosy, sword and famine. The fifth curse, in the midst of these four, is that "he" (every male of the family) מחזיק בפלך, an expression variously translated as "holds a spindle" (*NRSV*), "leaneth on a staff" (*JPS*), "whose strength is in the distaff" (*JB*), "afeminados" (*El Libro del Pueblo de Dios*). Except for this text, פלך appears only six times in Neh 3, where it is usually understood as a geographical district. A seventh occurrence, to which we turn now, is weighty.

This is the well-known poem on the Woman of Worth, whose large and rich household and her respected family owe her much (Prov 31:10–31). The mistress (or her servants?) makes blankets, belts and all kinds of textiles, either for her household or to be sold to the "Canaanite." She is described as putting her hands to the "distaff" (כישׁור) and holding "the spindle" (פלך). The problem is that the first term in this parallelism, כישׁור, is also a *hapax legomenon*, so biblical Hebrew does not help.[76] Among cognates, the Ugaritic *plk*, Sumerian/Akkadian [GIS]bala/*pilakku* apparently provide the best solution, not only because of their well-attested meaning of "spindle" but also because of associations with femininity, both divine and human.[77] If its translation is right, then, use here confirms the assertion already made of the predominance of textile work (spinning and weaving) as identified with women and adds one more instance of ideological diminishing of a warrior by feminization.[78]

Incidentally, Prov 7:16 brings up Egypt's long tradition of textile fine working. This, as female occupation, is also attested in their own ancient witnesses. According to Lesko, there is significant evidence that "in the earliest historical periods weaving workshops were filled exclusively by women,

---

[76] *BDB*, 507. Note that neither text uses טוה nor ארג. Another difficulty is that the lady in question is, in my view, not a real woman but Wisdom personified. All these facts notwithstanding, there is always an "agreement of truth" between writer and reader, so that the story is credible. How much this poem depicts a household; how much it is a compendium of female virtues and how much it intends only to point at Wisdom, are all open questions.

[77] Scott Layton, "A Chain Gang in 2 Samuel iii 29? A Rejoinder," *VT* 29 (1989): 84–85. He rejects Holloway's proposal ("Distaff, Crutch or Chain Gang: The Curse of the House of Joab in 2 Samuel iii 29") of translating חזק בפלך on the basis of Neh 3, as "become a corvée worker."

[78] As evidenced also in the blinding of prisoners and their ascription to the mills, see below. Hoffner, "Treatment," 67–70.

whereas men did not move into this important industry for several centuries."[79] Deborah Cassuto indicates that the incorporation of male workers at the beginning of the New Kingdom was

> contemporary with the newly developed vertical two-beam loom. It is most likely that this change in gender involvement occurred as part of the commercialization of textile production, a phenomenon, which according to O'Brian, is well known throughout history. However, there is no evidence that such changes would have occurred on the domestic level, as well.[80]

Reviewing evidence from Egyptian lower class women who complemented their income by different kinds of work, Armijo Navarro-Reverter reports as an example the village of Amarna. There, a large loom frame was unearthed. Since it is large enough to have covered almost a whole room, estimations are that it would have been used for extra-domestic work, with which women would have generated some income on their own.[81] On the other hand, as several scholars remind us, we should not think of individual enterprises but of people working in court, in small shops, or at home for the great institutions.

Also Israel's northern neighbors were expert weavers. Scholars affirm that textile production was mainly in woman's hands at least in ancient Mesopotamia, Nuzi, and Ugarit.[82] This is attested in seals, ration lists and titles

---

[79] Barbara S. Lesko, "Women's Monumental Mark on Ancient Egypt," *BA* 54 (1991): 5. Cited 20 December 2010. Online: http://www.jstor.org/stable/3210327.

[80] Deborah Cassuto, "Bringing the Artifact Home: A Social Interpretation of Loom Weights in Context," in *The World of Women in the Ancient and Classical Near East*, 68.

[81] Armijo Navarro-Reverter, "La vida de las mujeres egipcias," 131–32, quoting B. Kemp, "Amarna's Textile Industry," *Egyptian Archaeology* 11 (1997) 8 (7–9), unavailable to me. She mentions also the accumulation in a few rooms of moulds for bijouterie, in which, she supposes, beads were made and assembled (see below on pottery).

[82] See Stefania Mazzoni, "Having and Showing: Women's Possessions in the Afterlife in Iron Age Syria and Mesopotamia," in *Women and Property in Ancient Near Eastern and Mediterranean Societies: Conference Proceedings, Center for Hellenistic Studies, Harvard University* (ed. Deborah Lyons & Raymond Westbrook; n. p., 2005 [cited 25 November 2010]. Online: http://chs.harvard.edu/wb/1/wo/WnSQvul0ROgY8y7nVB1hqw/0.1) under "2. Women's Images and Death: the Portraiture of a Social Status" asserts that "Among the many objects shown, the distaff, the spindle and the basket of wool might have signaled at the same time symbolic and social values. They were certainly not new attributes of the role of women in family society, but it was undoubtedly only in the Syro-Hittite period that they began to play a role in female imagery and in monumental art. It seems significant that in the very same period and area specialized textile manufacture emerged with the adoption of the warp-weighted vertical draw loom, which made it possible to weave larger products. Moreover, artifacts for weaving, such as spindle whorls, distaff, spatulae, loom weights, and reels become ubiquitous in the domestic contexts of this period throughout the entire Levant (Cecchini 1992, 2000), attesting to a general increase in the production of textiles not only in industrial enterprises, such as the celebrated Phoenician ones, but also in households. As a consistent force of production in the household and in the community, women might have benefited from this process, eventually rising in rank and social status."

held by prominent women. Nemet-Nejat reasons about ancient Babylon's skilled workers:

> Many kinds of materials were woven, both coarse and fine, and with colors and bleaches. Both male and female washers, called fullers, were considered skilled workers. Sewing of clothing was probably done by women also. But it was apparently not considered a skilled craft as evidenced by the lack of an Akkadian word for the tailor, embroiderer, and producer of artificially fringed hems.[83]

The Mari archives also record several words for textiles, most of which cannot be identified any longer. According to S. Dalley's study of the ancient Babylonian cities of Mari and Karana, "fabric, clothes, trim for clothes such as fringes, tassels and ornamental strips, coverings and hangings, blankets and rugs —are among the commonest items manufactured and traded even in modern times."[84] There are also letters exchanged between husband (a merchant, far from home) and wife (the producer, at home, of "Akkadian textiles," a term for fine pieces); these show that, at least in certain periods, people could work independently from the state management.[85] Not only did they work for the state: "A Late Babylonian reference to female weavers is found in the temple archives, where they occasionally appear as workers charged with producing textiles that were needed for cultic services."[86] This information corresponds, perhaps, with a notice in the second book of Kings, the text to which I turn now.

As part of his religious reform—2 Kgs 23:7 reports—Josiah "tore down the houses of the *qedešim* that were in the house of Yahweh, where the women were weaving, where the houses of Asherah were."[87] I do not intend to get into the discussion on Asherah's popularity in pre-exilic Israel, for that is not our focus here. What concerns us is that here "the women," not just "some women," wove regularly for Asherah. Some think these women may have been the *qedešim*'s wives, having a joint function. Those who take this position are in general those who see these functionaries' tasks as related to sacred sex; a stand we have

---

[83] Nemet-Nejat, "Women," 107.

[84] Dalley, *Mari*, 51.

[85] Cassuto, "Bringing the Artifact," 67. Nemet-Nejat "Women," 107, affirms "After the Ur III period (2112–2004 B.C.E.), there was less evidence for large-scale, centrally controlled production."

[86] Marsman, *Women*, 407–8.

[87] Here I follow Tilde Binger, *Asherah* (JSOTSup 232; Sheffield: Sheffield Academic Press, 1997), 116. Most translations follow *BHS*'s Masoretic *rebia* at "the women" and then interpret "weaving there the houses" ארגות שם בתים לאשרה. Since that makes no sense, they attribute to it a meaning as "clothes, hangings" (for/of Asherah/ the asherah-pole") or some other term that would fit the context, although otherwise unattested. Binger prefers not to resort to an unknown meaning of a term in order to make sense of it, when moving the *rebia* solves the riddle.

already rejected.[88] Bird thinks the Dtr intended the term to be inclusive of male and female cultic functionaries, an ideological position she does not believe was true in reality.[89] They could have belonged to the priestly families, be Levites, slave families owned by the Jerusalem temple, or families of the land who wanted to contribute their work to the temple. The text is biased and brief. Whichever possibility, these weavers seem not to have been weaving commercially. For, as stated above, there seem not to have been independent craftsmen and craftswomen until late: "Also in Egypt, the artisans did not possess their own raw material. ... completely private artisans working for trade appear in Mesopotamia in large numbers only in Neo-Babylonian times."[90]

If I am right in my assumption that they did not weave commercially (at least, not as independent entrepreneurs), then they would have belonged to the temple personnel. This is all the Dtr let us know.

ENJOYING THE ARTS

As stated in our Introduction, Israel's life and relationship to God were accompanied by music, not only in the temple and holy festivals, but for entertainment and for mourning as well. While "music" involves several disciplines, such as writing, reading, performing, singing, and dancing, it is not always easy to differentiate them in our sources. On the one hand, pictorial material involves images about performance; there is no record available of musical notation in Egypt and there remains much to know about the musical systems of other peoples; sources are scarce and belong to long periods of times and cultures (and they are not bias-free either); finally, we encounter several biblical terms from which not much can be said. This is what we face.

In theory it should be easy also to differentiate between professional cultic singers and secular ones; however this becomes hard because of lack of concrete information. Mitchell notes that most references refer to cultic occasions: "While there is evidence in the Old Testament that music, particularly singing, was used on secular occasions ..., the majority of references suggest it played a significant part in religion, particularly in the worship of the Jerusalem

---

[88] For instance, P. Craigie, "Deuteronomy and Ugaritic Studies," in *A Song of Power and the Power of Song*, 115. Sweeney, *I & II Kings*, 447 says nothing about the women but keeps the "cultic prostitutes."

[89] Phyllis A. Bird, "The Place of Women in the Israelite Cultus," *Missing Persons and Mistaken Identities* (Philadelphia: Fortress, 1997), 99 n. 42: "I no longer believe that the term in these two verses [1 Kgs 15:12 and 2 Kgs 23:7] may be taken as evidence for women in this class, although I believe that the Deuteronomistic editor intends it as inclusive." She further refers to her "The End of the Male Cult Prostitute," already quoted. On the nouns of the stem קדש see the study of Deut 23:18–129 in chapter 7.

[90] Heltzer, "Royal Economy in Ancient Ugarit," 495 n.250.

Temple"[91] Yet, even with more evidence from the temple area, there is no agreement on what kind of service was that of the singers (שׁרים/תו but more commonly משׁררים/תו) listed, for instance, in 2 Chr 23:13; 35:25 or Ezra 2. Many scholars (including myself) take these quotations at face value and think there was temple personnel, male and female, whose function was performance; although, as Marsman pointedly remarks, the order of these female singers in Ezra 2:65 "in the list of those who returned from exile—between servants and horses—suggests they were of a low class and probably functioned as entertainers."[92] I agree with her about their low status, probably that of slaves. I wonder, however, whether they would not have been able to perform for the cultic realm just because they belonged to the lower echelons of society.

Johann Maier asserts that the people needed not be present during the sacrifices, but they usually were, responding by "acts of prostration, following signals and musical performances given by Levites from their position on the stairs ... The Levites, for their part, were led by priestly signals given from positions just inside the boundary of the priest's court."[93] Maier does not mention women, but perhaps his description would be applicable—one realm further, since women's courtyard was further from the priests than that of Israelite men. Wright argues that adding volume to the melody by horns and shouting was also an important aspect of cultic music making, so perhaps that is another task for these people.[94] Be it as it may, the question remains open as to what place, if any, women had in public cultic life in the post-exilic times.

Well attested in Egyptian sources is the long tradition of the "God's Wife."[95] Since the goddess Hathor had to do with music, major evidence from musician-priestesses comes from her cult. They are depicted with a *sistrum* (rattle) and occasionally a drum in their hands and in processions with other women (of whom we do not know much).[96] As divine woman, her main function

---

[91] T. C. Mitchell, "The Music of the Old Testament Reconsidered," *PEQ* 124 (1992):134, cited 2 September 2011. Online: http://www.biblicalstudies.org.uk/pdf/peq/music_ot_mitchell.pdf, referring to H. H. Rowley, *Worship in Ancient Israel: Its Forms and Meaning*, London, 1967, 202–12.

[92] Marsman, *Women*, 555.

[93] Johann Maier, "Self-Definition, Prestige, and Status of Priests towards the End of the Second Temple Period," *BTB* 23 (1993): 142.

[94] David P. Wright, "Music and Dance in 2 Samuel 6," *JBL* 121 (2002): 213–6, see below.

[95] One of the mixed blessings in this area is that Egyptian sources use mostly the masculine form of the noun "priest" both for males and females. They were looking at the function rather than the gender; on the other hand, it makes it more difficult to identify the female component.

[96] In her study on musicians in Egypt, Patricia Spencer, "Dance in Ancient Egypt," *NEA* 66 (2003): 117 brings up a "papyrus from the Twelfth Dynasty temple of Senwosret II at Lahun [which] describes in tabular form the occasions on which dances were performed with the name and nationalities of the singers and dancers/ acrobats concerned. From this we learn that the temple employed Asiatic and Nubian performers, in addition to Egyptians."

as priest was to bestow Hathor's blessings on the people in the pertinent ceremonies. These priests belonged to the aristocracy, at least in the Old Kingdom. In time, this function was taken away from the queen and given to unmarried daughters and, eventually, it could be taken up by women from the lowest social and economic echelons. One of the first modern scholars to contradict Herodotus on female priestesses in Egypt, traces their appearance in different mortuary documents and tombs, starting from the ones from the aristocracy to the humblest ones. He affirms:

> In the New Kingdom women of all classes, from the highest to the lowest, were attached as musician-priestesses to some temple or other. ...
>
> A woman, apparently unmarried, and of no particular standing, was a musician-priestess of Osiris, as were also two wives of weavers. A superintendent of craftsmen had five daughters who were musician-priestesses of Amūn. Such, too, was the wife of a shoe-maker."[97]

There were other priestly categories available to female priests, both for gods and goddesses, in several locations throughout the land. We do not know much about them except that their payment was the same for male and female alike;[98] and that "women with the title of *Mrt* held important responsibilities for real estate and agricultural personnel. They ultimately were responsible for the financial security of their cult centers, indicating that the position required considerable education."[99] In her study on banquet depictions in the Karnak and Amarna tombs, Lyn Green states that all musicians represented at royal banquet scenes,

> fall into one of two categories: all-female orchestras playing Egyptian instruments; or groups of musicians of indeterminate gender wearing "Asiatic" costume, and playing foreign instruments. ... A few of the female orchestras even wear the *modius*, a headdress reserved for high-ranking noblewomen. The

---

[97] Aylward Blackman, "On the Position of Women in the Ancient Egyptian Hierarchy," *JEA* 7 (1921): 22, referring to Auguste Mariette, *Catalogue général des monuments d'Abydos découverts pendant les fouilles de cette ville* numbers 1174, 1175, 1179 and 1187 on these wives of workers. He is one of the first modern scholars to contradict Herodotus on female priestesses in Egypt. Mariette's book is available on the web [cited 1 September 2011]. Online: http://www.archive .org/stream/cataloguegnr00mari#page/444/mode/2up.

[98] Sheldon L. Gosline, "Female Priests: A Sacerdotal Precedent from Ancient Egypt," *JFSR* 12 (1996): 39: "They received equal wages for equal services.[69] ... They were living in a society that appears to have been patriarchal in structure, yet flexible enough to adjust to individuals and sensitive to the needs of women to serve as fully participating members of organized religion", quoting (n.69) Barbara Lesko, *The Remarkable Women of Ancient Egypt* (2nd rev. ed.; Providence: Scribe, 1987), 19: "An Old Kingdom text reveals that a *w'b*-priestess of Hathor received the same payment for her services as a *w'b*-priest." See also Blakman, "On the Position of Women in the Ancient Egyptian Hierarchy," 29–30.

[99] Gosline, "Female Priests," 26.

instruments played, however, are the standard ones seen elsewhere in New Kingdom tombs: lutes, lyres and boat-shaped harps. The foreign musicians wear a wrapped garment which closely resembles that depicted on Syrian women. ... The "feminine" nature of their clothing originally led to suggestions that these foreign musicians were "transvestite" entertainers of the type who danced and made music at Babylonian temples. ... It is also possible that the musicians were eunuchs, and that their dress and caps were distinguishing marks similar to the distinctive hairstyles of eunuch musicians in Assyrian reliefs.[100]

Tomb depictions also show processions of female dancers, some of whom play the *sistrum* while others hold the "throw sticks" or dance without instruments in their hands, in groups of two or three, sometimes in two groups facing each other. Most of dancing recorded is religious in character, as in the Bible; however, "[d]ance in a domestic context is shown in [funerary] scenes from the Old Kingdom to the end of the New Kingdom."[101] Many of those dancing women are relatives of the deceased owner, thus not very likely professionals. What would have been the social standing of the professionals, then? Luckily, this is Spencer's last question:

> Can we say anything of the social status of professional entertainers, including dancers, in ancient Egypt? Today, professional dancers, though they may be admired for their skills, are not accorded high status in Egyptian village society. They travel around, often in the company of men to whom they are not related and may stay away from home at night—behavior on which society frowns. The fact that performers in ancient tomb-scenes are sometimes identified in the accompanying texts as members of the tomb-owner's family might suggest that to be a musician or a dancer was socially acceptable, but in such cases, these are unlikely to be professional performers. ...
>
> Temple performers—dancers, musicians and singers—would have been accorded high status in line with their dedication to the service of the gods but it is possible that professional performers might not have been so highly regarded in ancient Egyptian society.[102]

From Mesopotamian sources we learn that music (probably both composition and performance) were part of the *edubba* curriculum, where the sage got his education.[103] Rivka Harris also thinks that there might have been "a

---

[100] Lyn Green, "Some Thoughts on Ritual Banquets at the Court of Akhenaten and in the Ancient Near East," in Gary N. Knoppers & Antoine Hirsch, ed. *Egypt, Israel, and the Ancient Mediterranean World: Studies in Honor of Donald B. Redford* (Leiden/Boston: Brill, 2004), 216–17.

[101] Spencer, "Dance," 118.

[102] Spencer, "Dance," 119.

[103] Samuel N. Kramer, "The Sage in Sumerian Literature: A Composite Portrait," in *The Sage in*

kind of music academy for upper-class girls (and boys)," and for elite and slave adults as well, in which they would have "received instruction in singing and playing of musical instruments as part of their education (which in Mesopotamia did not usually include reading and writing)."[104] It is easy to overlook this possible tension between lower-rank performer, cultic performer and aristocratic poetess, because of the dearth of sources and the desire to make some sense of the little we have.[105] We also learn from Sargon's letter to Ashur that during his third campaign "Hezekiah, the Judean" had given him a considerable tribute:

> That Hezekiah, fear of the radiance of my majesty ... With 30 talents of gold, 800 talents of silver, precious stones, antimony, daggassu stone, wood, all that heavy treasure (along with) his daughters, his concubines, male and female musicians, he caused them to bring back to me to Nineveh, the city of my sovereignty, and in order to pay tribute and make obeisance, he sent his messenger.[106]

Pictographic and archival evidence also supports this activity, although it—obviously—does not acknowledge composers, unless they are also performing. John Franklin, a musicologist, mentions the following lists of musicians as "prizes of conquest or diplomatic gifts, to Nineveh from various subject states" as part of Assyrian ideological imperial propaganda:

> Records of wine rations from Nimrud, spanning perhaps half of the eighth century, show that as many as two hundred and forty musicians, both male and female, might be resident in the palace at any one time, including a large proportion of foreigners: Kassite, Chaldaean, Neo-(Hittite), Aramaean, Tabalites, Arpadites, and Kommagenes are all specified, and we have only a small fraction of the original records ... Similarly, one bread list from the palace of Sargon (ca. 721–705 BC) contains a large enough distribution for perhaps two hundred musicians ... A relief from the reign of Sennacherib (704–681 BC) shows three foreign lyre-players being driven into captivity; it is generally thought that these are the Judaean musicians mentioned in the emperor's annals, sent as tribute by Hezekiah after the campaign of 701. ... A propaganda piece from Ashurbanipal's reign shows the so-called Elamite

---

Israel and the Ancient Near East (ed. John G. Gammie & Leo G. Perdue; Winona Lake: Eisenbrauns, 1990), 32.

[104] Rivka Harris, "The Female 'Sage' in Mesopotamian Literature (with an Appendix on Egypt)" in *The Sage in Israel and the Ancient Near East*, 10.

[105] That is a point well taken by Bird, review of Engelken, 319: "...failing to recognize any conflict between the status of a performer or palace attendant and that of an aristocrat." I do not bring it here to be critical of Engelken, but as a reminder to myself of the danger of overlooking important differences in our sources.

[106] Brent A. Strawn, Sarah C. Melville, Kyle Greenwood & Scott Noegel, "Neo-Assyrian and Syro-Palestinian Texts II," in *The Ancient Near East: Historical Sources in Translation* (ed. Mark Chavalas; Malden: Blackwell, 2006), 347.

Orchestra—a large ensemble of vertical and horizontal harps, pipes, drum and possibly singers/dancers—celebrating the accession of Ummanigash, the emperor's appointee after the defeat of Teuman...[107]

This use of arts for ideological purposes during the Assyrian empire is also attested by Assante in her study of lead erotic reliefs found in what had been Tukulti-Ninurta's New Palace Terrace's workshops.[108] The majority of these depict couples or groups of two men and a woman in sexually-explicit positions. She demonstrates that, in contrast to the terracotta figures (found in all kinds of settings and across all archaeological levels and places), intended to prevent evil magic, these had the purpose of furniture decoration: "Their primary function was visual pleasure, although they carried political messages." Assante has been able to locate some reliefs in "the milieu of professional entertainment" due to "the inclusion of sexual props, musical instruments and what [she] recognize[s] as dancers' garments..."[109]

In short, information is not abundant considering the span in time and geography; and it is subject to constraints put by their society's taboos and artistic conventions; and written documents are reluctant because male scribes tended to be conservative and lessen women's "significance and recognized presence."[110] This reluctance repeats itself throughout time and space and it is not necessary to abound on it now, for it is the very reason that we are looking for hidden women throughout the Bible. It is true that pre-exilic sources—particularly pre- and early-monarchic—attribute to women an important role as musicians and singers, especially in exalting YHWH. The prime examples are Miriam and Deborah, introduced as prophetesses and authors of victory songs.

---

[107] John Franklin, "'A Feast of Music': The Greco-Lydian Musical Movement on the Assyrian Periphery," in *Anatolian Interfaces: Hittites, Greeks and their Neighbors: Proceedings of an International Conference on Cross-Cultural Interaction, September 17–19, 2004, Emory University, Atlanta, GA.* (ed. Billie J. Collins, M. R. Bachvarova & I. Rutherford. Oxford: Oxbow (2008), 195. Cited 8 August 2010. Online: http://www.kingmixers.com/FranklinPDFfilescopy/FeastofMusicWeb .pdf.

[108] Julia Assante, "The Erotic Reliefs of Ancient Mesopotamia" (Ph.D. diss., Columbia University, 2000), 179–209 (chapter V), especially conclusions on p. 208–9. Also Franklin, "Feast of Music," 196, speaking of the "famous relief of Ashurbanipal reclining in a one-man symposium among his women," states that " ...it is striking that all of the musical representations—with the exception of the banquet scene itself—feature Assyrian male musicians in the overtly public and nationalistic contexts of triumph, hunt, and religious ritual. If one may assume that the musical imagery is consistent with the ideology of the larger composition ... there emerges a picture of Assyrian music, with its classical Mesopotamian basis, in a dominant position. The music of subject nations, represented in large part by captive female musicians, is gathered, mingled fertilized by the emperor himself."

[109] Assante, "Erotic Reliefs," 2 and 4. More on her work below (on beer brewing).

[110] Gosline, "Female Priests," 34.

Although much has been discussed about their prophetic roles, especially that of Miriam, I believe one important chore, especially in Exod 15, is interpreting God's actions in their immediate setting—a clear prophetic task. At any rate, they should not be deeply discussed here, for their role belongs to the religious and political realms. Yes, it is important to recall their role as "mothers" of singing and processional dancing (Miriam), thus opening the way for female authors and performers from Israel's earliest times.

The semantic field of "music" includes many more terms than thought at first, including nouns related to musical notation (pausing, intonations, etc.), musical instruments, narratives about different moments and types of dancing or playing (processions, festivals, signals by trumpets and so forth); songs of different kinds, and verbs describing some action. What concerns us here is only what can tell us anything about professional musicians of any kind. And, if possible, in the DtrH. Perhaps the biblical lists leave other musicians' functions unattested. Two short references to musicians as enchanters have made me think of one of my favorite stories. In 2 Kgs 17:24 starts the story of the "idolatrous" origin of the Samaritans. Within this Deuteronomistically-charged story, verses 24–28 tell how, after Assyrian destruction of Samaria, a priest of YHWH had to be returned because there had appeared lions roaming and killing people; a fact interpreted to mean that the Lord of those lands was angry and required proper sacrifices. I just wonder whether a tradition of musicians who would control beasts could not lie behind the story, even though that is not in the returned priest's job-description. Amélie Kuhrt describes a plaque of Ur-nanshe of Lagaš (now in the British Museum), in which under each figure (the king, his wife and children, cup-bearer, musicians) the name or function is inscribed. One of the male figures is "a functionary entitled 'head snake-charmer' … The 'snake-charmer' appears in lists of musicians, and this is perhaps his titular court function; why this should be so is puzzling."[111] And Karen Nemet-Nejat asserts that "[m]usicians included among their ranks snake charmers and bear wardens as part of a ritual circus performance."[112] A quick perusal in the internet gives plenty of colorful stories about snake charmers in Egypt, who respond to drum beating and other techniques; these come, apparently, from very early times. I do not know whether lions were also tamed from early times in order to perform in circuses and, again, I cannot assert that is what lies behind the colorful story in 2 Kgs 17. The two quotations brought up, almost as an aside to their themes, have made me think that perhaps also in ancient Israel musicians (male or female?) might have acted as charmers.

The following terms and texts comprise the evidence available in the Hebrew Bible, to be briefly considered:

---

[111] Kuhrt, *Ancient Near East*, 1:36.
[112] Nemet-Nejat, "Women," 109.

- שרים ושרות, "male and female singers," 2 Sam 19:36, Qoh 2:8[113]

- משררים ומשררות, "male and female singers," Ezra 2:65 // Neh 7:67

- נגנים, "players of stringed instruments (lyres)," Isa 23:16; Ps 68:26

- תופפות, "drum players," Ps 68:26, (Exod 15:20)

- המחללות, very young women dancing in the vineyards, Judg 21:21–23

- מחלות, "dancers," 1 Sam 18:6

- משחקות, "performers," 1 Sam 18:6–7; 2 Sam 6:5, 20–23, 1 Chr 15:29

- רקד, "to leap," 1 Chr 15:29 (2 Sam 6:20–23)

A quick perusal shows already that DtrH did not find many occasions to mention musicians, especially women. Many other terms or texts will be of little use and thus, will not be taken up. For instance, if one takes translations of Judg 11:40, one finds nubile women celebrating a yearly remembrance of Jephthah's unnamed daughter. The verb, a *pi'el* infinitive construct from תנה II, is usually translated "to mourn." Its meaning seems to be "to recount" rather than sing or dance (it could involve repetition by singing or by processional dancing, but technically it would not belong to this semantic field); furthermore, it involves "all the women" and not necessarily professionals and thus it is excluded from the list. Likewise, "shouting [תרועה] is part of a larger musical expression that includes various musical instruments and singing."[114] It sounds funny that there would be professional shouters (see "the people" in Ezra 3:11). The idea would be to add volume and contrast to the melodic instruments, both with trumpets, horns, and voices.[115] At any rate, it would be a choir or group, not individuals. Wright makes a very interesting point in that one of the functions of such a shouting was to call the Deity's attention and engage him/her in the ceremony taking place; a function, he claims, similar to that of the *sistrum* players in Egypt.[116] If this was a priestly (Levitic?) function, then perhaps it was also part of the duties of the משררים בני אסף the singers from the sons of Asaph in Ezra 2:41. Alternatively, if we want to "downgrade" them, there are the משררים ומשררות mentioned in Ezra 2:65 and Neh 7:67, who are of very low rank (discussed in this same sub-section).

---

[113] Hebrew 2 Sam 19:33–37 = Eng 19:32–36.

[114] Wright, "Music," 213.

[115] Wright, "Music," 203–9; Mitchell, "Music," 130 affirms that the silver trumpets were played by the priests (this is confirmed by 2 Chr 13:14); therefore, the term מחצצרים (*Qere* מחצרים), *hip'il* from denom. חצר IV, "play the trumpet," would be exclusively masculine.

[116] Wright, "Music," 215, n. 33.

There are two *hapax legomena* (מפזז and מכרכר) used of David's dancing and leaping as the Ark of YHWH is brought back to Jerusalem (2 Sam 6:16), supplanted in its parallel in 1 Chr 15 with somewhat more common verbs.[117] I will start with the texts that provide less information and proceed to the more complex ones, those involving David. Finally, there is a specialized kind of song or poetry called "dirge," used for mourning rituals, which I will study at the end of this sub-section.

המחללות — *Dancers*

Judges 20–21 is the aftermath of that dark and violent story of the Levite's unnamed concubine given away to be gang-raped and dismembered (Judg 19); a story in many ways still so tangible, it is disquieting. Chapters 20 and 21 are far less known and studied and at first sight they do not seem so violent; yet, they are. One of Israel's tribes, Benjamin, is almost destroyed by the other tribes and, realizing what that would mean, it is replenished by abducting young, virgin women from Jabesh-Gilead (and killing their immediate families) and from Shiloh. The verses that concern us here are 21:19–23. From these we learn that there was an annual festival to YHWH, in which very young women danced in the vineyards. The story provides no data on the occasion, whether it was a vintage feast (my assumption) or any other occasion. There are no men mentioned, for the ones who could put a claim on the women after their abduction (fathers and brothers) would not be present and allow such a pillage. So, it seems to have been an occasion when very young women (still unmarried) and perhaps other older women (not the focus of the Benjaminites' interest, therefore unmentioned) would make music and dance in the fields.

Verse 21 speaks of the "daughters of Shiloh" who would come out "to dance in dances" or "in groups to dance" (*Jerusalem Bible*), לחול במחלות. Verse 23, after the deed, speaks of them as המחללות אשר גזלו, "the dancers they had robbed." This is a sad way to be remembered.

שרים ושרות — *Singers*

These two participles *qal* appear always in plural form; often as a pair, although the masculine appears also with other terms (Ps 87:7: שרים + חללים). For our research, the most interesting texts are the two identified in the list above, namely, 2 Sam 19:36 and Qoh 2:8. The latter is late and does not belong to the DtrH. Yet, it provides evidence that these groups (not defined in the text) could be someone's possession. The narrator poses as son of David, king in Jerusalem (Qoh 1:1), who, starting from 2:4, recounts all his great accomplishments.

---

[117] These texts in particular include more than one term and therefore will be studied in block, although they are listed above under each term separately.

Among these, v. 7 speaks of the acquisition (קנה) of slaves of different types and numerous herds. Then, in v. 8, categories change: first, gold and silver and treasures from the (conquered? looted?) kingdoms and provinces.

Next, three items belonging to some category to be loosely defined (human or male pleasure?), for which the verb עשׂה + the preposition לֹ + first singular suffix are added: "I made/got for myself." The three objects gotten: שׂרים ושׁרות male and female singers, תענוגת בני האדם, human luxuries, and שׁדה ושׁדת, a *hapax legomenon* of uncertain meaning, with several possible etymologies and translations proposed.[118] It is clear that singers go together with the pleasures of life for this "king."

The second pertinent text is 2 Sam 19:36. The story is part of the farewell conversation between David and Barzillai, as David and his followers fled Jerusalem and went over the Jordan river escaping from Absalom. Barzillai, already eighty, decides to go only a little way with him and then return home. His opening words are "I am eighty years old. Can I discern what is good from what is bad (or pleasant and unpleasant)? Can your servant taste what he eats or what he drinks? Can I still hear the voice of male and female singers?" Here, two word-pairs, eat-drink and male-female singers, are set as examples of his inability to discern the sensible world because of his age and thus, to enjoy it (alternatively, they could be three examples, more or less independent from each other).

Music is a symbol of the luxurious life of the wealthy and the wicked ones. It is striking that both texts in which the word pair under survey שׂרים ושׁרות appear in the whole Bible convey a similar idea, even though they belong to very different sections and possibly periods: Qoh 2:8 and 2 Sam 19:36. Male and female singers are a *topos* of enjoyment of the perceptions, which rich men can afford (see 2 Sam 19:33) although not always enjoy. This *topos* is also present in the prophetic literature, in which YHWH's punishment is often expressed as a cessation of all good things. One very important text in this line is Isa 5, the Song of the Vineyard (or the Sour Vine): in v. 11–12 those who pursue

---

[118] See *BDB*, 994. *NRSV* translates "and many concubines" with a note saying "Hebrew uncertain." R. Gordis, *Koheleth—The Man and His World* (New York: Jewish Theological Seminary of America, 5711/1951), 130 (translation of the text on 140) translates "of mistresses a good number"; the only note on the term being on the agreement of the *Peshiṭṭa* with LXX against MT. Oswald Loretz, *Qohelet und der alte Orient: Untersuchungen zu Still und theologischer Thematik des Buches Qohelet* (Freiburg: Herder, 1964), 159 translates "(Harems-) Frauen" and has a few notes on the verse, but does not explain the translation; Fox, *Ecclesiastes*, 14 translates as "male and female singers" and in the ensuing commentary brings up the Mishnah' translation as "coffer," Ibn Ezra's "women taken as booty" and also "a good number of concubines."

wine and feasts, including "lyre and harp, tambourine and flute and wine," (*NRSV*) will soon find themselves mourning.[119]

נגן — *Players of Stringed Instruments*

The term appears also in two Psalms, 33:3 and 68:26. In the first one, playing "skillfully amid shouts (again תרועה) of joy" (*JPS*) is paralleled to "singing a new song" and both occur in the summons to praise. Psalm 68 is a very complex, even though very interesting, text (dealt with as we discussed messengers). As several scholars have noted, resemblance of this Psalm to Judg 5 and some other internal clues make one wonder whether what is described in vv. 25–28 is a cultic or a military procession:

> Four tribes are mentioned next as marching in the procession ... Does our passage reflect premonarchical conditions? What does a concern like this for professional and political order of procession demonstrate? ... The Chronistic writings betray deep interest in liturgical personnel and procedures (cf. 1 Chr 16, etc.), but they do not employ the vocabulary and imagery found in Ps 68:25–28. And women marching with men toward the sanctuary seems to be an unusual arrangement, at least in strictly patriarchal setups. ... There is, however, a question of ranking in the tradition of leaving Mount Sinai (Num 10:11–28), and several strands emphasize the superior importance of the weak (cf. 1 Sam 9:21; Mic 5:1 ...). These references do not account for the professional and gender sequence in v. 26 that seems to imitate the order of troops on the warpath.[120]

For the issue that concerns us, it would make a difference whether the procession is called upon or narrated about; that is, whether the psalm evokes a cultic procession which includes female musicians or whether it allows it only insofar as it is an ancient vestige of a premonarchic "warpath." I do not intend to discuss "historicity" or "truth" here; the only important point for our discussion is whether the Psalm reflects any historically viable place for professional drummers, especially in the cultic setting. The answer is the usual and frustrating "We do not know for sure."

As to the precise instrument that כנור and נבל imply, there is consensus that they are stringed instruments framed by wood. There is also pictorial

---

[119] Isa 24:7–9 also combines these elements. A different mood is expressed by Job (21:11–12), in which his observation is not about the rich (he had been one himself) but about the wicked, whose children leap around (רקד) and who "sing to the drum and the lyre." Here a combination of these two lexemes, "leap" and "drum" occurs.

[120] Gerstenberger, *Psalms*, 41.

evidence for some of these "lyres."[121]   According to Wright, harps are "not attested in the ancient archaeological finds of the area for the general period of concern, though there are many examples of lyres" and "תפים are simple small round frame drums whose diameter would be about the length of a forearm, like a large modern tambourine but without jingles."[122] Mitchell concurs with the difficulty and considers that the LXX probably did not understand what the terms meant further than that they were stringed instruments. Thus,

> It seems clear, therefore, that both were stringed instruments, and though some doubt must exist as to whether the Septuagint translators really understood what the Hebrew names represented, there is a fair possibility that the Septuagint translation of *kinnôr* as *kithara*, "lyre", preserves a correct tradition, and that *nēbel* may reasonably be rendered "harp" … That the *nēbel*, in at least some cases, had ten strings is indicated by references to a *nēbel 'āśôr*, 'harp of ten', in the Psalms (33.2; 144.9), and it is probably reasonable to interpret a passage describing the accompaniment to praises of God in Psalm 92.3 (Hebrew 4) 'on a ten (*'āśôr*) and on a harp (*nēbel*) to the sound of a lyre (*kinnôr*)' as indicating two types of harp, one with ten strings, and, since ten was apparently worthy of special mention, the other with fewer strings.[123]

Were one to judge from the participles, one would conclude that only males played stringed instruments both in court and temple. The majority of terms (seven out of fifteen times) appears in the story of the search for someone to calm down Saul's evil spirit (1 Sam 16–19).[124] The only application to a woman uses the infinitive. It is the "Song of the forgotten prostitute" in Isa 23:16. The fact that it is used in such a generic way (it is not the typical "token" case) indicates that to the redactors and their audience it was at least not unthinkable

---

[121] In his study on the *marzeaḥ*, Jonathan S. Greer, "A *Marzeaḥ* and a *Mizraq*: A Prophet's Mêlée with Religious Diversity in Amos 6.4–7," *JSOT* 32 (2007): 248 attests that נבל appears almost exclusively in religious contexts.

[122] Wright, "Music," 203, although he does not specify exactly what is "the general period of concern."

[123] Mitchell, "Music," 130.

[124] R. Bowman, "The Fortune of King David/The Fate of Queen Michal: A Literary Critical Analysis of 2 Samuel 1–8," in *Telling Queen Michal's Story: An Experiment in Comparative Interpretation* (ed. David J. A. Clines & Tamara Cohn Eskenazi; JSOTSup 119; Sheffield: Sheffield Academic Press, 1991), 118, calls attention to identical hostile reactions by Saul and Michal toward David, especially in this episode (Saul) and as the ark is brought to Jerusalem (Michal). I only wonder whether Bowman is right in relation to Michal's reaction when stating (118): "Neither father nor daughter ultimately tolerate either the behavior David inspires in other women of Israel or the self-proclaimed, divinely inspired behavior he displays before them." Is Michal's concern really the reaction of the "maidservants"?

that a woman would play in the streets (Only a prostitute? Only in the streets?).[125]

תופפות — *Drummers*

The only time the denominative "play the tambourine" (*BDB*) appears is in Ps 68:26, a *qal* feminine plural participle, in which the processional order is prescribed:

> get to the front, you singers (קדמו שרים),
> (get to) the last, (you) lyre players (אחר נגנים)
> in the midst of (you?) the "young women" (בתוך עלמות) playing/players of
> the drum (תופפות)[126]

To note here is the fact that the subject is the noun עלמות, also a social category about which there is no agreed-upon translation.[127] At least one other text includes a young woman as drummer. Jephthah's daughter is said to meet her father "with timbrels and with dancing," בתפים ובמחלות (Judg 11:3). I would imagine she was at the front line of a group of friends of hers or other women from the household: it would have made a very poor welcome to come out alone, even if she was a gifted musician.

> The third instrument type specifically attested from Palestine, the tambour, is possibly to be identified with the Hebrew term *tōp* on the ground that the apparent use in Nahum 2.8 of *tāpap*, the verb derived from it, to describe women beating their breasts in mourning, suggests that the *tōp* was played by beating. This is supported by the Septuagint tradition where, out of its fifteen occurrences, it is rendered in all but one instance by *tumpanon*, 'tambourine'. This need only indicate that it was some kind of drum, but the pictorial evidence for the widespread use of the tambour favours this identification ...[128]

Support for this statement includes Miriam's leading in the Song of the Sea, Exod 15:20, where right upon her introduction as "Miriam, the prophetess, Aaron's sister," she "took a drum (תף) in her hand; and all the women went out

---

[125] See chapter 7 on this text.

[126] The preposition (בתוך עלמות) is in construct state and thus should be read "in the midst of the young women" (thus Alonso Schökel & Carnitti, *Salmos*, 888). If taken as absolute, the young women get between the two other groups (thus, *NRSV, JB, JPS*).

[127] Carolyn Pressler, *Joshua, Judges and Ruth* (Louisville: Westminster John Knox, 2002), 255: "young women;" Jost, *Gender, Sexualität und Macht*, 80: "Mädchen"; Engelken, *Frauen im Alten Israel*, 44–46 posits the עלמות (*Hofdamen* or *Palastfrauen*) belonged to the upper social echelons and served as accompanying people, played music, and in general were part of court life. Although one cannot make an argument out of silence when the subject is females in the Bible, it is notable that they are not paralleled to "your sons" taken to serve as officers in Samuel's warning (1 Sam 8).

[128] Mitchell, "Music," 130.

after her with drums and with dancing," again the same word-pair, בתפים
ובמחלות. Several Psalms also include the timbrel among its instruments. That,
however, does not tell us much about its performers, except that, being a small
instrument to be beaten, it could easily have been played by young and elderly
women alike.

Performing alongside King David

There are three additional texts to consider, all having David as their main
character. One is the victorious return to Jerusalem by Saul and David (1 Sam
18:6–16) and the other is the bringing back of YHWH's Ark after an earlier
attempt had turned into Uzzah being killed for—allegedly—touching the ark (2
Sam 6:12–16 // 1 Chr 15:25–29).[129] These are very interesting, because they
combine several elements related to these sub-sections: musical instruments,
singing, processions and rejoicing at the victors, and the questions about the
kind of women participating: Were these professional singers or is this an
expression of popular joy, informal and with no further consequences for our
study? We turn to these texts.

המחלות, הנשים המשׂחקות — Entertainers, Singers, and Dancers

Perhaps the story that people know best about David is his killing of the gigantic
Goliath in 1 Sam 17. After this victory over the mighty Philistines, the power
relationship between Saul, his children (particularly Jonathan and Michal), and
David will start to change. The first notice the reader is given is the different
reactions at his deed. Jonathan loved him like his very self and Saul started to be
jealous of his popularity. The text to consider comes right at this point. As they
return to Jerusalem, the good news of the victory over the Philistines has
preceded them and the people from every town come out in joy and
thanksgiving (1 Sam 18:6–7).

The first verse has some syntactic difficulties. Driver noted that והמחלות
and לשׁיר "correspond in form so imperfectly that the text can scarcely be in its
original form. The least change is to read with Bu[dde] בְּמְחֹלוֹת,"[130] a proposal

---

[129] Ingrid Haase, "Uzzah's Rebellion," *JHS*, Art. 3 (2004) n.p. [cited 20 May 2010]. Online:
http://www.jhsonline.org/Articles/article_33.pdf, "4.5 Uzzah's Death" is, however, very ironical
about this motif: "In other words, Uzzah who had lived in the presence of the Ark for about twenty
years, who had been assigned to drive the Ark to Jerusalem on the cart constructed exclusively for
this occasion, who, as the Bible says, in both the Samuel and the Chronicles passages, wanted to
protect the Ark from harm, which after all was his job as driver of the Ark, gets killed by God for
doing his job." This brings her to seek traces of a revolt against David's taking of the ark from the
Northern Kingdom to Jerusalem.

[130] Driver, *Notes*, 151.

he supports with some of the texts discussed here, see Exod 15:20; Judg 11:34; 21:21. Not only does it make sense: it is, as he states, the least change to the Masoretic text. That is the reading of most commentaries and translations, of which *NRSV* is one: "the women came out of all the towns of Israel, singing and dancing, to meet King Saul, with tambourines, with songs of joy, and with musical instruments."

I want to propose an alternative reading, which has two advantages. The first one is not to have to correct the text (except for the *Qere* reading of the infinitive); the second advantage, is that it rescues a term otherwise neglected as erroneous. I submit that there is a parallel structure, more evident when the words are set one below the other. Since v. 6a bears no weight on the discussion, I focus upon the issue that concerns us. The sentence reads:

i)	לשיר	הנשים מכל־ערי ישראל	ותצאנה
ii)	לקראת שאול המלך	והמחלות	
iii)		בתפים בשמחה ובשלשים	

The women came out of all the towns of Israel to sing/singing
The dancers   to meet/meeting King Saul,
with drums, with joy, and with musical instruments.

There is a verbal ellipsis in verse 6b.ii; the subjects of each sentence come in second place, parallel to each other: the women and the dancers. Then, in sentence i) we have a locative, from all the towns of Israel, also applicable to ii). The two infinitives are also in parallel and ii) adds the direct object of either both verbs ("to sing to, and to meet Saul the King") or the second verb ("to meet Saul (the King"). Finally, line iii), a complement of mode or instrumental, completes the information: the women/the dancers, came out with drums, manifestations of joy and musical instruments. The two sentences can be read as synonymous parallelism: the women, that is, the dancers; or as progressive parallelism: the women (perhaps the singers) and from them, the dancers.

I do not think choice of the *Qere* for the infinitive of שיר needs much explanation. The question is whether המחלות may be taken to mean the performers and not their actions, "dances." The major difficulty lies in the fact that the meaning I propose is highly unusual. There is partial support, however, for this claim in two other texts. The noun מחלה/ות has the clear meaning of an object in parallel to "tambourines" in Judg 21:21 (besides Exod 15:20 and Judg 11:34, already mentioned as we discussed drummers).[131] In these, "dances"

---

[131] The stem חול offers, according to *BDB*, at least the nouns מחול and מחולה, one masculine and one feminine, with the meanings "dance" and "dancing" respectively.

seems not to be the best translation either, at least as the parallel term for "timbrel"; perhaps it refers to some accompanying instrument, such as rattles.

In other texts, like 1 Sam 29:5, מחלות refers to the whole event and more precisely to singing rather than dancing. Perhaps, in the line of some notices about oral tradition of dirges for Saul or for Josiah (see below), there is here already the beginning of that tradition of David's growth against Saul's demise (that the latter would certainly not appreciate) carried on: "Is this not David, of whom they sing to one another in the dances, saying ..." (במחלות).

There are still two texts in which it is not clear whether the persons or the action are intended. On the one hand, because the saying could be understood as the literary device called "abstract for concrete," since there is no dancing without dancers (and it adds to gender-balance by having each a different plural form).[132] While I do not reject the traditional understanding of the term, I want to posit that "dancer/s" is another possibility at least as good as "dancing" in Exod 32:19 and in Song 7:1.[133]

Exodus 32:19. Here Moses approaches the camp after forty days with YHWH on the mountain and he sees את־העגל והמחלת "the calf and (some) *mĕḥōlōt*" (no article and no direct object marker in the second one, which most translations take to be "the dancing"). He sees "dancing." What prevents one from thinking that what he saw were "dancers"? What kind of dancing can be performed without dancers? Or are we to think that these were male dancers?

Song of Songs 7:1. Here, the Shulammite is compared to מחלת המחנים. This is a construct chain, the first noun being feminine singular (incidentally, the only singular of מחלת in the Bible) and the absolute, a dual term. Translations go in the line of "dancing between two lines of dancers" or "two choirs," "dancing in front of two camps or two armies," and other expressions. Here again, even though one may take the feminine singular מחלת to mean "dancing" of (whatever the two camps mean), it may as well mean "a dancer."[134]

I return now to the verse under scrutiny in 1 Sam 18. The main difficulty with my proposal is, as stated, that there is no irrefutable proof that the noun could mean "dancer" in addition to "dancing" or "dance," although there are two texts where this translation is equally possible. The second difficulty is the fact

---

[132] Wilfred Watson, *Classical Hebrew Poetry: A Guide to Its Techniques* (JSOTSS 26; repr. with corrections; Sheffield: Sheffield Academic Press, 1995), 314.

[133] Since the preposition ב is not that common accompanying persons, I have not included במחול/ות, with or without article vocalization, such as they appear in Ps 149:3 or Judg 21:21.

[134] See Exum, *Song of Songs*, 211–213 (translation) 228–230, who recognizes that part of the difficulty in understanding the intention of these lines is that "the comparison ... is difficult to fathom." (228) She opts for "the dance of two camps."

that hollow verbs tend to duplicate the third letter in order to compensate for the weak one in forms such as *po'lel*, etc.; thus, forms like (שיר) משררות or even from (חול) מחללות, as in Judg 21:23. However, since as a rule "identical or homorganic consonants do not appear in first and second positions; even though identical consonants can appear there, homorganic consonants do not appear in second and third positions (although this rule is not as strictly followed as the preceding one),"[135] perhaps we could explain the form מחלת (at least in the two plurals) as occurrences of "unrecognized defective participle," in which the form *mĕḥōlĕlōt* became *mĕḥollôt* in order to avoid as much as possible repetition of the ל and was taken to be the noun *mĕḥōlôt*.

In her study on the meaning of the stem זנה, Riegner explores how the biliteral stem *זנ adopted different by-forms, related to each other in meaning. If this principle can be also applied, then a biliteral stem *חל could be posited, evolving into different triliteral stems, such as (חלל II) חליל "flute," and its denominative verb (see 1 Kgs 1:4 והעם מחללים בחללים ושמחים שמחה גדולה "playing on pipes and rejoicing with great joy," *NRSV*); and even the vague על־מחלת (חלה II) in Psalm titles (53:1, 88:1). They all belong to the semantic field of dancing and playing the accompanying music, to which our terms belong. Since my interest lies elsewhere, I will not pursue further the philological argument; I content myself with opening up the possibility of imagining some more items for this semantic field.[136]

I move on to the next verse, 1 Sam 18:7, where the actual singing of these women is quoted, "Saul has killed his thousands, and David his myriads." Two verbs are used: they "answered" and "spoke or said," both *wayyiqtol* third feminine plural. In between, the subject: "the women who made merry," "the women, the merrymakers" or "the female entertainers" הנשים המשחקות. As Driver and other scholars have noticed, there are other narratives in which a procession or a group is said to "make merry" but none in which the verb is parsed in feminine (see 2 Sam 6:5, our next text; Jer 30:19; 31:4).[137] There are two important aspects of this verb to be discussed here. One is the connotation of the שחק *pi'el* and even of the English "merrymaking." Is it celebration or is it taunt? Was Saul too sensible to the women's celebration, misunderstanding the parallelism of their song or were they making sport of him?

In his study on 2 Sam 6, Rosenstock emphasizes the ritual aspect of the whole dancing event, including taunting by Michal as David dances and the ark is brought up to Jerusalem. He thus compares that episode with this other ritual משחק-ing in which the women taunt Saul and attributes Saul's reaction not to

---

[135] Angel Sáenz Badillos, *A History of the Hebrew Language* (Cambridge: Cambridge University Press, 1993), 21, comes to my attention thanks to Riegner.

[136] Riegner, "Vanishing Hebrew Harlot," 112–34, quoted abundantly in my chapter 6.

[137] Driver, *Notes*, 151.

paranoia or jealousy, but to his recognizing that this is plain mocking, permitted by, thus excused by, ritual practices known in their milieu:

> Women who are said to be "playing" (מְשַׂחֲקוֹת) in 1 Sam. 18.7 come out to greet the king (exactly as Michal does …) and seem to taunt him (that is how Saul understands it) with their chant, "Saul has killed his thousands, David his tens of thousands". Seow believes that the words of the women are not really abusive since "thousands" and "myriads" were, in Canaanite poetry, "not meant to be contrastive" (1989: 94). This leads Seow to attribute Saul's understanding of this verse as a taunt to his "paranoia". I would rather attribute Saul's understanding of the verse as a taunt to his awareness that the ritual context calls for mocking speech and, although the hemistichs can be read as simple parallelism, the poetics of the verse allows for reading the second hemistich as stepwise intensification of the first. The ambiguity of the verse (non-contrastive parallelism vs. intensification) is what makes it playfully abusive.[138]

From the various examples of שׂחק *pi᷉el* the Bible offers us, a few occur in contexts where dancing is not involved and מְשַׂחֵק-ing involves some kind of "abusive" occasion, to use Rosenstock's jargon. Others are less clearly negative. Prov 26:18–19 is a comparison between a "maniac who shoots deadly firebrands and arrows" (NRSV) and someone who shoots with his (her) tongue and intends to get away with it: "so is one who deceives his (her) neighbor and says, 'Was I not just joking?' " The participle translated "joking" is מְשַׂחֵק. It is not joking, but the deceiving, that is condemned.

A very interesting text in which the *pi᷉el* is used with the connotation of "entertainer" (left unsaid whether it included dancing) is Judg 16:25–27, in which the Philistines at the Dagon temple bring out the blinded and weakened Samson, that he may entertain them—which he does, to death. Also military "entertainment" involving death is that proposed and realized in 2 Sam 2:14.

The verb has also a negative connotation in Jer 15:17, where the prophet includes as part of his lament over his birth, this confession of innocence: "I did not sit in the company of the מְשַׂחֲקִים."[139] Another prophet includes boys and girls playing (merrymaking? dancing? all of these?) יְלָדִים וִילָדוֹת מְשַׂחֲקִים as a sign of the messianic times (Zech 8:5). I would like to think that the messianic sign is that boys and girls can dance together in the streets and there is no danger to (including despising of) anybody—unlike Judg 21 or 2 Sam 6.

---

[138] Bruce Rosenstock, "David's Play: Fertility Rituals and the Glory of God in 2 Samuel 6," *JSOT* 31 (2006): 71–72.

[139] There is also another text, 2 Chr 30:10, in which it is said of the messengers that they are made sport of, וַיִּהְיוּ מַשְׂחִיקִים עֲלֵיהֶם; the verb, however, is a *hip᷉il*, not a *pi᷉el*. It also appears in *qal*, especially in Job, with the meaning "laugh at."

Also a positive connotation of the verb (also *pi ʿel* participle, and this time feminine singular), is the pre-existent Wisdom in Prov 8:30–31. However, it is unclear whether it involves dancing or playing or both. Wisdom herself says "I was at his side, ואהיה אצלו playing/rejoicing before him at all times," משחקת לפניו בכל־עת; and in the next verse, again, "playing/rejoicing in/with the world, his earth (or the habitable world)... " משחקת בתבל ארצו.[140] Not only does Wisdom play: Leviathan does as well (Ps 104:26).

From this sampler it is clear that the *pi ʿel* conjugation of the verb may mean dancing or playing, and the latter with both a positive and a negative meaning. Although it might be used to speak of individuals (for instance, the "man" in Prov 26:18–19, to get away from his/her evil action by saying s/he was joking), and in most instances it involves a group, a company, whether as recipients (the Philistines vis-à-vis Samson) or as co-laughers or co-realizers (the merrymakers Jeremiah did not join). In fact, the plural participle occurs often. Even Wisdom, from the beginnings of time, is not alone in her משחק-ing but she is in the presence of YHWH and playing or playful with the inhabited world (בתבל, instrumental ב).

The second question is whether we can posit a particular group or occupation to which the title הנשים המשחקות would refer, or whether it is only descriptive of people generally rejoicing. From the examples just contemplated, it is clear that it is an activity not meant to be done alone; it involves someone performing or uttering something perceived by others as entertaining, amusing, subject to derision, or whatever "playing" or "merrymaking" might be understood to mean. Thus, in order to answer this question, we need to proceed.

Leaping and Dancing, in Two Versions (2 Samuel 6 and 1 Chronicles 15)

Second Samuel 6:1–11 recounts how YHWH's ark ended up at Gat, at Obed-Edom's home until it was deemed not dangerous anymore. In his first attempt to bring it to Jerusalem, David had gathered 30,000 of his chosen troops, every בחור; and "the whole people who were with him" דוד וכל־העם אשר אתו

---

[140] Opinions vary as to what is the exact meaning of the verb in these texts, as well as several other vexing riddles. From the several available resources, see Raymond N. Whybray's "Proverbs VIII 22–31 and Its Supposed Prototypes," *VT* 15 (1965): 504–14, already from 1965; R. Clifford, *Proverbs* (Norwich: SCM, 1999), 90–101 (with excursus on p. 98–99 on Jewish and Christian interpretations); N. Miura "A Typology of Personified Wisdom Hymns," *BTB* 34 (2004): 141–3. More recently and from a feminist perspective, see G. Baumann, *Die Weisheitsgestalt in Proverbien 1–9: Traditionsgeschichtliche und theologische Studien* (Tübingen: Mohr, 1996), 139; S. Gorges-Braunwarth, *"Frauenbilder—Weisheitsbilder—Gottesbilder" in Spr 1–9: Die personifizierte Weisheit im Gottesbild der nachexilischen Zeit* (Münster: LIT, 2002), 284–301; and Mercedes Lópes, "A mulher sábia e a sabedoria mulher – símbolos de co-inspiração:Um estudo sobre a mulher em textos de Provérbios" (Ph.D. diss., Universidade Metodista de São Paulo, 2007), 59–69.

(v.2). Would this "whole people" include women or would it be his army? If it did include women, they would be included with those in v. 5, said to be "making merry" (*NRSV*, same verb as in 1 Sam 18:7, see above), "dancing" (*JB*), "playing" (*JPS*) or "reveling" (Wright). In light of the second journey, it is likely that men and women would have come out to greet him and celebrate the ark's homecoming.[141] Bowman sees in 2 Sam 6:11b–23 "five interrelated parallel scenes which shift the focus of the story"[142] between David and YHWH (the first one), David and the people (second and fourth), and David and Michal.

Two characteristics of this procession are stressed by repetition in v. 12–19: joyous frenzy and sacredness. On the joy and the movements, already in v. 12 it is said that "David went and brought the ark … with rejoicing" (בשׂמחה); again in v. 14, "David was moving with all (his) strength before YHWH" (ודוד מכרכר בכל־עז לפני יהוה); and in v. 15, "David and all the house of Israel were bringing up YHWH's ark with shouting, and with the sound of the horn" (2 Sam 6:15). David Wright has compared both journeys, showing how in this second one David assumed a more priestly role and a more careful handling of God's ark, offering sacrifices at the very start of the journey, to ensure the Divinity's good will.[143] He concludes that

> it makes sense that the musical performance would be intensified in the second procession, to engage the deity more fully in the performance. But does David go too far? The music is one thing, but he also engages in a wild—even erotic—dance, a behavior that, if we give credit to Michal's criticism, seems to compromise the propriety of the ceremony. How does this fit into the ceremonial reforms?[144]

This wild dance in which David indulges is brought to the audience through his wife's eyes; looking through the window, she saw King David "jumping and dancing," מפזז ומכרכר (v. 16). The first of these two *hapax legomena* is taken to be related to "laid with gold" (1 Kgs 10:18) and its stem with "move with agility" (פזז). The second one, *pilpel* from כרר, might have originated from Arabic "move around" and then "recur." Driver states, "*leaping* (lit. *shewing agility) and circling about*. Both uncommon words … As Arabic shews, to *be active or agile*. I Ch. 15,30 substitutes more ordinary words … *skipping* (ψ.114,

---

[141] Haase, "Uzzah's Rebellion" explores the hidden rebellion by a sector of the leaders and priests against this move of the Northern symbol of YHWH's presence to Jerusalem; this rebellion is indicated by Uzzah's death, David's anger and fear; and the hint that it happened at the threshing-floor, a place for political and religious activities.

[142] Bowman, "Fortune," 114–5.

[143] Wright, "Music," 215.

[144] Wright, "Music," 216.

4.6; Job 21,11) and *playing...*"[145] Nonetheless, possibilities are high that its meaning is one relating to dance, because of the association in this chapter of each instance of dancing with "before YHWH;" because its "kindred verbs suggest that David's dance consisted of whirling or turning about;" and because of the Chronicles parallel, in which more common verbs are supplied.[146] Scholars have also pointed to the textual problems of the MT.

The motif of playing/dancing "before YHWH" is much stressed both by the narrator and by David, so that it serves as a criterion to pose that meaning for the verb מכרכר here, and to interpret the whole episode as a ritual one. It is also a notable intertextual reference to pre-existent Wisdom, playing before YHWH and rejoicing in God's creation (Prov 8:30–31, where the same verb and similar expression appear). It is perhaps possible to surmise that intertextual allusion is intended, in the light of Brueggemann's assertion, that,[147]

> [t]he entire exchange moves toward the Yahwistic claim at the center:
>
> Michal: honor
>   maids
>   shamelessly
> David: before Yahweh
>   chose me above ... above
>   prince over
>   before Yahweh
>   contemptible
>   maids
>   honor.

We turn now to the 1 Chr 15:29, where both *hapax legomena* have been "smoothed" or interpreted, as one prefers. Instead of מכרכר and מפזז we find here מרקד ומשחק. The stem רקד occurs nine times; five of these in poetic literature (Psalms, Job and Qoheleth), three in prophets, and here. Most of these appearances do not induce the reader to think literally of dancing, but rather of leaping or whirling: mountains, kids, and locusts are subjects of this verb. If we follow the LXX's emendation of the "vulgar fellows" or "shamelessly" הרקים of 2 Sam 6:20 to הרקדים, reading ονρcoume, nwn "dancers" we would add one

---

[145] Driver, *Notes*, 270. Wright, "Music," 209 prefers "leaping and prancing." Wright offers detailed analysis of every term, for which I am very grateful, for it helps in getting to the point that interests us through a smooth highway rather than having to open up a path through many bristles. So, I refer to his discussion for farther pondering on each of these *hapax legomena* and each textual difficulty.
[146] Wright, "Music," 221.
[147] Walter Brueggemann, *1 & 2 Samuel* (Interpretation; Louisville: Westminster John Knox, 1990), 252. McCarter, *2 Samuel*, 188–89, considers that Michal's might have been a different kind of Yahwism, less related to dancing and leaping and even to the Ark. Likewise, Lilian Klein, *Deborah to Esther* (Minneapolis: Augsburg Fortress, 2003), 92 notices the relationship of Michal to wooden idols, not (directly) to YHWH.

more occurrence to this participle and also explain the Chronicler's choice of this verb as one of both to replace the *hapax legomena*.[148]

Joy, contortions, or strong movements might not have been only David's to feel or to do, but he is the writers' focus, especially on the second journey. On the other hand, if Michal is right (v. 16) that David is dishonoring himself as king by his contortions, would females have been allowed ample movements? They are attested in Egyptian tombs, so they would not be unknown in court … Is Michal's implication that his are "feminine" movements? Or is she implying that a king would not have been moving as a contortionist or a "street dancer" would? Wright gives me an important clue by pointing at the connection between the "slave women" before whom David has dishonored himself (in Michal's view) and the proposed participle הרקדים:

> Did the people dance also in the second procession? There are a few affirmative clues in Michal's response to David. If the emendation of הרקדים, "the dregs," to הרקדים, "the dancers," at the end of v. 20 is correct, the definite article may indicate that Michal here is referring not just to dancers in abstract but to dancers that were in the witnessed procession. Moreover, Michal's criticism that David revealed himself to the slave women of his servants may indicate that these women were not simply in the parade audience, but dancing along with David.[149]

A more recent article by Rosenstock looks at David's actions in this chapter in a tension with ancient Near Eastern royal practices destined to bring fertility to the land by the King's representing the corresponding Deity. In contraposition to those rituals, David has sought to dishonor himself, as both Michal's words and his answer to her confirm.

> Her words highlight what might be called David's play as a form of *carnivalization*. I use this term in the sense proposed by Michael Bakhtin in his book on Rabelais (Bakhtin 1984). Bakhtin speaks of the way that medieval and early modern popular festivals, such as the "east of fools", *uncrown* the king and in his stead present a mocking and often grotesque parody of royal authority in the figure of the jester. David, in effect, has staged his own carnivalesque "uncrowning". Michal's words make this self-carnivalization apparent by comparing the king's glory to that of "the worthless fellows" who

---

[148] Singular genitive participle from ovrce, omai, "dance." Followed by McCarter, *2 Samuel*, 185: "some dancer." Driver, *Notes*, 272 mentions it, but since he adds "Judg 9,4. 11,3" (which are on the רקים), it is not clear to me which one he would adopt.

[149] Wright, "Music," 222–23.

expose themselves. This is perhaps a reference to other participants in the procession whose social status is lower than that of the king and his retinue.[150]

According to this proposal, Michal's utterance is not a rebuke or criticism, but ritual taunt, also a fairly common element in several rituals. It should be noted, however, that this near Eastern ritual has been adapted not only to exalt David despite his self-abasement, but to eject Michal from the biblical record with a very negative portrayal—and this is especially clear in the Chronicler's version, in which her contempt for her husband are the last words about her at all (1 Chr 15:29).

The end result of this angry marital encounter between Michal and David is the notice in 2 Sam 6:23 that Michal never became a mother, which indicates serious consequences for both the Saulide and the Davidic lines. Whether this lack of children is God's punishment (a likely possibility, since it is YHWH who opens the womb) and/or David's avoidance of his wife or (the least likely possibility considering the biblical mindset, but why not?), Michal's refusal of David, is left unsaid, for it is not within the narrator's focus.[151] And since it is also outside ours, I will deal very briefly with it, posing more questions than answers.

The narrator's implication that Michal's barrenness is a consequence of this encounter requires some untying. For this discussion, it would matter whether it is *YHWH's* punishment (the redactor's mind) for it would confirm David's side on the discussion, that is, that his dancing and contortions were done in the presence of YHWH rather than in view of the lowly women around him—whether musicians themselves, servants or servants' wives. Since, as already stated (this text was studied in reference to the אמהות),[152] neither David nor Michal contest these women's low status, would the narrator contest it by his statement? Would YHWH through barrenness? But then, what about David's concurrence that these women were of lowly status? Where is *his* punishment if Michal's is due to this assumption? To what extent would his erotic dance match Michal's barrenness?

Rosenstock has been amply quoted. While I remain unconvinced by some of his arguments, especially in what refers to the *hieros gamos* between David and Michal, I agree with his perception of a role exchange.[153] This misplacement of Michal's roles should not surprise as, since, as exposed by Berlin, her gender-

---

[150] Rosenstock, "David's Play," 70.

[151] Bowman, "Fortune," 116 rightly argues that this fact's reasons are not the narrator's concern.

[152] See chapter 4 (ideological use of the term "slave women" or "maidservants" עבדיו אמהות by both Michal and David to refer depreciatively to the women who had come out to celebrate).

[153] Rosenstock, "David's Play," 72. Reference to *hieros gamos* between David and Michal, 74–76.

related roles had already been exchanged from the very beginning with her brother Jonathan.[154] Sad thing, always to be on the wrong place!

Another clue may come from Bowman's study. Looking at Michal's fate more broadly, Bowman relates two political decisions by David to gain control over the whole people by seeking allegiance from the "Saulide," northern regions, namely, bringing the ark to Jerusalem and claiming devolution of his former wife Michal. Neither had YHWH's approval, thus bringing the ark to a stalemate and Michal to eternal barrenness. He asserts that,

> ...both efforts result in failure so long as David is acting upon his own initiative. Whereas God eventually authorizes David's regaining possession of the ark, he apparently does not authorize his regaining possession of Michal. The narrative contains no story of birth to this barren woman...
> This suggests that God himself will legitimate the monarchy of David. Legitimation will not come through an alliance with the house of Saul, nor will it continue through its progeny.[155]

This is also, needless to say, the official view, since the hero is David and not Saul nor, even less, Michal. Literary work or piece of reality, it is sad that the woman's body and sexuality are the battlefield between father and husband and between them and God. Not the first time, neither the last one.

מקוננות — Wailing Women or Lamenters

The term in question, מקוננות is the po'lel feminine plural participle of a denominative verb קין, "to sing a dirge, lament, wail." The verb is parsed in different forms along six texts, of which two acknowledge female performers, none in the DtrH. Ezekiel 32:16 closes a lamentation on Egypt by indicating that the "daughters of the nations" will sing it. The other occurrence of the term is also a prophetic invective, this time not against a foreign nation, but directed towards Judah itself. YHWH warns, it is time to call upon the wailing women over the general destruction of Zion. In typical Hebrew poetry, two terms are set in synonymic parallelism, with repetition of one verb (varying its spelling) and internal chiasmus:

---

[154] Adele Berlin, "Characterization in Biblical Narrative: David's Wives," in *Telling Queen Michal's Story*, 91–93; Lilian Klein, "Michal, The Barren Wife," in *A Feminist Companion to Samuel and Kings* (ed. Athalya Brenner; 2nd series; Sheffield: Sheffield Academic Press, 2000), 38 n.5 however, believes it is, rather than a gender issue, one of docility and control. Bowman, "Fortune," 99, affirms that "David's is a flawed but favored character, while Michal's is ever victimized but never vindicated."

[155] Bowman, "Fortune," 117. Also Haase does a political analysis of the episode.

Consider (התבוננו)![156]

and call	for the מקוננות		to come;
	for the חכמות	send	to come (Jer 9:16).

The second term is the feminine plural of the adjective "wise," which has two different meanings, one related to practical, handicraft skills and one that has to do with political (in its broadest sense) ability to maneuver, particularly to negotiate. Thus, two possible translations are "skilled women" and "female counselors."[157] The question to ask is whether the second term reflects also a profession or is only a fitting adjective to complement the parallel construction. In order to answer this question, we move on.

In her review of the sage in the ANE material, Harris makes a very important distinction in terms of learning between those few who could read and write and thus, make musical compositions, and those who could perform—a different kind of art but no less skilled, in my view. This difference is also recognized in the Bible, as the following examples show:

Second Samuel 1:17–18. As news came that these men had perished in battle against the Philistines, David not only intoned a lamentation (קינה) honoring Saul and Jonathan, but he ordered that it be taught to "the sons of Judah." Translations vary greatly as they attempt to deal with the last part of the verse, between "the Song of the Bow" (*NRSV, El Libro del Pueblo de Dios*), "teaching archery" (*JB*), "to teach the bow" (*JPS*) or ignoring the bow altogether (*Reina Valera*). Be it as it may, the important point is that David composes the lament and commands the people to learn it. Here, the people (or a group of people, whether the archers, the children or whatever we understand by "בני־יהודה") are passive receptors of the song. The song was recorded in the Book of the Just/Jashar (available for further reference?).[158] Note should be taken, on the other hand, of the recognition of the daughters of the Philistines in parallel to the daughters of the uncircumcised as those who should not rejoice at Saul's and Jonathan's death in v. 20.[159]

---

[156] The first imperative, introducing the divine announcement, is a *hitpoʿel* of the verb בין, "consider, discern." In his study on the נתינים Levine translates the participle masculine plural of this stem (*hipʿil*, not *hitpoʿel*, however) as "*mebinim* ('expert musicians')." I wonder if the use of this particular verb bears any weight on the semantics of these two feminine nouns.

[157] On this term see Camp, *Wisdom and the Feminine*, 120–3 and "The Wise Women of 2 Samuel."

[158] The other Dtr narrative in which the stem appears is 2 Sam 3:22–39, where the people are even more passive, following David's mourning signs in the face of Abner's murder.

[159] Noted and shortly discussed by Laniak, *Shame*, 98 in his study of mourning practices, shame and public scrutiny (although quotation is wrongly given as I Sam 1:20).

Second Chronicles 35:25. It is agreed among scholars that trying to explain Josiah's untimely death is one of the main concerns of the *golah*. In its later version in Chronicles, this astonishment is expressed by a dirge composed in his honor by Jeremiah:

> And Jeremiah lamented (ויקונן) over Josiah, and all the male and female singers (כל־השרים והשרות) told (it) in their lamentations (בקינותיהם) about Josiah until today. They made it a practice over Israel; these are written in the (book of) Laments (הקינות).

This piece of information is even more interesting than the one on David's arts as composer, for here there is, besides or after Jeremiah, a tradition of male and female singers (Heb. שיר). Thus, the Chronicler recognizes two distinct associations of singers. Not only that. They might have gotten the "script" from Jeremiah; but they "talked" about him and in his honor in their קינות—that is, as they performed—"until today" which is, if we read Chronicles narratively, until after the *golah* came back home or at least considered coming back (2 Chr 36:22).

Oral performance is never mere repetition (and it could never be throughout so long a time) and this is better known by oral cultures than by literate ones; thus, I assume it is not unwittingly that the narrators tell us so. It is a recognition of both Jeremiah's skills and of male and female performers. Notice also how the motif of having been written in a book supposedly available has been shifted here from the original poet to the school created by him.

Now I return to the question left open above and state that, in my opinion, the use of the adjective חכמות in parallel to מקוננות in Jer 9:16 intends to convey a deeper meaning than the aesthetic one of completing the parallel. The lexeme חכמה, with or without "אשה," singular or plural, evokes a semantic range of occupations and abilities by trained and recognized women. Among these, to be able to compose or to adapt a קינה in the manner of 2 Chr 35:25 would be but a little thing.[160] We have encountered them in relation to conception and pregnancy and to healing (at least, healing of women but probably also children if not males), as singers and poets, as skilled weavers in its more practical acceptation; and, as several scholars have pointed out and we have mentioned in our Introduction, there is a political office also called by this lexeme.

---

[160] Amico, "Status of Women," 239–40: "There is a mythological healer named Š'tqt, who is created by El to cure Keret of his illness (KTU 1. 16. V:26–VI:10). In fact, part of what she does is to weep and sob. Healing and mourning thus seem intimately connected." See also Marsman, *Women*, 526–27.

Summing Up the Evidence for Musicians

The question that concerned us here was whether there is reasonable evidence to posit the existence of some kind of an organized group of female "entertainers" in the general sense of the term, including singers, dancers, even contortionists and/or "taunters" who would be hidden under the participles usually translated as verbs and thus, less noticed as possible "guilds," sisterhoods or associations. There are several terms identifying music players, dancers and performers of some type of dance or contortions (perhaps referring originally to malabarists as a different group?), most of which fall outside our block of material and do not focus on women. Three texts, two in the DtrH and one parallel in Chronicles, combine many of these terms and specifically mention women as mocking-singers, musicians, and dancers. In all three the main character is not they, but David. In other texts there is evidence of regular female involvement in music and performance.

The nature of the stories studied does not allow for a clear statement for or against female sacred participation. First, because there are no ancient criteria for us to decide whether what is described is sacred or not—a puzzle for each term included or left out. Many celebrations, including that one that brought Michal to despise David, are done "before YHWH": would that be enough to make them sacred? Then, women had a clear leadership alongside men in many of them. However, evidence is scarce and, to a certain point, circumstantial: Jephthah's daughter coming out is the first one to come—yet, does she come because she has a function or because it is her father's victory?[161] Miriam or Deborah, recognized leaders, have a profession; the entertainers המשחקות, coming out to sing about David and Saul (and bring the latter to utter jealousy and murderous intent, 1 Sam 18) seem, at least, to have belonged (maybe only some of them) to some choir or company.

I stated above that Dtr did not find many occasions to let their audiences hear there were female musicians, including players of instruments, singers, and dancers. How to assess these situations? Were they normal, despite the lack of biblical evidence? Or, on the contrary, are they present only as token or accidental evidence, as part of the *scenario*? It seems to me that it is possible to make a case for the Dtr's expurgation of their presence. For even in occupations or realms elsewhere clearly related to women, such as drummers or mourners

---

[161] Pamela Tamarkin Reis, "Spoiled Child: A Fresh Look at Jephthah's Daughter," *Prooftexts* 17 (1987): 279–98, argues that the teen-ager knew about her father's promise to offer to YHWH the first one to come out; that it was her decision, not his hurried vow, that brought about the issue and that it is about celibacy and not death. Donna Nollan Fewell, *The Children of Israel* (Nashville: Abingdon, 2003), 78–80 gives several possible reasons, among them perhaps "that no one else's death would make him [her father] stop and realize that his disregard for innocent life made him no better than the Gileadites who had treated him like garbage to be discarded." (79)

(and, more generally outside music, as health advisors or midwives) they sought circumlocutions, mentioned them just in passing, or set them in a secondary role, under the authorship of a renowned male (Moses above Miriam, David as composer of dirges, and so forth). This is a trend that, unfortunately, cannot be ascribed only to these particular sages, but is evident in the whole corpus of ANE sources. It comes as no surprise, therefore, that Harris would observe:

> The term "sage" when preceded by the adjective female must be put in quotations marks, for it is highly questionable whether women in the ancient Near East were ever considered to be culture creators, or whether any mirrored "in themselves the ideals of wisdom" or were "folk heroes of the wisdom tradition.[6] … Indeed, "female" and "sage" were contradictions in terms in the ancient Near Eastern world.
>
> A more fruitful and probably the only viable approach to the topic for now is by way of the rich vocabulary for wisdom and its derivatives, as it was actually used *or might be inferred* in reference to women and their activities.[162]

Were it not for welcome, outstanding exceptions, we would not have been able to trace the singers, music players, performers, poets, and lamenters; that we have partially uncovered. They might not have been sages, but they were wise. The question posed earlier, whether it is possible to imagine that at least some of them belonged to recognized associations of musicians or singers, such as many men did, cannot be definitely answered, although we lean towards a shy "yes." Notice should be taken that they are often mentioned by the participle determined by the article, without previous introduction, performing precisely as doers—one function the participle has, in the style of "the singers, the heads of the Levites' families… "המשררים ראשי אבות ללוים" (1 Chr 9:33) or ותקום מרים הנביאה אחות אהרן את־התף "Miriam, the prophetess, Aaron's sister, took the drum…". What we have is, then, the minimal evidence that allows us to say "at least there were all of these associations." How much more there was depends on our optimism and our luck with future discoveries, and on our ability as scholars to glean further fruit from our sources. Were we to count only with Deuteronomy to 2 Kings, we would even miss what has been presented above, since we needed often to resort to other bodies of material. Even so, it is not much to know about women in ancient Israel, is it?

---

[162] Harris, "Female 'Sage'," 4, quoting G. Buccellati, "Wisdom and Not: The Case of Mesopotamia," *JAOS* 101 (1981): 42.

SECTION III: NOTABLE ABSENTEES FROM DTRH

In this section I turn to notable absentees. By this is meant occupations that belong to everyday life, from a small to a large household, in all probability part and parcel of a woman's chore, at the domestic level and also professionally. Thus, finding them mentioned in the DtrH would not have come as a surprise, but not once are they recognized. Since "could have been mentioned" is very subjective, it may help set three questions as criteria:

- Could ancient Israelites have lived without "it" (e.g., midwifery, spinning, dentistry, divination, hairdressing, etc.)?
- Is there a term in the Bible that hints at this occupation?
- Is it probable that a woman would have professionally performed this activity?

When the answers to all these are affirmative, they come in this section, provided their realm is not specifically political or religious, such as the prophetess, the judge, the queen or the diviner, left untreated on purpose.

מילדת — *Midwife and Health-Care Giver*

The Hebrew term for midwife is מילדת, *pi'el* feminine participle of ילד.[163] Midwifery involved several activities and skills, many of which can easily be lost to today's reader, since the term is not stated in many texts, and the characteristics of the occupation have changed. No other professional was so much in contact primarily with women as a midwife was. According to studies by Matthews and Benjamin, the midwife played a key role in monitoring the whole process leading to a child, starting from finding out what would be the right moment for conception and making it as propitious as possible, conducting pre-natal care, helping during delivery and finally presenting the baby to the father or disposing of it if the father did not want it.[164] In spite of the fact that practically every woman was assisted by a midwife, "מילדת" is not mentioned once in the laws, in DtrH, in wisdom literature or in the prophets. Where do we find them? Midwives appear twice in Genesis and once in Exod 1. This is telling, considering that "the woman's most important role was the bearing of numerous children (Gen. 1:28; 9:1), while the man hoped to produce many progeny who would contribute needed labor and continue the household into the

---

[163] The *pi'el* stem is the only one with the meaning "to act as a midwife." ילד *hip'il* appears in Isa 55:10 with YHWH bringing forth life from the rain, and in 66:9 with YHWH as the one who opens the womb and delivers. Other instances have to do with conception. See J. Kühlewein, "ילד," in *TLOT* (ed. Ernst Jenni & Claus Westermann; 3 vol.; Peabody: Hendrickson, 1997), 2.546; GK II.393.

[164] Matthews & Benjamin, *Social World of Ancient Israel*, 67–74; Don C. Benjamin, "Israel's God: Mother and Midwife," *BTB* 19 (1989): 117; see also 115.

future (Gen 15:4–6)."[165] At any rate, numerous progeny was more exception than rule, since children under six were at high risk and several pregnancies usually resulted in about two to three surviving children.[166]

In Gen 35:17 the midwife המילדת appears, comforting Rachel while she delivers Ben-oni and dies. In Gen 38:28, a midwife binds a red crimson around one of Tamar's twin sons. Finally, two midwives, Puah and Shiphrah appear in Exod 1, where they are called to task because the Hebrew babies are not being killed, as Pharaoh had ordered them to do. The general ideological assumption is that Egyptian and Hebrew women are different.[167] But while Pharaoh assumes Egyptian superiority, the Hebrew writer builds upon that same assumption of difference to state that Hebrews are better. The Hebrew nationality of the two midwives locates them among those persecuted by a Pharaoh who was afraid of the possible growth of the Israelites.[168] For the writer, Shiphrah and Puah do not challenge the system's assumption that Egyptians and Hebrews *are* different, but turn it around to justify their refusal to participate in the babies' killing, in a tactic of survival and resistance often used by minorities or oppressed groups.[169]

Funny as Pharaoh's fear of newborn children might seem to us, he joins other rulers in their fear of people's ways. Amico states: "The role of midwife/wise woman is strongly attested in Hittite texts, where the practitioners were known as the 'Old Women.' Thirteen of them are known by name, and at least one Hittite king, Hattušili I, expressed strong disapproval for their activities, perhaps because they were so powerful among the people."[170] One reason why they would be feared is that they, as wise women, ensured a safe birth for mother and child through the use of proper incantations and other "dark" practices and mysterious remedies, which sometimes would help and sometimes would seem to have killed the mother or the child.[171] Furthermore,

---

[165] Leo Perdue, "The Israelite and Early Jewish Family: Summary and Conclusions," in *Families in Ancient Israel*, 170.

[166] Stager, "Archaeology of the Family," 18; Gruber, "Breast-Feeding," 61–2, quoting anthropologist H. Granqvist, *Child Problems among the Arabs* (Helsinki: n.e., 1950), 52–5. Carol Meyers, "The Roots of Restriction: Women in Early Israel," *BA* 41 (1978): 91–103.

[167] Weems, "Hebrew Women," 28.

[168] The grammar of the text is ambiguous as to the nationality of Shiphrah and Puah; I am assuming they would be Hebrew because in general people have midwives from their same people –actually, they usually learned by training, starting with their own families and with no formal preparation. It would make sense that a people who are being enslaved and persecuted would have their own midwives from among their own women.

[169] Weems, "Hebrew Women," 29–30; D. Knight, "Political Rights and Powers in Monarchic Israel," in *Ethics and Politics in the Hebrew Bible* (ed. D. Knight & C. Meyers. *Semeia* 66. Atlanta: Scholars Press, 1995), 104.

[170] Amico, "Status of Women," 240.

[171] Nancy R. Bowen, "The Daughters of Your People: Female Prophets in Ezekiel 13:17–23," *JBL*

men would not want to have anything to do with them, being easier to condemn them than to learn from them or being challenged by their expertise. Marsman speaks about midwives in the Hittite sources:

> First, of course, there are the actual physical tasks involved in any birth: The midwife prepares the equipment ...
>
> Secondly, the midwife recites incantations on behalf of the new-born, beseeching the gods to remove evil influences and to grant a desirable fate to the child.
>
> As a spokesperson for the new-born babies, the task of the midwife, in her capacity as incantation priestess, could sometimes be expanded to include magician on behalf of those suffering from some sort of illness.[172]

Rivka Harris thinks that Mesopotamian midwifery (in her view, carried on by the *qadištu*s rather than the *nadītu*s) "was a profession that may well have covered the services of a modern gynecologist, obstetrician, and pediatrician. Perhaps they also served to advise and help with family problems. Their knowledge was presumably taught by mothers to daughters and other relatives."[173] Also Egyptian sources are very restricted about midwifery, since tombs especially are very stereotyped, and again they focus on the male's worldview. Nonetheless, there are data available from documents, medico-magical papyri, arts and archaeological pieces on their understanding of conception, pregnancy, childbirth, and childcare.

> [S]ome Ptolemaic temple scenes show the birth of a divine child. Usually one goddess stands behind the mother holding her, and one kneels in front to receive the child. A Middle Kingdom story records the miraculous birth, as triplets, of the first three kings of the Fifth Dynasty. The mother Rudjedet is attended at the birth by the four goddesses, Isis, Nephthys, Meskhenet, and Hekat. Each birth is described in a similar manner, apart from words spoken by Isis punning on the child's name: "Isis placed herself before her [Rudjedet], Nephthys behind her, Hekat hastened the birth .... The child slid into her [Isis's] arms .... They washed him, having cut his navel cord, and laid him on a pillow of cloth."[174]

Sifting the story out of mythological elements, the midwives' task during labor of any common woman is still easily perceptible. Medical papyri also contain instructions with regard to this process, even though they cannot be

---

118 (1999): 423–28. Worthy of note is also Bowen's warning that we should not different so sharply between prophecy and divination or magic.

[172] Marsman, *Women*, 412 quoting G. M. Beckman, *Hittite Birth Rituals* (StBT, 29), Wiesbaden 1983, 234 (unavailable to me).

[173] Harris, "Female 'Sage,'" 12.

[174] Robins, *Women*, 82.

easily comprehended. In her work Robins does not use once the term "midwife" and one wonders if that reflects in some way the absence of a term for "midwife" in Egyptian sources, or whether it is just an accident. Robins mentions remnants of paintings from Deir el-Medina where women suckle newborn babies and are waited upon by young women. She states, however, that these are thought to refer to the mother's purification after fourteen days, in which case it is harder to assume that those waiting upon her are midwives.[175] Considering that most surviving documents represent the male world in which there is no personal experience of midwives and delivery, it is not surprising that there are in general so few references to midwives in ancient writings. Ugarit is yet another example of this scarcity of sources for our study:

> Unless the Kotharot are divine midwives as well as conception goddesses, there is no attestation of midwifery at Ugarit, although it is inconvievable [*sic*] that it did not exist, providing occupation for a number of women. A related role is that of wetnurse, ordinarily a rather lowly occupation, although at Ugarit it is glorified by being attributed to goddesses.[176]

Female physicians are also very rare in the sources available today, although an Old Kingdom Egyptian text mentions Peseshet, "Overseer of the female physicians."[177] Considering how little evidence there is, perhaps Marsman is right in that "professional healers normally were men, both in Mesopotamia and Egypt."[178] But perhaps there are other factors as well, such as considering their service more on the side of divination, witchcraft and other unacceptable (for orthodoxy) practices thus not recognizing their services on an equal footing with their male colleagues. This unequal status ascription is confirmed also for the workers' village of Deir el-Medina, where, according to sources, there appears

> the feminine title of *rḫy.t*, the knowing or divining woman, who, as Joris F. Borghouts has concluded from a few mentions in the ostraca, seemingly had the power to predict events and was consulted to explain "manifestations of the god": illnesses, accidents, or divine oracles. Whether such a woman (she is never named) was paid for helping others we do not know. "Wise" women in other cultures often prepared herbal medicines and assist at the sickbed or as midwives, but in this village one of the workmen was paid extra and given time off to practice as a physician.[179]

---

[175] Robins, *Women*, 87–88.

[176] Amico, "Status of Women," 241.

[177] Marsman, *Women*, 411; Lesko, "Women's Monumental Mark," 5.

[178] Marsman, *Women*, 411.

[179] Barbara S. Lesko, "Ranks, Roles, and Rights," in *Pharaoh's Workers: The Villagers of Deir el Medina* (ed. Leonard H. Lesko; Ithaca: Cornell University Press, 1994), 26, quoting Joris Borghouts,

Why was it not "medicine" on equal footing with that of a male physician when a wise woman recommended an herbal tea, for instance? Sorting out plants, preparing them correctly, storing them, and knowing which ones to use for which ailment was also part of their job description, for sure. This quotation from a male specialist in ancient Mesopotamia is illustrative; I arrive at his opinion through Harris's analysis, which I quote at length because she puts it more nicely than I could:

> Female healers are "more likely to define themselves as informal practitioners, to operate within the home and not fit the model of medical knowledge, practice, and advancement."[41]
>
> For Leo Oppenheim, "Mesopotamian medicine is shown to be a typical folk medicine ... the *materia medica* consists mainly of native herbs of many kinds ..." [42] He points out that the two medical traditions and schools of Mesopotamia can be divided into the "scientific" and the "practical." Women may safely be assigned only to the latter; the former presupposes a modicum of literacy. But once again we are at the mercy of the anonymity and the elusiveness of the women we seek.[180]

Still today patriarchy has difficulties to ascribe equal honor and salary (for instance, through recognition of capacities, allocation of resources, respect for a particular viewpoint, etc.), to people who are not at the center of their worldview (i.e., not only women, but to all who do not conform to the heterosexual male from dominant social class and adequate skin-color model). Just as today there are still so many glass ceilings, and just as the Dtr forgot to mention the midwives and other women they must have seen working even in their own families, so could our sources just ignore female physicians.

Pottery Making

Above, I mentioned several areas in which women had the main responsibility (and to a large degree, we still have), to name a few: nourishing (including everyday feeding, care of infants, elderly, and sick members of the family), pregnancy and birthing, textiles, and pottery making.[181] When studying pottery,

---

"Divine Intervention in Ancient Egypt and Its Manifestation (*b3w*)," in Robert Demarée and Jac. J. Janseen (ed. *Gleanings from Deir el-Medina*, Leiden: Instituut voor het Nabije Oosten, 1982), 1–70.

[180] Harris, "Female 'Sage,'" 11, quoting S. A. Sharp, "Women as Keepers and Carriers of Knowledge," *Women's Studies International Forum* 9/3 (1986) 247–48 and Oppenheim, *Ancient Mesopotamia*, 292.

[181] I have only come across one book on care of the sick in the ANE, *The Care of the Elderly in the Ancient Near East*, edited by Marteen Stol & Sven P. Vleeming (Leiden: Brill, 1998). It is only partially available to me through the internet [cited 1 September 2011]. Online: http://books.google.com.ar/books?hl=en&lr=&id=C5kVfVwHmm4C&oi=fnd&pg=PP9&dq=marteen+stol,+elderly&ots=VP8pdRjbuw&sig=J-iHTFIncAlCYmVUo8k2s0wX0Qg#v=onepage&q&f=false.

one should make a distinction between large industrial complexes, located especially in areas in which access to metal and to furnaces was possible—in which case it would seem logical that men (or more men than women) would be involved—and domestic production of pots, vessels, and beads for bijouterie (and perhaps small amulets and also seals?). The evidence for this type of "small" pottery is hard to be made visible. This does not preclude their existence, of course.

There is evidence for the spreading of a particular kind of hand-made ceramic artifacts called "Negevite," left behind by nomadic autochthonous Negevite and Transjordanian groups as they migrated within the region. This kind of pottery is found in archaeological sites ranging from the Bronze to the Early Islamic periods and is especially typical of the Iron Age. A recent dissertation has proposed that, rather than presupposing a "guild" of specialized producers of this pottery for commercial purposes, it was domestically manufactured as needed.[182] It served local and momentary needs and it was left behind as the seminomadic groups moved or as it broke. In my opinion, there is no reason to exclude female activity in this task, especially if men were involved with cattle, commercial activity, or defense.

In one of her articles on ethno-archaeology applied to ceramics, Gloria London tells how it is still customary for potters in the Philippines and in Cyprus to allocate the domestic space according to pressing needs. During the summer months, hundreds of pots were produced, dried, and stored wherever they could store them. Afterwards, the same rooms were used for other needs and there remained no evidence of the production after the season. "If women in antiquity were responsible for making pottery, and they carried out the work in the confines of their house exteriors or courtyards as they undertook myriad other daily and seasonal chores, it will be difficult for archaeologists to recognize pottery production areas."[183] This means, for our study, that women would be the primary pottery-makers, at least of domestic artifacts, since they would work at home, while realizing and supervising other tasks. Armijo Navarro-Reverter reports on archaeological findings of beads and molds used for necklaces and other uses (perhaps amulets?) concentrated specifically in the "T33, T35 and T36 quadrants, where the humble houses abound" in the village of Amarna, which indicate to her a localized working spot, with which women would generate some extra income.[184]

---

[182] Juan M. Tebes, "Tribus, Estados, cobre e incienso" (Ph.D. diss., Facultad de Filosofía y Letras, Universidad de Buenos Aires: Buenos Aires, 2010), 190–8.

[183] Gloria London, "Fe(male) Potters as the Personification of Individuals, Places, and Things as Known from Ethnoarchaeological Studies," in *The World of Women in the Ancient and Classical Near East*, 160. Papers in this collection come from conferences between 2000 and 2007.

[184] Armijo Navarro-Reverter, "La vida de las mujeres egipcias," 132.

Studying women's socialization of cooking and weaving spaces in Iron Age Syro-Palestine, Baadsgaard makes good use of the concept of "heterarchy." These networks [women's roles and powers] were crucial for maintaining political and economic stability among and between families and communities and entail female power over and control of certain technologies, such as bread and textile production. Thus it seems that Iron Age society might be better understood as a flexible heterarchy, an organizational system with multiple and overlapping individuals and groups existing in different kinds of power relationships."[185]

If I understand Janet Levy (whom Baadsgaard refers to) correctly, the concept challenges the exclusive hierarchical (gendered and homogenizing) look at any phenomenon (be it family, labor, even brain activity); for there are several cross-cutting relationships, which defy or at least qualify such a hierarchy. Levy applies this concept to labor in this way: "A heterarchical approach to division of labor will emphasize cross-cutting boundaries, lateral relationships as well as vertical ones, and multiple scales of analysis. That is, rather than assume a specific division of labor or specific trajectory of increasing specialization over time, we should consider evidence for variable organization of labor within family, community, and region."[186]

In short, the evidence collected in traditional villages allows us to posit the probability that women would be involved in pottery manufacturing, although not many remains have survived. Nor has it survived in the Bible, where only masculine terms appear, the majority of which refers to divine action.[187]

OUR DAILY BREAD

Barley, made into a porridge, bread or beer was, together with some fruits, olives, and yoghurt, staple food in ancient Israel. Bakers and cooks or butchers, male and female, are recognized in the DtrH as occupations expected by the wealthy: 1 Sam 8 includes these female workers among those taken from the Israelite families to serve the political apparatus; bakers are ordered to provide Jeremiah daily bread (Jer 37:21), and Joseph orders the butcher at Pharaoh's palace to prepare a meal for him and his brothers (Gen 43:16).

Intermingled in narratives about various issues, a few very interesting references to different moments in the process of turning grain into bread can be

---

[185] Aubrey Baadsgaard, "A Taste of Women's Sociality: Cooking as Cooperative Labor in Iron Age Syro-Palestine," in *The World of Women in the Ancient and Classical Near East*, 17.

[186] Levy, "Gender," 226. According to Levy, 219, Carole L. Crumley introduced the term into archaeology in 1979.

[187] As human activity see Isa 29:16; 30:14; 45:9b; Ps 2:9; 1 Chr 4:23; Jer 18:11 (YHWH presenting God-self as the potter אנכי יוצר).

gathered. Starting by harvesting, we find dependent men and women, working for a rich landowner at harvest time, either permanently or, like Ruth, as a seasonal laborer (Ruth 2:22–23). Ruth starts as a poor widow who asks for her right to glean after the harvesters and is incorporated by Boaz throughout the season. "Boaz's generosity is evident. Ruth is poor and she is hungry. But there is more. Ruth is invited to eat with men (the harvesters), which is unusual. ... Boaz has just taken a step in the direction of liberalism. Besides, Ruth's gleaning is transformed by Boaz's wishes. She now has access to the very harvest, no longer just to what the harvesters leave behind."[188] Not only is she incorporated, so that she needs no longer worry about eating every day, but Boaz's generosity is also evident in his twofold instructions to protect her from harassment. These instructions are addressed directly to her, "Don't leave anywhere, stay with my dependents" (2:8–9, replicated by Naomi in v. 22) and to his workers, not to molest her (reported by Boaz himself). Most scholars note the tension between gleaners and harvesters evidenced in these dialogues; I would stress also the ever-present possibility that even the female dependents, working under Boaz's patronage, would be molested by their male co-workers and bosses. This would apply not only to workers in the field like Ruth, but everywhere, especially in the palace and the temple, where status and power would have played a larger role.[189]

Inadvertently, Num 11 gives us some clues as to the process involved in preparing a cake or bread, boiled or baked. The story is about the people's complaint that, day in and day out, they only have manna to eat. The narrator recalls women's every-day task. Here, since manna fell from heaven, it needed not be harvested nor gleaned among the sheaves, but just gathered: "The people went around and gathered it, ground it in mills or beat it in mortars, then boiled it in pots and made cakes of it; and the taste of it was like the taste of cakes baked with oil." (Num 11:8, *NRSV*).

טוֹחֲנ/וֹת — *Grinders at the Mill*

There are also a few, really few, references to grinding, so that there would be flour: nine verses altogether, including verb and noun, figurative and literal, for food and for gold. One masculine singular and one feminine plural participle are recorded, and they refer to people being put in this occupation permanently. Interestingly, the only reference to this activity in DtrH is to Samson, blinded and put to work as grain grinder at the Gaza prison mill (Judg 16:21, וַיְהִי טוֹחֵן). Blinding of prisoners is attested also in other, biblical and extrabiblical sources.

---

[188] André LaCocque, *Ruth* (Minneapolis: Fortress, 2004), 74.

[189] See John C. Whittaker, "Alonia and Dhoukanes: The Ethnoarchaeology of Threshing in Cyprus," *NEA* 63 (2000): 62–69 for an approximation to ancient threshing floors and techniques.

Harry Hoffner, a specialist on Hittite material, reports on lists of blinded men among prisoners; since some of them had fled, it is not clear whether they had been totally blinded (in which case, they would have counted with accomplices) or only from one eye. Blinding prisoners was a humiliation device, as well as a security measure—to the extent that people can be kept imprisoned against their will. "From the Maşat letters it is clear that persons captured in battle were employed in various forms of public labor until such time as some might be reclaimed by their own people through ransom. One form of such public labor was mill work. And it was performed chiefly, if not exclusively, by captives who had been blinded."[190] Evidently, there was also the possibility, at least in theory, that some of these men would be ransomed by family or village, especially if they had been valiant soldiers. However, many practical hindrances would often make this a very remote possibility. Not only was blinding humiliating: setting them at the mill was, even though very necessary for everybody's table, a typically feminine job, thus adding to their humiliation.[191] To be noted in Samson's story is how this gender-related activity becomes a permanent condition, his identity: he became grinder—not "he was obliged to grind" or "was conscripted to work at the mill." He became טוחן.This low status of the occupation can also be perceived in Isa 47:1–4, where the lofty position of Queen Babylon/Chaldea will be no more. In her reversal of fate, she is commanded: קחי רחים וטחני קמח, take the millstones and grind flour, v. 2. The Lady will take her slave's place, will lose her privileges and will no longer do her will, but the slave's work, unveiled, nude, ashamed and abused.[192]

The remaining text to be dealt with is Qoh 12:1–7. In this book we have already encountered lists of male and female slaves, male and female singers, and probably war captives among the acquisitions by the "king." Here, in verses

---

[190] Hoffner, "Treatment," 70.

[191] It is true that archeological evidence is not conclusive as to gendered ascription of roles, since there are figurines both of men and women grinding with the two stones. However, ethno-archaeology and some texts allow us to assume that food processing was mostly carried out by women. Carol Meyers, "Archaeology—A Window to the Lives of Israelite Women" in *Torah* (ed. Irmtraud Fischer & Mercedes Navarro Puerto; Atlanta: SBL, 20011), 83 enumerates "drying or soaking, grinding, sifting, kneading, heating and often leavening" as some of the tasks required daily to make cereal into edible items.

[192] Another oblique reference to grinding as slavish activity is provided by Job 31:10. In verses 7–12 pious Job makes his disclaimer about any intention or realization of adultery on his participle He swears, "if my heart was seduced by a woman... may my wife grind for another one and over her may others kneel." Norman Habel, *The Book of Job* (OTL; Louisville: Westminster John Knox, 1985), 433–4 (and other scholars, of course) has commented on the sexist character of this passage, in which Job would not be punished by his own sin had he sinned, but his wife would—or would he? Since the passage is plagued with double-entendres, it is not clear to what extent the allusion to grinding intends to be taken literally. Habel also refers the readers to Exod 11:5, in which again the female slave in charge of grinding (השפחה אשר אחר הרחים) is at the opposite extreme in the social scale than the Pharaoh.

3 and 4 appear the only feminine plural participle and one of the two nouns from this same stem (טחנה).[193] The Sage does not say much about the grinders themselves; however, when the noise of their grinding (קול הטחנות) fades because their number has faded, it signals disaster. The context does not allow for an unambiguous decision for a domestic or a professional allusion here; the "voice of grinding" to cease could either be that of the women of the household or the slaves working for the large households. References to "guardians" or "strong men" and to the door-gates in the streets (דלתים בשוק) make one think larger than the household, at least the village is in focus here.

Aside from being eaten as porridge or bread, barley was fundamental for the whole industry of beer brewing. In the Bible there is the noun שכר, which often appears in translations and commentaries as "strong drink." Noteworthy is also the total absence of terms for males as performers and for expenditure centers (taverns or inns) in the Hebrew Bible. Unless, as discussed in the previous chapter, several references to זונה/ות would be to tavern keepers and inn keepers, together with or instead of, "harlots." We go for a drink now.

Beer Brewing

Beer is well attested both as a staple food and as an offering to the deities.[194] Beer was the daily drink of most people for several reasons, from its caloric and proteinic value to the fact that water was usually not very safe to drink. Bread and beer went together, since brewing "was an offshoot of bread production. Beer was a dietary staple in this region...."[195] Since much of bread and beer preparation was women's work, such as grinding grain, fetching water, and

[193] In Lam 5:13 there is a complaint that involves, again, a reversal of fate: the young men, who would usually be the young Lords or warriors, are obliged to take mill-stone (בחורים טחון נשאו) and the dependents (ונערים) stumble under the weight of wood. Another expression is "the two stones" (רחים, dual).

[194] Gary Beckman, "Hittite Literature," in *From an Antique Land: An Introduction to Ancient Near Eastern Literature* (ed. Carl S. Ehrlich; Lanham: Rowman & Littlefield Publishers, 2009), 247 translates what he calls (245) "arguably the single most moving piece of surviving Hittite literature, ... the better part of The Prayer of Kantuzzilito the Sun-god," from which the pertinent line is: "O Sun-god, sustain this mortal, your servant, so that he might begin to offer bread and beer to the Sun-god regularly. O Sun-god, take him, your just servant, by the hand." In Egypt, an ancient legend attributes its origins to Osiris, as part of civilization's gift, but Hathor held the title of goddess of beer and wine. That beer and other supplies were provided to the dead is attested in the first chapter of the Book of the Dead and by archaeologists; see Ildefonso Robledo Casanova, "Los misterios de los egipcios. El hombre, sus componentes y el Más Allá," *Antigua: Historia y Arqueología de las Civilizaciones* (web), n. p. [cited: 20 December 2010]. Online: http://213.0.4.19/servlet/SirveObras/13538363212820165754491/021575.pdf#search=%22cerveza%20osiris%22&page=15.

[195] Ebeling & Homan, "Baking and Brewing Beer," 46.

preparing the dough, this would be yet another area in which women labored and which for many was their job. According to a scholar, "[b]eer drinking, like the bed, is inextricably linked to sexual activity and arousal in the world of poetry. In the real world, beer drinking and sex were the two chief pleasures available to non-elite Mesopotamians."[196] And "[s]ince women were the brewers of beer in antiquity, it should come as no surprise that the earliest deities associated with alcohol in the Near East and Egypt were female," reason two specialists on the issue.[197] There are two Sumerian goddesses of beer; the best known is Ninkasi, who looked over its manufacture, as one old poem shows.[198] In Mesopotamia, the goddess of beer and patroness of tavern keepers was Inanna. According to Frymer-Kensky, Sumerian goddesses "were in charge of the three activities that the Mesopotamians considered basic to a civilized life: the wearing of cloth, the eating of grain, and the drinking of beer."[199] Each of these activities was overseen by its corresponding goddess, who were eventually marginalized and replaced by male gods. "The diminishing role of the goddesses thereby, in itself, served as a paradigm for the recession of women. And since this paradigm of male monopolizing was projected onto the divine sphere, it both modeled and provided sacred warrant for the ongoing cultural displacement of women."[200] No wonder, then, that the professional tavern keeper or "alewife" *sābītu*, "'disappears from the scene at the end of the Old Babylonian Period.' …. With very few exceptions, their tasks [those of women at the Neo-Babylonian Ebabbar temple at Sippar] were humble, like grinding flour and weaving."[201] Note should be taken that Marsman is very careful not to say that there were no more women in these professions, but that they disappear from records. They might have disappeared from several positions, particularly those more visible such as running a tavern; but experience even today says lower-class people continue to do the hard work, even though they never appear in records or awards.

Beer brewing is, in fact, well attested in the whole ANE (including Israel, see below), not only in writing (ration lists, legal documents, ritual regulations,

---

[196] Assante, "Erotic Reliefs," 232.

[197] Ebeling & Homan, "Baking and Brewing Beer," 50.

[198] In a report appearing in 1991, "Modern Brewers Recreate Ancient Beer" (n. p. [cited 1 July 2011]. Online: http://oi.uchicago.edu/research/pubs/nn/fal91_civil_hymn.html, Miguel Civil recounts how his earlier paper in honor of A. Leo Oppenheim on two Sumerian drinking songs from the eighteenth century B.C. turned to be the recipe for a "Ninkasi Beer." After research on terms and trying several possibilities, the San Francisco located Anchor Brewery successfully produced the "Ninkasi Beer" after this old recipe. cited (see also http://www.cromwell-intl.com/brewing/brewing-links.html).

[199] Frymer-Kensky, *Wake*, 32.

[200] Frymer-Kensky, *Wake*, 44. See also Ebeling & Homan, "Baking and Brewing Beer," 50–52.

[201] Marsman, *Women*, 405–6, quoting Harris, "Independent Women," 148. Furthermore, Nemet-Nejat, "Women," 107 states that date-beer brewing sets are recorded in dowries until the Neo-Babylonian period.

myths), but also in pictorial evidence. Among the Egyptian treasures, one finds wooden painted statuettes of women kneading dough or filtering barley bread in a deep, bucket-type, container. Several depictions of different classes (figurines, seal impressions) of people drinking beer, alone, two at a time, and even during sexual intercourse, have been unearthed.[202] Beer was drunk from a jar through a long strainer and it was not kept for long.[203] "Breweries from Egypt to Mesopotamia created beer by lightly baking dough composed of ground germinated cereals, and these loaves along with yeast were placed in jars of water, where the maltose sugars were converted to alcohol."[204] The strainer would prevent little pieces from being swallowed with the drink, since it was not filtered. This explanation is both confirmed and deepened by microscopic research on Egyptian food remains. Conducted in the 1990s, it showed that "ancient Egyptians brewed using a two-part process of coarsely ground, well-heated malt or grain and unheated malt ... This technique explains well the morphology of starch in ancient Egyptian beer residues. The process does not resemble modern brewing, and the microstructural data do not match the use of lightly baked bread for brewing."[205]

In other words, what these experiments show is that beer consumption was very common, including offerings to the Gods and to the dead; therefore, brewing was also widespread. Through microscope observation, researchers have found different types of molecular remains which, they assert, proves that beer brewing involved several processes, some with and some without heating. At least in Egyptian remains, no proof of added flavor was found. Questions remain about the variety of names for "beer" and what can be observed with a microscope, but this avenue takes us too far from our interests and expertise.

Questions also remain as to why, being so common a female occupation in Mesopotamia, "[t]here is no record of women brewers (or any brewers for that matter) from Ugarit. The only allusion to a female who might be an artisan is an

---

[202] Assante, "Erotic Reliefs," 217, shows that these terracota figures were made after Inanna's depictions in literature, following two basic models. That of the "single woman" who "goes to the tavern in search of sexual companionship" is the one that tells us something here, for the figures depict the woman drinking beer during sex. See especially 74–107 (chapter III, Typologies and the Visual Inscription of Gender) and 210–55 (chapter VI, Sources and Magical Uses of Terracota Plaques); see also her "Sex, Magic."

[203] Ebeling and Homan, "Baking and Brewing Beer," 48–50; Joan Pilsbury Alcock, *Food in the Ancient World* (Westport: Greenwood, 2006), 136–8.

[204] Michael Homan, "Beer Production by Throwing Bread into Water: A New Interpretation of Qoh. xi 1–2,"*VT* LII (2002): 275; see also his other contributions.

[205] Delwen Samuel, "Investigation of Ancient Egyptian Baking and Brewing Methods," *Science* 273 (1996): 489. Cited 20 May 2011. Online: http://sbli.ls.manchester.ac .uk/fungi/21st_ Century_Guidebook_to_Fungi/REPRINT_collection/Samuel_ancient_Egyptian_baking+brewing19 96.pdf.

intriguing line in KTU 4.175, a distribution to a number of people …"[206] Neither is there anyone in the Bible, male or female, attested as "brewer" nor is there any description or any scene involving a brewery. Thus, there is as yet no consensus as to its existence, literary or otherwise, in biblical Israel. With many scholars, I believe the noun שכר, usually translated "strong drink," but more properly, "fermented drink" refers to beer.[207] It must be recognized that the biblical occurrences of the term (as well as post-biblical) are not totally clear on their meaning. This is why several scholars think that, on the basis of texts like Num 6:1–8, it "can only be a grape product"[208] and thus they keep the traditional translation or choose "*grappa*" or some other particular term. Perhaps its more descriptive original meaning of "fermented drink" would explain its ambiguous use. The noun appears often in parallel to wine, in prohibitions or sayings and even in ritual prescriptions that require that YHWH's altar be poured daily an amount of שכר, together with two kids and bread (Num 28:3–8). The nominative verb is of no help here, because it has to do with making drunk or becoming drunk, not with preparing beer.

One is tempted to think this dearth of participles or descriptions has to do with the fact that its primary location would be domestic. It is a noteworthy silence, nevertheless, because there must have been industrial preparation as well. The law passed by YHWH to Moses regarding daily libations of שכר indicates already that the temple compound also needed large amounts of beer, probably brewed in its precincts by its own personnel.

The other large household was the palace. Proverbs 31:4 admonishes kings not to let heavy drinking (שכר) influence their judgment. One may, of course, not take it literally, although usually there is a layer of experience behind sayings, especially when they involve institutional injustice—even if uttered by a queen! Why would one think that those closely related to the king would not enjoy abundant food and drink, especially when it would have been seen as a sign of prosperity and divine blessing? Once again, whether brewing was made in the palace kitchens by slaves or corvée laborers, or whether it was brought in as supplies from elsewhere, still large amounts of beer would have been produced and still, silence about brewers in the Bible is noteworthy.

---

[206] Amico, "Status of Women," 233.

[207] Milgrom, *Leviticus*, 240 accepts also the renderings "beer" and "ale."

[208] Philip J. King and Lawrence E. Stager, *Life in Biblical Israel* (Louisville: Westminster John Knox, 2001), 102. The book is partially available online [cited 26 July 2011] Online: http://books.google.com.ar/books?id=OtOhypZz_pEC&pg=PA97&dq=olive+oil+press&hl=es&ei=P68pTYrXD1G78gaxm7nEBQ&sa=X&oi=book_result&ct=result&resnum=4&ved=0CD0Q6AEwAw#v=onepage&q=olive%20oil%20press&f=false. Their argument is the regulation of Nazirites in Num 6:1–8. This controversy is already evident in the different translations of the ancient versions.

Unwittingly, Matthews responds to our question about the dearth of data from another perspective. He considers that the Syro-Palestinian geography allowed nearly every village (of the hill country) to have its vineyards and therefore,

> wine was able to serve as the common beverage in Syro-Palestine and also became an aspect of everyday social life (Ruth 2:14; Hos 2:7; Dan 10:3). It serves as a libation offering... Wine also had the potential to become a source of social comment if it were used intemperately (Isa 56:12). Its value could also become a form of evidence of injustice to the poor, as it does in Amos' indictment of those who profit from unfair fines (Amos 2:8).[209]

Wine must have been, indeed, quite common in the hill country and there is plenty of evidence on that. On the other hand, I am unconvinced by his argument that wine served as common beverage in Syro-Palestine, unless "common" implies only well-to-do people. Boaz was not precisely amongst the poor of the land; Daniel could be considered poor in the sense that he had been exiled, but the table at his disposal was that of the king. The third example he puts, that of Hosea's indictment, if taken literally, means again, rich women with rich lovers. The last sentence in his quotation above signals, I think, precisely my contention that wine was not so accessible to the lower classes. In terms of the archaeological and literary imbalance in favor of wine against beer, Matthews's statement of course explains it, for both ancient literary sources and much of archaeology have been interested in luxurious and elite items.

Ebeling and Homan go in this same line of mine, focusing on gender and archaeology. They find that, even though men, women and children drank large amounts of this drink,

> biblical scholars and archaeologists have focused on wine, not beer, because wine is associated with industry, trade, inheritance, ritual and status while beer is associated with the domestic sphere. Moreover, the remains of wine are more common than those concerning beer, because beer was typically produced for immediate consumption, and, unlike wine, it does not improve with age; in general, people traded wine and grain as opposed to beer and grapes.[210]

Their analysis is important, because they manage to use gender sensibility to interpret the archaeological milieu in which they work: not only are there loops in our information, due to reasons such as longer presence of wine over beer in archaeological remains; but also the importance that traditional

---

[209] Victor Matthews, "Treading the Winepress. Actual and Metaphorical Viticulture in the Ancient Near East," *Semeia* 86 (1999): 22. He further states that Ahlström discovered "117 winepresses of various types at small sites radiating from the urban center of Megiddo."

[210] Ebeling and Homan, "Baking and Brewing Beer," 46.

scholarship has placed on macro-economic and prestige-laden objects (i.e., wine international trade, inheritance) over against family-related and domestic aspects. This is not new, although there start to appear works on gender archaeology, ethno-archaeology, and other areas besides those specifically theological.

> Since iconographic and textual sources from the ancient Near East and Egypt show that beer was often produced from bread cakes, the spatial correlates of brewing in the areas where bread production was carried out can now be identified. In the "four-room houses" found in Iron Age sites in Israel, for example, the central open space on the lower level may have been the main locus of baking and brewing activities.[211]

Behind these words, there is what could be termed "household archaeology" or "domestic archaeology," which pays special attention to particular areas and corners usually neglected in reports and journals and reads them with an interest on gender issues, especially on gendered use of space. For instance, some studies relate the four-room houses with female needs and constrictions:

> More recently a third proposal suggests that the layout of the "four-room" house reflects the Israelites' ethnic behaviors that evolved from the laws of impurity that applied to the relationship between a man and his wife during her menses. Hence, the spatial division of the dwelling enables a woman to move more freely while avoiding contact with the men of the house. A contextual study of artifacts can shed light on domestic gender-interactions and their meanings, including the ways in which inhabitants of the "four-room" house used their space, and divided their activity areas.[212]

Around them, several women and children met and shared resources, knowledge, concerns, and time—much time—daily. These remains help understand how domestic space could be variously used according to needs and resources, locating grinding, food processing, cooking, brewing, child-care activities, all at once at the center of women's networking spaces. Because women spent so much time and effort on these joint activities, they could also spatially shape the domestic space and social relationships.[213] And—as is still the case around the globe—most of them could, if chance allowed, make a little extra income by selling the best products of their hands.

In summary, I have included "beer brewing" for the reason that bread was the first step in brewing this popular drink according to ancient technology. Since this is not a philological study on Hebrew terms for professions or

---

[211] Ebeling and Homan, "Baking and Brewing Beer," 61.

[212] Cassuto, "Bringing the Artifact," 71–2.

[213] See Meyers, "Archaeology—A Window" 83–91 on evidence for shared spaces and tools and 103–106 on women's networks.

occupations, it seemed to me that the weight of evidence in favor of beer as a staple food in the region warrants consideration of its makers among workers— even if one contested the meaning of שֵׁכָר—and even if no mention of such workers has found its way into the Hebrew Bible.

We do not have access to other external information, such as laws referring to tavern owners, contracts, or narratives in which it is clear that someone would run a tavern; possibilities are high that Rahab (Josh 2 and 6) and also the unknown woman whom Samson visited in Gaza (Judg 16) would have run taverns and/or inns. Whether this was the case or not, it is rather safe to assume there were several people, men and women, working as brewers, either for the palace, for the temple, for their own households, or for thirsty customers.

CONCLUDING REMARKS

Child rearing, water drawing, cooking, pottery, and textile activity were and are woman's responsibilities throughout time and space. This is not to say they were *exclusively* women's responsibilities, nor that they have remained unchanged, even within the same cultural milieu.[214] Furthermore, societies have also changed and with them, their gender roles. This pervasive assignment of roles related to household and family services notwithstanding, the Bible in general does not abound in information on women's work; in fact, being mostly the writing of the scribal and religious leadership, it pays little attention also to much of what were men's working activities.

In this chapter I have looked at evidence for women under categories that escape much categorization. The main cause of their quasi-invisibility is the Deuteronomist's partial or total ignorance of them (midwives, singers, attendants) or their extraordinary location (women weaving for Asherah but otherwise unrecorded as textile workers). The chapter is comprised of three quite independent sections. The first one, "Women Hidden in Occupations Denoted by Masculine Terms" looks at "brotherhoods" whose membership was likely hereditary. The question is, then, what would have been the relationship and social status of their women. The second section, "The Dtr Redactors Fall Short of the Mark," looks at indications of professional services understated by general terms or under religious activities only. Finally, the last section looks at "Notable Absentees" from DtrH and the Bible in general (such as women grinding grain or brewing beer).

---

[214] Dosch, "Non-Slave Labor in Nuzi," 230–1. On Egypt see Robins, *Women*, 949–6, 103–4, 119–20. Amico, "Status of Women," 235, states that at Ugarit "the words for 'spinner' and 'weaver' are masculine in gender," and indeed it seems to reflect a male occupation.

One could, of course, limit oneself to those terms and texts in the Hebrew Bible offering some information on female working conditions: it would still be a valid contribution to a subject not much studied among biblical scholars. On the other hand, if we want to build a working model that would involve as much of the lower socio-economic echelons as possible, seeking hidden or rather forgotten workers—especially female workers—seemed to be inescapable. Even though it is a slippery task, arguing from bits and pieces and at times even stretching the imagination, it is a worthy attempt at broadening our intellectual horizons. To what extent our informed guesses will pass the test of time and criticism is not for me to say.

CHAPTER 6

FEMALE WORKERS RELATED TO THE ROYAL HOUSEHOLD

Chapter 4 studied most appearances of the terms denoting a woman on an economic and social dependency from a household (institutional or private) other than her own; in other words, slaves and other people subject to an owner. The next two chapters study women according to the occupation they perform. In this chapter, we will look at occupations DtrH relates to the royal household; then in chapter seven, we will look at one occupation located elsewhere, that of the sex worker (in a broad sense).[1]

The question asked in this chapter of each professional is not "Is her legal status that of a slave, of a dependent, or of a free woman?" but "What is the social location of, for instance, the wet nurse? How is she portrayed by Dtr? How much can be known about her occupation?" It will be seen that the texts show a strong bias against female workers, expressed in the lack of interest for these women, in their literary and ideological use for purposes other than talking about them or their occupation, in the writer's easy discharge of them, in the fact that only those women who attend to male needs are mentioned, and in their

---

[1] This division reflects the occupations and locations as they appear in DtrH. There could have been, at least in theory, women who served in the same capacity in the village, but DtrH does not mention them. On the one hand, this reflects an arbitrary division of work, while on the other hand personal assistants or perfumers are not professions the common Israelite could have afforded for him or herself. In charts IV–VII I have listed all terms (that I recall) according to appearance in DtrH or elsewhere, in service-type occupations (those treated in this book) and for religious and political occupations.

being used as foils to contrast with high-ranking people. Several scholars have long recognized that biblical texts look at issues from the male's perspective and interests. This is also expressed in that many kings are blessed with several children, but many of their mothers, not to mention their midwives, are ignored or just absent. Despite these drawbacks, the writer leaves in certain clues about female labor, which deserve to be brought into the picture.

רקחות — *Perfumers,* טבחות — *Cooks, and* אפות — *Bakers*

Mention of perfumers, cooks, and bakers as female occupations outside the domestic realm occurs only in 1 Sam 8:13, as part of Samuel's speech against a king for Israel.[2] Samuel's report of YHWH's answer to the petition for a king is based on the socio-economic cost of a king for the same Israelite families who are requesting a king. Some authors have noticed how often the word "king" appears, either explicitly or through a suffix: he is the subject of fourteen out of seventeen sentences.[3] This, and the repeated use of the passive voice, signal the focal point of the passage. Thus, people are not the focal point, but the king's object of interest, presented as his "law," "justice" or "custom."[4] People are mentioned in distinct groups. First appears "your sons." Young Israelite men are enlisted to take care of war paraphernalia and agricultural chores for the palace. It is unclear whether the men who serve in war and the ones who serve in agricultural tasks are the same people who work for the royal household all year long or, more likely, whether they would serve for a certain amount of time and then go home for the rest of the year (corvée). From the peasant's standpoint, in either case they are needed hands absent in the farm.

In literary parallel to "your sons" appears "your daughters." Young Israelite women are recruited to provide for food and perfume, which are some of the items that characterize palace life.[5] Recruitment of women does not seem to be temporary. If parallelism applied not only to social categories (your sons/your daughters) but also to their social evaluation, for an Israelite woman to be cook

---

[2] Crüsemann, *Widerstand,* 61–73; Klein, *1 Samuel,* 72–79, especially74 (anti-monarchic). Cf. R. Polzin, "The Monarchy Begins:1 Samuel 8–10," *SBLSP* 26 (1987): 120–43; Gerbrandt, *Kingship,* 140–50.

[3] Miguel Alvarez Barredo, *Los orígenes de la monarquía en Israel: Tradiciones literarias y enfoques teológicos de 1 Sam 8–12.* Murcia: Instituto Teológico de Murcia OFM/Espigas, 2009, 122.

[4] Klein, *1 Samuel,* 74 chooses "claim of right," following Timo Veijola, *Das Königtum in der Beurteilung der deuteronomistischen Historiographie* (Annales Academiae Scientiarum Fennicae, series B 198. Helsinki: Suomalainen Tiedeakademia, 1975). The wordplay created by משפט is irreproducible. One possible translation would be to use "justice," with a non-literal tone given by quotation marks and by translating with Crüsemann the verbs in present tense: the problem the text addresses is contemporary, although it is put in the past.

[5] Peter Ackroyd, *The First Book of Samuel* (CBC on the NEB; Cambridge: At the University Press, 1971), 72 takes "perfumers" as euphemism for concubines. Quoted by Klein, *1 Samuel,* 77.

or aesthetician at the palace should entail as much honor as for an Israelite man being enlisted to work at the palace. One is left to wonder whether cooks or perfumers fared on the same level as commanders and craftsmen or as farmers and horse keepers.

The text reads as follows:

[11]So [Samuel] said:
These are the (claims of) right (משפט) of the king who rules over you:
Your sons he takes,
> and sets them for his chariotry, and his cavalry, and they run ahead of his chariotry,

[12] to put them as captains of thousand, and captains of fifty,
> and they will plow his ground, and reap his harvest,[6]
> and make the tools for his war and for his chariotry.

[13] And your daughters he takes (ואת־בנותיכם יקח)
> as perfumers, and as cooks, and as bakers (ולאפות לרקחות ולטבחות).

[14] And your fields, vineyards, and olive groves, the best ones, he takes,
> and gives to his courtiers,

[15] and grain and your vineyards he tithes
> and gives to his officers and his courtiers.

[16] And your male slaves (ואת־עבדיכם),
your female slaves (ואת־שפחותיכם),
and your dependents (ואת־בחוריכם),[7] the best ones,
and your donkeys he takes, and sets (them) for his tasks,

[17] and your flocks he tithes.
> So you will be his slaves (עבדיכם)!

[18] Then you will cry out on account of your king, which you have chosen for yourselves, but YHWH will not answer you then.

The parallel between service by men and women should not be stretched. First, in this text men are recruited to work outside, and women to work inside the household; second, since work is divided along gender lines but there is no job description, one cannot assess to what extent—if at all—men and women

---

[6] P. Kyle McCarter, *1 Samuel*, 155 considers that "MT and LXX[B] are haplographic, each in its own way. LXX[L], then, preserves the primitive reading." Klein, *1 Samuel*, 73 retains MT.

[7] בחורים, "young men, youth." Crüsemann thinks the "sons" in v 12 are the married ones, while the single ones, who remain at home still have a dependent status. Cf. McCarter, *1 Samuel*, 155, who considers that "youngsters" is out of place here, since חמרים, asses, comes next. However, as McCarter himself points out, חמרים is probably a later addition, after the adjective טובים. Considering also how awkward v 17a stands in the picture, it seems better to retain בחורים (v. 16) as "youth" and consider the addition of חמרים an attempt to ameliorate its meaning.

found themselves doing the same tasks; and third, there is no table of correspondences of honor for men and for women, and thus one does not know how closely they describe parallel labor. It is evident, however, that in this text a woman's honor, however low or high, is related neither to staying at her own home nor to her sexual faithfulness, which is not mentioned at all here.

A second group of people, "the best of your male slaves, female slaves and your dependents" (v. 16) is also taken from the people to attend to royal needs, probably of a more menial character. One can just imagine the amount of work needed in carrying water, cooking, cleaning, attending to the palace children, milling grain, doing laundry, perhaps preparing paper or clay tablets for the scribes, and many other daily tasks for the royal court to function. Warburton speaks of more than thirty employments enumerated by an Egyptian scribe:

> Before the end of the Ramesside era in Egypt (about 1200 BCE), a scribe recorded a list of possible subordinates: "craftsmen, manual laborers, office workers, administrative officials, time-servers, stewards, mayors, village headmen, empowered district officers, department heads, scribes of offering tables, commissioners, envoys, administrative messengers, brewers, bakers, butchers, servants, confectioners, cake bakers, wine tasters, project managers, supervisors of carpenters, chief craftsmen, deputies, draftsmen, sculptors, miners, masons, wreckers, stone workers, guardians . . . statue sculptors . . . wood workers, . . . " (Gardiner 1937: 136–7; Caminos 1954: 497–501). The author clearly decided not to make a comprehensive account, and yet it should be evident that the urban world of the Ancient Near East was familiar with more than the essentials. It should be borne in mind that it is not entirely clear that all of the professions listed by the scribe meant that these people were "working," even if they held down jobs. In fact, many of those whose titles are recorded in the documents might not have been working at all but just holding an official position which might or might not involve any effort.[8]

Even considering his warning that these represent official positions but not necessarily "work," the list shows the enormous machinery the more sophisticated ANE states set up. Samuel's speech does not regard a cook or perfumer with contempt. Rather, it strongly criticizes the economic hardship monarchy imposes on the people, and the naiveté of most people in not realizing how the system exploited them—a naiveté even worse after the people's own experience of tyrannical states at the time of the final compilation of the DtrH.[9]

---

[8] Warburton "Working," 170.

[9] Whatever we think of the thorny issue of dating the DtrH, even of considering there was something we call today the DtrH, the fact is that the text was edited within the book at a much later date than the one it portrays and, thus, the editors' and the people's experience of monarchic burden makes it even stronger Samuel's charge of naiveté, even of ideological blindness.

People may feel proud of being captains or bakers, but they are no less dependent, no less enslaved.

Notable in this list brought up by Warburton is the absence of perfume-makers, unless they are included in the more general craftsmen or manual laborers terms. Besides the fact, already stated by Warburton, that it is not intended to be exhaustive, the list is noteworthy in that there are more supervisory-oriented (male's domain) than production- or service-oriented occupations (traditionally female's domain).

Perfume-Makers or Cosmeticians

Regrettably, most writers, ancient and modern, do not differentiate between male and female labor in their descriptions. In fact, Armijo Navarro-Reverter asserts that the Egyptian language has no female terms for laborers, even for the most menial ones![10] On the other hand, at least some Babylonian texts ascribe this profession to women. And there is "Overseer of Funerary Priests" among the titles held by females in the Egyptian Old Kingdom; perhaps preparation of cosmetics was part of these priest(ess)'s duties.[11]

In the Bible, expertise in perfume preparation in connection with ritual is, of course, a man's occupation. Apart from our text in which perfumery is a female occupation, we hear of "an early maker of perfumes ... Bezalel, a skillful and versatile craftsman (Ex. 37:29)."[12] The expression used is מעשה רקח, "the perfumer's doing, action, work." Similar expressions with the participle appear in Exod 30:25 and in 1 Chr 9:30 (רקחי המרקחת לבשמים "prepared the mixing of spices") both describing priestly responsibilities. There is also another task for some perfumers. In his study on perforated tripodal vessels, Nicolae Roddy calls attention to the use of herbs for burial purposes, as described in 2 Chr 16:14. King Asa from Judah was buried "on a bier that had been filled with various kinds of spices prepared by the perfumer's art" (*NRSV*). As the author notes, this is "a rare biblical insight into the use of aromatics in funerary rituals."[13] Finally, we also find among those reconstructing the wall of Jerusalem a certain Hananiah, from the "guild" of the perfumers (בן־הרקחים Neh 3:8).[14]

---

[10] Armijo Navarro-Reverter, "La vida de las mujeres egipcias," 132.

[11] Lesko, "Women's Monumental Mark," 5.

[12] King and Stager, *Life in Biblical Israel*, 281. Unfortunately, they do not refer to female perfumers at all.

[13] Nicolae Roddy, "Perforated Tripodal Vessels at Iron II Bethsaida-Tzer," *BN* NF141 (2009): 98. On several powdered herbs used in ritual offerings, 96–99.

[14] Gendolyn Leick, *Mesopotamia: la invención de la ciudad* (Barcelona: Paidós, 2002), 229, mentions luxurious oils and aromatic plants among the items bought and sold by Sippar *naditus* during the Old Babylonian period. On perfumers at Ugarit see Yamashita, "Professions," 68, #36. *rqh šmn*, perfumer's oil, "a profession of a special skill."

Thus, one finds confirmation here that occupations were passed along from father to son; perhaps also from mother to daughter. Otherwise we hear about consumption (people bathing and using oils, women perfuming their beds, and so forth) but not much about its production, neither domestic nor industrial.

This rich tradition of ointment and perfume consumption involves women and men, rich and poor, in the sanctuary and in everyday life, including skin-care, ritual anointing, medicinal use and burial preparations.[15] Olive oil, animal fat, and aromatic herbs were used by everybody, while other oils and fragrances (sesame, acacia, spikenard, almond, and others) are also attested in Syria, Mesopotamia, Egypt, or Somalia. These were articles of commerce and a sign of royal wealth, as also attested in Ezek 27:22. Likewise, pigmenting and cosmetic products were expensive. Technically they are not perfumes but were also produced (according to Graham), by the "Judean 'plowmen' or workmen" who were also responsible for perfumes.[16] Frankincense and myrrh were also used in medicine, since their many properties for diverse ailments are well-known in Greco-Roman sources.[17] And, according to Song 4:10, 14, also for pleasure.

Since there were so many different uses and locations for ointments and cosmetics, from everyday household needs to luxury items, professions related to perfume- and ointment-making must have been rather common, starting from nursing the different plants needed or collecting and drying them, processing them for fragrance and getting to a quality end-product. Because of such a specialization in the Iron Age II, some scholars think workers ascribed to these jobs were not corvée laborers, but permanent specialized people who worked all

---

[15] Concerning the use of perfume or frankincense in the temple see Exod 25:6; 30:22–25; 37:29; Lev 2:1–15; 24:7; Num 5:15; 1 Chr 9:29–30; Neh 13:5–9; Ps 45:9; as "beauty" product see Isa 3:24; Esth 2:12; Cant 4:14–16; 5:1; 6:2; 8:14; Prov 7:17. Spices are also mentioned on the occasion of the burial of King Asa, 2 Chr 16:14 for the preparation of his corpse and among the treasures shown by Hezekiah (2 Kgs 20). See also C. Rabin, "The Song of Songs and Tamil Poetry," *SR* 3 (1973/4): 205–19; Athalya Brenner, "Aromatics and perfumes in the Song of Songs," *JSOT* 25 (1983): 75–81; Moshe Elat, "The Monarchy and the Development of Trade in Ancient Israel," in *State and Economy in the Ancient Near East*, 2:527–34.

[16] Nira Karmon & Ehud Spanier, "Remains of a Purple Dye Industry Found at Tel Shiqmona," *IEJ* 38 (1988): 184–86 report about archaeological findings also in the Northern territory.

[17] Cf. Gus van Beek, "Frankincense and Myrrh," in *The Biblical Archaeological Reader* (ed. D. Freedman & E. Campbell, Jr.; Garden City: Doubleday Anchor, 1964), 2:114–5 (frankincense, little used in cosmetics, very much used in burners, in temples and houses); 2:116–7 (myrrh, used much in cosmetics and for corpse preparation, and in medicine). According to Dorothea Bedigian's and Jack R. Harlan's abstract, "Evidence for Cultivation of Sesame in the Ancient World," *Economic Botany* 40 (1986): 137–54, "New evidence suggests that the Mesopotamian oil plant še-giš-ì is sesame, and that the crop and one name for its oil, *ellu*, were introduced from India. A cuneiform text indicates that the barley harvest [in spring] was followed by the sowing of še-giš-ì, a summer crop in Mesopotamia. Sesame can be distinguished clearly from flax, a cool-season crop, and their growing seasons differ as would be expected." Cited 9 January 2011. Online: http://www.springerlink.com/content/t083363t84120143/.

year long at particular locations (such as the Dead Sea and Ein-Gedi areas).[18] We do not know, however, whether these would have been women like the ones referred to in Samuel's speech or only men, or both. One can well imagine that, the larger the production needed, the more people working on it. Even though small households needed oil every day and every night, it would have been costly to produce it individually. As it still happens in different parts of the world, production of different items tends to be concentrated in different villages and then exchanged for other products.[19] These considerations notwithstanding, Frick asserts that the range of oil presses unearthed run from private ones to those belonging to political authorities, even within the same village:

> Oil presses have been found in all kinds of settlements: in towns ranging from three to six hectares, in smaller sites, and on agricultural farms. Eitam maintains that the location of olive oil installations at a site illumines the character of both the olive oil industry and the site itself (27). He observes, for example, that at Khirbet Bint-Bar … olive oil installations were clustered in two areas. Some were located at a central, high point of the settlement while others were spread out on terraces between houses. This type of distribution hints at two types of ownership of oil presses—some were probably privately owned while others belonged to the town authorities.[20]

Furthermore, there is a development factor to be considered (although that is not our focus here), which explains differences in oil production even within the (comparatively limited) time period covered by the Bible.[21] Scholars affirm

---

[18] Wolfgang Zwickel, *Frauenalltag im biblischen Israel* (Verlag Katholisches Bibelwerk: Stuttgart, 1980), 45, 94; Karen Nemet-Nejat, *Daily Life in Mesopotamia* (Westport: Greenwood Press, 1998), 157 asserts that "a woman was listed as the author of a series of recipes for making perfumes."

[19] So also King and Stager, *Life in Biblical Israel*, 192.

[20] Frank S. Frick, "'Oil from Flinty Rock' (Deuteronomy 32:13): Olive Cultivation and Olive Oil Processing in the Hebrew Bible—A Socio-Materialist Perspective," *Semeia* 86 (1999): 11. Scholars (including Frick) rely on Rafael Frankel's works on wine and oil production. Frankel's works are unavailable to me; see, however, Marilyn M. Schaub, review of Frankel, Rafael, *Wine and Oil Production in Antiquity in Israel and Other Mediterranean Countries*, *CBQ* 62 (2000): 724–5; David John Jordan, Review of Rafael Franklin[sic], *Wine and Oil Production in Antiquity in Israel and Other Mediterranean Countries*, *Review of Biblical Literature* [http://www.bookreviews.org] (2000). Hans M. Barstad, "After the 'Myth of the Empty Land': Major Challenges in the Study of Neo-Babylonian Judah," in *Judah and the Judeans in the Neo-Babylonian Period* (ed. Oded Lipschits & Joseph Blenkinsopp; Winona Lake: Eisenbrauns, 2003) looks at the Neo-Babylonian need of keeping Judah as oil and wine producer; see especially n.25 on p.10 on other bibliography on agriculture, and more generally, 10–13.

[21] Frick, "'Oil," 5–11 for a very helpful summary. See, for instance, Seymour Gitin and Trude Dotan, "The Rise and Fall of Ekron of the Philistines: Recent Excavations at an Urban Border Site," *BA* (1987): 207–9 for a detailed description of unearthed oil press rooms and altars. In 2008, a Byzantine olive press was accidentally discovered, according to this newspaper report: Hana Levi

the industry took on new proportions during the Iron Age II, when the monarchy allocated material and human resources to industrial production of luxury items.[22] The activity continued even when "Israel" disappeared. In this line argues Graham, who thinks the "vinedressers and plowmen" left by Nebuzaradan after killing or deporting to Babylon the Judahite elite, were skilled workers continuing the cosmetic industry. He states that around the Dead Sea have been unearthed

> remains of a perfume industry dating from the end of the seventh and the beginning of the sixth centuries. The hypothesis has been formulated that the workshops there were staffed by a guild of workers under royal control. The main product was balm. How the estate began and what befell it after the Babylonian invasion is reflected in a Talmudic tradition relating to one of our texts, Jeremiah 52:16:
>
> > *Nebuzaradan the captain of the guard left of the poorest of the land to be vinedressers . . . and husbandmen* [plowmen].... R. Joseph learnt: This means balsamum gatherers from En Gedi to Ramah. (Shabbath *26a*, Freedman 1938)
>
> This source reveals that after the anointing oil had been hidden by Josiah, kings were anointed with this balm oil. The possibility exists, therefore, that during Josiah's reign, En-gedi became a royal estate manufacturing balm. The Babylonians, realizing the estate's potential and the market for balm (it had been a major Judean export according to Ezekiel 27:17), took it over.[23]

According to this author, the linking element in this Rabbinic explanation between the Jeremiah text and ointment (*balsamum*) from Ein-gedi to Ramah of Benjamin is Josiah's anointing oil. King Josiah had set the balm industry in the Ein-gedi region and the Babylonians kept it working under a man they trusted, Governor Gedaliah, after the destruction of Judah in 586 B.C.E. They would have left also some of the poorest people in the land as vinedressers and plowmen. Likewise, Barstad has called attention to "the *enormous* economic significance

---

Julian, "Ancient Olive Oil Press Unearthed in Galilee," (Published: 08/07/08, 10:02 AM/Last Update: 08/08/08, 9:22 AM, n. p. [cited 9 June 2010]. Online: http://www.israelnationalnews. com/News/News.aspx/127106. For modern reconstructions of oil pressing, see Ruth Hestrin and Zeev Yeivin's account, "Oil From The Presses of Tirat-Yehuda," *BA* 40 (1977); 29–31, of the reconstruction of an oil press from the second century B.C.E. At least this press was managed by human labor, since there was no room for an animal: "At first we thought that an animal had been harnessed to the crosspiece to turn the *memel*, [the crushing stone, acting as a wheel] but since the space between installation and walls was so narrow, we decided that human labor had been employed. The wheel, however, proved easy to turn and after two or three rotations the olives were ready for the press." (31) They conclude: "The squeezing process took us ten hours, weight-loading included."

[22] Frick, "Oil," 10.

[23] J. N. Graham, "'Vinedressers and Plowmen' 2 Kings 25:12 and Jeremiah 52:16," *BA* 47 (1984): 56.

of wine and olive oil production in ancient Palestine and in the Mediterranean countries," particularly at Tell en-Naṣbeh/Mizpah and Gibeon after 586 B.C.E.[24]

Both terms employed for workers in these verses are *qal* participle masculine plural; one is a nominative from the stem כרם, "vineyard," while the other term יגב appears only in the verse quoted (Jer 52:16 // 2 Kgs 24:14) and in Jer 39:10, where it reproduces the same information turning the two participles into nouns: "Nebuzaradan ... left in the land of Judah some of the poor people ... and gave them vineyards and fields (כרמים ויגבים)."[25] If this reconstruction is true, these people (probably men) would have been forced laborers under imperial rule—yet another variation in the fulfillment of Samuel's warning in 1 Sam 8. Graham's reconstruction is very plausible but one should also contemplate the possibility that, besides the poorest, they also left some skilled perfumers—male or female—to ensure quality and to provide continuity with the previous industry. Perhaps these were called (רקחה(ים, while those working the land were the vinedressers and plowmen (כרמים ויגבים).

Butchers or Cooks

The stem טבח denotes animal or human slaughtering (see Gen 41:12; Exod 21:37; Jer 51:40; 2 Kgs 25) and thus it applies to butchers as well as murderers and royal guards—and even to YHWH's allowance of Jerusalem's disaster (Lam 2:21). The feminine plural noun appears only in 1 Sam 8:13, but in Prov 9:2 the verb is used of Wisdom preparing a feast.[26] According to Driver, the intensified form "denotes one who possesses an *established character* (as ... *given to butting*, ... *jealous*), or *capacity* (as ... *cook* [lit. *slaughterer*], ... *thief*, ... *judge*."[27] It may also be understood as "express[ing] an intensification of the idea of the stem, either emphasizing the energy of the action or else indicating a longer continuance of the relation or state."[28] Perhaps this continuance is the reason why these intensified participles are used for professions, even though this is grammatically irregular. As repeated too often in this work, information on workers and particularly on female cooks and millers is scant; it is traceable in the Old and Middle (Egyptian) Kingdoms in tomb depictions and in some Levantine lists, for instance, from Ebla. Archi reports cooks among the many

---

[24] Barstad, "After the 'Myth," 12.

[25] Willliam Holladay, *Jeremiah* (Hermeneia; Philadelphia: Fortress, 1986), 2:441 referring to Graham's translation and meaning.

[26] Camp, *Wisdom and the Feminine*, 133–8, 261–5.

[27] Driver, *Notes*, 67.

[28] GK §84[b]; see also *b*: "*Nomina opifcum* also, curiously enough, are so treated in Hebrew (at least in the constr. state of the sing.), although the corresponding Arabic form *qăttâl* points to an original (unchangeable) *â* in the second syllable…"

workers included in the latter. Of importance is also his reflection on the gender division of work:

> There were wardrobe mistresses (dam lúdam lí [é] ti-túg), those who prepared the clothes (dam gada-TÚG / íb+III-TÚG), who dyed clothes (dam dar), who wove baskets (dam GÁxGI-GÁxGI), prepared perfumes (dam GIŠ-šim), oil (dam [é] ì-giš), beer (dam lú [é] ŠE+TIN), bread (dam lú ninda) and baked it (*dam a-bi-a-tum* lú ninda) and cooks (dam muhaldim-mí). Different groups of these women came under male overseers.
>
> While some tasks, such as weaving and grinding grains, were held to be typically feminine work, others were undoubtedly entrusted to women because they had to be performed in areas reserved for women. This is the case of the gardeners, cooks, wardrobe mistresses, and possibly also those concerned with bread and oil.[29]

What would a female cook or butcher do? Zwickel thinks the women referred to in this text would have been enlisted under corvée service, would have been temporary workers and would have cooked for the corvée men in the countryside or wherever they worked.[30] That is, certainly, a possibility. Keeping up with court life, feeding all the king's entourage, guests, soldiers, and family would also require a large amount of kitchen work. Thus, there would also be permanent cooks and bakers around. Perhaps they travelled with the army as they went to war.

Descriptions of Egyptian tombs state that among the lower-class daily depictions, women work in agriculture (harvest, but without any cutting tool), grinding grain, trapping birds and brewing beer. I am not sure whether trapping birds was a cook's task or whether those birds were kept alive for entertainment or both. Today, nobody would think of a *chef* running after a hen to kill it; however, butchering hens is still very much within rural women's domestic tasks and, in those rural, poor areas, the butcher is also the cook—or the *chef*, depending on how much one wants to upgrade the profession and its practitioners.

Bakers

The participle feminine (plural) of אפה only appears in 1 Sam 8:13; unlike its accompanying terms, this one takes on the *qal* conjugation. There are a few scattered references through the Hebrew Bible to people baking bread, but in most cases the masculine form is used, presumably including women.[31] As a

---

[29] Alfonso Archi, "The Role of Women in the Society of Ebla," in *Sex and Gender in the Ancient Near East*, 2.

[30] Zwickel, *Frauenalltag*, 44–45 uses the term "decentralized."

[31] The *qal* singular masculine participle appears in Hos 7:4–6, where Hosea accuses the leaders of Israel of being "like a heated oven, whose fire the baker does not need to stir." Since folk proverbs

group האפים are mentioned in Jer 37:21, where King Zedekiah orders that Jeremiah be fed daily a loaf of bread from the bakers' street. Leviticus 24:5 stipulates how to do the baking of the bread for the tabernacle, but it is not clear whether this bread is to be brought in by the people or baked at the temple. The instructions for bread preparation—verbs in second masculine singular—could apply to anyone, while the priest is the only one to set them on the table, at least with regard to the Jerusalem temple. The text probably combined diverse traditions, so that at this point the reader cannot know what was intended by the text, and can only choose one or another explanation.[32] If loaves were made in the temple, questions arise concerning the degree to which this task belonged to a specialized group (like the Levites or temple slaves) and the degree to which women from the priestly families had any ritual responsibility.[33]

Research conducted in two other fields also sheds light on this ancient occupation. One of them has to do with non-Yahwist rituals (variously interpreted in the Bible as "whoring," "vain," "abominable," and so forth). These were particularly attractive to women, because the official religious system left no room for their active performance. Since religious occupations are not our goal here, this will be a very short mention. Jeremiah is one of the prophets whose voice raises against adoration of the Queen of Heaven (Jer 7:18). Perhaps his accusation that "the women knead dough, children gather wood and fathers kindle fire" reflects what was normally the distribution of household chores.[34] Apparently, this would not be "work" in the sense we are studying here; on the other hand, perhaps it was not required or even common practice that every family would knead and bake their own cake—and there were, for sure, many families with shortage of hands or ability, that perhaps

---

are often masculine in form but not in intention, it is hard to determine whether the baker of the saying is only intended to be a male.

[32] Gerstenberger, *Leviticus*, 358–60 stresses lay participation. It seems to us, however, that these loaves would have been baked in the temple, since the temple would have had control over the bread's quality and would also have had easy access to resources, both material and human. Noth, *Leviticus*, 177 points out that the original "thou" addressed Moses and not the priests. He leaves open the question, who fulfilled Moses' role in post-exilic times, when Moses is obviously not the addressee? On women as participants in ritual, see Mayer I. Gruber, "Women in the Cult According to the Priestly Code," in Mayer I. Gruber, *The Motherhood of God and Other Studies* (South Florida Studies in the History of Judaism; Atlanta: Scholars Press, 1992), 49–68; Phyllis A. Bird, "The Place of Women in the Israelite Cultus," 81–102; "Israelite Religion and the Faith of Israel's Daughters," *Missing Persons and Mistaken Identities* (Philadelphia: Fortress, 1997), 103–20.

[33] Cf. L. Díez Merino, "XI Congreso de la Organización Internacional para el Estudio del Antiguo Testamento (IOSOT) (Salamanca, 28 agosto–2 septiembre 1983)," *EstBibl* 42 (1984): 166–67. Quoting M. Gruber, "Women in the Cult According to the Priestly Code."

[34] See also Isa 44:9–20, especially v. 19.

bought the required cakes from accredited religious specialists or from neighbors.

This intermingling of the religious and the secular can be observed also from the other side. Starting from Old Babylonian texts speaking of building house shrines to ensure good businesses "such as a physician's practice, a tavern, a bakery, etc.," Assante has a similar appreciation with regard to how some occupations could be easily located in one realm or another:

> Some were erected in the "house of the tavernkeeper" (the *bīt sabiti* for female tavern keepers or the *bīt sabī* for males), a term meaning both the personal dwelling as well as the public place of business. One home then had a religious function as well as a public secular function. ... To compound the issue, some taverns (usually the *aštammu* type) were within temple complexes. Similarly, a baker, a brewer, physician or even plaque maker might well be included in the personnel of a temple or a palace that in turn sold his or her proceeds or services to the outside community.[35]

Adrien Bledstein has drawn a very telling parallel between the women baking cakes for the Queen of Heaven and Tamar the daughter of David baking cakes for his half-brother Amnon. These stories have in common more than evident at first hand, such as a ritual performance led by a(n) authorized or appointed woman, for the benefit of (a member of) the family, including kneading and baking special cakes or breads.[36] Similar actions (slaughtering a calf, kneading and baking cakes for a sacrifice) are performed by the medium who had invoked Samuel's spirit for Saul, 1 Sam 28:24, the only other appearance of the verb אפה with a feminine subject (cf. ויאפו, Exod 12:39). The main reason for bringing up the last issue is the fact that there seem to have been more opportunities than the Hebrew Bible recognizes for women to exercise their occupation as bakers. Ovens, like olive presses, were usually shared and, according to estimations, could hold the bread production of between seven and ten women.[37] This would not, then, have been an impediment if opportunity arose for women to sell their product, either in the secular market or as a religious offering.

---

[35] Assante, "Erotic Reliefs," 116, last paragraph and note 20.

[36] Adrien Bledstein, "Was *Habbiryâ* a Healing Ritual Performed by a Woman in King David's House?" *BR* 37 (1992): 15–31, draws attention to ritual healing practices from Mesopotamia and Ugarit as well. I take the opportunity to heartily thank her for sending me her paper.

[37] In Lev 26:26, one clear instance of the *verb* in feminine form, Israel is warned that disobedience brings war, pestilence, and hunger, to the point that one oven will be enough to be shared by ten women.

סכנת — *Personal Assistant*

A fascinating woman appears in 1 Kgs 1:1–4, opening the book of Kings and concluding David's life. The story is quite simple in its argument: David is too old to keep himself warm, so his assistants choose a beautiful young, virgin woman, Abishag the Shunammite, who sleeps with him to keep him warm.[38] Despite the simplicity of the biblical text, her social location and her identity remain very much open to guesswork, especially in terms of her legal status (free or slave?), her sexual status (virgin or sex partner?), the use of the verb שרת to explain her ministry to David (distinguished or menial?) and her unique characterization as סכנת. Two additional elements to consider are the contrast between her voicelessness in the texts and the fact that she is never referred to as שפחה or אמה; and the even briefer mention of her presence with King David in 1 Kgs 1:15 when Bathsheba visits him. These elements will now be evaluated in order to assess the narrator's depiction of Abishag.

The first, ambiguous characterization of Abishag is her lack of clear family ties. It is well known that women are identified in the Bible in terms of males to whom they are related.[39] Abishag, however, is referred to only by her gentilic. Her only other denomination is נערה, a woman outside the protection of a *paterfamilias*. These facts make of her at least a woman on her own, and very likely (we do not know for sure) of foreign descent.[40] Being of foreign descent did not automatically imply low status during the monarchy, as is obvious from some of the closer helpers of David and Solomon, but it imposed certain restrictions on their rights, on participation in the assembly of YHWH's people, as well as protection and safety. A second fact that characterizes Abishag is ambivalence as to her status. There is a physical closeness to David, which is perceived differently by the narrator (who makes clear that they did not have sexual intercourse), and by others (while this fact is apparently not public knowledge, it gives Solomon the excuse to kill his brother Adonijah soon after

---

[38] See Garsiel, "Puns," 379–86.

[39] For instance, Michal, daughter of Saul (2 Sam 6); Rizpah, referred to as daughter of Aiah (2 Sam 21:8) and for a period also as Saul's concubine (2 Sam 21:11); Bathsheba remains "Uriah's wife" until Solomon's birth (2 Sam 12:15b), and then she is recognized as David's wife (2 Sam 12:24) or Solomon's mother (1 Kgs 1:11).

[40] According to Patricia Franklin, "The Stranger within Their Gates: How the Israelite Portrayed the Non-Israelite in Biblical Literature" (Ph.D. diss., Duke University, 1990), 21 a man had to possess patrimonial land to become an Israelite. Thus a גר (male) could never become part of Israel while Israel was in the land. He and his family would not, therefore, acquire a name, but only a gentilic (Uriah the Hittite, Barzillai the Gileadite, and others). Since the woman married into another family, Franklin continues, a foreign woman could become an Israelite. Since Abishag is not married, her name cannot come from her husband's tribe, so she must have been the descendant of a גר.

his accession to the throne, 2:13–25).[41] As the dispute between Solomon and Adonijah comes to a close with Adonijah's death and Solomon's rise as monarch, she disappears from the record.

A third fact unique to this woman is the use of the participial form of the stem שׁרת to express her service to the king (v. 4, 15). The verb applies in general to ministerial service, including higher domestic service such as that of Joseph in Egypt and of Gehazi for Elisha, royal officers (1 Chr 27:1, 28:1), royal domestics such as those the Queen of Sheba saw in Solomon's palace (1 Kgs 10:5), and angelic service to YHWH (Ps 103:21). It also applies to worship by priests and Levites (Exod 28:35, Num 3:6, 8:26, Ezek 44:17–27). The only woman of whom it is specifically used is Abishag the Shunammite.[42] As if these ambivalences were not enough for Dtr, he adds still another note. Abishag is said to be a סכנת, *qal* participle from the verb "to be of use or service," therefore in participial form "steward" (Isa 22:15) or "stewardess" (1 Kgs 1:2–4).[43] The ambivalence of this term originates in the fact that its cognates point to officials of varied responsibilities and status, and since the origins of the word are unclear, it is hard to determine what would have been the most likely meaning of the term in biblical Hebrew. The following examples will illustrate the problem. In Ugarit, the masculine term *skn* appears as an epithet of the king of Ugarit, high above other titles: "Thus the *skn* office may be seen to be higher than that of the crown prince .... This statement accords with that of M. Heltzer ... that the *skn/sākinu* held the second highest office in the kingdom."[44] In Assyria it also applied to a high officer in the administration of the kingdom. As Heltzer points out, then "the most important question is a) did the office of the *sokenet* reach Israel from Assyria? b) was it a result of the local independent development? or c) is the office of the *sōkenet* in Sargonid Assyria a loan from

---

[41] It is also differently perceived by scholars. For instance John van Seters, "Love and Death in the Court History of David," in *Love and Death in the Ancient Near East: Essays in Honor of Marvin H. Pope* (ed. J. Marks and R. Good; Guildford: Four Quarters, 1987), 121, takes her as a concubine: "Finally, in 1 Kgs 2:13ff., Adonijah becomes infatuated with Abishag, the former concubine of David, and makes a request for her from Solomon through Bathsheba."

[42] One could argue that her brief appearance happens in the story and perhaps not in real life. This is true, but all the writer allows us to know (all her existence in a sense) is what the story tells us. On the other hand, although perhaps long in years, if she had a historical existence after her life together with David, it would have been in the "harem," as so many other examples in these books tell us. Elna K. Solvang, "Classifying Women: The 'Harem' and What it Does and Doesn't Tell us about Women," in *Proceedings of the 51st Rencontre Assyriologique Internationale Held at the Oriental Institute of the University of Chicago, July 18–22, 2005* (ed. Robert D. Biggs, Jennie Myers & Martha T. Roth; Studies in Ancient Oriental Civilization 62; Chicago: The University of Chicago, 2008), 415–20.

[43] The Aramaic cognate, *sgn*, appears in Dan 2:48; 3:2,3,27, with *BD* 's translation of "prefect."

[44] Cutler and Macdonald, "The Unique Ugaritic Text UT 113 and the Question of 'Guilds,'" 33. Reference to M. Heltzer, 33 n.19: "Problems of the Social History of Syria in the Late Bronze Age," in *La Siria nel Tardo Bronzo* (Rome, 1969), 41. See also Yamashita, "Professions," 64–65 #29: *skn*.

the West-Semitic area?"[45] The answer to this question determines whether one would expect the biblical סכנת, Abishag, to have been a bedroom attendant or whether she was accorded, even if only by the narrator, a higher status, as the *šakintu* had in Ugarit and later in the Neo-Assyrian period.

> As Dalley and Postgate point out, the *šakintu*, according to the texts of fort Shalmaneser was the female housekeeper of the queen i.e. of the MÍ.É.GAL or MÍ.KUR .... At her disposal were also the queen's scribes and according to the texts 39 and 40 also a female scribe (A.BA-*tú*) as also ... "the deputy (female) of the *šakintu*". But naturally not all the staff of the *šakintu* was female. ...
>
> A text from Ugarit from the XIII cent. B.C.E. U.V, 161 dealing with land-transactions of the queen of Ugarit lists among the witnesses... "Matenu, the *sākinu* of the palace (household) of the queen". In another land-transaction of the same queen the same Matenu is called ... "the *abarakku* of the queen". From here we learn, that at least in this case the *abarakku* and *sākin bîti* were identical. Otherwise we know that the female counterpart of the *abarakku* - *abarakkatu* is often mentioned among the palace-personell [*sic*] in the texts of Mari of the XVIII cent. B.C.E., which also belongs to the West-Semitic area. The *abarakkatu* belonged to the senior palace-personell [*sic*] also there. Therefore, it is possible that we have here an old West-Semitic parallel to biblical *sōkenet* and this was the position of *Abîšag* (var. *bat 'Abîšag*)[46]

If one opted for the latter possibility, there are still further questions for which there are no answers. These concern the narrator's choice; since he chose a term that points to an officer and not a bedroom attendant, was he serious or ironic? Was he exalting or despising Abishag? What kind of ideological intention should one attribute to Dtr?

In his narrative study on the Samuel cycle, Fokkelman has noted a chiastic structure, which leaves at the center "she will be his *sōkenet*."[47] Around this center, her "job description" is enclosed by three references to "the king" and the fourth one, to "lie on his bosom." Such a crafty combination of diverse

---

[45] M. Heltzer, "The Neo-Assyrian *Šakintu* and the Biblical *Sōkenet* (I Reg. 1,4)," in *La Femme dans le Proche-Orient Antique: XXXIIIe. Rencontre Assyriologique Internationale*. Edited by Jean-Marie Durand. Editions Recherche sur les Civilisations: Paris, 1987, 89. According to Heltzer, 89, "the *šakintu* does not appear in Old- and Middle Assyrian texts, and in Neo-Assyrian the term appears only in the Sargonide period. Therefore it is not impossible that the office of the *šakintu* came to Assyria from the West, but the word by itself is not of West-Semitic origin." See also R. Henshaw, "The Office of *Šaknu* in Neo-Assyrian Times;" Edward Lipiński, "*Škn* et *Sgn* dans Le Sémitique Occidental du Nord," *UF* 5 (1973): 191–207.

[46] Heltzer, "Neo-Assyrian *Šakintu*," 87, 89–90. References not included in this quotation.

[47] J. P. Fokkelman, *Narrative Art and Poetry in the Books of Samuel: A Full Interpretation Based on Stylistic and Structural Analyses, I: King David (II Sam. 9–20 & I Kings 1–2)* (Assen: Van Gorcum, 1981), 347.

elements (serve the king, stand at his service, be his officer, lie at his bosom) makes it hard to rescue her from the bedroom and have her at an office. All the harder since the connection with the only other term of the same stem in the Hebrew Bible has recently been challenged. To this connection we turn next.

Unlike Abishag, the one סכן mentioned in the Hebrew Bible has nothing to do with the king's bed (Isa 22:15–16):

> [15] Thus says YHWH, the Lord of hosts:
> Come, go אל־הסכן הזא
> to Shebna, who is supervisor of the household, and say,
> [16] "What are you doing here and whom do you have here,
> that you have hewn here a tomb for yourself,
> cutting a tomb on the heights, carving in the rock a dwelling place?"

Recent bibliography on this passage is scant. Between 1901 and 1905 three articles dealt with Shebna. Although their main concern was the relationship of the Shebna of Isa 22 with the one in Isa 36–37, some hints can be picked up from their view of this official. Kamphausen opined that they all refer to the same person, "he having been first the manager of Hezekiah's household and afterward state secretary"; and "an exalted secular official," as biblical examples such as 2 Kgs 15:5 show.[48] Fullerton proposed that there was a general consensus as to the meaning of the text, namely that Shebna had no claim ("what do you have here? whom do you have here?") perhaps because he was a foreigner. The title, he stated, "seems to be a general title, and does not allow us to determine what particular office he filled."[49] One year later Koenig complemented Fullerton's analysis by stating that where he disagreed was that "this" in God's command to Isaiah "cannot 'suggest that the personality of the official was well known,'" but it "rather has the function here of pointing toward a contemptible personage," which Koenig expressed in this characterization.

> The arrogant character of Shebna is also probably expressed by the choice of the phrase *ha-sôkhēn*,[1] for סכן in the Phoenician means "to care for, to administer,"[2] and *sakânu* in the Tell-el-Amarna letters has the sense of "to care for."[3] If *sôkhēn* had been "a general title" (Fullerton, p. 622), it would probably occur more frequently ....
>
> I may say, in passing, that the idea that Shebna was a foreigner who possibly had been brought from Damascus by Ahaz (cf. II Kings 16:10ff.; Isa. 2:6) may be indicated by the א in שבנא.[50]

---

[48] A. Kamphausen, "Isaiah's Prophecy concerning the Major-domo of King Hezekiah," *AJT* 5 (1901): 50, 51. See also his review of earlier scholarship, 57–8.

[49] K. Fullerton, "A New Chapter Out of the Life of Isaiah," *AJT* 9 (1905): 622.

[50] E. Koenig, "Shebna and Eliakim," *AJT* 10 (1906): 675–6. His notes refer to: [1] "*hasokheneth* Abishag of Shunem (I Kings 1:2).," [2] to "Bloch, *Phoenisisches Glossar, sub voce.*," and [3] to

Most present-day scholars follow the same line of thought as the one just described. Hayes and Irvine, however, understand Isaiah's rebuke metaphorically. The prophet uses the tomb image in reference to Shebna's abuse of authority in digging the Siloam tunnel.[51] Key in these arguments has been the deciphering by Avigad of a tomb inscription found in Siloam in 1870. The inscription records that "...yahu, who is over the house" lies there, buried together with his אמה.[52] As Avigad himself reminds his readers, his guess on the incomplete name remains a conjecture, because he searches only among the seven stewards mentioned in the Bible.[53] Among them, Shebna, Hezekiah's minister, is a very likely candidate, because of the paleographic similitude of the tomb inscription with the Siloam tunnel inscription and with Phoenician inscriptions (facts which locate the inscription very strongly in the eighth century), because of the tomb location not in a cave but up in what from the valley would have appeared as a hill, and because of the evidence of names ending א is a shortened version of names ending in יהו. Worthy of note are the concluding words of his article.

> In the light of the former interpretation, the somewhat surprising occurrence of *amah* and the Phoenician-style formula of our inscription could be regarded from a different angle. But this would lead us too far into discussion of a matter which, after all, is based on conjecture alone.
>
> Whatever the name of the owner of the tomb, he was without doubt one of the king's ministers, and his sepulchre stands in the midst of a necropolis where persons of rank and high distinction were laid to rest.
>
> The inscription discussed here is, in the words of its discoverer, the first "authentic specimen of Hebrew epigraphy of the period of the Kings of Judah", for it was discovered ten years before the Siloam tunnel inscription. Now, after its decipherment, we may add that it is (after the Moabite Stone and the Siloam tunnel inscription) the third longest monumental inscription in Hebrew and the

---

"*Keilinschriftliche Bibliotek*, Vol. V, Brief 105, l. 3: *tiskin*, "thou carest;" Brief 105, 34, 38: *liskin*, "may he care."

[51] John Hayes and Stuart Irvine, *Isaiah, the Eighth-century Prophet: His Time and Preaching* (Abingdon: Nashville, 1987), 284–5.

[52] Nahman Avigad, "The Epitaph of a Royal Steward from Siloam Village," *IEJ* 3 (1953): 146, n. 21 reads: "A different opinion, worthy of notice, was expressed to the writer by Maj.-Gen. Y. Yadin. In his view, the designation *amah*, both on the above-mentioned seal [discussed in n. 19, which refers to Avigad, 'A Seal of a Slave-Wife (Amah)' *PEQ*, 1946, 125–132] and in our inscription, applies to a legally married wife and not to a slave-wife, that is to say אמה equals אשה. Mr Yadin observes that in Assyrian literary sources Zukûtu, the wife of Sennacherib, king of Assyria, is referred to as the *amtu* of Sennacherib. Cf. Hildegard Lewy: Nitokris Naqî'a, *JNES* 11, 1952, p. 282, n. 92." This is yet another suggestion on the term אמה, which cannot be further discussed here. What we are dealing with here is not the meaning of אמה but the probable identification of Shebna in the inscription.

[53] Avigad, "Epitaph," 144–45.

first known text of a Hebrew sepulchral inscription from the pre-Exilic period.[54]

Finally, mention should be made of an article that appeared in 2010, in which Christopher Hays raised again the issue of the translation and meaning of the stem סכן in Isa 22:15–19. His proposal is to read this oracle paying much more attention to its tomb setting; that is, highlighting (and understanding literally) its pertinent jargon in the pericope. Thus, he takes סכן not as meaning "steward" or the like, but—with the vocalization *sikkān* or *sikkōn*—as meaning mortuary stela, probably from the Emar Akkadian *sikkānu*.[55] His proposal makes sense to me, even though that makes Abishag's description as *sōkenet* a *hapax legomenon*. At any rate, he accepts this term's derivation from a West-Semitic stem attested in Akkadian *šakānu*, Ugaritic *skn* and even in the Amarna letters from Jerusalem, with a basic meaning of "care for" and a derived meaning of "prefect, governor, mayor, manager, administrator."[56]

In summary, there is much that is uncertain here. The social location of Abishag in the Bible (and, on another lexical basis of Shebna, if Hays is right) thus remains open to much pondering, since there are enough elements, biblical and extra biblical, to argue for a high-status political office or for a low-status bed attendant; even to argue for the first possibility for Shebna and the second one for Abishag. The opposite could also be theoretically possible; unfortunately, this study has again and again found traces of male bias in the treatment of female workers, thus precluding a potentially more positive view of Abishag.[57]

Elsewhere I have tried to demonstrate that, despite all efforts to diminish her position by locating her at the king's bedchamber to keep him warm and try his sexual potency, this woman was no "nobody" but must have come from a renowned family. The narrator is at pains to make her election a national event: they chose her out of the whole territory of Israel. Since Shunem holds no particular previous importance in the Hebrew Bible, she would not have been chosen because of her provenance from Shunem.[58] On the other hand—perhaps somewhat aside from this discussion or perhaps pertinent to it—Shunem is

---

[54] Avigad, "Epitaph," 152.

[55] Christopher B. Hays, "Re-Excavating Shebna's Tomb," 558 n.2 and 564–5.

[56] Hays, "Re-Excavating," 564 n.33, referring to John T. Willis, "אב As an Official Term" (*SJOT* 10 [1996] 115–36, unavailable to me).

[57] Michael Heltzer, "The Neo-Assyrian *Šakintu* and the Biblical *Sōkenet* (I Reg. 1,4)," in *La Femme*, 89, states that according to documents from Nimrud from the Neo-Assyrian period, the *šakintu* could own considerable property and probably also have responsibility for supervision of the royal harem. The biblical text does not give us any hint in this line.

[58] See Mercedes L. García Bachmann, "What Is in a Name? Abishag the Shunammite as *sokenet* in 1 Kings 1:1–4," in *Out of Place: Doing Theology on the Crosscultural Brink* (ed. Jione Havea & Clive Pearson; London: Equinox, 2011), 233–54.

recorded in one of the Amarna letters as one area related to conscripted labor well before David. According to Na'aman, that is the second oldest attestation after Alalakh, in which Biridiya, ruler of Megiddo and apparently in charge of paying their wages, reports: "In fact, only I am cultivating in Shunem, and only I am furnishing conscripted laborers (*amīlūti massa*)."[59] Perhaps the region had been some kind of "no man's land" with much geographic mobility and that favored election of someone from the region. Or perhaps the region had become loyal to David and it would therefore have been a natural area where to look for someone.

In my opinion, Abishag stood at a crucial place, where only someone capable, totally reliable, and faithful could stand. Notice is given the readers that, as Bathsheba enters the chamber to convince David that he should not delay any longer appointing Solomon as his successor, Abishag was there. She must have been there most of the time, hearing and seeing more than Nathan or Bathsheba themselves would. She had the chance—if needed and if desired or required—to pass on every information about David's last decisions and conversations. She must have been chosen because of these qualities, besides her characterization as a beautiful young virgin from Shunem. That there were high expectations for this job can be corroborated by two independent facts. The first one is the evidence from Isa 22 and from the Neo-Assyrian evidence for an office of the same name with a high responsibility for the person over it (Shebna or any *šakintu*). The second element appears in the narrative itself: twice in the story there appears a possibility for her to become a king's concubine (David's) or a prince's wife (Adonijah's), neither of which is finally realized. It is interesting that neither failure is attributed to her (nobody vetoes her candidacy to be a concubine or a wife), but to David's impotence and Solomon's assassination of his brother Adonijah. This tells us something about Abishag's place in court, at least in principle (perhaps there were other, unstated reasons).

All this considered, at least the possibility that this worker would have held an honorable status and not just "bedfellow" should be estimated. Of course, we cannot rule out the possibility that *šakintu*, *sōkēn* and *sōkenet* shared an office called in the same manner but with disparate working conditions.

מינקת — *Wet Nurse*

In the Bible, the Hebrew term translated "wet nurse" is the *hipʿil* participle feminine of ינק, "nurse, breast-feed," and in DtrH it only appears in 2 Kgs 11:2 (= 2 Chr 22:11), when Joash is taken with his unnamed (wet) nurse from among the king's children about to be killed by Athaliah, and both are hidden away for

---

[59] Na'aman, "From Conscription," 748. The letter's reference is EA 365:8–29.

six years. Those other children in the palace, whose fate was not so fortunate, also had unnamed nurses. These, however, like many others for several generations of children in the Israelite and Judean court (not to mention other rich families or other courts), are taken for granted and never mentioned in our texts.[60]

This is as much as DtrH lets the reader know. Important clues come from Exod 2:1–10, where Pharaoh's daughter takes in Moses and seeks a way to have him safely raised. Perhaps because it is Moses' mother herself who is hired, most commentaries overlook the fact that she is formally hired by Pharaoh's daughter to do the job:

> His sister told Pharaoh's daughter, "Shall I go and call for you a breastfeeding woman (אשה מינקת) from the Hebrews? She will breast-feed the baby for you." And Pharaoh's daughter told her "Go!" and the youngster (העלמה) went and called the baby's mother. Pharaoh's daughter told her: "Take this baby and breast-feed him for me (והינקהו לי), and I will give you your wages (שכרך)." So the woman took the baby and nursed him (ותניקהו). (Exod 2: 7–9)

Gruber has noted yet another element: "It is taken for granted by all the characters in the narrative of Exod 2:6–9 that, even when enslaved, the Hebrew women in Egypt continued to employ wet nurses."[61] Does this signal how common it was for women to seek these professionals' services or is it only a historical error? It is hard to assess.

The stem שׂכר (verb, two nouns and an adjective) has the meaning "hire," "hired," and "wages," applying to soldiers, mercenaries, oxen, servants, and in one figurative case, the husband's sexual favors.[62] The term appears often in texts protecting hired laborers' rights, who depend on their daily payment to survive, who have lost their means of subsistence, and who in all probability owe others and therefore walk constantly on the brink between debt and permanent slavery. The only explicit reference to a woman happens in our text. In a story where Israelites are increasingly suffering oppression and being enslaved, and where persecution reaches to the point of male infanticide in order to control their growth, it is natural that Israelite women would work as much as men would. That the first chapters of Exodus are a social and theological

---

[60] Yamashita, "Professions," 52 #13: *ynq* (CTA 15 II:28; 128 II:28).The *hip'il* as verb appears in a few texts, neither of which refers to a hired nurse, except, perhaps, 1 Kgs 3:21.

[61] Mayer I. Gruber, "Hebrew Women in Egypt: Bible," in *Jewish Women: A Comprehensive Historical Encyclopedia*(1 March 2009; Jewish Women's Archive) n. p. Cited 22 September 2011. Online: http://jwa.org/encyclopedia/article/hebrew-women-in-egypt-bible.

[62] Jeremiah 46:21; 2 Kgs 7:6 (soldiers); Exod 22: 14 (ox); Gen 30:28–33 (Jacob to Laban); Deut 15:18 (wage of a hired man); Gen 30:16 (husband). In some texts it carries the meaning of "reward," see Gen 15:1; Isa 40:10.

construct does not matter here, because within the text-world it is taken for granted that a Hebrew woman should breast-feed a Hebrew baby.[63]

It is estimated the nursing period lasted about three years. While in the Bible the only reference is the one just mentioned with unspecified "wages," several contracts as well as laws have been discovered from ancient Mesopotamia. These regulate both parties' responsibilities and costs, including payment of food, barley, oil, wood, or clothing (three of these items at a time are mentioned) to the wet nurse; prohibition to take on another suckling without express consent from the first child's parents; and prohibition to engage in sexual intercourse, lest the milk turns bitter and thinner. Often, wet nurses were slaves or free poor women, who could in this way make ends meet. Apparently, they raised the child in their own home (this is also implied in the story of Moses' upbringing, where his mother takes him to his adoptive mother, Pharaoh's daughter, when she weans him). Other documents speak of wet nurses who receive rations from the palace; these ones would probably have lived also in the palace, taken care of sucklings and later educated these children or taken up other tasks, caring for the women—one can also imagine that, if their "milk son" became king, they would hold a special position and would perhaps enjoy leisure, rather than performing other domestic tasks.[64] S. Dalley asserts that, because of Shibtu, King Zimri-Lim's wife's many responsibilities and children, "[t]he wet-nurse *mušēniqtum* for infants and the nanny or governess *tārītum* for weaned children were established in society."[65] One should imagine, also, that even in the palace everybody worked, either administering or gardening or in whatever capacity. Perhaps the major difference would be in the kind of work they did and in the honor ascribed to it.[66]

According to Archi, in the Ebla court, wet nurses retained this title long after their function as such had finished.

Two monthly documents relating to rations of cereals (*ARET* IX 41, 42), to be dated to the very last years of Ebla, list: a) 11 "women of the king," dam en; b)

---

[63] See M. Lefkowitz & M. Fant, *Women's Life in Greece and Rome. A Source Book in Translation* (Baltimore: Johns Hopkins University Press, 1982.) 28 §54, 29 §59 (epitaph and tomb inscription), 29 §58(i), (wet-nurses in inscriptions of manumission), and 110–11 §111 (letter on how to hire a wet-nurse). On breast-feeding in antiquity and in rural societies today, see Mayer I. Gruber, "Breast-Feeding Practices in Biblical Israel and in Old Babylonian Mesopotamia," *JANES* 19 (1989): 61–83.

[64] So Stol, *Birth*, 188 on Mari women.

[65] Stephanie Dalley, *Mari and Karana* (Piscataway, N.J.: Gorgias, 2002² [1984]), 98–9.

[66] Dalley, *Mary and Karana*, 73, mentions the following occupations in the ration lists: "the drawers of water, at Mari two girls ...; and two men who 'carried wood'. There was a doorkeeper (women were doorkeepers at Chagar Bazar), a barber, a throne bearer and a reed worker who would have made baskets, mats and fencing. There were gardeners ... Two potters are found in the ration lists of Chagar Bazar."

141 women involved in various tasks, that is to say: 12 "wet-nurses," ga-du, "singers," ..."stable-hands," ..."doorkeepers," "gardeners," ...; c) approximately 900 "weavers," túg-nu-tag and "grinders of grain," dan kikken. All of these women "were residents" (al$_6$-tuš), that is worked in the Palace (SA.ZA$_x$^{ki}), while a far smaller number were active in the lower city or in its surroundings (uru-bar)[67]

Listing the different types of women, working both in the palace and in the city, being paid rations by the palace, he asserts in a footnote about these twelve wet nurses: "They continued to belong to this group of women even when they could no longer assure their function as wet-nurses" and continued receiving rations from the palace supplies. What exactly these women did in Ebla and elsewhere, after their small patrons had grown up, is open to discussion. In some records it is clear from the appellatives the same woman receives, that a wet nurse continued as dry nurse or "nanny."[68] That the relationship continued well past childhood is often attested, both in the position such a woman or her immediate male relatives enjoyed when that child became king, and from the memorials erected to commemorate them at their death (including mourning, laments or, in some extreme cases, a tomb at the King's Valley in Egypt).[69] In Egypt, wet nurses did belong to the upper-classes: "while the majority of women probably suckled their own children, wetnurses are attested for royal children and also in elite scribal families. Royal nurses were themselves members of elite families, often the wives or mothers of high officials."[70] That is also the reason why several of them appear in tomb depictions, either on their own or prominent in their husbands' tombs. They appear with the child on their knees, being the only occurrences in a tomb depiction "of physical contact between a particular and royalty" according to one scholar.[71] In a few instances, even their names have survived. Since in Egypt wet nurses remained in court and helped educate the future kings, queens and princes(ses), this extended relationship (and the fact that they belonged to the ruling elite) must have deepened the impact they made on the children. Recently, Cynthia Chapman has traced the importance of breast-feeding as identity giver in several cultures as a contribution to a deeper understanding on our part in biblical texts. That the breast milk would carry personality characteristics to the child explains the continuation of the relationship to the wet nurse past weaning. On the other hand, it would indicate

---

[67] Archi, "Role of Women," 2 (text and note 5, next quotation above).

[68] Stol, *Birth*, 189 about prince Jagid-Lim's nurse (kingdom of Mari), about Rabbatum, princess Me-Sataran's wet nurse and nurse, and about Deborah, Rebekah's nurse.

[69] Stol, *Birth*, 189–90; Marsman, *Women*, 414–5.

[70] Robins, *Women*, 89.

[71] Armijo Navarro-Reverter, "La vida de las mujeres egipcias," 129.

that, whenever possible, the wet nurse would belong to the upper social echelons, so that her milk would enhance the child's assets.[72]

Perhaps that would explain also why Deborah was so important to Rebekah the matriarch that even her burial place became an etiological name—and one related to grief: "And Deborah, Rebekah's nurse (מינקת), died. And she was buried below Bethel, under the oak tree; so they named it the Oak of Tears or Allon-bakuth" (Gen 35:8). Shaul Bar has proposed that Deborah was also a professional crier and thus her burial place got a name related to her duties.[73]

She is the only other biblical מינקת recorded (Gen 24 and 35), always "Rebekah's wet nurse," even when her mistress travels to get married to Isaac.[74] As it happens also in 2 Kgs 11, it is not clear what were their responsibilities after they ceased to breast-feed. Whether Deborah belonged to the lower classes or not is never attested; besides this lack of information, the Genesis narratives are notably difficult to locate and thus, we do not risk making assertions on this issue.

Assante and other scholars have called to our attention that the Akkadian term *qadištu*, usually interpreted to mean "sacred prostitute," meant "wet nurse" in some texts. In other texts, she seems to be responsible for childbirth, rather than wet nursing. Although there remains much to be understood, at least for the time being some data seem clear. In his book on birth in ancient Babylon, Stol enumerates several groups of religious women acting in different functions during childbirth:

> A hymn extolling the free citizens of Babylon, records these lines about the three well known classes of religious women: "Women who have learned insight at their work: the *entu*-votaries (nin.dingir.ra) who are faithful (?) to their husbands, the *nadītu*-women who give the womb life by wisdom, the *qadištu*-women who ... in purification water. They respect the taboo, they observe the interdict, they pray ... They are reverent, observant, minding the good. Daughters of the gods ...". The second and third classes of these women are here involved in childbirth.[75]

---

[72] This would be confirmed by some kings' claim to have been breast-fed by deities. Debora or Moses' mother did not belong to the governing élite: perhaps that is why they are singled out. Cynthia R. Chapman, "'Oh that you were like a brother to me, one who had nursed at my mother's breasts.' Breast Milk as a Kinship-Forging Substance," *JHS* 12 art. 7 (2012), n. p. [cited 2 January 2013]. Online: http://epe.lac-bac.gc.ca/100/201/300/journal_hebrew/pdf/2012/article_169.pdf.

[73] Shaul Bar, "The Oak of Weeping," *Bib* 91 (2010): 259–274. He notes that usually trees served as burials in emergency situations and were not worship places (at least, not to the religious orthodoxy).

[74] The other instances of the participle *hip ʿil* do not refer to "real" women: Isa 49:23 uses the figure of the מינקת in an oracle of reversal of fate, when the queens of far lands will nurse Israel.

[75] Maarten Stol, *Birth in Babylonia and the Bible: Its Mediterranean Setting* (with a chapter by F.A.

Stoll recognizes that *qadištu*s were also, somehow, related to wet nursing and child rearing. So, after reviewing some texts, he proposes another possibility, which may be the best one to be made for now:

> The role of the *qadištu* remains obscure. We remind the reader of the "house /room of the *qadištu*" in the myth of Atra-ḫasīs where the first human being was born. We have noted in the section on the midwife that it has been interpreted by some as "house of the tabooed woman." Everything we have learned about the *qadištu* suggests another possibility: this house may have been a nursery.[76]

This means, *qadištu*s would have run nurseries or medical centers in which they would have perhaps performed themselves certain tasks. More importantly, they would have, above all, ensured the whole process was accomplished properly, both medically and legally. We do not know whether there was any system resembling our state offices, in which peoples' names, family ties and other information would be consigned (except for ration lists, in which some information was poured, especially how many they were at a certain time and space and how much they "cost" the system). Polls were not uncommon, but oriented toward males apt for military service, rather than newborn children.

Regarding the Greco-Roman sources, the situation is a little different in that there is more material for study. Sarah Pomeroy compares the lives of slaves in Greece and in Rome, showing that their possibilities depended on their education, which in turn very much depended on several factors, extending from house-born slaves with some training to peasant women with only basic household skills, kidnapped as adults and set to serve at someone else's household as slave:

> Owing to the limitations of women's education, a freshly captured woman may have been at most a midwife, an actress, or a prostitute. Most women did not have any training beyond the traditional household skills. In slavery, as in freedom, they could work as spinners, weavers, clothesmakers, menders, wetnurses, child nurses, kitchen help, and general domestics. The household duties of female slaves in Rome differed from those we observed in Greece. Because Roman engineers devised mechanical methods for transporting large quantities of water, Roman slave women did not carry water to the same extent that Greeks had done. Moreover, in Rome, unlike Greece, all clothing was not made at home. In addition, female slaves were given special training in the

---

M. Wiggermann); Cuneiform Monographs; Groningen: Styx, 2000), 172. Quotations here are from online version. Cited 1 July 2011. Online: http://books.google.com.ar/books?hl=es&lr=&id=-n4LQNeU1ckC&oi=fnd&pg=PP11&dq=maarten+stol+%26+birth&ots=IhHOJ9EXz4&sig=DjAueB Mr3vsgzvniSTPsfbgDOdl#v=onepage&q&f=false.
[76] Stol, *Birth*, 188.

wealthy Roman home and worked as clerks, secretaries, ladies' maids, clothes folders, hairdressers, haircutters, mirror holders, masseuses, readers, entertainers, midwives, and infirmary attendants. Children born into slavery in a wealthy Roman home thus stood a fair chance of receiving some education.[77]

In this sub-section I have reviewed briefly the information available on wet nurses. Not every contract or every name recorded has been brought up, especially because these are not biblical or Syro-Palestinian; furthermore, they belong to diverse cultures, times and locations, even if they provide much helpful information. The evidence revised allows me to draw a few conclusions:

First, there is far less information than there were wet nurses.

In the Hebrew Bible, our best source is Exod 2, because it portrays wet nursing as a job stipulated by a contract between the adoptive mother, Pharaoh's daughter and the wet nurse. When the contract is over, the wet nurse returns the infant to his mother's place. It is not clear when the wet nurse receives her wages. Genesis 24 confirms information encountered in other sources, that the relationship between wet nurse and suckling child lasted well beyond breast-feeding; we cannot know what percentage of relationships lasted, of course, but at least in a few instances it is well attested.

Extra-biblical material attests to the variety of situations in which one finds these women, from women ascribed to a court well past their wet nursing service, receiving daily rations, to women serving as particulars for about a three-year period; from upper-class to lower-class women; from beloved and mourned nurses to provisos about breach of contract or death of a baby.

With regard to DtrH, only one of them appears in a narrative. As a side-commentary to Queen Athaliah's murder of the royal lineage, 2 Kgs 11:1–3 tells that the king-to-be was hidden by his aunt, with his wet nurse, for six years. That's it. This matter-of-fact way of recognizing there were wet nurses in the palace attests to the low consideration they enjoyed for this historian. They belong to service personnel, like several others, unworthy of much attention.

On the positive side, nothing at all of what is said in the three biblical stories has to do with their sexual purity or fidelity. If anything, they are appreciated by their being present as accompanying, trusted persons in case of danger (hidden child in court, long journey to an unknown land and husband in the case of Rebekah). Exodus 2 is more complicated in this regard for its legendary character and as a trickster story. Here nothing is said about the wet nurse's conditions as such, because being the child's biological mother and being the whole thing a ruse to protect him, what other credentials would she

---

[77] Pomeroy, *Goddesses*, 191–2; see also above, n. 136 on Keuls' *The Reign of the Phallus*. See also Vogt, *Ancient Slavery*, 105–9.

need? As with several biblical stories in which lower-class women appear (they are foreign oppressed slaves) here her wit, the princess's connivance and the older sister's courage are exalted. Nothing, again, about proper sexuality.

אמנת — *Guardian, Child-Care Giver*

The *qal* participle of אמן is translated in different ways, with the meaning of "one who supports, nourishes." All those "foster parents, guardians" have in common their tutoring and nourishing responsibilities for a minor, although in the end Ahab's sons' tutors turn out to be their killers, following Jehu's orders. One אמן is Esther's cousin Mordecai, becoming her tutor after her parents' death.

Two of these texts are interesting for another reason. They set in parallel this masculine participle with a feminine form from ינק considered above; one is Num 11:12 (where Moses, fed up with the peoples' complaints and worried about food for them in the desert, asks God "Did *I* conceive all this people? Did *I* give birth to it, that you say to me, 'Carry it in your bosom as the nurse carries כאשר ישא האמן a sucking child את־הינק) ...?'"). The second one is Isa 49:23, an oracle about a restoration time, when the kings of the nations will be their guardians and their princesses, their wet nurses. They do not provide much information, but the very context in which they appear, especially the Isaiah oracle, indicates that kings and queens/princesses are diametrically opposite to the guardians and wet nurses.

From the seven occurrences of the participle, only two refer to women. One is Naomi taking care of her grandson Obed in Ruth 4:16. Besides the family link, it does not go deeper into any detail that would help us know anything about this task.[78] The remaining story is the only one in DtrH, except for the one already mentioned about Ahab's sons' guardians—a telling contrast, it may be said.

Saul's son, Ishbaal the king of Israel, was murdered by Rechab and Baanah, sons of Rimmon the Beerothite (2 Sam 4:1–3). Then, v 4 states that "Jonathan, son of Saul, had a crippled son, who was five years old when news had come to palace about Saul and Jonathan at Jezreel; so his (female) guardian had lifted him up and had fled. And in her haste to flee he had fallen and became lame. His name was Mephibosheth."[79] The story of Mephibosheth continues through

---

[78] Naomi's taking of Obed at the end of the book of Ruth could be studied in the light of a merger of two originally independent tales in the book—as Brenner has suggested—but it does not add any element to how society would see a guardian, and it does not refer to a lower-class dependent worker, since Ruth's child is said to build Naomi's family. A. Brenner, "Naomi and Ruth," in *A Feminist Companion to Ruth* (ed. A. Brenner; Sheffield: Sheffield Academic Press, 1993), 77–79.

[79] With Z. Zevit, *The Anterior Construction in Classical Hebrew* (SBLMS 50; Atlanta: Scholars Press, 1998), 27, as pluperfect. The verse refers the reader back to 1 Sam 31.

several of David's regnal years, with tensions on both parts.[80] However, the story of the child-care giver ends as soon as her action saves the royal child. What does the text say about her? She goes unnamed and forgotten. This verse tells more about Dtr's disinterest in or lack of concern for people who serve royal personages than it says about the child-care giver herself.

I would like at this point to make some concluding remarks concerning female labor taking care of children. Although general statements about how people looked at their children's needs cannot be made from these texts because the only stories concern royal sons, Dtr gives his readers the idea that in the palace—to which war captives and indentured Israelites would be brought for service—dependents took special care in the nourishment and upbringing of the royal children. The two stories preserved concern only royal boys. Although one would not know it from DtrH, royal daughters were usually brought up to serve as ambassadors, through marriage alliances at their husband's family or kingdom.[81] Thus, one may surmise they would have been cared for, breast-fed, educated, and so forth.

On the social location of these care-takers, very little can be said. Since both cases in DtrH (2 Sam 4:4, 2 Kgs 11:2) concern royal children (Mephibosheth, and Joash) brought up in the palace, conditions under which female laborers served and were paid must have been under the direction of some administrator at the palace. In all cases one can presume a low social status of the woman involved, since she was a dependent, very likely a slave, as Moses' biological mother.

Children were very important to the Hebrews, but everyday concerns such as their upbringing or feeding were not the center of the biblical writers' attention. A careful look at the stories shows that attendants are focused upon when the child they are in care of is in danger, because of the political implications of the danger of murder of a royal heir.[82]

---

[80] Mephibosheth is later brought in to eat at the king's table every day, as a sign of loyalty from David to his friend Jonathan. Loyalty expects loyalty, so Jonathan is in this way more controlled by David. When David flees from Jerusalem at the time of Absalom's revolt, Mephibosheth's נער, Ziba, takes the opportunity to prejudice David against his master. All these events point to mixed feelings on both sides, which is not surprising considering that they represent two dynasties, one in power and one ruined. On Ziba's location as נער, see Leeb, *Away from the Father's House*, 54–62.

[81] There are no biblical records of particular aspects of such upbringing. See, however, B. Batto's *Studies on Women at Mari* (Baltimore: The Johns Hopkins University Press, 1974), where the correspondence between King Zimri-Lin and his daughters is analyzed.

[82] Moses' situation can be likened to those of Mephibosheth and Joash in that as an adopted son of Pharaoh's daughter, he became an heir to the throne. This preoccupation with the throne does not cancel out personal feelings of love and fear when a child was sick or died.

CONCLUDING REMARKS

As the proverbial half-full or half-empty glass, the reader can look at the Bible's depiction of economically dependent women working for the household with very different eyes. It is fair to first locate oneself in the social world of the texts and their recognition of woman's contribution to society, and only in a second moment explore how today's paradigms of contribution would be different. Allowing for a margin of error (not every text was studied in detail), one may conclude that women serving in general, non-gendered tasks (bakers, cooks, perfumers, weavers), appear in such a faded light that one hardly recognizes their presence. The masculine form is used, and the reader is left to interpret whether by the masculine both genders or only men are intended to be understood.[83] Only when dealing with gendered services one finds a clearer picture of what was woman's realm. One has to keep in mind that occupations studied here are only part of the spectrum of occupations recognized in the Bible (which, in turn, are minimally acknowledged), and since the ones chosen here deal with the household, it is to be expected that they were closer to family issues—traditionally the female realm—than occupations related to religious or political services, which were male strongholds. On the other hand, DtrH, the body of text chosen as the primary referent for this research, is concerned with Yahwist-religious and political issues. Thus what appear as household occupations refer overwhelmingly to the royal household or to prominent leaders, all of them the locus of androcentric historiography. The same trend can be seen in the guardian for Mephibosheth and the wet nurse for Joash, whose appearance and disappearance are only determined by the royal children who are in their care. Even more telling is the lack of recognition of any occupation that would serve female needs exclusively.

In drawing conclusions one must also remember that there is no evidence that allows us to generalize a situation in one text into a general Israelite practice. One should also leave some room for chance in the occurrence of terms, especially since some texts (like the anti-monarchic speech of 1 Sam 8:11–18) only point to some examples of what it meant to be under a monarch.

Nothing else is known of the fate of Rizpah daughter of Aiah, Abishag, the medium at Endor, the unnamed wet nurses, the harlots who washed in Ahab's blood, the weavers at the temple prior to Josiah's reform, the woman who threw a millstone on Abimelech's head, and so many other female laborers. Dtr's

---

[83] Other occupations attested for females in extra-biblical sources, appearing in the Bible only in masculine form, with no hint of female participation (potters, scribes, beer-brewers), have been dealt with in chapter 5. See Yamashita, "Professions," 68 # 37 (notes feminine participles); Amico, "Status of Women at Ugarit," 248 (231–51 on occupations and lack of evidence in sources for female names); Dalley, *Mari*, 73–74. More generally, Carol Meyers, "Archaeology—A Window," elaborates on women's important socio-economic and religious roles during the Iron Age.

interest in these women goes only as far as they are part of important males' lives, so their record is left empty after the events the narrator recounts, with two exceptions. Rahab lived happily ever after (although later tradition has her married, as befits a worthy woman who has joined Israel!).[84] And the ten concubines raped by Absalom with David's complicity were locked up in a house (David never had sex with them again), where they lived (unhappily?) ever after.[85]

---

[84] See Matt 1:5.
[85] The fate of the unnamed women in Judg 19–21 is well-known, but that is part of the story itself.

CHAPTER 7

PROSTITUTES AND OTHER SEX WORKERS

CONCEPTUAL DIFFICULTIES

At least these main conceptual difficulties may be identified when seeking the sex workers of the ANE (including Israel):one difficulty lies in the wide range of meanings of the stem זנה, from the exercise of prostitution to idolatry. Secondly, there is the added difficulty of centuries-long biased translations and interpretations, which have found secular and sacred prostitutes in every reference to women unaccounted for. Thus, it is one of the feminist scholar's tasks to undo some well-established trends. A third difficulty lies in the fact that even marriage involved the exchange of gifts for sex! In societies in which there are dowries involved, and in which money was not the main means of exchange, there is a very thin line between different situations in which women would have received some kind of sex for pay. Finally, even if taking only those texts which arguably speak of "an organized form of sexual extramarital commerce," there would be disagreement among us as to which of today's categories would best apply, being sex tourism, exploitation of girls and boys for pornography, traffic of women and girls for "accompaniment" during events such as the soccer world championship, and an international web of brothels in which abducted girls and women are kept captive for prostitution, some of the darkest modes of this trade. Modes of which we do not hear in our sources, although it is not hard to imagine that some of them would have been already part of a captive's fate, for instance. At any rate, it is important to determine *if and when* an accusation of "playing the harlot" refers to a "sex worker," to a woman committing adultery, or to some other perception and, once identified as prostitute(d), to keep in mind the wide gap between the ANE world and ours.

WHAT DO I TAKE TO BE PROSTITUTION

Prostitution is understood here as "an organized form of sexual extramarital commerce, both despised and tolerated by society"; thus a prostitute is a person of either gender who exercises a trade, exchanging sex for wages.[1] According to Christine Stark, prostitution involves a second characteristic: promiscuity. Both aspects together differentiate prostitution from other non-marital sexual activities:

> Prostitution kann wesentlich durch das Ineinander der beiden Aspekte Profit und Promiskuität beschrieben werden... Folgende Definition sei vorgeschlagen: Prostitution ist Angebot und Ausübung sexueller Handlungen gegen materialle (meist finanzielle) Vorteilnahme, wobei die Bindung den Beteiligten in der Regel zeitlich auf die vereinbarte Handlung befristet ist. Die anbietende Person wird Prostituierte/r genannt.[2]

In his treatment of prostitution in late Roman antiquity, Thomas McGinn proposes what he calls a "sociological definition" of prostitution, "contain[ing] three components: promiscuity, payment for sex, and lack of an emotional bond between the partners."[3] Clearly, adultery is a different issue, involving a male whose rights to exclusive possession of the female's sexuality are violated. Or, to borrow someone's incisive precision, "[a]dultery activates retribution,

---

[1] Francisco Gomezjara, "Hablemos más claro sobre la prostitución," in *Sociología de la Prostitución* (México, DF: Fontamara [Nueva Sociología], 1982), 27 "una forma organizada de comercio sexual extraconyugal, menospreciada y tolerada por la sociedad." Quoting anthropologist Estanislao Barrera, but with no references. Theoretically, prostitution could be exercised by men as well, but restrictions of gender make it highly improbable that there would have been professional male prostitutes.

[2] Christine Stark, *"Kultprostitution" im Alten Testament? Die Qedeschen der Hebräischen Bibel und das Motiv der Hurerei* (OBO 221; Academic Press Fribourg, Vandenhoeck & Ruprecht, Göttingen, 2006) 57: "Prostitution kann wesentlich durch das Ineinander der beiden Aspekte Profit und Promiskuität beschrieben werden... Folgende Definition sei vorgeschlagen:
Prostitution *ist Angebot und Ausübung sexueller Handlungen gegen materialle (meist finanzielle) Vorteilnahme, wobei die Bindung den Beteiligten in der Regel zeitlich auf die vereinbarte Handlung befristet ist. Die anbietende Person wird* Prostituierte/r *genannt."* Stark differentiates also *Prostitution* from *Hure(rei)* (harlot[ry]) and both from "cultic prostitution."

[3] Thomas A. J. McGinn, "The Legal Definition of Prostitute in Late Antiquity," *Memoirs of the American Academy in Rome* 42 (1997): 74, quoting Kingsley Davis, "The Sociology of Prostitution," *American Sociological Review* 2 (1937): 744–55 (unavailable to me).

prostitution does not."[4] A prostitute might have an owner or "pimp" who profits from her activity, but she is legally endowed to exercise her occupation.

However clear this categorization between different types of female sexual and relational behaviors may seem at first sight, we concur with Laura McClure when she asserts that

> ... clear boundaries between nonmarital sexual relations, such as concubinage and adultery and sex for pay, are often elusive. The promiscuous woman often has the same social meaning whether an adulteress or prostitute ... terms for prostitutes are much contested in nearly every ancient language, not only in Greek, where the exact relation of *hetaira* (courtesan) and *pornê* (brothel worker) has long been debated, but also in the languages of ancient Mesopotamia and in biblical Hebrew. ... The problem of terminology reflects in part our inadequate access to the social practices depicted by the literary accounts, even as it reveals the ambiguous status of such socially outcast and marginal figures in the ancient world.[5]

One should not be surprised that there is such "inadequacy" in ancient vocabulary; besides the wide distance in time and culture that separates us (and the happenstance of archaeological discoveries) it reflects social life and social living, which are never static.[6] There is still today a tendency to clothe raw prostitution with nice terms, especially when it involves other services besides sex—and when it involves higher class patrons. Avaren Ipsen tells in her book that one motivation for discussing this topic is her own upbringing in a USA inner-city ghetto in the 1960s. Her mother was not a harlot, but she was a divorcee who worked as a "scantily clad cocktail waitress who occasionally modelled lingerie—considered a form of sex work by SWOP [Sex Worker Outreach Project] readers." She can further reflect on her own experience and those of her neighborhood with the academic tools provided by her doctoral work, but more importantly, with an awareness of their social location: "When I

---

[4] Irene E. Riegner, "The Vanishing Hebrew Harlot: A Diachronic and Synchronic Study of the Root *znh*" (Ph.D. diss., Temple University, 2001), 140. See also Jost, "Hure/Hurerei," 1. Begriffliche Definitionen.

[5] Laura K. McClure, Introduction," in *Prostitutes and Courtesans in the Ancient World* (ed. Christopher A. Faraone & Laura K. McClure; Madison: University of Wisconsin Press, 2006), 6.

[6] Perhaps here is useful Stark's differentiation between prostitution and "whoring" ("Hure[rei]," both different from "cultic prostitution"). According to her ("Kultprostitution", 60), "whoring" involves social condemnation and pejorative stand and no commercial exchange: "Hurerei bezeichnet nicht-eheliche sexuelle Beziehungen mit geringem gesellschaftlichen Ansehen bzw. unter gesellschaftlicher Ächtung. Die beteiligten Personen können Hure bzw. Hurer genannt werden. Überdies wird der Begriff Hurerei diffamierend verwendet und kann in metaphorischer Übertragung allgemein untreues Verhalten bezeichnen." If I understand her correctly, this term would apply to accusations of deviation from an orthodox cult.

think about it further, many of the neighbourhood women who helped raise me were sexual outlaws of some sort—they were guilty of miscegenation, lesbianism, a wide variety of sex-work, and lots of non-marital childbearing—which has made me think there must be a *big* sexual component to class."[7] I find it particularly valuable that she make explicit her own interests, concerns, and suspicions, which link sexual work with class, and that she can thus open a way for academic readers to engage in contemporary social issues. Some of these ambiguities or rather ideological differences in assessing certain practices surface also when scholars assess ancient sources.

WHAT DO I TAKE NOT TO BE PROSTITUTION

There are some other words which have suffered from centuries of academic conceptual misunderstandings and misuse in expressions such as "cultic prostitute," "temple prostitution," "hierodule," "votive sex," and others; and from all sorts of imaginative descriptions of their (supposed) functions and actions. Until such a time comes when they are ascribed their proper social value (starting from translation), it seems unavoidable to discuss time and again their association or disassociation with "whoring." Thus, I should explain why *qadištu*/קדשה is not discussed in connection with the women who worked as prostitutes זונה/ת. There is, in the first place, an increasing number of scholars who have studied the texts dealing with different Mesopotamian and classic feminine terms and have come to conclude that, whatever they were, they were *not* cultic prostitutes—or, if we want to side with the most prudent ones, there is no proof as to their existence.[8] Just one scholar's contribution on this matter may suffice to state my position:

> Because of the dearth of information concerning the status of *ḫarimūtu* and our lack of knowledge concerning the temple's part in the regulation of the tavern/brothel and the prostitutes that congregated there, it might be better to give a more generalized definition of "prostitution" in Mesopotamia. Consequently, I would suggest that a "prostitute" is one who is outside the culturally defined bounds of controlled sexuality.
>
> If prostitution is defined as occurring outside the cultural bounds of controlled sexuality, then controlled coitus within the sacred sphere is not prostitution. ...

---

[7] Avaren Ipsen, *Sex Working and the Bible* (London: Equinox, 2009), 36.

[8] Thus Mayer I. Gruber, Review of Stephanie Budin, *The Myth of Sacred Prostitution in Antiquity*, *Review of Biblical Literature* (2009), 1 (Budin's book is unavailable to me). On *qdšm/ qdšt* and other problematic (female) terms, there are several references; I have taken, among the most representative, those available to me; see especially Assante, Baumann, Bird, Goodnick Westenholz, Gruber (one of the few men to write on this issue), Riegner, Stark, van der Toorn, and Wacker in the bibliography.

"Sacred prostitution" is an amalgam of misconceptions, presuppositions, and inaccuracies.[9]

Second, even though the terms designate some occupation or office involving "controlled sexuality" they would belong to the religious realm together with the prophetess, the priestess, the singer, and others whom I have left out of my research. It is clear, then, that it would be inappropriate to include the קדשה/תו in an assessment of the sex worker in ancient Israel.[10]

A BRIEF TRIP THROUGH THE ANE MATERIAL

When trying to answer the question about prostitution in the ANE, one may presuppose that there are plenty of literary, juridical, and administrative sources. Just as "sacred prostitution" was born in those exotic eastern lands, so holds Mesopotamia the doubtful honor of being the cradle of "the oldest profession of the world" and the well from which biblical scholars have "proved" its existence in Israel. However, there are important voices alerting us that this is not "the oldest profession of the world." Notably, sexual commerce is clearly identifiable in only one Mesopotamian text:

---

[9] Joan Goodnick Westenholz, "Tamar, *Qědēšā, Qadištu,* and Sacred Prostitution in Mesopotamia," *HTR* 82 (1989): 262, 263. Other scholars take a different position; see James E. Miller, "A Critical Response to Karin Adams's Reinterpretation of Hosea 4:13–14,"*JBL* 128 (2009): 503–6 studies Hos 4 and, partially supported by Gen 38 and Deut 23, concludes that it is sacred prostitution because of its religious character, but voices also a note of caution with regard to its fallacies: "Because a writer attributes to Canaanite/pagan religion the practice of sacred prostitution does not mean we must therefore believe such practices were part of the ancient cultures indicated. It is at least possible that such claims were part of a polemical package that had only partial identity with the real world. Recognition of this factor could change the tone of some scholarly polemics on the issue of ancient sacred prostitution." (506)

[10] There are also some works contesting traditional interpretations that made prostitutes of every group of women not under the authority of a male in Mesopotamia. Harris, "Organization," 121–57 has studied the evidence of *naditu* cloisters in Mesopotamia and has demonstrated they were *not* harlots. A. Taggar-Cohen, "The Prince, the KAR.KID Women and the *arzana*-house: A Hittite Royal Festival to the Goddess *Katahha* (CTH 633)," *AoF* 37, No. 1 (2010): especially 118–20, has just developed the thesis that the ritual described in the Hittite document CTH 633 (and other fragments), thought to be the rite of passage of the prince into adulthood, in fact is a political rite for conferring political legitimacy to the prince assuming rulership. Within this ritual, twelve KAR.KID women participate in a banquet with the prince, whom they later prepare for a night at the *arzana*-house. Contrary to earlier interpretations that made prostitutes of these twelve women, she manages to show their cultic role in setting up an appropriate encounter between the prince and the goddess, who might visit him during the night he spends alone in the temple compound. Of course, Taggar-Cohen does not disprove the possibility that certain *harīmtu*s might have been prostitutes; what she does prove, however, is that one of the Hittite sources for their existence as such is rather referring to a completely different type of woman.

In the vast corpus of millions of legal, administrative, economic, and literary cuneiform texts from Mesopotamia, prostitution—that is, sex in exchange for wealth—is clearly documentable in only one passage: a song (or songs) addressed to the goddess Inanna (as Nanaja) known from a number of near-duplicates, all dating to the Old Babylonian period ... and we are, remember, still talking about the price for the goddess Inanna here, not about that for a mortal whore.[11]

The Sumerian text referred to by Roth is the *balbale* to Inanna/Nanaja, in which a provocative goddess offers herself to a patron ("farmer") and stipulates her price; the lines in question (19–20), however, do not appear in all versions of the poem and they are not equally assessed by all scholars. At any rate, it could teach us more on "womanly" manners and male fantasies on goddesses and women, than on the real life of poor women who made a living by selling drinks and/or sex. One thing, however, seems to be confirmed by the scenario of this poem, namely, that "the wall" is one place where men are eroticized by accessible women:

[16–20] Your hand is womanly, your foot is womanly. Your conversing with a man is womanly. Your looking at a man is womanly. ... As you rest against the wall, your patient heart pleases. As you bend over, your hips are particularly pleasing.
[20A–29] (*mss. a and c add 2 lines:* My resting against the wall is one lamb. My bending over is one and a half *gij*.) Do not dig a canal, let me be your canal. Do not plough a field, let me be your field. ...[12]

What is the significance of "the wall" and which wall is it? And, what other element/s or space/s could be posted as more comfortable? A room or a tent somewhere? The inner-city as opposed to the garbage disposal? Both are possible locations for harlots, homeless, impure, "untouchable" and other people, falling out of the social system. Also the Gilgamesh hero Enkidu curses his initiator Shamhat, invoking upon her "the shadow of the city wall" as the place where she will stand!

---

[11] Roth, "Marriage, Divorce, and the Prostitute in Ancient Mesopotamia," 24–25. Also Julia Assante, "What Makes a 'Prostitute' a Prostitute? Modern Definitions and Ancient Meanings," *Historiae* 4 (2007): 129, and "Erotic Reliefs," 70, who even states that both cuneiform and Egyptian languages lacked any vocabulary for "prostitute" or "brothel." Cf. Steele, "Women and Gender," 305, who states that "in only two literary texts is a *harīmtu* explicitly identified as a sex professional." Unfortunately she does not identify these texts.
[12] I have taken it from the *ETCSL* project, referred to by Roth. Cited 25 November 2010. Online: http://www-etcsl.orient.ox.ac.uk/section4/tr4078.htm. Roth's translation, "Marriage, Divorce, and the Prostitute in Ancient Mesopotamia," 24–25, is a bit different, but the general sense is the same: "When you stand against the wall your nakedness is sweet,/When you bend over, your hips are sweet ... When I stand against the wall it is one shekel, /When I bend over, it is one and a half shekels."

May the ground defile your finest garment!
May the drunkard stain your festive gown with dirt!
May you never acquire a well-equipped household! . . .
May the shadow of the city wall be where you stand! . . .
May drunk and sober strike your cheek![13]

That here the city wall stands for all the undesirable places of city life can be seen both in his other curses and in the contrast to "a well-equipped household" never to be achieved (the fantasy of a wealthy man's household, who would divorce his wife for the harlot).[14] It should be remembered that, as in the text studied by Roth, these dealings happen in the realm of myth, not everyday life or even a list of incomes for a prostitute's service, for instance; and notably, the commercial transaction itself is either implicit (Shamhat was asked by the hunter to bring Enkidu into civilization, not by her patron himself) or it is lacking in some versions (the Inanna/Nanaja myth). Yet, the city-wall, the drunkard and the filth reflect the social and economic reality of poor women, rather than of Godheads; as we shall discuss below, some biblical texts confirm this same impression.

The Egyptian evidence is scantier than the Mesopotamian one. In his chapter on work, Warburton mentions prostitutes among many other professions: "Among the professional classes were merchants, barmaids, prostitutes, physicians, barbers, priestesses, managers, governors, and scribes. Sailors and soldiers wandered between the various professions, acting at times as merchants and farmers."[15] Unfortunately, except for the priestess and the

---

[13] Roth, "Marriage, Divorce, and the Prostitute in Ancient Mesopotamia," 27 (on note 11 she states she follows M. G. Lambert, "Prostitution," in V. Haas, ed., *Aussenseiter und Randgruppen: Beiträge zu einer Sozialgeschichte des Alten Orients,* Konstanz, 1992, 127–31 and A. George, ed., *The Babylonian Gilgamesh Epic,* vol1, 299); E. Speiser, "Akkadian Myths and Epics," in *ANET,* 86 translates: "[...] shall cast into thy house./[...] the road shall be thy dwelling place,/[The shadow of the wall] shall be thy station,/[...] thy feet,/[The besotted and the thirsty shall smite] thy cheek!". Bird, "The Harlot as Heroine," 201 reconstructs the poem as follows: "[Dark corners] of the street shall be your home, / The shadow of the city's wall shall be your station. / [Men shall piss there in front of] your feet, / The drunken and thirsty shall slap your face."

[14] Roth, "Marriage, Divorce, and the Prostitute in Ancient Mesopotamia," 27; see also her n.10 on p. 36. Marsman, *Women,* 418–9 believes this is one of the texts that quite obviously refers to prostitution. Marsman quotes also Rivka Harris (419, n.102) who, however, by avoiding the term "prostitute" leaves room for other possibilities, such as "courtesan": "The term *harimtu* in the Enkidu episode is, in my view, a non-judg[e]mental term for a woman who uses her sexuality to support herself. In Enkidu's curse the *harimtu* becomes an object of male control and male violence." ("Images of Women in the Gilgamesh Epic," in T. Abusch et al., ed., *Lingering over Words: Studies in Ancient Near Eastern Literature in Honor of William L. Moran,* Atlanta: 1990, 222 n.14, unavailable to me).

[15] Warburton, "Working," 170.

prostitute, he does not differentiate professions by gender, so we cannot know whether any of the other professions were also held by female personnel. Deborah Sweeney shares also the impression that it is likely that there would have existed prostitution in ancient Egypt, even though it is not clear-cut in the available sources before the Ptolemaic period. In this field of study there are also controversies when it comes to interpreting the evidence, out of lack of explicit evidence.[16]

Dearth of evidence does not mean non-existence; there is evidence that foreign prisoners, men and women, were used for sex at least during the Assyrian empire;[17] and one ancient wisdom text advises men not to seek sex with "indigenous slave girls because of their disobedient natures."[18] Perhaps not all these involved prostitution, but some might very well have involved sex for pay, and thus, prostitution, even though pay landed not on the harlot herself. These loose ends leave open a breach that has enabled feminist scholars to doubt the traditional renditions of Sumerian KAR.KID, Akkadian ḫarīmtu and qadištu, and Hebrew זונה and קדשה as "prostitute" and "sacred prostitute or hierodule" respectively. It should be said that there is a growing skepticism on the whole existence (as described by Herodotus and several of his followers up to date) of the qadištu/קדשה. Skepticism which I share, as expressed already when stating what do I consider prostitution and what I do leave out (chapter 1). There is far less acceptance of the proposals that question the terminology for prostitutes.

This poses a particular problem to our study, for how are we to study a profession when the term on which the study stands, זונה, is contested? After much pondering and having enjoyed scholarly exchange with several colleagues, mentors, and friends, I am convinced that the evidence is far from clear and thus, it allows for divergent opinions, especially in the muddy waters of possible developments in the meaning of terms along the centuries. One main problem seems to be that of presuppositions and worldviews—the proverbial half-empty or half-full glass: Was there room for women to live on their own and *not* be prostitutes? How much variation should we allow in our interpretation of ancient sources? How much do our own preconceptions interfere in our interpretations?

---

[16] Debora Sweeney, personal communication. I take the chance to thank her heartily for bibliography and email communication.

[17] Assante, "Erotic Reliefs," 94: "The [soft-pointed] caps unfailingly identify the males in the scenes as westerners, or, more properly, at the time of Tukulti-Ninurta I, as people from the modern region of Syria ... The cap was the chief visual means by which westerners, especially captives, were distinguished from Assyrians." K. Lawson Younger, Jr. "'Give Us Our Daily Bread.' Everyday Life for the Israelite Deportees," in *Life and Culture in the Ancient Near East* (ed. Richard Averbeck, Mark W. Chavalas and David B. Weisberg; Bethesda: CDL Press, 2003), 271, asserts that taking spoils and raping conquered peoples were part of the Assyrian pay to its army.

[18] Assante, "What Makes a Prostitute," 127, referring to the "Instructions of Shuruppak" from approx. 2500 B.C.E.

The line between a refined prostitute, a woman who lived alone and accepted occasional sex partners (and gifts), and a woman who became someone's permanent lover and enjoyed her own home are not very clearly distinguishable today (at least seen from outside) and much less when dealing with ancient evidence, which we may easily misunderstand, since vocabulary and evidence are so scant. Furthermore, some of these ambiguous terms may have acquired a different connotation as time went on. That would explain why there are at least some texts in which it is quite obvious that the terms refer to what we call today "prostitution" while others leave an open door into divergent interpretations.[19]

One of the key elements in this analysis is the recognition that categories of women were far more diverse and more complicated to grasp than just "good girls" and "bad girls." This tension is recognized by most scholars, independently of how they translate particular terms. A small sampler is enough: "Promiscuity in the world of the Bible is not simply a lack of sexual discretion, but a symptom of the risks that a household is taking with its land and children. Husbands and fathers are responsible for the honor of their women, which is associated with sexual purity."[20] There were, however, other women who, for whatever circumstances, "deviated, to varying degrees, from the norm represented by free, adult, married, domestic women."[21] And even though they seem to have been persecuted or at least despised by society, the very fear that those texts transpire show their "prestige" or allure. I am thinking here, for instance, of Proverbs' repeated warnings against loose women, variously depicted as adulterous harlots, ready to walk the street. The same may be said of Mesopotamian texts:

> These promiscuous women—whether prostitutes, adulteresses, or merely sexually active females operating outside male control—occasioned fear because they did not submit to men and could disrupt legitimate marriages. They were of interest in the construction of Mesopotamian legal documents because of their impact on private and economic issues, such as inheritance devolution, rather than out of desire to regulate morality.[22]

---

[19] Marsman, *Women*, 417. Assante, "Erotic Reliefs," 72: "In general, the label of common prostitute was one that Mesopotamians themselves did not recognize. It is a monumental creation of coordinated modern scholarship that required ancient Mesopotamia and its single women to champion 'the oldest profession in the world.'"

[20] Matthews, "Honor and Shame in Gender-Related Situations," 104.

[21] Steele, "Women and Gender," 300.

[22] Laura K. McClure, "Introduction," 9. One should note that the terminology of "promiscuous women," applies here because the author is reviewing sexually active women outside wedlock, not every instance of a woman outside the patriarchal hold.

If—as I assume with McClure—it is true that the fear reflected in some Mesopotamian (and biblical) texts available to us is due to economic issues, a valid question to ask is: How would they endanger established homes? How would lose women make a living outside their immediate patriarchal household? Where would they find the sustenance and protection a household would have afforded other women? Here is where prostitution could be one of several possibilities, depending on other factors, such as whether these women would have owned land and/or a house (in which they could grow a garden and have some animals), whether they would have dwelled with other women to share resources (like the two women in 1 Kgs 3), would have run a tavern, practiced midwifery or divination, worked on some craft that they could sell or whether they would have been totally disenfranchised. The important point here is that many might have ended up as prostitutes but prostitution would not have been the only option. And by only option I mean also that perhaps—like many women today—disenfranchised women would have made a living out of a combination of occupations and income-sources.

There is much more we do not know than what we have been able to grasp. That large amount of information that lies in the shadows could support the established views or could confirm those scholars who intuit one single translation for so many situations does not suffice. It is hard to demonstrate that women in ancient Israel, Mesopotamia, or Egypt could live on their own, away from a patrimonial estate, and not be prostitutes. On the other hand, several texts witness to cracks in the social system that would drag many women to the edges. And while sex has been and still remains a way for those women to generate some income, it is not their only resource. Furthermore, the very fact that any woman who is loose from control has throughout the centuries—and still is—labeled a prostitute, makes me wary of class and gender stereotyping. Thus, my approach to the biblical texts on the זונה/תו is to ask, first and foremost, whether the traditional translation as "harlot" is the only possible one or even the most likely in that text's context.

The short trip taken through some Near Eastern material has prepared the ground for an examination of the pertinent biblical texts on the זנה. Scholarship is like building a memorial on which we add one stone or brick to those already set by others before us. I have included some controversial opinions along with well-established scholars. Some of today's scholarship will not stand the trial of time and peer discussion, but at least, it is hoped, it will have opened new avenues. As to my own position, I am unable to take a definite stand. It seems to me there is evidence for prostitution both in the Hebrew Bible and the ANE sources; but there is also much scholarly make-up around them as well, which makes me wonder how much earlier interpretations reproduce vicious circles: because זנה is translated "harlot," it is a harlot, even though nothing in the particular story would prevent considering her a bartender or a woman living on her own.

BIBLICAL TEXTS OUTSIDE DTRH

A WIDE RANGE OF MEANINGS

References to a woman "זנה-ing" or to a זונה (-woman) call for assessment in order to establish whether they apply in the field of work or whether they refer to a non-professional "fornicator woman,"[23] to a woman outside a patriarchal family structure, or to the (mostly male) Israelite/Judean elite and their covenant breaches. Even though the line between the fornicator and the prostitute might have been thin in ancient people's minds, it is important for us at least to be aware of the fundamental difference, namely, the commercial aspect of it (and, perhaps the lack of emotional attachment, which is the third component of our definition). Ancient versions reflect this variety by choosing several words to translate the stem זנה. Scholars have attempted to delve deeper into this conundrum and have proposed social locations for these women and several processes by which it acquired differing meanings in different texts. I am, myself, not totally at ease with those proposals. Neither am I happy with my own conclusions, but at the present stage of scholarship I cannot find a better solution.

Some of the first studies on prostitution in the Bible are those by Phyllis Bird, published since 1989. One is a study on their social location, the other traces the consequences of the use of the harlot as a metaphor for Israel's religious and ethical infidelity in the prophetic literature, thus opening the way for further studies of prostitution in the Hebrew Bible. Yet a third one was earlier mentioned, in which she proves why the religious ministry of the *qadištu*/קדש (whatever its job description) is not to be considered (secular) prostitution.

In 1992, Hannelis Schulte took up an earlier approach. She posits a development of the concept from a pre-monarchic or early monarchic *binah* (a matrilineal household, co-existing alongside the *baʿal*, patriarchal household, into a patrilineal system alone. Women attached to a matrilocal marriage were

---

[23] The expression is used by Phyllis Bird in order to be faithfull to the Hebrew language, in which the same stem is used to refer to a professional harlot and to a woman having extramarital relations (as English "whore" is also verb and noun). My expression "loose woman" keeps the same vagueness in terms of categorization of women, although formed by an adjective, not a verb. See especially Bird's "'To Play the Harlot'," 219–25 and "Prostitution in the Social World and the Religious Rhetoric of Ancient Israel," 44.

זונות. With the disappearance of this type of family, the concept took on a more negative connotation, that of a harlot. This view is hardly considered today.[24]

A couple of years later yet another response at the dissatisfaction with the meanings and assumptions about these terms appeared. Starting from the *impasse* in the academic discussion on the above-mentioned question and since "sacred prostitution" cannot offer any help in understanding the Hebrew term זנה, Irene Riegner posits a process which starts with Hosea's condemnation of illicit religious praxis and moves into sexual semantics and not *vice-versa*. In her conclusion she states:

> The network of words surrounding the stem זנה "participate in illicit religious practices" consisted of pejorative language appropriate to the social and theological worlds. Using parallelism, Hosea blended זנה "illicit religious praxis," with נאף "adultery" (Hos 4.134b–14a), language from Israelite social life and a criminal offense. About one hundred fifty years later, Jeremiah did the same (Jer 3.9;3.27). With Hosea, זנה acquired a criminal complexion and assumed a sexual dynamic. The sexual became the dominant meaning but as used in Hosea and Jeremiah and in the Holiness Code, זנה refers to illicit religious practices.[25]

This transference of meaning runs opposite to the usual assumption that the use of זונה to speak of idolatry, insofar as it is a symbolic development, must derive from the sexual meaning. On the other hand, suspecting illicit sexual practices has been and still is a way of undermining a woman's professional (and personal) authority; and there is always a cloud of suspicion on female religious practices. Thus, the transfer of meanings between a religious and a sexual one, both with negative connotations from the holders of orthodoxy, should not surprise us. No doubt, these issues, particularly the possible development of concepts vis-à-vis the dating of the biblical material, needs further study and it needs also be incorporated into ongoing discussions.[26]

---

[24] Hannelis Shulte, "Beobachtungen zum Begriff der Zônâ im Alten Testament," *ZAW* 104 (1992): 262, takes a clue from Gen 38 and Hos 4:13–19, with the parallel between קדשה and זנה and concludes that "[w]ir haben hier also eine Begriffsverschiebung vor uns, die mit einer sozialen Umwandlung parallel geht. Die mit dem Patriarchat neu entstehende Lebensweise der Hure, der Prostituierten, schafft sich keinen neuen Begriff, sondern übernimmt die Bezeichnung einer aussterbenden Lebensweise von Frauen. Das wird dadurch erleichtert, daß sich in einer Übergangszeit diese beide Lebensweisen von außen gesehen kaum unterscheiden lassen, obwohl sie von innen her wie Feuer und Wasser verschieden sind."

[25] Riegner, "Vanishing Hebrew Harlot," 347.

[26] This dissertation has been published (Peter Lang, 2009) but so far I have not seen any review. Unfortunately, I have no access to the published version.

WHICH BIBLICAL TEXTS TO CONSIDER?

We will start with a short detour through Gen 38, some prophetic utterances and the pertinent Proverbs texts in order to arrive at DtrH. Since many good and detailed studies—even feminist ones in many cases—are available on each of these texts, I shall concentrate on what I consider of weight for my argument and leave other aspects.

Genesis 38

The only biblical story including a commercial transaction for sex is that of Judah and Tamar, in which a kid is accepted as the price. Aside from the difficulties in locating socially and chronologically the Genesis narratives, the reader knows from the beginning what Judah ignores to the very end of the story, namely, that Tamar is concealing herself behind a veil, so that he may take her for a זונה and give her deceased husband, Judah's own elder son, the heir that he has refused her by sending her away with a promise he intends to postpone indefinitely. She is not a prostitute, the narrator tells us, but she dresses herself as זונה, a "loose woman" who can be approached, at least in the eyes of Judah. So, by the place called "the opening of the eyes" he sees a prostitute and approaches her. Or is she another type of זונה, a "loose woman"? Or, taking Riegner's assertion, is what characterizes her as זונה her relationship with cultic praxis (illicit from the Yahwist's viewpoint), especially through sacrifice, for which kids are required? Would Judah or anyone else have been able, on the road, to differentiate a זונה who was a "loose woman" (say, for instance, a diviner) from a זונה working as a harlot? Perhaps this uncertainty makes Judah ask politely; perhaps the narrator wanted to "save" both from a purely commercial transaction. Be it as it may, the narrator puts a polite request on Judah's lips, "Let me come in to you!" and an equally polite counter-request on hers: "What shall you give me if you come in to me?" (v. 16). Noteworthy is the fact that the term "wage" (אתנן), which would make it certain that it is a professional transaction, is not used in this one story in which there is some evidence of commercial sex.[27] Or is it not? As stated above, all occurrences of אתנן save Deut 23:19 are figurative.

Assante wonders about the ancient near Eastern societies in general, in which there is scarcely any description about prostitution and brothels. One of her contentions deserves further reflection, namely, that "individual bartering for sexual favors might have been culturally too normative to be regarded as an

---

[27] It is all the more notorious since *BDB* offers no provenance for the noun, gives two doubtful stems תנה II and תנן II, with no relation to their respective first meanings.

official profession. The exchange of sex for financial security was basic to arranged marital alliances."[28] If I interpret her correctly, ancient categories would not (or not only) categorize women according to whether they did or did not receive gifts. This is both a very complex and a very important issue. Here, it could explain both the narrator's need to protect Judah and Tamar from incest (and thus, their purported commercial deal) and also the lack of further descriptions in most of our sources.

In any story there is a tacit agreement between storyteller and audience: one is to believe the "scenery" of the story. And in this one a woman who is sitting alone by the road close to the city gates can, at least, be approached by a patriarch for sex and be paid for sex—and in case someone thinks this unbelievable even to this very day—he should only ask the women around him, or just read the police reports or the newspaper about unwelcome advances to women! Although the narrator makes sure that all flanks are covered (Judah is past his mourning period as a widower, Tamar is not "playing the whore" but seeking her right, there are no further sexual encounters), the fact that a patriarch seeks a prostitute by the road is depicted matter-of-factly, nothing is extraordinary in the approach (extraordinary is his recognition that his daughter-in-law is more righteous than him!), thus giving us a clue that, at least in a certain period of Israel's story, it was not unthinkable to approach a street-walker for sex.[29]

The Prophetic Corpus

In the prophetic corpus and the book of Proverbs there are a few references to זנה which, while referring probably to Israel/Judah, liken their behavior or attitudes to those of a prostitute, although oftentimes they jump back and forth into the realm of the household and the promiscuous wife. I turn now to this and other texts from the prophetic corpus.

Isaiah 23:15–18. Verses 15–16 and 17–18 are two post-exilic readings of an oracle against Tyre, which is best dated at Assyrian times. Tyre will be punished during seventy years, after which it will be restored.[30] The image is that of a forgotten זונה, who must go about the city playing music with a lyre in order to be remembered and thus, be able to come back to life. Of course, there is nothing particularly "whorish" in this text that would prevent us from reading any "loose woman" in the allusion. Nonetheless, it makes sense that the woman

---

[28] Assante, "Erotic Reliefs," 70–72.
[29] The use of the term "קדשה" to refer to Tamar (38:21–22) has complicated scholars and there is as yet no agreed-upon explanation.
[30] J. Severino Croatto, *Isaías 1–39* (Comentario Bíblico Ecuménico; Buenos Aires: La Aurora, 1989), 135.

who so needs to call attention would be a prostitute, not a fornicator: she would need to earn a living. The association of "her wages" אתננה with the verb זנה in verse 18 contributes to this association, although in fact by now the oracle has moved once again to Tyre.

Furthermore, one tends to think (and so also many commentaries) that this is an old prostitute, although the text only uses "forgotten" (זונה נשכחה). The older they became, the harsher work and living conditions and the less room for negotiating they would have had. Thus also Jost: "Das Lied von der vergessenen *zônāh* in Jes 23,16f, die aufgefordert wird zu singen und zu spielen, um auf sich aufmerksam zu machen, lässt die Situation der alternden Prostituierten erahnen."[31]

Leaving aside the war context of the oracle and looking only at the reality conveyed by the image, one can suppose that a forgotten prostitute would not have many chances to make a living, unless she had other resources. Fokkelien van Dijk-Hemmes has noted that, even though the actual sung text is not recorded, they "had their own repertoire of songs."[32] Music performance would be such an extra resource, as a way to attract patrons as well as an extra income per se. While it can be supposed that taverns, banquets, and other occasions attracted male and female entertainers (musicians, dancers, perhaps storytellers, clowns, acrobats) it should not be assumed that all artists worked also as prostitutes.

We do not know whether there were female music teachers who would make a living by teaching girls (or boys) to play an instrument and to sing. However, some scholars believe that at least certain Mesopotamian texts refer to young slave girls being trained to work as musicians. It is impossible to assert whether this training was conducted by other female musicians or not.[33] This association of both music and sexual arts is otherwise well attested.[34]

Some prophetic texts are very difficult to take, for two reasons. First, they mix metaphors into something new that is quite difficult to categorize. These metaphors involve improper female behavior (here is where "זנה" appears) and improper—mainly male—behavior (Israel/Judah's leaders' idolatry and the nations' cruelty). The second reason why they become unbearable is the degree of violence against women they show. Even if it is anachronistic to accuse the biblical authors with the charge of being gender violent, that is what these texts are and they should be studied very carefully. Here only some of these will be

---

[31] Jost, "Hure/Hurerei (AT)," under 2.1.

[32] Van Dijk-Hemmes, "Traces," 82.

[33] Dalley, *Mari*, 99.

[34] See Assante, "Erotic Reliefs," 98–99.

reviewed, considering especially whether they may add any information, albeit oblique, to prostitution.

Ezekiel 16:30–34. It is clear that its concern is not prostitution *per se*, but the fate of Jerusalem at very troubled and troubling times, particularly for the priesthood. The violence of this chapter has been denounced enough and it is not our intention to deal with it here. For a study on prostitution, what is interesting is that, as said, it is one of the few texts in which paid-for sex is explicitly mentioned. Ironically, the whole chapter speaks of a very unlikely situation: first, a woman who seems to be זנה-ing but not quite, because she "scorns" her payment: ולא־היית כזונה לקלס אתנן; and, so the argument runs, a harlot would not do that.[35] So, is she a harlot, a זונה, who refuses to charge for her service or is she an אשה זונה (v. 30), whatever that means? Then, to make issues even worse, this woman, a fornicator, brings other men to her husband's household and even pays herself אתנן! So she is hiring male harlots: an utter inversion of gender roles![36]

Out of the concern shared by several scholars to counter gender violence in the prophetic texts, Erin Runions maps the relationships between the three characters of the text and realizes that there are inconsistencies. To name just one, "[b]ecause the sexual imagery cannot account on its own for the lovers' violence, the metaphor relies on a third, inordinately violent, deity figure."[37] The real issue, asserts this scholar, is between YHWH and the nations, who share the same object of desire (control over Jerusalem), while the woman becomes the scapegoat. It is no wonder that the metaphor chosen is that of the prostitute, since scapegoats and harlots are at the fringe of their community, so that they both belong but are vulnerable. The harlot is, in Ezekiel, "marginal to it by virtue of her 'deviant' sexual behaviour and by virtue of her gender."[38]

---

[35] *Pi˓el* infinitive construct of קלס is rare and refers to mockery (for instance, of Elisha's boldhead, 2 Kgs 2:23).

[36] S. Tamar Kamionkowski, "Gender Reversal in Ezekiel 16," in *Prophets and Daniel. A Feminist Companion to the Bible* (ed. Athalya Brenner; 2nd series; Sheffield Academic Press/Continuum: London & New York (2001), studies in detail this reversal of traditional gender roles and calls attention (182) to the use of הפך, "an overturning" precisely, in v. 34. In the same book, Erin Runions "Violence and the Economy of Desire in Ezekiel 16.1–45,"156–69, explores the function of these metaphors (violence against women, woman's free sexuality) with the help of Rene Girard's study on mimetic violence. The real issue, she asserts, is between YHWH and the nations, who share the same object of desire, while the woman becomes the scapegoat.

[37] Runions, "Violence," 163.

[38] Runions, "Violence," 168. Runion's appreciation regarding the weak social location of the prostitute, can also be said of many loose women, especially if they had been expelled from their father's household for whatever conflict or scandal. Runions also calls attention to the fact that the only verse that speaks of נאף "commit adultery" does so in an image, changing the verbs from the second to the third person.

Nahum 3:1–7. This is a two-part prophetic oracle against Nineveh with accusation (v. 1–4) and judgment (v. 5–7). In a kind of summary of Assyria's characterization, appears the זונה as term of comparison (v. 4). But what is she? She is characterized by a set of practices and power hardly attributable to the "common streetwalker" or the notorious "loose woman" of the village, to name:

- the many "fornications of the fornicator," זנוני זונה,

- the "quality of her grace" טובת חן,

- the "mistress of sorcery" (*NRSV*: "gracefully alluring" בעלת כשפים,

- "the one who sells nations through her fornications and families/tribes through her sorcery" המכרת גוים בזנוניה ומשפחות בכשפיה.

Assyrian cruelty and power are the main concerns here presented through the mixing of at least two sets of images: those of heteropraxis ("sorceries") and those related to the wiles of a זונה–woman (the "fornications of the fornicator" and the "quality of her charm") in v. 4. In the following verses, the lifting up of her skirt to her face (וגליתי שוליך על־פניך) and her shame (קלונך) are mentioned as part of her punishment. While these could be associated with prostitution, discovering a woman's nakedness and her shaming are, judging from other prophetic invectives, more related to other types of women rather than to the prostitute. The oracle against Babylon in Isa 47 comes to mind, where nakedness and humiliation also happen and are the fate of the mistress who becomes a slave rather than the prostitute. It should be conceded, however, that both texts do not share the same vocabulary and that female slaves (even former mistresses downgraded to slaves) could be put to work as prostitutes for their masters or mistresses.

Nahum has chosen a polemical term, שקצים, which appears often in the prophetic litigations against other deities, especially Jeremiah and Ezekiel, and thus, contexts where charges of "זנה-ing" are conspicuous.[39] According to Riegner, the term שקצים "refers primarily to the contents of the rural, religious sites, their artifacts and, especially, their deities. The noun שקוץ in the singular is associated with gods of foreign countries or with local deities other than Yahweh."[40]

The second noun קלון, is also connected to the polemics of the prophets, notably Jer 13:26, almost parallel to our Nahum verse, with which it shares the

---

[39] Except for 2 Kgs 23:24, in DtrH it always appears in singular (1 Kgs 11:5, 7 on the abominations Solomon allowed and 2 Kgs 23:13 on Josiah's cleansing of "detestable things").

[40] Riegner. "Vanishing Hebrew Harlot," 308.

words שׁוּלַיִךְ עַל־פָּנָיִךְ and the verb רָאָה in connection with קְלוֹנֵךְ.[41] At any rate, even though we cannot take the metaphor of the זוֹנָה too far, we can learn something about the fate of the weakest segments of society.

> In the strongest possible metaphor, the beauty that was Assyria's is shown to be sordid and ugly. The nakedness of the alluring whore is exposed, perhaps shown to be covered with the harlot's sores. Verse 6 may refer to the merciless treatment to which such women were subjected, and it is to be emphasized that Nahum is carrying through the metaphor of the harlot here. She is made the object of scorn and an example to all who see her.
>
> Indeed, finally the harlot will be done to death, and verse 7b is a dirge: "Destroyed is Nineveh!" (*RSV*: Wasted.)[42]

I share Achtemeier's insight that, by likening Nineveh to a זוֹנָה to the very end of the oracle, it is very violent toward women. I am not convinced, however, that the significant would be the prostitute and not the "loose woman," the unfaithful wife or the "sorcerer" that sells the land away with her doings. Images are, anyway, too knit with each other to give us a clear answer on this issue.[43]

Another example appears in Jer 3:1–6, which uses זוֹנָה to speak of political and social issues.[44] Judah is likened to an אִשָּׁה זוֹנָה who refuses to look ashamed. One could, of course, understand the term to refer either to a "loose woman" (especially if she has done nothing wrong) or to a prostitute who boldly seeks out patrons. It would make sense that a woman obliged to work in the "sex industry" would have looked bold and "unashamed." It would be part of her characterization, together with some other cosmetic aspects (clothing, make-up, hair). The biblical text, however, likens this type of attitude, "unashamed," to that of the (occasional) fornicator or the adulterer rather than the prostitute.

---

[41] The term also appears in Hos 4:18; a verse that presents several difficulties; for an alternative view to that of "tavern and sex" see Riegner 220–3.It also has a more general nuance, appearing in several Psalms and Proverbs and once in Job.

[42] Elizabeth Achtemeier, *Nahum-Malachi* (Interpretation. Atlanta: John Knox, 1986), 24. On the term רָאִי in v. 6, see Aron Pinker, "A Note on כְּשָׂאִי in Nahum 3:6," *HipⁱⁱⁱⁱIl* 5(2008), n. p. Cited 11 June 2011. Online: http://www.see-j.net/index.php/hiphil/article/view/39/36.

[43] Thus also Jost, "Hure/Hurerei," under *2.2*, speaking of Jeremiah and Ezekiel: "Eine Unterscheidung zwischen hurerischem Treuebruch und Prostitution ist hier nicht möglich, da die Liebschaften der Frau auch mit materiellen Vorteilen in Verbindung gebracht werden."

[44] Scholars divide the text into sections very differently. Holladay, *Jeremiah* I:57, considers 3:1, with its strange beginning לֵאמֹר, a direct continuation from 2:4–9. Robert Carroll, *Jeremiah: A Commentary* (OTL. London: SCM, 1986), 140–41 takes 3:1–5 as a unit. Verse 6 continues the theme of unfaithfulness through the harlot image, but this verse is considered an exilic comment on the earlier verses and does not add anything to the social location of זוֹנָה.

The Book of Proverbs

Finally, four texts in Proverbs use the זונה image, but it is doubtful whether any or all of them talk about the prostitute. They use once the lexeme אשה זונה, twice זנה/תו as absolute to a construct noun, and once זונה as attributive. All of them are undetermined. My own inclination is to locate two of them (Prov 7:10, 29:3) on the "prostitute side" of my spectrum. The remaining two sayings lean toward the "loose-woman side" of the spectrum (Prov 6:26, 23:27). Be it as it may, Roth's warning about the difficulties in using cuneiform literary sources to learn something about women's categories applies also to the biblical proverbs:

> There are many references in the cuneiform sources that refer to sexual activities involving nonwives, but literary texts, omens, proverbs, and so on, need to be read and understood within the limitations of their genres; further, allusions to sexual behavior in such texts serve functions that are far too multifaceted and complex to yield simple conclusions about moral or legal attitudes. Such documents rarely inform us about that intersection of prostitution—whose practitioners were, in some sense, free agents in the sexual and reproductive market—and recognized marriage—the locus of controlled, regulated, and legitimate sexual activities resulting in recognized inheritance devolution.[45]

Not only are our sources difficult to assess: they do not add much information, but only confirm the tendency already perceived of fear of any woman other than the faithful wife. Whether the danger is perceived as coming from a prostitute is what these texts do not say easily; again, perhaps in the ancient writers' minds there was no such clear difference.

I will not follow the canonical order, but will start with the two texts that I have located closer to the "harlot" side of the spectrum.

Proverbs 7. This passage warns young men against the woman who is a "temptress." The majority of scholars remain convinced that this אשה זרה and נכריה (v. 5) is an adulterous, married woman. Noteworthy is the excuse or reason adduced by the woman: she must pay her vows that very day and needs money. With McKane, Karel van der Toorn reads the verb שלמתי in v. 14 as modal: "I must provide a sacrificial meal, / today I am to fulfill my vows."[46]

---

[45] Roth, "Marriage, Divorce, and the Prostitute in Ancient Mesopotamia," 25.

[46] Karel van der Toorn, "Female Prostitution in Payment of Vows in Ancient Israel," *JBL* 108 (1989): 197. His proposal, already almost thirty years old, is often quoted but not much taken into consideration. He is right that the laws in Num 30:2–17 and Deut 23:19 reflect this tension on the fulfillment of vows by women and, perhaps, recourse to sex was used as a means of pressure on the husband but, in my opinion, probably not put often into practice. It is to Van der Toorn's credit, also,

Since "the man" is away, he is not to come back soon and has taken the "cash" with him she must take recourse to prostitution in order to pay her vows. Van der Toorn thinks she is a married woman trying to pay her vows by raising money through sex. One should note, however, that the depiction of this woman (called various names besides אשה זרה and נכריה in Prov 1–9) is a composite one. Taken by itself, chapter 7 does not indicate her clear married status, since the expression usually taken to mean "my husband" (אין האיש בביתו, v. 19) is far from clear.[47]

In short, there is presently no consensus on the precise meaning of this expression; this is not surprising, given the literary history and symbolic load of the expression.[48] For our study it does not matter much, for she would not be a professional harlot; recourse to prostitution to pay vows would still be sporadic. According to the above definitions of prostitution, it would be sex for pay. The question—which we cannot answer—is whether it would lack its second component, promiscuity. The real concern is not a harlot who raises her money, but a promiscuous woman who seeks extramarital sex.

The verse that concerns us here is v. 10, because of the descriptions of the woman who comes to "meet him," characterized by two, divergent, elements: one calls attention to her and one keeps her mysterious. The question to be answered is whether these two characterizations, which at best are used for comparison with an adulteress, refer to a harlot or to an unattached woman.

The first description is "the garment of a זונה." I take this to be a comparison with a prostitute, because it is unlikely that a woman who lived alone or an adulterous woman would dress in special ways, lest she wanted to attract sexual partners (Tamar in Gen 38). Furthermore, the talk is probably about adultery and it would make sense to have another stock-image as a way of comparison.[49]

The second element is נצרת לב. BDB translates it "secret, wily minded" but considers it dubious; NRSV chooses "wily of heart" and Scott reads $n^e\ṣ\ôrat$

---

to have resisted the trend to have put this *nokriyâ* with the *qĕdēšâ* all in one package on "sacred prostitution."

[47] See among others, studies by Gale A. Yee and Harold C. Washington in *A Feminist Companion to Wisdom Literature* (Athalya Brenner, ed. Sheffield: Sheffield Academic Press).

[48] Herbert Robinson Marbury, "The Strange Woman in Persian Yehud: A Reading of Proverbs 7," in *Approaching Yehud* (ed. Jon L. Berquist; Atlanta: SBL, 2007), especially 168–72, calls attention to the different words to depict the strange woman, mostly in chapters 6 and 7. Mieke Heijerman, "Who Would Blame Her? The 'Strange' Woman of Proverbs 7," in *A Feminist Companion to Wisdom* Literature (ed. A. Brenner; Sheffield: Sheffield Academic Press, 1995), 104–7 sees at least three possible portraits within this text, (the mother's rival, the male's scapegoat, and the woman in financial need), depending on whose voice one imagines is that of the teacher.

[49] There is some discussion on whether she is married, because v. 19 does not state "my husband" but "there is no man at his home, he has gone…"

lot "heavily veiled."[50] McKane notes how the meaning of the terms deteriorates from "guarded" to "sly":

> The meaning of *n^{e}ṣūrat lēb* has been well elucidated by G. R. Driver (*VT* i, 1950, p. 250) in terms of the parallel semantic development of *ṣn* ʿand *nṣr* from "guarded", "reserved" to "crafty", "sly" (Syriac *ṣnī*, "sly"). She has an easy and assured mastery over all the devices of seduction. She has a house, but not a home; she is a woman without roots in her family and community who can only live at fever temperature and whose wanderlust is the index of her homelessness and her alienation from authentic social experience. She is flighty, a rover and wanderer whose feet do not stay in her house (on *sōreret*, which is to be explained with reference to Accadian *sarāru*, "to be unstable", as well as "to be rebellious", see G. R. Driver, *ZAW* 50, 1932, pp. 141f.).[51]

Although different translations are possible here, the image of the woman remains secretive, dangerous, promiscuous, and stereotyped, to brand the warning against adultery in the young man's mind.[52] These can be characteristics either of a loose woman or of a prostitute, both of which are, for whatever reasons, outside the patriarchal household. The use of a garment to identify her is the main reason to suppose her a harlot.

Proverbs 29:3. This verse marks the last occurrence in that book and uses the plural form. Here the anonymous speaker of the *mashal* "contrasts two loves,"[53] stating very shortly that,

> a man who loves wisdom makes his father glad,
> but a friend/companion of זונות blots out his wealth.

---

[50] R. Scott, *Proverbs, Ecclesiastes* (AB; Garden City: Doubleday, 1965), 63, calls her "Temptress." Raymond N. Whybray, *Wisdom in Proverbs* (London: SCM Press, 1965), 50, calls attention to how different the portraiture of the danger of "the temptress" is from other chapters. "Features which are entirely lacking in the discourses play a prominent part here: the sacrificial feast, the absence of a husband ..." Several authors have also noticed the relationship that the text (in direct speech by the woman) establishes between her sexual offer and cultic aspects; see Jost, "Hure/Hurerei," under *2.3*.

[51] William McKane, *Proverbs: A New Approach* (London/ Philadelphia: SCM/Westminster, 1970), 336.

[52] Several scholars have noted the fact that we have access to her words only through the narrator/teacher/father/mother. See Scott C. Jones, "Wisdom's Pedagogy: A Comparison of Proverbs VII and 4Q184", *VT* 53 (2003), 65–80; Heijerman, "Who Would Blame Her?," 100–9, shows there are at least three different ways to read her speech, namely, the mother's speech against a possible rival, the father's in search of a scapegoat and an economically-deprived woman's speech seeking her lover or a patron.

[53] Bird, "Prostitution in the Social World," 45.

The pursuit of זנות is first contrasted to the pursuit of wisdom, perhaps as an exhortation to young men to concentrate on what really matters in life. And a young man spending all his wealth with harlots, fornicators or loose women is contrasted to his parents' unhappiness. Arguments for one or the other translation weigh about the same, thus making it extremely hard to make a decision. On the one hand, the financial dimension of the concern would point to her being a prostitute, as several scholars have shown. The following is a typical analysis:

> An aspect of indiscipline which looms large in Prov. 1–9 is sexual promiscuity. The prostitute is seen as the largest single threat to the young man; this is an all too familiar way of death and her house can be described as the very entrance to the realm of death. [3] In v. 3 such behaviour is described as ruinous, and, in view of the antithetic parallelism, the implication is that nothing is more calculated to break a father's heart than that his son should make himself a pauper through his fondness for prostitutes.[54]

On the other hand, as is common knowledge, the sages' and/or parents' concern in Proverbs is not with money spent on prostitutes, but with liaisons that would be dangerous to the household and thus, to society at large. And in this regard, married women seeking extramarital sex (adulterous) were the most dangerous because of further consequences to the offenders, followed by loose women who could eventually "steal" away a wealthy man from his wife. Only in the last place comes a prostitute who would charge a wage or a fee for sex and who belonged generally to the lower classes. If my analysis is right, then it is highly unlikely, though not impossible, that the professional prostitute would mean such a danger to a young man. Is this a sign that the term does not denote a harlot? Or do we have here a class prejudice?

The next texts, Prov 6:26 and 23:27, lean more probably toward the "loose-woman" side of the spectrum, rather than the professional sex worker.

Proverbs 6:20–35 contrasts the two types of woman to seek, the אשה זונה and the אשת איש, "a man's wife." The comparison appears in v. 26: כי בעד־אשה זונה עד־ככר לחם. Added to the complexity of the construction is the fact that the lexeme under discussion is, precisely, the compound one, which seems not to refer to a harlot. Nevertheless, most translations follow this line of thought:

> A prostitute's price, a loaf of bread,[55]
> But a woman with husband hunts with costly desire.[56]

---

[54] McKane, *Proverbs*, 336.

[55] Taking בעד as a construct noun, "exchange, price" instead of preposition "for, in exchange for" with G. Driver, "Problems and Solutions," *VT* 4 (1954): 244.

The two contrasting concepts "loaf of bread" and "costly desire" seem to be understood literally, implying that the prostitute's price is pennies compared to the luxuries a married woman would expect from a lover—and perhaps the wronged husband too.

> The meaning of *nepeš yᵉqārāh* (*RSV*'s a man's very life, literally "a precious life") is disputed. *nepeš* has many meanings including "soul", "person" and "life". However, Driver argues that it sometimes means "abundance", and that since *yaqār* (this word is not directly translated by *RSV*) means "precious", the phrase should be rendered by "costly abundance": that is, the adulteress, unlike the prostitute who is satisfied with a little bread, demands a life of luxury from her lover. Thomas (VTSuppl. 3, 1955, pp. 283–4) renders *nepeš yᵉqārāh* by "a weighty person": that is, she will only accept a wealthy man as her lover. But Driver's and Thomas's interpretations agree in seeing here a contrast between the prostitute's modest demand and the excessive cost of a liaison with a married woman, who may ruin her lover by her excessive demands.[57]

That prostitution is safer than adultery is the general biblical view, based on the fact that for the male it carries a monetary compensation to the woman for her occupation, with no further ado, while adultery carries all the dangers of a jealous husband and further problems between families or clans. The teaching does not consider whether a prostitute needs more than some pennies thrown at her, especially in terms of health care, provisions for her elderly years (if she survived), children, safety, and affection.

On the other hand, the *JPS* translation offers us a window into another interpretation for the terms אשה זונה. They translate Prov 6:26, "for on account of a harlot a man is brought to a loaf of bread, but the adulteress hunteth for the precious life." Let us put on hold the harlot since that is, precisely, our discussion. What concerns me here is the other part of the first sentence. The subject of the sentence is not, in this translation, the poor prostitute who contents herself with a loaf, but the man who, on account of her, loses everything. If it is the man who loses everything, then the proverb is not setting antonyms but rather similar situations, that of losing everything. The fact that the verses immediately preceding and following this one are all of synonymic parallelism would support this interpretation. This translation helps, of course, our contention that the phrase אשה זונה can mean a woman other than a "harlot." For a man can spend all his fortune on a harlot's bed; but it is more likely that

---

[56] Taking נפש יקרה as "costly abundance," on the basis of נפש as "abundance" in Isa 58:10; W. McKane, *Proverbs*, 329; Scott, *Proverbs*, 61: "But a married woman hunts with keener appetite." *NRSV*: "but the wife of another stalks a man's very life."

[57] Raymond N. Whybray, *Proverbs* (NCBC. Grand Rapids: Eerdmans, 1994), 105–6.

such an אשה זונה, like the אשת איש of the other member of the parallelism, be a lover on whom this man showers his richness. Although not every אשה זונה would be an adulteress, in people's imagination and in practice it is possible that unattached women would accept some man/men's favors and at times his whole "wallet"—or at least that would be the family's fear.

Prov 23:26–28 is a short teaching in which the "son" is warned against two types of women, set in a parallel saying in v. 27: the זונה and the נכריה, over against the speaker (apparently, Wisdom, see v. 22–25). Like the other short saying of Prov 29:3, we could see this one as a "contrast of two loves," that of wisdom against danger, here expressed by two female terms and two terms with underworld overtones:

> My son, give me your heart,
> and may your eyes delight in my ways.
> For/that, a deep pit is the זונה,
> a narrow well a female outsider נכריה.
> Yes! She lies in wait like a thief
> and increases the (number of) the treacherous.

Or, to take Phyllis Bird's proposal,

> A fornicator is a deep pit;
> an "alien woman" is a narrow well.
> She too lies in wait for prey.[58]

The first thing that calls attention is that a prostitute would have so much power, quasi-cosmic power. Several explanations are possible. One is that, in view of the sages' preoccupation with the fornicator-adulterous woman and not the paid harlot (a preoccupation further stressed by mentioning here the נכריה, alien, outsider or "other" woman), the connotation of the term here would be that of the "fornicator," rather than the professional harlot. Another possible explanation would be that the writer is actually thinking of the harlot, "a woman without morals, who will rob a man, and eventually bankrupt him. The warning is to stay away from such women, who may appear to offer easy pleasure, without the legal censure, but turn out to be a 'deep pit.'"[59] I had initially not considered this possibility of a literal prostitute in this text, but it complements well Solomon's assumption, on which 1 Kgs 3 is built, that at least one of the two *zōnôt*-women seeking his verdict on the child claimed by both is a liar. Finally, a third possible explanation would be that the author used hyperbole

---

[58] Bird, "Prostitution in the Social World," 45.
[59] Bird, private communication.

(exaggeration) to bring his warning home: "Any 'loose' woman, whether professional or amateur, is dangerous: Watch out, young man!'"

This text, then, could be interpreted to contradict the trend I have detected, which uses the noun on its own for the professional prostitute and the compound אשה זונה for the "loose woman."

CONCLUDING REMARKS ON TEXTS OTHER THAN DTRH

The information gleaned throughout these texts about a particular group of female workers is not abundant. This is the case also about other professions; but unlike studying these, the major difficulty in searching for the harlot has been to decide what certain texts (and their interpreters) do *not* say.

References to the commercial transaction of sex are rare and oblique but are present in the story of Tamar's ruse and in some prophetic and wisdom texts. The song of the forgotten harlot in Isa 23 seems to indicate what was the fate of an old prostitute, but this is also not totally clear. Other indications as to her profession" would only be those alluded to in "the garment of a זונה," in associations with music, and with going around the city attracting men's attention to her (Isa 23:16); or perhaps in the description in Prov 7:11 that she is "loud and wayward; her feet do not stay at home" (*NRSV*), although it is not clear, in that text, where the comparison ends and the allusion moves to the unfaithful wife.

With regard to her social location and ascription of honor, assessment is partly dependent on the selection of texts and on the degree to which we believe the descriptions that follow the metaphor apply to her. This is especially important—together with the ideological-theological criticism of such utterances—in the prophetic oracles studied and the many other left aside (especially Hosea, Jeremiah, Ezekiel).

If the four occurrences in Proverbs were taken to refer to a sex worker, then the image of the harlot would show a shift from the harmless woman who is treated as a poorly paid service provider to the object of the parents' concern that the family inheritance not be spent on them. If, as I believe, only some texts say something about the harlot, her social location is with the lower class: she is done with a few coins (a flat bread), she is easily forgotten and needs to attract patrons in order to survive; there is no concern for her well-being or for her life at all.

On the other hand, precisely because she does not belong with the "people like us," the danger that she might become wealthy through exploitation (!) of a patron might have made its way into a popular saying. Not very likely, and rather class-biased, at any rate.

One should note the scarcity of occurrences of either noun in the Torah.[60] A זונה is a woman a man visits to get comfort after his wife's death, while on the road, and one deals fairly with her, as accorded in the transaction. But that same man sees things differently when his daughter-in-law has been "harloting." As Bird reflects, "what a man desires for himself may be quite different from what he desires for his daughter or wife" or, as the case may be, daughter-in-law (Gen 38).[61] And precisely the fact that the prostitute is not accountable to any male makes her harmless to men, and very vulnerable, as shown.

TEXTS IN THE DTRH

We turn now to the texts in the Deuteronomistic History in which the participle *qal* of זנה could mean a harlot. The participle appears in the following texts:

- Deut 23:19, prohibition of a זונה's wages as offering at the temple;

- Josh 2:1; 6:17–25, Rahab, called רחב הזונה and אשה זונה;

- Judg 11:1, Jephthah's mother, אשה זונה;

- Judg 16:1, an unnamed "*zônâ*-woman" אשה זונה sought by Samson;

- 1 Kgs 3:16, two "*zōnôt* women" נשים זונות fight for one living baby;

- 1 Kgs 22:38, הזנות wash where Ahab's blood fell, at the Samaria pool.

Only two texts use the participle זונה functioning as noun with no added reference (once with and once without an article); besides these, it appears twice together with a proper noun, Rahab. In all other instances to be studied, it is always adjectival/appositional to "woman/women." We will start with the most likely candidates to tell us something about the profession.

DEUTERONOMY 23

Prostitutes and prostitution are neither forbidden nor punished in the Bible (unlike adultery, cf. Gen 38). Judging from the legal material, Israel was not very worried about them, since they are mentioned only in our text and in Lev

---

[60] I leave out Gen 34, whose last verse likens Dinah's treatment at the hands of the Shechemites to that of a זונה. Although translations use the term "prostitute," it is clear from the story that she was not one, nor was she taken for one. Furthermore, the final, rhetorical question by Dinah's brothers fits well, in my opinion, with Assante's contention ("What Makes a Prostitute" 130) that the זונה (like the *ḫarīmtu*) would be an "unmarried woman", a woman (perhaps momentarily) outside a patriarchal household—certainly not the message that Simeon and Levi would want to convey to the inhabitants of the region!

[61] Bird, "The Harlot as Heroine," 201.

21:1–15.[62] Deuteronomy 23 contains several, miscellaneous laws, more or less loosely put together under general rubrics such as "belonging to the assembly of Israel" (v. 2–9), "purity within the camp" (v. 10–15), "run-away slaves" (v. 16–17), "abominable practices" (v. 18–19), "lending" (v. 20–21), "vows" (v. 22–24), and "the right to eat from a neighbor's field" (v. 25–26).[63] Their character is not uniform: some of them have the casuistic and others the apodeictic formulations; some of them include theological justifications supporting the prohibition or the command; some are very dry and others wholly expanded. As discussed earlier on the slave legislation, there is no consensus on the intent of the laws in terms of their judicial weight; there is also no consensus as to the relationship between legal corpora and other bodies, especially narratives. Here they are of interest only because of what they reveal about the social and theological ideals of "YHWH's people."

The first thing to note is that it does not provide much information about the life, working conditions, or even social status of a sex worker. For its focus is, in fact, temple income, not prostitution itself. Details are not provided, except that "these two are an abomination to YHWH."[64] The amount of space that we need to apportion this law is not proportional to its length nor to the information we might be able to glean from it; but it is so much "tainted" by other issues (issues on the sacred and on sex), both in the text itself and in scholarship, that it would not be possible to simply state our opinion on it.

A short review of the main reasons for such a variety of interpretations follows:

(a) The larger context: Can this law, studied with other laws in the chapter, acquire meaning from a broader, structural arrangement (for instance, in relation to other laws on vows)?

(b) The immediate context: Is the law under revision related to the previous one, in which Israelites, men and women, are forbidden to take active part in

---

[62] Leviticus 21:1–15 will be briefly discussed below (legal material).

[63] References are to Hebrew verses; Deut 23:2–26 = Eng 23:1–25.

[64] תועבה, "abomination," is a typically, but not exclusively, Dtr evaluation of objects, practices or persons unfit for YHWH, in a ritual as well as in an ethical sense. Weinfeld, *Deuteronomy and the Deuteronomic School*, 226 states, "The 'abomination' belongs to that category of things which the delicate find odious and abhorrent, which is why we find injunctions against such disparate practices as self-mutilation, head-shaving as a sign of mourning, and the eating of unclean animals or the remains of animals that died naturally (נבלה), all grouped together in one section (Deut. 14)." Erhard Gerstenberger, "תעב *tʿb* pi. **to abhor**," in *TLOT*, 3.1431, sees the term as indicating "originally that which was deemed dangerous on the basis of group norms and hence that which aroused anxiety and repulsion. Cultic usage may have preceded legal and ethical usages; the word may have also been used simultaneously, however, in several areas of life to guard against that which was foreign or strange."

non-Yahwist cult? Or are both independent laws and should not be read one in light of the other?

(c) The two elements of the law itself: Does the law speak of two kinds of "dirty money" that are not to be brought to the temple or does it speak of prostitutes and animals?

Although items (b) and (c) are theoretically separable from each other, their interpretation depends on several issues. Amongst these, what the law itself says (item c), which in turn depends on the meaning of both words זונה and כלב, and whether these meanings depend on קדשה and קדש (item b)! Thus both will be studied together, trying to avoid the trap of thinking in circles.

The Larger Context

The vast majority of scholars considers this chapter a collection of miscellaneous laws and thus interpret v. 18–19 in the light of what each term, קדשה and קדש in v. 18, and זונה and כלב in v. 19, is thought to hint at, with no regard for a general structure, since no general structure is perceived in this chapter. Luckily, there are a few exceptions. Bird notes, for example, that v. 18 interrupts the chain of second person commands: "Its formulation as an absolute prohibition in impersonal third-person form contrasts with the second-person series into which it has been introduced."[65] Studying the laws in Deut 22:5, 9–12, Georg Braulik concludes that: "together with the cultic-sexual rules concerning acceptance into the assembly of YHWH (23:1–8), the purity of the armed camp (23:9–14), and the prohibition of cult prostitution (23:17–18), they form a redactional 'frame' around the laws for marriage and family (22:13–30)."[66] Additionally, Nelson notes that Deut 23:19's "evaluation [of both items prohibited] as *tôʿēbâ* and a similar twofold gendered format link v. 19 [Eng 18] to 22:5 (cross-dressing)."[67]

Whoever placed one law next to the other intended some connection between these four elements. What is under discussion is whether the only or even the strongest connection is the prevalent one in scholarship, clustering קדשה with זונה, and קדש with כלב, based on that scholarly invention called

---

[65] Phyllis Bird, private communication, based on the preliminary draft of a forthcoming publication. I take the chance to thank her heartily for sending me her draft.

[66] Georg Braulik, "The Sequence of the Laws in Deuteronomy 12–26 and in the Decalogue," in *A Song of Power and the Power of Song*, 332. Jeffrey Tigay, *Deuteronomy* (JPS Torah Commentary; Philadelphia: JPS, 5756/1996), 456 speaks of "Article f. 23:10–25:19 various subjects" (see also on p. 452–459 the excursus on the arrangement of the laws in Deuteronomy).

[67] Richard D. Nelson, *Deuteronomy: A Commentary* (OTL; Louisville: Westminster John Knox, 2002), 281.

"sacred prostitution."[68] Our contention is that Deut 23 shows an arrangement of several, originally independent laws around the overall theme of boundaries to the Israelite community. This overall theme is divided into two major clusters, which respond to the questions "Who is in the community and who is not?" (v. 1–15), and "What are some of our financial responsibilities to each of these?" (v. 16–26). Failing to see the inter-connectedness of the chapter, accomplished through the use of repetition of catch-words and the weaving of issues, leads to seeing only isolated sets of terms.

Structure. The diagram on next page should make some of these elements (laws arranged in clusters, repetition of catch-words, and weaving of issues) more easily apparent. It covers the whole chapter, but it only records those words that are important or repeated. One should not do much of this arrangement, for it is only very loose; its main purpose is to stress the association through monetary pursuits unacceptable to the Yahwists, rather than the sexual component of it. Nelson calls this section "Ritual and Social Boundaries." He also considers that "[t]he clearest linkages are of a catchword nature: '(not) enter' … the root *yšb* … the root *nṣl* …'holy' … 'vow'… Verses 16–26 fall into the pattern that alternates relationships in the human realm with duties associated with Yahweh."[69]

The text shows alternation of apodeictic and casuistic laws (v. 2–4, 6–8, 16, 18–20 start with לֹא " [you shall] not" and v. 10, 11, 22–23, 25–26 start with כִּי, "if"), and verbal alternation between second and third person masculine forms. Aside from the rhythm produced by such an alternation, which appears at the beginning of each verse, there are several other threads, all of which contribute to the final weaving of these verses. In order to see them, one ought not to look at the laws themselves in terms of their topics, but rather at particular ideas and lexemes working as connectors from one general topic to another, so that various laws were arranged in this chapter. First, the repetition of the verb בוא (often with the negative particle) helps determine "who is in and who is out."

The verb appears thirteen times in this chapter, mostly accompanied by לֹא.[70] In turn, the negative particle לֹא also provides a link with other, apodictic laws, in

---

[68] See Mayer I. Gruber, "Hebrew *Qĕdēšāh* and Her Canaanite and Akkadian Cognates," *UF* 18 (1986): 133–48; Goodnick Westenholz, "Tamar," 245–65; Paul Dion, "Did Cultic Prostitution Fall into Oblivion during the Post Exilic Era? Some Evidence from Chronicles and the Septuagint," *CBQ* 43 (1981): 41–48. Cf. von Rad, *Deuteronomy*, 147–8; Hans W. Wolff, *Hosea* (Hermeneia. Philadelphia: Fortress, 1974), 87.

[69] Nelson, *Deuteronomy*, 277.

[70] Most occurrences of the verb without the negative particle are not in laws but in further regulations: v. 9 allows the Edomites to join YHWH's assembly; v. 12 is on an unclean man joining the camp again; and v. 21 is a typical Dtr expression.

v. 7, 8, 16, 18 and 20. This leaves us with a rather uniform set of laws, where very few laws and explanations appear with the verb without the negative particle.

The divine name יהוה אלהיך, and יהוה in construct with קהל, appears repeatedly in v. 2–6 and 19–22, once each time in v. 9, 15, and 24.

There is also the use of relational terms: sons and daughters of Israel (v. 9, 18), "your brother" v. 20; "you/your" throughout the chapter, and "YHWH your God" (v. 6 [3x], 19, 21, 22, 24). Additionally, there is a distinction between these "you" who belong, and the ones who do not belong because of various categories (especially v. 1–8, 18–19, 20–21).

The semantic field of cultic purity for Israel is expressed also by the use of קדש in v. 15 and twice in v. 18; the קהל יהוה ("assembly of those belonging to YHWH, or YHWH's assembly" in v. 2–4, 9), and the words תעב ("abhor" v. 8 [2x], 19), חשא ("guilt" v. 22–23), דבר רע ("bad thing, impropriety" v. 10) and ערות דבר ("anything indecent," v. 15) to express what is unacceptable behavior for those within. This separation is further stressed by the use of אחיך (v. 20 "your brother") and רעך (v. 25–26 "your neighbor"), with whom you deal rightly, and איביך (v. 15 "your enemy"), עבד (v. 16–17, "the slave"), and נכרי (v. 21 "the alien").

The law on protection of the run-away slave (v. 16–17) serves as a buffer between both parts of the chapter, which then turns into issues clustered together because of their financial implications. Although it is not clear what type of run-away slaves are protected by this law, in all likelihood they are Israelites sold abroad who managed to return and should be accepted into the Israelite community once again rather than being returned to their owners abroad.[71] Thus, they are included at the end of the section on those who belong to Israel, and at the beginning of the section on financial obligations.

This law is followed in Deut 23:19 by the first law on vows, which regulates payment of vows—a financial issue—through prostitution, another financial issue.[72] The chapter continues with regulations on lending money with or without interest. This law is followed by another one on vows again. Vows had serious consequences for daily life and for relations, and had to be regulated.[73] Finally the last law concerns the right to eat from the neighbor's field, but not to take more than that (v. 25–26).

---

[71] See above, chapter 3, on legal material on slaves.

[72] Prostitution is foremost not a sexual issue, no matter how fulfilling, safe, or deviating it is to be seen, but it is, as our definition above already emphasized, "an organized form of sexual extramarital *commerce,"* and as such it is a financial issue. Emphasis added. See definitions, above.

[73] The seriousness of the issue can be seen in the power of the father and then the husband to confirm or veto a vow made by a woman (Num 30); in the laws in Lev 27, and in stories concerning, for instance, Jephthah's vow (Judg 11), and Hannah's vow (1 Sam 1). See van der Toorn, "Female

All these facts considered, the separation of v. 18–19 from the other laws, as virtually all commentaries attempt, appears to be more determined by a pre-conception of what these four terms mean, and how each pair relates (if they relate at all) to the other pair, rather than by a careful analysis of the text itself, as we have attempted to prove. Worthy of notice is the particular location of these laws in the second part of the chapter, together with other laws on financial issues. These data notwithstanding, the connection between the different issues dealt with in this chapter remains loose.

The Immediate Context

Up to this verse the chapter dealt with the boundaries to membership in YHWH's assembly, including momentary separation from the camp of those male fighters under uncleanness. Run-away slaves are "borderline" in this respect, as just stated. And now, verse 18 reverses the focus, looking at those who belong and some of the financial and other consequences of belonging.

The first law of this series states that those who are Israel's "daughters" and "sons" cannot be also קדש; a term that indicates some kind of religious office, whose characteristics elude us. In the Ugaritic material, the term *qdšm* appears in lists. But lists do not tell us much about their status or tasks, and are subject to interpretation as well. "The word occurs in three texts in lists of guilds or corporations and in two of these three texts it follows immediately the word *khnm* ('priests'). ... A tiny tablet [*CTA* 77 (*UT* 63) 3], thought to be an inventory or census, but probably a bill of lodging, mentions both *khnm* and *qdšm* in such a way as to suggest that the two offices were approximately equal in status."[74]

Whether females were equal in status to their male partners is quite another discussion and the answer is probably "no." Unfortunately, the קדשה and קדש cannot be compared for there is no trace of her in the Ugaritic sources![75] This is also applicable to Israel's socio-political and religious organization, where females found, at best, "a glass-ceiling" and, at worse, were barred from certain offices like priesthood.[76] Indeed, despite this law's total parallelism between men and women, there is a great imbalance in the appearance of the masculine

Prostitution;" Katharine Doob Sakenfeld, "Numbers," in *The Women's Bible Commentary*(ed. Carol Newsom & Sharon Ringe; Louisville: Westminster/John Knox, 1992), 49–50.

[74] Craigie, "Deuteronomy," 113–4.

[75] Noted by Marsman, *Women*, 519–20. That is also Amico's conclusion in her dissertation ("Status of Women," 417), although she takes a longer road, discussing whether Ugaritic myths support the often found contentions of *hyeros gamos* and sexualized rituals. "It seems that the greatest evidence for ritual sexuality in Canaan comes nor from Ugarit but from the Bible..."

[76] Bibliography on this issue is too abundant to be covered here. See Marsman, *Women*, 473–572 on women as religious specialists in Ugarit and Israel.

and feminine, singular and plural, forms of the stem קדש; a phenomenon even more evident with the term זונה, for which there is not even a masculine participle whose meaning is to be taken literally. Thus, Cheryl Anderson observes,

> In spite of these laws' apparent inclusivity, some features of gender construction may remain. For example, if women tend to be associated with worship practices that deviate from those approved by the official cult, then gender construction is implicated. ... Even the law, (supposedly) against cultic prostitution may have an underlying gender bias. As Bird argues, the use of the term *qdš* in Deut. 23.18 is 'by itself insufficient to establish either the existence of a class of male hierodules or the nature of their activity'. [77]

Since Dtr never labels orthodoxy with "קדש/ה," all that can be said from this verse is that the term implies some belonging or practice which Israelites are forbidden to be and/or to do. Their practices might or might not be the product of Yahwists' ideological imagination. As to their status, as Craigie carefully states, "[t]he principal conclusion concerns the close association between *khnm* and *qdšm*, and therefore the natural assumption that the *qdšm* were associated with the temple. Little more than this can be established with any certainty."[78]

The Two Elements of the Law Itself

Both prohibitions use the verb היה "to be, become" in the third person singular, each paralleling the other:

There will be no	קדשה	amongst the daughters of Israel
There will be no	קדש	amongst the sons of Israel

Note that, contrary to custom, the female is mentioned before the male, perhaps because autochthonous religion was a much more common practice amongst women than men. Or because, just like in modern scholarship, anything that smelled of heterodoxy or heteropraxis was first ascribed to women, even though the evidence points also to males.[79] Worthy of note is also the fact that, contrary

---

[77] Cheryl B. Anderson, *Women, Ideology and Violence: Critical Theory and the Construction of Gender in the Book of the Covenant and the Deuteronomic Law* (New York: T&T Clark, 2004 [2005]), 64, quoting Bird, "The End of the Male Cult Prostitute; A Literary-Historical and Sociological Analysis of Hebrew *Qādēš/Qĕdēšim*," 51.

[78] Craigie, "Deuteronomy," 114.

[79] Just some examples will indicate my point. In the HB, there are far more references to the קדשה than to the קדש; in modern scholarship, as stated, presumption of "sacred prostitution" with all kinds of imaginative behaviors, starting with Herodotus, involve far more females than males; Hosea and Jeremiah accuse women of taking an active part in non-Yahwist religious practices variously named with the lexemes זנה, while men are accused of following their wives' lead. Riegner's thesis is, precisely, that the original meaning of the term in the pre-exilic prophets is that of a female leader

to other Deuteronomic laws and statutes, there is no punishment prescribed for breach of law (nothing like Deut 13).

Verse 19 changes to second person masculine singular and makes a parallel double prohibition followed by an emphatic causal statement that links both:

> You shall not bring a prostitute's wage (אתנן זונה)
> nor a dog's price (מחיר כלב)
> to the house of YHWH your God for any vow,
> for it is an abomination to YHWH your God—these two.

The word אתנן "hire, wage" (already mentioned above, when Gen 38 was discussed) appears in Isa 23:17–18, Mic 1:7, Ezek 16:31–41, and Hos 9:1, all texts where a "woman" (Israel, Judah, or Tyre) is accused of actions described as fornication or prostitution, but the action condemned is idolatry, not prostitution. The only instance where the word intends to be literal is Deut 23:19.[80] The second prohibition in v. 19 is set in parallel to the first one through the term "price," a noun which in the Hebrew Bible applies to several situations, from horses acquired by Solomon (2 Chr 1:16) to YHWH giving away Israel for a bargain (Ps 44:13), and from the invitation to eat and drink at no cost (Isa 55:1) to recrimination of the city rulers for bribery (Mic 3:11). It is evident that it has a literal as well as a theological meaning, and its use is traced through very different texts (prophetic utterances, wisdom sayings, narratives). Both are not exactly parallel terms, since מחיר denotes the price for an item of goods, while אתנן, the wages for a service.[81]

It has also been noticed that the addressee(s) are male, while usually prostitution is associated with women. One explanation offered is that here the law is concerned with "male instigators" of vow fulfillment through prostitution.[82] Whether these instigators would be priests interested in better

---

in cultic acts involving sacrifices: "First, זנה was found to be a superordinate category with a diversified content comprising illicit religious practices, deities other than Yahweh, and the artifacts associated with these practices. ... Second, I looked at the semantic environment. The network of words surrounding the stem זנה 'participate in illicit religious practices' consisted of pejorative language appropriate to the social and theological worlds." ("Vanishing Hebrew Harlot," 345, 347, both in the concluding chapter).

[80] According to *BDB*, 87, 1072, it stems from תנן II; referring also to another "hire" from תנה I (Hos 2:14, where Israel is also accused of זנה–ing and of going after her lovers' gifts).

[81] Elaine Adler Goodfriend, "Could *keleb* in Deuteronomy 23:19 Actually Refer to a Canine?" in *Pomegranates and Golden Bells: Studies in Biblical, Jewish, and Near Eastern Ritual, Law, and Literature in Honor of Jacob Milgrom* (ed. D. Wright, D. Freedman & A. Hurvitz. Winona Lake: Eisenbrauns, 1995), 392–3.

[82] Bird, "Prostitution in the Social World," 49. Riegner notes the peculiarity but offers no explanation.

income to the temple, or whether they would be male relatives of women, who would thus instigate their female relatives into prostitution is unstated. Bird thinks likewise:

> "Understanding this prohibition as targeting income derived from recognized prostitutes seems preferable. The term *zonah* fits the professional prostitute better than a married woman who engages in prostitution for a limited time and purpose, as does the term *ʾetnan* for her earnings. Might we not then assume that the target of this law is in fact a man, who pays a vow by engaging a prostitute under temple patronage."[83]

The next difficulty in interpreting this law comes from the term set in parallel to זונה, namely, כלב "dog." Apart from signifying the animal,[84] it is used of people waiting to prey on their victims[85] and of someone in a servant position, denoting submission.[86] The word also appears with the meaning of servant of a deity in Akkadian, Phoenician, Ugaritic, Arabic, Aramaic, Syriac, and Ethiopic, thus providing a framework for etymology and for comparison.[87]

Together with self-abasement towards a superior, the כלב is expected to watch after his master's interests as a watch-dog. In the Amarna letters a certain Abdi-Ašratu writes to the Pharaoh, "I am the servant of the king and the dog of his house," and also "the whole of Amurru-land I watch for the king, my lord."[88] From calling oneself in self-abasement in a prayer "your dog" to be institutionalized as a "dog" because of one's watch in the temple over the deity's interests there is only one, very logical, step. Thus one finds evidence, for example, from Neo-Babylonian and Phoenician documents, of temple personnel who are called servants and dogs, and who are in no way patronized or diminished in their rank, except when they come under the Dtr's eye.

> Our conclusion then is that כֶּלֶב, when it refers to temple servants, while it has the normal meaning "dog", has attained the idea of the faithful dog of god, his humble slave and devotee. The term כֶּלֶב was the ordinary term to describe such a servant, and was not a term deliberately aimed at him in contempt. And so he could be officially listed at Kition in company with other persons with honourable functions to perform ....What was respectable elsewhere in the

---

[83] Phyllis Bird, private communication, based on the preliminary draft of a forthcoming publication.

[84] See, for example, Prov 26:11, 17; Job 30:1; 1 Kgs 14:11; 16:4; 21:2, 6, 15; 22:38; 2 Kgs 9:10.

[85] See, for example, Ps 22:17, 21; 59:7–15; Isa 56:10–11.

[86] See, for example, 1 Sam 17:43; 2 Sam 3:8; 9:8; 16:9; 2 Kgs 8:13.

[87] D. Winton Thomas, "*Kelebh* 'dog': Its Origin and Some Usages of It in the OT," *VT* 10 (1960): 414.

[88] Thomas, "*Kelebh*," 424. He also recalls a prayer to Marduk, where his suppliant calls himself his "little dog." See also 2 Kgs 8:13, 2 Sam 7:21 and 1 Chr 17:19, the latter of which has been proposed to be emended to read "for the sake of thy servant and thy dog," a reading which is possible according to the consonantal text.

Semitic world did not pass muster with the Deuteronomist, and the כֶּלֶב (קָדֵשׁ) and the קְדֵשָׁה were banned, together with other features of pagan worship.[89]

Other authors have understood the term to refer to male prostitutes, although it is not clear whether there would be any etymological or textual reason aside from interpretation based on its close association with זונה in this verse. Bird, for instance, states very carefully:

> "The sole reference (if correctly interpreted) is found in a prohibition in Deuteronomy 23:18 [Heb. 23:19] … It is generally accepted that "dog" in this passage refers to a male prostitute. If this is in fact the case, the order in this gender-paired reference further emphasizes the secondary character of the male class; in contrast to the normal male-female order, the term for the female practitioner is the leading and defining term."[90]

Richard Nelson rejects this association out of lack of evidence from the ANE, that would suggest that the term is related to homosexual male prostitution. Thus, he prefers to understand "dog" as related to "'a devoted follower' (cf. *ANET*, 322) in the service of a pagan god. The payment forbidden here might even involve a real dog, either fulfilling a vow with money acquired from selling a dog or an attempt to substitute a monetary equivalent or another animal to satisfy a vow promising a dog to the temple, since a canine could not itself be sacrificed."[91] Adler Goodfriend, on the other hand, vindicates the traditional Mishnaic literal understanding of this law, whereby what is forbidden is to bring in a canine instead of a stipulated animal for a sacrifice. "Among common animals, though asses were not edible or acceptable for sacrifice, they also were not predatory. Canines, therefore, were regarded with particular disgust because of their unique status as urban carnivores."[92] She calls attention to the fact that also the story of Ahab's blood being licked by dogs by the Samaria pool links dogs and prostitutes. Thus, what is at first sight an unlikely pair, could have been more common than expected.[93]

In short, the question remains whether the two laws in Deut 23:18 and 19 are so closely related that their meaning should be taken from each other. This is what a majority of commentaries and translations does, referring them all to sex

---

[89] Thomas, "*Kelebh*," 426.

[90] Very doubtfully, Bird, "Prostitution in the Social World," 49 states so: "It is generally accepted that 'dog' in this passage refers to a male prostitute. If this is in fact the case, the order in this gender-paired reference further emphasizes the secondary character of the male class; in contrast to the normal male-female order, the term for the female practitioner is the leading and defining term."

[91] Nelson, *Deuteronomy*, 281.

[92] Adler Goodfriend, "Could *keleb*," 389.

[93] Adler Goodfriend, "Could *keleb*," 395.

(sacred and secular). However, there are dissonant old and new voices as well. For one, Riegner's thesis that זונה originally meant "participate in illicit religious practice," would fit well with a theory that would put together v. 18–19: "The קְדֵשׁוֹת of Deut 23.18 are frequently paired with the זנות of Deut 23.19; however there is no compelling reason to link the two verses. Neither the surface syntax nor the morphology nor the semantics point to parallel lines and continuity of thought. The first addresses the occupation of Israelite women and the second, illicit offerings."[94]

One understands also why, somewhere along the redactional process, these laws were put one next to the other. Reflecting on the diminished male status from "faithful devotee" to "dog," Thomas attributed such a process to the biblical mistrust of non-Yahwist cult—a mistrust we have often perceived also with regard to female cultic personnel.[95] And while not denying the Bible's biased perspective on other cults, Frymer-Kensky finds very different reasons for the confusion of the prostitute with the non-Yahwist cultic devotees:

> Two women stand completely outside the family structure—the *qedeshah* and the *zonah*. The *zonah* is a prostitute, someone who has sex for a price. The *qedeshah* was probably *not* a sacred prostitute, that is, someone who has sex as part of her duties to the temple .... Despite the fact that the *qedeshah* was not a prostitute, they had one characteristic in common. Both were women outside the family, and they could therefore make their own decisions about their sexual activity.[96]

For the time being, until new evidence would clearly change the current *impasse*, I cannot add much, except that the association of temple personnel with sexual activity still rings a warning bell in my ears.

Concluding Remarks on Deuteronomy 23:19

The wealth of recent research and the variety of opinions with regard to the independent meaning of each of the four words and in combinations is such that at this point it is impossible to bring them all into a coherent discussion. Perhaps this is one of those issues that needs further study and time to settle down. The

---

[94] Riegner, "Vanishing Hebrew Harlot," 214.

[95] Thomas, "*Kelebh*", 424–427.

[96] Tikva Frymer-Kensky, "Deuteronomy," in *The Women's Bible Commentary* (ed. Carol A. Newsom & Sharon Ringe; Louisville: Westminster John Knox, 1992), 59–60. A similar opinion is held by Angelika Engelmann, "Deuteronomium. Recht und Gerechtigkeit für Frauen im Gesetz," in *Kompendium feministische Bibelauslegung* (ed. Luise Schottroff & Marie-Theres Wacker; Gütersloh /Chr. Kaiser, Gütersloher Verlaghaus, 1999), 77: "Probably that was the reason [the *qĕdēšōt*'s belonging to the temple personnel] why they did not have their own family and thus perhaps were perceived as sexually available."

question remains, then, whether the law in v. 19, the one that concerns us here, is to be read together with the previous law or not and our tendency is to reject such association. Perhaps the most that can be said is that "the two parts of this verse would have in common the disallowance of gifts to the temple that come from objectionable sources."[97]

A second, to us more important, question posed by the text is whether the זונה of the law can be taken to mean a sex worker or whether it has here another meaning. There remains a grey zone that makes it impossible to give a one hundred-percent sure answer. On account of the particular literary genre (a law, not a poetic piece), of the use of the term זונה rather than אשה זונה, and on the financial character of the law, I take this to be one instance in which the reference is to a sex worker, a professional prostitute, harlot or whore, as one might want to name her.

The information about the life and work conditions of the prostitute is not highly informed by this law. Contrary to קדשה/תו, prostitution is not banned and neither are its practitioners. What is banned is the use of wages coming from prostitution as money brought in to the temple in fulfillment of vows. What would this really mean in terms of the social location of the professional prostitute and with regard to Dtr's assessment of lower-class female workers remains to be seen.

FIRST KINGS 22:38

This verse is the only one of the narrative of 1 Kgs 22:29–38 where "the זונות" come in, and only obliquely. This story concludes King Ahab's fate, complicated by the factors of a plot by Ahab and Jehoshaphat to regain lost territory through war against Syria, Ahab's enmity against Micaiah ben-Imlah, the four hundred prophets who predict victory against the one (Micaiah) who first predicts doom and then lies, the enmity between Micaiah and Zedekiah (Elijah does not appear), God's sending of a lying spirit, and finally the battle, to which Ahab goes in disguise only to get killed anyway. Verse 38 confirms Elijah's prophecy against Ahab because of his misappropriation of Naboth's vineyard. Elijah had proclaimed to him that where the dogs had licked up Naboth's blood they would lick up Ahab's too (1 Kgs 21:19). Fulfillment comes to pass in a rather awkward way: after being wounded and dying in battle against the Arameans, Ahab's corpse is carried back to Samaria "and they (lit. he) washed the chariot by the pool of Samaria. And the dogs licked his blood—

---

[97] Tigay, *Deuteronomy*, 216.

and the prostitutes washed—according to the word of YHWH, which he had spoken" (v. 38).[98]

The *wayyiqtol* chain proceeds uninterrupted from the shout going through the camp that everyone should go home (v. 35),[99] continues with Ahab's dying, being brought to Samaria and being buried and still goes into the washing of the chariot and the licking of the blood by the dogs at the pool. Then, in order to signal a change, the narrative chain is interrupted and a new subject precedes the next verb, והזנות רחצו, and the *zōnôt* washed (themselves). The whole story comes to an end with the narrator confirming these events as the fulfillment of YHWH's word.[100]

What about prostitutes? Information about prostitutes is rather scant here, but also unchecked in the sense that, not being the focus of attention, they are paid little attention by the narrative and therefore, are not subject to "politically correct" jargon. The focus is on the most shameful end of a powerful and evil king, whose death in battle is not bad enough. Thus, the fact that prostitutes bathe or wash in the pool of Samaria, where his royal blood ended, signals both the sorry fate of someone who does not die in peace and the sorry fate (the low status) of women who did not have their own home to bathe and needed to do so at the public pool. As stated earlier, there are no irrefutable proofs that these זנות were prostitutes and not "loose" or "single women" unattached to a patriarchal household; they do not appear in a typically business-like transaction. And there might have been single women who were also homeless and needed to wash themselves (and their clothes) at the public pool.

That the term is generic (article + plural participle) and that it does not appear as appositional or adjectival complement to the noun "woman," indicate

---

[98] The unity of the chapter is highly disputed. Burke O. Long, *1 Kings with an Introduction to Historical Literature* (FOTL 9; Grand Rapids: Eerdmans, 1984), 232–3, 237–9 takes it to be a unit. S. McKenzie *The Trouble with Kings* (VTSup 42. Leiden: Brill, 1991), 89, 92, notes several inconsistencies, among them the irregularity that Ahab is said to have "slept with his ancestors." The phrase "slept with his ancestors" is used, according to G. Hölscher, "Das Buch der Könige, seine Quellen und seine Redaktion," *Eucharisterion* (FRLANT NF 19. I. Göttingen, 1923, quoted by McKenzie), 185 only of kings who died in peace; thus, the notice in 1 Kgs 22:40 does not know of 22:38. McKenzie further calls attention to a later addition, 21:27–29, the postponement of Ahab's punishment announced by Elijah. Since these two texts contradict 22:1–38, they are seen as a later addition to the book of Kings. More recently, see Patrick Cronauer, OSB, *The Stories about Naboth the Jezreelite: A Source, Composition, and Redaction Investigation of 1 Kings 21 and Passages in 2 Kings 9* (T&T Clark: New York, 2005) on all the texts related to Naboth, King Ahab and Jezebel.

[99] Marvin Sweeney, *1 & II Kings* (OTL; Louisville: Westminster John Knox, 2007), 261 interprets the cry as a sign of victory.

[100] Marian Broida, "Closure in Samson," *JHS* 10, art. 2 (2010), n.p. [cited 22 January 2011]. Online: http://www.arts.ualberta.ca/JHS/jhs-article.html, under "Literary Features Enhancing Closure" discusses, among other devices, interruption of a *wayyiqtol* chain by introduction of a *qatal* SVO (subject, verb, object) sentence and death as closure indications. In our particular text, v. 39 also serves such a function by referring to the Book of the Deeds or Annals of the Kings of Israel.

a recognizable group. Riegner notes that this is the only text in which the Targum retains the Masoretic זונות; a term which "in this case, delineates a distinctive, social group, a group of outcaste women, not a specific person."[101]

Not only do we lack information about some type of group comprised of "single women," but they would probably also make a less spectacular foil to a king than poor prostitutes. These reasons make me think that it is safe here to understand the term as referring to those harlots who were lower in the social and economic ladder, who worked in the streets or taverns, the literal "street walkers": women of low status or low self-consciousness—or both.

Not by chance Shamhat, the woman appointed to domesticate Enkidu (another ambivalent figure because she could be either a courtesan or a harlot, as pointed out above) operates also outside the city by open water. And the place Tamar chooses to induce Judah to have sex with her is called *Petaḥ ʿênayim*, which may be translated "Entrance to Enayim," but also "Opening of the eyes" or "of the wells." So, while we should not put too much weight on this place name, it is noteworthy that it should also be related to the town's well. Yes, wells are apt places for one to find danger or adventure (or even the husband-to-be in some stories), because of their location between "civil" and "wild" life, where females and males meet, between "home" and "field"—even battlefield. The city pool is then a likely place for an encounter between Ahab's blood after battle and harlots after the day's work.[102]

That "loose women" would be liminal figures, related both to the city and also to the wild, both to the bedroom and to the tavern or the open space, has been pointed out by several scholars. While that would not make a difference in the assessment of these זנות as either unmarried women or professional sex workers, it is an element to consider in how the narrative (the worldview of both narrator and audience) imagines the living space of הזנות.

The two texts studied, the law in Deut 23 and the notice on the prostitutes at the pool of Samaria in 1 Kgs 22 are, together with Judg 16, the only ones that use the single participle (ה)זונה. Except for Rahab, in whose story two

---

[101] Riegner, "Vanishing Hebrew Harlot," 167.

[102] This separation between outer space as the "manly" space of battle and the city as "woman space" appear already in the Akkadian *Erra* poem, according to Mobley, *Samson and the Liminal Hero* (New York: T&T Clark, 2006), 56–57: "When the Sibitti [the warrior Erra's personified weapons] awaken, they attempt to rouse Erra by challenging his manhood. Their speech in *Erra* I 46–91 contrasts the 'manly virtue' ... of the warrior in the battlefield with the effeminate and shameful state of the warrior in the city. Houses and towns, they say, are for 'feeble old men' (*šībbi muqqi*) and 'a lisping child' (*šerri laʾî*) (I 47–48). The urban environment is the realm of women, where one consumes 'women's bread' (*akal sinniš*), 'city food' (*akal ali*), and 'sweet *našpu* beer' (*šikar našpi duššupi*). Cities are places for festivals, palaces, fine food, and clothing."

denominations appear, "Rahab, the זונה" and "האשה הזונה," all other texts prefer the compound formula אשה זונה (singular or plural).

Although inconvenient because one must go back and forth through the Bible from one text to the next one, the reason why I have started with these is the likelihood that they say something, albeit little, about the sex-worker. The next texts could refer to sex workers, but it is equally possible that they refer to tavern keepers or innkeepers. In all instances, they are "loose women"— independent, unmarried, free from paternal control, women. Women who can be linked to any specific work or just dwellers? None are clear enough to allow for a decision, despite centuries of interpretation.

I arrange them according to the likelihood that they would refer to a worker. The first two stories are set in pre-monarchic times, both in war-like or settlement contexts (Joshua and Judges) and both located at an (אשה) זונה's own place, on foreign, enemy land: Gaza and Jericho. The third one is located in the monarchic period, at the beginning of Solomon's reign in Jerusalem and the last one goes again to the book of Judges and to Israelite territory, Galaad. Also the amount of pages given each text dwindles according to the pertinence of the subject-matter.

JUDGES 16:1–3

Judges 14–16 tells the story of Samson, from his miraculous birth announcement by a divine messenger to his death at the temple of Dagon, blind and made sport of by a multitude of Philistines. The Samson story can be (and has been) studied with reference to the women to whom he related, namely, his unnamed mother ("Manoah's wife"); his Timnite wife, also unnamed; the unnamed אשה זונה "zônâ-woman" from Gaza whom Samson visited; and lastly, the woman he loved, Delilah. The verses that concern us are 16:1–3. Most commentaries take them as part of chapter 16, with "Gaza" enclosing both ends of it.[103] The question we are dealing with is, once again, twofold. First, whether the woman so named can be considered, even with a margin of error, a sex worker; secondly, if the answer is positive or at least not negative, what can we know about her.

The first verse situates geographically the scene and goes immediately into Samson's reasons for an incursion into dangerous territory: "And Samson went to Gaza and saw there an אשה זונה and went in to her." Verse 2 points at the narrator's real concern, which is not the "prostitute," but the enmity between Samson and the men from the region. Finally, v. 3 tells the outcome of the narrative. Again, the interest is not on the woman, although incidentally a little

---

[103] Jichan Kim, *The Structure of the Samson Cycle* (Kampen: Kok Pharos, 1993), 303–4 locates them in his *"canto* II" (14:1–16:3); Broida, "Closure," n.55, considers they belong to no larger pericope.

piece of information is provided: "Samson lay there until midnight and at midnight he got up, took hold of the town gate and its two posts."

Broida calls attention to the summary note at the end of chapter 15 on Samson's period as a judge. That is a "boundary marker" which leads the reader to think Samson's story is over; thus the surprise a new beginning causes.[104] Furthermore, the new beginning brings the audience back to his fateful marriage with the Timnite at the beginning of chapter 14:

וירד שמשון תמנתה וירא אשה בתמנתה מבנות פלשתים: ויעל ויגד ...

וילך שמשון עזתה וירא־שם אשה זונה ויבא אליה:

Judg 14: 1–2	verb of movement (וירד)	personal name (Samson)	city name (Timnah)	verb of perception (וירא)	direct object (אשה a woman)	local adverb (at Timnah)
Judg 16:1	verb of movement (וילך)	personal name (Samson)	city name (Gaza)	verb of perception (וירא) + local adverb (שם)	direct object, (זונה-a woman)	
Judg 14: 1–2	Further information on the woman (she was a Philistine)	Further action by Samson (he came up...)				
Judg 16:1		Further action by Samson (he went to her)				

A careful audience would perceive these similarities and would imagine both a new beginning and a *dejá-vue* situation: "How much is this new desire for a Philistia-located (Philistine or foreigner, we do not know) woman going to cost him?" and it would probably also perceive differences: Are "wages" of an אשה זונה higher or lower than a relationship to a Timnite, with whom wedding

---

[104] Broida, "Closure," under "Unit Three: Judg 16:1–3"; on next page she also calls attention to elements linking this short unit to unit IV.

arrangements went awry?[105] How much weight should the audience put on her being an אשה זונה? I will try to address these questions from two different directions. Several scholars have noticed the appearance of the verb ראה "see" both with the sexual connotation of "seeing leads to desiring" and as one structuring device in this story. So, there is on the one hand, Samson's eyes (and desire) posed on this unnamed woman and that could signal danger to the audience. But there are many more eyes staring than Samson's!

> On the other hand, the narrator succeeds in convincing his audience of the potential threat posed by the fact that the eyes of the Philistines meanwhile are constantly glued to Samson. Thus balanced symmetry highlights the contrast between Samson and the Philistines: Samson is busy with searching for *a woman* whereas the Philistines are determined to overpower *Samson*. That is why the Delilah affair is decisive.[106]

Kim's comment is particularly helpful here because he takes up the narrator's concern and by so doing, puts the weight of the story where the narrator wants it (which is not where *we* would want it) and thus makes a lesser character of "a woman" Samson is searching for. On the other hand, as it will be seen below, her inferiority derives not from her profession but from the contest between warriors. And, in such a contest, women are polluting if not outright dangerous.[107] Besides, in such a contest between warriors, any woman would not be a subject but an object to be used, if possible.

The second avenue for an answer on her status comes from Gregory Mobley's study of Samson as a liminal hero, alternating between civilization and wild life, "home" and foreign territory. According to him, there are several aspects of this judge which can be studied, together with other ANE literature, in terms of the thematic oppositions between which he moves. This liminal wild man comes and goes between field and house, "home" and "foreign territory," rest and agitation, gender roles, city and open space. In this process, like the mythical Enkidu, he encounters animals and some liminal female figures.

Scholars concur that, since a wild man needs to be taught to live socially it is necessary that a liminal, at times mother-like figure teach him the basics of becoming human: how to eat and drink, to dress himself, and to know the city. Since Samson had a mother and a father who taught him, among other things, to live up to his Nazirite vows and to search for a wife from within Israel—lessons

---

[105] Of course, one could (as has been done) blame the women and ask "How much are these women going to cost him?" Both from the narrative itself (especially the Timnah affair) and out of gender fairness, that would be the wrong question.

[106] Kim, *Structure*, 390–2; quotation from p. 392.

[107] Mobley, *Samson*, 56–58 on cities as "women's places" in the *Erra* epic; 59–63 on warriors abstaining from women and city life in the Bible; Kim, *Structure*, 304–5 recalls Samson's mission to deliver Israel from the Philistines was holy war and he should presumably have to abstain from sex.

that he didn't learn very well, I am afraid—I would rather refer to Delilah and, to a lesser degree, to the anonymous אשה זונה from Gaza as teachers of culture, in the same manner as Shamhat had taught Enkidu. According to Asher-Greve, "[a]s seductress, instructor (adviser), and temporary caretaker Shamhat symbolizes woman in two cultural aspects, the unknown but desirable feminine and the mother/socializer."[108] Shamhat, our woman from Gaza and also Delilah are liminal, as far as we know unmarried, unattached-to-a-patriarchal-household women and because of this, good candidates for bringing a wild man into city life. Delilah will not be included in this study, although she has earned an honorary degree of אשה זונה. She is "an unattached woman who is not defined through a relationship with a husband, even though the word [זונה] does not appear in the text. She has her proper name and an independent identity."[109] She shares many characteristics with both anonymous women related to Samson.[110] "As a 'prostitute,' ḥarimtu, Shamhat has a liminal role in society since she is an extra-domestic woman who supports herself. Further, as a prostitute, she is the quintessential representative of the city, sent on a mission to tame the wild man."[111] Since, as stated, Samson had already been born into civilization, perhaps one should not make much of such similitudes. Perhaps there is behind these characterizations the awareness of a higher, more sophisticated, urbanite, "technological" Philistine society, in contrast to a more "primitive," rural, poorer, "developing" Israelite society.

What makes the "Gazite" also a liminal figure are her location in foreign territory, her condition of unmarried, unattached woman (and also, although not exclusively, her namelessness), her association with the city gates, and her role as intermediary. According to Mobley, "[w]omen are intermediaries who lead men from one state to another: from wildness to calm, from nature to culture, and from the battlefield to civilian life."[112]The two latter are rather indirect in our text, through the male contest between Samson and the "men from Gaza" waiting for him and assuming he will come out weakened. This זונה could be a

---

[108] Asher-Greve, "Decisive Sex," 14–5.

[109] Jost, Gender, Sexualität und Macht, 251, also quoting H. Schulte, "Beobachtungen," (ref. to both these, thanks to Mrs. T. Binder and Mr. J. Leipziger from Augustana Hochschule, Germany). My reason for excluding Delilah from this study is that she is an unacknowledged אשה זונה but probably not a prostitute, at least not during her relationship with Samson.

[110] Notably, L. Daniel Hawk, Joshua (Berit Olam; Collegeville: Liturgical Press, 2000), 35 assumes Delilah is a prostitute(-like?) figure: "In this role [of trickster] she [Rahab] resembles other biblical prostitutes (also outsiders): Delilah, who seduces Samson through the power of her words (Judg 16:4–22), and Tamar, who masquerades as a prostitute (Gen 38:1–30) in order to secure her place within Israel."

[111] Mobley, Samson, 96. Mobley compares the Samson story with the Gilgamesh Epic and Erra and Ishum.

[112] Mobley, Samson, 84.

harlot, an innkeeper or a "loose woman" and she would still be liminal, because of her unattachment to a father or husband. Liminal, it is good to remind ourselves, is not "bad" or evil. Weak? Yes, often. And also necessary precisely because of both belonging and not belonging.

Apparently, some of the early Rabbis saw in this adventure the beginning of Samson's misadventures, and this for three reasons: the first one is that, by surviving the attack, he headed toward "the crowning feat of his career, his encounter with Delilah...;" the second one, that Samson is perceived as "engaged in the satisfaction of his base inclination, without any benefit to Israel." This is true and if the focus is on Israel's salvation, one can at least question Samson's strange ways of bringing them to happen. Thirdly, the Rabbis noted, "prior to this event, we are told that *he led Israel in the days of the Philistines for twenty years* (15:20), possibly hinting that until the incident in Gaza Samson was considered a judge, and what he did in Gaza was entirely irrelevant to his function and purpose to be the first to deliver Israel from the Philistines."[113] The point is well taken and it is only logical that the Rabbis would be harsh on such an individualistic, tragic hero. Yet, even agreeing with their evaluation, Samson's achievement and the playful character of the story do not load any judgment on the unnamed אשה זונה or on her profession. "This story is not a cautionary tale about the dangers of foreign women or prostitutes but instead celebrates Samson's bawdiness and larger-than-life potency."[114]

So, is this "*zônâ*-woman" a prostitute? In my opinion, one could equally argue for or against her being a sex worker. As in all stories observed, there is no record of transaction, no indication of a "house of a זונה" and no information as to how he knew she was an אשה זונה when he saw her. All these holes leave ample room for speculation. There is also abundant proof that Samson would have had chances to have gotten to know a woman, somebody unattached to a household, in Gaza. The two encounters recorded in chapters 14 and 16 are just two (of other possible) examples of a man who is—for Israelite standards (whatever that is in Judges!)—unusually fond of foreign lands, women and quarrels. It would not be impossible, therefore, that the unnamed woman whom he visits (16:1) be not a professional harlot, but a free woman whom he had met or seen earlier. Since 14:1 and 16:1 are so similar, I believe the narrator intended his audience to associate both stories and think of them as possible attachments to Samson. In this sense, an unmarried woman would be far riskier than a prostitute.

It is also very likely that, like Rahab in Josh 2, this woman would run a tavern or inn. This is the option of the Targum. And, supposing what Samson saw was her at her inn's door (not explicit in the text), it would explain why he

---

[113] Shimon Bakon, "Samson: A Tragedy in Three Acts," *JBQ* 35 (2007): 38.

[114] Mobley, *Samson*, 88.

knew she was a *zōnâ*-woman and he could go to her. Besides these reasons, it would be an easy place to identify and, eventually, to hide—realistically, neither the spies at Jericho nor Samson are very successful at that. Unlike that story, however, the text does not say that he entered the house of an אשה זונה, but that he saw one and came (in) to her. So, perhaps she did not have a private space she would call "house" or perhaps it is only a redactional detail.

All matters considered, I have included her amongst the likeliest cases of a sex worker because it would explain more easily how it is that Samson ended up on (one of) her bed(s); why the ambushed men thought he would stay the whole night and not for a couple of drinks only; and what are the similarities and differences with his failed relationship with his Timnite wife, indicated by similar beginnings of both stories in 14:1 and 16:1. At the same time, since the term used is אשה זונה, the likeliest probability is that she would be a tavern keeper and/or an innkeeper, who could, eventually, be included among the sex workers in the broadest sense of the term: Inducing patrons to drink or to stay overnight? Promoting prostitution? Accepting patrons herself? Only flirting with them?

I recognize both the danger of circular reasoning as well as the stereotyping involved in thinking that any woman who ran a tavern must have been herself a harlot. On the other hand, like Rahab's story to be studied following this one, half of the fun is taken away when one chooses one meaning over its ambiguity.

Whatever one ends up choosing, one may safely commend her, on whose bed Samson spent at least one memorable night –memorable because of the city gates, of course!

JOSHUA 2

Another אשה זונה is the main character in Josh 2 and, with a passive role, in Josh 6. The differences between both chapters are well researched and they are brought here only in what pertains to their information on Rahab or the זונה figure.

It is to be noted that the first and fullest reference to a זונה comes in 2:1 and it refers to her home: the spies went to "a house of a *zōnâ*-woman," and her name was Rahab/Wide" בית־אשה זונה ושמה רחב. The term זונה does not appear again in this chapter, where she is called once Rahab (2:3) and otherwise "the woman," "she," or by the feminine singular pronoun. The expression בית + אשה זונה is unique, as far as I have been able to trace it.[115] In chapter 6, she is

---

[115] The closest association, "and they trooped into a house of a זונה" appears in Jer 5:7, a text actually speaking of adultery = idolatry. Note similarities of Jer 5:7 with Josh 2 are closer than between Josh 2 and 6.

alternatively called רחב הזונה (v. 17, 25) and האשה הזונה in v. 22. One should note that, unlike Josh 2, in chapter 6 the participle appears always with the article, giving it a more fixed character. This confirms historico-critical analyses showing redactional work (including references to the earlier story in chapter 2).[116]

Since the story is well-known, it is not necessary here to dwell long on its details. Scholars view the text in different manner, as reflecting a historical narrative; as a saga of a people who are on their way to the promised land; as a satire, where none less than a foreign prostitute has two Israelite men hanging from a rope and exacts from them life for her and her family; as a critique of an enterprise where YHWH had not been sought first; and as a remnant of those early memories of an internal revolution by the lower class against the powerful landlords of the Canaanite city-states.[117]

The intentionally multivalent portrait of Rahab in chapter 2 is tied to the several possible interpretations of the purpose and message of the book of Joshua and to a long redaction history. For example, in holy war, Israel is to conquer and utterly destroy the enemy in order to prevent religious contamination (Deut 7:2, 20:17; Josh 6; 23:11–13; Judg 2). Yet Rahab (and even more the Gibeonites, Josh 9) are presented as managing to exert a promise from the Israelites in a way that opens questions as to whether this is what YHWH had in mind. Or we may read her, following Nelson, as the only point of contact between two groups of men, those commissioned by the king of Jericho and those commissioned by Joshua, whose agendas are opposed to each other and in which Rahab's "actions are fundamental to the success of one and the failure of the other."[118] Women as both pivotal to, and used by, contending men is not a new phenomenon.

---

[116] J. Alberto Soggin, *Joshua* (OTL. Philadelphia: SCM, 1972), 38 observes that "the version of events given in ch. 2 seems older, and more historically probable, than that attested by ch. 6, which is simply a liturgical and cultic transfiguration of the events, retold as history at a later period"; Richard Nelson, *Joshua* (OTL; Louisville: Westminster John Knox, 1997), 87–91 considers several indications of redactional work; in his opinion, the Divine Warrior image is stronger (and earlier) here than the liturgical one.

[117] Nelson, *Joshua*, 42, calls it "a typical ethnological saga in which a wily ancestor helps herself and her kinfolk through shrewdness." Tikva Frymer-Kensky, "Reading Rahab," in *Tehilla le-Moshe: Biblical and Judaic Studies in Honor of Moshe Greenberg* (ed. Mordechai Cogan, Barry Eichler, & Jeffrey Tigay; Winona Lake: Eisenbrauns, 1997) 57–60 shows the close parallel between the first seven chapters of Joshua and events in Moses' life. For example, the sending of the spies (Num 13), the use of the uncommon verb צפן for "hiding" of the men by Rahab and of Moses by his mother; the miraculous crossings of the Reed Sea and the Jordan, and the reaction these produce in Israel's enemies; an angel appearing to Joshua (Josh 5:15) and the burning bush experience in Moses' life; and Rahab and her family's shelter in her home while the city is destroyed, and the Passover narrative. J. Alberto Soggin, *Joshua* (OTL; Philadelphia: SCM, 1987 [1972]), 42, notes the use of a red signal in the Rahab story as a reminder of the Passover night.

[118] Nelson, *Joshua*, 40.

What needs to be asked here is, first, whether there are elements that would indicate the probability or even the possibility that this אשה זונה was a prostitute. In case we can answer positively this question, the second question is about her social location, how she is depicted, and what the text tells about the writer's perception of prostitutes as part of lower-class women. We start with a doubt, which prompted one of the earliest available papers on this issue, namely, whether a woman who has her own paternal family so close by (who, incidentally, is referred to from the point of reference of Rahab and not of her father, ואת־בית אביה ואת־כל־אשר־לה), would need to (or would be able to) sell herself as a harlot in the same city where her family dwelt.

> Mich hat schon immer gewundert, warum eine Frau, die inmitten ihrer Sippe lebt—Vater, Mutter und Brüder werden genannt—das Leben einer Hure führen sollte. Sie war doch nicht aus Not gezwungen, ihren Körper zu verkaufen. Allerdings stellt sich der Erzähler eine für ihn und seine Zeit „normale" patriarchale Familie vor. Der Verlauf der Handlung weist sie jedoch als frei in ihrem Hause lebende Frau aus. Auch die resolute Art, wie sie die Kundschafter rettet, spricht für eine selbständige Frau.[119]

Since people at times had to sell a daughter in order to escape debt, slavery or death, and since up to this day women often end up in prostitution for the most varied economic and social reasons, even having their own partner or husband, in principle it would not be impossible that Rahab would be a prostituted woman. She does not dwell with her family prior to Jericho's destruction, although from both chapters 2 and 6 one gathers she wanted to save them. At any rate, I concur with Schulte that Rahab seems to live alone and that there are no clear hints that she was a prostitute rather than some other unattached woman.

One has to remember that, in order for the story to be credible, Rahab had to be some kind of "public woman," (and often "public woman" is—at least in Spanish—an euphemism for a harlot, but not necessarily so). Several writers have noticed that "the assurance with which the spies go to Rahab's house is striking."[120] Further, they would have needed a place in which to lodge without raising misgivings (on which they fail, but that is another important point in the plot). The unlikely possibility would be, then, that an unmarried, unattached,

---

[119] Schulte, "Beobachtungen," 256. One of Schulte's proposals is the existence of an earlier (pre-monarchic) form of marriage, later overrun by the patriarchal marriage or *Baal*-marriage, which centered on the woman and her location. Somehow this issue is no longer in the scholar's agenda; since it would not be a professional term, we need not deal further with it here.

[120] Soggin, *Joshua*, 39. There is also a theological reason, of course. As the writer himself notes, Rahab also knows who they are.

non-public woman would have fit this role more easily than a "bartender," an innkeeper or a harlot. An innkeeper is also the earliest reading. Cohen keeps both meanings: "*harlot*. Hebrew *zonah*, which the Targum and Jewish commentators connect with *mazon*, 'food,' and render 'an innkeeper.' It may be that she was both. ...strangers would not normally be noticed where travellers were constantly coming and going."[121]

Still, there is one important aspect of this story, which several commentaries note, to wit: its purposeful ambiguity and even picaresque character, evident in the association of Rahab's name with the "open place, open court, *plaza;*"[122] the recognition that the men "came in to her" and slept there (2:1,3–4); the folkloric nature of the tale; and the very use of the ambiguous אשה זונה. In my view, precisely this ambiguity, especially the *double entendres*, take away at least half of the fun of the story if one tries to decide whether Rahab was or was not a prostitute.

Some facts are clear in the text no matter how one chooses to interpret them. Rahab is not an upper-class citizen. She lives close to the city gates at the city walls, the most exposed area in case of a breakthrough, not only due to physical proximity, but also because within the preindustrial walled city there were additional walls, enclosing and protecting particular neighborhoods. Preindustrial cities show a pattern characterized by a concentration of the most prominent institutions at the core of the city, going increasingly far from the center as they decrease in importance. Neighborhoods both determine and reveal status, so that there is control over who lives where, and people do not move as they wish, but as they are allowed to mainly by socio-economic, ethnic, and family position.[123]

On the other hand, since city gates were strategic as both the weakest point of access and as a post of control over its movements, we may surmise it was too important to have been left unattended. Perhaps part of Rahab's tasks as Jericho's innkeeper (if that is what she was) was, precisely, to inform about foreigners coming in. There is no evidence, of course; not even a distinctive biblical term for "innkeeper" as far as I know. Yet, there is Babylonian evidence

---

[121] Cohen, *Joshua & Judges*, 7. He translates it with the term "prostitute" and adds a note that "perhaps she was both."

[122] Schulte, "Beobachtungen," 256 n.9 quoting Noth: "Haus am freien Platz." Soggin, *Joshua*, 40–41: "good example of a West Semitic name, no doubt linked with a divine name or title, e.g. *rāḥāb-'el*."

[123] Sjoberg, *Preindustrial City*, 95–96 mentions "1) the pre-eminence of the 'central' area over the periphery; 2) certain finer spatial differences according to ethnic, occupational, and family ties, and 3) the low incidence of functional differentiation in other land use patterns." On fortification of cities and importance of walls and gates, see Borowski, *Daily Life*, 46–49; Aaron Burke, "The Architecture of Defense: Fortified Settlements of the Levant during the Middle Bronze Age" (Ph.D. diss., University of Chicago, 2004), especially 325–30 on social complexity and fortifications and his concluding chapter, 331–5.

for women owing taverns and earning enough to be able to give loans to other people. Here I have to rely on Assante's assertion that "[u]nlike the *bīt aštammi* or inn, the *bīt sabîm/sabîtim* [local tavern usually run by a woman] did not offer lodging and hence had no beds."[124] Zwickel asserts that, since there were no hotels or pensions in the modern sense of the word, women who offered lodging to foreigners soon offered also sex.[125] I think that is one possibility, not the only one, though. Furthermore, "from laws and literature copulation seems to have taken place nearly everywhere outside the home: the main thoroughfare, the city square, the city wall, the granary, the sheep hut, the storehouse, the canebrake and the garden."[126]

Would that have been Rahab's status? The construction את־כל־אשר־לה appears at least three times in Josh 6 (v. 22, 23, 25 and slightly different in chapter 2: once in Rahab's mouth in first singular and once in second feminine singular in the spies' response). It may be translated "everything that pertained to her" or "everybody who belonged to her." The first interpretation would insinuate that she was (more or less) well-off and she was taken out of Jericho with her possessions. While such possibility would accord with at least some Babylonian women, it is unlikely, given the theological framework of the book of Joshua: since the Israelites are to dedicate the city to *ḥerem*, I interpret they would take out "everybody who belonged to her," that is, the family, but no Canaanite possessions.

In short, the story is ambivalent as to Rahab's profession, economic means, and social status, because of the lack of concrete data. If Rahab was an innkeeper, her social standing could have been a little higher or at least perhaps better considered. But, again, maybe not better financially. Not all innkeepers owned their business. Or she could be a harlot, as so many translations and commentaries still affirm. Scholars consider that prostitutes and people (especially single women) whose house was close to or in the city walls, had to be of a low social standing. Prostitution is not and was not a safe, well-paid occupation, and often women were exposed to degrading or violent treatment by their customers and perhaps by their "owners" as well. Typically, social attitudes are ambivalent because, as Bird expresses it, "[f]emale prostitution is an accommodation to the conflicting demands of men for exclusive control of

---

[124] Assante, "Sex, Magic, and the Liminal Body in the Erotic Art and Texts of the Old Babylonian Period," in *Sex and Gender in the Ancient Near East*, 31. See also Ebeling and Homan, "Baking and Brewing Beer," 47, who mention evidence in the Hammurabi Code concerning their obligation to "police their establishments and turn in conspirators."

[125] Zwickel, *Frauenalltag*, 125.

[126] Assante, "Sex, Magic," 31 n.17.

their wives' sexuality and for sexual access to other women."[127] In the Gilgamesh Epic, Enkidu first curses the ḫarīmtu (courtesan?) who introduced him to culture and then proceeds to bestow also a blessing on her. While in the Hebrew Bible nothing condemns the person who exercises commercial sex, on the other hand the same stem זנה is used to condemn to death certain women and to regret the people's forsaking of their God.[128] In any case, blessed or cursed, sought after or despised, by implicit definition the prostitute belonged and still belongs to the lowest echelons of society.

These stereotypes contribute in Josh 2 to making Rahab a surprising character, doing far more for the Israelites than expected from her (חסד), precisely because she is despised by society. Her professional service does not include hiding men in danger, lying to the king, and devising a plan to send them back to their camp safely; and it is a welcome, ironic twist that an "underdog" would outsmart both the Jericho king and the spies. And in Josh 6, Rahab is yet another non-Israelite used by the biblical writers in order to strengthen Israel's right to the land at the cost of their earlier inhabitants, in exchange for which she and her family can stay on the land "until this day." From an ideological hermeneutical analysis, these chapters complement each other in presenting Rahab as the lowly woman who saw God's purpose for Israel and seized a share of it, when other, "greater" people, such as her own king, did not; as an outcome of which, she was able, together with her family, to dwell within Israel (and according to other traditions, even marry a worthy Israelite!). Not only are these two stories combined to portray a "harlot of golden heart" (as someone has depicted her) who chooses the right warring faction; as Hawk notes, [t]he reader who has come to Joshua by way of Deuteronomy is prepared to view the peoples of Canaan as the primary threat to Israelite existence and identity in the land (Deut 7:1–5, 17–26; 9:4–5)." And the first Canaanitess they meet is Rahab, who happens, however, not to be the threat Deuteronomy would imagine:

> Rahab the prostitute, who ostensibly epitomizes the threat represented by the peoples of Canaan, takes the Israelites in; the king of Jericho, however, wants to take them out. The contrast between king and people becomes more pronounced when Rahab returns to speak to the spies (2:9b–14). Whereas the king has responded aggressively to the presence of the Israelites, she reveals that the *people* are no threat at all; they are terror-stricken and their hearts have melted (2:9).[129]

[127] Bird, "The Harlot as Heroine," 200; Gomezjara, "Hablemos más claro," 39–40 (and charts on 42–44, 46) shows how she is called anything but "harlot" when she moves in a wealthy environment.
[128] Ipsen, *Sex Working*, 37–38.
[129] L. Daniel Hawk, "Conquest Reconfigured: Recasting Warfare in the Redaction of Joshua," in

Hawk's statement that Rahab epitomizes the (supposed) threat to Israelites from Canaanite peoples can be read in different ways. His study concerns the increasing differentiation in Joshua between the peoples and their kings and their "humanization" and Rahab's is the first encounter as one comes out of Deuteronomy; I think this is what he means. One can go a step further, however, and take this statement to confirm, with sadness, that she would epitomize danger because of a common prejudice, that certain disenfranchised, unbound people—especially women—are tricky, liars, and so not to be trusted.[130] That reading would surely add to the contrast between this Deuteronomic pessimistic assessment and the reality encountered by the spies in Joshua. And it is, unfortunately, not uncommon. In 1 Kgs 3 there is another story about two *zōnôt*-women based, precisely, on this bias. The two OT stories yet to be studied include *zōnôt*-women, mothers of male children, whose status is low, whatever the exact meaning of "*zōnâ*-woman" be.

FIRST KINGS 3:16–28

There were once two women living alone in the same house (no "stranger" or relative present), each one mother of a newborn son. One night one mother inadvertently killed her own child and replaced him with the other woman's living son. A quarrel over the living son ensued, for which they requested the king's wisdom. These two women are introduced as two *zōnôt*-women (1 Kgs 3:16 נשים זנות). Now, were they prostitutes? Again, we do not know, for the story is concerned with Solomon's wisdom, to be verified in the solution to a seemingly domestic impenetrable problem, rather than on any of the claimants. While one cannot exclude the possibility that a harlot would conceive and carry her pregnancy through, one must also remember that it would have meant severe restrictions in, if not outright impossibility of working, and then yet another mouth to feed. And for several poor women, who could not earn their livelihood otherwise, pregnancy and a baby would have been "bad business." Could these children have been an economic asset?[131] They could, for instance, be an

---

Writing and Reading War, 147.

[130] Hawk, *Joshua*, 41 sees an additional allusion to the danger she represents to Israel in the use of the term זונה, elsewhere referring to idolatry. To his credit, Borowski, *Daily Life*, 38 speaks of "Rahab, the woman who helped the spies" without further adjectivating her.

[131] So also Jost "Hure/Hurerei (AT)," under 2.1. posits: "Die Prostituierten in 1Kön 3,16ff streiten um ihren Sohn. Waren (männliche) Kinder auch für die Versorgung und Zukunft von Prostituierten bedeutsam? Oder ist davon auszugehen, dass Kinder als geschäftsschädigend galten? (Schulte, 257)." So also Zwickel, *Frauenalltag*, 127. Since, as Jost reminds us, prostitution has an economic component, there is also the possibility that these children would be seen as an economic asset for their future.

"insurance policy" for the mother's old age. Yet, in this story we have not one but two (presumed) harlots with child; would that have been an unlikely situation? Granted, one may argue that the whole situation is very unlikely, with the children being of so similar characteristics as to be confused, the wisest king granting judgment, and so forth. Yet, it would not be that unlikely if two pregnant women outside other patriarchal structures would have pooled their resources together and shared a common living space. Yet, once again, these are just attempts at an explanation we do not have.

The story is told neither from the women's point of view nor for their sake, but for the sake of affirming Solomon's reign and his access to it: "their profession does not prevent them from appealing to the king himself for judgment. They are socially inferior but legally equal to their fellows. Finally, they display maternal instincts similar to those of other (decent) women,"[132] according to Brenner. The final words, "And all Israel heard of the judgment that the king had rendered; and they stood in awe of the king" (NRSV) (ויראו מפני המלך) is an auspicious beginning for a king whose rule was anything but wholly accepted. Or is the Dtr, rather, making sport of "the wisest king" by having him propose something even more outrageous than the problem itself? Humor is very difficult to agree upon, especially in stories like this one. For, as Ipsen reminds her readers, there is so much violence in prostitutes' real lives and in this story, that it is hard to laugh about it. For "justice" finds a solution and identifies "*the* mother" at the price of renouncing justice![133] Then, the final words ויראו מפני המלך would go more towards fear than awe: "And all Israel heard of the judgment which the king had judged; and they feared the king" (JPS).

Solomon's truce to bring to light the "true mother," that is, the mother with true maternal instinct (instinct that puts the child's welfare even above her loss of her child) is based upon those polarities between good mother *vs.* bad mother, good woman *vs.* bad woman, truth-telling mother *vs.* lying זונה. Note that their first description is not that of "two mothers, both bereaved because of the (actual and potential) loss of their children" but "two *zōnôt*-women." But at the end, Solomon refers to "his (the baby's) mother."

First Kings 3:16–28 stands or falls on the veracity of two stereotypes, that of the "true and good mother who gives anything for the sake of her child" and that of the "bad woman" (harlot or single mother?) who is not a real mother and does not deserve a living child. In this mutually-supporting stereotyping (and

---

[132] Brenner, *Israelite Woman*, 81–82.

[133] Ipsen, *Sex Working*, 100–102. Starting from her prostituted co-readers' own experiences with police and court, she exposes how violent the "justice" system actually is: had not one of the women (really the true mother?) contested his "wisdom" and renounced her own right to the living baby, what would Solomon have done?

trying to give an answer to our leading question), would the case be stronger were the נשים זונות harlots and not "single women" or would it not?

JUDGES 11

With this question we come to the last DtrH text where אשה זונה appears, Judg 11:1: "And Jephthah the Gileadite was a mighty man of valor and/but he was an אשה זונה's son; Gilead begat/was the father of Jephthah." The conflict develops after Gilead's death, or at least in his absence. His other sons, called "his wife's sons," drove him out, so that Jephthah would not inherit anything from their father's house, "because you are the son of another אשה." Since this term means both woman and wife, we could as well translate this last expression, "you are another wife's son." And it would be most accurate in this case, for there is nothing in the text that would indicate that this anonymous and uncharacterized woman, his mother, would have been a prostitute rather than another type of unattached woman.

The accompanying adjective אחרת appears twenty-six times in feminine (singular or plural) and in four of these it refers to "another" woman. In two of these texts, it clearly refers to another wife; one is a law on the rights of the first wife in Exod 21:10: "If he takes another wife to himself, he shall not diminish the food, clothing, or marital rights of the first wife" (*NRSV*). The other one is a notice in 1 Chr 2:26 "Jerahmeel also had another wife, whose name was Atarah; she was the mother of Onam" (*NRSV*). The remaining one (apart from the one we are studying) is the reference to "this woman ... and this other woman" in the story just reviewed of Solomon's judgment, 1 Kgs 3:22. In this story nothing speaks of co-wives (or any other relationship between them, except for the shared house). Yet, even in that text the term אחרת clearly indicates that both women are on an equal footing, be it as co-wives or co-plaintiffs before the judge.

I am assuming this applies also to the two women in Judg 11:1. I take it also that this is what Schulte means with her question: "Warum wird die Mutter Jiptahs in der Rede der Brüder ‚andere Frau' genannt? ... Denn er wird durch diesen Ausdruck als Vollbürger mit allen Rechten und Pflichten eines solchen ausgewiesen."[134] In Judg 11, furthermore, there is no reference to any sexual, fornicating or adulterous activity by the woman: in fact, there is no reference to her social and geographical location, family connections, or even whether she is alive or dead. Finally, there is no doubt as to Gilead's paternity, an unlikely fact were she a prostitute. This fact—assurance of paternity—is seldom taken into

---

[134] Schulte, "Beobachtungen," 255.

account in discussing and translating these terms. Yet, it is decisive since promiscuity is essential to prostitution, as seen above. Of course, one could resort to other options, such as adoption of the child by a well-to-do *paterfamilias* (whether biological father or not, impossible to say); a "leave of absence" from prostitution by the woman involved previous to her pregnancy and until providing the father with an heir, and so on. Tikva Frymer-Kensky states that in Mesopotamia prostitutes made a contract to conceive a child for a childless couple, so that the father would have an heir.[135] Since Jephthah has brothers, he could have been the oldest one, conceived through this arrangement with a loose woman previous to the main wife's pregnancy; or there might be another family situation behind the story, of which we do not hear further. In short, any of these options is possible and cannot be ruled out. In my opinion, the most probable case for situations like this one of Jephthah's family is one where the expression אשה זונה in reference to her mother does *not* mean a professional sex worker but a single mother.

There is at least one other story in the book of Judges, in which somebody is rejected by his half-brothers because of his mother's lower status. Both stories share several characteristics, such as expulsion of the brother who will eventually become a mighty warrior and a judge over Israel, and recourse to banditry or violence by this rejected brother. One notable element is the *paterfamilias*' absence; in the case of Jephthah, since the rejection is related by the other brothers to inheritance, perhaps Gilead was already deceased. In the story of Gideon's sons, Abimelech's rejection as "son of a slave woman" (Jotham's words, 9:18) happens after the notice of Gideon's death (8:33) and chapter 9 builds on this information but it does not clearly state that the problem between brothers was that of inheritance. Apparently, Abimelech and his mother had always lived away from Gideon's other offspring, with her Shechemite relatives (8:31).

Another, less noted, absence in both stories is that of the corresponding mother. Both are unnamed and both have a secondary status *vis-à-vis* another wife or wives. Both are only referred to, neither of them is present in her son's story and there is no notice of her death either. Worse, neither name nor description concerns them directly, but their sons are called "son of a ..." The main difficulty with comparing these two women in our survey is the fact that they are called by different names:

---

[135] Tikva Frymer-Kensky, *Reading the Women of the Bible* (New York: Schocken, 2002), 103, states that "[i]n the Ancient Near East, prostitutes could be hired as surrogate wombs as well as sexual objects. Laws and contracts regulated the relationship between the child of such a prostitute and children of the first wife. ... Jephthah has been wronged, but he has no recourse. He must leave home. The biblical audience, knowing that his brothers' action was improper, will be sympathetic to Jephthah."

Abimelech's mother is a אמה "slave" or "servant" (9:18).[136]

Jephthah's mother is a אשה זונה *zônâ* woman" (11:1).

Would these two have been recognizable social categories to the first audience, or are they abusive inventions of the narrator? One should not forget that, in a manner similar to that of Abimelech's lineage in Judg 8–9, disqualification of Jephthah's mother is put on the other party's lips: the "right sons" for inheritance are the ones who name the other half-brother's mother as a "nobody" by name-calling her with the still-well-and-alive "son of a …" This happens not by chance, of course. There is an ideological war here, the need to discredit others who are seen or expected to be seen as socially inferior. At least from the other sons' perspective, being the "son of an אשה זונה" would have qualified Jephthah for lesser rights than their own. But not quite, otherwise they would not have needed to drive him out! These facts point to the wisdom of looking at the use of the term and its translation with great suspicion.

AGAIN: AN INTRIGUING COMBINATION OF TERMS

I come back now to a point advanced in my chapter 1, on differentiating (or not) between זונה and אשה זונה. Let us quickly review our sources. From the thirty-five appearances of the feminine participle of זונה, all are absolute, six are plural, half of these are determined by article and only one is in apposition to נשים.[137] Of the singular participles, four are determined by article, (three of them in Josh 6); and two by preposition + vocalization of article (כ and ב); all others are undetermined.[138] Seven are the appearances of the phrase אשה זונה, all undetermined except for Josh 6:22.[139] In three texts the participle appears in conjunction with the construct "house of" in slightly different forms: בית־זונה (Jer 5:7), בית־אשה זונה (Josh 2:1), and בית־אשה זונה (Josh 6:22).[140]

I am increasingly convinced that there is a difference in meaning between both expressions, even though that difference is not immediately obvious and, frankly, I am unable to pin it down. I am aware of the doubts I myself hold, all

---

[136] As discussed in chapter 3, however, the term may be translated into several different social categories.

[137] 1 Kings 3:16. The other ones, 1 Kgs 22:38; Prov 29:3; Ezek 16:9, 33; Hos 4:14.

[138] The other is the "song of the forgotten זונה" in Isa 23; with preposition: Ezek 16:31; Joel 3:3.

[139] These are Lev 21:7; Judg 11:1; 16:1; Prov 6:26; Jer 3:3; Ezek 16:30; 23:44. Five appear in the Torah, eight in the DtrH; four in the book of Proverbs and all others, seventeen in total, in the prophetic corpus, mostly in Jeremiah and Ezekiel.

[140] From all occurrences, those in the prophets are the largest group (seventeen); the most pertinent ones are reviewed below.

the more so anybody else. Yet, it seems to be an issue worth bringing to the fore and further exploring.

To make issues worse, most women named either אשה זונה or זונה do not appear in situations that permit us easily to identify them as harlots and this becomes clear once we are alert to the weight traditional translations still bear on our minds as we read those texts. And most of the scant examples in which אתנן, "fee, wage" appears are metaphoric.[141] And when a dialogue indicates a transaction (Gen 38), the term "wage" does not appear and the woman is *not* a prostitute! These "anomalies make it very hard to come to conclusions; why, then, is so strong the association in people's minds between these terms (or these women) and harlotry as the only possibility? One of the best examples to try these biases is Rahab: Why do we assume she is a prostitute, when the only thing the text says is that the spies, sent to observe the land and the city, came in to the house of an אשה זונה called Rahab and they lodged/lay there. Why is she immediately associated to a harlot? Is it because the only woman who would accept foreign men at her place would be a prostitute? Is this not a bias? Could she not run a "bed and breakfast" or a tavern? In the story she does not offer herself up nor ask for payment for sex. Instead, she asks for retribution for her kindness in hiding them and lying to the soldiers.[142]

If we try to order the terms graphically according to their degree of certainty as to their meaning, a few can be located at the safer sides of this spectrum and others fall in between. I propose here some points to be considered.[143]

Legal Material

Starting on the safer side, I set the law in Deut 23 as one of the cases in which זנה means a prostitute. The law establishes a parallel between two types of "dirty money" not to be brought to the sanctuary in payment of vows. Laws avoid polysemy and are literal in their intention in order to be applied—although this law itself is evidence that today we cannot agree on its terms' meaning any more. Furthermore, the association of זונה + אתנן, as well as the financial dimension of several other laws in this chapter, calls for a prostitute.

The only other legislation that concerns us is Lev 21:1-15, about purity concerns for the priesthood. Among these varied laws, a few are concerned with types of women a priest is allowed or forbidden to marry. On the positive side,

---

[141] As noted by Assante, "What Makes a Prostitute," 129, when she wonders why there is so little written evidence about prostitutes in antiquity, many women beside prostitutes received gifts from prospective husbands (or their families) and perhaps lovers; this would have made it very hard even to those who observed them, to distinguish them from professional sex workers.

[142] It is true that she is also called רחב הזנה in 6:17,25; however, her identification with a harlot occurs much earlier than those verses in the readers' mind. Is this not due to traditional interpretations?

[143] Most of these texts will be further studied below, so not all arguments are offered here.

v. 13 states that he is to marry an אשה בבתוליה, usually understood "a wife in her virginity." [144] As to negative expressions, priests are forbidden to marry any of these women: "a loose woman or a profaned woman they shall not take as wife; neither shall they take a woman expelled by her husband..." אשה זנה וחללה לא יקחו ואשה גרושה מאישה לא יקחו (v. 7). Finally, v. 14 combines both the prohibition and the positive command: "A widow, or a divorced woman, or a woman who has been defiled, a זונה—these he shall not marry. He shall marry a virgin of his own kin..." אלמנה וגרושה וחללה זנה את־אלה לא יקח. The expression אשה זנה וחללה in v. 7 may be taken as two terms, "a prostitute or a woman who has been defiled," (NRSV) or as hendyadis, "a woman profaned by prostitution" (NJB). In either case, an "unattached woman" (Schulte, Assante) or "a woman engaged in non-Yahwist worship" (Riegner) makes at least so much sense as a prostitute. As to v. 14, similar terms appear, but in reverse order: אלמנה וגרושה וחללה זנה. Since the second part of the law indicates what kind of a woman is allowed, perhaps mention of אשה closing the law does double duty: כי אם־בתולה מעמיו יקח אשה "but a virgin of his own people shall he take as wife/woman." Also here the enumeration comprises three family-related terms united by the conjunction. These are forbidden women in contraposition to the virgin; to those three, זנה, without conjunction after two other nouns with conjunction (אלמנה וגרושה וחללה), seems to have been added as an afterthought rather than a hendyadis and its meaning as "harlot" is, to me, far from clear. [145]

In short, a case may be made to consider the scant legal material in the Pentateuch to confirm our suspicion as to a differentiated meaning of both expressions.

Pay For Sex

The term usually translated "wages" אתנן only appears associated with a זונה, never with אשה זונה or with any other professional, male or female. The problem is, however, that all occurrences of אתנן save Deut 23:19 are

---

[144] However, not every בתולה is "a woman who has known no man." The term seems to point more toward what we would call "a teenager" or "a young adult"; obviously, her genital virginity would have been expected (and preserved as much as possible).

[145] Just two verses further the subject is not the priests' possible wives but any priest's daughters. Here the proscription is to profane herself (nip̄'al of חלל) by "playing the whore" (King James Version) or "through prostitution" (NRSV). Since the stem is used not as a participle but infinitive, לזנות, and no context is provided, it is virtually impossible to determine whether it means "by prostitution" or, in a non-literal sense, "by idolatry." At any rate, the impression remains that the exercise of "the oldest profession in the world" was not of serious concern to ancient Israel.

figurative, so that we should at least suspect such a definition and leave yet another open-ended road in what refers to commercial transactions, wages, and negotiations.[146]

Term of Comparison

זונה/תו appears in those stories or proverbs in which it is a term of comparison with (an)other person/s. Except for Jer 3:3 (the "זונה אשה's forehead") in all these זונה alone is used (even though it is not always clear whether the woman so named is a harlot or a fornicator). Those comparisons include varied genres:

* a rhetorical question by Dinah's brothers (Gen 34:31);

* a narrative on Tamar and her father-in-law Judah (Gen 38:15);

* some prophetic utterances against the people of Judah or Israel (some rather too obscure to know whether they compare them to a prostitute or a fornicator, such as Isa 1:21, Ezek 16:33, Hos 4:14);

* a song (Isa 23:15); and

* the wisdom saying in Prov 29:3, where the company with harlots serves as foil to pursuit of wisdom.

Today's use of expressions such as "son of a ...," where the meaning is not to be taken literally, should alert us that some of these comparisons might have made use of the figure of the loose woman instead of, or together with, that of the harlot. Other comparisons (the song in Isa 23:15, for instance), would be enhanced by the use of the harlot imagery rather than that of a loose woman.

Special Attire

Proverbs 7:10 speaks of the "שית זונה," a זונה's attire. What this would consist of is not clear. Tamar is taken to be a harlot precisely because of her attire (38:15). In Ps 73:6 (together with Prov 27:23, the only other instance of the noun שית), it means some kind of garment or veil to cover the face. Also Enkidu's curse involves nice garments.[147]

Although not preceded by the comparative particle, Prov 7:10 uses this image as a device to downplay the fornicator who is never at home, but on the

---

[146] *BDB*, 1072.

[147] See Heather McKay, "Gendering the Discourse of Display in the Hebrew Bible," in *On Reading Prophetic Texts: Gender-Specific and Related Studies in Memory of Fokkelien van Dijk-Hemmes* (ed. Bob Becking and Meindert Dijkstra; Leiden: Brill, 1996), especially 178–81, where she summarizes the anthropological background to understanding the different symbolic connotations of dressing (and undressing).

contrary, is always looking for a fool to entrap. Since the comparison is between a woman who dresses with a special attire and a fornicating woman who wanders around, it seems likely that the comparison has the harlot in mind—unless, of course, one would think of a loose woman dressed to call attention.

Out-of-Wedlock Motherhood

Those who are "single mothers," i.e., mothers who live alone or whose children's right of inheritance are questioned by use of this term, are always called אשה זונה, never זונה alone. These are Jephthah's mother (Judg 11:1) and the two women who seek Solomon's court of justice (1 Kgs 3:16).

Innkeepers?

There are a few narratives in which an אשה זונה is notoriously difficult to locate professionally. These are those in Josh 2 and in Judg 16:1–3 (and to a certain extent, Josh 6, although also רחב הזונה appears). What these have in common is that each has her own home into which they can take foreign men (men presumably unknown to them, but that is unclear in Judg 16). They do not have a husband nor children as far as we know; Rahab has a family, which does not live with her. Both appear in the Targum as "innkeeper" and this seems to be the best solution to the dilemma, although, as Riegner notes in reference to Rahab, the term מלון "food, sustenance" is absent.[148]

Perhaps these two texts reflect a situation (a period or a region) in which זונה did not achieve its technical use and thus it was tantamount to one of the meanings of אשה זונה. I am suggesting that this compound lexeme אשה זונה meant several things, namely, a woman unattached to a patriarchal household, an innkeeper and, sometimes, a prostitute.

TEXTS THAT SEEM TO CONTRADICT ALL THESE CONCLUSIONS

Finally, I should mention that some texts contradict these conclusions. Among these, there are those prophetic texts in which it is not very clear what their intent is and what they mean, particularly Joel 4:3. Also, the remaining texts from the book of Proverbs require some explanation, for they seem to contradict each other. Two texts compare two kinds of women who are dangerous to the family's patrimony. Proverbs 6:26 compares the אשה זונה with the אשת איש, the married woman, a man's woman or wife. In this sense, the use of the compound lexeme stresses our case, for it is not the harlot but the single woman

---

[148] Riegner, "Vanishing Hebrew Harlot," 164.

who may be dangerous to an established household.[149] On the other hand, Prov 23:27, states that "a זונה is a deep ditch and an alien woman, a narrow pit." If we stay with the previous examples, here comparison of the alien woman would gain weight if the second term were אשה זונה rather than זונה. Zwickel offers a different explanation with regard to the diverse perceptions in Proverbs on these women's danger: "While the prostituted [*Prostituerte*] was an unproblematic component of society, because visiting her must not have been that frequent, the prostitutes of post-exilic times appear to have sought a commitment by the men, so that to have access to their monies. That must have had consequences for her place in society."[150]

In summary, there seems to be a semantic range that goes from the prostitute to the "non-prostitute," the unattached; "loose woman," or to the fornicator. Legal material, use of the term "wage," comparisons and wisdom sayings point to the harlot on one end of the spectrum. But אשה זונה points to the single woman whose life, including her sexual life, is not regulated by a male relative—although at least one of them bore a child of recognized paternity (Judg 11:1). This non-attachment could mean freedom or lack of protection, or both. At any rate, it was feared by established households, as evident in some proverbial sayings.

At any rate, it is worth repeating my admonition that this whole proposal should be seen as provisory and worthy of further checking before it may be adopted, modified, or rejected.

CONCLUDING REMARKS

All texts in the DtrH and several others in which the term זונה appears have been studied, with two basic questions, to wit: Can the term be understood to refer to a sex worker with any degree of probability? And in case this was affirmatively answered: What can we know about her, especially about her social status? I presented the texts ordered from those I saw more probably speaking of a harlot to those less likely to mean that. A quick mention of Delilah was also made, since she belongs with several other biblical women to those living on her own and thus, not subject to a male authority and often taken to be a prostitute.

If my analysis holds true, some conclusions may be taken as to prostitution in ancient Israel, with particular focus on the Dtr angle to it. While the stem discussed is relatively common in the Hebrew Bible, its meaning varies, referring to a professional sex worker, to fornication, to illicit religious praxis,

---

[149] On the other hand, traditional translation of the verse speaks of the harlot's wages as a bread-loaf; if this is the right translation, אשה זונה for "harlot" weakens our case.

[150] Zwickel, *Frauenalltag*, 125.

and to some form of unattached life outside the patriarchal household (which could include sex). An added difficulty is that there are two forms to be considered, זונה and אשה זונה, which so far have defied classification.

I have not addressed the issue of the connection between the terms זונה (אשה) and religious practices, especially sacrifices. This relationship, explored among other scholars by Bird, Riegner, Stark, and Wacker, is more evident in the prophetic corpus and Gen 38; texts which I have only touched upon tangentially. I do not deny this could be the meaning of the term in some of the texts studied—particularly in those where it is not clear what אשה זונה means, such as references to Rahab, to the Gazite woman, and to Jephthah's mother in Judges. Were that the case, they would not be harlots. Then, we would have come full circle and would need to start this discussion ("harlot or not harlot"?) all over again.

In general, prostitutes are not fully developed characters, but agents: they advance the plot and contribute to someone else's development and fame. Sometimes they lie between warring parties, like the woman visited by Samson (and Delilah, who is however not called an אשה זונה but shares many of her characteristics). Sometimes they become the tool for a king's experiment on wisdom, power, and prestige, like the two who sought Solomon's judgment over their babies' loss.

Harlots belong to the lower echelons of society, live close to the city wall or by its gates and wash themselves in the public pool. Not only do these elements point to their low status; such low status is part and parcel of the narratives in which they appear in order to serve as foil in favor of their counterparts. The Israelite spies at Jericho are given a theological speech on YHWH's mighty acts by an אשה זונה who is, contrary to the king and other important figures of the city, a "nobody." On the other hand, it is precisely this condition of nobody or underdog that makes her a favorite of all times, including DtrH itself. For, in the final redaction, it is she, a poor and perhaps despised woman of Canaan, a trickster folkloric character, the one who pronounces YHWH's name and predicts Israel's wonderful future in the promised land.

When two נשים זונות bring their judicial case to a recently appointed wise king, it is again unclear whether the idea behind it is to show how open and wide-ranging his court was or whether it is ironic. In any case, the contrast between the king and the plaintiffs is stronger if these two women (again, we do not know whether they are prostitutes or single women) belong to the lower strata. Were they refined women, familiar with the court and belonging to high-ranking or influential families, there would have been some male to put their affairs in order without airing their internal quarrels. Unfortunately, we hear nothing about family, a *paterfamilias*, their social and racial status and the like;

we only hear they share a house, have babies, live by themselves, and quarrel with each other.

We have studied several texts which, in the end, might later prove not to be that directly pertinent for a study on prostitution. At any rate, one thing is clear. Those characterized by the participial form of this stem, either as אשה זונה or plainly as זונה, may be richer or poorer, more or less despised by their society, more or less feared as *femme fatale* by the very fact of living alone; might be liminal and even dangerous liars; might be women whom men sought, desired, paid or even gave lavish presents. Since they do not belong to a patriarchal household to which they must respond, at least in the mind of the Deuteronomistic authors, they are not judged according to their use of their sexuality and even less, according to a supposedly regulated code of honor and shame, that would tell them to stay at home.

This concludes the study of the pertinent texts for the female workers in the DtrH, with particular attention to service-type labor.

CHAPTER 8

REASSESSING THE SOCIAL LOCATION OF FEMALE LABOR IN DTRH

"Although the sexes were equal at creation, this is not reflected in the gender system." Writing on normative genders in ancient Mesopotamia, Asher-Greve intends to convey a panoramic assessment of that ancient culture's attitude toward gender stratification. I have quoted her poignant assessment at the beginning of this paragraph to speak, in general terms, of the Bible's tension between recognition of the theological value of each human being as God's plan and rampant examples of increasing inequality and injustice as one goes down the social ladder.[1]

The Deuteronomistic History, Isaiah, Jeremiah, and other biblical works are all children of the exile; they were concerned with YHWH's plans and promises, all having experienced the fall of the monarchy and the apparent defeat of YHWH.[2] In a new geographical, political, and religious situation the sages reflected on themes such as the fall of the monarchy, Yahwism, religious orthodoxy, God's promises, land, what had gone wrong and why, and how it could have been prevented. The fruitfulness of this period speaks of their need to

---

[1] Asher-Greve, "Decisive Sex," 16. She proceeds to affirm that in ancient Mesopotamia the only source of procreation was attributed to semen and thus, men became the first gender and women the second one.

[2] Chronology of the "Deuteronomist/s" and of Joshua–2 Kings is highly debated and no consensus exists at the moment. We take the position that there was a Dtr school and that it used pre-exilic material, but shaped it in the light of their own experience of deportation and deprivation, and the return to Judea of an elite.

make sense of their new reality. And even though it would be silly to deny these privileged groups their share of suffering, humiliation, and death in the face of those gloomy events, they were not the only ones to suffer. Men and women standing on the lower socio-economic layers also suffered the consequences of invasion and exile, as had earlier suffered their own fellow Israelites' oppression, humiliation, and neglect. And in these, women fared worse than men.

Ideally every Israelite family would have had its inheritance, which would be a home for several generations and a source of income and satisfaction. With the growth of the monarchy an urban elite also grew in power, controlled military, political, and economic decisions, and was closely allied to those in charge of religion and education. Peasants fed these elites, paying with increasing loss of patrimonial land through indebtedness, high taxes, rent, and interests on loans. Natural disasters, invasion, and war were always possible, inviting destruction of fields and trees, heavier drainage of material and human resources, siege, starvation, and slavery or death. Even if the city was miraculously spared—as the Bible itself recounts—rebuilding the country, crops growing, and heavier tribute also took a toll on peasantry. If, as feared, the city was taken and destroyed, numerous deaths and slavery for the survivors were sure to result. These events did not happen all at the same time for the same family, but they were not extraordinary for preindustrial societies and they form the background to the biblical world. When one only reads about the royal household and the king's political and religious behavior, it is easy to forget that peasants and workers are the backbone of the whole system.

A MODEL FOR WOMEN AND CLASS

Normally, preindustrial societies are drawn as formed by three social classes, namely upper, lower, and the outcasts, each one with distinctive marks. In our view as laid out in chapter 1, the best way to depict society is as a continuum from one extreme to the other, since there are several factors (gender, age, family ties, military record, religion, purity, type of occupation, mobility) which determine boundaries and subclasses, and thus create several overlapping areas between groups.[3] This continuum model has important consequences for the study of women in the Bible, as it promotes sensitivity to forms of privilege or discrimination within each class, besides those between classes. Certain women were powerful and rich, others were independent and recognized by their community, and others were unprotected and abused. As *groups,* all women

---

[3] These overlapping areas are lost in a layered model of society, of the pyramidal kind, for instance. See Lenski, *Power and Privilege,* 74–75. Furthermore, there is much missing information in our sources, thus preventing us from a clear-cut categorization of people.

were behind the men of their respective class in privilege and authority, but aside from this fact, their lives were probably very different from those of other women in other aspects.[4]

Any model used to explain an ancient society such as the one reflected in the Hebrew Bible belongs to our time, not to the time or society it intends to understand. To the extent that it be faithful to its sources and not made "after our own image and likeness" it will gain acceptance from other observers of those same sources. We have posited that a model focusing on women in the ANE should value them for their socio-economic, political, and cultural contributions to society. Not only is a model in which work is one important factor more faithful to real life; it fosters revision of other aspects of ancient society and of current scholarship. As one scholar states,

> The work patterns and authority structures that characterize the reality of daily life in premodern societies are rarely hierarchical along gender lines, even if such hierarchies do exist in certain political, religious, or jural aspects of the society. A rich assortment of recent studies of the family and household in traditional societies is especially cognizant of the range of women's contributions to and also control of household economic functions. ...
>
> Just as important, the newer ethnographies examine the articulation of the household with wider community functions. They have discovered that the modern conceptual separation between domestic and public spheres cannot hold up to nuanced evaluations of women's extra-domestic activities. The two domains, it is now understood, are not necessarily separate. ... Rather, in most premodern, village-based societies, the lines between such hypothetical spheres blurred.[5]

A consequence of this approach may be, for instance, a model that considers women's contribution in socio-economic terms, that values them not for their virginity, marital faithfulness, or sex appeal. Then, by suggesting such a model we want also to challenge some very popular social-scientific models focusing too much on women's value (= shame) as avoidance of contact with

---

[4] According to M. Chaney, "Systemic Study of the Israelite Monarchy," in *Social Scientific Criticism of the Hebrew Bible and Its Social World: The Israelite Monarchy* (ed. Norman K. Gottwald; *Semeia* 37; Atlanta: Scholars Press, 1986), 56, "it is a simple fact that the lives of the ruling elite in Israel and Judah had more in common with the ruling elite of other Near Eastern monarchies than with the peasants, artisans, and expendables of their homelands. Elites understood each other and their world on the same basic terms. ... For modern social historians to be content with such a perspective, however, is to leave the experience of ninety-five to ninety-eight percent of the population of those societies out of account."

[5] Meyers, "Everyday Life," 189–90.

males other than the immediate family members (father, brothers and, later husband, sons).[6]

VISIBLE WOMEN

שפחה/ות, אמה/ות, and נערה/ות — Slaves and Dependents

From the first major group of female workers studied in chapter 4 (that comprising occurrences of the women called שפחה/תו, אמה/תו, and נערה/תו), the following conclusions deserve notice. First, Engelken's claim that the אמה is closer to the household and the שפחה is of lower social status is correct, but there is no room for details on conditions of these two groups. In fact, since in the whole DtrH אמה is used literally only in the Deuteronomic laws concerning festivals and the prohibition to covet the neighbor's property, and only 2 Sam 17:17 refers to a שפחה in a concrete, albeit atypical situation, it would be hard to substantiate further claims about differences between these terms in what concerns DtrH.[7]

Second, Leeb's conclusions about the social location of the נערה taken and applied to women in DtrH allowed us to choose from among them those dependent women who were under the authority of another "father."

Third, by also adding to our "continuum of powerlessness" model free women who would have been at risk of becoming someone's slave, or of being seduced or abducted as concubines or wives, the picture of women in ancient Israelite society becomes more nuanced and complex.[8]

Chart I shows references to slaves and dependent women in DtrH. The first two rows refer to female slaves and indentured servants seen in chapter 4 (except for those in self-debasement, which are presented in Chart II). The שפחה/ות, אמה/ות, and נערה/ות of Deut 22:15–29 and Judg 21:12 are free women; those of 1 Sam 25:42, 1 Kgs 1–2, and 2 Kgs 5:2–4 are dependents; and for those of Judg 19 and 1 Sam 9 there is not enough information.

One should notice that many of the texts are considered part of earlier sources used for DtrH, although there is considerable debate among scholars concerning dating of sources.[9] Deuteronomy is by far the book with more

---

[6] Available models from the social sciences applied to the biblical world were discussed in chapter 1.

[7] All other instances of the term are general, theoretical statements about slaves (Deut 28:68, 1 Sam 8:16, 2 Kgs 5:26). Noticeable also is the lack of overlapping of both terms, except for those instances in which a woman uses alternatively both terms in self-debasement.

[8] Like Dinah (Gen 34) or the women taken for the Benjaminites (Judg 21).

[9] G. von Rad, *Deuteronomy*, 21–23 (generally, on the use of earlier sources), 59–60 (on Deut 5), 147–8 (on Deut 23); R. Rendtorff, *The Old Testament: An Introduction* (Philadelphia: Fortress, 1986), 155. Judges 9 is considered to have been collected in the eighth century B.C.E., while 19–21 belong to the exilic redaction; see Boling, *Judges,* 29–32, 182–5; Rendtorff, *Old Testament,* 167–70.

references (all in laws except for Deut 28:68). Joshua does not contain one single term. Here what can be safely said is that Dtr used early material, part of which recognizes the existence of women working as slaves or servants, and thus they *could* have been in his sources.

Texts do not spell out what was like to be a bound person in Israel. Nothing is said about origin, marital status, everyday situation, or other elements that would help locate them socially.[10] On the one hand, this lack of information is due to their appearance according to the needs of the narrative.[11] On the other, it points to their being part of a familiar picture to writers and readers alike, so that they did not need much introduction. One knows that in any community there were several "maintenance activities" and we also know that in Israel there was a patriarchal distribution of power.[12] These facts lead one to think that, if nothing else, the basic household chores were carried on by dependent personnel, male or female, when they were available and affordable. We also know from the texts that slaves and dependents had to obey and do whatever task they were called upon to perform, and thus they are found accompanying their mistress in her trip or passing on information.

Second Samuel 6:20–23 is the end of the ark narrative. Since this end is debated, most commentaries leave open the question of their date; see Klein, *1 Samuel*, 38–40. First Samuel 8–12 dates to the time of David or Solomon; see Crüsemann, *Widerstand*, 87–8; Klein, *1 Samuel*, 74; Rendtorff, *Old Testament*, 170–2. First Kings 1–2 form the end of the Succession Narrative, which justifies Solomon's accession to the throne instead of his brother Adonijah's. Long, *1 Kings*, 33–4 sees at least "three redactional patterns"; for Rendtorff, *Old Testament*, 172–4, they form a literary unit. Finally, 2 Kgs 5, a unity in itself, is part of the Elisha cycle, again dated differently by scholars (Long, *2 Kings*, 66–79; Cogan & Tadmor, *2 Kings*, 66–68, Rendtorff, *Old Testament*, 178–9).

[10] There are hints about their situation, for instance in laws like Exod 21:20–21, which limits the right of the master on beating the male or female slave, and Exod 21:26–27, which limits the right of a creditor to abuse a distrainee. These laws do not prohibit punishment, only limit it in extreme cases.

[11] In Genesis slaves appear as surrogate mothers, used in the matriarchs' struggle with barrenness and jealousy, because that is the main concern of the story. Likewise, in stories concerned with an important female character (Pharaoh's daughter or Esther), the focus is on their safety, well being, and honor, and therefore slaves are present only to accompany their mistresses.

[12] Meyers, "Archaeology—A Window," 82 n.46, quoting Margarita Sánchez Romero, "Women, Maintenance Activities, and Space," in *SOMA 2001: Symposium on Mediterranean Archaeology: Proceedings of the Fifth Annual Meeting of Postgraduate Researchers, the University of Liverpool, 23 – 23 [sic?] February 2001* (ed. Georgina Muskett, Aikaterini Koltsida, & Mercourios Georgiadis; BAR International Series 1040; Oxford: Archaeopress, 2002), 178. I have been unable to get this article; see, however, her "Actividades de mantenimiento en la Edad del Bronce del sur peninsular: el cuidado y la socialización de individuos infantiles," *Complutum* [Online], Vol. 18 (10–25–2007), http://revistas.ucm.es/index.php/CMPL/article/view/CMPL0707110185A.

Belittled Women

Responding to the need to determine what information is trustworthy in terms of the social location of a slave and what information should not be taken literally, considerable attention was paid to texts in DtrH in which אמה or שפחה are used with the ideological intention of diminishing the person thus named, in self-reference or by other persons (Chart III). The first two rows are those in which a person uses "your slave" (with one or the other term studied) to denote her subjection to the higher authority of the person addressed, i.e., a man or YHWH (for which, only אמתך is attested). The last row is that in which the term אמה or the expression בן־אמה are used by a third person (the narrator or Michal or David in their dialogue) to insult or dismiss someone thus named. Second Samuel 6:20–23 reflects the view of Michal and David with reference to the women who saw David dance. Since no other voice is brought up about that event, no sure information can be extracted about their social location.

Far more interesting is the case of the two women who are named אמה in Judg 8–9 and 19–20. Both of them are unnamed; both are "concubines" פילגש (one of Gideon, the other of a Levite); both are still strongly connected to their own family; and both are foreign to the husband's clan (one lives with her own kindred, the Shechemites; the other leaves her husband in the remote areas of the hill-country of Benjamin and goes to her father at Bethlehem of Judah). They also share the fact that these are the only two instances in which the characterizations of אמה and פילגש are applied to the same woman *in the same text*.[13] In short, these women have material and psychological resources available to them, a fact that points to their social location as secondary wives, rather than chattel slaves.

WOMEN AND OCCUPATIONS

Women subject to slavery or dependency were very likely taken for granted if not humiliated as workers, used as breeders, sold or rented out, and perhaps hardly taken care of. The Bible, as a product of its time, does not take a stand against these facts (also inflicted on men), which for us today constitute clear abuses of basic human rights.[14] At the same time, the Hebrew Bible envisions

---

[13] Bilhah is also described as אמה in Gen 30:4 and as פילגש in 35:22.

[14] There are biblical examples of a reversal of fate. Isaiah 47 is a wonderful example, because it depicts all the humiliation and suffering of the "slave" (the exiled community) as punishment to be brought on Assyria. See J. Severino Croatto, *Isaías: la palabra profética y su relectura hermenéutica: II: 40–55: La liberación es posible* (Buenos Aires: Lumen, 1994) chapter 10; on a slightly different subject, Norman K. Gottwald, "Social Class and Ideology in Isaiah 40–55: An Eagletonian Reading," in *Ideological Criticism of the Bible*, 43–57 (and responses in the same volume).

another reality, at least for the Israelites. Its God is, precisely, a God who rescued them from slavery and humiliation to make of them a great nation!

Throughout the Bible, women perform several tasks, many of them in a professional manner. Often, texts do not pause to give us detailed information (they often do not even remember them), as has become clear in our study. Many terms occur in pre-exilic sources (notably, in the books of Samuel), and some of them, such as the song of Deborah (Judg 5), are considered by most scholars as part of the earliest material that we have, even though reworked and integrated into that post-exilic meta-narrative that is the "Deuteronomistic History" or the "Former Prophets," as one chooses to look at Joshua–2 Kings. Except for references to the זונה (sex worker) and "concubines" (more a relational term than that of an occupation, as already discussed) all other occupations appear only once in this whole block Joshua–2 Kings (and only the זונה is mentioned in a law in Deut 23) as evident in our Chart IV.

Besides these, we have traced several other professions, such as grinders, singers, music performers, messengers, weavers, and advisers. Since they are ignored or even somehow misplaced in the biblical record, they are located with other women made invisible. Charts VIII (DtrH) and IX (elsewhere) reflect the texts in which they appear.[15]

INVISIBLE WOMEN

In chapter 5, several associations or "brotherhoods" were studied. Since many if not all of these were hereditary (priests, temple servants, donated people, water drawers, wood hewers, and others), they were literally born from women. We cannot know, however, whether these women belonged to those "guilds" and even in case they did, what that means in terms of work. It is our assumption that at least in the case of groups belonging to the lower socio-economic echelons, whether legally free or slaves, active members of the hereditary guilds or not, their lives did probably suffer restrictions: they usually lived on the edge of survival and must have worked to help out the family.[16] DtrH also states that at least certain groups of Canaanites who survived Israel's settlement were permanently bound to the state and temple. These groups included women whose living standards are unknown to us. Furthermore, people serving in tasks such as grain-grinding at the mill, beer-brewing, midwifery, music and arts,

---

[15] By "misplaced" I mean that they appear in unusual contexts (such as weaving for Asherah, but nowhere else) or their recognized female-related profession is ascribed to a male in DtrH (such as the composers and singers of songs of war and of laments).

[16] Women were also affected by their relatives' absence due to corvée or war, but they probably remained free. See above, chapter 3.

performance, or textiles are notably absent from most biblical sources, including the DtrH.

Also, a few words should be said about the term זונה and its translation (chapter 7, one of the longest in this book). Traditional interpretations in the sense that the original meaning of the term is the sexual one (fornication, prostitution), later re-signified to mean "idolatry," have been recently challenged. Although there is as yet no agreement between the diverse proposals (in the sense that different proposals from several scholars cannot be put together into a coherent system), these revisions pose a question on our assumptions on prostitution and its range of activities. A further consequence of our study on זונה in the Hebrew Bible is the proposal, advanced in chapter 1, that the constructions of participle with and without the terms for "person" vary in their meaning and are not exactly synonymous.

Two other types of people, the freed persons who entered into clientship with the former owner (חפשי) and those born in the house, were mentioned almost in passing because of the scant information about them. But these have to be considered also when one locates people in social categories, since they also were part of the socio-economic picture.

All these data indicate that the number of female workers was percentage-wise higher than one tends to think. Vast areas of the socio-economic and political life of Israel influenced women's lives. Distribution of land, increasing pauperization of peasants and of debt-slaves, consolidation of the state bureaucracy and of a wealthy elite, remission of debts, natural phenomena, and warfare are some of the socio-economic factors pervasive in biblical Israel as well as in today's world. These might be areas in which the prophets' concern for social justice and Dtr's depiction of lower-class people might cross paths.[17]

Considering our continuum model for society, working women came from at least these situations: free Israelites in economic duress (due, for instance, to a drought, to absence of males because of sickness, war or corvée service); corvée service (perhaps applicable also to women, we do not know, but see 1 Sam 8:13); indentured slaves working for their families' creditors; abducted people; members of the temple and court staff (some probably slaves, others members of the guilds), and Canaanites made permanent state-slaves. Although social location and particular situations were different for women of these groups in terms of inheritance, honor, or rights, they all probably knew what financial difficulties meant, at least from time to time.[18]

---

[17] The difference in terminology for the oppressed and poor between DtrH and the prophets needs further research. Much of the Hebrew Bible is related to the monarchy, either as a corrective voice to excesses (the "classical" prophets), as part of Israel's history (DtrH or Chronicles), or as sponsor of wisdom (Psalms or Proverbs ascribed to David and Solomon). There are, however, very few references to female slaves or dependents in the prophets.

[18] Unfortunately examples are not abundant. One might think of Ruth and Naomi's difficulties upon

REDEFINING HONOR

Even though not the main interest of this study, we contest the widespread contention among biblical scholars that honor and shame constitute a pair of comparable values and that in the Mediterranean basin this meant that men provided safety and sustenance and women made sure their behavior and especially their sexuality were properly guarded or kept. Apart from arguments from anthropologists, which show that honor and shame do not work in people's lives in similar manners and are not comparable categories, we resist that model because it is too general to account for poor women (and poor families as well). We have demonstrated that several texts evaluate women by very different standards than sexual faithfulness to a husband or restriction to their home.[19]

Wikan's conclusions from her field work in Oman, that there are two parallel worlds, each embraced by both men and women but in different manners, illumine the research conducted here. "In the male world, females are interesting mainly in terms of their sexual trustworthiness, because this is where they so strongly affect the lives of men," including proper inheritance and access to other women as well.[20] Several texts in DtrH demonstrate these preoccupations, such as the birth of Eli's grandson Ichabod, the quarrels in the book of Judges between proper heirs and other sons (Abimelech, Jephthah), and the use of concubines as signs of political power.

"In the female world, hospitality and a number of other qualities are highly relevant and have priority," continues Wikan. These qualities are harder to find among lower-class women, because most of them are either part of the master's household in which they cannot offer hospitality, or their depiction is too brief to allow the reader to check Wikan's contention. There are, however, a few hints in texts where the woman is mistress of her household. For instance, the medium of Endor whose profession Saul had banned is depicted as butchering her fatted calf and baking to comfort Saul after the bad news he had heard from Samuel's spirit (1 Sam 28).[21] Abigail saves the day by sending David food and drinks (1 Sam 25:18). In many stories, as stated earlier, nurturing is the role of women, for which cooks and bakers are brought to the palace (1 Sam 8). The woman depicted in Prov 31:10–31 as far worthier than jewels is praised for her

---

their return to Judah, and the widow whom Elisha met (2 Kgs 4:1–7) as examples of free women under economic pressure. There are no particular examples of women among the remaining Canaanites, except for the note about Rahab's and the Gibeonites' offspring (Josh 6:25; 9:27). One might surmise that their social status was low.

[19] One could have attempted an answer from the perspective of the loss of honor for the males who are responsible for the family's honor in the public world, but that search would not have taken us close to the female workers.

[20] Wikan, "Shame and Honour," 636.

[21] Cf. Tamarkin Reis, "Eating the Blood," who contends that this is a sacrificial meal.

industriousness and in general good social behavior, with no reference to her sexual life. Being hard-working for one's own benefit and giving as little as possible as a means of resistance to working for others are values of peasantry and lower-class, while owning workers and making them work for *their owners'* benefit are values of the upper-class. Since, then, honor is not only gender defined but also class defined, it is important to ask the texts how lower-class women were assessed by their peers. This is more easily asked than answered, since DtrH preserves the view of the religious and political leadership. There are, however, a few clues in the texts to discern how some workers were looked upon.

The Prostitute

It was stated above that judging from her appearance in DtrH, the prostitute was one of the lowest women among the outcasts, at least in the elite's appreciation. One text in which the profession of the woman matters is Deut 23:19, whose wages are forbidden as offering to the sanctuary; Josh 2, Josh 6 and 1 Kgs 3:16–28 need their lack of family to advance the plot.[22] First Kings 22:38 uses them as an illustration of shamelessness or perhaps impurity. In Judg 16:1, Samson's visit to an אשה זונה has the aim of creating suspense and having him come out unaware of the dangers that await him; she could equally well function in the story as a single, unattached woman, a bartender or a prostitute. From time immemorial, this is a profession to be associated with innkeepers and taverns; an association not easy to prove in the Bible, where there is not even a noun for this other occupation. Nonetheless, one could imagine a combination of activities at the city's "pub," which could have involved lodging and also prostitution. Again, in a patriarchal system to imagine these chances available to men is not to be too far from reality, but it is still imagination.

After Judg 16:1, the זונה appears in her professional role only to imply a certain social location. Her services were requested by commoners, and while she is still mentioned in 1 Kings and in the prophetic books, her appearances there are not as performer of the service she is supposed to provide.[23] The king has a harem of his own, the priest is forbidden to marry a זונה, and in the prophets she is often a foil for Israel.[24] This clearly bans her from access to the higher social ranks, at least as far as laws are concerned.

---

[22] And some of them are called אשה זונה and not just זונה. Another אשה זונה is Jephthah's mother (Judg 11), a story in which her condition invalidates Jephthah as heir to Gideon's, his father's, inheritance (but in the story Gideon's paternity is never questioned; a difficulty were she a harlot).

[23] Except for the song of the זנה in Isaiah, already studied; for even in Ezek 16 and 23, if she is to be taken literally as a harlot (which is dubious), it is an image to speak of Israel, especially its males.

[24] Why a man would require the services of a prostitute is a question that goes beyond the interest of this work. One can surmise, however, that the elite (priests, sages, king, officials) had at hand

What the assessment of the prostitute was among women is extremely difficult to infer from the texts. Admonitions to sons against the temptation of an adulterous woman or spending too much on a harlot might reflect concerns shared by father and mother, but they also show class biases. As observed in chapter 7, at least in the Hebrew Bible prostitutes do not enjoy palace life, where the king has access to several wives of different rank and characteristics. They are usually associated with the poorer areas of the city or its vicinities, the city wall, its gates and the public pool. Incidentally, the notice about King Ahab's blood at the pool of Samaria lowers his status and honor by identifying the pool at which his blood was rinsed off as the place where also the prostitutes wash themselves.

We find no elements for a more precise assessment of the biblical prostitute. She was sought by some men, despised by the elite and perhaps ignored by others. What is sure is that everyone in her society would have known she belonged to the outcasts.

Women Brought into the Harem

How Abishag got to serve king David reflects the elitist and androcentric assumptions that the king's needs come first and can be solved by a pretty virgin girl in his bed. Since she is never mentioned by a patronymic, it is hard to say what kind of a family she had, where she stemmed from, and whether her move to the palace was seen as a promotion or not. The book of Esther assumes this type of event—beauty contest, one night with the king, the chance of being called again—as desirable for women, but again, nobody asked the women what they felt.[25] Furthermore, Esther's beauty contest led to her being designated as queen and saving her people, a fate totally unlike that allotted Abishag the Shunemite.

Samuel's speech on the liabilities of the monarchy (1 Sam 8) might be useful in this discussion. Samuel warns of the consequent exodus of Israelite youngsters from their family farms to join the court in tasks such as the military

---

women whom they could control better than the prostitute. The king made political alliances through marriage and concubinage and would not need a harlot. In Prov 29:3 the preoccupation is that the young man would not spend his inheritance in prostitutes, hardly a concern of a king or a courtier. Thus, there is a drastic decline in the appearance of the harlot as the DtrH progresses, which is not to be read chronologically, but socially. This means that the explanation is not that with the advancement of the monarchy prostitution disappears, but that as the Dtr becomes more immersed in court-related issues, prostitutes are increasingly left in the margins, as they serve the man who is also in the periphery of political life.

[25] Scholarship is divided since Rabbinic times as to whether Esther was taken forcefully or voluntarily to King Ahasuerus's harem. At any rate, she seems not to bother much about questioning the system until Mordecai's pivotal challenge in 4:13–14.

or agriculture (men) and cooking and preparing perfumes (women). In an agrarian society such a movement would not be perceived as job openings for adventurers—there might have been individuals (particularly younger children in large families) who saw them in that way, but the system did not. It was a drainage of farm hands in favor of the system, which besides sons and daughters exacted fields, tithes, male and female slaves, and animals and which also regulated prices, interest on loans, and taxes. As demonstrated in the corresponding analysis of the text, there might have been large sectors of the traditional society who did not see their daughters' going into the palace as a social promotion.[26] Considering also some of the events in the palace which eventuated in rape, and considering that honor for females is supposedly connected to their sexual purity, one misses any warning in 1 Sam 8 about their integrity such as appears in the complaints about the daughters in Neh 5.

Even less concern is expressed for foreign women taken as captives into Israel, whether into palace, temple or private households. Even though there is in Deut 21:10–14 a law foreseeing the transition of a young, attractive woman from captive to bride, as Pressler contended, it intends to ensure harmony in the captor's household by providing a mechanism through which a new wife is incorporated. Even interpretation of the rites in the least humiliating way (as mourning signs for her beloved ones) does not erase the shame and the anomy of a woman whose family has been killed, who has been picked up from the spoils, and has been uprooted and transferred to her conqueror's house to become his wife. The law on the captive bride and the abduction of women as booty, reflected for instance in Judg 5:30; 21:10–12 and in Gen 34:29, seems to have in mind the common Israelite, the man who fights YHWH's battle, besides the king and his court. This means that the common man and perhaps the common woman considered at least certain women as possessable.[27] All these women were requested or taken as sexual objects (all terms have to do with their sexual service to men); while in Judg 21:12 a point is made that the abducted girls still be virgins, in other texts that condition might be supposed but it does not come up explicitly. It should be noted, however, that these are texts dealing with men (wrongfully) seeking wives, not (at least, not primarily) workers.

The Midwife

Assessment of the midwife might have been very much gender-determined. The very fact that the term מילדת does not appear once in DtrH despite the number

---

[26] See analysis of 1 Sam 8 and of 1 Kgs 1 in chapter 5.

[27] How women would look upon other women would depend on various factors. If one takes Deborah's song to be a female voice, as van Dijk-Hemmes, "Traces," 42–48 does, then a female voice uses an image of spoils and forced marriage to mock a fallen mighty warrior. The interpretation preferred by this study was that of a male voice co-opting a female voice in the poem.

of children born is a sign that her role was regarded by some at least as "a woman thing." Above we discussed some of the possible tasks the midwife took before and after delivery. Supposing for a moment she did not have a key role in determining the appropriate time for conception and prenatal care and that all she did was to be present and help during delivery, it must have been obvious even to men that the lives of mother and newborn depended on her; a power also recognized to Shiphrah and Puah in their encounter with Pharaoh in Exod 1.

And if that story can be believed in any way as to midwives' social location, their reply to Pharaoh shows the popular theme of the underdog's wit to trick the powerful. Of course, one could argue that this was necessary for the Exodus scenario (being slaves in Egypt under a powerful ruler) but did not apply to Israelite midwives in Israel's later times. I would rather argue that both that story and the Dtr's neglect of their contributions reflect the androcentric perspective by which only issues élite *men* deem important were/ are recorded as universally valid. From the woman's perspective the midwife must have been a welcome and needed comfort at a time of danger as delivery was. According to Tikva Frymer-Kensky, Gula, the Sumerian patroness of healing, continued to share this privileged position with her son and co-worker Damu. What is indicative of the prominence of women in healing is the process, evident along the centuries, by which several goddesses lost their place as men took over the profession.[28]

At any rate, midwives are never judged according to their sexuality, neither on their faithfulness to a husband, nor on their "shame" as related to staying home, secluded from strange men. It is quite obvious that a midwife worked often at her patroness's home. Perhaps it would be fruitful to look at her as someone who, because of her contact with blood, kept men away from her.

The Wet Nurse

Judging from those stories in the Bible from which some information can be gleaned about wet nurses, they seem to have belonged to the lower echelons of society. The close relationship they established with the children they fed often lasted as long as they lived, thus possibly adding to the honor ascribed them. As Rebekah left her homeland to marry Isaac, she goes accompanied by her wet nurse, whose name and burial place are recorded (Gen 24:59; 35:8). The story seems to imply that Deborah had remained a servant or slave at Rebekah's household. The dialogue between Moses' mother and Pharaoh's daughter points to a different type of service, in which the child was taken to the wet nurse's home and raised in exchange for a hire. Second Kings 11:2 involves a dependent

---

[28] Frymer-Kensky, *Wake*, 42–44.

working at the palace, in charge of one (perhaps more) of the king's heirs. How common all these services were in Israel or neighboring countries we are unable to say. The advantage of the wet nurse over other women was her influence, especially if the child she had fed was now a powerful man. In the biblical texts, neither the midwife nor the wet nurse are assessed in relation to their sexual honor, although elsewhere contracts attest to sexual restrictions on the wet nurse while she is in service (but those would be due to the danger that she would conceive and have to wean her little patron).

The Performer or Singer

Several terms denote women involved in musical and perhaps other forms of bodily performance, such as acrobatics and recitation. A special category of singing is that of the lamentation or dirge composition and recitation. Information in general on musicians and performers is scant and most terms appear only in passing or are ascribed illustrious *men*, such as David's composition of dirges. At any rate, nothing relates these women with sexual purity or faithfulness or with staying enclosed at home; on the contrary, they play in the streets or as groups with the corresponding male category ("male and female singers"), even in religious events.

Other women are even less assessable than these ones, and it would be too daring to advance further conclusions about them. This research involves a certain degree of chance, since at times only a mention in passing is available. In this sense any conclusion has to remain very much restricted to what can be said from the texts as they stand, unless other evidence illumines the biblical text.

CONCLUDING REMARKS

The texts chosen as primary referents for this research are a reflection on the political and social process of Israel's rise into two (relatively) independent kingdoms and their dilution into exile and loss. And, since both processes are seen as caused by their God, their main arenas are the political and the religious, rather than the every-day function of the household or village. What appear as household or community occupations, especially in the books of Samuel and Kings, refer to the royal household or to prominent leaders—the locus of androcentric historiography—except for the sexual workers, who are located elsewhere (when located at all). Women appear to fulfill needed roles and tasks, especially in problematic situations in which these roles and tasks are necessary, but also unusual, at least to our standards (women passing on information on Absalom's revolt, nannies hiding children from slaughter or weaving for Asherah). Nevertheless, they show time and again that women were not secluded; or, to be more precise, as Marsman puts it:

The degree of seclusion of women was correlated to their social status. The higher women's status was, the more secluded they were. Royal and upper class women had their personnel to do the work. Social status and living conditions thus intertwined. Servants would do the tasks that required going out, while the mistress stayed in. Moreover, there was enough space in larger houses to make a distinction between male (public) and female (private) quarters.

It also mattered whether a woman lived in a rural or an urban context. The Bible describes the circumstances of women living in a rural context, where they went out to perform tasks of animal husbandry and agriculture. Moreover, both in towns and villages women went out to draw water. According to archaeological data on household units in the Cisjordan hill country at the beginning of the Iron Age, women were involved in all aspects of economic life, although a certain gender distinction always existed.[29]

We concur with her analysis and applaud her distinction between urban and rural environments (although these are sometimes blurred by the stories themselves, especially when they have to do with palace personnel located somewhere else). From our viewpoint, her assessment that social status intertwined with living and working conditions is especially important, for it has not been that clear in a body of texts where the preoccupation with religious and political matters seemed to be universal preoccupations.

In the DtrH, the private is political—political and religious decisions impact on the familiar and vice versa, since even the most private actions are read through the political and religious lenses of the Dtr. A couple of examples suffice to make the point. The appearance and disappearance of the only two women guarding children—Mephibosheth in 2 Sam 4:4, Joash in 2 Kgs 11:2— are determined by the royal children of whom they are in charge. Not only are they determined by the children, but the only information about them is how they are hidden for years with the child in danger. Otherwise, we would never learn there were "nannies" in court.[30]

In the first two chapters of Exodus concern for women's and children's needs is apparent; and, for a change, midwives, and wet nurses are active parts of a story. However they made their way into the Bible mainly because of the broader picture of Israel's struggle for survival in slavery and as pre-condition for Moses' exalted role. The role of the midwives in Pharaoh's court and not in

---

[29] Marsman, *Women*, 709–10.

[30] Even more evident are some of David's undertakings and their consequences for the whole nation, such as his adultery and murder involving Bath-sheba and Uriah (2 Sam 11) and following and his census (2 Sam 24).

the delivery room shows especially that they intervene because of a situation considered out of the ordinary.

Meager as this evidence is for a history of women, it deserves to be evaluated upon its own merit, as witness from a world largely ignored or depreciated. To recognize these women in their own merit would at least imply a recognition of their contribution to society, not only as women whose sexuality belonged to a man and had to be fiercely protected against improper advances, but as persons recognized for their contribution to society, most noticeably in social and economic terms.

CHARTS

I. FEMALE TERMS FOR "SLAVE" AND "DEPENDENT" IN DtrH

	Josh	Judg	1 Sam	2 Sam	1 Kgs	2 Kgs[1]
אמה/תו		9:18; 19:19		6:20–22[2]		
שפחה/תו			8:16	17:17		5:26
נערה/תו		19:3–9; 21:12	9:11; 25:42		1:2–4	5:2–4
רחמתים/ רחם womb/s		5:30				
פילגש[3] concubine		8:31; 19:1–20:6		3:7; 5:13; 15:16; 16:21–22; 19:6; 20:3; 21:11	11:3	

---

[1] I follow Hebrew verse references.

[2] This reference appears twice, see next chart and also discussion in chapter 3.

[3] פילגש is a tern which does not belong exactly to the professional field. However, several women thus called are also slaves or dependants and therefore are here included.

II. TERMS USED WITH IDEOLOGICAL INTENTION IN DTRH

	Josh	Judg	1 Sam	2 Sam	1 Kgs	2 Kgs
אמתך/ו			1:11, 16; 25:24–41	14:15, 16; 20:17	1:13, 17; 3:20	
שפחתך			1:18; 25:27–41; 28:21–22	14:15, 17		4:2, 16
אמה/תו (as naming)		9:18; 19		6:20–22		

III. FEMALE TERMS FOR "SLAVE" AND "DEPENDENT" ELSEWHERE

	Torah	Prophets	Chronicles, Ezra-Neh	Other Writings
אמה/תו	Deut 5:14–21; 12:12–18; 15:17; 16:11–14			
שפחה/תו	Gen 12:16; 20:14; 29:24, 29; 30:43 Exod 11:5 Lev 19:20 Deut 28:68, etc.	Isa 14:2; 24:2 Jer 34:9–16 Joel 3:2	2 Chr 28:10	Ruth 2:13 Esth 7:4 Qoh 2:7 Ps 123:2 Prov 30:23
נערה/תו	Gen 24:14–61; 34:3,12; Exod 2:5 Deut 22:15–29	Am 2:7	1 Chr 4:5–6	Ruth 2:5–8, 22–23; 3:2; 4:12 Esth 2 (x 11); 4:4, 16 Prov 9:3; 27:27; 31:15 Job 40:29

IV. FEMALE TERMS FOR SERVICE-TYPE OCCUPATIONS IN DTRH

	Joshua	Judges	1 Sam	2 Sam	1 Kgs	2 Kgs
שרות				19:36		
זונה prostitute	Chapters 2 (x 4) and 6 (x 3)	11:1; 16:1			3:16–28; 22:38	
מינקת wet nurse						11:2
אפות bakers			8:13			
רקחות perfumers			8:13			
טבחות cooks			8:13			
אמנת nurse				4:4		
סכנת assistant					1:1–4	

V. FEMALE TERMS FOR SERVICE-TYPE OCCUPATIONS ELSEWHERE

	Torah	Prophets	Chr, Ezra-Neh	Other Writings
שרות singer			2 Chr 35:25	Qoh 2:8
שדה ושדות				Qoh 2:8
טוחנות (grain) grinder		(Isa 47:2)		Qoh 12:3
משררות Singer			Ezra 2:65 // Neh 7:67	
תופפות drum player	Exod 15:20	(Nah 2:8)		Ps 68:26
זונה prostitute[1]	Gen 34:31; 38:15 Lev 21:7,14 Deut 23:19	Isa 1:21; 23:15–16 Jer 2:20; 3:3 Ezek 16 (x5); 23:44 Hos 4:14 Joel 4:3, etc.		Prov 6:26; 7:10; 23:27; 29:3
מילדת midwife	Gen 35:17; 38:28 Exod 1 (x 7)			
מינקת (wet) nurse	Gen 24:59; 35:8 Exod 2:7, 9	Isa 49:23	2 Chr 22:11	
רעה shepherdess	Gen 29:9			
מקוננות wailing women / lamenters		Jer 9:16 Ezek 32:16		
מבשרת/תו messenger		Isa 40:9		Ps 68:12
פילגש concubine	Gen 22:24; 25:6; 35:22; 36:12		1 Chr 1:32; 2:46– 48; 3:9 2 Chr 11:21, etc.	Esth 2:14 Cant 6:8–9

[1] Here I have included all feminine references, even those that have the religious connotation of idolatry and not that of the sexual worker.

VI. FEMALE TERMS FOR RELIGIOUS AND POLITICAL OCCUPATIONS IN DTRH[2]

	Josh	Judg	1 Sam	2 Sam	1 Kgs	2 Kgs
שפטה judge		4:4				
נביאה prophetess		4:4				22:14
אבות necromancers?			28:3, 9			23:24
ידענים acquainted (with the unseen world)			28:3, 9			23:24
גבירה queen-mother					11:19–20; 15:13	10:13
מלכה queen					10:1–13	
אשה חכמה counselor, negotiator[3]		(5:29)		Chapters 14 and 20		

---

[2] Some offices, such as that of prophets/esses and judges should be considered religious and political occupations. To a certain extent, the same could be said of the queen mother; after all, many of them were banished because of their allegiance to Asherah. These are the occupations I have not dealt with in this book.

[3] The term has also the connotation of a skilled craftswoman, see Exod 35:25. This is apparently the meaning it has also in Jer 9:16 [Eng 9:17]; note there, however, its parallelism with the מקוננות, the singers of dirges or mourners.

VII. FEMALE TERMS FOR RELIGIOUS AND POLITICAL OCCUPATIONS ELSEWHERE

	Torah	Prophets	Chronicles, Ezra-Neh	Other Writings
נביאה prophetess	Exod 15:20	Isa 8:3	2 Chr 34:22 Neh 6:14	
אבות necromancers ?	Lev 19:31; 20:6	Isa 8:19; 19:3		
ידענים "acquainted (with secrets of unseen world)"	Lev 19:31; 20:6	Isa 8:19; 19:3		
קדשה/תו devotee	Gen 38:21–22 Deut 23:18	Hos 4:14		
שׁגל (queen) consort			Neh 2:6	Ps 45:9–10 Dan 5:2–3, 23

VIII. INVISIBLE WOMEN IN THE DTRH

	Josh	Judg	1 Sam	2 Sam	1 Kgs	2 Kgs
בני מחול member of the orchestral guild?					5:11	
חטבים/חטבי עצים wood hewer	9:21–27					
שאבות/שאבי מים water drawers	9:21–27		(9:11)			
בני/חבל־נביאים company of prophets			10:5–10			2:3–15; 4:1; 6:1
חפשי freed/client			17:25			
(ה)נצבות women on duty			4:19–22			
(הנשים) הצבאות women on duty			2:22			
ארגות weaving		(16:13)				23:7
משׂחקות[1] "merrymaker," singer?			18:6–7	6:20–23		

---

[1] The stem has several meanings; in these texts it refers to some form of (antiphonal) singing or dancing, or some other kind of response to the victors' homecoming. Also, see in chapter 5 the discussion on the use of רקד "to leap" in 2 Sam 6:20–23 and 1 Chr 15:29 as something of a performance or dance.

IX. INVISIBLE WOMEN ELSEWHERE

	Torah	Prophets	Chronicles, Ezra-Neh	Other Writings
נתינים donated ones			Ezra 2:43–70; 7:7, etc. Neh 3:26, 31, etc. 1 Chr 9:2	Qoh 2:8
בני מחול members of the orchestral guild?				Qoh 2:8
בני עבדי שלמה company of Solomon's servants			Ezra 2:55 // Neh 7:57	
חטבים/חטבי עצים wood hewer	Deut 19:5; 29:10	Jer 46:22 Ezek 39:10	2 Chr 2:29	
שאבות/שאבי מים water drawer	Gen 24:11 Deut 29:10 (Gen 24:13–43)			
חפשי freed / client	Exod 21:5 Deut 15:12–18	Jer 34:14		
הצבאות women on duty	Exod 38:8			
מנחמ(ים) comforter			1 Chr 19:3	
נגנים player of stringed instruments (lyres)		Isa 23:16		Ps 68:26
(טוה) spinning, that spun	Exod 35:20–29			
משחקות "merrymaker" singer?			1 Chr 15	

SOURCES CONSULTED

Achtemeier, Elizabeth. *Nahum-Malachi.* Interpretation. Atlanta: John Knox, 1986.

Ackroyd, Peter R. *Exile and Restoration.* OTL. London: SCM, 1968.

———. *The First Book of Samuel.* CBC on the NEB. Cambridge: Cambridge University Press, 1971.

———. "The Historical Literature." Pages 297–323 in *The Hebrew Bible and Its Modern Interpreters.* Edited by Douglas A. Knight and Gene M. Tucker. Philadelphia/Chico, Calif.: Fortress Press/ Scholars Press, 1985.

Adler Goodfriend, Elaine. "Could *keleb* in Deuteronomy 23:19 Actually Refer to a Canine?." Pages 381–97 in *Pomegranates and Golden Bells: Studies in Biblical, Jewish, and Near Eastern Ritual, Law, and Literature in Honor of Jacob Milgrom.* Edited by David P. Wright, David N. Freedman, and Avi Hurvitz. Winona Lake: Eisenbrauns, 1995.

Ahlström, Gösta. *The History of Ancient Palestine.* Minneapolis: Fortress, 1993.

Albenda, Pauline "Woman, Child, and Family: Their Imagery in Assyrian Art." Pages 17–21 in *La Femme dans le Proche-Orient Antique: XXXIIIe. Rencontre Assyriologique Internationale.* Edited by Jean-Marie Durand. Editions Recherche sur les Civilisations: Paris, 1987.

Albright, William "Notes on Early Hebrew and Aramaic Epigraphy." *JPOS* 6 (1926): 75–102.

———. "The Lachish Cosmetic Burner and Esther 2:12." Pages 361–68 in *Studies in the Book of Esther.* Edited by Carey A. Moore. New York: Ktav, 1982.

Alcock, Joan Pilsbury. *Food in the Ancient World.* Westport: Greenwood, 2006.

Alonso Schökel, Luis and Cecilia Carniti. *Salmos.* 2 vols. Estella: Verbo Divino, 1992.

Alt, Albrecht. "Menschen ohne Namen." Pages 198–213 in vol. 3 of *Kleine Schriften zur Geschichte des Volkes Israels.* Edited by Martin Noth. 3 vols. Munich: Beck, 1959 (1953–1963).

Alter, Robert. *The Art of Biblical Narrative.* New York: Basic Books, 1981.

Alvarez Barredo Miguel. *Los orígenes de la monarquía en Israel: Tradiciones literarias y enfoques teológicos de 1 Sam 8–12*. Murcia: Instituto Teológico de Murcia OFM/ Espigas, 2009.

Ames, Frank Ritchel. "The Meaning of War: Definitions for the Study of War in Ancient Israelite Literature." Pages 19–31 in *Writing and Reading War: Rhetoric, Gender, and Ethics in Biblical and Modern Contexts*. Edited by Brad E. Kelle and Frank Ritchel Ames. SBL Symposium Series. SBL: Atlanta, 2008.

Amico, Eleanor "The Status of Women at Ugarit." Ph.D. diss., University of Wisconsin-Madison, 1990.

Amit, Yairah. "The Jubilee Law—An Attempt at Instituting Social Justice." Pages 47–59 in *Justice and Righteousness*. Edited by Henning Graf Reventlow and Yair Hoffman. JSOTSup 137. Sheffield: Sheffield Academic Press, 1992.

————. "Literature in the Service of Politics: Studies in Judges 19–21." Pages 28–40 in *Politics and Theopolitics in the Bible and Postbiblical Literature*. Edited by H. Reventlow, Y. Hoffman, and B. Uffenheimer. Sheffield: JSOT Press, 1994.

Andersen, Francis I. and David N. Freedman. *Amos*. AB. Garden City: Doubleday, 1989.

————. *Hosea*. AB. Garden City: Doubleday, 1980.

Anderson, Cheryl B. *Women, Ideology and Violence: Critical Theory and the Construction of Gender in the Book of the Covenant and the Deuteronomic Law*. New York: T&T Clark, 2004.

Archi, Alfonso. "The Role of Women in the Society of Ebla." Pages 1–9 in *Sex and Gender in the Ancient Near East: Proceedings of the 47th Rencontre Assyriologique Internationale, Helsinki, July 2–6, 2001*. Edited by Simo Parpola and R. M. Whiting. Helsinki: ©Neo-Assyrian Text Corpus Project, Institute for Asian and African Studies, University of Helsinki (2002).

Arensberg, C. and S. Kimball. "The Small Farm Family in Rural Ireland." Pages 19–42 in *Sociology of the Family: Selected Readings*. Edited by Michael Anderson. Penguin Modern Sociology Readings. Middlesex, England: Penguin, 1971. Reprinted from *A Reader from Family and Community in Ireland*. 2nd edition, 59–60, 45–56, 63–147. Harvard: Harvard University Press, 1968 (1940).

Arlandson, James M. *Women, Class, and Society in Early Christianity: Models from Luke-Acts*. Peabody, Mass.: Hendrickson, 1997.

Armijo Navarro-Reverter, Teresa. "La vida de las mujeres egipcias durante la Dinastía XVIII." *Boletín de la Asociación Española de Orientalistas* XXXVIII (2002) 113–36. Cited 8 September 2011. Online: http://www.cervantesvirtual.com/obra/la-vida-de-las-mujeres-egipcias-durante-la-dinasta-xviii-0/.

Asher-Greve, Julia M. "Decisive Sex, Essential Gender." Pages 11–26 in *Sex and Gender in the Ancient Near East: Proceedings of the 47th Rencontre Assyriologique Internationale, Helsinki, July 2–6, 2001*. Edited by Simo Parpola and R. M. Whiting. Helsinki: ©Neo-Assyrian Text Corpus Project, Institute for Asian and African Studies, University of Helsinki, 2002.

————"Feminist Research and Mesopotamia." Pages 218–37 in *A Feminist Companion to Reading the Bible: Approaches, Methods and Strategies*. Edited by Athalya Brenner and Carol Fontaine. Sheffield: Sheffield Academic Press, 1997.

————. *Frauen in altsumerischer Zeit*. Bibliotheca Mesopotamica 18. Malibu: Undena, 1985.

————"The Oldest Female Oneiromancer." Pages 27–32 in *La Femme dans le Proche-Orient Antique: XXXIIIe. Rencontre Assyriologique Internationale*. Edited by Jean-Marie Durand. Editions Recherche sur les Civilisations: Paris, 1987. Ashley, Timothy. *The Book of Numbers*. NICOT. Grand Rapids: Eerdmans, 1993.

Assante, Julia. "Sex, Magic, and the Liminal Body in the Erotic Art and Texts of the Old Babylonian Period." Pages 27–52 in *Sex and Gender in the Ancient Near East: Proceedings of the 47th Rencontre Assyriologique Internationale, Helsinki, July 2–6, 2001*. Edited by Simo Parpola and R. M. Whiting. Helsinki: ©Neo-Assyrian Text Corpus Project, Institute for Asian and African Studies, University of Helsinki, 2002.

————. "The Erotic Reliefs of Ancient Mesopotamia." Ph.D. diss., Columbia University, 2000.

————. "What Makes a 'Prostitute' a Prostitute? Modern Definitions and Ancient Meanings." *Historiae* 4 (2007): 117–32.

Avigad, Nahman. "A Seal of a Slave-Wife (Amah)." *PEQ* 78 (1946), 125–32.

————. "The Epitaph of a Royal Steward from Siloam Village." *IEJ* 3 (1953): 137–52.

Azzoni, Annalisa. "Women and Property in Persian Egypt and Mesopotamia." In *Women and Property in Ancient Near Eastern and Mediterranean Societies:Conference Proceedings, Center for Hellenistic Studies, Harvard University*. Edited by Deborah Lyons Deborah and Raymond Westbrook. ©2005, Center for Hellenic Studies, Trustees for Harvard University. Cited 25 May November 2010. No pages. Online: http://chs.harvard.edu/wb/1/wo/WnSQvuI0ROgY8y7nVB1hqw/0.1.

Baadsgaard, Aubrey. "A Taste of Women's Sociality: Cooking as Cooperative Labor in Iron Age Syro-Palestine." Pages 13–44 in *The World of Women in the Ancient and Classical Near East*. Edited by Beth Alpert Nakhai. Newcastle upon Tyne: Cambridge Scholars Publishing, 2008.

Bailey, Randall C. *David in Love and War: The Pursuit of Power in 2 Samuel 10–12*. JSOTSup 75. Sheffield: Sheffield Academic Press, 1990.

Bakir, Abd El-Mohsen. *Slavery in Pharaonic Egypt*. Cairo: Institut Français d'Archéologie Orientale, 1952.

Bakon, Shimon. "Samson: A Tragedy in Three Acts." *JBQ* 35 (2007): 34–40.

Bal, Mieke. *Death and Dissymmetry: The Politics of Coherence in the Book of Judges*. Chicago: University of Chicago Press, 1988.

Baltzer, K. "Liberation from Debt Slavery after the Exile in Second Isaiah and Nehemiah." Pages 477–84 in *Ancient Israelite Religion: Essays in Honor of Frank Moore Cross*. Edited by Patrick D. Miller, Jr., Paul D. Hanson, and S. Dean McBride. Philadelphia: Fortress, 1987.

Bamberger, B. J. "*Qetanah, Naʿarah, Bogereth*." *HUCA* 32 (1961): 281–94.

Bar, Shaul."The Oak of Weeping." *Bib* 91 (2010): 259–74.

Barr, James. "Ancient Biblical Laws and Modern Human Rights." Pages 21–33 in *Justice and the Holy: Essays in Honor of Walter Harrelson*. Edited by Douglas A. Knight and Peter J. Paris. Atlanta: Scholars Press, 1989.

————. *The Semantics of Biblical Language*. Oxford: Oxford University Press, 1961.

Barstad, Hans M. "After the 'Myth of the Empty Land': Major Challenges in the Study of Neo-Babylonian Judah." Pages 1–20 in *Judah and the Judeans in the neo-Babylonian Period*. Edited by Oded Lipschits and Joseph Blenkinsopp. Winona Lake: Eisenbrauns 2003.

———. "The Old Testament Personal Name Rahab: An Onomastic Note." *Svensk Exegetisk Årsbok* 54 (1989): 43–49.

———. *The Religious Polemics of Amos: Studies in the Preaching of Am. 2:7b–8; 4:1–13; 5:1–27; 6: 4–7; 8:14*. VTSup 34. Leiden: Brill, 1984.

Bass, Dorothy C. "Women's Studies and Biblical Studies: An Historical Perspective." *JSOT* 22 (1982): 6–12.

Batto, Bernard F. "Land Tenure and Women at Mari." *JESHO* 23 (1980): 209–39.

———. *Studies on Women at Mari*. Baltimore and London: The Johns Hopkins University Press, 1974.

Baumann, Gerlinde. *Die Weisheitsgestalt in Proverbien 1–9: traditionsgeschichtliche und theologische Studien*. Tübingen: J. C. B. Mohr, 1996.

Baumann, Gerlinde and Louise Schottroff. "Prostitution." Pages 450–54 in *Sozialgeschichtliches Wörterbuch zur Bibel*. Edited by Frank Crüsemann, Kristian Hungar, Claudia Janssen, Rainer Kessler, and Luise Schottroff. Gütersloh: Gütersloher Verlagshaus, 2009.

Bechtel, Lyn M. "Shame as a Sanction of Social Control in Biblical Israel: Judicial, Political, and Social Shaming." *JSOT* 49 (1991): 47–76.

———. "The Perception of Shame within the Divine-Human Relationship in Biblical Israel." Pages 79–92 in *Uncovering Ancient Stones: Essays in Memory of H. Neil Richardson*. Edited by Lewis M. Hofpe. Winona Lake: Eisenbrauns, 1994.

———. "What if Dinah is not Raped?" *JSOT* 62 (1994): 19–36.

Becking, Bob and Meindert Dijkstra, eds. *On Reading Prophetic Texts: Gender-Specific and Related Studies in Memory of Fokkelien van Dijk-Hemmes*. Leiden: Brill, 1996.

Beckman, Gary. "Hittite Literature." Pages 215–54 in *From an Antique Land: An Introduction to Ancient Near Eastern Literature*. Edited by Carl S. Ehrlich. Lanham: Rowman & Littlefield, 2009.

Beek, Gus W. van. "Frankincense and Myrrh." Page 126 in *Biblical Archaeological Reader, II*. Edited by David N. Freedman and Edward Campbell, Jr. 2 vols. Garden City: Doubleday Anchor, 1964.

Bellis, Alice Ogden. *Helpmates, Harlots, and Heroes: Women's Stories in the Hebrew Bible*. Louisville: Westminster John Knox Press, 1994.

Benjamin, Don C. *Deuteronomy and City Life*. Lanham, Md.: University Press of America, 1983.

———. "Israel's God: Mother and Midwife." *BTB* 19 (1989): 115–20.

Berg, Sandra Beth. *The Book of Esther: Motifs, Theme, and Structure*. SBLDS 44. Missoula: SBL, 1979.

Berlin, Adele. "Characterization in Biblical Narrative: David's Wives." Pages 91–93 in *Telling Queen Michal's Story: An Experiment in Comparative Interpretation*. Edited by David J. A. Clines and Tamara Cohn Eskenazi. JSOTSup 119. Sheffield: Sheffield Academic Press, 1991.

———. *Poetics and Interpretation of Biblical Narrative*. Winona Lake: Eisenbrauns, 1994.

Bernstein, Henry and Terence J. Byres. "From Peasant Studies to Agrarian Change." *Journal of Agrarian Change* 1 (2001): 1–56.

Bertholet, Alfred. *Die Stellung der Israeliten und der Juden zu den Fremden.* Freiburg: Moor, 1896.

Beuken, W. A. M. "No Wise King without a Wise Woman (I Kings iii 16–28)." *OTS* 25 (1989): 1–10.

Binger, Tilde. *Asherah: Goddesses in Ugarit, Israel and the Old Testament.* JSOTSup 232. Sheffield: Sheffield Academic Press, 1997.

Birch, Bruce C. *Let Justice Roll Down.* Louisville: Westminster John Knox, 1992.

Bird, Phyllis A. "Images of Women in the Old Testament." Pages 13–51 in *Missing Persons and Mistaken Identities: Women and Gender in Ancient Israel,* Minneapolis: Fortress, 1997. Repr. from pages 41–88 in *Religion and Sexism: Images of Woman in the Jewish and Christian Traditions.* Edited by Rosemary Radford Ruether. New York: Simon & Schuster, 1974.

———. "Israelite Religion and the Faith of Israel's Daughters." Pages 103–20 in *Missing Persons and Mistaken Identities: Women and Gender in Ancient Israel.* Minneapolis: Fortress, 1997. Repr. from pages 97–108, 311–17 in *The Bible and the Politics of Exegesis: Essays in Honour of Norman K. Gottwald on His Sixty-Fifth Birthday.* Edited by David Jobling, Peggy L. Day, and Gerald T. Sheppard. Cleveland: Pilgrim, 1991.

———. "'Male and Female He Created Them': Gen 1:27b in the Context of the Priestly Account of Creation." Pages 123–54 in *Missing Persons and Mistaken Identities: Women and Gender in Ancient Israel.* Minneapolis: Fortress, 1997.. Repr. from *HTR* 74 (1981): 129–59.

———. "Poor Man or Poor Woman: Gendering the Poor in Prophetic Texts." Pages 67–78 in *Missing Persons and Mistaken Identities: Women and Gender in Ancient Israel.* Minneapolis: Fortress, 1997. Repr. from pages 37–51 in *On Reading Prophetic Texts: Gender-Specific and Related Studies in Memory of Fokkelien van Dijk-Hemmes.* Edited by Bob Becking and Meindert Dijkstra. Leiden: Brill, 1996.

———"Prostitution in the Social World and the Religious Rhetoric of Ancient Israel." Pages 40–58 in *Prostitutes and Courtesans in the Ancient World.* Edited by Christopher A. Faraone and Laura K. McClure. Madison: University of Wisconsin Press, 2006.

———. Review of Karen Engelken, *Frauen im Alten Israel: Eine begriffsgeschichtliche und sozialrechtliche Studie zur Stellung der Frau im Alten Testament. JBL* 112 (1993): 319–21.

———. "The End of the Male Cult Prostitute: A Literary-Historical and Sociological Analysis of Hebrew *qādēš-qĕdēšîm.*" Pages 37–80 in *Congress Volume, Cambridge, 1995.* Edited by John Emerton. VTSup. 66. Leiden: Brill, 1997.

———. "The Harlot as Heroine: Narrative Art and Social Presupposition in Three Old Testament Texts." Pages 197–218 in *Missing Persons and Mistaken Identities: Women and Gender in Ancient Israel,* Minneapolis: Fortress, 1997. Repr. from pages 119–39 in *Narrative Research on the Hebrew Bible.* Edited by Miri Amihai, George Coats, and Anne Solomon. *Semeia* 46. Chico: Scholars Press, 1989.

————. "The Place of Women in the Israelite Cultus." Pages 81–102 in *Missing Persons and Mistaken Identities: Women and Gender in Ancient Israel*, Minneapolis: Fortress, 1997. Repr. from pages 397–419 in *Ancient Israelite Religion: Essays in Honor of Frank Moore Cross*. Edited by Patrick Miller, Jr., Paul Hanson and S. Dean McBride. Philadelphia: Fortress, 1987.

————. "'To Play the Harlot': An Inquiry into an Old Testament Metaphor." Pages 219–36 in *Missing Persons and Mistaken Identities: Women and Gender in Ancient Israel*, Minneapolis: Fortress, 1997. Repr. from pages 75–94 in *Gender and Difference in Ancient Israel*. Edited by Peggy L. Day. Minneapolis: Fortress, 1989.

————. "Women (Old Testament)." Pages 52–66 in *Missing Persons and Mistaken Identities: Women and Gender in Ancient Israel*. Minneapolis: Fortress, 1997. Repr. from pages 951–57 in *Anchor Bible Dictionary*. Edited by David Noel Freedman. 6 vol. New York: Doubleday, 1992.

Black, J. A., Cunningham, et al. *Electronic Text Corpus of Sumerian Literature*. Oxford: 1998. Cited 8 September 2011. Online: http://etcsl.orinst.ox.ac.uk/.

Blackman, Aylward M. "On the Position of Women in the Ancient Egyptian Hierarchy." *JEA* 7 (1921): 8–30.

Bledstein, Adrien. "Was *Habbiryâ* A Healing Ritual Performed by a Woman in King David's House?" *BR* 37 (1992): 15–31.

Blenkinsopp, Joseph. *Ezekiel*. Interpretation. Louisville: John Knox, 1990.

————. *Ezra-Nehemiah*. OTL. Philadelphia: Westminster, 1988.

————. "The Family in First Temple Israel." Pages 48–103 in *Families in Ancient Israel*. Edited by Leo Perdue, et al. Louisville: Westminster John Knox, 1997.

————. "The Household in Ancient Israel and Early Judaism." Pages 169–85 in *Blackwell Companion to the Hebrew Bible*. Edited by Leo G. Perdue. Molden: Blackwell, 2001.

————. "The Social Context of the 'Outsider Woman' in Proverbs 1–9." *Bib* 72 (1991): 457–73.

Block, Daniel. *The Book of Ezekiel Chapters 1–24*. NICOT. Grand Rapids: Eerdmans, 1997.

Bodner, Keith. *1 Samuel: A Narrative Commentary*. Sheffield: Sheffield Phoenix Press, 2009.

Boecker, Hans Jochen. *Law and the Administration of Justice in the Old Testament and Ancient East*. Minneapolis: Augsburg, 1980.

Boer, P. A. H. de. "Research into the Text of 1 Samuel xviii–xxxi." *OTS* 6 (1949): 1–100.

Boer, Roland. "The Sacred Economy of Ancient 'Israel.'" *SJOT* 21 (2007): 29–48.

Boling, Robert. *Judges*. AB. Garden City, N.Y.: Doubleday, 1975.

Borowski, Oded. "Animals in the Religions of Syria-Palestine." Pages 405–24 in *A History of the Animal World in the Ancient Near East*. Edited by Billie Jean Collins. Leiden: Brill, 2002.

————. *Daily Life in Biblical Times*. Atlanta: SBL, 2003.

Botterweck, G. Johannes, Helmer Ringgren, and Heinz-Josef Fabry, eds. *Theological Dictionary of the Old Testament*. 9 vols. John T. Willis, David E. Green, and Douglas W. Scott, translators. Grand Rapids: Eerdmans.

Bowen, Nancy R. "The Daughters of Your People: Female Prophets in Ezekiel 13:17–23." *JBL* 118 (1999): 417–33.

Bowman, Glenn Walker. "'Migrant Labour': Constructing Homeland in the Exilic Imagination." *Anthropological Theory* 2 (2002): 447–68. Cited 7 September 2011. Online: http://kar.kent.ac.uk/152/1/Migrant_Labour,_Anthropological_Theory.pdf.

Bowman, Richard G. "The Fortune of King David/The Fate of Queen Michal: A Literary Critical Analysis of 2 Samuel 1-8." Pages 97–120 in *Telling Queen Michal's Story: An Experiment in Comparative Interpretation*. Edited by David J. A. Clines and Tamara Cohn Eskenazi. JSOTSup 119. Sheffield: Sheffield Academic Press, 1991.

Bradley, Keith. *Slavery and Society at Rome*. Cambridge: Cambridge University Press, 1994.

———. *Slaves and Masters in the Roman Empire: A Study in Social Control*. New York: Oxford University Press, 1987.

Braulik, Georg. "Das Deuteronomium und die Menschenrechte." *TQ* 166 (1986): 8–24.

———. "The Sequence of the Laws in Deuteronomy 12–26 and in the Decalogue." Pages 313–35 in *A Song of Power and the Power of Song*. Edited by Duane Christensen. Winona Lake: Eisenbrauns, 1993.

Brayford, Susan Ann. "To Shame or Not to Shame: Sexuality in the Mediterranean Diaspora." *Semeia* 87 (1999): 163–76.

Brekelmans, C. "Deuteronomy 5: Its Place and Function." Pages 164–73 in *Das Deuteronomium: Entstehung, Gestalt und Botschaft*. Edited by Norbert Lohfink. BETL 68. Leuven: Leuven University Press, 1985.

———. "Wisdom Influence in Deuteronomy." Pages 123–34 in *A Song of Power and the Power of Song*. Edited by Duane L. Christensen. Winona Lake: Eisenbrauns, 1993.

Brenner, Athalya. "Aromatics and Perfumes in the Song of Songs." *JSOT* 25 (1983): 75–81.

———. "Naomi and Ruth." Pages 70–84 in *A Feminist Companion to Ruth*. Edited by Athalya Brenner. Sheffield: Sheffield Academic Press, 1993.

———. *The Intercourse of Knowledge: On Gendering Desire and "Sexuality" in the Hebrew Bible*. Leiden: Brill, 1997.

———. *The Israelite Woman. Social Role and Literary Type in Biblical Narrative*. Sheffield: JSOT Press, 1985.

———, ed. *A Feminist Companion to the Song of Songs*. Sheffield: Sheffield Academic Press, 1993.

———. *A Feminist Companion to Exodus to Deuteronomy*. Sheffield: Sheffield Academic Press, 1994.

———. *A Feminist Companion to Judges*. Sheffield: Sheffield Academic Press, 1993.

———. *A Feminist Companion to Ruth*. Sheffield: Sheffield Academic Press, 1993.

———. *A Feminist Companion to Samuel to Kings*. Sheffield: Sheffield Academic Press, 1994.

———. *A Feminist Companion to the Latter Prophets*. Sheffield: Sheffield Academic Press, 1995.

Brenner, Athalya and Fokkelien van Dijk-Hemmes. *On Gendering Texts: Female and Male Voices in the Hebrew Bible*. Leiden: Brill, 1993.

Brenner, Athalya and Carol Fontaine, eds. *A Feminist Companion to Reading the Bible: Approaches, Methods and Strategies*. Sheffield: Sheffield Academic Press, 1997.

Brettler, Marc. "The Composition of 1 Samuel 1–2." *JBL* 116 (1997): 601–12.

Bridge, Edward J. "Female Slave vs Female Slave: אָמָהand שִׁפְחָה in the HB." *JHS* 12 article 2 (2012). No pages. Cited 22 January 2013. Online: http://ejournals.library .ualberta.ca/index.php/jhs/article/view/16440/13145.

———. "Self-Abasement as an Expression of Thanks in the Hebrew Bible." *Bib* 92 (2011): 255–73. Cited 22 January 2013. Online: http://www.bsw .org/Biblica/Index-By-Authors/Self-Abasement-As-An-Expression-Of-Thanks-In-The-Hebrew-Bible/470/.

Briggs, Sheila. "The Deceit of the Sublime: An Investigation into the Origins of Ideological Criticism of the Bible in Early Nineteenth-Century German Biblical Studies." Pages 1–23 in *Ideological Criticism of the Bible*. Edited by David Jobling and Tina Pippin. *Semeia* 59. Atlanta: Scholars Press, 1992.

Brinkman, John A. "A Preliminary Catalogue of Written Sources for a Political History of Babylonia: 1160–722 B. C." *JCS* 15 (1961): 83–109.

———. "Sex, Age and Physical Condition Designations for Servile Laborers in the Middle Babylonian Period." Pages 1–8 in *Zikir sumim: Assyriological Studies Presented to F. R. Kraus on the Occasion of His Seventieth Birthday*. Edited by G. van Driel, Th. J. H. Krispijn, M. Stol, and K. R. Veenhof. Leiden: Brill, 1982.

Britt, Brian. "Death, Social Conflict, and The Barley Harvest in the Hebrew Bible." *JHS* 5, art. 14 (2005). No pages. Cited 2 January 2011. Online: http://www.arts.ualberta .ca/JHS/Articles/article_45.pdf.

Broida, Marian. "Closure in Samson." *JHS* 10, article 2 (2010). No pages. Cited 22 January 2011. Online: http://www.arts.ualberta.ca/JHS/jhs-article.html.

Brueggemann, Walter. *1 and 2 Samuel*. Louisville: John Knox Press, 1990.

———. "2 Samuel 6." Pages 121–3 in *Telling Queen Michal's Story: An Experiment in Comparative Interpretation*. Edited by David J. A. Clines and Tamara Cohn Eskenazi. JSOTSup 119. Sheffield: Sheffield Academic Press, 1991.

———. *A Commentary on Jeremiah: Exile and Homecoming*. Grand Rapids: Eerdmans, 1998.

———. *A Social Reading of the Old Testament: Prophetic Approaches to Israel's Communal Life*. Edited by Patrick D. Miller, Jr. Minneapolis: Fortress, 1994.

———. *Isaiah 1–39*. Louisville: Westminster John Knox, 1998.

———. "Life and Death in Tenth Century Israel (Gen 37, 39–48, 50; 2 Sam 9–20, 1 Kings 1–2)." *JAAR* 40 (1972): 96–109.

———. "On Trust and Freedom: A Study of Faith in the Succession Narrative (2 Sam 9–20, 1 Kings 1–2)." *Int* 26 (1972): 3–19.

Brun, Jean-Pierre. "The Production of Perfumes in Antiquity; The Cases of Delos and Paestum." *AJA* 104 (2000): 277–308.

Budd, Philip J. *Leviticus*. NCBC. London/Grand Rapids: Pickering/Eerdmans, 1996.

Burgh, Theodore W. "'Who's the Man?' Sex and Gender in Iron Age Musical Performance." *NEA* 67 (2004): 128–36.

Burke, Aaron Alexander. "The Architecture of Defense: Fortified Settlements of the Levant during the Middle Bronze Age." Ph.D. diss., The University of Chicago, 2004.

Butting, Klara. *Die Buchstaben werden sich noch wundern: Innerbiblische Kritik als Wegweisung feministischer Hermeneutik*. Berlin: Alektor, 1993.

Callaway, Mary. *Sing, O Barren One: A Study in Comparative Midrash.* SBLDS 91. Atlanta: Scholars Press, 1986.

Cameron, Averil and Amelie Kuhrt, eds. *Images of Women in Antiquity.* Detroit: Wayne State University Press, 1983.

Camp, Claudia V. "1 and 2 Kings." Pages 96–109 in *The Women's Bible Commentary.* Edited by Carol Newsom and Sharon Ringe. Louisville: Westminster John Knox, 1992.

——. "The Wise Women of 2 Samuel: A Role Model for Women in Early Israel?" *CBQ* 43 (1981): 14–29.

——. "What's So Strange About the Strange Woman?" Pages 17–31 in *The Bible and the Politics of Exegesis: Essays in Honor of Norman K. Gottwald on the Occasion of His Sixty-Fifth Birthday.* Edited by David Jobling, Peggy L. Day, and Gerald T. Sheppard. Cleveland: Pilgrim, 1991.

——. *Wisdom and the Feminine in the Book of Proverbs.* Decatur, Ga.: Almond, 1985.

Campbell, Anthony F. *Of Prophets and Kings: A Late Ninth-Century Document (1 Samuel 1–2 Kings 10).* CBQMS. Washington: Catholic Biblical Association, 1986.

——. *The Ark Narrative (1 Sam 4–6; 2 Sam 6): A Form-Critical and Traditio-Historical Study.* SBLDS 16. Missoula, Mont.: SBL, 1975.

Campbell, Edward F., Jr. *Ruth: A New Translation with Introduction, Notes, and Commentary.* AB. New York: Doubleday, 1975.

Campbell, K. M. "Rahab's Covenant. A Short Note on Joshua II 9–21." *VT* 22 (1972): 243–44.

Carasik, Michael. "Why the Overseer Was Embarrased." *ZAW* 107 (1995): 493–94.

Cardellini, Innocenzo. *Die biblischen "Sklaven"-Gesetze im Lichte des keilschriftlichen Sklavenrechts.* BBB 50. Bonn 1981.

Cardoso Pereira, Nancy. "La profecía y lo cotidiano: La mujer y el niño en el ciclo del profeta Eliseo." *RIBLA* 14 (1993): 7–21. Cited 4 September 2012. Online: http://www.ribla.org/.

Carlson, Rolf A. *David, the Chosen King: A Traditio-Historical Approach to the Second Book of Samuel.* Stockholm: Almqvist & Wiksell, 1964.

Carney, T. F. *The Shape of the Past: Models and Antiquity.* Lawrence, Kan.: Coronado, 1975.

Carroll, Robert P. *Jeremiah: A Commentary.* OTL. London: SCM, 1986.

Carter, Charles. "Social Scientific Approaches." Pages 36–57 in *The Blackwell Companion to the Hebrew Bible.* Edited by Leo G. Perdue. Molden: Blackwell, 2001.

Cassuto, Deborah. "Bringing the Artifact Home: A Social Interpretation of Loom Weights in Context." Pages 63–77 in *The World of Women in the Ancient and Classical Near East.* Edited by Beth Alpert Nakhai. Newcastle upon Tyne: Cambridge Scholars Publishing, 2008.

Chance, John K. "The Anthropology of Honor and Shame: Culture, Values, and Practice." Pages 139–51 in *Honor and Shame in the World of the Bible.* Edited by Victor H. Matthews and Don C. Benjamin. *Semeia* 68. Atlanta: Scholars Press, 1996.

Chaney, Marvin L. "Ancient Palestinian Peasant Movements and the Formation of Premonarchic Israel." Pages 39–90 in *Palestine in Transition: the Emergence of Ancient Israel.* Edited by David. N. Freedman and D. F. Graf. SWBA 2. Sheffield: Almond, 1983.

———. "Debt Easement in Israelite History and Tradition." Pages 127–39 in *The Bible and the Politics of Exegesis: Essays in Honor of Norman K. Gottwald on the Occasion of His Sixty-Fifth Birthday.* Edited by David Jobling, Peggy L. Day, and Gerald T. Sheppard. Cleveland: Pilgrim, 1991.

———. "Systemic Study of the Israelite Monarchy." Pages 53–76 in *Social Scientific Criticism of the Hebrew Bible and Its Social World: The Israelite Monarchy.* Edited by Norman K. Gottwald. *Semeia*37. Atlanta: Scholars Press, 1986.

Chapman, Cynthia R. "'Oh that you were like a brother to me, one who had nursed at my mother's breasts.' Breast Milk as a Kinship-Forging Substance," *JHS* 12 article 7(2012). No pages. Cited: 2 January 2013. Online: http://epe.lac-bac.gc.ca/100/201/300/journal_hebrew/pdf/2012/article_169.pdf.

Charpin, Dominique. "L'Andurârum à Mari." Pages 253–70 in *La Femme dans le Proche-Orient Antique: XXXIIIe. Rencontre Assyriologique Internationale.* Edited by Jean-Marie Durand. Editions Recherche sur les Civilisations: Paris, 1987.

Charvát, Petr. "Social Configurations in Early Dynastic Babylonia (*c.* 2500–2334 BC)." Pages 251–64 in *The Babylonian World.* Edited by Gwendolyn Leick. New York: Routledge, 2007.

Chirichigno, Gregory. *Debt-Slavery in Israel and the Ancient Near East.* JSOTSup 141. Sheffield: JSOT Press, 1993.

Christensen, Duane L. "Form and Structure in Deuteronomy 1–11." Pages 135–44 in *Das Deuteronomium: Entstehung, Gestalt und Botschaft.* Edited by Norbert Lohfink. BETL 68. Leuven: Leuven University Press, 1985.Civil, Miguel. "Modern Brewers Recreate Ancient Beer." *The Oriental Institute News and Notes* 132 (1991), rev. Feb 7, 2007. No pages. Cited 1 July 2011. Online: http://oi.uchicago.edu/research/pubs/nn/fal91_civil.html.

———, ed. *A Song of Power and the Power of Song: Essays on the Book of Deuteronomy.* Winona Lake: Eisenbrauns, 1993.

Clark, D. "Sex-Related Imagery in the Prophets." *BT* 33 (1982): 409–13.

Clements, Ronald E. *Deuteronomy.* OTG. Sheffield: JSOT Press, 1989.

———. *Ezekiel.* WBC. Louisville: Westminster John Knox, 1996.

———. "Solomon and the Origins of Wisdom in Israel." *PRSt* 15 (1988): 23–35.

———, ed. *The World of Ancient Israel: Sociological, Anthropological and Political Perspectives.* Cambridge: Cambridge University Press, 1989.

Clifford, Richard. *Deuteronomy, with an Excursus on Covenant and Law.* Wilmington: Glazier, 1989.

———. *Proverbs: A Commentary.* Norwich/Louisville: SCM/Westminster John Knox, 1999. Clines, David J. A. *Ezra, Nehemiah, Esther.* NCBC. Grand Rapids: Eerdmans; London: Marshall, Morgan & Scott, 1984.

———. *The Esther Scroll: The Story of the Story.* JSOTSup30. Sheffield: JSOT Press, 1984.

Clifford, Richard and J. Cheryl Exum. "The New Literary Criticism." Pages 11–25 in *The New Literary Criticism and the Hebrew Bible*. Edited by David J. A. Clines and J. Cheryl Exum. Valley Forge: Trinity Press International, 1993.

Coates, George W. "Theology of the Hebrew Bible." Pages 239–62 in *The Hebrew Bible and Its Modern Interpreters*. Edited by Douglas A. Knight and Gene M. Tucker. Philadelphia/Chico: Fortress/ Scholars Press, 1985.

Cogan, Mordechai and Hayim Tadmor. *II Kings*. AB. Garden City: Doubleday 1988.

Cohen, A., ed. *Joshua and Judges: Hebrew Text and English Translation with Introductions and Commentary*. Soncino Books of the Bible. Rev. ed. London: Soncino, 1982.

Cole, Sally. *Women of the Praia: Work and Lives in a Portuguese Coastal Community*. Princeton: Princeton University Press, 1991.

Collins, Billie Jean. "Animals in the Religions of Ancient Anatolia." Pages 309–34 in *A History of the Animal World in the Ancient Near East*. Edited by Billie Jean Collins. Leiden: Brill, 2002.

Collins, John J. "Marriage, Divorce, and Family in Second Temple Judaism." Pages 104–62 in *Families in Ancient Israel*. Edited by Leo G. Perdue, et al. Louisville: Westminster John Knox, 1997.

Conroy, Charles. "A Literary Analysis of 1 Kings 1:41–53, with Methodological Reflections." Pages 54–66 in *Congress Volume: Salamanca, 1983*. Edited by John Emerton. VTSup 36. Leiden: Brill, 1983.

————. "Methodological Reflections on Recent Studies of the Naaman Pericope (2 Kings 5): Some Backgrounds to Luke 4:27." Pages 32–47 in *Luke and Acts*. Edited by Gerald O'Collins, Emilio Rasco, Gilberto Marconi, and Matthew J. O'Connell. New York: Paulist Press, 1993.

Coote, Robert and Keith Whitelam. "The Emergence of Israel: Social Transformation and State Formation Following the Decline in Late Bronze Age Trade." Pages 107–47 in *Social Scientific Criticism of the Hebrew Bible and Its Social World: The Israelite Monarchy*. Edited by Norman K. Gottwald. *Semeia* 37. Atlanta: Scholars Press, 1986.

————, eds. *The Emergence of Early Israel in Historical Perspective*. SWBA 5. Sheffield: Almond Press, 1987.

Craigie, Peter. "Deuteronomy and Ugaritic Studies." Pages 109–22 in *A Song of Power and the Power of Song*. Edited by Duane L Christensen. Winona Lake: Eisenbrauns, 1993.

————. *Ezekiel*. Philadelphia: Westminster, 1983.

Croatto, José Severino. *Isaías 1–39*. Comentario Bíblico Ecuménico. Buenos Aires: La Aurora, 1989.

————. *Isaías: la palabra profética y su relectura hermenéutica. II: 40–55: La liberación es posible*. Buenos Aires: Lumen 1994.

————. "La deuda en la reforma social de Nehemías (Un estudio de Nehemías 5:1–19)." *RIBLA* 5–6 (1990): 27–37. Cited 4 September 2012. Online: http://www.ribla.org/.

Cronauer, Patrick T., O.S.B., *The Stories about Naboth the Jezreelite: A Source, Composition, and Redaction Investigation of 1 Kings 21 and Passages in 2 Kings 9*. T&T Clark: New York, 2005.

Crook, Zeba A. "Honor, Shame, and Social Status Revisited." *JBL* 128 (2009): 591–611.

Cross, Frank Moore. *Canaanite Myth and Hebrew Epic: Essays in the History of the Religion of Israel*. Cambridge: Harvard University Press, 1973.

Crüsemann, Frank. *Der Widerstand gegen das Königtum: die anti-Königliche Texte des Alten Testament und der Kampf um den frühen israelitischen Staat*. WMANT 49. Neukirchen-Vluyn: Neukirchener Verlag, 1978.

———. *The Torah*. Minneapolis: Fortress, 1996.

———. "Zwei alttestamentliche Witze: I Sam 21 11–15 und II Sam 6 16.20–23 als Beispiele einer biblischen Gattung." *ZAW* 92 (1980): 215–27.

Cutler, B. (Collaboration of J. Macdonald). "Identification of the *Naʿar* in the Ugaritic Texts." *UF* 8 (1976): 27–36.

Cutler, B. and John Macdonald. "The Unique Ugaritic Text UT 113 and the Question of 'Guilds.'" *UF* 9 (1977): 13–30.

Dalley, Stephanie. *Mari and Karana: Two Old Babylonian Cities*. Piscataway, N.J.: Gorgias, 2002[2] (1984).

Dandamayev, Muhammad A. "Free Hired Labor in Babylonia during the Sixth through Fourth Centuries BC." Pages 271–9 in *Labor in the Ancient Near East*. Edited by Marvin A. Powell. AOS 68. New Haven: American Oriental Society, 1987.

———. "Neo-Babylonian and Achaemenid State Administration in Mesopotamia." Pages 373–98 in *Judah and the Judeans in the Persian Period*. Edited by Oded Lipschits and Manfred Oeming. Winona Lake: Eisenbrauns, 2006.

———. *Slavery in Babylonia from Nabopolassar to Alexander the Great (626–331 BC)*. Rev. ed. DeKalb: Northern Illinois University Press, 1984.

———. "State and Temple in Babylonia in the First Millennium B.C." Pages 589–96 in volume 2 of *State and Temple Economy*. Edited by Edward Lipiński. 2 volumes. OLA 5–6. Leuven: Departement Oriëntalistiek, 1979.

———. "The Late Babylonian Ambaru." *JANES* 16–17 (1984–1985): 39–40.

Darr, Katheryn Pfisterer. "Asking at Abel: A Wise Woman's Proverb Performance in 2 Samuel 20." Pages 102–21 in *Women of the Hebrew Bible and Their Afterlives*. Edited by Peter S. Hawkins and Lesleigh Cushing Stahlberg. Volume 1 of *From the Margins*. Sheffield: Sheffield Phoenix, 2009.

———. "Two Unifying Female Images in the Book of Isaiah." Pages 17–30 in *Uncovering Ancient Stones: Essays in Memory of H. Neil Richardson*. Edited by Lewis M. Hofpe. Winona Lake: Eisenbrauns, 1994.

Daube, David. *Studies in Biblical Law*. Cambridge: Cambridge University Press, 1947.

David, A. Rosalie. *The Ancient Egyptians*. London: Routledge, 1982.

David, M. "The Manumission of Slaves under Zedekiah." *OTS* 5 (1948): 63–79.

Davies Eryl W. "Land: Its Rights and Privileges." Pages 349–69 in *The World of Ancient Israel: Sociological, Anthropological and Political Perspectives*. Edited by Ronald E. Clements. Cambridge: Cambridge University Press, 1989.

———. *Numbers*. NCBC. Grand Rapids: Eerdmans, 1995.

Day, Linda. *Three Faces of a Queen: Characterization in the Books of Esther*. JSOTSup 186. Sheffield: Sheffield Academic Press, 1995.

Day, Peggy L. ed. *Gender and Difference in Ancient Israel.* Minneapolis: Fortress, 1989.

De Pina-Cabral, João. "The Mediterranean as a Category of Regional Comparison: A Critical View." *Current Anthropology* 30 (1989): 399–406.

Deurloo, K. A. "The King's Wisdom in Judgment. Narration as Example (I Kings 3)." Pages 11–21 in *New Avenues in the Study of the Old Testament:Fs. M. J. Mulder.* Edited by A. S. van der Woude. OTS 25, Leiden 1989.

Diakonoff, Igor M., ed. *Ancient Mesopotamia: Socio-Economic History: A Collection of Studies by Soviet Scholars.* Moscow: Nauka Publishing House, Central Department of Oriental Literature, 1969.

———. "Slave-Labour vs. Non-Slave Labour: The Problem of Definition." Pages 1–3 in *Labor in the Ancient Near East.* Edited by Marvin Pope. AOS 68. New Haven: American Oriental Society, 1987.

———. *Structure of Society and State in Early Dynastic Sumer.* Los Angeles: Undena, 1974.

Díez Merino, Luis. "XI Congreso de la Organización Internacional para el Estudio del Antiguo Testamento (IOSOT) (Salamanca, 28 agosto–2 septiembre 1983)." *EstBibl* 42 (1984): 137–98.

Dijk-Hemmes, Fokkelien van. "Traces of Women's Texts in the Hebrew Bible." Pages 17–112 in *On Gendering Texts: Female and Male Voices in the Hebrew Bible.* Edited by Athalya Brenner and Fokkelien van Dijk-Hemmes. Leiden: Brill, 1993.

Dion, Paul. "Did Cultic Prostitution Fall into Oblivion during the Post Exilic Era? Some Evidence from Chronicles and the Septuagint." *CBQ* 43 (1981): 41–48.

Dollinger, André. "Scents—incense and perfume." no pages. Cited: 11 March 2011. Online: http://www.reshafim.org.il/ad/egypt/trades/perfume_makers.htm.

Dorothy, Charles V. *The Books of Esther: Structure, Genre, and Textual Integrity.* JSOTSup 187. Sheffield: Sheffield Academic Press, 1997.

Dosch, Gudrun. "Non-Slave Labor in Nuzi." Pages 223–35 in *Labor in the ANE.* Edited by Marvin Powell. AOS 68. New Haven: American Oriental Society, 1987.

Driver, G. "Problems and Solutions," *VT* 4 (1954): 225–45.

Driver, Samuel. *Notes on the Hebrew Text and the Topography of the Books of Samuel, with an Introduction on Hebrew Paleography and the Ancient Versions and Facsimiles of Inscriptions and Maps.* 2nd rev. enl. ed. Oxford: Clarendon, 1960 (1913).

Duke, Rodney K. "A Model for a Theology of Biblical Historical Narratives: Proposed and Demonstrated with the Books of Chronicles." Pages 65–77 in *History and Interpretation: Essays in Honour of John H. Hayes.* Edited by M. Patrick Graham, William P. Brown, and Geoffrey K. Kuan. JSOTSup 173; Sheffield: JSOT Press, 1993.

Durand, Jean-Marie, ed. *La Femme Dans le Proche-Orient Antique: XXXIIIe Rencontre Assyriologique Internationale.* Paris: Editions Recherche sur les Civilisations, 1987.

Eagleton, Terry. *Criticism and Ideology: A Study in Marxist Literary Theory.* London: Verso, 1976.

Ebeling, Jennie R. "Archaeological Remains of Everyday Activities. Ground Stone Tools in Bronze and Iron Age Palestine." Pages 311–24 in *Life and Culture in the Ancient*

Near East. Edited by Richard Averbeck, Mark W. Chavalas, and David B. Weisberg. Bethesda: CDL Press, 2003.

Ebeling, Jennie R. and Michael M. Homan. "Baking and Brewing Beer in the Israelite Household: A Study of Women's Cooking Technology." Pages 45–62 in *The World of Women in the Ancient and Classical Near East.* Edited by Beth Alpert Nakhai. Newcastle upon Tyne: Cambridge Scholars Publishing, 2008.

Ebeling, Jennie R. and Yorke M. Rowan. "The Archaeology of the Daily Grind: Ground Stone Tools and Food Production in the Southern Levant." *NEA* 67 (2004): 108–17.

Edelman, Diana Vikander. *King Saul in the Historiography of Judah.* JSOTS 121. Sheffield: JSOT Press, 1991.

Eisenstadt, S. N. *The Political Systems of Empires.* New York: Free Press of Glencoe, 1963.

Eissfeldt, Otto. *The Old Testament: An Introduction Including the Apocrypha and Pseudepigraha, and also the Works of Similar Type from Qumran.* Trad. Peter R. Ackroyd. New York: Harper & Row, 1965.

Elat, Moshe. "The Impact of Tribute and Booty on Countries and People within The Assyrian Empire." *AfO* 19 (1982): 244–51.

———. "The Monarchy and the Development of Trade in Ancient Israel." Pages 527–46 in volume 2 of *State and Economy in the Ancient Near East.* Edited by Edward Lipiński. 2 vols. OLA 5–6. Leuven: Departement Oriëntalistiek, 1979.

Elliott, John H. *What Is Social-Scientific Criticism?* GBS. Minneapolis: Fortress, 1993.

Emmerson, Grace. *An Israelite Prophet in Judean Perspective.* JSOTSup 28. Sheffield: JSOT Press, 1984.

———. "Women in Ancient Israel." Pages 371–94 in *The World of Ancient Israel: Sociological, Anthropological and Political Perspectives.* Edited by Ronald E. Clements. Cambridge: Cambridge University Press, 1989.

Engelken, Karen. *Frauen im Alten Israel:Eine begriffsgeschichtliche und sozialrechtliche Studie zur Stellung der Frau im Alten Testament.* BWANT 7th series, 10. Stuttgart: Kohlhammer, 1990.

Engelmann, Angelika. "Deuteronomium. Recht und Gerechtigkeit für Frauen im Gesetz." Pages 67–79 in *Kompendium Feministische Bibelauslegung.* Edited by Luise Schottroff and Marie-Theres Wacker. Gütersloh/ Chr. Kaiser, Gütersloher Verlaghaus, 1999.

Epsztein, Leon. *Social Justice in the Ancient Near East and the People of the Bible.* London: SCM, 1986

Eskenazi, Tamara Cohn. "Exile and the Dreams of Return." *CurTM* 17 (1990): 192–200.

———. "Out from the Shadows: Biblical Women in the Postexilic Era." *JSOT* 54 (1992): 25–43.

Eslinger, Lyle M. *Kingship of God in Crisis: A Close Reading of 1 Samuel 1–12.* Decatur, Ga.: Almond Press, 1985.

Exum, J. Cheryl. "Feminist Criticism: Whose Interests are Being Served?" Pages 65–90 in *Judges and Method.* Edited by Gale Yee. Minneapolis: Fortress, 1995.

Eyre, Christopher J. "Work and the Organisation of Work in the Old Kingdom." Pages 5–47 in *Labor in the Ancient Near East.* Edited by Marvin Powell. AOS 68. New Haven: American Oriental Society, 1987.

Falk, Z. W. "Law and Ethics in the Hebrew Bible." Pages 82–90 in *Justice and Righteousness: Biblical Themes and Their Influence.* Edited by Henning Graf Reventlow and Yair Hoffman. JSOTSup 137. Sheffield: Sheffield Academic Press, 1992.

———. "Manumission by Sale." *JSS* 3 (1958): 127–28.

———. "The Deeds of Manumission in Elephantine." *JJS* 5 (1954): 114–17.

Falkenstein, Adam. *The Sumerian Temple City.* Translated by Maria Dej. Ellis. Monographs in History: ANE 1/1. Los Angeles: Undena, 1974.

Faust, Avraham and Shlomo Bunimovitz. "The Four-Room House. Embodying Iron Age Israelite Society." *NEA* 66 (2003): 22–31.

Feeley-Harnick, Gillian. "Naomi and Ruth: Building Up the House of David." Pages 163–84 in *Text and Tradition: The Hebrew Bible and Folklore.* Edited by Susan Niditch. Atlanta: Scholars Press, 1990.

Fensham, F. Charles. "Exodus 21:18–19 in the Light of Hittite Law # 10." *VT* 10 (1960): 333–35.

———. "Malediction and Benediction in Ancient Near Eastern Vassal-Treaties and the Old Testament." Pages 247–55 in *A Song of Power and the Power of Song.* Edited by Duane L. Christensen. Winona Lake: Eisenbrauns, 1993.

———. "The Son of the Handmaid in North West Semitic." *VT* 19 (1969): 312–21.

Fewell, Danna Nolan. "Joshua." Pages 63–66 in *The Women's Bible Commentary.* Edited by Carol Newsom and Sharon Ringe. Louisville: Westminster John Knox, 1992.

———. "Judges." Pages 67–77 in *The Women's Bible Commentary.* Edited by Carol Newsom and Sharon Ringe. Louisville: Westminster John Knox, 1992.

Fewell, Danna Nolan and David Miller Gunn. *Compromising Redemption: Relating Characters in the Book of Ruth.* Louisville: Westminster John Knox Press, 1990.

———. *Gender, Power, and Promise: The Subject of the Bible's First Story.* Nashville: Abingdon, 1993.

Fields, Weston. "The Motif 'Night as Danger' Associated with Three Biblical Destruction Narratives." Pages 17–32 in *Shaarei Talmon: Studies in the Bible, Qumran, and the Ancient Near East presented to Shemaryahu Talmon.* Edited by Michael Fishbane and Emanuel Tov. Winona Lake: Eisenbrauns, 1992.

Finkelstein, Israel, and Nadav Na'aman (eds). *From Nomadism to Monarchy: Archaeological and Historical Aspects of Early Israel.* Washington: Biblical Archaeology Society, 1994.

Finkelstein, J. J. "Amisaduqa's Edict and the Babylonian 'Law Codes.'" *JCS* 15 (1961): 91–104.

———. "Sex Offenses in Sumerian Laws." *JAOS* 86 (1966): 355–72.

Finley, Moses. *Ancient Slavery and Modern Ideology.* New York: Penguin Books, 1983.

———. "Was Greek Civilization Based on Slave Labour?" In *Historia* 8 (1959): 145–64.

Finley, Moses, ed. *Slavery in Classical Antiquity: Views and Controversies.* Cambridge: Heffer, 1960.

Flanagan, J. W. "Court History or Succession Document? A Study of 2 Sam 9–20 and 1 Kings 1–2." *JBL* 91 (1972): 172–81.

Fokkelman, J. P. *Narrative Art and Poetry in the Books of Samuel*, 4 vols. Assen: van Gorcum, 1981–1993.

―――. "Structural Remarks on Judges 9 and 19." Pages 33–45 in *Shaarei Talmon: Studies in the Bible, Qumran, and the Ancient Near East presented to Shemaryahu Talmon*. Edited by Michael Fishbane and Emmanuel Tov. Winona Lake: Eisenbrauns, 1992.

Fontaine, Carole R. *With Eyes of Flesh: The Bible, Gender and Human Rights*. The Bible in the Modern World 10; Sheffield: Sheffield Phoenix Press, 2008.

Foster, Benjamin. "Notes on Women in Sargonic Society." Pages 53–61 in *La Femme dans le Proche-Orient Antique: XXXIIIe. Rencontre Assyriologique Internationale*. Edited by Jean-Marie Durand. Editions Recherche sur les Civilisations: Paris, 1987.

Fox, Michael V. *Character and Ideology in the Book of Esther*. Columbia: University of South Carolina Press, 1991.

―――. *Ecclesiastes: The Traditional Hebrew Text with the New JPS Translation Commentary by Michael V. Fox*. Philadelphia: Jewish Publication Society, 2004.

―――. "Ideas of Wisdom in Proverbs 1–9." *JBL* 116 (1997): 613–33.

Franklin, John Curtis. "'A Feast of Music': The Greco-Lydian Musical Movement on the Assyrian Periphery." Pages 193–203 in *Anatolian Interfaces: Hittites, Greeks and their Neighbors: Proceedings of an International Conference on Cross-Cultural Interaction, September 17–19, 2004, Emory University, Atlanta, GA*. Edited by Collins, Billie J., M. R. Bachvarova, and I. Rutherford. Oxford: Oxbow (2008). Cited 8 August 2010. Online: http://www.kingmixers .com/FranklinPDFfilescopy/FeastofMusicWeb.pdf.

Franklin, Patricia N. "The Stranger within Their Gates: How the Israelite Portrayed the Non-Israelite in Biblical Literature." Ph.D. diss., Duke University, 1990.

Freedman, David Noel, ed. *Anchor Bible Dictionary*. 6 volumes. New York: Doubleday, 1992.

Freund, Yosef. "The Marriage and the Dowry (1 Kgs 3:1)." *JBQ* 23 (1995): 248–51.

Frey, Christopher. "The Impact of the Biblical Idea of Justice on Present Discussions of Social Justice." Pages 91–104 in *Justice and Righteousness: Biblical Themes and Their Influence*. Edited by Henning Graf Reventlow and Yair Hoffman. Sheffield: JSOT, 1992.

Frick, Frank S. "*Cui Bono?*—History in the Service of Political Nationalism: The Deuteronomistic History as Political Propaganda." Pages 79–92 in *Ethics and Politics in the Hebrew Bible*. Edited by Douglas A. Knight. *Semeia* 66. Atlanta: Scholars Press, 1994.

―――. "Ecology, Agriculture, and Patterns of Settlement." In *The World of Ancient Israel: Sociological, Anthropological and Political Perspectives*. Edited by Ronald E. Clements, 67–93. Cambridge: Cambridge University Press, 1989.

―――. "'Oil from Flinty Rock' (Deuteronomy 32:13): Olive Cultivation and Olive Oil Processing in The Hebrew Bible—A Socio-Materialist Perspective." *Semeia* 86 (1999): 3–17.

―――. "Social Science Methods and Theories of Significance for the Study of the Israelite Monarchy: A Critical Review Essay." Pages 9–52 in *Social Scientific Criticism of the Hebrew Bible and Its Social World: The Israelite Monarchy.*Edited by Norman K. Gottwald. *Semeia* 37. Atlanta: Scholars Press, 1986.

———. "Sociological Criticism and Its Relation to Political and Social Hermeneutics." Pages 225–38, 346–50 in *The Bible and the Politics of Exegesis: Essays in Honour of Norman K. Gottwald on His Sixty-Fifth Birthday.* Edited by David Jobling, Peggy L. Day, and Gerald T. Sheppard. Cleveland: Pilgrim, 1991.

———. *The City in Ancient Israel.* Missoula, Mont.: Scholars Press, 1977.

———. *The Formation of the State in Ancient Israel: A Survey of Models and Theories.* Sheffield: Almond, 1985.

Frymer-Kensky, Tikva. "Deuteronomy." Pages 52–62 in *The Women's Bible Commentary.* Edited by Carol A. Newsom and Sharon Ringe. Louisville: Westminster John Knox, 1992.

———. *In the Wake of the Goddesses.* New York: The Free Press, 1992.

———. "Law and Philosophy: The Case of Sex in the Bible." Pages 89–102 in *Thinking Biblical Law.* Edited by Dale Patrick. *Semeia* 45. Atlanta: Scholars Press, 1989.

———. "Near Eastern Law and the Patriarchal Family." *BA* 44 (1981): 209–14.

———. "Reading Rahab." Pages 57–67 in *Tehilla le-Moshe: Biblical and Judaic Studies in Honor of Moshe Greenberg.* Edited by Mordechai Cogan, Barry Eichler, and Jeffrey Tigay. Winona Lake: Eisenbrauns, 1997.

———. *Reading the Women of the Bible.* New York: Schocken, 2002.

———. "The Family in the Hebrew Bible." Pages 55–73 in *Religion, Feminism, and the Family.* Edited by Anne Carr and Mary Stewart Van Leewven. Louisville: Westminster John Knox Press, 1996.

———. "Tit for Tat: The Principle of Equal Retribution in Near Eastern and Biblical Law." *BA* 43 (1980): 230–34.

———. "Virginity in the Bible." Pages 79–96 in *Gender and Law in the Hebrew Bible.* Edited by Victor H. Matthews, Bernard M. Levinson, and Tikva Frymer-Kensky. JSOTSup 262. Sheffield: Sheffield Academic Press, 1998.

Fuchs, Esther. "The Literary Characterization of Mothers and Sexual Politics in the Hebrew Bible." Pager 117–36 in *Feminist Perspectives on Biblical Scholarship.* Edited by Adela Yarbro Collins. SBL Centennial Publications. Chico, Calif.: Scholars Press, 1985.

Fullerton, Kemper. "A New Chapter Out of the Life of Isaiah." *AJT* 9 (1905): 621–42.

Gabbay, Uri. "The Akkadian Word for 'Third Gender': The *kalû* (gala) Once Again." Pages 49–56 in *Proceedings of the 51st Rencontre Assyriologique Internationale held at the Oriental Institute of The University of Chicago, July 18–22, 2005.* Edited by Robert D. Biggs, Jennie Myers, and Martha T. Roth. Studies in Ancient Oriental Civilization 62. Chicago: The University of Chicago, 2008.

Gafney, Wilda C. *Daughters of Miriam: Women Prophets in Ancient Israel.* Minneapolis: Fortress, 2008.

Galán, José M. "The Ancient Egyptian Sed-Festival and the Exemption from Corveé." *JNES* 59 (2000): 255–64.

Galpaz-Feller, Pnina. "David and the Messenger—Different Ends, Similar Means in 2 Samuel 1." *VT* 29 (2009): 199–210.

García Bachmann, Mercedes L. "'Little Women': Female Labor in the Deuteronomistic History. Ph.D. diss., The Lutheran School of Theology at Chicago, 1999.

————. "La ley y el orden. Una apreciación del material legal y cultual en el libro del Éxodo." Pages 215–63 in *Relectura del Éxodo.* Edited by Isabel Gómez Acebo. Bilbao: Desclée de Brower, 2006.

————. "What is in a Name? Abishag the Shunammite as *Sokenet* in 1 Kings 1:1–4." Pages 233–54 in *Out of Place: Doing Theology on the Crosscultural Brink.* Edited by Jione Havea and Clive Pearson. London: Equinox, 2011.

Garnsey, Peter. *Ideas of Slavery from Aristotle to Augustine.* Cambridge: Cambridge University Press, 1996.

Garsiel, Moshe. "Puns upon Names as a Literary Device in 1 Kings 1–2." *Bib* 72 (1991): 379–86.

Gass, Erasmus. "Topographical Considerations and Redaction Criticism in 2 Kings 3." *JBL* 128 (2009): 65–84.

Gelb, Ignace J. "Approaches to the Study of Ancient Society." *JAOS* 87 (1967): 1–8.

————. "Definition and Discussion of Slavery and Serfdom." *UF* 11 (1979): 283–97.

————. "From Freedom to Slavery." *CRRA* 18 (1972): 81–92.

————. "Household and Family in Early Mesopotamia." Pages 1–97 in volume 1 of *State and Temple Economy in the Ancient Near East.* Edited by Edward Lipiński. 2 vols. OLA 5–6. Leuven: Departement Oriëntalistiek, 1979.

————. "Prisoners of War in Early Mesopotamia." *JNES* 32 (1973): 70–98.

————."Quantitative Evaluation of Slavery and Serfdom." Pages 195–207 in *Kramer Anniversary Volume: Cuneiform Studies in Honor of Samuel Noah Kramer.* Edited by Barry L. Eichler, with the assistance of Jane W. Heimerdinger and Åke Sjöberg. AOAT 25. Kavalaer: Butzon & Bercker, 1976.

————. "Socio-Economic Classes in Babylonia and the Babylonian Concept of Social Stratification." *CRRA* 18 (1972): 41–52.

Geoghegan, Jeffrey C. *The Time, Place, and Purpose of the Deuteronomistic History: The Evidence of "Until This Day."* Providence: Brown University, 2006.

Gerbrandt, Gerald. *Kingship according to the Deuteronomistic History.* SBLDS 87. Atlanta, : Scholars Press, 1986.

Gerstenberger, Erhard. *Leviticus: A Commentary.* OTL. Louisville: Westminster John Knox, 1996.

————. *Psalms, part 2, and Lamentations.* The Forms of the Old Testament Literature XV. Grand Rapids: Eerdmans, 2001.

————. "The Religion and Institutions of Ancient Israel." Pages 261–76 in *Old Testament Interpretation: Past, Present, and Future. Essays in Honor of Gene M. Tucker.* Edited by James Luther Mays, David L. Petersen, and Kent H. Richards. Nashville: Abingdon Press, 1995.

————. *Yahweh The Patriarch: Ancient Images of God and Feminist Theology.* Minneapolis: Fortress, 1996.

Gestoso Singer, Graciela. *El intercambio de bienes entre Egipto y Asia Anterior: Desde el reinado de Tutmosis III hasta el de Akhenaton.* Ancient Near Eastern Monographs/ Monografías sobre el Antiguo Cercano Oriente. 2nd ed. Buenos Aires: SBL/Centro de Estudios de Historia del Antiguo Oriente, UCA, 2008.

Gitin, Seymour and Trude Dotan. "The Rise and Fall of Ekron of the Philistines: Recent Excavations at an Urban Border Site." *BA* (1987): 197–222.

Glass, Zipporah G. "Land, Labor and Law: Viewing Persian Yehud's Economy through Socio-Economic Modeling." Ph.D. diss., Vanderbilt University, 2010.

Gomezjara, Francisco. "Hablemos más claro sobre la prostitución." Pages 11–103 in *Sociología de la Prostitución.* Edited by Francisco Gomezjara. México: Fontamara (Nueva Sociología), 1982.

Goodnick Westenholz, Joan. "Tamar, *Qĕdēšā, Qadištu,* and Sacred Prostitution in Mesopotamia." *HTR* 82 (1989): 245–65.

Goody, Jack. "Marriage Prestations, Inheritance and Descent in Pre-Industrial Societies." *Journal of Comparative Family Studies* 1 (1970): 37–54.

———. *Production and Reproduction: A Comparative Study of the Domestic Domain.* Cambridge: Cambridge University Press, 1976.

Gordis, Robert. *Koheleth—The Man and His World.* New York: Jewish Theological Seminary of America, 5711/1951.

———. *The Song of Songs.* New York: Bloch, 1954.

Gordon, Robert P. "A House Divided: Wisdom in Old Testament Narrative Traditions." Pages 94–105 in *Wisdom in Ancient Israel: Essays in Honor of J. A. Emerton.* Edited by John Day, Robert P. Gordon, and H. G. M. Williamson. Cambridge: Cambridge University Press, 1995.

Gorges-Braunwarth, S. *"Frauenbilder— Weisheitsbilder— Gottesbilder" in Spr 1–9: Die personifizierte Weisheit im Gottesbild der nachexilischen Zeit.* Münster: LIT, 2002.

Gorman, Frank, Jr. *Leviticus: Divine Presence and Community.* ITC. Grand Rapids/ Edinburgh: Eerdmans/ Hansel, 1997.

Gosline, Sheldon L. "Female Priests: A Sacerdotal Precedent from Ancient Egypt." *JFSR* 12 (1996): 25–39.

Gottwald, Norman K. "Biblical Theology or Biblical Sociology?" *Radical Religion* 2 (1975): 46–57.

———. "Social Class and Ideology in Isaiah 40–55: Ideological Criticism of the Biblical Text." Pages 43–57 in *Ideological Criticism of Biblical Texts.* Edited by David Jobling and Tina Pippin. *Semeia* 59. Atlanta: Scholars Press, 1992.

———. "Social Class as an Analytic and Hermeneutical Category in Biblical Studies." *JBL* 112 (1993): 3–22.

———. "Sociological Method in the Study of Ancient Israel." Pages 26–37 in *The Bible and Liberation: Political and Social Hermeneutics.* Edited by Norman K. Gottwald. Maryknoll: Orbis, 1983.

———. *The Hebrew Bible: A Socio-Literary Introduction.* Philadelphia: Fortress, 1985.

———. *The Hebrew Bible in Its Social World and in Ours.* SBLSS. Atlanta: Scholars Press, 1993.

———. "The Participation of Free Agrarians in the Introduction of Monarchy to Ancient Israel: An Application of H. A. Landsberger's Framework for the Analysis of Peasant Movements." Pages 77–106 in *Social Scientific Criticism of the Hebrew Bible and Its Social World: The Israelite Monarchy.* Edited by Norman K. Gottwald. *Semeia* 37. Atlanta: Scholars Press, 1986.

———. *The Tribes of Yahweh: A Sociology of the Religion of Liberated Israel.* Maryknoll: Orbis, 1979.

374 | Women at Work in the DtrH

Gowan, Donald E. *Ezekiel.* Knox Preaching Guides. Atlanta: John Knox, 1985.
Grabbe, Lester L. *Priests, Prophets, Diviners, Sages: A Socio-Historical Study of Religious Specialists in Ancient Israel.* Valley Forge: Trinity International, 1995.
Graham J. Nigel. "'Vinedressers and Plowmen' 2 Kings 25:12 and Jeremiah 52:16." *BA* 47 (1984): 55–58.
Gray, John. *I and II Kings: A Commentary.* London/Philadelphia: SCM/Westminster, 1963.
———. "Feudalism in Ugarit and Early Israel." *ZAW* 64 (1952): 49–55.
———. "Israel in the Song of Deborah." Pages 421–55 in *Ascribe to the Lord: Biblical and Other Studies in Memory of Peter C. Craigie.* Edited by Lyle Eslinger and Glen Taylor. JSOTSup 67. Sheffield: JSOT Press, 1988.
———. *The Legacy of Canaan: The Ras Shamra Texts and Their Relevance to the Old Testament.* VTSup 5. Leiden: Brill, 1957.
———. "Traditional Composition in the 'Succession Narrative.'" *VT* 26 (1976): 214–29.
Green, Lyn. "Some Thoughts on Ritual Banquets at the Court of Akhenaten and in the Ancient Near East." Pages 203–22 in *Egypt, Israel, and the Ancient Mediterranean World: Studies in Honor of Donald B. Redford.* Edited by Gary N. Knoppers and Antoine Hirsch. Leiden: Brill, 2004.
Greenberg, Moshe, "Some Postulates of Biblical Criminal Law." Pages 283–300 in *A Song of Power and the Power of Song: Essays on the Book of Deuteronomy.* Edited by Duane L. Christensen. Winona Lake: Eisenbrauns, 1993.
Greenfield, Jonas. "Some Neo-Babylonian Women." Pages 75–80 in *La Femme dans le Proche-Orient Antique: XXXIIIe. Rencontre Assyriologique Internationale.* Edited by Jean-Marie Durand. Editions Recherche sur les Civilisations: Paris, 1987.
Greengus, Samuel. "Some Issues Relating to the Comparability of Laws and Coherence of the Legal Tradition." Pages 60–87 in *Theory and Method in Biblical and Cuneiform Law.* Edited by Bernard Levinson. JSOTSup 181. Sheffield: Sheffield Academic Press, 1994.
Greenstein, Edward L. "On Feeley-Harnick's Reading of Ruth." Pages 185–91 in *Text and Tradition: The Hebrew Bible and Folklore.* Edited by Susan Niditch. Atlanta: Scholars Press, 1990.
Greer, Jonathan S. "A *Marzeah* and a *Mizraq:* A Prophet's Mêlée with Religious Diversity in Amos 6.4–7." *JSOT* 32 (2007): 243–62.
Gressmann, Hugo. "The Oldest History Writing in Israel." Pages 9–58 in *Narrative and Novella in Samuel: Studies by Hugo Gressmann and Other Scholars 1906–1923.* Edited by David M. Gunn. JSOTS 116. Sheffield: Almond Press, 1991.
Grosz, Katarzyna. "Some Aspects of the Position of Women in Nuzi." Pages 167–80 in *Women's Earliest Records from Ancient Egypt and Western Asia.* Edited by Barbara Lesko. BJS 166. Atlanta: Scholars Press, 1989.
Gruber, Mayer I. "Breast-Feeding Practices in Biblical Israel and in Old Babylonian Mesopotamia ," *JANES* 19 (1989): 61–83.
———. "Hebrew *Qĕdēšāh* and Her Canaanite and Akkadian Cognates." *UF* 18 (1986): 133–48.
———. "Hebrew Women in Egypt: Bible." *Jewish Women: A Comprehensive Historical Encyclopedia.* 1 March 2009. Jewish Women's Archive. No pages. Cited 22

September 2011. Online: http://jwa.org/encyclopedia/article/hebrew-women-in-egypt-bible.

————. Review of Stephanie Budin, *The Myth of Sacred Prostitution in Antiquity*. RBL [http://www.bookreviews.org] (2009). Published 28 March 2009.

————. *The Motherhood of God and Other Studies*. South Florida Studies in the History of Judaism. Atlanta: Scholars Press, 1992.

Guillaume, Philippe. "Nehemiah 5: No Economic Crisis." *JHS* 10, article 8 (2010). No pages. Cited 22 January 2011. Online version: http://www.arts.ualberta.ca/JHS/Articles/article_136.pdf.

Gunn, David M. "New Directions in the Study of Biblical Hebrew Narrative." Pages 412–22 in *Beyond Form Criticism: Essays in OT Literaty Crististicsm*. Edited by Paul R. Hose. Eisenbrauns, Winona Lake, 1992. Repr. from *JSOT* 39 (1987): 65–75.

————. *The Story of King David: Genre and Interpretation*. JSOTSup 6. Sheffield: JSOT, 1978.

————, ed. *Narrative and Novella in Samuel: Studies by Hugo Gressmann and Other Scholars 1906–1923*. Transl. David E. Orton. Sheffield: Almond Press, 1991.

Haase, Ingrid M. "Uzzah's Rebellion." *JH5*, Article 3 (2004). No pages. Cited 20 May 2010. Online: http://www.jhsonline.org/Articles/article_33.pdf.

Habel, Norman C. *The Book of Job*. OTL. Louisville: Westminster John Knox, 1985.

————. "The Future of Social Justice Reasearch in the Hebrew Scriptures: Questions of Authority and Relevance." Pages 277–91 in *Old Testament Interpretation: Past, Present, and Future. Essays in Honor of Gene M. Tucker*. Edited by James Luther Mays, David L. Petersen and Kent H. Richards. Nashville: Abingdon Press, 1995.

————. *The Land Is Mine: Six Biblical Land Ideologies*. Minneapolis: Fortress, 1994.

Hackett, Jo Ann. "1 and 2 Samuel." Pages 85–95 in *The Women's Bible Commentary*. Edited by Carol Newsom and Sharon Ringe. Louisville: Westminster John Knox, 1992.

————. "In the Days of Jael: Reclaiming the History of Women in Ancient Israel." Pages 15–38 in *Immaculate and Powerful: The Female in Sacred Image and Social Reality*. Edited by Clarissa W. Atkinson, Constance H. Buchanan, and Margaret R. Miles. Boston: Beacon Press, 1985.

————. "Rehabilitating Hagar: Fragments of an Epic Pattern." Pages 12–27 in *Gender and Difference in Ancient Israel*. Edited by Peggy L. Day. Minneapolis: Fortress, 1989.

————. "Women's Studies and the Hebrew Bible." Pages 141–64 in *The Future of Biblical Studies: The Hebrew Scriptures*. Edited by Richard Elliot Freedman and H. G. M. Williamson. SBLSS. Atlanta: Scholars Press, 1987.

Hallo, William W., James C. Moyer, and Leo G. Perdue, eds. *Scripture in Context II: More Essays on the Comparative Method*. Winona Lake: Eisenbrauns, 1983.

Halpern, Baruch. "The Centralization Formula in Deuteronomy." *VT* 31 (1981): 20–38.

Hals, Ronald M. *Ezekiel*. FOTL XIX. Grand Rapids: Eerdmans, 1988.

Hamilton, Jeffries M. "Caught in the Nets of Prophecy? The Death of King Ahab and the Character of God." *CBQ* 56 (1994): 649–63.

Hanson, K. C. "*BTB's* Reader's Guide to Kinship." *BTB* 24 (1994): 183–94.

Harris, Rivka. "Independent Women in Ancient Mesopotamia?" Pages 145–56 in *Women's Earliest Records from Ancient Egypt and Western Asia.* Edited by Barbara Lesko. BJS 166. Atlanta: Scholars Press, 1989.

———. "The Female 'Sage' in Mesopotamian Literature (with an Appendix on Egypt)." Pages 3–17 in *The Sage in Israel and the Ancient Near East.* Edited by John G. Gammie and Leo G. Perdue. Winona Lake: Eisenbrauns, 1990.

———. "The Organization and Administration of the Cloister in Ancient Babylonia." *JESHO* 6 (1963): 121–57.

Hauer, Chris, Jr. "The Economics of National Security in Solomonic Israel." *JSOT* 18 (1980): 63–73.

Hawk, L. Daniel. "Conquest Reconfigured: Recasting Warfare in the Redaction of Joshua." Pages 145–60 in *Writing and Reading War: Rhetoric, Gender, and Ethics in Biblical and Modern Contexts.* Edited by Brad E. Kelle and Frank Ritchel Ames. SBL Symposium Series 42. Atlanta: SBL, 2008.

———. *Joshua.* Berit Olam. Collegeville: Michael Glazier/Liturgical Press, 2000.

———. "Strange Houseguests: Rahab, Lot, and the Dynamics of Deliverance." Pages 89–97 in *Reading between Texts.* Edited by Danna Nolan Fewell. Louisville: Westminster John Knox Press, 1992.

Hayes, John and Irvine Stuart. *Isaiah, the Eighth-century Prophet: His Time and Preaching.* Nashville:, Abingdon, 1987.

Hays, Christopher B. "Re-Excavating Shebna's Tomb: A New Reading of Isa 22,15–19 in its Ancient Near Eastern Context." *ZAW* 122 (2010): 558–75.

Heffelfinger, Katie M. "'My father is king': Chiefly Politics and the Rise and Fall of Abimelech." *JSOT* 33 (2009): 277–92.

Heijerman, Mieke. "Who Would Blame Her? The 'Strange' Woman of Proverbs 7." Pages 100–109 in *A Feminist Companion to Wisdom* Literature. Edited by Athalya Brenner. Sheffield: Sheffield Academic Press, 1995.

Heinisch, P. "Das Sklavenrecht in Israel und im Alten Orient." *SC* 11 (1934–5): 201–18.

Heltzer, Michael. "Royal Economy in Ancient Ugarit." Pages 459–96 in volume 2 of *State and Temple Economy.* Edited by Edward Lipiński. 2 vols. OLA 5–6. Leuven: Departement Orientalistiek, 1979.

———. "The Neo-Assyrian *Šakintu* and the Biblical *Sōkenet* (I Reg. 1, 4)." Pages 87-90 in *La Femme dans le Proche-Orient Antique: XXXIIIe. Rencontre Assyriologique Internationale.* Edited by Jean-Marie Durand. Editions Recherche sur les Civilisations: Paris, 1987.

Henshaw, Richard A. "The Office of *Šaknu* in Neo-Sumerian Times, I." *JAOS* 87 (1967): 517–25.

———. "The Office of *Šaknu* in Neo-Sumerian Times, II." *JAOS* 88 (1968): 461–83.

Hens-Piazza, Gina. *Of Methods, Monarchs, and Meanings: An Approach to Sociorhetorical Exegesis.* Studies in Old Testament Interpretation 3. Macon, Ga.: Mercer University Press, 1997.

Hertzberg, H. W. *I and II Samuel.* OTL. London: SCM, 1964.

Herzfeld, Michael. "Honour and Shame: Problems in the Comparative Analysis of Moral Systems." *Man,* New Series 15 (1980): 339–51.

Hestrin, Ruth and Zeev Yeivin. "Oil from the Presses of Tirat-Yehuda." *BA* 40 (1977): 29–31.

Hill, Andrew. "On David's 'Taking' and 'Leaving' Concubines (2 Samuel 5:13; 15:16)." *JBL* 125 (2006): 129–50.

Hobbs, T. R. "An Experiment in Militarism." Pages 457–80 in *Ascribe to the Lord: Biblical and Other Studies in Memory of Peter C. Craigie*. Edited by Lyle Eslinger and Glen Taylor. JSOTSup 67. Sheffield: JSOT Press, 1988.

———. "*BTB* Readers Guide: Aspects of Warfare in the First Testament World." *BTB* 25 (1995): 79–90.

———. "Reflections on Honor, Shame, and Covenant Relations." *JBL* 116 (1997): 501–503.

———. "Reflections on 'The Poor' and the Old Testament." *ExpTim* 100 (1989): 291–94.

Hobsbawm, E. J. *Bandits*. Rev. ed. New York: Pantheon, 1981.

Hoffner, Harry A., Jr. "Daily Life among the Hittites." Pages 95–118 in *Life and Culture in the Ancient Near East*. Edited by Richard Averbeck, Mark W. Chavalas, and David B. Weisberg. Bethesda, Md.: CDL Press, 2003.

———. "Oil in Hittite Texts." *BA* 58 (1995): 108–14. Cited 2 April 2011. Online: http://www.bu.edu/asor/pubs/nea/back-issues/ba/hoffner.html.

———. "The Treatment and Long-Term Use of Persons Captured in Battle according to the Maşat Texts." Pages 61–71 in *Recent Developments in Hittite Archaeology and History: Papers in Memory of Hans G. Güterbock*. Edited by Harry A. Hoffner, Jr. and A. Yener. Winona Lake: Eisenbrauns, 2002.

Holladay, William. *Jeremiah*. 2 volumes. Hermeneia. Philadelphia: Fortress, 1986.

Holloway, Steven W. "Distaff, Crutch or Chain Gang: The Curse of the House of Joab in 2 Samuel 3:29." *VT* 37 (1987): 379–75.

Homan, Michael M. "Beer and Its Drinkers: An Ancient Near Eastern Love Story" *NEA* 67 (2004): 84–95.

———. "Beer Production by Throwing Bread into Water: A New Interpretation of Qoh. xi 1–2." *VT* 52 (2002): 275–78.

———. "Did the Ancient Israelites Drink Beer?" *BAR* 36 (2010):48–56, 78.

Hopkins, David C. *The Highlands of Canaan: Agricultural Life in the Early Iron Age*. SWBA 3. Sheffield: Almond, 1985.

Hopwood, Keith. "Bandits, Elites and Rural Order." Pages 171–87 in *Patronage in Ancient Society*. Edited by A. Wallace-Hadrill. London: Routledge, 1989.

Hubbard, Robert L. Jr. "Theological Reflections on Naomi's Shrewdness." *TB* 40 (1989): 283–92.

Ipsen, Avaren. *Sex Working and the Bible*. London: Equinox, 2009.

Jobling, David. "'Forced Labor': Solomon's Golden Age and the Question of Literary Representation." *Semeia* 54 (1991): 57–76.

Jones-Warsaw, Koala. "Toward a Womanist Hermeneutic: A Reading of Judges 19–21." Pages 172–86 in *A Feminist Companion to Judges*. Edited by A. Brenner. Sheffield: Sheffield Academic Press, 1993.

Jordan, David John. Review of Rafael Franklin [*sic*], *Wine and Oil Production in Antiquity in Israel and Other Mediterranean Countries*. RBL [http://www.bookreviews.org] (2000). Published 21 April 2000.

Jost, Renate. *Gender, Sexualität und Macht in der Anthropologie des Richterbuches.* Kohlhammer: Stuttgart, 2006.

———. "Hure/Hurerei (AT)." In *WiBiLex* 2011, no pages. Cited 3 June 2011. Online:www.wibilex.de/stichwort/Hure/.Kaiser, Otto. *Isaiah 13–39.* London: SCM, 1974.

Kalugila, Leonidas. *The Wise King: Studies in Royal Wisdom as Divine Revelation in the Old Testamen and Its Environment.* ConBOT 15. Lund: LiberLaromedel/Gleerup, 1980.

Kamionkowski, S. Tamar. "Gender Reversal in Ezekiel 16." Pages 170–85 in *Prophets and Daniel. A Feminist Companion to the Bible (Second Series).* Edited by Athalya Brenner. London/New York: Sheffield Academic Press/Continuum,(2001).

Kamphausen, A. "Isaiah's Prophecy Concerning the Major-domo of King Hezekiah." *AJT* 5 (1901): 43-74.

Karmon, Nira and Ehud Spanier. "Remains of a Purple Dye Industry Found at Tel Shiqmona." *IEJ* 38 (1988): 184–86.

Kaufman, Stephen A. "A Reconstruction of the Social Welfare Systems in Ancient Israel." Pages 277–86 in *In the Shelter of Elyon: Essays on Ancient Palestinian Life and Literature in Honor of G. W. Ahlström.* Edited by W. Boyd Barrick and John R. Spencer. JSOTSup 31. Sheffield: JSOT Press, 1984.

———. "Deuteronomy 15 and Recent Research on the Dating of P." Pages 273–76 in *Das Deuteronomium: Entstehung, Gestalt und Botschaft.* Edited by Norbert Lohfink. BETL 68. Leuven: Leuven University Press, 1985.

Kauz, Sophie. "Frauenräume im Alten Testament am Beispiel der Siedlung." *lectio difficilior* 2/2009. No pages. Cited: 28 August 2011. Online: http://www.lectio.unibe .ch/09_2/pdf/kauz_frauenraeume.pdf

Kelle, Brad E. and Frank Ritchel Ames, eds. *Writing and Reading War: Rhetoric, Gender, and Ethics in Biblical and Modern Contexts.* SBL Symposium Series 42. Atlanta: SBL, 2008.

Kenyon, Kathleen. *Royal Cities of the Old Testament.* New York: Schocken Books, 1971.

Keuls, Eva. *The Reign of the Phallus: Sexual Politics in Ancient Athens.* New York: Harper & Row, 1985.

Kiesow, Anna Christine. *Löwinnen von Juda: Frauen als Subjekte politischer Macht in der judäischen Königszeit.* Digitale Dissertation, Humboldt-Universität zu Berlin, 1998.

Kim, Jichan. *The Structure of the Samson Cycle.* Kampen: Kok Pharos, 1993.

King, Philip J. and Lawrence E. Stager. *Life in Biblical Israel.* Louisville: Westminster John Knox, 2001. Partially available online. Cited 26 July 2011. Online: http://books .google.com.ar/books?id=OtOhypZz_pEC&pg=PA97&dq=olive+oil+press&hl=es& ei=P68pTYrXDIG78gaxm7nEBQ&sa=X&oi=book_result&ct=result&resnum=4&v ed=0CD0Q6AEwAw#v=onepage&q=olive%20oil%20press&f=false

Kitchen, K. "Egypt and Israel during the First Millennium B.C." Pages 107–23 in *Congress Volume, Jerusalem, 1986.* Edited by John Emerton. VTSup 40. Leiden: Brill, 1988.

Klein, Lillian R. *From Deborah to Esther: Sexual Politics in the Hebrew Bible.* Minneapolis: Augsburg Fortress, 2003.

————. "Honor and Shame in Esther." Pages 149–75 in *A Feminist Companion to Esther, Judith, and Susanna*. Edited by Athalya Brenner. Sheffield: Sheffield Academic Press, 1995.

————. "Michal, The Barren Wife." Pages 37–46 in *A Feminist Companion to Samuel and Kings*. Edited by Athalya Brenner. 2nd Series. Sheffield: Sheffield Academic Press, 2000.

Klein, Ralph W. *1 Samuel*. WBC 10. Waco: Word Books, 1983.

————. *Ezekiel: The Prophet and His Message*. Columbia: University of South Carolina Press, 1988.

————. *Israel in Exile*. Philadelphia: Fortress, 1979.

————. "Israel/Today's Believers and the Nations: Three Test Cases."*CurTM* 24 (1997): 232–37.

————. "Reflections on Historiography in the Account of Jehoshaphat." Pages 643–57 in *Pomegranates and Golden Bells: Essays in Honor of Jacob Milgrom*. Edited by David Noel Freedman and Avi Hurvitz. Winona Lake: Eisenbrauns, 1995.

Klengel, Horst. "Non-Slave Labour in the Old Babylonian Period: The Basic Outline." Pages 159–66 in *Labor in the Ancient Near East*. Edited by Marvin Powell. AOS 68. New Haven:, American Oriental Society, 1987.

Kletter, Raz, Irit Ziffer and Wolfgang Zwickel. "Cult Stands of the Philistines. A Genizah from Yavneh." *NEA* 69 (2006): 146–59.

Knight, Douglas A. "Political Rights and Powers in Monarchic Israel." Pages 93–117 in *Ethics and Politics in the Hebrew Bible*. Edited by Douglas Knight. *Semeia* 66. Atlanta: Scholars Press, 1994.

Koenig, Eduard. "Shebna and Eliakim." *AJT* 10 (1906): 149–64.

Korpel, Marjo. "The Female Servant of the LORD in Isaiah 54." Pages 153–67 in *On Reading Prophetic Texts: Gender-Specific and Related Studies in Memory of Fokkelien van Dijk-Hemme*. Edited by B. Becking and M. Dijkstra. Leiden: Brill, 1996.

Kramer, Samuel Noah. "The Sage in Sumerian Literature: A Composite Portrait." Pages 31–44 in *The Sage in Israel and the Ancient Near East*. Edited by John G. Gammie and Leo G. Perdue. Winona Lake: Eisenbrauns, 1990.

————. *The Sumerians: Their History, Culture, and Character*. Chicago: University of Chicago Press, 1963.

————. "The Woman in Ancient Sumer: Gleanings from Sumerian Literature." Pages 107–12 in *La Femme dans le Proche-Orient Antique: XXXIIIe. Rencontre Assyriologique Internationale*. Edited by Jean-Marie Durand. Editions Recherche sur les Civilisations: Paris, 1987.

Kuhrt, Amélie. "Non-Royal Women in the Late Babylonian Period: A Survey." Pages 215-39 in *Women's Earliest Records from Ancient Egypt and Western Asia*. Edited by Barbara Lesko. BJS 166. Atlanta: Scholars Press, 1989.

————. *The Ancient Near East, c.3000–330 BC*. 2 volumes. London: Routledge, 1997 (repr. 2003).

Lacheman, E. R. "Note on the Word *Hupšu* at Nuzi." *BASOR* 86 (1942): 36–37.

LaCocque, André. *Ruth: A Continental Commentary*. Minneapolis: Fortress, 2004.

Laffey, Alice. *An Introduction to the Old Testament: A Feminist Perspective.* Philadelphia: Fortress, 1988.

Lambert, W. "Goddesses in the Pantheon: A Reflection of Women in Society?" Pages 125–30 in *La Femme dans le Proche-Orient Antique: XXXIIIe. Rencontre Assyriologique Internationale.* Edited by Jean-Marie Durand. Editions Recherche sur les Civilisations: Paris, 1987.

———. "Old Testament Mythology in its Ancient Near Eastern Context." Pages 124–43 in *Congress Volume, Jerusalem 1986.* Edited by John Emerton. VTSup 40. Leiden: Brill, 1988.

Landsberger, B. "Zu den Frauenklassen des Kodex Hammurabi." *ZA* 30 (1915–16): 67–73.

Landy, Francis. "The Ghostly Prelude to Deutero-Isaiah." *BibIn* 14 (2006): 332–63.

Lang, Bernhard. "Arbeit (AT)." In: *WiBiLex* 2011. No pages. Cited 3 February 2012. Online: www.wibilex.de/stichwort/Arbeit/.

———. "Introduction: Anthropology as a New Model for Biblical Studies." Pages 1–20 in *Anthropological Approaches to the Old Testament.* Edited by Bernhard Lang. IRT 8. Philadelphia/London: Fortress/SPCK, 1985.

———. *Monotheism and the Prophetic Minority: An Essay in Biblical History and Sociology.* Sheffield: Almond Press, 1983.

———. "The Social Organization of Peasant Poverty in Biblical Israel." Pages 114–27 in *Monotheism and the Prophetic Minority.* Edited by Bernhard Lang. Sheffield: Almond, 1983. Repr. in *Anthropological Approaches to the Old Testament.* Edited by Bernhard Lang, 83–99. IRT 8. Philadelphia/London: Fortress/ SPCK, 1985.

Langlamet, F. "Pour ou contre Salomon? La redaction prosalomonienne de I Rois." *RB* 83 (1976): 321–79, 481–528.

Laniak, Timothy S. *Shame and Honor in the Book of Esther.* Atlanta: Scholars Press, 1998.

Layton, Scott C. "A Chain Gang in 2 Samuel 3:29? A Rejoinder." *VT* 29 (1989): 81–86.

Lasine, Stuart. "Judicial Narratives and the Ethics of Reading: The Reader as Judge of the Dispute between Mephibosheth and Ziba," *HS* 30 (1989): 49–69.

Lebacqz, Karen. *Six Theories of Justice.* Minneapolis: Augsburg, 1986.

Leeb, Carolyn. *Away from the Father's House: The Social Location of na ʿar and na ʿarah in Ancient Israel.* Sheffield: Sheffield Academic Press, 2000.

Lefkowitz, M. and M. Fant, *Women's Life in Greece and Rome: A Source Book in Translation.* Baltimore: Johns Hopkins University Press, 1982.

Leick, Gwendolyn. *Mesopotamia: La invención de la ciudad.* Barcelona: Paidós, 2002.

Lemaire, Andre. "Wisdom in Solomonic Historiography." Pages 106–18 in *Wisdom in Ancient Israel: Essays in Honour of John A. Emerton.* Edited by John Day, Robert P. Gordon and R. P. Williamson. Cambridge: Cambridge University Press, 1995.

Lemche, Niels P. *Ancient Israel: A New History of Israelite Society.* Sheffield: JSOT, 1988.

———. *Early Israel: Anthropological and Historical Studies on the Israelite Society before the Monarchy.* VTSup 37. Leiden: Brill, 1985.

———. "Kings and Clients: On Loyalty between the Ruler and the Ruled in Ancient 'Israel.'" Pages 119–32 in *Ethics and Politics in the Hebrew Bible.* Edited by Douglas Knight. *Semeia* 66. Atlanta: Scholars Press, 1994 (1995).

————. "The Hebrew and the Seven Year Cycle." *BN* 25 (1984): 65–76.

————. "The Hebrew Slave. Comments on the Slave Law, Ex. xxi 2–11." *VT* 25 (1975): 129–44.

————. "חפשי in 1 Sam. XVII 25." *VT* 24 (1974): 373–74.

Lenski, Gerhard E. *Human Societies: A Macrolevel Introduction to Society* New York: McGraw-Hill Book Company, 1970.

————. *Power and Privilege: A Theory of Social Stratification.* Chapel Hill: University of North Carolina Press, 1984.

Lenski, Gerhard and Jean Lenski. *Human Societies: An Introduction to Macrosociology.* New York: McGraw-Hill, 1974.

Lerner, Gerda. *The Creation of Patriarchy.* New York: Oxford University Press, 1986.

Lesko, Barbara S. "Ranks, Roles, and Rights." Pages 15–40 in *Pharaoh's Workers: The Villagers of Deir el Medina.* Edited by Leonard H. Lesko. Ithaca: Cornell University Press, 1994.

————. *The Remarkable Women of Ancient Egypt.* 2nd rev. ed. Providence: Scribe, 1987.

————. "Women's Monumental Mark on Ancient Egypt." *BA* 54 (1991): 4–15. Cited 20 December 2010. Online: http://www.jstor.org/stable/3210327.

————, ed. *Women's Earliest Records from Ancient Egypt and Western Asia.* BJS 166. Atlanta: Scholars Press, 1989.

Leuchter, Mark. "The Manumission Laws in Leviticus and Deuteronomy: The Jeremiah Connection." *JBL* 127 (2008): 635–53.

Levi Julian, Hana. "Ancient Olive Oil Press Unearthed in Galilee." Published: 08/07/08, 10:02 AM/Last Update: 08/08/08, 9:22 AM. No pages. Cited 9 June 2010. Online: http://www.israelnationalnews.com/News/News.aspx/127106.

Levenson, Jon D. *Esther: A Commentary.* OTL. Louisville: Westminster John Knox, 1997.

Lever, Alison. "Honor as a Red Herring." *Critique of Anthropology* 6/3 (1986): 83–106.

Levine, Amy-Jill. "Ruth." Pages 78–84 in *The Women's Bible Commentary.* Edited by Carol Newsom and Sharon Ringe. Louisville: Westminster John Knox, 1992.

Levine, Baruch. *Leviticus.* JPS Torah Commentary. Philadelphia: JPS, 5749/1989.

————."The *Netînîm.*" *JBL* 82 (1963): 207–12.Levinson, Bernard M. "The Birth of the Lemma: The Restrictive Reinterpretation of the Covenant Code's Manumission Law by the Holiness Code (Leviticus 25:44–46)." *JBL* 124 (2005): 617–39.

Levy, Janet. "Gender, Heterarchy, and Hierarchy." Pages 219–46 in *Handbook of Gender in Archaeology.* Edited by Sarah Milledge Nelson. Lanham: AltaMira, 2006. Cited 10 June 2011. Online: http://books.google.com .ar/books?id=EtIQUpgo2cEC&printsec=frontcover&dq=Handbook+of+gender+in+ archaeology&hl=en&sa=X&ei=vcsFUcOZLee- 0QHVwoGgCQ&ved=0CCoQ6AEwAA#v=onepage&q=Handbook%20of%20gend er%20in%20archaeology&f=false.

Lewy, J. "The Biblical Institution of *deror* in the light of Akkadian Documents." *EI* 5 (1958): 21–31.

Limburg, James. *Hosea-Micah.* Interpretation. Atlanta: John Knox, 1988.

————. *Psalms*. Louisville: Westminster John Knox, 2000.

————. *The Prophets and the Powerless*. Atlanta: John Knox, 1977.

Linafelt, Tod. "Taking Women in Samuel: Readers/Responses/Responsibility." Pages 99–113 in *Reading between Texts*. Edited by Danna Nolan Fewell. Louisville: Westminster John Knox, 1992.

Lindenberger, James M. "How Much for a Hebrew Slave? The Meaning of Mišneh in Deut 15:18." *JBL* 110 (1991): 479–98.

Lindhagen, Curt. *The Servant Motif in the Old Testament*. Uppsala: Lundequistska, 1950.

Lipiński, Edward. "*škn* et *sgn* dans le Sémitique Occidental du Nord." *UF* 5 (1973): 191–207.

————, ed. *State and Temple Economy in the Ancient Near East*. 2 vols. OLA 5–6, Leuven: Departement Oriëntalistiek, 1979.

Llagostera Cuenca, Esteban. "La importancia socio-política de la mujer en el Antiguo Egipto." No pages. Cited: 7 January 2011. Online: http://www.egiptologia .com/mujer-en-el-antiguo-egipto/360-la-importancia-socio-politica-de-la-mujer-en-el-antiguo-egipto.html.

Lofthouse, William. *Israel after the Exile: Sixth and Fifth Centuries, B.C.* Oxford: Clarendon Press, 1928.

Lohfink, Norbert, S.J. "Poverty in the Laws of the Ancient Near East and of the Bible." *TS* 52 (1991): 34–50.

————. *Theology of the Pentateuch*. Minneapolis: Augsburg Fortress, 1994.

London, Gloria. "Fe(male) Potters as the Personification of Individuals, Places, and Things as Known from Ethnoarchaeological Studies." Pages 155–80 in *The World of Women in the Ancient and Classical Near East*. Edited by Beth Alpert Nakhai. Newcastle upon Tyne: Cambridge Scholars Publishing, 2008.

Long, Burke O. *1 Kings with an Introduction to Historical Literature*. FOTL 9. Grand Rapids: Eerdmans, 1984.

————. *2 Kings*. Grand Rapids: Eerdmans, 1991.

————. "Framing Repetitions in Biblical Historiography." *JBL* 106 (1987): 385–99.

Lopes, Mercedes. *A mulher sábia e a sabedoria mulher— símbolos de co-inspiração. Um estudo sobre a mulher em textos de Provérbios*. Ph.D. diss., Universidade Metodista de São Paulo (Brazil), 2007.

————. "A sabedoria artista do universo: Provérbios 8, 22–31." Pages 135–50 in *Ecce mulier: Homenaje a Irene Foulkes*. Edited by Rebeca Montemayor *et al.* San José: UBL, 2005.Loretz, Oswald. *Qohelet und der alte Orient: Untersuchungen zu Still und theologischer Thematik des Buches Qohelet*. Freiburg: Herder, 1964.

Lowery, R. H. *The Reforming Kings: Cults and Society in First Temple Judah*. JSOTSup 120, Sheffield: Sheffield Academic Press, 1991.

Mace, D. *The Hebrew Marriage: A Sociological Study*. New York: Philosophical Library, 1953.

Macdonald, J. "The Status and Role of the Na'ar in Israelite Society." *JNES* 35 (1976): 147–70.

————. "The Status and Role of the Suharu in the Mari Correspondence." *JAOS* 96 (1976): 57–68.

MacDonald, Elizabeth. *The Position of Women as Reflected in Semitic Codes of Law*. Toronto: University of Toronto Press, 1931.

Maidman, Maynard Paul. *Nuzi Texts and Their Uses as Historical Evidence*. Edited by Ann K. Guinan. Atlanta: SBL, 2010.

Maier, Christl M. "Daughter Zion as Queen and the Iconography of the Female City." Pages 147–62 in *Images and Prophecy in the Ancient Eastern Mediterranean*. Edited by Martti Nisinen and Charles E. Carter. Göttingen: Vandenhoeck & Ruprecht, 2009.

Maier, Johann. "Self-Definition, Prestige, and Status of Priests towards the End of the Second Temple Period." *BTB* 23 (1993): 139–50.

Malamat, Abraham. "Is There a Word for the Royal Harem in the Bible? The *Inside Story*." Pages 785–87 in *Pomegranates and Golden Bells: Festschrift Jacob Milgrom*. Edited by D. P. Wright, D. N. Freedman, and A. Hurvitz. Winona Lake: Eisenbrauns, 1995. Repr. in his *Mari and the Bible*. Leiden: Brill, 1998, 172–74.

———. "Pre-Monarchical Social Institutions in Israel in the Light of Mari." Pages 165–76 in *Congress Volume Jerusalem 1986*. Edited by J. A. Emerton. VTSup 40. Leiden: Brill, 1988.

———. "The Last Kings of Judah and the Fall of Jerusalem." *IEJ* 18 (1968): 377–92.

Malina, Bruce J. "Patron and Client: The Analogy behind Synoptic Theology." FF 4 (1988): 2–31.

———. *The New Testament World: Insights from Cultural Anthropology*. Rev. ed. Louisville: Westminster John Knox, 1993.

———. "Understanding New Testament Persons." Pages 46–49 in *The Social Sciences and New Testament Interpretation*. Edited by Richard Rohrbaugh. Peabody, Mass.: Hendrickson, 1996.

———."The Social Sciences and Biblical Interpretation." Pages 11–25 in *The Bible and Liberation: Political and Social Hermeneutics*. Edited by Norman K. Gottwald. Maryknoll, N.Y.: Orbis, 1983.

Malina, Bruce J. and Richard L. Rohrbaugh. *Social-Science Commentary on the Synoptic Gospels*. Minneapolis: Fortress, 1992.

Malina, Bruce J. and C. Seeman. "Envy." Pages 55–59 in *Biblical Social Values and Their Meaning: A Handbook*. Edited by Bruce J. Malina and John Pilch. Peabody, Mass.: Hendrickson, 1993.

Maloney, R. "Usury and Restriction on Interest-taking in the Ancient Near East." *CBQ* 36 (1974): 1–20.

Mandelkern, Solomon. *Veteris Testamenti Concordantiae Hebraicae atque Chaldaicae*. Edited byF. Margolin. Graz: Akademische Druck- und Verlagsanstalt, 1925.

Marbury, Herbert Robinson. "The Strange Woman in Persian Yehud: A Reading of Proverbs 7." Pages 167–82 in *Approaching Yehud: New Approaches to the Study of the Persian Period*. Edited by Jon L. Berquist. Atlanta: SBL, 2007.

Mariette, Auguste. *Catalogue général des monuments d'Abydos découverts pendant les fouilles de cette ville*. Paris: L'Imprimerie Nationale, 1880. Cited 1 September 2011. Online: http://www.archive.org/stream/cataloguegnr00mari#page/444/mode/2up.

Marsman, Hennie J. *Women in Ugarit and Israel: Their Social and Religious Position in the Context of the Ancient Near East*. Brill: Leiden, 2003.

Martin, J. D. "Israel as a Tribal Society." Pages 95–115 in *The World of Ancient Israel: Sociological, Anthropological and Political Perspectives.* Edited by Ronald E. Clements. Cambridge: Cambridge University Press, 1989.

Massynbaerdeford, J. "Bookshelf on Prostitution." *BTB* 23 (1993): 128–134.

Matthews, Victor H. "Honor and Shame in Gender-Related Situations." Pages 97–112 in *Gender and Law in the Hebrew Bible.* Edited by Victor H. Matthews, Bernard M. Levinson, and Tikva Frymer-Kensky. Sheffield: Sheffield Academic Press, 1998.

———. "Social Sciences and Biblical Studies." Pages 7–21 in *Honor and Shame in the World of the Bible.* Edited by Victor H. Matthews and Don C. Benjamin. *Semeia* 68. Atlanta: Scholars Press, 1996.

———. "Treading the Winepress: Actual and Metaphorical Viticulture in the Ancient Near East." *Semeia* 86 (1999): 19–32.

Matthews, Victor H. and Don C. Benjamin. *Social World of Ancient Israel, 1250–587 BCE.* Peabody, Mass.: Hendrickson, 1993.

Mattila, Sharon Lea. "Jesus and the 'Middle Peasants'? Problematizing a Social-Scientific Concept." *CBQ* 72 (2010): 291–313.

Mayer, Walter. *Nuzi-Studien I: Die Archive des Palate und die Prosopographie der Berufe.* AOAT 205/1. 1978.

Mayer, Walter, and Mayer-Opificius, Ronald. "Die Schlacht bei Qadeš: Der Versuch einer neuen Rekonstruktion."*UF* 26 (1994): 321–68.

Mayes, A. D. H. *Deuteronomy.* NCBC. Grand Rapids / London: Eerdmans / Marshall, Morgan, & Scott, 1981.

———. *Judges.* OT Guides. Sheffield: JSOT Press, 1985.

Mays, James L. *Amos: A Commentary.* OTL. Phidadelphia: Westminster Press, 1969.

Mazzoni, Stefania. "Having and Showing: Women's Possessions in the Afterlife in Iron Age Syria and Mesopotamia." In *Women and Property in Ancient Near Eastern and Mediterranean Societies:Conference Proceedings, Center for Hellenistic Studies, Harvard University.* Edited by Deborah Lyons and Raymond Westbrook. ©2005, Center for Hellenic Studies, Trustees for Harvard University. Cited 25 May November 2010. No pages. Online: http://chs.harvard .edu/wb/1/wo/WnSQvuI0ROgY8y7nVB1hqw/0.1.

McBride, S. Dean, Jr. "Polity and the Covenant People: The Book of Deuteronomy." Pages 62–77 in *A Song of Power and the Power of Song: Essays on the Book of Deuteronomy.* Edited by Duane L. Christensen. Winona Lake: Eisenbrauns, 1993.

McCaffrey, Kathleen. "Reconsidering Gender Ambiguity in Mesopotamia: Is a Beard Just a Beard?" Pages 379–91 in *Sex and Gender in the Ancient Near East: Proceedings of the 47th Rencontre Assyriologique Internationale, Helsinki, July 2–6, 2001.* Edited by Simo Parpola and R. M. Whiting. Helsinki: ©Neo-Assyrian Text Corpus Project, Institute for Asian and African Studies, University of Helsinki, 2002. McCarter, P. Kyle. *1 Samuel.* AB. Garden City: Doubleday, 1980.

———. *2 Samuel.* AB. Garden City: Doubleday, 1984.

———. "'Plots, True or False.' The Succession Narrative as Court Apologetic." *Int* 35 (1981): 355–67.

McCarthy, D. J. *Treaty and Covenant.* AnBib 21. Rome: Pontifical Biblical Institute, 1963.

McClure, Laura K. "Introduction." Pages 3–18 in *Prostitutes and Courtesans in the Ancient World*. Edited by Christopher A. Faraone and Laura K. McClure. Madison: University of Wisconsin Press, 2006.

McConville, J. G. *Law and Theology in Deuteronomy*. JSOTSup 33. Sheffield: JSOT Press, 1986.

McDaniel, Thomas F. *The Song of Deborah: Poetry in Dialect. A Philological Study of Judges 5 with Translation and Commentary*. Palmer Theological Seminary, Wynewood, PA, 2003. (A rev. edition of *Deborah Never Sang: A Philological Study of the Song of Deborah (Judges Chapter V), with English Translation and Comments*. Jerusalem: Makor, 1983. No pages. Cited 11 June 2011. Online: http://tmcdaniel.palmerseminary.edu.

McDonald, Elizabeth. *The Position of Women as Reflected in Semitic Codes of Law*. Toronto: University of Toronto Press, 1931.

McEvenue, Sean. "The Basis of Empire. A Study of the Succession Narrative (2 Sam. 9–20; 1 Kings 1–2)." *ExAud* 2 (1986): 34–45.

———. "The Old Testament, Scripture or Theology." *ExAud* 1 (1985): 115–24.

———. "Who Was Second Isaiah?" Pages 213–22 in *Studies in the Book of Isaiah: Festschrift for Willem A. M. Beuken*. Edited by J. van Ruiten, and M. Vervenne. Leuven: Leuven University Press, 1997.

McGinn, Thomas A. J. "The Legal Definition of Prostitute in Late Antiquity." *Memoirs of the American Academy in Rome* 42 (1997): 73–116.

McGovern, Arthur. "The Bible in Latin American Theology." Pages 74–85 in *The Bible and Liberation: Political and Social Hermeneutics*. Edited by Norman K. Gottwald. Maryknoll, N. Y.: Orbis, 1983.

McIntosh, M. "Stages of Curricular Re-Vision." Wellesley College Center for Research on Women, Working Paper # 124, 1983.

McKane, William. *I and II Samuel*. London: SCM, 1963.

———. *Proverbs: A New Approach*. London / Philadelphia: SCM / Westminster, 1970.

———. *The Book of Micah: Introduction and Commentary*. Edinburgh: T&T Clark, 1998.

McKay, Heather A. "Gendering the Discourse of Display in the Hebrew Bible." Pages 169–200 in *On Reading Prophetic Texts: Gender-Specific and Related Studies in Memory of Fokkelien van Dijk-Hemmes*. Edited by Bob Becking and Meindert Dijkstra. Leiden: Brill, 1996.

———. "She Said to Him, He Said to Her: Power Talk in the Bible *or* Foucault Listens at the Keyhole." *BTB* 28 (1998): 46–48.

McKenzie, Steven. *The Trouble with Kings: The Composition of the Book of Kings in the Deuteronomistic History*. VTSup 42. Leiden: Brill, 1991.

McNutt, Paula M. *The Forging of Israel: Iron Technology, Symbolism, and Tradition in Ancient Society*. JSOTSup 108. SWAB 8. Sheffield: Almond, 1990.

Meek, Theophile J. "The Code of Hammurabi." Pages 163–80 in *Ancient Near Eastern Texts Relating to the Old Testament*. Edited by James B. Pritchard. Rev. and enl. ed. Princeton: Princeton University Press, 1955.

Meier, Samuel A. "Women and Communication in the Ancient Near East." *JAOS* 111 (1991): 540–47.

Melville, Sarah C., Brent A. Strawn, Brian B. Schmidt, and Scott Noegel. "Neo-Assyrian and Syro-Palestinian Texts I." Pages 280–330 in *The Ancient Near East: Historical Sources in Translation*. Edited by Mark W. Chavalas. Malden: Blackwell, 2006.

Mena López, Maricel. "Raíces Afro-Asiáticas en el mundo bíblico. Desafíos para la exégesis y hermenéutica latinoamericana." *RIBLA* 54 (2006): 17–34. Cited 4 September 2012. Online: http://www.ribla.org/.

Mendelsohn, Isaac. *Legal Aspects of Slavery in Babylonia, Assyria and Palestine: A Comparative Study (3000–500 B. C.)*. Williamsport: Bayard, 1932.

———. "New Light on the *Hupšu*." *BASOR* 139 (1955): 9–11.

———. "On Corvée Labor in Ancient Canaan and Israel." *BASOR* 167 (1962): 31–35.

———. "On Slavery in Alakakh." *IEJ* 5 (1955): 65–72.

———. "Samuel's Denunciation of Kingship in the Light of the Akkadian Documents from Ugarit." *BASOR* 143 (1956): 17–22.

———. *Slavery in the Ancient Near East*. New York: Oxford University Press, 1949.

———. "State Slavery in Ancient Israel." *BASOR* 85 (1942): 14–17.

———. "The Canaanite Term for 'Free Proletarian.'" *BASOR* 83 (1941): 36–39.

———. "The Conditional Sale into Slavery of Free-Born Daughters in Nuzi and in the Law of Ex 21, 7–11." *JAOS* 55 (1935): 190–95.

———. "The Family in the ANE." *BA* 11 (1948): 24–40.

Menu, Bernadette. "Women and Business Life in the First Millennium B.C." Pages 193–205 in *Women's Earliest Records from Ancient Egypt and Western Asia*. Edited by Barbara Lesko. BJS 166. Atlanta: Scholars Press, 1989.

Meyers, Carol. "Archaeology—A Window to the Lives of Israelite Women." Pages 61–108 in *Torah*. Edited by Irmtraud Fischer and Mercedes Navarro Puerto. Atlanta: SBL, 2008.

———. *Discovering Eve: Ancient Israelite Women in Context*. New York: Oxford University Press, 1988.

———. "Everyday Life in Biblical Israel: Women's Social Networks." Pages 185–204 in *Life and Culture in the Ancient Near East*. Edited by Richard Averbeck, Mark W. Chavalas, and David B. Weisberg. Bethesda, Md.: CDL Press, 2003.

———. "Fumes, Flames or Fluids? Reframing the Cup-and-Bowl Question." Pages 30–39 in *Boundaries of the Ancient Near Eastern World: A Tribute to Cyrus H. Gordon*. Edited by Meir Lubetski. Sheffield: Sheffield Academic Press, 1998.

———. "Procreation, Production, and Protection: Male-Female Balance in Early Israel." *JAAR* 51 (1983): 569–93.

———. "The Family in First Temple Israel." Pages 48–103 in *Families in Ancient Israel*. Edited by Leo G. Perdue, et al. Louisville, Kentucky: Westminster John Knox, 1997.

———. "The Roots of Restriction: Women in Early Israel." *BA* 41 (1978): 91–103.

———. "'To Her Mother's House': Considering a Counterpart to the Israelite *Bet 'ab*." Pages 39–51 in *The Bible and the Politics of Exegesis: Essays in Honor of Norman K. Gottwald on the Occasion of His Sixty-Fifth Birthday*. Edited by David Jobling, Peggy L. Day, and Gerald Sheppard. Cleveland: Pilgrim, 1991.

————. "Women and the Domestic Economy of Early Israel." Pages 265–78 in *Women's Earliest Records from Ancient Egypt and Western Asia*. Edited by Barbara Lesko. BJS 166. Atlanta: Scholars Press, 1989.

Milgrom, Jacob. "H_R in Leviticus and Elsewhere in the Torah." Pages 24–40 in *The Book of Leviticus: Composition and Reception*. Edited by Rolf Rendtorff and Robert A. Kugler (with the assistance of Sarah Smith Bartel). Leiden: Brill, 2003.

Miller, James E. "A Critical Response to Karin Adams's Reinterpretation of Hosea 4:13–14." *JBL* 128 (2009): 503–6.

————. *Raw Material: Studies in Biblical Sexuality*. 2nd rev. ed. 2010 (2006). Unpublished. No pages. Cited 2 January 2011. Online: http://www.othersheep .org/Writings_James_E_Miller_Raw_Material_Studies_in_Biblical_Sexuality_2nd_ Edition_2010.html.

Miller, Marvin Lloyd. "Nehemiah 5: A Response To Philippe Guillaume." *JHS* 10, article 13 (2010). No pages. Cited 22 January 2011. Online: http://www.arts.ualberta.ca/JHS/Articles/article_141.pdf.

Mitchell, T. C. "The Music of the Old Testament Reconsidered." *PEQ* 124 (1992): 124–43. Cited 2 September 2011. Online: http://www.biblicalstudies.org .uk/pdf/peq/music_ot_mitchell.pdf.

Miura, Nozomi. "A Typology of Personified Wisdom Hymns." *BTB* 34 (2004): 138–49.

Mobley, Gregory. *Samson and the Liminal Hero in the Ancient Near East*. London: T&T Clark, 2006.

Moore, Michael S. Review of Claus Wilcke, *Early Ancient Near Eastern Law: A History of Its Beginnings: The Early Dynastic and Sargonic Periods*. *Review of Biblical Literature* [http://www.bookreviews.org] (2008). Published 19 April 2008.

Myers, Jacob M. *1 Chronicles*. AB. Garden City: Doubleday, 1965

————. *Ezra. Nehemiah*. AB. Garden City: Doubleday, 1965.

————. "Sociology and the Old Testament." Pages 39–63 in *The World of Ancient Israel: Sociological, Anthropological and Political Perspectives*. Edited by Ronald E. Clements. Cambridge: Cambridge University Press, 1989.

Na'aman, Nadav. "From Conscription of Forced Labor to a Symbol of Bondage: *Mas* in the Biblical Literature." Pages 746–58 in *"An Experienced Scribe Who Neglects Nothing": Ancient Near Eastern Studies in Honor of Jacob Klein*. Edited by Yitschak Sefati *et al*. Bethesda, Md.: CDL Press, 2005.

Nakhai, Beth Alpert. "Daily Life in the Ancient Near East: New Thoughts on an Old Topic." *RelSRev* 31 (2005): 147–53.

————. "Introduction: The World of Women in the Ancient and Classical Near East." Pages ix–xviii in *The World of Women in the Ancient and Classical Near East*. Edited by Beth Alpert Nakhai. Newcastle upon Tyne: Cambridge Scholars Publishing, 2008.

Nash, Manning. *Primitive and Peasant Economic Systems*. San Francisco: Chandler, 1966.

Nelson, Richard D. *Deuteronomy: A Commentary*. OTL. Louisville/London: Westminster John Knox, 2002.

————. *Joshua*. OTL. Louisville: Westminster John Knox, 1997.

Nemet-Nejat, Karen Rhea. *Daily Life in Ancient Mesopotamia*. Westport: Greenwood, 1998.

———. "Women in Ancient Mesopotamia." Pages 85–114 in *Women's Roles in Ancient Civilizations: A Reference Guide*. Edited by Bella Vivante. Westport, Conn.: Greenwood, 1999.

Neufeld, E. "The Prohibitions against Loans at Interest in Ancient Hebrew Laws." *HUCA* 26 (1955): 355–412.

———. "The Rate of Interest and the Text of Nehemiah 5.11." *JQR* 44 (1953/54): 194–204.

Neumann, Hans. "Bemerkungen zu Ehe, Konkubinat und Bigamie in neusumerischer Zeit." Pages 131–37 in *La Femme dans le Proche-Orient Antique: XXXIIIe. Rencontre Assyriologique Internationale*. Edited by Jean-Marie Durand. Editions Recherche sur les Civilisations: Paris, 1987.

Newsom, Carol A. "Reflections on Ideological Criticism and Postcritical Perspectives." Pages 541–60 in *Method Matters: Essays on the Interpretation of the Hebrew Bible in Honor of David L. Petersen*. Edited by Joel M. LeMon and Kent Harold Richards. Resources for Biblical Study. Atlanta: SBL, 2009.

Newsom, Carol A. and Sharon Ringe, eds. *The Women's Bible Commentary*. Louisville: Westminster John Knox, 1992.

Newsome, J. D., Jr. *By the Waters of Babylon: An Introduction to the History and Theology of the Exile*. Atlanta: John Knox, 1979.

Neyrey, Jerome H. "Loss of Wealth, Loss of Family, and Loss of Honour: The Cultural Context of the Original Makarisms in Q." Pages 139–58 in *Modeling Early Christianity: Social-scientific Studies of the New Testament in Its Context*. Edited by Philip Esler. London: Routledge, 1995.

Nicholson, E. W. "Covenant in a Century of Study since Wellhausen." Pages 78–93 in *A Song of Power and the Power of Song: Essays on the Book of Deuteronomy*. Edited by Duane L. Christensen. Winona Lake: Eisenbrauns, 1993.

Niditch, Susan. "Genesis." Pages 10–25 in *The Women's Bible Commentary*. Edited by Carol Newsom and Sharon Ringe. Louisville: Westminster John Knox, 1992.

———. "The 'Sodomite' Theme in Judges 19–20: Family, Community, and Social Disintegration." *CBQ* 44 (1982): 365–78.

———. *War in the Hebrew Bible: A Study on the Ethics of Violence*. New York, Oxford: Oxford University Press, 1993.

Nielsen, Kirsten. *Ruth: A Commentary*. OTL. Louisville: Westminster John Knox, 1997.

Nixon, Lucia. "Gender Bias in Archaeology." Pages 1–23 in *Women in Ancient Societies: An Illusion of the Night*. Edited by Léonie Archer, Susan Fischler, and Maria Wyke. New York: Routledge, 1994.

North, R. *Sociology of the Biblical Jubilee*. AnBib 4. Rome, 1954.

Noth, Martin. *A History of Pentateuchal Traditions*. Trans. and introd. by Bernhard W. Anderson. Englewood Cliffs, N. J.: Prentice Hall, 1972.

———. *Leviticus*. London: SCM, 1965.

———. *The Laws in the Pentateuch and Other Studies*. Philadelphia: Fortress, 1967.

———. *The Chronicler's History*. Trans. and intr. by H. Williamson. JSOTSup 50. Sheffield: Sheffield Academic Press, 1987.

O'Brien, D. P. "'Is This the Time to Accept ...?' (2 Kings V 26B): Simply Moralizing or Yahweh's Rejection of Israel (MT)?" *VT* 46 (1996): 448–57.

O'Connell, Robert H. "Proverbs VII 16–17: A Case of Fatal Deception in A 'Woman and the Window' Type-Scene." *VT* 41 (1991): 235–41.

Oded, Bustenay. "Judah and the Exile." Pages 435–88 in *Israelite and Judean History*. Edited by J. H. Hayes and J. M. Miller. London: SCM, 1977.

O'Hara Graff, Ann, ed. *In the Embrace of God: Feminist Approaches to Theological Anthropology*. Maryknoll, N. Y.: Orbis, 1995.

Olmo Lete, Gregorio del. *Mitos y leyendas de Canaán según la tradición de Ugarit*. Madrid: Cristiandad, 1981.

Olson, Dennis T. *Numbers*. Interpretation. Louisville: John Knox, 1996.

Olyan, Saul M. "Honor, Shame, and Covenant Relations in Ancient Israel and Its Environment." *JBL* 115 (1996): 201–18.

Oppenheim, A. Leo. *Ancient Mesopotamia: Portrait of a Dead Civilization*. Rev. ed. completed by Erica Reiner. Chicago: University of Chicago Press, 1977.

———. "'Siege-Documents' from Nippur." *Iraq* 17 (1955): 69–89.Osiek, Carolyn. "The Feminist and the Bible: Hermeneutical Alternatives." Pages 93–105 in *Feminist Perspectives on Biblical Scholarship*. Edited by Adela Yarbro Collins. SBL Centennial Publications. Chico, Calif.: Scholars Press, 1985.

———. "Slavery in the Second Testament World." *BTB* 22 (1992): 174–79.

———. *What Are They Saying About the Social Setting of the New Testament?* Rev. and exp. ed. New York: Paulist, 1992.

Otto, Eckart. "Aspects of Legal Reforms and Reformulations in Ancient Cuneiform and Israelite Law." Pages 160–96 in *Theory and Method in Biblical and Cuneiform Law*. Edited by Bernard Levinson. JSOTSup 181. Sheffield: Sheffield Academic Press, 1994.

———. "False Weights in the Scales of Biblical Justice: Different Views of Women from Patriarchal Hierarchy to Religious Equality in the Book of Deuteronomy." Pages 128–46 in *Gender and Law in the Hebrew Bible*. Edited by Victor H. Matthews, Bernard M. Levinson, and Tikva Frymer-Kensky. Sheffield: Sheffield Academic Press, 1998.

———. "Rechtssystematik im altbabylonischen 'Codex Esnunna' und im altisraelitischen 'Bundesbuch'. Eine Redaktionsgeschichtliche und rechts-vergleichende Analyse von CE §§ 17; 18; 22–28 und Ex 21,18–32; 22,6–14; 23, 1–3.6–8." *UF* 19 (1987): 175–97.

———. Review of John Van Seters, *A Law Book for the Diaspora: Revision in the Study of the Covenant Code*. *Review of Biblical Literature* [http://www.bookreviews .org] (2004). Published 10 July 2004.

Otzen, B. "The Promoting Mother. A Literary Motif in the Ugaritic Texts and in the Bible." Pages 104–14 in *History and Traditions of Early Israel. Studies Presented to Eduard Nielsen*. Edited by Andre Lemaire and Benedikt Otzen. VTSup 50. Leiden: Brill, 1993.

Overholt, Thomas W. *Cultural Anthropology and the Old Testament*. Minneapolis: Fortress, 1996.

Parker, B. "The Nimrud Tablets, 1952–Business Documents." *Iraq* 16 (1954): 29–58.

Parker, Kim Ian. "Repetition as a Structuring Device in 1 Kings 1–11." *JSOT* 42 (1988): 19–27.

Parsons, Talcott. *Essays in Sociological Theory.* Glencoe, Ill.: Free Press, 1957.

Patai, Raphael. *The Hebrew Goddess.* 3rd. enlarged ed. Detroit: Wayne State University Press, 1990.

Patrick, Dale. *Old Testament Law.* Atlanta: John Knox, 1985.

Patte, Daniel, ed. *Narrative and Discourse in Structural Exegesis. John 6 and 1 Thessalonians. Semeia* 26. Chico, Calif.: Scholars Press, 1983.

Patterson, Orlando. "Slavery." *Annual Review of Sociology* 3 (1977): 407–49.

———. *Slavery and Social Death: A Comparative Study.* Cambridge: Harvard College, 1982.

Paul, Shalom M. "Biblical Analogues to Middle Assyrian Law." Pages 333–50 in *Religion and Law: Biblical-Judaic amd Islamic Perspective.* Edited by Edwin B. Firmage, Bernard G. Weiss, and John W. Welch. Winona Lake: Eisenbrauns, 1990.

———. *Studies in the Book of the Covenant in the Light of Near Eastern Law.* VTSup 18. Leiden: Brill, 1970.

Pearce, Laurie E. "The Scribes and Scholars of Ancient Mesopotamia." Pages 2265–78 in volume 4 of *Civilizations of the Ancient Near East.* Edited by Jack M. Sasson. 4 volumes. New York: Scribner, 1995.

Pedersen, Johannes. *Israel, Its Life and Culture.* 2 vols. London: Oxford University Press, 1926.

Penchansky, David. "Staying the Night: Intertextuality in Genesis and Judges." Pages 77–88 in *Reading between Texts.* ed. D. Nolan Fewell. Louisville: Westminster John Knox, 1992.

Perdue, Leo G. "The Household, Old Testament Theology, and Contemporary Hermeneutics." Pages 223–57 in *Families in Ancient Israel.* Edited by Leo G. Perdue et al. Louisville: Westminster John Knox, 1997.

———. "The Israelite and Early Jewish Family: Summary and Conclusions." Pages 163–222 in *Families in Ancient Israel.* Edited by Leo G. Perdue et al. Louisville: Westminster John Knox, 1997.

Peristiany, J. G. and J. Pitt-Rivers. "Introduction." Pages 1–17 in *Honor and Grace in Anthropology.* Edited by J. G. Peristiany and J. Pitt-Rivers. Cambridge: at the University Press, 1992.

Pham, Xuan Huong Thi. *Mourning in the Ancient Near East and the Hebrew Bible.* JSOTSup 302. Sheffield: Sheffield Academic Press, 1999.

Phillips, Anthony. "Some Aspects of Family Law in Pre-Exilic Israel." *VT* 23 (1973): 349–61.

———. "The Decalogue: Ancient Israel's Criminal Law." Pages 225–46 in *A Song of Power and the Power of Song: Essays on the Book of Deuteronomy.* Edited by Duane L. Christensen. Winona Lake: Eisenbrauns, 1993.

———. "The Laws of Slavery: Exodus 21.2–11." *JSOT* 30 (1984): 51–66.

Pigott, Susan M. "Wives, Witches and Wise Women: Prophetic Heralds of Kingship in 1 and 2 Samuel."*RevExp* 99 (2002): 145–73.

Pilch, John J. and Bruce J. Malina. *AHandbook of Biblical Social Values.* Peabody, Mass.: Hendrickson, 2009.

Pinker, Aron. "A Note on בשא in Nahum 3:6." *Hip̄l* 5(2008). No pages. Cited 11 June 2011. Online: http://www.see-j.net/index.php/hiphil/article/view/39/36.

Pirenne-Delforge,Vinciane. Review of Stephanie Budin, *The Myth of Sacred Prostitution in Antiquity*. *Bryn Mawr Classical Review* 2009.04.28. No pages. Cited 23 November 2010. Online: http://bmcr.brynmawr.edu/2009/2009-04-28.html.

Pitt-Rivers, Julian. *The Fate of Shechem or The Politics of Sex: Essays in the Anthropology of the Mediterranean*. Cambridge: Cambridge University Press, 1977.

Plevnik, J. "Honor/Shame." Pages 95–104 in *Biblical Social Values and Their Meaning*. Edited by John J. Pilch and Bruce J. Malina. Peabody. Mass.: Hendrickson, 1993.

Ploeg, van der, J. P. M. "Slavery in the Old Testament."Pages72–87 in *Congress Volume: Uppsala 1971*. Edited by H. S. Nyberg *et al*. VTSup 22. Leiden: Brill, 1972.

Pollock, Susan. "Women in a Men's World: Images of Sumerian Women." Pages 366–87 in *Engendering Archaeology: Women and Prehistory*. Edited by Joan M. Gero and Margaret W. Conkey. Oxford: Basil Blackwell, 1991.

Polzin, "The Monarchy Begins: 1 Samuel 8–10." *SBLSP* 26 (1987): 120–43.

Pomeroy, Sarah B. *Goddesses, Whores, Wives, and Slaves: Women in Classical Antiquity*. 20th anniversary ed. New York: Schocken, 1995.

———. *Women in Hellenistic Egypt: From Alexander to Cleopatra*. New ed. Detroit: Wayne State University Press, 1984.

Powell, Marvin A., ed. *Labor in the Ancient Near East*. AOS 68. New Haven: American Oriental Society, 1987.

Pope, Marvin H. *Song of Songs*. AB. Garden City: Doubleday, 1977.

Postgate, J. N. "Employer, Employee and Employment in the Neo-Assyrian Empire." Pages 256–70 in *Labor in the Ancient Near East*. AOS 68. New Haven: American Oriental Society, 1987.

Pressler, Carolyn. *Joshua, Judges and Ruth*. Louisville: Westminster John Knox, 2002.

———. *The View of Women Found in the Deuteronomic Family Laws*. BZAW 216. Berlin: de Gruyter, 1993.

———. "Wives and Daughters, Bond and Free: Views of Women in the Slave Laws of Exodus 21.2–11." Pages 147–72 in *Gender and Law in the Hebrew Bible*. Edited by Victor H. Matthews, Bernard M. Levinson, and Tikva Frymer-Kensky. JSOTSup 262. Sheffield: Sheffield Academic Press, 1998.

Pyper, Hugh S. "Judging the Wisdom of Solomon: The Two-Way Effect of Intertext." *JSOT* 59 (1993): 25–36.

———. "Surviving Writing: The Anxiety of Historiography in the Former Prophets. Pages 227–49 in *The New Literary Criticism and the Hebrew Bible*. Edited by David J. A. Clines and J. Cheryl Exum. Valley Forge: Trinity International; Sheffield Academic Press, 1993.

Rabin, Chaim. "The Origin of the Hebrew Word *Pīlegeš*." *JJS* 25 (1974): 353–64.

———. "The Song of Songs and Tamil Poetry." *SR* 3 (1973/4): 205–19.

Rad, Gerhard von. *Deuteronomy: A Commentary*.OTL. Philadelphia: Westminster, 1966.

———. *Genesis*. Rev. ed. OTL. London: SCM, 1972 (1961).

Rand, H. "Figure-vases in Ancient Egypt and Hebrew Midwives." *IEJ* 20 (1970): 209–12.

Raitt, T. M. *A Theology of Exile: Judgment/Deliverance in Jeremiah and Ezekiel.* Philadelphia: Fortress, 1977.

Rainey, Anson F. "Compulsory Labor Gangs in Ancient Israel." *IEJ* 20 (1970): 191–202.

Reade, Julian. "Was Sennacherib a Feminist?" Pages 139–45 in *La Femme dans le Proche-Orient Antique: XXXIIIe. Rencontre Assyriologique Internationale.* Edited by Jean-Marie Durand. Editions Recherche sur les Civilisations: Paris, 1987.

Reinhartz, Adele. "Anonymity and Character in the Books of Samuel." *Semeia* 63 (1993): 117–41.

———. "Anonymous Women and the Collapse of the Monarchy: A Study in Narrative Technique." Pages 43–65 in *A Feminist Companion to Samuel and Kings.* Edited by Athalya Brenner. Sheffield: Sheffield Academic Press, 1994.

Reis, Pamela Tamarkin. "Eating the Blood: Saul and the Witch of Endor." *JSOT* 73 (1997): 3–23.

———. "Killing the Messenger: David's Policy or Politics?" *JSOT* 31 (2006): 167–91.

———. "Spoiled Child: A Fresh Look at Jephthah's Daughter." *Prooftexts* 17 (1987): 279–98.

Rendtorff, Rolf. *The Old Testament: An Introduction.* Philadelphia: Fortress, 1986.

Renger, Johannes. "Comment on: On Economic Structures in Ancient Mesopotamia." *Orientalia* 63 (1994): 157–208.

———. "Economy of Ancient Mesopotamia: A General Outline." Pages 187–97 in *The Babylonian World.* Edited by Gwendolyn Leick. New York: Routledge, 2007.

Reventlow, Henning Graf and Yair Hoffman. *Justice and Righteousness: Biblical Themes and Their Influence.* Sheffield: JSOT, 1992.

Reynolds, Frances. "Food and Drink in Babylonia." Pages 171–84 in *The Babylonian World.* Edited by Gwendolyn Leick. New York: Routledge, 2007.

Riegner, Irene. "The Vanishing Hebrew Harlot: A Diachronic and Synchronic Study of the Root *znh*." Ph.D. diss., Temple University, 2001.

Robins, Gay. *Las mujeres en el antiguo Egipto.* Madrid: Akal, 1996.

———. "Some Images of Women in New Kingdom Art and Literature." Pages 105–16 in *Women's Earliest Records from Ancient Egypt and Western Asia.* Edited by Barbara Lesko. BJS 166. Atlanta: Scholars Press, 1989.

———. *Women in Ancient Egypt.* Cambridge: Harvard University Press, 1993.

Robbins, Vernon K. *Exploring the Texture of Texts: A Guide to Socio-Rhetorical Interpretation.* Valley Forge: Trinity Press International, 1996.

———. "Social-scientific Criticism and Literary Studies: Prospects for Cooperation in Biblical Interpretation." Pages 274–89 in *Modelling Early Christianity.* Edited by Philip Esler. London: Routledge, 1995.

Robledo Casanova, Ildefonso. "Los misterios de los egipcios. El hombre, sus componentes y el Más Allá." *Antigua: Historia y Arqueología de las Civilizaciones* (Web). Alicante: Biblioteca Virtual Miguel de Cervantes. No pages. Cited: 20 December 2010. Online: http://213.0.4 .19/servlet/SirveObras/13538363212820165754491/021575.pdf#search=%22cerveza%20osiris%22&page=15

Roddy, Nicolae. "Perforated Tripodal Vessels at Iron II Bethsaida-Tzer." *BN* NF 141 (2009): 91–100.

Rodney, Nanette B. "Ishtar, the Lady of Battle." *The Metropolitan Museum of Art Bulletin*, New Series. 10, N° 7 (1952): 211–16.

Rofé, Alexander. "Family and Sex Laws in Deuteronomy and the Book of the Covenant." *Henoch* 9 (1987): 131–60.

Rogers, J. S. "Narrative Stock and Deuteronomic Elaboration in 1 Kings 2." *CBQ* 50 (1988): 398–413.

Rogerson, J. W. "Anthropology and the Old Testament." Pages 17–37 in *The World of Ancient Israel: Sociological, Anthropological and Political Perspectives.* Edited by Ronald E. Clements. Cambridge: Cambridge University Press, 1989.

Rohrbaugh, Richard, ed. *The Social Sciences and New Testament Interpretation.* Peabody. Mass.: Hendrickson, 1996.

Rosenstock, Bruce. "David's Play: Fertility Rituals and the Glory of God in 2 Samuel 6." *JSOT* 31 (2006): 63–80.

Roth, Ann Macy. "The Absent Spouse: Patterns and Taboos in Egyptian Tomb Decoration." *Journal of the American Research Center in Egypt* 36 (1999): 37–53. Cited 15 June 2011. Online: http://www.jstor.org/pss/40000201.

Roth, Martha. *Babylonian Marriage Agreements, 7th–3rd Centuries B.C.* AOAT 222. Neukirchen-Vluyn: Verlag Butzon & Bercker Kevelaer/Neukirchener Verlag, 1989.

———. *Law Collections from Mesopotamia and Asia Minor.* SBL Writings from the Ancient World. Atlanta: SBL, 1997[2] (1995).

———. "Marriage and Matrimonial Prestations in First Millennium B.C. Babylonia." Pages 245–55 in *Women's Earliest Records from Ancient Egypt and Western Asia.* BJS 166. Atlanta: Scholars Press, 1989.

———. "Marriage, Divorce, and the Prostitute in Ancient Mesopotamia." Pages 21–39 in *Prostitutes and Courtesans in the Ancient World.* Edited by Christopher A. Faraone and Laura K. McClure. Madison: University of Wisconsin Press, 2006.

Rowlett, Lori. *Joshua and the Rhetroric of Violence: A New Historicist Analysis.* JSOTSup 226. Sheffield: Sheffield Academic Press, 1996.

Ruether, Rosemary Radford. "Feminism and Patriarchal Religion: Principles of Ideological Critique of the Bible." *JSOT* 22 (1982): 54–66.

———, ed. *Religion and Sexism.* New York: Simon and Schuster, 1974.

Runions, Erin. "Violence and the Economy of Desire in Ezekiel 16.1–45." Pages 156–69 in *Prophets and Daniel. A Feminist Companion to the Bible.* Edited by Athalya Brenner. 2nd series. Sheffield Academic Press/Continuum: London/New York, 2001.

Ruwe, Andreas. "The Structure of the Book of Leviticus in the Narrative Outline of the Priestly Sinai Story (Exod 19:1–Num 10:10)." Pages 55–78 in *The Book of Leviticus: Composition and Reception.* Edited by Rolf Rendtorff and Robert A. Kugler (with the assistance of Sarah Smith Bartel). Leiden: Brill, 2003.

Sacon, Kiyoshi K. "A Study of the Literary Structure of 'The Succession Narrative.'" Pages 27–54 in *Studies in the Period of David and Solomon and Other Essays.* Edited by Tomoo Ishida. Winona Lake: Eisenbrauns, 1982.

Sáenz Badillos, Angel. *A History of the Hebrew Language.* Cambridge: Cambridge University Press, 1993.

Sakenfeld, Katharine Doob. *Journeying with God: A Commentary on the Book of Numbers*. Grand Rapids/Edinburgh: Eerdmans/Handsel, 1995.

―――. "Numbers." Pages 45–51 in *The Women's Bible Commentary*. Edited by Carol Newsom and Sharon Ringe. Louisville: Westminster John Knox, 1992.

―――. "Old Testament Perspectives: Methodological Issues." *JSOT* 22 (1982): 13–20.

Saller, Richard. "Patronage and Friendship in Early Imperial Rome: Drawing the Distinction." Pages 49–62 in *Patronage in Ancient Society*. Edited by A. Wallace-Hadrill. London: Routledge, 1989.

Samuel, Delwen. "Investigation of Ancient Egyptian Baking and Brewing Methods by Correlative Microscopy." *Science* 273 (1996): 488–90. Cited 20 May 2011. Online: http://sbli.ls.manchester.ac.uk/fungi/21st_Century_Guidebook_to_Fungi/REPRINT_collection/Samuel_ancient_Egyptian_baking+brewing1996.pdf.

Sarna, Nahum. *Exodus*. The JPS Torah Commentary. Philadelphia: The Jewish Publication Society, 5751/1991.

―――. *Genesis*. JPS Torah Commentary. Philadelphia: JPS, 5749/1989.

―――. "Zedekiah's Emancipation of Slaves and the Sabbatical Year." Pages 143–49 in *Orient and Occident: Essays Presented to Cyrus H. Gordon on the Occasion of His Sixty-fifth Birthday.* Edited by Harry A. Hoffner, Jr. AOAT 22. Butzin & Bercker: Kevelaer/ Neukirchener Verlag: Neukirchener-Vluyn, 1973.

Sasson, Jack M. *Ruth: A New Translation with a Philological Commentary and A Formalist-Folklorist Interpretation*. Baltimore: The Johns Hopkins University Press, 1979.

Sasson, V. "*šmn rḥṣ* in the Samaria Ostraca." *JSS* 26 (1981): 1–5.

Sawyer, J. F. A. "Daughter of Zion and Servant of the Lord in Isaiah: A Comparison." *JSOT* 44 (1989): 89–107.

Schäfer-Bossert, S. "Den Männern die Macht und der Frau die Trauer? Ein Kritischer Blick auf die Deutung von אוֹן—oder: Wie nennt Rahel ihren Sohn?" Pages 106–25 in *Feministische Hermeneutik und Erstes Testament: Analysen und Interpretationen*. Edited by H. Jahnow et al. Stuttgart: Kohlhammer, 1994.

Schaub, Marilyn M. Review of Frankel, Rafael, *Wine and Oil Production in Antiquity in Israel and Other Mediterranean Countries*, *CBQ* 62 (2000): 724–25.

Schenker, Adrian. "The Biblical Legislation on The Release of Slaves: The Road From Exodus To Leviticus." *JSOT* 78 (1998): 23–41.

Schneider, Tammi. *Judges*. Berit Olam. Studies in Hebrew Narrative and Poetry. Collegeville: Liturgical Press, 2000.

Schniedewind, William. "Prolegomena for the Sociolinguistics of Classical Hebrew." Volume 5, article 6. No pages. Cited 23 June 2010. Online: http://www.arts.ualberta.ca/JHS/Articles/article_36.pdf.

―――. "Prophets and Prophecy in the Books of Chronicles." Pages 215–20 in *The Chronicler as Historian*. Edited by M. Patrick Graham, Kenneth G. Hoglund, and Steven L. McKenzie. JSOTSup 238. Sheffield: Sheffield Academic Press, 1997.

Scholz, Susanne. *Sacred Witness: Rape in the Hebrew Bible*. Minneapolis: Fortess, 2010.

Schottroff, Louise, Silvia Schroer, and Marie-Theres Wacker, eds. *Feminist Interpretation: The Bible in Women's Perspective*. Minneapolis: Fortress, 1998.

Schottroff, Louise and Marie-Theres Wacker, with collaboration by Claudia Janssen and Beate Wehn, eds. *Kompendium feministische Bibelauslegung*, Gütersloh: Chr. Kaiser-Gütersloher, 1998.

Schroer, Silvia. "Toward a Feminist Reconstruction of the History of Israel." Pages 85–176 in *Feminist Interpretation: The Bible in Women's Perspective.* Edited by Louise Schottroff, Silvia Schroer, and Marie-Theres Wacker. Minneapolis: Fortress, 1998.

———, ed. *Images and Gender: Contributions to the Hermeneutics of Reading Ancient Art.* Fribourg/ Göttingen: Fribourg Academic Press/ Vandenhoeck & Ruprecht, 2006.

Schulte, Hannelis. "Beobachtungen zum Begriff der *Zônâ* im Alten Testament." *ZAW* 104 (1992): 255–62.

Schulz, Alfons. "Narrative Art in the Books of Samuel." Pages 119–70 in *Narrative and Novella in Samuel: Studies by Hugo Gressmann and Other Scholars 1906–1923.* Edited by David M. Gunn. JSOTS 116. Sheffield: Almond Press, 1991.

Schüngel-Straumann, Helen. *Denn Gott bin ich, und kein Mann.* Mainz: Matthias Grünewald-Verlag, 1996.

Schwantes, Milton. "Hagar and Sarah." Pages 76–83 in *Faith Born in the Struggle for Life: A Re-reading of Protestant Faith in Latin America Today.* Edited by D. Kirkpatrick. Grand Rapids: Eerdmans, 1988.

Scott, R. *Proverbs, Ecclesiastes*. AB. Garden City: Doubleday, 1965.

Scullion, John J., S.J. *Genesis: A Commentary for Students, Teachers, and Preachers.* Collegeville, Minn.: Liturgical Press, 1992.

Scurlock, Joanne. "On Some Terms for Leatherworking in Ancient Mesopotamia." Pages 171–76 in *Proceedings of the 51st Rencontre Assyriologique Internationale Held at the Oriental Institute of the University of Chicago, July 18-22, 2005.* Edited by Robert D. Biggs, Jennie Myers, and Martha T. Roth. Studies in Ancient Oriental Civilization 62. Chicago: The University of Chicago, 2008.

Seibert, Ilse. *Woman in Ancient Near East.* Leipzig: Edition Leipzig, 1974.

Selms, A. van. "The Root k-ṯ-r and Its Derivatives in Ugaritic Literature." *UF* 11 (1979): 739–44.

Selz, Gebhard J. "Power, Economy and Social Organization in Babylonia." Pages 276–87 in *The Babylonian World.* Edited by Gwendolyn Leick. New York: Routledge, 2007.

Seow, C. L. *Ecclesiastes.* AB. New York: Doubleday, 1997.

Setel, T. Drorah (O'Donnell). "Exodus." Pages 26–35 in *The Women's Bible Commentary.* Edited by Carol Newsom and Sharon Ringe. Louisville: Westminster John Knox, 1992.

———. "Feminist Insights and the Question of Method." Pages 35–42 in *Feminist Perspectives on Biblical Scholarship.* Edited by Adela Yarbro Collins. SBL Centennial Publicarions. Chico, Calif.: Scholars Press, 1985.

———. "Prophets and Pornography: Female Sexual Imagery in Hosea." Pages 143–55 in *A Feminist Companion to the Song of Songs.* Edited by Athalya Brenner. Sheffield: JSOT Press, 1993.

Shanin, Theodor. "Introduction: Peasantry as a Concept." Pages 1–4 in *Peasants and Peasant Societies: Selected Readings*. Edited by Theodor Shanin. Oxford: Blackwell, 1987.

Shargent, Karla G. "Living on the Edge: The Liminality of Daughters in Genesis to 2 Samuel." Pages 26–42 in *A Feminist Companion to Samuel and Kings*. Edited by Athalya Brenner. Sheffield: Sheffield Academic Press, 1994.

Sherwood, Aaron. "A Leader's Misleading and a Prostitute's Profession: A Re-examination of Joshua 2." *JSOT* 31 (2006): 43–61.

Silver, Morris. *Economic Structures of the Ancient Near East*. Totowa, N. J.: Barnes and Noble, 1986.

Sjoberg, Gideon. *The Preindustrial City*. Glencoe, Ill.: The Free Press, 1960.

Smith, Michael E. "The Archaeological Study of Neighborhoods and Districts in Ancient Cities." *Journal of Anthropological Archaeology* 29 (2010): 137–54.

———. "The Archaeology of Ancient State Economies." *Annual Review of Anthropology* 33 (2004):73–102.

Snell, Daniel C. *Flight and Freedom in the Ancient Near East*. Culture and History of the Ancient Near East 8. Leiden: Brill, 2001. Partially available online, quotations here are from this version. Cited 21 September 2011. Online: http://books.google.com.ar/books?id=sxvk2iGhcioC&printsec=frontcover&dq=snell,+flight+and+freedom&hl=es&ei=qhFfTdWxHIP88AbjhomoDA&sa=X&oi=book_result&ct=result&resnum=1&ved=0CCwQ6AEwAA#v=onepage&q&f=false.

———. "The Ordinarity of the Peculiar Institution." Pages 3–22 in *The Babylonian World*. Edited by Gwendolyn Leick. New York: Routledge, 2007.

Snaith, Norman H. *2 Samuel XVI–XIX*. London: Epworth, 1945.

———. *Notes on the Hebrew Text of 1 Kings XVII–XIX and XXI–XXII*. London: Epworth, 1954.

Soden, Wolfram von. *The Ancient Orient: An Introduction to the Study of the Ancient Near East*. Grand Rapids: Eerdmans, 1994.

Soggin, J. Alberto. "Compulsory Labor under David and Solomon." Pages 259–67 in *Studies in the Period of David and Solomon and Other Essays*. Edited by T. Ishida. Winona Lake: Eisenbrauns, 1982.

———. *Introduction to the Old Testament: From Its Origins to the Closing of the Alexandrian Canon*. 3rd ed. Louisville: Westminster John Knox, 1989.

———. *Joshua: A Commentary*. OTL. Philadelphia: SCM, 1987.

———. "The Davidic-Solomonic Kingdom." Pages 332–80 in *Israelite and Judean History*. Edited by John H. Hayes and J. Mawxell Miller. Philadelphia: Westminster Press, 1977.

Solvang, Elna K. "Classifying Women: The 'Harem' and What It Does and Doesn't Tell Us about Women." Pages 415–20 in *Proceedings of the 51st Rencontre Assyriologique Internationale Held at the Oriental Institute of the University of Chicago, July 18–22, 2005*. Edited by Robert D. Biggs, Jennie Myers, and Martha T. Roth. Studies in Ancient Oriental Civilization 62. Chicago: The University of Chicago, 2008.

Spencer, Patricia. "Dance in Ancient Egypt." *NEA* 66 (2003) 111–21.

Speiser, E. A. "Akkadian Myths and Epics." Pages 60–119 in *Ancient Near Eastern Texts Relating to the Old Testament*. Edited by James B. Pritchard. Rev. and enl. ed. Princeton: Princeton University Press, 1955.

―――. *Genesis*. AB. Garden City, N.Y.: Doubleday, 1982.

Sprinkle, Joe M. *"The Book of the Covenant": A Literary Approach*. JSOTSup 174. Sheffield: JSOT Press, 1994.

Stager, Lawrence E. "The Archaeology of the Family in Ancient Israel." *BASOR* 260 (1985): 1–35.

―――. "The Finest Olive Oil in Samaria." *JSS* 28 (1983): 241–45.

Stähli, H.-P. *Knabe-Jüngling-Knecht: Untersuchungen zum Begriff Na ʿar im Alten Testament*. Edited by J. Becker and H. Reventlow. BBET. Frankfurt: Lang, 1978.

Stark, Christine. *"Kultprostitution" im Alten Testament? Die Qedeschen der Hebräischen Bibel und das Motiv der Hurerei*. OBO 221. Fribourg/Göttingen: Academic Press/Vandenhoeck & Ruprecht, , 2006.

Starr, Susan Sered. *Women as Ritual Experts*. New York: Oxford University Press, 1992.

Ste. Croix, G. E. M. de. "Slavery and Other Forms of Unfree Labour." Pages 19–32 in *Slavery and Other Forms of Unfree Labour*. Edited by Leonie J. Archer. London: Routledge, 1988.

Steele, Laura D. "Women and Gender in Babylonia." Pages 299–316 in *The Babylonian World*. Edited by Gwendolyn Leick. New York: Routledge, 2007.

Steinberg, Naomi. "Gender Roles in the Rebekah Cycle." *USQR* 39 (1984): 175–76.

―――. *Kinship and Marriage in Genesis: A Household Economics* Perspective. Minneapolis: Augsburg Fortress, 1993.

―――. "Romancing the Widow: The Economic Distinctions between the ʾalmānâ, the ʾiššâ-ʾalmānâ and the ʾēšet-hammēt." Pages 327–46 in volume 1 of *God's Word for Our World: Biblical Studies in Honor of Simon John De Vries*. Edited by J. Harold Ellens et al. 2 volumes. JSOTSup. London: T&T Clark, 2004. Also available at *Women and Property in Ancient Near Eastern and Mediterranean Societies: Conference Proceedings, Center for Hellenistic Studies, Harvard University*. Edited by Deborah Lyons and Raymond Westbrook. Center for Hellenic Studies, Trustees for Harvard University, 2005. Cited 25 Nov 2010. Online: http://www.chs.harvard .edu/wa/pageR?tn=ArticleWrapper&bdc=12&mn=1219.

―――. "Social Scientific Criticism: Judges 9 and Issues of Kinship." Pages 45–64 in *Judges and Method*. Edited by Gale A. Yee. Minneapolis: Fortress, 1995.

―――. "The Deuteronomic Law Code and the Politics of Cult Centralization." Pages 161–70 in *The Bible and the Politics of Exegesis: Essays in Honor of Norman K. Gottwald on the Occasion of His Sixty-Fifth Birthday*. Edited by David Jobling, Peggy L. Day, and Gerald Sheppard. Cleveland: Pilgrim, 1991.

Steiner, Franz. "Enslavement and the Early Hebrew Lineage System." Pages 21–25 in *Anthropological Approaches to the Old Testament*. Edited by Bernhard Lang. London/Philadelphia: SPCK/Fortress, 1985.

Steiner, Gerd. "Die 'Femme Fatale' in alten Orient." Pages 147–53 in *La Femme dans le Proche-Orient Antique: XXXIIIe. Rencontre Assyriologique Internationale*. Edited by Jean-Marie Durand. Paris: Editions Recherche sur les Civilisations, 1987.

Steinkeller, P. "The Foresters of Umma: Toward a Definition of Ur III Labor." Pages 73–115 in *Labor in the Ancient Near East.* Edited by Marvin Powell. AOS 68. New Haven: American Oriental Society, 1987.

Stek, John H. "Rahab of Canaan and Israel. The Meaning of Joshua 2." *CTJ* 37 (2002): 28–48.

Stol, Maarten. *Birth in Babylonia and the Bible: Its Mediterranean Setting* (with a chapter by F. A. M. Wiggermann). Cuneiform Monographs. Groningen: Styx, 2000. Partially available online. Cited 1 July 2011. Online: http://books.google.com .ar/books?hl=es&lr=&id=4LQNeU1ckC&oi=fnd&pg=PP11&dq=maarten+stol+%2 6+birth&ots=IhHOJ9EXz4&sig=DjAueBMr3vsgzvniSTPsfbgDOdI#v=onepage&q &f=false.

———. "Women in Mesopotamia." *JESHO* 38 (1995): 123–44.

Stone, Ken. "Gender and Homosexuality in Judges 19: Subject—Honor, Object—Shame?" *JSOT* 67 (1995): 87–107.

———. "How A Woman Unmans A King: Gender Reversal and The Woman of Thebez in Judges." Pages 71–85 in *Women of the Hebrew Bible and Their Afterlives.* Edited by Peter S. Hawkins and Lesleigh Cushing Stahlberg. Volume 1 of *From the Margins.* Sheffield: Sheffield Phoenix, 2009.

———. *Sex, Honor, and Power in the Deuteronomistic History.* JSOTSup 234. Sheffield: Sheffield Academic Press, 1996.

Strawn, Brent A. et al. "Neo-Assyrian and Syro-Palestinian Texts II." Pages 331–81 in *The Ancient Near East: Historical Sources in Translation.* Edited by Mark W. Chavalas. Malden: Blackwell, 2006.

Suriano, Matthew. "A Fresh Reading for 'Aged Wine' in the Samaria Ostraca." *PEQ* 139 (2007): 27–33.

Sweeney, Deborah. "Walking Alone Forever, Following You: Gender and Mourners' Laments from Ancient Egypt." *NIN: Journal of Gender Studies in Antiquity* 2 (2002): 27–48.

Sweeney, Marvin A. *I and II Kings.* OTL. Louisville: Westminster John Knox, 2007.

———. "The Critique of Solomon in the Josianic Edition of the Deuteronomistic History." *JBL* 114 (1995): 607–22.

Taggar-Cohen, Ada. "The Prince, the KAR.KID Women and the *arzana*-house: A Hittite Royal Festival to the Goddess *Katahha* (CTH 633)." *AoF* 37 (2010): 113–31.

Tamez, Elsa. "The Woman Who Complicated the History of Salvation." Pages 5–17 in *New Eyes for Reading.* Edited by J. Pobee and B. von Wartenberg-Potter. Geneva: World Council of Churches, 1986.

Tapp, A. M. "An Ideology of Expendability: Virgin Daughter Sacrifice in Genesis 19:1–11, Judges 11:30–39 and 19:22–26." Pages 157–74 in *Anti-Covenant: Counter-Reading Women's Lives.* Edited by Mieke Bal. Sheffield: JSOT Press, 1989.

Tate, Marvin E. *Psalms 51–100.* Word Biblical Commentary 20. Waco: Word Books, 1990.

Tatu, Silviu. "Jotham's Fable and The Crux Interpretum in Judges." *VT* 56 (2006): 105–24.

Tavares, A. Augusto. "*L'Almanah* hebraique et *l'Almattu* des textes akkadienes." Pages 155–62 in *La Femme dans le Proche-Orient Antique: XXXIIIe. Rencontre*

Assyriologique Internationale. Edited by Jean-Marie Durand. Editions Recherche sur les Civilisations: Paris, 1987.

Tebes, Juan Manuel. "Tribus, estados, cobre e incienso. El Negev y Edom durante la Edad del Hierro." Ph.D. diss., Facultad de Filosofía y Letras, Universidad de Buenos Aires, 2010.

Teubal, Savina. *Hagar the Egyptian: The Lost Tradition of the Matriarchs.* San Francisco: Harper & Row, 1990.

Thiel, W. *Die soziale Entwicklung Israels in vorstaatlicher Zeit.* WMANT 52. Neukirchen-Vluyn: Neukirchener Verlag, 1985.

Thomas, D. Winton. "*Kelebh* 'dog': Its Origin and Some Usages of It in the OT." *VT* 10 (1960): 410–27.

Tigay, Jeffrey. *Deuteronomy.* JPS Torah Commentary. Philadelphia: JPS, 5756/1996.

Toivari, Jaana. "Man Versus Woman. Interpersonal Disputes in the Workmen's Community of Deir El-Medina." *JESHO* 40 (1997): 153–73.

Toorn, Karel van der. "Female Prostitution in Payment of Vows in Ancient Israel." *JBL* 108 (1989): 193–205.

———. *From Her Cradle to Her Grave.* Sheffield: JSOT Press, 1994.

———. "Saul and the Rise of Israelite State Religion." *VT* 43 (1993): 519–42.

———. "The Significance of the Veil in the Ancient Near East." Pages 327–39 in *Pomegranates and Golden Bells: Studies in Biblical, Jewish, and Near Eastern Ritual, Law, and Literature in Honor of Jacob Milgrom.* Edited by David P. Wright, David N. Freedman, and Avi Hurvitz. Winona Lake: Eisenbrauns, 1995.

Townsend, Theodore. "The Kingdom of God as a Reality: Israel in the Time of the Judges." *IJT* 32 (1983): 19–36.

Trebolle, Julio. "En torno a las adiciones y omisiones de Samuel y Reyes (1 Sam 8,18 y 1 Re 21,29)." *EstBib* 44 (1986): 253–62.

Trible, Phyllis. *God and the Rhetoric of Sexuality.* Philadelphia: Fortress, 1978.

———. *Texts of Terror: Literary-feminist Readings of Biblical Narratives.* Philadelphia: Fortress, 1984.

Troyer, Kristin De. "An Oriental Beauty Parlour: An Analysis of Esther 2.8–18 in the Hebrew, the Septuagint, and the Second Greek Text." Pages 47–70 in *A Feminist Companion to Esther, Judith and Susanna.* Edited by Athalya Brenner. Sheffield: Sheffield Academic Press, 1995.

Tsevat, Matitiahu. "Alalakhiana." *HUCA* 29 (1958): 109–34.

———. "Studies in the Book of Samuel." *HUCA* 36 (1965): 49–58.

———. "The Hebrew Slave According to Deuteronomy 15:12–18: His Lot and the Value of His Work, with Special Attention to the Meaning of *mšnh*." *JBL* 113 (1994): 587–95.

Tucker, Gene. "The Rahab Saga (Joshua 2): Some Form-Critical and Traditio-Historical Observations." Pages 66–86 in *The Use of the Old Testament in the New and Other Essays: Studies in Honor of William Franklin Steinspring.* Edited by James M. Efird. Durham, N.C.: Duke University, 1972.

Turnham, Timothy. "Male and Female Slaves in the Sabbath Year Laws of Exodus 21:1." *SBLSP* 26 (1987): 545–49.

Tyree, E. Loeta and Evangelia Stefanoudaki. "The Olive Pit and Roman Oil Making." *BA* 59 (1996): 170–78.

Uchitel, Alexander. "Women at Work: Weavers of Lagash and Spinners of San Luiz Gonzaga." Pages 621–31 in *Sex and Gender in the Ancient Near East: Proceedings of the 47th Rencontre Assyriologique Internationale, Helsinki, July 2–6, 2001.* Edited by Simo Parpola and R. M. Whiting. Helsinki: ©Neo-Assyrian Text Corpus Project, Institute for Asian and African Studies, University of Helsinki (2002).

Van de Mieroop, Marc. *A History of the Ancient Near East, ca. 3000–323 BC.* Blackwell History of the Ancient World. Malden: Blackwell, 2004.

———. "Women in the Economy of Sumer." Pages 53–66 in *Women's Earliest Records from Ancient Egypt and Western Asia.* Edited by Barbara Lesko. BJS 166. Atlanta: Scholars Press, 1989.

Van Seters, John. *A Law Book for the Diaspora: Revision in the Study of the Covenant Code.* Oxford: Oxford University Press, 2003.

———. "Love and Death in the Court History of David." Pages 121–4 in *Love and Death in the Ancient Near East: Essays in Honor of Marvin H. Pope.* Edited by J. Marks and R. Good. Guildford, Conn.: Four Quarters, 1987.

Vaux, Roland de. *Ancient Israel: Its Life and Institutions.* 2 vols. New York: McGraw-Hill, 1961.

Veenhof, K. R. "A Deed of Manumission and Adoption from the Later Old Assyrian Period." Pages 359–85 in *Zikir Sumim. Assyriological Studies Presented to F. R. Kraus on the Occasion of His Seventieth Birthday.* Edited by G. van Driel, T. J. H. Krispijn, M. Stol, and K. R. Veenhof. Leiden: Brill, 1982.

Veloso, Mario. "Rut: Tres Mujeres Frente a Una Crisis." *RB* 38 (1976): 59–66.

Vermeylen, J. "Les sections narratives de Deut 5–11 et leur relation a Ex 19–34." Pages 174–207 in *Das Deuteronomium: Entstehung, Gestalt und Botschaft.* Edited by Norbert Lohfink. BETL 68. Leuven: Leuven University Press, 1985.

Vervenne, M. and J. Lust, eds. *Deuteronomy and Deuteronomic Literature. Festschrift C. H. W. Brekelmans.* Leuven: Leuven University Press, 1997.

Vieira Sampaio, Tânia Mara. *Movimentos do corpo prostituído da mulher: Aproximações da profecia atribuída a Oséias.* São Paulo: Loyola, 1999.

Vílches Líndez, José. *Sapienciales III: Eclesiastés o Qohelet.* Estella: Verbo Divino, 1994.

Virolleaud, C. "Les Villes et les Corporations du Royaume d'Ugarit." *Syria* 21 (1940): 123–51.

———. "Lettres et Documents Administratifs de Ras Shamra." *Syria* 21 (1940): 245–76.

Vogt, H. *Studie zur nachexilischen Gemeinde in Esra-Nehemia.* Werl: Komissionsverlag D. Coelde, 1966.

Vogt, Joseph. *Ancient Slavery and the Ideal of Man.* Cambridge: Harvard University Press, 1975.

Vries, Simon J. de. *1 and 2 Chronicles.* FOTL 11. Grand Rapids: Eerdmans, 1989.

Vorster, Willem S. "Readings, Readers and the Succession Narrative: An Essay on Reception." *ZAW* 98 (1986): 352–62.

Wacker, Marie-Theres. "Historical, Hermeneutical, and Methodological Foundations." Pages 3–82 in *Feminist Interpretation: The Bible in Women's Perspective.* Edited by

Louise Schottroff, Silvia Schroer, and Marie-Theres Wacker. Minneapolis: Fortress, 1998.

————. "'Kultprostitution' im Alten Israel? Forschungsmythen, Spuren, Thesen." Pages 55–84 in *Tempelprostitution im Altertum: Fakten und Fiktionen*. Edited by Tanja S. Scheer and Martin Lindner. Berlin: Antike, 2009.

Waetzoldt, Hartmut. "Compensation of Craft Workers and Officials in the Ur III Period." Pages 117–41 in *Labor in the Ancient Near East*. Edited by Marvin Powell. AOS 68. New Haven: American Oriental Society, 1987.

Waldow, H. Eberhard von. "Social Responsibility and Social Structure in Early Israel." *CBQ* 32 (1970): 182–204.

Wallace-Hadrill, Andrew. "Introduction." Pages 1–13 in *Patronage in Ancient Society*. Edited by A. Wallace-Hadrill. London: Routledge, 1989.

Walsh, Jerome T. "The Characterization of Solomon in First Kings 1–5." *CBQ* 57 (1995) 471–93.

Warburton, David A."Working." Pages 169–82 in *A Companion to the Ancient Near East*. Edited by Daniel Snell. Malden: Blackwell, 2005.

Ward, William A.. "Non-Royal Women and Their Occupations in the Middle Kingdom." Pages 33–43 in *Women's Earliest Records from Ancient Egypt and Western Asia*. Edited by Barbara Lesko. BJS 166. Atlanta: Scholars Press, 1989.

————. "Relations between Egypt and Mesopotamia from Prehistoric Times to the End of the Middle Kingdom." *JESHO* 7 (1964): 1–45, 121–35.

Washington, C. H. "Lest He Die in the Battle and Another Man Take Her: Violence and the Construction of Gender in the Laws of Deuteronomy 20–22." Pages 185–213 in *Gender and Law*. Edited by Victor H. Matthews, Bernard Levinson, and Tikva Frymer-Kensky. JSOTSup 262. Sheffield: Sheffield Academic Press, 1998.

Waters, John. "Who Was Hagar?" Pages 187–205 in *Stony the Road We Trod: African American Biblical Interpretation.* Edited by Cain Hope Felder. Minneapolis: Fortress, 1991.

Watson, Wilfred G. E. "Archaic Elements in the Language of Chronicles." *Bib* 53 (1972): 191–207.

————. *Classical Hebrew Poetry: A Guide to Its Techniques*. JSOTSS 26. Reprinted with corrections. Sheffield: Sheffield Academic Press, 1995.

————. "Daily Life in Ancient Ugarit." Pages 121–52 in *Life and Culture in the Ancient Near East*. Edited by Richard Averbeck, Mark W. Chavalas, and David B. Weisberg. Bethesda, Md.: CDL Press, 2003.

————. "Gender-matched Synonymous Parallelism in the OT." *JBL* 99 (1980) 321–41.

————. "Recent Work on Daily Life in the Ancient Near East." *Historiae* 6 (2009): 87–99.

Weems, Renita J. *Battered Love: Marriage, Sex, and Violence in the Hebrew Prophets*. Minneapolis: Fortress, 1995.

————. "Do You See What I See? Diversity in Interpretation." *Church and Society* 82 (1991): 28–43.

————. "Re-Reading for Liberation: African American Women and the Bible." Pages 19–32 in *Feminist Interpretation of the Bible and the Hermeneutics of Liberation*.

Edited by Silvia Schroer and Sophia Bietenhard. Sheffield: Sheffield Academic Press, 2003.

———. "The Hebrew Women Are Not Like the Egyptian Women: The Ideology of Race, Gender and Sexual Reproduction in Exodus 1." Pages 225–34 in *Ideological Criticism of the Bible*. Edited by David Jobling and Tina Pippin. *Semeia* 59. Atlanta: Scholars Press, 1992.

Wegner, Judith Romney. "Leviticus." Pages 36–44 in *The Women's Bible Commentary*. Edited by Carol Newsom and Sharon Ringe. Louisville: Westminster John Knox, 1992.

Weinfeld, Moshe. *Deuteronomy and the Deuteronomic School*. Oxford: Clarendon Press, 1972.

———. "Deuteronomy: The Present State of Inquiry." Pages 21–35 in *A Song of Power and the Power of Song: Essays on the Book of Deuteronomy*. Edited by Duane L. Christensen. Winona Lake: Eisenbrauns, 1993.

———. "'Justice and Righteousness'—משפט וצדקה—The Expression and Its Meaning." Pages 228–46 in *Justice and Righteousness: Biblical Themes and Their Influence*. Edited by Henning Graf Reventlow and Yair Hoffman. JSOTSup 731. Sheffield: Sheffield Academic Press, 1992.

———. "The Emergence of the Deuteronomic Movement: The Historical Antecedents." Pages 76–98 in *Das Deuteronomium: Entstehung, Gestalt und Botschaft*. Edited by Norbert Lohfink. BETL 68. Leuven: Leuven University Press, 1985.

———. "Traces of Assyrian Treaty Formulae in Deuteronomy." *Bib* 46 (1965): 417–27.

Weisman, Zvi. *Political Satire in the Bible*. Atlanta: SBL, 1998.

Wenham, Gordon. *The Book of Leviticus*. NICOT. Grand Rapids: Eerdmans, 1992.

Westbrook, Raymond. "Biblical and Cuneiform Law Codes." *RB* 92 (1985): 247–64.

———. "Lex Talionis and Exodus 21:22–25." *RB* 93 (1986): 52–69.

———. *Property and the Family in Biblical Law*. JSOTS 113. Sheffield: Sheffield Academic Press, 1991.

———. *Studies in Biblical and Cuneiform Law*. Cahiers de la Revue Biblique, 1988.

———. "The Female Slave." Pages 214–38 in *Gender and Law in the Hebrew Bible and the Ancient Near East*. Edited by Victor Matthews, Bernard Levinson and Tikva Frymer-Kensky. JSOTSup 262. Sheffield: Sheffield Academic Press, 1998.

———. "What is the Covenant Code?" pages 15–36 in *Theory and Method in Biblical and Cuneiform Law*. Edited by Bernard Levinson. JSOTSup 181. Sheffield: Sheffield Academic Press, 1994.

Westermann, Claus. *Genesis 1–11: A Commentary*. Minneapolis: Augsburg, 1984.

———. *Genesis 12–36: A Commentary*. Minneapolis: Augsburg, 1986.

———. *Genesis 37–50: A Commentary*. Minneapolis: Augsburg, 1986.

———. *Roots of Wisdom. The Oldest Proverbs of Israel and Other Peoples*. Louisville: Westminster John Knox, 1995.

Westermann, William L. "Slavery and the Elements of Freedom in Ancient Greece." Pages 17–32 in *Slavery in Classical Antiquity: Views and Controversies*. Edited by Moses Finley. Cambridge: Heffer, 1960. Repr. from *Quarterly Bulletin of the Polish Institute of Arts and Sciences in America* (1943): 1–16.

———. *The Slave System of Greek and Roman Antiquity*. Philadelphia: The American Philosophical Society, 1955.

Whitelam, Keith. "Israelite Kingship. The Royal Ideology and Its Opponents." Pages 119–39 in *The World of Ancient Israel: Sociological, Anthropological and Political Perspectives.* Edited by Ronald E. Clements. Cambridge: Cambridge University Press, 1989.

———. *The Just King.* JSOTSup. 12. Sheffield: JSOT Press, 1979.

Whittaker, John C. "Alonia and Dhoukanes: The Ethnoarchaeology of Threshing in Cyprus." *NEA* 63 (2000): 62–69.

Whybray, Raymond N. *Proverbs.* NCBC. Grand Rapids: Eerdmans, 1994.

———. "Proverbs VIII 22–31 and Its Supposed Prototypes." *VT* 15 (1965): 504–14.

———. *The Book of Proverbs.* Cambridge: Cambridge University Press, 1972.

———. *The Book of Proverbs: A Survey in Modern Study.* Leiden: Brill, 1995.

———. "The Sage in the Israelite Royal Court." Pages 133–39 in *The Sage in Israel and the Ancient Near East.* Edited by J. G. Gammie and L. G. Perdue. Eisenbrauns: Winona Lake, 1990.

———. "The Social World of the Wisdom Writers." Pages 227–50 in *The World of Ancient Israel: Sociological, Anthropological and Political Perspectives.* Edited by Ronald E. Clements. Cambridge: Cambridge University Press, 1989.

———. *The Succession Narrative: A Study of 2 Samuel 9–20 and 1 Kings 1 and 2.* SBT, 2nd series, 9. Naperville, Ill.: Allenson, 1965.

———. *Wealth and Poverty in the Book of Proverbs.* JSOTSup 99. Sheffield: JSOT Press, 1990.

———. *Wisdom in Proverbs.* London: SCM Press, 1965.

———. "Wisdom Literature in the Reigns of David and Solomon." Pages 13–26 in *Studies in the Period of David and Solomon and Other Essays.* Edited by Tomoo Ishida. Winona Lake: Eisenbrauns, 1982.

Whyte, Martin King. *The Status of Women in Preindustrial Societies.* Princeton: Princeton University Press, 1978.

Wiedemann, Thomas. *Greek and Roman Slavery.* Baltimore: Johns Hopkins University Press, 1981.

Wikan, Unni. "Shame and Honour: A Contestable Pair." *Man* 19 (1984): 635–52.

Wilcke, Claus. *Early Ancient Near Eastern Law: A History of Its Beginnings: The Early Dynastic and Sargonic Periods.* Rev. and enlarged version. Winona Lake: Eisenbrauns, 2007 [2003]. Cited 8 November 2012. Online: http://books.google.com .ar/books?hl=es&lr=&id=nwlbg0MqmYoC&oi=fnd&pg=PA7&dq=claus+wilcke,+ Sargonic&ots=wf2Zj6sMm5&sig=iW3iU4h2uk2YPPvDUS3V2Pm9nS8#v=onepag e&q=slave&f=false.

Willesen, Folker. "The *Yālīd* in Hebrew Society." *ST* 12 (1958): 192–210.

Williamson, H. G. M. "The Concept of Israel in Transition." Pages 141–61 in *The World of Ancient Israel: Sociological, Anthropological and Political Perspectives.* Edited by Ronald E. Clements. Cambridge: Cambridge University Press, 1989.

Williams, James G. "The Beautiful and the Barren: Conventions in Biblical Type-Scenes." *JSOT* 17 (1980): 107–19.

Wilson, Robert. *Sociological Approaches to the Old Testament.* Philadelphia: Fortress, 1984.

Windisch, Hans. "Zur Rahabgeschichte (Zwei Parallelen aus der klassischen Literatur)." *ZAW* 37 (1917/18): 188–98.

Winter, Irene. "Women in Public: The Disk of Enheduanna, the Beginning of the Office of En-Priestess, and the Weight of Visual Evidence." Pages 189–201 in *La Femme dans le Proche-Orient Antique: XXXIIIe. Rencontre Assyriologique Internationale.* Edited by Jean-Marie Durand. Paris: Editions Recherche sur les Civilisations, 1987.

Winters, Alicia. "La Memoria Subversiva de Una Mujer: II Samuel 21:1–14."*RIBLA* 13 (1992): 77–86. Cited 4 September 2012. Online: http://www.ribla.org/.

———. "Una Vasija de Aceite: Mujer, Deudas y Comunidad (II Reyes 4:1–7)." *RIBLA* 14 (1993): 53–59. Cited 4 September 2012. Online: http://www.ribla.org/.

Wolde, Ellen van. "Who Guides Whom? Embeddedness and Perspective in Biblical Hebrew and in Kings 3:16–28." *JBL* 114 (1995): 623–42.

Wolf, Erik. *Peasants.* Englewood Cliffs, N.J.: Prentice-Hall, 1966.

Wolff, Hans Walter. *Hosea.* Hermeneia. Philadelphia: Fortress, 1974.

———. "Masters and Slaves." *Int* 27 (1973): 259–72.

Wright, Benjamin G., III. "ʿebed/Doulos: Terms and Social Status in the Meeting of Hebrew Biblical and Hellenistic Roman Culture." *Semeia* 93–94 (1998): 83–111.

Wright, David P. "Music and Dance in 2 Samuel 6." *JBL* 121 (2002): 201–25.

Wright, J. W. "The Fight for Peace: Narrative and History in the Battle Accounts in Chronicles." Pages 150–77 in *The Chronicler as Historian.* Edited by M. Graham, K. Hoglund, and S. McKenzie. JSOTSup 238. Sheffield: Sheffield Academic Press, 1997.

Wyatt, N. "The Story of Dinah and Shechem." *UF* 22 (1991): 433–58.

Yamashita, T. "Professions." Pages 41–68 in *The Ras Shamra Parallels II.* Edited by Loren R. Fisher, Duane E. Smith, and Stan Rummel. 3 volumes. AnOr 50. Rome: Pontificium Institutum Biblicum, 1975.

Yee, Gale A. "Ideological Criticism: Judges 17–21 and the Dismembered Body." Pages 146–70 in *Judges and Method.* Edited by Gale Yee. Minneapolis: Fortress, 1995.

———. "'Take This Child and Suckle It for Me': Wet Nurses and Resistance in Ancient Israel." *BTB* 39 (2009): 180–89.

Yee, Gale A., ed. *Judges and Method.* Minneapolis: Fortress, 1995.

Yon, Marguerite. *The City of Ugarit at Tell Ras Shamra.* Winona Lake: Eisenbrauns, 2006. It is partially available online. Cited 2 September 2011. Online: http://books .google.com.ar/books?id=2YWQZ6x56dAC&printsec=frontcover&dq=Yon&hl=es &ei=IdJiTbj1HsP88AbszeHsCw&sa=X&oi=book_result&ct=result&resnum=5&ve d=0CDwQ6AEwBA#v=onepage&q&f=false.

Younger, K. Lawson, Jr. "'Give Us Our Daily Bread.' Everyday Life for the Israelite Deportess." Pages 269–88 in *Life and Culture in the Ancient Near East.* Edited by Richard Averbeck, Mark W. Chavalas and David B. Weisberg. Bethesda: CDL Press, 2003.

———, ed. *Ugarit at Seventy-five.* Winona Lake: Eisenbrauns, 2007.

Zagarell, Allen. "Trade, Women, Class, and Society in Ancient Western Asia." *Current Anthropology* 27 (1986): 415–30.

Zakovitch, Yair. "Humor and Theology or the Successful Failure of Israelite Intelligence: A Literary-Folkloric Approach to Joshua 2." Pages 75–98 in *Text and Tradition:*

The Hebrew Bible and Folklore. Edited by Susan Niditch. Atlanta: Scholars Press, 1990.

Zevit, Ziony. *The Anterior Construction in Classical Hebrew.* SBLMS50. Atlanta: Scholars Press, 1998.

Zipor, M. "Restrictions on Marriage for Priests." *Bib* 68 (1987): 259–67.

Zwickel, Wolfgang. *Frauenalltag im biblischen Israel (mit einem Beitrag von Sabine Kersken).* Stuttgart: Verlag Katholisches Bibelwerk, 1980.

INDEX OF BIBLICAL REFERENCES

20:3	28, 347	11:26–28	106	17:24	198
20:16	29	12	305	22:14	10, 352
20:17	118, 348	14:11	301	23:7	12, 109, 188,
20:24	171	14:24	12		191, 192
21:8	249	15:12	12	23:13	283
21:11	249, 347	15:13	10, 352	23:7	109, 354
21:19	188	16:4	301	23:24	11, 283, 352
23:16	170	20:13–22	124	24:12	167
		21:2	301	24:14	162, 245
1 Kings		21:6	301	24:15	10
1	342	21:15	301		
1–2	334	21:19	304	*Isaiah*	
1:1–4	20, 123, 125,	21:27–29	305		
	249, 350	22	306	1:21	325, 351
1:2–4	74, 119, 120,	22:1–38	305	3:24	242
	250, 347, 350	22:29–38	304	5	12, 201
1:4	7, 208	22:38	292, 301, 304,	7:20	176
1:11	249		305, 306, 322,	8:3	10, 353
1:13	118, 348		347, 350	8:19	11, 353
1:15	7, 249	22:40	305	14:2	349
1:17	118, 348	22:47	12	19:3	11, 353
1:42–43	183			19:9b	188
2:13–25	250	*2 Kings*		22	252, 255
3	276, 290, 318			22:15	250
3–11	105	2:3–15	10, 354	22:15–16	252
3:16	26, 292, 318,	4:1–7	165, 173, 339	22:15–19	254
	326, 340	4:1	10, 354	23	291, 322
3:16–28	326, 347, 350	4:2	119, 348	23:15	325
3:20	118, 348	4:16	119, 348	23:15–16	280, 351
3:21	256	4:8	123	23:15–18	280, 281, 282
3:22	320	5	2, 120,	23:16	199, 203, 291,
4:5	26, 179		125,160, 335		355
4:6	171	5:1	127	23:17–18	280, 300
4:7	179	5:2	119, 120	24:2	349
5:7 [4:27]	26, 179	5:2–4	334, 347	24:7–9	202
5:11[4:31]	164, 167,	5:4	119	29:7–8	27
	154	5:26	118, 120, 125,	29:16	226
5:27–32			334, 347	30:14	226
[5:13–18]	106	6:1	354	36–37	252
9:15–22	173	6:24–30	89	38:12	188
9:15–28	106, 169	7:6	256	40	184
9:21	172	8:1–6	123	40:9	184, 351
9:21–22	171, 172	8:13	301	40:10	256
10:1–13	352	9:10	301	41:27	184
10:5	250	10:13	10, 352	44:5	106
10:18	211	11	259	44:9–20	247
11:3	28, 347	11:2	255, 263, 343,	44:19	247
11:5	283		345, 350	45:9b	226
11:7	283	11:1–3	261	47	115, 283, 336,
11:19–20	10, 352	15:5	252		366
		17:34	149	47:1–4	228

34:22	10, 353
35:25	193, 217, 351
36:22	217

Luke

| 1:46–55 | 50 |
| 2:34 | 50 |

John

| 4 | 126, 170 |

CPSIA information can be obtained at www.ICGtesting.com
Printed in the USA
LVOW062156170513

334361LV00001B/53/P